# Contents

❋   ❋   ❋   ❋

Tunguska Event ✦ What Really Killed John Wayne? ✦ Shroud of Turin: Real or Fake? ✦ The Champion of American Lake Monsters ✦ The Guy Who Killed the Guy Who Killed Abraham Lincoln ✦ 9 of History's Coldest Cases ✦ William Desmond Taylor ✦ Dream Weaver ✦ Who Betrayed Anne Frank? ✦ Whatever Happened to D. B. Cooper ✦ Who Cracked the Liberty Bell? ✦ An Open Secret ✦ Gone Without a Trace ✦ The Mystery of the Missing Comma ✦ Giant Frogman Spotted in Ohio! ✦ A Superior Tragedy: The Edmund Fitzgerald ✦ The Anasazi

The Hidden History of the Jockstrap ✦ What Is the "7" in 7-Up? ✦ How Did I Get My Birthmark? ✦ How Do Dogs Remember Where They Bury Their Bones? ✦ Top-Secret Locations You Can Visit ✦ America's Only King ✦ Who Says Dinosaurs Are Extinct? ✦ The Mystery of the Lost Dauphin of France ✦ Who Reads All Those Letters to Santa? ✦ Undiscovered Animals ✦ Waiter, There's Meat in My Mincemeat ✦ The "Moon Illusion" ✦ The Doubleday Myth ✦ How Did Houdini Die? ✦ Pressing Ye Issue ✦ Who Really Discovered the 'Way to a Man's Heart'? ✦ The Boston Tea Party ✦ Illinois's Little-Known Black Codes ✦ Washington's Tab ✦ Tale of a Fateful Trip ✦ Show Me the Money ✦ On the Autobahn ✦ Milk for Cats ✦ Brains and Brawn ✦ Bible Translations You've Probably Never Heard of ✦ Point Me to the Welsh Rabbits ✦ No Cats Were Harmed ✦ The Cat Toss ✦ Stealing the President ✦ Tracking Tektite Truths ✦ Baby Ruth's Truth? ✦ Civil War Myths ✦ Some Registered Tax-Exempt Religions You've Never Heard of ✦ Oh the Calamity!

The Day King Tut's Tomb Was Opened ✦ Millions of Mummies ✦ The Mystery of the 700-Year-Old Piper ✦ The Catacombs of Paris ✦ Sandstone Gateway to Heaven ✦ The Mound Builders: Mythmaking in Early America ✦ The Library of the Muses ✦ Identities Lost: The Druids and the Picts ✦ Are You Related to Genghis Khan? ✦ Treasures Lost and Found ✦ The Tomb in Washington Square Park ✦ Prehistoric Hollywood ✦ Why Didn't the Vikings Stay in North America? ✦ Sorry, Mates, but Aussies Didn't Invent the Boomerang ✦ Nostradamus: Seer of Visions ✦ A Discovery of Biblical Proportions ✦ The News Is What the President Says It Is ✦ The Truth and the Myth of the Ninja ✦ Sacajawea's Story ✦ The Earl of Sandwich's Favorite Snack ✦ Ahead of His Time ✦ History's Little Mystery ✦ Reward: One Lost Island ✦ Aztalan: A Prehistoric Puzzle ✦ The Mystery of Easter Island ✦ The Fast-Draw Myth ✦ Labor of Love: The Taj Mahal

## Explore a World of Secrets

✳ ✳ ✳ ✳

Welcome to *The Big Book of Big Secrets*. If you're one of those people who find themselves wondering whether a crazy conspiracy theory might really be true, how a certain celebrity really died, or how a bizarre convention originated, then you're sure to find ample entertainment in this book. In these pages, we'll pull back the curtains on classic media hoaxes, identity scams, and clandestine organizations rumored to rule the world. We'll unmask secret identities, reveal forgeries, and investigate myths, urban and otherwise.

Each chapter takes an intriguing subject—secret societies, the art world, the Bible, UFOs, paranormal phenomena—and ferrets out the secret stories and lesser known truths. Whether it's a world-changing event or something local and obscure, every story is sure to pique your interest. Did John Lennon see a UFO above New York City in 1974? Read about it on page 403. Where do fortune cookies really come from? Find out on page 596. How many people has the tomb of King Tut supposedly killed? Turn to page 205 . . .

# Chapter 1

# The Art World

## Cracking the Code of da Vinci's Masterpiece

*After centuries of beguiling viewers—and maddening artists and scientists who tried to uncover its secrets—Leonardo da Vinci's Mona Lisa may have finally revealed her secret code.*

✳   ✳   ✳   ✳

THE RENAISSANCE GENIUS began his portrait of Lisa del Giocondo, a Florentine gentlewoman, in 1503 and is believed to have finished the painting just before his death in 1519. Using a process of brushwork he called *sfumato* (from the Italian fumo, meaning smoke), da Vinci said his technique created a painting "without lines or borders, in the manner of smoke or beyond the focus plane." Although he left many notes on his other projects, Leonardo never explained how he created the subtle effects of light and shadow that give his masterwork an unworldly, three-dimensional quality.

Although the painting has been studied extensively over the centuries, even the most modern scientific instruments have been unable to uncover its secrets. Much of the brushwork on the portrait's face and hands is too small to be studied by X-ray or microscope. French artist and art historian Jacques Franck, however, believes he has discovered da Vinci's methods through his own trial and error. According to Franck, after completing a conventional sketch of his subject, da Vinci applied a base coat of pale yellow imprimatura—a diluted semi-opaque wash—then began one of history's greatest creative marathons. Using minute crosshatching techniques, da Vinci spent more than 15 years brushing on 30 successive layers of paint. Apparently requiring a magnifying glass, the process took 30 to 40 small dots of oil paint smaller than the head of a pin to cover one square millimeter of canvas. Franck believes da Vinci applied additional layers of imprimatura between each layer of paint to further soften lines and blend colors, creating successively finer layers of shading and tones.

Although Franck's conclusions have been disputed by some art historians, he has convincingly reproduced the effects with his own copies of small sections of the painting. A recent exhibit at the Uffizi Gallery in Florence displayed six panels by Franck re-creating one of Mona Lisa's eyes, illustrating the step-by-step process of how Leonardo may have worked. Though his artistic sleuthing remains controversial, Franck points out that the use of minute dots of paint—similar to the pointillism developed by modern artists—had been used since Roman times and is clearly evident in some of da Vinci's earlier paintings. With the Mona Lisa, Leonardo apparently took the technique to an unmatched level of virtuosity.

# John Myatt, Master Forger

*When people hear the word forgery, they usually think of money. But legal currency isn't the only thing that can be faked.*

✳    ✳    ✳    ✳

"**M**ONET, MONET, MONET. Sometimes I get truly fed up doing Monet. Bloody haystacks." John Myatt's humorous lament sounds curiously Monty Pythonesque, until you realize that he can do Monet—and Chagall, Klee, Le Corbusier, Ben Nicholson, and almost any other painter you can name, great or obscure. Myatt, an artist of some ability, was probably the world's greatest art forger. He took part in an eight-year forgery scam in the 1980s and '90s that shook the foundations of the art world.

Despite what one might expect, art forgery is not a victimless crime. Many of Myatt's paintings—bought in good faith as the work of renowned masters—went for extremely high sums. One "Giacometti" sold at auction in New York for $300,000, and as many as 120 of his counterfeits are still out there, confusing and distressing the art world. But Myatt never set out to break the law.

Initially, Myatt would paint an unknown work in the style of one of the cubist, surrealist, or impressionist masters, and he seriously duplicated both style and subject. For a time, he gave them to friends or sold them as acknowledged fakes. Then he ran afoul of John Drewe.

## The Scheme Begins

Drewe was a London-based collector who had bought a dozen of Myatt's fakes over two years. Personable and charming, he ingratiated himself with Myatt by posing as a rich aristocrat. But one day he called and told Myatt that a cubist work the artist had done in the style of Albert Gleizes had just sold at Christies for £25,000 ($40,000)—as a genuine Gleizes. Drewe offered half of that money to Myatt.

The struggling artist was poor and taking care of his two children. The lure of Drewe's promise of easy money was irresistible. So the scheme developed that he would create a "newly discovered" work by a famous painter and pass it along to Drewe, who would sell the painting and then pay Myatt his cut—usually only about 10 percent. It would take Myatt two or three months to turn out a single fake, and he was only making about £13,000 a year (roughly $21,000)—hardly worthy of a master criminal.

One of the amazing things about this scam was Myatt's materials. Most art forgers take great pains to duplicate the exact pigments used by the original artists, but Myatt mixed cheap emulsion house paint with a lubricating gel to get the colors he needed. One benefit is that his mix dried faster than oil paints.

## The Inside Man

But Drewe was just as much of a master forger, himself. The consummate con man, he inveigled his way into the art world through donations, talking his way into the archives of the Tate Gallery and learning every trick of *provenance*, the authentication of artwork. He faked letters from experts and, on one occasion, even inserted a phony catalog into the archives with pictures of Myatt's latest fakes as genuine.

But as the years went by, Myatt became increasingly worried about getting caught and going to prison, so at last he told Drewe he wanted out. Drewe refused to let him leave, and Myatt realized that his partner wasn't just in it for the money. He loved conning people.

## The Jig Is Up

The scam was not to last, of course. Drewe's ex-wife went to the police with incriminating documents, and when the trail led to Myatt's cottage in Staffordshire, he confessed.

Myatt served four months of a yearlong sentence, and when he came out of prison, Detective Superintendent Jonathan Searle of the Metropolitan Police was waiting for him. Searle suggested that since Myatt was now infamous, many people would love to own a real John Myatt fake. As a result, Myatt and his second wife Rosemary set up a tidy business out of their cottage. His paintings regularly sell for as much as £45,000 ($72,000), and Hollywood has shown interest in a movie—about the real John Myatt.

# The Vanishing Treasure Room

*In the Age of Enlightenment, kings and emperors built immense palaces to outdo one another—each one bigger and more gilded and bejeweled than the last. But one of Russia's greatest 18th century treasures became one of the 20th century's greatest unsolved mysteries.*

✳   ✳   ✳   ✳

THE STORIED HISTORY of the Amber Room begins in 1701, when it was commissioned by Frederick I of Prussia. Considered by admirers and artists alike to be the "Eighth Wonder of the World," the sparkling, honey-gold room consisted of a series of wall panels inlaid with prehistoric amber, finely carved and illuminated by candles and mirrors. In 1716, Prussian King Freidrich Wilhelm I made a gift of the panels to his then-ally Russian Tsar Peter the Great to ornament the imperial palace at his new capital, St. Petersburg.

After sitting at the Winter Palace for four decades, the Amber Room was relocated to Tsarskoye Selo, the Romanov palace just south of St. Petersburg. During the mid-18th century, Prussia's King Frederick the Great sent Russia's Empress Elizabeth more of the amber material from his Baltic holdings, and Elizabeth ordered her court's great Italian architect, Bartolomeo Rastrelli, to expand the Amber Room into an 11-foot-square masterpiece.

The golden room was not finished until 1770, under the reign of Catherine the Great. Incorporating more than six tons of amber and accented with semiprecious stones, the fabled room became not only a prized imperial showpiece of the Russian empire, but a symbol of the long-standing alliance between Prussia and Russia.

## From Peace to War

Two centuries after the Amber Room was removed to the Catherine Palace, the world was a much darker place. Prussia and Russia, formerly faithful allies, were locked in a deadly struggle that would bring down both imperial houses. By 1941, the former dominions of Frederick and Peter were ruled by Adolf Hitler and Joseph Stalin.

In a surprise attack, Hitler's armies advanced across the Soviet border in June 1941 to launch the most destructive war in history. German panzers rumbled from the Polish frontier to the gates of Moscow in a harrowing six-month campaign, laying waste to some of the most fertile, productive territory in Eastern Europe.

One of the unfortunate cities in the path of the Nazi onslaught was St. Petersburg, renamed Leningrad by its communist conquerors. Frantic palace curators desperately tried to remove the Amber Room's antique panels, but the fragile prehistoric resin began to crack and crumble as the panels were detached. Faced with probable destruction of one of Russia's greatest treasures or its abandonment to the Nazis, the curators attempted to hide the room's precious panels by covering them with gauze and wallpaper.

Although Leningrad withstood a long, bloody siege, German troops swept through the city's suburbs, capturing Tsarskoye Selo intact in October 1941. Soldiers discovered the treasure hidden behind the wallpaper, and German troops disassembled the room's panels over a 36-hour period, packed them in 27 crates, and shipped them back to Königsberg, in East Prussia.

The fabled Amber Room panels were put on display in Königsberg's castle museum. They remained there for two years—until the Third Reich began to crumble before the weight of Soviet and Anglo-American miltary forces. At some point in 1944, the room's panels were allegedly dismantled and packed into crates, to prevent damage by British and Soviet bombers. In January 1945, Hitler permitted the westward movement of cultural treasures, including the Italo-Russo-German masterpiece.

And from there, the Amber Room was lost to history.

## The Great Treasure Hunt

The world was left to speculate about the fate of the famous imperial room, and dozens of theories have been spawned about the room's whereabouts. Some claim the Amber Room was lost—sunk aboard a submarine, bombed to pieces, or perhaps burned in Königsberg itself. This last conclusion was finally accepted by Alexander Brusov, a Soviet investigator sent to find the Amber Room shortly after the war's end. Referring to the destruction of Königsberg Castle by Red Army forces on April 9, 1945, he concluded: "Summarizing all the facts, we can say that the Amber Room was destroyed between 9 and 11 April 1945."

An in-depth hunt by two British investigative journalists pieced together the last days of the Amber Room and concluded that its fate was sealed when Soviet troops accidentally set fire to the castle compound during the last month of combat, destroying the brittle jewels and obscuring their location.

Other treasure hunters, however, claim the room still sits in an abandoned mine shaft or some long-forgotten Nazi bunker beneath the outskirts of Königsberg. One German investigator claimed former SS officers told him the room's panels were packed up and hidden in an abandoned silver mine near Berlin; a Lithuanian official claimed witnesses saw SS troops hiding the panels in a local swamp. Neither has been able to prove his claims.

## The Trail Goes Cold

The hunt for the Amber Room has been made more difficult because its last witnesses are gone—several under mysterious circumstances. The Nazi curator in charge of the room died of typhus the day before he was scheduled to be interviewed by the KGB, and a Soviet intelligence officer who spoke to a journalist about the room's whereabouts died the following day in a car crash. In 1987, Georg Stein, a former German soldier who had devoted his life to searching for the Amber Room, was found murdered in a forest, his stomach slit open by a scalpel.

In 1997, the world got a tantalizing glimpse of the long-lost treasure when German police raided the office of a Bremen lawyer who was attempting to sell an amber mosaic worth $2.5 million on behalf of one of his clients, the son of a former German lieutenant. The small mosaic—inlaid with jade and onyx as well as amber—had been stolen from the Amber Room by a German officer and was separated from the main panels. After its seizure, this last true remnant of the legendary tsarist treasure made its way back to Russia in April 2000.

Decades of searches by German and Soviet investigators have come up empty. The fate of the fabled room—worth over $250 million in today's currency—has remained an elusive ghost for treasure seekers, mystery writers, and investigators looking for the Holy Grail of Russian baroque artwork.

## Picking up the Pieces

In 1979, the Soviet government, with help from a donation made by a German gas firm in 1999, began amassing old photographs of the Amber Room and pieces of the rare amber to create a reconstructed room worthy of its predecessor. Carefully rebuilt at a cost exceeding $7 million, the reconstructed room was dedicated by the Russian president and German chancellor at a ceremony in 2003, marking the tricentennial of St. Petersburg's founding. The dazzling Amber Room is now on display for the thousands of tourists who come to Tsarskoye Selo to view the playground of one of Europe's great dynasties.

# 7 Notorious Art Thefts

*Some people just can't keep their hands off other people's things—including the world's greatest art. Art thieves take their loot from museums, places of worship, and private residences. Because they would have trouble selling the fruits of their labor on the open market—auction houses and galleries tend to avoid stolen works—art burglars often either keep the art for themselves or try to ransom the hot property back to the original owner. Among the major robberies in the past hundred years are these daring thefts of very expensive art (values estimated at the time of the theft).*

❋ ❋ ❋ ❋

1. **Boston, March 1990: $300 million:** Two men dressed as police officers visited the Isabella Stewart Gardner Museum in the wee hours of the morning. After over-powering two guards and grabbing the security system's surveillance tape, they collected Rembrandt's only seascape, *Storm on the Sea of Galilee,* as well as Vermeer's *The Concert,* Manet's *Chez Tortoni,* and several other works. Authorities have yet to find the criminals despite investigating everyone from the Irish Republican Army to a Boston mob boss!

2. **Oslo, August 2004: $120 million:** Two armed and masked thieves threatened workers at the Munch Museum during a daring daylight theft. They stole a pair of Edvard Munch paintings, *The Scream* and *The Madonna,* estimated at a combined value of 100 million euros. In May 2006, authorities convicted three men who received between four and eight years in jail. The paintings were recovered three months later.

3. **Paris, August 1911: $100 million:** In the world's most notorious art theft to date, Vincenzo Peruggia, an employee of the Louvre, stole Leonardo da Vinci's *Mona Lisa* from the storied museum in the heart of Paris. Peruggia simply

hid in a closet, grabbed the painting once alone in the room, hid it under his long smock, and walked out of the famed museum after it had closed. The theft turned the moderately popular *Mona Lisa* into the best-known painting in the world. Police questioned Pablo Picasso and French poet Guillaume Apollinaire about the crime, but they found the real thief—and the *Mona Lisa*—two years later when Peruggia tried to sell it to an art dealer in Florence.

4.  **Oslo, February 1994: $60–75 million:** *The Scream* has been a popular target for thieves in Norway. On the day the 1994 Winter Olympics began in Lillehammer, a different version of Munch's famous work—he painted four—was taken from Oslo's National Art Museum. In less than one minute, the crooks came in through a window, cut the wires holding up the painting, and left through the same window. They attempted to ransom the painting to the Norwegian government, but they had left a piece of the frame at a bus stop—a clue that helped authorities recover the painting within a few months. Four men were convicted of the crime in January 1996.

5.  **Scotland, August 2003: $65 million:** Blending in apparently has its advantages for art thieves. Two men joined a tour of Scotland's Drumlanrig Castle, subdued a guard, and made off with Leonardo da Vinci's *Madonna of the Yarnwinder*. Alarms around the art were not set during the day, and the thieves dissuaded tourists from intervening, reportedly telling them: "Don't worry . . . we're the police. This is just practice." Escaping in a white Volkswagen Golf, the perpetrators have never been identified—and the painting remains missing.

6.  **Stockholm, December 2000: $30 million:** Caught! Eight criminals each got up to six and half years behind bars for conspiring to take a Rembrandt and two Renoirs—all of them eventually recovered—from Stockholm's National

Museum. You have to give the three masked men who actually grabbed the paintings credit for a dramatic exit. In a scene reminiscent of an action movie, they fled the scene by motorboat. Police unraveled the plot after recovering one of the paintings during an unrelated drug investigation four months after the theft.

7. **Amsterdam, December 2002: $30 million:** Robbers used a ladder to get onto the roof of the Van Gogh Museum, broke in, and stole two of the Dutch master's paintings, *View of the Sea at Scheveningen* and *Congregation Leaving the Reformed Church in Nuenen*, together worth $30 million. Police reported that the thieves worked so quickly that, despite setting off the alarms, they had disappeared before police could get there. Authorities in the Netherlands arrested two men in 2003, based on DNA from hair inside two hats left at the scene, but they have been unable to recover the paintings, which the men deny taking.

# Deadly Bling?: The Curse of the Hope Diamond

*Diamonds are a girl's best friend, a jeweler's meal ticket, and serious status symbols for those who can afford them. But there's one famous diamond whose brilliant color comes with a cloudy history. The Hope Diamond is one of the world's most beautiful gemstones—and one that some say causes death and suffering to those who possess it. So is the Hope Diamond really cursed? There's a lot of evidence that says "no," but there have been some really strange coincidences.*

✳   ✳   ✳   ✳

### The Origin of Hope

IT'S BELIEVED THAT this shockingly large, blue-hued diamond came from India several centuries ago. At the time, the exceptional diamond was slightly more than 112 carats, which is enormous. (On average, a diamond in an engagement ring ranges from a quarter to a full carat.) According to legend, a thief stole the diamond from the eye of a Hindu statue, but scholars don't think the shape would have been right to sit in the face of a statue. Nevertheless, the story states that the young thief was torn apart by wild dogs soon after he sold the diamond, making this the first life claimed by the jewel.

## Courts, Carats, and Carnage

In the mid-1600s, a French jeweler named Tavernier purchased the diamond in India and kept it for several years without incident before selling it to King Louis XIV in 1668, along with several other jewels. The king recut the diamond in 1673, taking it down to 67 carats. This new cut emphasized the jewel's clarity, and Louis liked to wear the "Blue Diamond of the Crown" around his neck on special occasions. He, too, owned the gemstone without much trouble.

More than a hundred years later, France's King Louis XVI possessed the stone. In 1791, when the royal family tried to flee the country, the crown jewels were hidden for safekeeping, but they were stolen the following year. Some were eventually returned, but the blue diamond was not.

King Louis XVI and his wife Marie Antoinette died by guillotine in 1793. Those who believe in the curse are eager to include these two romantic figures in the list of cursed owners, but their deaths probably had more to do with the angry mobs of the French Revolution than a piece of jewelry.

## Right this Way, Mr. Hope

It is unknown what happened to the big blue diamond from the time it was stolen in France until it appeared in England nearly 50 years later. When the diamond reappeared, it wasn't the same size as before—it was now only about 45 carats. Had it been cut again to disguise its identity? Or was this a new diamond altogether? Because the blue diamond was so unique in color and size, it was believed to be the diamond in question.

In the 1830s, wealthy banker Henry Philip Hope purchased the diamond, henceforth known as the Hope Diamond. When he died (of natural causes) in 1839, he bequeathed the gem to his oldest nephew, and it eventually ended up with the nephew's grandson, Francis Hope.

Francis Hope is the next person supposedly cursed by the diamond. Francis was a notorious gambler and was generally bad with money. Though he owned the diamond, he was not allowed to sell it without his family's permission, which he finally got in 1901 when he announced he was bankrupt. It's doubtful that the diamond had anything to do with Francis's bad luck, though that's what some believers suggest.

## Coming to America

Joseph Frankel and Sons of New York purchased the diamond from Francis, and by 1909, after a few trades between the world's most notable jewelers, the Hope Diamond found itself in the hands of famous French jeweler Pierre Cartier. That's where rumors of a curse may have actually originated.

Allegedly, Cartier came up with the curse concept in order to sell the diamond to Evalyn Walsh McLean, a rich socialite who claimed that bad luck charms always turned into good luck charms in her hands. Cartier may have embellished the terrible things that had befallen previous owners of his special diamond so that McLean would purchase it—which she did. Cartier even inserted a clause in the sales contract, which stated that if any fatality occurred in the family within six months, the Hope Diamond could be exchanged for jewelry valued at the $180,000 McLean paid for the stone. Nevertheless, McLean wore the diamond on a chain around her neck constantly, and the spookiness surrounding the gem started picking up steam.

Whether or not anything can be blamed on the jewel, it certainly can't be denied that McLean had a pretty miserable life starting around the time she purchased the diamond. Her eldest son died at age nine in a fiery car crash. Years later, her

25-year-old daughter killed herself. Not long after that, her husband was declared insane and was committed to a mental institution for the rest of his life. With rumors swirling about the Hope Diamond's curse, everyone pointed to the necklace when these terrible events took place.

In 1947, when McLean died (while wearing the diamond) at age 60, the Hope Diamond and most of her other treasures were sold to pay off debts. American jeweler Harry Winston forked over the $1 million asking price for McLean's entire jewelry collection.

### Hope on Display

If Harry Winston was scared of the alleged curse, he didn't show it. Winston had long wanted to start a collection of gemstones to display for the general public, so in 1958, when the Smithsonian Institute started one in Washington, D.C., he sent the Hope Diamond to them as a centerpiece. These days, it's kept under glass as a central figure for the National Gem Collection at the National Museum of Natural History. So far, no one's dropped dead from checking it out.

# The Mysterious Voynich Manuscript

*Dubbed the "World's Most Mysterious Book," the Voynich manuscript contains more than 200 vellum pages of vivid, colorful illustrations and handwritten prose. There's only one small problem: No one knows what any of it means. Or whether it means anything at all.*

✳  ✳  ✳  ✳

IT WAS "DISCOVERED" in 1912 after being hidden from the world for almost 250 years. An American antique book dealer named Wilfried Voynich came across the medieval manuscript at an Italian Jesuit College. Approximately nine inches by six inches in size, the manuscript bore a light-brown vellum cover, which was unmarked, untitled, and gave no indication as to when it had been written or by whom. Bound inside were approximately 230 yellow parchment pages, most of which contained richly colored drawings of strange plants, celestial bodies, and other scientific matter. Many of the pages were adorned by naked nymphs bathing in odd-looking plumbing and personal-size washtubs. Handwritten text written in flowing script accompanied the illustrations.

Although Voynich was an expert antiquarian, he was baffled by the book's contents. And today—nearly a century later—the manuscript that came to bear his name remains a mystery.

## Weird Science

The mystery surrounding the Voynich manuscript begins with its content, which reads (so to speak) like a work of weird science presented in six identifiable "sections":

✳ a botanical section, containing drawings of plants that no botanist has ever been able to identify

✳ an astronomical section, with illustrations of the sun, moon, stars, and zodiac symbols surrounded by nymphs bathing in individual washtubs

✳ a "biological" section, showing perplexing anatomical drawings of chambers or organs connected by tubes—and which also features more nymphs swimming in their inner liquids

✳ a cosmological section, consisting mostly of unexplained circular drawings

✳ a pharmaceutical section, depicting drawings of plant parts (leaves, roots) placed next to containers

✳ a recipe section, featuring short paragraphs "bulleted" by stars in the margin

Weirder still are the ubiquitous nymphs—a nice touch perhaps, but how they relate to the subject is anyone's guess.

## Many Mysteries, Still No Answers

And then there's the manuscript's enigmatic text. The world's greatest cryptologists have failed to unravel its meaning. Even the American and British code breakers who cracked the Japanese and German codes in World War II were stumped. To this day, the Voynich manuscript has not been deciphered.

This, of course, has led to key unsolved questions, namely:

✳ Who wrote it? A letter found with the manuscript, dated 1666, credits Roger Bacon, a Franciscan friar who lived from 1214 to 1294. This has since been discredited because the manuscript's date of origin is generally considered to be between 1450 and 1500. There are as many theories about who wrote it as there are nymphs among its pages. In fact, some believe Voynich forged the whole thing.

✳ What is it? It was first thought to be a coded description of Bacon's early scientific discoveries. Since then, other theories ranging from an ancient prayer book written in a pidgin Germanic language to one big, elaborate hoax (aside from that supposedly perpetrated by Voynich) have been posited.

✳ Is it real writing? Is the script composed in a variation of a known language, a lost language, an encrypted language, an artificial language? Or is it just plain gibberish?

## What Do We Know?

Despite the aura of mystery surrounding the manuscript, it has been possible to trace its travels over the past 400 years. The earliest known owner was Holy Roman Emperor Rudolph II, who purchased it in 1586. By 1666, the manuscript had passed through a series of owners to Athanasius Kircher, a Jesuit scholar who hid it in the college where Voynich found it 250 years later.

After being passed down to various members of Voynich's estate, the manuscript was sold in 1961 to a rare-book collector who sought to resell it for a fortune. After failing to find a buyer, he donated it to Yale University, where it currently resides—still shrouded in mystery—in the Beinecke Rare Book and Manuscript Library.

## The Search for Meaning Continues

To this day, efforts to translate the Voynich manuscript continue. And still, the manuscript refuses to yield its secrets, leading experts to conclude that it's either an ingenious hoax or the ultimate unbreakable code. The hoax theory gained some ground in 2004 when Dr. Gordon Rugg, a computer-science lecturer at Keele University, announced that he had replicated the Voynich manuscript using a low-tech device called a Cardan grille. According to Rugg, this proved that the manuscript was likely a fraud—a volume of jibberish created, perhaps, in an attempt to con money out of Emperor Rudolph II. Mystery solved? Well, it's not quite as simple as that. Many researchers remain unconvinced. Sure, Rugg may have proven that the manuscript might be a hoax. But the possibility that it is not a hoax remains. And thus, the search for meaning continues.

# A Portrait of Oils

*The unique characteristics of oil paint contributed to the accomplishments of the Renaissance—and still inspire artists today.*

✳   ✳   ✳   ✳

PAINTINGS ARE AMONG the most ancient of artworks. More than 30,000 years ago, Neolithic painters decorated caves with patterns and images of animals. All paints include two elements: pigment and a liquid binder. Pigments from charred wood and colored minerals are ground into a fine powder. Then they are mixed into the binder; linseed oil is the most popular, but other oils, including walnut oil, are common.

The idea of using oil as a binder for pigment is very old, but oil paints as we know them are relatively modern. In the 12th century, a German monk named Theophilus wrote about oil paint in his *Schoedula Diversarum Artium* and warned against paint recipes using olive oil because they required excessively long drying times. The Italian painter and writer Cennino Cennini described the technique of oil painting in his encyclopedic *Book of Art*. Oil paints came into general use in northern Europe, in the area of the Netherlands, by the 15th century and, from there, spread southward into Italy. Oils remained the medium of choice for most painters until the mid-20th century.

Oil paintings are usually done on wood panels or canvas, although paintings on stone and specialty paper are not uncommon. In any case, the support material is usually prepared with a ground to which oil paint easily adheres. Oil paints dry slowly, an advantage to artists, who adjust their compositions as they work. When the painting is done, a protective layer of varnish is often applied. In the 19th century, oil paint in tubes simplified the painter's work. A rainbow of innovative, synthetic colors contributed to the emergence of new approaches to art and, in particular, modern abstract painting.

# I Know It When I See It

*What makes something "art"?*

✳    ✳    ✳    ✳

IF YOU WANT to see a name-calling, hair-pulling intellectual fight (and who doesn't?), just yell this question in a crowded coffee shop. After centuries of debate and goatee-stroking, it's still a hot-button issue.

Before the fourteenth century, the Western world grouped painting, sculpture, and architecture with decorative crafts such as pottery, weaving, and the like. During the Renaissance, Michelangelo and the gang elevated the artist to the level of the poet—a genius who was touched by divine inspiration. Now, with God as a collaborator, art had to be beautiful, which meant that artists had to recreate reality in a way that transcended earthly experience.

In the nineteenth and twentieth centuries, artists rejected these standards of beauty; they claimed that art didn't need to fit set requirements. This idea is now widely accepted, though people still disagree over what is and isn't art.

A common modern view is that art is anything that is created for its own aesthetic value—beautiful or not—rather than to serve some other function. So, according to this theory, defining art comes down to the creator's intention. If you build a chair to have something to sit on, the chair isn't a piece of art. But if you build an identical chair to express yourself, that chair *is* a piece of art.

Marcel Duchamp demonstrated this in 1917, when he turned a urinal upside down and called it "Fountain." He was only interested in the object's aesthetic value. And just as simply as that: art.

This may seem arbitrary, but to the creator, there is a difference. If you build something for a specific purpose, you measure success by how well your creation serves that function. If you make pure art, your accomplishment is exclusively determined by how the creation makes you feel. Artists say that they follow their hearts, their muses, or God, depending on their beliefs. A craftsperson also follows a creative spirit, but his or her desire for artistic fulfillment is secondary to the obligation to make something that is functional.

Many objects involve both kinds of creativity. For example, a big-budget filmmaker follows his or her muse but generally acquiesces to studio demands to try to make the movie profitable. (For instance, the movie might be trimmed to ninety minutes.) Unless the director has full creative control, the primary function of the film is to get people to buy tickets. There's nothing wrong with making money from your art, but purists say that financial concerns should never influence the true artist.

By a purist's definition, a book illustration isn't art, since its function is to support the text and please the client—even if the text is a work of art. The counter view is that the illustration *is* art, since the illustrator follows his or her creative instincts to create it; the illustrator is as much an artistic collaborator as the writer.

Obviously, it gets pretty murky. But until someone invents a handheld art detector, the question of what makes something art will continue to spark spirited arguments in coffee shops the world over.

# The Secret Origin of Comic Books

*Today's graphic novels have a long history that stretches back to newspaper comic strips.*

\* \* \* \*

IN THE 1920S and '30s, comic strips were among the most popular sections of newspapers and were often reprinted later in book form. Generally, these were inexpensive publications that looked like newspaper supplements, though other formats were tried (including "big little books" in which the comic panels were adapted and text was added opposite each panel).

These so-called "funny books" were often given away as premiums for products such as cereal, shoes, and even gasoline. Then, in 1933, a sales manager at the Eastern Color Printing Company in Waterbury, Connecticut, hit on a winning format: 36 pages of color comics in a size similar to modern comics. *Famous Funnies: A Carnival of Comics*, considered the first true comic book, featured reprinted strips with such cartoon characters as Mutt and Jeff. It was still a giveaway, but it was a hit.

The next year, Eastern Color published *Famous Funnies #1* and distributed the 68-page comic book to newsstands nationwide with a cover price of 10 cents.

As the demand for reprinted strips outpaced supply, publishers began introducing original material into comic books. One publisher, searching for features to fill the pages of a new book, approached a young creative team made up of writer Jerry Siegel and artist Joe Shuster, who had been trying for years to sell a newspaper strip about an invincible hero from another planet. Siegel and Shuster reformatted the strips into comic book form, and Superman debuted in *Action Comics #1*. It was an instant smash hit. The "Golden Age" of comics followed, introducing many of the popular heroes who are still with us today, including Batman, Wonder Woman, Captain America, and The Flash. In the 1960s, the "Silver Age" introduced new, more emotionally flawed heroes such as Spider-Man, Iron Man, and the Hulk. The comic book has certainly come a long way since Mutt and Jeff.

# Salvador Dalí and Harpo Marx: A Match Made in Surrealist Heaven

*The great 20th-century surrealist artist Salvadore Dalí knew how to put a brush to canvas, but after making fast friends with Harpo Marx of the Marx Brothers, Dalí was inspired to try his hand at writing comedy. Thus was born a surrealist comedy script that was deemed unmarketable—even by Hollywood standards.*

❋   ❋   ❋   ❋

## Dalí the Filmmaker

SALVADOR DALÍ WAS never one to paint a dull picture. From melting watches to roses that float in the middle of the desert, Dalí painted the world as he imagined it, not as it was. And Dalí did not limit this dreamlike vision to painting—he designed clothing, furniture, and stage settings in Broadway productions. In effect, Dalí transferred his unique vision to whatever media would hold it. "Painting is an infinitely minute part of my personality," he said.

From a young age, Dalí had a particular interest in the surrealist potential of film. He grew up watching silent film comedic greats such as Charlie Chaplin and Buster Keaton. Slapstick comedic acts often had a distinct surrealist slant—after all, how many pie fights can a person encounter in a day? Dalí saw the potential inherent in cinema's ability to place one image right on top of another in time, thus allowing for the juxtaposition of bizarrely disconnected images, such as, say, a slashed human eye followed by a pink teddy bear. Dalí once described the epitome of film as "a succession of wonders."

At age 25, Dalí set to work making his imagined succession of wonders a sur-reality. He paired with friend and famed surrealist filmmaker Luis Bunuel to make a short film called *Un Chien Andalous* (1929), which is now considered a groundbreaking first in avant-garde cinema. His film career may have begun with this bang, but *Un Chien Andalous* and *L' Âge d'or*, (1930) proved to be the only Dalí films to make it into production. In 1946, he collaborated with Walt Disney on a short six-minute animated film, *Destino*, that was abandoned as too strange and unmarketable. Eventually, *Destino* was released in 2003 after Dalí's death. He also made a short dream sequence for Hitchcock's *Spellbound*, but for the most part Dalí's film projects were nipped in the bud.

## Dalí the Comedian

The inspiration behind Dalí's wackiest unmade film script was his friendship with Harpo, the Marx brother who consistently hid crazy gags up his sleeve. Harpo's very persona was surreal: His character refused to speak, instead relying on the art of pantomime, whistles, and props to communicate. He wore outrageous outfits topped by his wild mat of curly clown hair and was a self-taught virtuoso harpist.

Dalí was enthralled with Harpo. After the two met in Paris in the summer of 1936, they strummed up an appropriately peculiar friendship. Dalí sent Harpo a gift: A gilded harp with barbed-wire strings and teaspoon tuning knobs. Delighted, Harpo returned the favor by sending Dalí a photograph of himself playing the harp with cut-up, bandaged fingers.

The following year, Dalí traveled to California to see Harpo. As he noted in a postcard, "I'm in Hollywood, where I've made contact with the three American Surrealists: Harpo Marx, Disney, and Cecil B. DeMille." According to the always-dramatic Dali, upon arrival, he found Harpo lying "naked, crowned with roses, and in the center of a veritable forest of harps." During their vacation, Dalí drew sketches of Harpo at his harp, grinning with a lobster on his head. The two also began collaboration on a surrealistic film called *Giraffes on Horseback Salad*. The film followed the misadventures of a Spanish businessman who comes to America and falls in love with a woman, to be played by Dalí's wife, Gala. The script also calls for burning giraffes wearing gas masks and Harpo catching Little People with a butterfly net. The film was never realized as MGM, the Marx Brothers's studio, refused to make it. The script does, however, still exist in a private collection—perhaps someday Dalí and Harpo's inimitable dream will come to fruition.

# Who Invented the Printing Press?

*Sure, Johannes Gutenberg's development of the printing press in 15th-century Germany led to mass-market publishing. But innovations in printing technology were around long before Gutenberg revolutionized the industry.*

✳ ✳ ✳ ✳

## The Stamp of Uniformity

ALTHOUGH PRINTING IS usually associated with reading materials, the original impetus behind printing technology was the need to create identical copies of the same thing.

Printing actually began with coining, when centralized states branded their coins with uniform numbers and symbols. In those days, written manuscripts were copied the old-fashioned way, letter by letter, by hand. Only the upper echelons of society were literate, books were costly, and the laborious and artistic method of copying matched the rarity of books.

The first major innovation in printing came with the Chinese invention of block printing by the eighth century AD. Block printing involved carving letters or images into a surface, inking that surface, and pressing it on to paper, parchment, or cloth. The method was used for a variety of purposes, from decorating clothes to copying religious scrolls. The blocks were usually made of wood, which posed a problem as the wood eventually decayed or cracked. Oftentimes entire pages of a manuscript, complete with illustrations, were carved into a single block that could be used again and again.

The Chinese also invented movable type, which would prove to be the prerequisite to efficient printing presses. Movable type is faster than block printing because individual characters are created by being cast into molds. Once this grab bag of individual characters is made, they can then be reused and rearranged in infinite combinations by changing the typeset. Movable type characters are also more uniform than the carved letters of block printing. Pi-Sheng invented this method in 1045 using clay molds. The method spread to Korea and Japan, and metal movable type was created in Korea by 1230.

## Supply and Demand

The Chinese didn't use movable type extensively because their language consists of thousands of characters, and movable type makes printing efficient only in a language with fewer letters. Meanwhile, Europeans used the imported concept of block printing to make popular objects like playing cards or illustrated children's books. During the Middle Ages, serious secular scholarship had all but disappeared in Europe, and the reproduction of new and classical texts was mostly confined to the Asian and Arab worlds. That is, until literacy began to spread among the middle classes, and lay people, especially in Germany, showed an interest in reading religious texts for themselves. Thus, German entrepreneur Johannes Gutenberg, the son of a coin minter, began to experiment with metal movable type pieces. It's believed Gutenberg was unfamiliar with the previously invented Chinese method, but at any rate, several other Europeans were experimenting with similar methods at the same time as Gutenberg.

By the 1440s, Gutenberg had set up a printing shop, and in 1450, he set out to produce a Bible. Gutenberg perfected several printing methods, such as right justification, and preferred alloys in the production of metal types. By 1455, Gutenberg's press had produced 200 copies of his Bible—quite the feat at the time, considering one Bible could take years to copy by hand. These Bibles were sold for less than hand-copied ones yet were still expensive enough for profit margins equivalent to modern-day millions.

Presses soon popped up all across Europe. By 1499, an estimated 15 million books had been produced by at least 1,000 printing presses, mostly in Germany and then throughout Italy. For the first time ever, ideas were not only dreamed up and written down—they were efficiently reproduced and spread over long distances. The proliferation of these first German printing presses is commonly credited with the end of the Middle Ages and the dawn of the Renaissance.

# Worth a Fortune: Very Rare U.S. Coins

*Why are certain coins so valuable? Some simply have very low mintages, and some are error coins. In some cases (with gold, in particular), most of the pieces were confiscated and melted. Better condition always adds value.*

✳  ✳  ✳  ✳

THE CURRENT MINTS and marks are Philadelphia (P, or no mark), Denver (D), and San Francisco (S). Mints in Carson City, Nevada (CC); Dahlonega, Georgia (D); and New Orleans (O) shut down long ago, which adds appeal to their surviving coinage. Here are the most prized and/or interesting U.S. coins, along with an idea of what they're worth:

**1787 Brasher gold doubloon:** It was privately minted by goldsmith Ephraim Brasher before the U.S. Mint's founding in 1793. The coin was slightly lighter than a $5 gold piece, and at one point in the 1970s it was the most expensive U.S. coin ever sold. Seven known; last sold for $625,000.

**1792 half-disme (5¢ piece):** Disme was the old terminology for "dime," so half a disme was five cents. George Washington supposedly provided the silver for this mintage. Was Martha the model for Liberty's image? If so, her hairdo suggests she'd been helping Ben Franklin with electricity experiments. Perhaps 1,500 minted; sells for up to $1.3 million.

**1804 silver dollar:** Though actually minted in 1834 and later, the official mint delivery figure of 19,570 refers to the 1804 issue. Watch out—counterfeits abound. Only 15 known; worth up to $4.1 million.

**1849 Coronet $20 gold piece:** How do you assess a unique coin's value? The Smithsonian owns the only authenticated example, the very first gold "double eagle." Why mint only one?

It was a trial strike of the new series. Rumors persist of a second trial strike that ended up in private hands; if true, it hasn't surfaced in more than 150 years. Never sold; literally priceless.

**1870-S $3 gold piece:** Apparently, only one (currently in private hands) was struck, though there are tales of a second one placed in the cornerstone of the then-new San Francisco Mint building (now being renovated as a museum). If the building is ever demolished, don't expect to see it imploded. One known; estimated at $1.2 million.

**1876-CC 20-cent piece:** Remember when everyone confused the new Susan B. Anthony dollars with quarters? That's what comes of ignoring history. A century before, this 20-cent coin's resemblance to the quarter caused similar frustration. Some 18 known; up to $175,000.

**1894-S Barber dime:** The Barber designs tended to wear quickly, so any Barber coin in great condition is scarce enough. According to his daughter Hallie, San Francisco Mint director John Daggett struck two dozen 1894-S coins, mostly as gifts for his rich banker pals. Dad gave little Hallie three of the dimes, and she used one to buy herself the costliest ice cream in history. Twenty-four minted, ten known; as high as $1.3 million.

**1907 MCMVII St. Gaudens $20 gold piece:** This is often considered the loveliest U.S. coin series ever. Its debut featured the year in Roman numerals, unique in U.S. coinage. The first, ultra-high-relief version was stunning in its clarity and beauty, but it proved too time-consuming to mint, so a less striking (but still impressive) version became the standard. About 11,000 minted, but very few in ultra-high relief; those have sold for $1.5 million.

**1909-S VDB Lincoln cent:** It's a collectors' favorite, though not vanishingly rare. Only about a fourth of Lincoln pennies from the series' kickoff year featured designer Victor D. Brenner's initials on the reverse; even now, an occasional "SVDB" will show up in change. There were 484,000 minted; worth up to $7,500.

**1913 Liberty Head nickel:** This coin wasn't supposed to be minted. The Mint manufactured the dies as a contingency before the Buffalo design was selected for 1913. Apparently, Mint employee Samuel W. Brown may have known that the Liberty dies were slated for destruction and therefore minted five of these for his personal gain. One of the most prized U.S. coins—and priced accordingly at $1.8 million.

**1913-S Barber quarter:** Forty thousand of these were made—the lowest regular-issue mintage of the 20th century. Some Barbers wore so flat that the head on the obverse was reduced to a simple outline. Quite rare in good condition; can bring up to $24,000.

**1915 Panama-Pacific $50 gold piece:** This large commemorative piece was offered in both octagonal and round designs. Approximately 1,100 were minted; prices range from $40,000 to $155,000.

**1916 Liberty Standing quarter:** This coin depicts a wardrobe malfunction... except by design! Many were shocked when the new coin displayed Lady Liberty's bared breast. By mid-1917, she was donning chain mail. Like the Barber quarter before it, the Liberty Standing wore out rapidly. With only 52,000 minted in 1916, the series' inaugural year, a nice specimen will set you back nearly $40,000.

**1933 St. Gaudens $20 gold piece:** This coin is an outlaw. All of the Saint's final mintage were to be melted down—and most were. Only one specific example is legal to own; other surviving 1933 Saints remain hidden from the threat of Treasury confiscation. The legal one sold in 2002 for an incredible $7.6 million.

**1937-D "three-legged" Buffalo nickel:** A new employee at the Denver Mint tried polishing some damage off a die with an emery stick. He accidentally ground the bison's foreleg off, leaving a disembodied hoof. No telling exactly how many were struck, but they sure look funny. Up to $30,000.

# Bird on a Wire

*Few names call to mind a love of birds more than that of John Audubon, but any bird with a brain would have done well to steer clear of him!*

✳  ✳  ✳  ✳

THERE IS NO doubt that 19th-century wildlife illustrator John James Audubon cared about his feathered friends. He devoted his life to their study, observing and drawing them from the time he was a child. However, Audubon's shotgun was as important a tool as his paintbrush. He may have loved birds, but he had no qualms about killing them.

In the era before photography, most wildlife illustrators used stuffed carcasses as their models. That's how Audubon, a self-taught artist, began drawing birds. Frustrated by the lack of vibrancy in his illustrations, he set out to find new ways to draw the birds he had shot. His goal was to "represent nature . . . alive and moving!" It was at this time that he began piercing freshly killed birds, securing them to boards and using wires to pose them into "lifelike" positions. Eventually, Audubon mastered the technique of manipulating fresh carcasses like puppets and was able to draw birds as they had never been rendered before. His paintings showed animals in lifelike situations—nesting, hunting, and even feeding one another.

# Chapter 2

# A Question of Identity

## Controversial Queen

*In establishing the identity of the Egyptian queen Nefertiti, scholars find themselves up to their necks in conflicting info.*

✳ ✳ ✳ ✳

LIKE CLEOPATRA, NEFERTITI is one of the most famous queens of ancient Egypt. She's also often referred to as "The Most Beautiful Woman in the World," largely due to the 1912 discovery of a painted limestone bust of Nefertiti depicting her stunning features: smooth skin, full lips, and a graceful swanlike neck—quite the looker! Now housed in Berlin's Altes Museum, the likeness has become a widely recognized symbol of ancient Egypt and one of the most important artistic works of the pre-modern world. But the bust, like almost everything about the famous queen, is steeped in controversy.

### Conflicting Accounts

It wasn't until the bust surfaced in the early 20th century that scholars began sorting out information about Nefertiti's life. Her name means "the beautiful one is come," and some think she was a foreign princess, not of Egyptian blood. Others believe she was born into Egyptian royalty, that she was the niece or daughter of a high government official named Ay, who later became pharaoh. But basically, no one knows her origins for sure.

When the beautiful one was age 15, she married Amenhotep IV, who later became king of Egypt. Nefertiti was thus promoted to queen. No one really knows when this happened—other than that it was in the 18th Dynasty—but it's safe to say that it was a really long time ago (as in, the 1340s BC). Nefertiti appears in many reliefs of the period, often accompanying her husband in various ceremonies—a testament to her political power.

An indisputable fact about both Nefertiti and Amenhotep IV is that they were responsible for bringing monotheism to ancient Egypt. Rather than worship the vast pantheon of Egyptian gods—including the supreme god, Amen-Ra—the couple devoted themselves to exclusively worshipping the sun god Aten. In fact, as a sign of this commitment, Amenhotep IV changed his named to Akhenaten. Similarly, Nefertiti changed her name to Neferneferuaten-Nefertiti, meaning, "The Aten is radiant of radiance [because] the beautiful one is come." (But we're guessing everyone just called her "Nef.") Again, it's unclear as to why the powerful couple decided to turn from polytheism. Maybe there were political reasons. Or perhaps the two simply liked the idea of one universal god.

## Disappearance/Death?

In studying Egyptian history, scholars discovered that around 14 years into Akhenaten's reign, Nefertiti seems to disappear. There are no more images of her, no historical records. Perhaps there was a conflict in the royal family, and she was banished from the kingdom. Maybe she died in the plague that killed half of Egypt. A more interesting speculation is that she disguised herself as a man, changed her named to Smenkhkare, and went on to rule Egypt alongside her husband. But—all together now—*no one knows for sure!*

During a June 2003 expedition in Egypt's Valley of the Kings, an English archeologist named Joann Fletcher unearthed a mummy that she suspected to be Nefertiti. But despite the fact that the mummy probably is a member of the royal family from the 18th Dynasty, it was not proven to be female. Many Egyptologists think there is not sufficient evidence to prove that Fletcher's mummy is Nefertiti. So, that theory was something of a bust.

In 2009, Swiss art historian Henri Sierlin published a book suggesting that the bust is a copy. He claimed that the sculpture was made by an artist named Gerard Marks on the request of Ludwig Borchardt, the German archeologist responsible for discovering the bust in 1912. Despite the mysteries surrounding Nefertiti, there's no question that she was revered in her time. At the temples of Karnak are inscribed the words: "Heiress, Great of Favours, Possessed of Charm, Exuding Happiness . . . Great King's Wife, Whom He Loves, Lady of Two Lands, Nefertiti."

# Crockefeller

*What began as a search to find a missing girl uncovered 30 years of fraud, fake identities, and possible foul play. Before Christian Karl Gerhartsreiter was a convict, he was a con artist.*

✳   ✳   ✳   ✳

IT STARTED AS a case of parental kidnapping not uncommon in custody battles: In July 2008, Clark Rockefeller, a descendant of the moneyed oil family, absconded with his seven-year-old daughter during a court-supervised visitation in Boston.

But oddly, FBI databases showed no record of a Clark Rockefeller, and the Rockefeller family denied any connection. His ex-wife, millionaire consultant Sandra Boss, confessed he had no identification, no social security number, and no driver's license. *So who was this guy?* The FBI released his picture, hoping for information. And that's when the stories—and aliases—began pouring in.

## Fake Foreign Exchange

His real identity is Christian Karl Gerhartstreiter, a German national who came to the United States in 1978 at age 17, claiming to be a foreign exchange student. In truth, he showed up unannounced on the doorstep of a Connecticut family he'd met on a train in Europe, who'd suggested he look them up if he ever visited the States.

After living with them briefly, he posted an ad describing himself as an exchange student in search of a host and was taken in by the Stavio family. They threw him out after it became clear he expected to be treated like royalty. During this time, Gerhartstreiter allegedly became enamored with the *Gilligan's Island* character Thurston Howell III, the ascot-wearing millionaire, and even adopted Howell's snobbish accent.

## Bogus Brit

In 1980, "Chris Gerhart" enrolled at the University of Wisconsin-Milwaukee as a film major and persuaded another student to marry him so that he could get his green card. Shortly after the wedding, he left school and headed to Los Angeles to pursue a film career—this time posing as the dapper British blue-blood Christopher Chichester (a name he borrowed from his former high school teacher).

He settled in the swanky town of San Marino, living in a building with newlyweds John and Linda Sohus. The couple went missing in 1985, around the same time Chichester moved away; allegedly, he went back to England following a death in the family.

Chichester resurfaced in Greenwich, Connecticut, as former Hollywood producer and business tycoon Christopher Crowe. It was under this name that, in 1988, he tried to sell a truck that had belonged to the Sohuses. Police investigators traced the Sohus's missing truck to Connecticut, and they soon realized that Crowe and Chichester were the same person. But by then, he'd already vanished.

## Mock Rock

Now he was Manhattan's Clark Rockefeller, the new darling of the elite. It was here that he met and married the Ivy League-educated business whiz Sandra Boss. For most of their 12-year marriage, Sandra believed his elaborate stories. She even believed he'd filed the paperwork for their marriage to be legal (it appears he hadn't).

Eventually, however, Sandra grew suspicious. She filed for divorce and won full custody of their seven-year-old daughter, Reigh, and the two moved to London. Clark was limited to three court-supervised visits per year. It was on the first of these visits that he kidnapped her.

## Conclusion

In August 2008, the con man was arrested in Baltimore, and Reigh was returned to her mother. In June 2009, a judge sentenced him to four to five years in prison.

Gerhartsreiter says he has no recollection of his life before the 1990s. And he insists on being called Mr. Rockefeller because that's his name, thank you very much.

# "Fifteen Women on a Dead Woman's Chest..."

*If Calico Jack had heard the famous pirate song sung this way, would he have declared it blasphemous? Don't bet your booty.*

✳ ✳ ✳ ✳

## Women of the Sea

THROUGHOUT HISTORY, WOMEN have received more than their share of omissions, and this certainly was the case during the Golden Age of Piracy. Although it's true that men were the predominant players in this high-seas melodrama, women had important roles. Most people have heard of Captain Kidd, Blackbeard, and Calico Jack, but those same people might scratch their heads while trying to recall Anne Bonny, Lady Mary Killigrew, and Mary Read.

Despite their relative anonymity, female swashbucklers were as much a part of the pirate experience as garish costumes and hand-held telescopes. In fact, the story of female pirates is at least as captivating as buried treasures or mutinous uprisings.

Female pirates date back at least as far as the fifth century, but the most notable figures appeared long after that. Mary Killigrew, a lady under Queen Elizabeth I, operated in the late 16th century. In her most celebrated outing, Killigrew and her shipmates boarded a German vessel off of Falmouth, Cornwall. Once on deck, they killed the crew and stole their cargo. When later brought to trial for the murders, Killigrew was sentenced to death. With some well-placed bribes and a queen sympathetic to her plight, however, she was eventually acquitted. Her bold tale is said to have inspired female pirates yet to come.

## The Story of Mary and Anne

The exploits of pirates Mary Read and Anne Bonny rank among those of their male counterparts. Read was born in London in the late 17th century and spent her entire childhood disguised as a boy. The reasons for her unusual dress are lost to time, but Read's thirst for adventure has never been in question.

Working as a "footboy" for a wealthy French woman, "Mark" Read eventually grew tired of such drudgery and signed on for sea duty aboard a man-o'-war. From there, the cross-dressed woman joined the Flemish army, where she served two stints. Eventually, Read booked passage on a ship bound for the West Indies. While on this fateful journey, her vessel was attacked and captured by none other than Captain (Calico) Jack Rackham.

A dashing figure in her male persona, Read drew the amorous gaze of Bonny, who was Calico Jack's mistress and a pirate in her own right. Upon the discovery of Read's gender, the two became friends, and they struck a deal to continue the ruse. The game wouldn't last long. A jealous Calico Jack confronted the pair, and he too learned the truth. Finding appeal in the prospect of having two female pirates on his crew, the captain let things stand.

Adventure-loving Read took well to her life of piracy and soon fell in love with a young sailor. This upset a veteran crewmate, who challenged the would-be Lothario to a duel. Fearful that her man would be killed by the strapping seaman, Read demanded her own showdown. She was granted her wish. After the combatants discharged their pistols, both stood unscathed. When they reached for their swords, Read cunningly ripped her shirt open and exposed her breasts. The stunned seaman hesitated, and Read, in classic pirate fashion, swung her cutlass. It found its mark.

## Courageous Buccaneers

Read's victory would be short lived. Charged with piracy after their ship was seized by Jamaican authorities in 1720, Read, Bonny, and Calico Jack were tried and sentenced to hang. When asked in court why a woman might wish to become a pirate and face such a sentence, Read cockily replied, "As to hanging, it is no great hardship, for were it not for that, every cowardly fellow would turn pirate and so unfit the seas, that men of courage must starve." Read could easily have added "women of courage" to her answer. She and other female pirates had pillaged at least that much.

# Male Impersonators

*A young girl nowadays has a lot more freedom to choose what she wants to be when she grows up. This hasn't always been the case, but the women on this list didn't let that stop them: These fearless females did what they wanted to do, even if that meant masquerading as men for most of their lives.*

✳ ✳ ✳ ✳

## Charley Parkhurst

TIMES WERE ROUGH for ladies in the Wild West, so this cracker-jack stagecoach driver decided to live most of her life as a man. Born in 1812, Parkhurst lived well into her sixties, though how she managed to do it is the stuff of miracles. She is remembered to have been a hard-drinking, tobacco-chewing, one-eyed brute with a taste for adventure. Parkhurst gave birth at one point, but the child died. She lived out the rest of her life pursuing her stagecoach career until she died in December 1879. It was then that her true identity was revealed, much to the surprise of her friends.

## Dr. James Barry

The life of James Barry, M.D., is proof positive that truth is often stranger than fiction. A vegetarian, teetotaler, and gifted doctor with skills ahead of his time (he performed one of the first successful cesarean sections while serving as a military surgeon), Dr. Barry was also quite possibly a female. If you lived in 19th-century Britain and happened to be a girl, you could kiss your dreams of being a surgeon goodbye. Barry, whose real name may have been Miranda, allegedly assumed a male identity to become an army physician. Barry's voice was high and he reportedly challenged those who made fun of it to a duel on the spot. When Barry died in 1865, the woman who was preparing the body for burial was said to be the first to discover his secret.

## Billy Tipton

Born in Oklahoma in 1914, Dorothy Lucille Tipton was a gifted musician from the start. Her love of the saxophone and the piano was bittersweet, as the school she was attending wouldn't let girls play in the band. After escaping high school, Tipton decided to do whatever it took to pursue her passion. She started going by "Billy," wore suits, and bound her chest with tape to create the illusion that she was one of the guys. It worked, and Tipton's musical career was on its way. Tipton performed with some of the era's jazz greats and even recorded an album with The Billy Tipton Trio. Tipton married a woman, adopted three sons, and was reportedly a good father. Tipton died in 1989, and it was then that Tipton's sons learned of their father's true identity.

## Pope Joan

Long held as a hero for feminists and anti-Catholics alike, Pope Joan's story is a debatable one. Even if the story is purely fictional, it's a good one nonetheless. "John Anglicus" was an Englishman in the ninth century who traveled to Rome where his fame as a lecturer led to his becoming a cardinal in the church. According to the story, when Pope Leo IV died in AD 855, Anglicus was unanimously elected Pope. Legend has it that during a citywide processional, the Pope stopped by the side of the road complaining of a stomachache and suddenly gave birth to a child. The jig was up: Pope John was actually a woman. Was it true? The Catholic Church denies that any "John Anglicus" was ever pope—according to their documents, Benedict III succeeded Leo IV.

## John Taylor

Mary Anne Talbot was a troublemaker, but she was also a brave soldier, a hard worker, and a true talent in the art of male impersonation. Born in Britain in 1778, Talbot was orphaned when her mother died during childbirth. She was the mistress of a naval officer and accompanied him on trips across the Atlantic by posing as his footboy. When the naval officer died in battle in 1793, she had no choice but to continue posing as a man—John Taylor. She was wounded in the leg in 1794 and suffered from complications from the injury for the rest of her life. During her life, Talbot was a prisoner of war in France, an officer aboard an American merchant vessel, a highway worker, a London pensioner, a jewelry maker, an actor, and a nurse.

## William Cathay

Born in Missouri in the midst of slavery, Cathay Williams served as a house slave until Union soldiers freed her during the Civil War. The soldiers employed her after that, and she worked for them for a while before wanting to see more action firsthand. Since women weren't allowed in the army, Williams dressed as a man in order to enlist. Of the approximately 5,000 black infantrymen and cavalry who served in the frontier army, "William Cathay" was the only woman to serve as a Buffalo Soldier (the nickname given to members of the U.S. 10th Cavalry Regiment of the U.S. Army, which now often refers to soldiers in any of the six black regiments that served in the war). Williams was examined by an army surgeon who discovered her true identity. She was discharged and retired to New Mexico where she passed away at age 82.

## Joan of Arc

Born in France in 1412, 17-year-old Jeanne d'Arc disguised herself as a page when journeying through enemy territory so as to go unnoticed by soldiers. Before she was burned at the stake for being a heretic, Joan allegedly claimed that she was "doing a man's work" and therefore had to dress the part. The Catholic Church finally took back all the nasty things it said about Joan and recognized her as a saint in 1920.

# The Real "Man Who Never Was"

*When a drowned corpse washed ashore in Spain holding a briefcase of plans to invade Sardinia and Greece, the Nazis thought they'd made an astounding catch. They couldn't have been more wrong.*

✻ ✻ ✻ ✻

THE ROUGH TIDES rolled up against the southern Spanish coast in the spring of 1943, carrying the dishevelled corpse of a British major who appeared to have drowned after his plane crashed somewhere offshore. The body, one of thousands of military men who had met their end in the Mediterranean waters, floated atop a rubber life jacket as the current pulled it slowly toward Huelva, Spain. With a war raging in Tunisia just across the sea, a drifting military corpse was not such an unusual event.

But this body was different, and it drew the immediate attention of Spanish authorities sympathetic to German and Italian Fascists. Chained to the corpse was a briefcase filled with dispatches from London to Allied Headquarters in North Africa concerning the upcoming Allied invasions of Sardinia and western Greece. The information was passed on to the Nazis, who accepted their apparent stroke of good luck, and now anticipated an Allied strike on the "soft underbelly of Europe."

Unfortunately for them, the whole affair was a risky, carefully contrived hoax.

## Rigging the "Trojan Horse"

Operation Mincemeat was conceived by British intelligence agents as a deception to convince the Italians and Germans that the target of the next Allied landings would be somewhere other than Sicily, the true target. To throw the Fascists off the trail, British planners decided to find a suitable corpse—a middle-aged white male—put the corpse in the uniform of a military courier, and float the corpse and documents off the coast of Huelva, Spain, where a local Nazi agent was known to be on good terms with local police.

The idea of planting forged documents on a dead body was not new to the Allies. In August 1942, British agents planted a corpse clutching a fake map of minefields in a blown-up scout car. The map was picked up by German troops and made its way to Rommel's headquarters. He obligingly routed his panzers away from the "minefield" and into a region of soft sand, where they quickly bogged down.

This deception, however, would be much grander. If the planted documents made their way up the intelligence chain, Hitler and Mussolini would be expecting an invasion far from the Sicilian coast that Generals Eisenhower, Patton, and Montgomery had targeted for invasion in July 1943.

## The Making of a Major

Operation Mincemeat, spearheaded by Lieutenant Commander Ewen Montagu, a British naval intelligence officer, and Charles Cholmondeley of Britain's MI5 intelligence service, found its "host" in early 1943 when a single Welshman living in London committed suicide by taking rat poison. The substance produced a chemical pneumonia that could be mistaken for drowning.

The two operatives gave the deceased man a new, documented identity: "Major William Martin" of the Royal Marines. They literally kept the "major" on ice while arrangements for his new mission were made. To keep Spanish authorities from conducting an autopsy—which would give away the body's protracted post-mortem condition—the agents decided to make "Major Martin" a Roman Catholic, giving him a silver cross and a St. Christopher medallion.

They dressed the body, complete with Royal Marine uniform and trench coat, and gave him identity documents and personal letters (including a swimsuit photo of his "fiancée," an intelligence bureau secretary). With a chain used by bank couriers, they fixed the briefcase to his body.

Martin's documents were carefully prepared to show Allied invasions being planned for Sardinia and Greece (the latter bearing the code name Operation Husky). They also indicated that an Allied deception plan would try to convince Hitler that the invasion would take place in Sicily (the site of the real Operation Husky). With everything in order, the agents carefully placed the corpse into a sealed container—dry ice kept the body "fresh" for the ride out to sea.

The submarine HMS *Seraph* carried "Major Martin" on his final journey. On April 28, the *Seraph* left for the Andalusian coast, and two days later the body of a Royal Marine officer washed ashore. Within days, photographs of the major's documents were on their way to Abwehr intelligence agents in Berlin.

## Taking the Bait

Abwehr, Hitler, and the German High Command swallowed the story. After the war, British intelligence determined that Martin's documents had been opened and resealed before being returned by the Spanish. The German General Staff, believing the papers to be genuine, had alerted units in the Mediterranean to be ready for an invasion of Sardinia and Greece. They moved one panzer division and air and naval assets off the Peloponnese, and disputed Italian fears of an impending invasion of Sicily.

The Allies captured Sicily in July and August 1943, and after the war, Commander Montagu wrote a bestselling account of Operation Mincemeat titled, *The Man Who Never Was*. The book was made into a film thriller a few years later.

Who was Major William Martin? The original body appears to have been a 34-year-old depressed Welsh alcoholic named

Glyndwr Michael, and "Major Martin's" tombstone in Spain bears Michael's name. Historians have debated the identity of "Major Martin," however, theorizing that a "fresher" corpse from a sunken aircraft carrier was substituted closer to the launch date.

Whoever the real "Major Martin" may have been, one thing is certain: He saved thousands of lives, and became a war hero and action movie star in the process—quite an accomplishment for a dead man!

# A Gay Time in the Oval Office?

*Before he became U.S. president, the unmarried James Buchanan enjoyed a long, close association with his housemate, William R. King—so close that unconfirmed speculation about the pair still swirls after more than 150 years. Was Buchanan—the nation's only bachelor chief executive—also its first homosexual president?*

✳    ✳    ✳    ✳

THE YEAR 1834 WAS a momentous one for 42-year-old politician James Buchanan. Already a veteran political leader and diplomat, Buchanan managed to win a seat in the U.S. Senate and formed a friendship with the man who would be his dearest companion for the next two decades.

Buchanan and his chum, William Rufus de Vane King, a U.S. senator from Alabama, became virtually inseparable. They shared domestic quarters in Washington, D.C., for over 15 years—though it should be said that having a roommate was not uncommon at the time. Capitol wits referred to the partners—who attended social events together—as "the Siamese twins."

Buchanan's bond with Senator King was so close that the future president described it as a "communion." In praising his friend as "among the best, purest, and most consistent public men I have ever known," Buchanan also added that King was a "very gay, elegant-looking fellow." The adjective "gay," however, didn't mean "homosexual" back in those days. It commonly meant "merry."

It's also useful to understand that it was not unusual for educated men to wax rhapsodic about other men during the 19th century. Admiring rather than sexual, this sort of language signified shared values and deep respect.

Historians rightly point out a lack of evidence that either of the bachelors found men sexually attractive. They note that when Buchanan was younger, he asked a Pennsylvania heiress to marry him. (She broke off the engagement.) Later, he was known to flirt with fashionable women.

## Buchanan's "Wife"

Whatever the nature of his relationship with Buchanan, King seemed to consider it something more than casual. After the Alabaman became U.S. minister to France in 1844, he wrote home from Paris, expressing his worry that Buchanan would "procure an associate who will cause you to feel no regret at our separation."

Buchanan did not find such a replacement, but it was apparently not for want of trying. He wrote to another friend of his attempts to ease the loneliness caused by King's absence: "I have gone a wooing to several gentlemen, but have not succeeded with any one of them."

Sometimes the pair drew derisive jibes from their peers. The jokes often targeted King, a bit of a dandy with a fondness for silk scarves. In a private letter, Tennessee Congressman Aaron V. Brown used the pronoun "she" to refer to the senator, and called him Buchanan's "wife." President Andrew Jackson mocked King as "Miss Nancy" and "Aunt Fancy."

## High-Flying Careers Derailed

Despite the childish jokes, both Buchanan and King advanced to ever-more-important federal posts. President James K. Polk selected Buchanan as his secretary of state in 1845. King won the office of U.S. vice president (running on a ticket with Franklin Pierce) in 1852. Voters elected Buchanan to the White House four years later.

Unfortunately, neither of the friends distinguished himself in the highest office he reached. King fell ill and died less than a month after taking the oath as vice president.

Erupting conflicts over slavery and states' rights marred Buchanan's single term in the Oval Office. Historians give him failing marks for his lack of leadership as the Civil War loomed. The pro-slavery chief executive (he was a Pennsylvania Democrat) opposed secession of the Southern states but argued that the federal government had no authority to use force to stop it. As a result, Buchanan made no effort to save the Union, leaving that task to his successor, Abraham Lincoln.

## What's Sex Got to Do with It?

Would Buchanan have risen to the highest office in the land if his peers honestly believed he was homosexual? It's hard to say. Today's perception is that 19th-century Americans were more homophobic than their 21st-century descendants. Yet in an era when sexuality stayed tucked beneath Victorian wraps, there was a de facto "don't ask, don't tell" policy for virtually any profession. Whatever their private proclivities, Buchanan and King clearly excelled in their public lives—at least until Buchanan got into the White House. Based on what little evidence history provides, neither man's sexual orientation had much, if any, bearing on what he accomplished, or failed to accomplish, in his career.

# Edward Hyde: Cross-dresser or Double-crossed?

*Edward Hyde, Viscount Cornbury, Third Earl of Clarendon, was governor of New York and New Jersey from 1701 to 1708, yet his legacy is one that politicians wouldn't want to touch with a ten-foot pole. Aside from doing a generally terrible job, rumors of Hyde's cross-dressing ways landed him a sullied spot in the annals of political history.*

✳ ✳ ✳ ✳

## Here, Have a Job!

AS THE STORY goes, being of noble English lineage, Edward Hyde was able to buy an officer's commission in the British army. While in that position, he helped overthrow his commander (and uncle), King James II. The king who replaced James was William III, who was quite pleased with Hyde's assistance in getting him the throne, so in 1701, William made Hyde governor of New York as a way of saying thanks. Later, William's successor (and Hyde's first cousin), Queen Anne, also threw in the governorship of New Jersey for Hyde. Suddenly, a woefully underqualified guy from England was in charge of two of the most prominent colonies in the New World.

## Corruption, Colonial Style

When Hyde arrived in New York in 1703 to assume his new post, he didn't make a very good impression with the struggling, toiling colonists. His luxurious house was filled with sumptuous linens, curtains, silverware, furniture, and art. To make matters worse, he soon found it necessary to divert public defense funds toward his new country house on what was then christened "Governor's Island."

It didn't take long for the bribery to start. At first, Hyde reportedly turned down a bribe from a New Jersey proprietor, but it appears he only passed because the bribe wasn't big enough.

The man, hoping to get preferential treatment of some kind, then upped the ante. Hyde accepted the bribe the second time around and did the businessman's bidding. Soon, a group of the governor's favorites controlled tax and rent collections across the area. The bribes were constant, and the governor sank deeper and deeper into corruption. He was described at one point as "a spendthrift, a grafter, a bigoted oppressor and a drunken vain fool."

By 1707, a desperate New Jersey assembly wrote to Queen Anne to take Hyde back to Britain. One assembly member, Lewis Morris, made a list of Hyde's crimes and added a juicy bit: He claimed the corrupt governor was actually fond of dressing up in women's clothing. That item of gossip didn't sit well with the queen, and Hyde lost his job. What isn't often mentioned is that Hyde, thrown into disgrace (and into debtor's prison) for some time, actually rallied later in life and held office in England where he was a respected diplomat of the Privy Council.

## Right This Way, Mrs. Hyde?

The question remains whether Hyde really was a cross-dresser or just the victim of salacious rumor drummed up by his enemies to help shove him out of power. One story tells of Hyde costumed as Queen Anne in order to show deference and respect—but could that really be true?

According to certain historians, there is no compelling evidence that Hyde was fond of wearing dresses. Only four contemporary letters contain any information pertaining to his cross-dressing, and they don't include eyewitness accounts. Experts maintain that if the governor of New York and New Jersey really did don full petticoats and silk taffeta, it would have been plastered across every newspaper in the Western Hemisphere—people in the 18th century loved a scandal as much as people do now.

Still, the rumors persisted for years and stories of his behavior grew—there is even a period portrait of a scruffy man in women's clothing that is said to be Hyde. Yet, art historians say there's no proof that the painting is of anyone other than an unfortunate-looking young woman.

# The Catcher Was a Spy

*When it comes to character assessments, you gotta listen to Casey Stengel. And the Ol' Perfessor claimed Moe Berg was "the strangest man ever to put on a baseball uniform." But Berg wasn't just strange in a baseball uniform, he was strange and mysterious in many ways—some of them deliberate.*

✳　✳　✳　✳

MOE BERG LIVED a life shrouded in mystery and marked by contradictions. He played alongside Babe Ruth, Lefty Grove, Jimmie Foxx, and Ted Williams; he moved in the company of Norman Rockefeller, Albert Einstein, and international diplomats; and yet he was often described as a loner. He was well-liked by teammates but preferred to travel by himself. He never married, and he made few close friends.

## "The Brainiest Guy in Baseball"

Moe was a bright kid from the beginning, with a special fondness for baseball. As the starting shortstop for Princeton University, where he majored in modern languages, Moe was a star. He was fond of communicating with his second baseman in Latin, leaving opposing base runners scratching their heads.

He broke into the majors in 1923 as a shortstop with the Brooklyn Robins (later the Dodgers). He converted to catcher and spent time with the White Sox, Senators, Indians, and Red Sox throughout his career. A slow runner and a poor fielder, Berg nevertheless eked out a 15-season big-league career. Pitchers loved him behind the plate. They praised his intelligence and loved his strong, accurate arm. And while he once went 117 games without an error, he rarely nudged his batting average much past .250. His weak bat often kept him on the bench and led journalists to note, "Moe Berg can speak 12 languages flawlessly and can hit in none." He was, however, a favorite of sportswriters, many of whom considered him "the brainiest guy in baseball."

He earned his law degree from Columbia University, attending classes in the off-seasons and even during spring training and partial seasons with the White Sox. When Berg was signed by the Washington Senators in 1932, his life took a sudden change. In Washington, Berg became a society darling, delighting the glitterati with his knowledge and wit. Certainly it was during his Washington years that he made the contacts that would serve him in his espionage career.

## Time in Tokyo and on TV

Berg first raised eyebrows in the intelligence community at the start of World War II when he shared home movies of Tokyo's shipyards, factories, and military sites, which he had secretly filmed while on a baseball trip in 1934. While barnstorming through Japan along with Ruth, Lou Gehrig, and Foxx, Berg delighted Japanese audiences with his fluency in their language and familiarity with their culture. He even addressed the Japanese parliament.

But one day he skipped the team's scheduled game and went to visit a Tokyo hospital, the highest building in the city. He sneaked up to the roof and took motion picture films of the Tokyo harbor. Some say those photos were used by the U.S. military as they planned their attack on Tokyo eight years later. Berg maintained that he had not been sent to Tokyo on a formal assignment, that he had acted on his own initiative to take the film and offer it to the U.S. government upon his return. Whether or not that was the case, Berg's undercover career had begun.

On February 21, 1939, Berg made the first of several appearances on the radio quiz show *Information, Please!* He was an immense hit, correctly answering nearly every question he was asked. Commissioner Kenesaw Mountain Landis was so proud of how intelligent and well-read the second-string catcher was that he told him, "Berg, in just 30 minutes you did more for baseball than I've done the entire time I've been commissioner." But Berg's baseball time was beginning to wind down; 1939 was his last season.

## Secret Agent Man

Berg's intellect and elusive lifestyle were ideal for a post-baseball career as a spy. He was recruited by the Office of Strategic Services (predecessor to the CIA) in 1943 and served in several capacities. He toured 20 countries in Latin America early in WWII, allegedly on a propaganda mission to bolster the morale of soldiers there. But what he was really doing was trying to determine how much the Latin countries could help the U.S. war effort.

His most important mission for the OSS was to gather information on Germany's progress in developing an atomic bomb. He worked undercover in Italy and Switzerland and reported information to the States throughout 1944. One of his more daring assignments was a visit to Zurich, Switzerland, in December 1944, where he attended a lecture by German nuclear physicist Werner Heisenberg. If Heisenberg indicated the Germans were close to developing nukes, Berg had been directed to assassinate the scientist. Luckily for Heisenberg, Berg determined that German nuclear capability was not yet within the danger range.

## Life After the War

On October 10, 1945, Berg was awarded the Medal of Freedom (now the Presidential Medal of Freedom) but turned it down without explanation. (After his death, his sister accepted it on his behalf.)

After the war he was recruited by the CIA. It is said that his is the only baseball card to be found in CIA headquarters. After his CIA career ended, Berg never worked again. He was often approached to write his memoirs. When he agreed, in 1960 or so, the publisher hired a writer to provide assistance. Berg quit the project in fury when the writer indicated he thought Berg was Moe Howard, founder of the Three Stooges. But his unusual career turns were later immortalized in the Nicholas Dawidoff book *The Catcher Was a Spy*. At age 70, Berg fell, injuring himself. He died in the hospital. His last words were to ask a nurse, "What did the Mets do today?"

# Fugitive Nazis in South America

*Nazi leaders were sentenced to death after the war, but a few managed to escape the grip of Nuremberg and sneak into South America.*

✳   ✳   ✳   ✳

IN JULY 1972, an old man complaining of intense abdominal pain checked himself into a hospital in Sao Paulo, Brazil. The admitting physician noted that the man, obviously a foreigner, looked much older than the 46 years listed on his identity card but accepted the excuse that the date was misprinted. The man had an intestinal blockage: He had a nervous habit of chewing the ends of his walrus mustache, and over the years the bits of hair had accumulated in his digestive tract. The man had good reason to be nervous. He was Josef Mengele, a Nazi war criminal, who had been hiding in South America since the end of the Second World War.

After the war, many Nazi war criminals escaped to start new lives in non-extraditing countries like Argentina, Brazil, Uruguay, Chile, and Paraguay. They lived in constant danger of discovery, though in several cases, friendly dictatorships turned a blind eye in exchange for services. Many were found and kidnapped by the Israeli Mossad, tried, and sentenced for their crimes. Some, including Mengele, the cruel concentration camp doctor, eluded capture until their deaths. Mengele died by accidental drowning in 1979.

South America was a refuge from the net of international justice that swept Europe at war's end. Several of the countries had enjoyed friendly prewar relations with the Reich— Argentina, in particular, was sympathetic to the plight of the fugitive Nazis. Many found positions in Argentina's Fascist government, controlled by Juan Perón. His wife, Evita, later traveled to Europe, ostensibly on a goodwill tour. However, she was actually raising funds for the safe passage of war criminals.

In Argentina, Uruguay, Chile, Bolivia, and Paraguay, scores of Nazis found familiar traditions of elitism and militarism. Perhaps most importantly, corruption in those countries made it easy to obtain false identification papers through bribery.

## Nazis Who Slipped Overseas

* Walter Rauff invented the Auschwitz "death trucks" that killed more than half a million prisoners. Rauff was arrested in Santiago, Chile, in 1963, but the Chilean authorities released him after three months in jail. Many believe that Rauff designed the concentration camps where Chilean political prisoners were killed under the Pinochet regime.

* Paul Schäfer served in the Hitler Youth. Years later, he was arrested for pedophile activities while working at an orphanage in postwar Germany. Schaefer fled to Chile where he established a settlement known as Colonia Dignida, in which abuse, torture, and drugs were used to control followers. The adults were taught to call Schaefer "Führer"; the colony's children called him "Uncle." Schaefer sexually abused hundreds of children in the decades that followed. The colony prospered and, despite information from escaped members, it remained in operation until 1993 when Schaeffer went into hiding. He managed to escape justice until 2006 when he was sentenced to 20 years in prison.

* Klaus Barbie, the notorious "Butcher of Lyon," became a counterintelligence officer for the U.S. military which helped him to flee to Bolivia soon after the war. In 1971, he assisted in a military coup that brought the brutal General Hugo Banzar to power. Barbie went on to head the South American cocaine ring called Amadeus that generated funds for political activity friendly to U.S. interests in the region. When a more moderate government came to power in 1983, Barbie was deported to France, where he was tried and convicted of war crimes. He died of cancer after spending four years in prison.

## Nueva Germania

German colonists had settled in South America long before the start of the Second World War. One of the more outlandish attempts occurred in the late-nineteenth century when Elisabeth Nietzsche-Forster and her husband Bernhard Forster led a group of 14 families to Paraguay. They founded a utopian village dedicated to anti-Semitism and an "authentic rebirth of racial feeling." They called their remote settlement Nueva Germania. Within two years, many of the colonists had died of disease, Bernhard drank himself to death, and Elisabeth returned to Europe where she successfully worked to have her husband's writings adopted as the favorite philosophy of the Nazi Party. After the Second World War, many fugitive Nazis were rumored to have sheltered in Nueva Germania, including Josef Mengele.

## Submarines Full of Nazi Gold

Despite evidence suggesting that Hitler's secretary, Martin Bormann, died in the streets of Berlin in 1945, rumors persist about his escape to South America. According to the same accounts, Bormann witnessed his Führer's suicide and then followed prearranged orders to escape to Argentina, where he had been transporting large amounts of Reich gold and money using submarines. In the final days of the war, go the stories, Bormann and dozens of other Nazi officials left Germany in ten submarines, five of which arrived safely in Argentina. Waiting for them was a friendly government and the stolen wealth of Europe, safely deposited by the Peróns in Swiss bank accounts. Some estimates place the accumulated wealth at $800 million.

# What Was Dr. Pepper a Doctor of?

*And how did he come up with his famous soda anyway?*

❋ ❋ ❋ ❋

THERE WERE NO postgraduate degrees involved in the creation of Dr Pepper (the company dropped the period from "Dr." in the 1950s), and it was never considered a health drink. But soda lore does tell of a real doctor who inspired the name.

Charles Alderton—a pharmacist at Morrison's Old Corner Drug Store in Waco, Texas—invented the drink in 1885. (In those days, a drugstore often featured well-stocked soda fountains.) Alderton loved the smell of various fruit syrups mixed together and experimented to create a drink that captured that aroma. Customers eagerly gulped down the result, which was initially called a "Waco." Alderton's boss, Wade Morrison, renamed the beverage "Dr. Pepper" and started selling it to other soda fountains.

A long-standing legend holds that Morrison named the drink after Dr. Charles T. Pepper, a physician and druggist who had been Morrison's boss back in his home state of Virginia. One version of the story claims that Morrison was simply honoring the man who had given him his start in the business.

However, the more popular variation contends that Morrison was in love with Pepper's daughter, but that Pepper didn't approve. Heartbroken, Morrison moved to Texas. He eventually called his popular beverage Dr. Pepper—either to flatter Pepper and perhaps get another shot at his daughter, or just as a joke.

This was the official story for years, but researchers eventually uncovered evidence that largely debunked it. Census records show a Dr. Charles Pepper living in Virginia at the time, but his daughter would have been only eight years old when Morrison left the state, and it's not clear whether Morrison actually worked for Pepper. However, census records also show that when Morrison was a teenager, he lived near another Pepper family, which included a girl who was just one year younger than him. The star-crossed-lovers story might be true—just with a different Pepper.

Another possibility is that Morrison simply came up with a marketable name. "Doctor" could have suggested that the drink was endorsed by a physician for its health benefits, while "Pepper" may have indicated that it was a good pick-me-up, as well.

So the original good doctor was either an MD or a figment of a pharmacist's imagination. In any case, the name worked well—Dr Pepper is the oldest soda brand in the world. It just goes to show that people like a drink with nice credentials.

# Canada's Cryptic Castaway

*This mute amputee has a foothold in Nova Scotian folklore—nearly a century after his death.*

✳ ✳ ✳ ✳

### Who Is This Man?

ON SEPTEMBER 8, 1863, two fishermen in Sandy Cove, Nova Scotia, discovered an unusual treasure washed ashore: a lone man in his twenties with newly amputated legs, left with just a loaf of bread and jug of water.

There were a few clues, such as his manner of dress, that led the townspeople to speculate on whether the fellow was a gentleman or an aristocrat. But there was no point in asking him—he didn't speak. In fact, he was said to have uttered only three words after being found: "Jerome" (which the villagers came to call him), "Columbo" (perhaps the name of his ship), and "Trieste," an Italian village.

Based on these three words, the villagers theorized he was Italian and concocted various romantic stories about his fate: that he was an Italian nobleman captured and mutilated by pirates (or perhaps a pirate himself), a seaman punished for threatening mutiny, or maybe he was an heir to a fortune who had been crippled and cast away by a jealous rival.

## Charity Case

Jerome was taken to the home of Jean and Juliette Nicholas, a French family who lived across the bay in Meteghan. There was still a chance Jerome could be French and Jean was fluent in five languages. (Although none of which proved successful in communicating with Jerome.)

In 1870, the Nicholases moved away. The town, enthralled with their mysterious nobleman, rallied together and paid the Comeau family $140 a year to take him in. On Sundays after mass, locals would stop by and pay a few cents for a look at the maimed mute. Jerome lived with the Comeaus for the next 52 years until his death on April 19, 1912.

Records suggest Jerome was no cool-headed castaway. Though he never spoke intelligibly, hearing some words (specifically "pirate") would put him in a rage. It's also been said that he was particularly anxious about the cold, spending winters with his leg stumps shoved under the stove for warmth. Though in his younger days he enjoyed sitting in the sun, he allegedly spent the last 20 years of his life as a shut-in, huddled by the stove.

## Mystery Revealed

Jerome's panic about the cold makes sense—if the latest hypotheses about him are true. Modern historians have posited a couple of different theories, both of which trace Jerome to New Brunswick.

One group of scholars uncovered a story in New Brunswick about a man who was behaving erratically and couldn't (or wouldn't) speak. To rid themselves of him, members of his community put him on a boat to New England—but not without first chopping off his legs. The man never made it to New England but instead wound up on the beach at Sandy Cove.

Another theory links Jerome to a man—probably European—who was found in 1861, pinned under a fallen tree in Chipman, New Brunswick, with frozen legs. Without a doctor nearby, the man was sent down the St. John River to Gagetown and then shipped back to Chipman, where he was supported for two years by the parish and nicknamed "Gamby" (which means "legs" in Italian). At that point, the parish got tired of taking care of him and paid a captain to drop him across the bay in Nova Scotia. Another account suggests that after the surgery, the man wasn't returned to Gagetown but put right on a boat.

Regardless of which theory is more accurate, all suggest that the reason for Jerome's arrival in Nova Scotia is that an entire town disowned him.

But New Brunswick's loss has been Nova Scotia's gain. There, Jerome is a local legend. He has been the subject of a movie (1994's *Le secret de Jérôme*), and a home for the handicapped bears his name. Tourists can even stop by his grave for a quick snapshot of the headstone, which reads, quite simply, "Jerome."

# Molly Pitcher: Rebel Militiawoman

*Historians disagree about Molly; not over whether she lived, but over her true identity. Did a cannon-cocker's wife truly step up and serve a gun under fire in the American Revolution?*

✳   ✳   ✳   ✳

**Was Molly Pitcher real?** A couple of Revolutionary women's stories sound a lot like Molly's. Because women have "pitched in" during battle in just about every war, that's neither surprising nor a revelation. It wasn't rare in that era for wives to accompany their husbands on military duty, to say nothing of those daring few women who masqueraded as men. So who was Molly? Many historians say she was an Irish immigrant named Mary Hays (later McCauly). Some believe that Molly was Margaret Corbin, a Pennsylvania native. The most likely case is that both were real women who did pretty much as history credits them and that the legend of Molly Pitcher commingles the two.

**What did Mary Hays do?** The story, likely accurate, credits her first with bringing water (the "pitcher" part explained) to the artillery gunners at the Battle of Monmouth (1778). It wasn't just drinking water; a soldier had to wet-sponge a cannon after a shot in order to douse any residual embers. If he or she didn't, the person pushing in the next powder charge would suffer the consequences. Accounts describe Mary as a woman who was always ready with a choice profanity and was as brave as any man, and she is widely credited with evacuating wounded men. After her husband fell wounded, she stepped forward to help crew his gun. Mary died around 1832.

**And Margaret Corbin?** Her tale enters focus at the Battle of Fort Washington (1776) and has her first helping her husband crew a cannon, then firing it unassisted after his death in action. (That would be possible, but very slow.) Taken out of action by grapeshot—a cannon firing musket balls as a super shotgun—she was evacuated and given a military pension by the Continental government. Considering said government's notorious poverty and lousy credit, there's doubt whether poor Margaret ever collected any money in time to help her. She died in 1789, a partly disabled veteran.

**How did the stories get so muddled together?** One must consider the times. No one videotaped Mary or Margaret; eyewitnesses spoke or wrote of their deeds. Others retold the tales, perhaps inflating or deemphasizing them. As the war lingered on, people who had heard both stories probably assumed they were variants of the same story, and they retold it in their own words. Regardless, dozens of American women besides Mary and Margaret fought for independence; many thousands more helped the cause with all their strength. Molly Pitcher is an emblem, a Rosie the Riveter of her era.

# Santa Is a New Yorker

*Everyone knows that old St. Nick lives at the North Pole. The problem is, there is overwhelming evidence that Santa actually lives in New York City! Even if he spends some of the year in the Arctic Circle, the fact that there are so many solid connections between the Big Man and the Big Apple can't be a coincidence.*

❋ ❋ ❋ ❋

MACY'S HAS LONG laid claim to hosting the one true Santa Claus. Every year since 1924, the start of the Christmas season has been marked by the arrival of Santa Claus at the end of Macy's Thanksgiving Day Parade held in New York. Now, considering all the work Santa has to do before Christmas Eve, it would only make sense for him to spend the last month he has to prepare for his annual voyage in Macy's parade if he happened to be a New Yorker. Some might argue that this just isn't the case, that he is just another chubby old man with a beard in a red suit, but that question was resolved in 1947!

In fact, it was decided in 1947, and then again in 1955, 1959, 1973, and 1994, in the film *Miracle on 34th Street*. Sure, there are plenty of 34th streets around the world, but Santa only ever calls the one in New York City his home. After all, what is really on trial in that film is Santa himself, and the court, of course, rules on the side of Kris Kringle every time. If that isn't enough, keep in mind that the original film was nominated for a Best Picture Oscar, and actually won three Academy Awards, so it must have merit—and be true.

Then of course, there are those who will argue that the film(s) got it all wrong, and that there is no such thing; that Santa simply does not exist. New York, as we should expect, is also source to the most famous rebuttal to that argument, the "Yes, Virginia . . ." letter. In 1897, Virginia O'Hanlon wrote to the *New York Sun* at the suggestion of her father, to ask if Santa Claus was real. Her father's reasoning, according to legend, was "If you see it in the *Sun*, it's so." She received a response in the form of an editorial by Francis Pharcellus Church on the morning of September 21 that same year. In it, Church made one of the greatest arguments for the existence of Santa, leaving out only the part about his living in New York. The article would be reprinted numerous times, and the catchphrase "Yes, Virginia, there is a Santa Claus" has become prevalent in popular culture even today.

Still, for some that may not be enough, so we need to look at the other evidence. For example, according to NORAD's 2008 tracking of St. Nick's journeys, Santa's reindeer have an affinity for the Statue of Liberty, and they spend extra time in the Big Apple. This indicates that while Santa lives in New York, he must keep the reindeer up north at his Arctic base of operations. Speaking of the reindeer, the famous poem "'Twas the Night Before Christmas" was first published in a New York newspaper about three hours north of Santa's American home. It was an ingenious way of revealing the names of Nick's beloved beasts of burden, as well as other secrets, to the world.

## Before Santa Drank Coke

Evidence further suggests that Santa moved from this smaller New York town to the big city a few decades later. He enlisted the help of New York City artist Thomas Nast in the 1860s to reveal his image, red suit and all, to the public via illustrations in *Harper's Weekly*. As the center of world commerce and communication, only a city like New York could help him stage such a revelation. Besides, who but a resident of the "city that never sleeps" would even dare to take on the task of delivering all those presents to the entire world in one night? No, dear readers, consider the North Pole story a refuted myth. Santa Claus, without a doubt, hearts New York.

## How Many Ronald McDonalds Have There Been?

*And what is their strange relationship with Bozo the Clown?*

✳  ✳  ✳  ✳

**M**CDONALD'S GUARDS THIS bit of information even more closely than its secret sauce recipe. The company won't even acknowledge the existence of multiple Ronalds, though McDonald's obviously would need many actors to keep up with store openings, hospital visits, and other events around the world. The company forbids Ronald actors from revealing what they do.

The only specific Ronald actor that McDonald's happily acknowledges is the original one, Willard Scott, who went on to become the world's most famous weatherman. The story began in 1960, when Scott played Bozo the Clown in the Washington, D.C., version of *Bozo's Circus*. A local McDonald's franchisee sponsored the show, and Scott also appeared as Bozo at McDonald's restaurants as part of the promotion. He was a big hit, so when the station dropped *Bozo's Circus* in 1963, a franchisee hired Scott to play a new McDonald's clown character in local ads.

The ads were a success, and McDonald's decided in 1965 to feature the character in nationwide TV spots as part of its sponsorship of the Macy's Thanksgiving Day parade. Instead of using Scott, McDonald's hired a thinner actor, reasoning that it would be easier to find lean actors rather than heavy actors to play Ronald around the nation. (Guess the obesity epidemic hadn't yet gripped America.)

The history gets fuzzy there, but we know that McDonald's was working through the 1970s on its clown army. In 1972, it published *Ronald and How*, a training manual for new Ronalds. In a 2003 *Wall Street Journal* article, marketing experts who were familiar with McDonald's said that there were about 250 active Ronalds, which could mean that there have been several thousand over the years. Every two years, current and prospective Ronalds attend a secret Ronald McDonald convention, where they have to pass inspection. It's heady stuff, to be sure.

Scott is the only person confirmed by McDonald's to have appeared as Ronald in television ads. There are Internet rumors about other TV Ronalds, but these actors are unconfirmed. Mayor McCheese could not be reached for comment.

# Walt Disney: FBI Man or Mouse?

*As the creator of the most famous cartoon mouse in the world, Walt Disney carefully protected and shielded the rodent and his friends from anything that could put their world in a bad light. But it seems that Disney, whose entertainment empire was as pure as Snow White, may have protected and shielded other facets of his life from public view—ones that might have darkened his squeaky clean image.*

✳  ✳  ✳  ✳

## Young Walter

WALT DISNEY WAS born in Chicago on December 5, 1901, to parents Elias and Flora. His father was a farmer and carpenter, running the household with an overly firm hand. Walt and his siblings, working the Disney land near Kansas City, often found themselves on the receiving end of a strap as their dad doled out the discipline. As a young boy, Walt took advantage of his infrequent free time by drawing, improvising his supplies by using a piece of coal on toilet paper. When the Disneys moved back to Chicago in 1917, Walt attended art classes at the Chicago Academy of Fine Arts.

Armed with forged birth records, Walt joined the American Red Cross Ambulance Corps and entered World War I in 1918, just before it ended. He returned to Kansas City, where two of his brothers continued to run the Disney farm. Although he was rejected as a cartoonist for the *Kansas City Star*, Walt soon began to create animated film ads for movie theaters, working with a young Ub Iwerks, who eventually became an important member of Disney Studios.

In 1922, Disney started Laugh-O-Gram Films, producing short cartoons based on fairy tales. But the business closed within a year, and Walt headed to Hollywood, intent on directing feature films. Finding no work as a director, he revisited the world of film animation. With emotional and financial support from his brother Roy, Walt slowly began to make a name for Disney Brothers Studios on the West Coast. The company introduced "Oswald the Lucky Rabbit" in 1927 but lost the popular character the next year to a different company. Disney was left in the position of having to create another cute and clever cartoon animal.

## The Tale of the Mouse

According to Disney, the Kansas City office of Laugh-O-Gram Films was rampant with mice. One mouse was a particular favorite of Walt. This rodent became the inspiration for Disney's next cartoon character. Working with Iwerks, and borrowing copiously from their former meal ticket Oswald, Disney Studios produced *Steamboat Willie* in November 1928. With a voice provided by Disney himself, Mickey Mouse quickly became a hit in movie theaters. The animated star introduced additional Disney icons, including girlfriend Minnie Mouse, the always-exasperated Donald Duck, faithful hound Pluto, and dim-but-devoted pal Goofy. Disney's cartoons won every Animated Short Subject Academy Award during the 1930s.

## A Dark Side of Disney

As Disney Studios moved into animated feature films (which everyone said would never work), Walt began to wield the power he'd gained as one of Hollywood's most prominent producers. What's more, his strict upbringing and harsh bouts of discipline had left him with a suspicious, ultraconservative mindset. Bad language by employees in the presence of women resulted in immediate discharge—no matter the inconvenience. Disney was prone to creating a double standard between himself and his employees. For example, although Walt kept his dashing mustache for most of his life, all other Disney workers were prohibited from wearing any facial hair. While he considered his artists and animators "family," he treated them in the same way Elias Disney had treated his family—unfairly. Promised bonuses turned into layoffs. Higher-paid artists resorted to giving their assistants raises out of their own pockets. By 1941, Disney's animators went on strike, supported by the Screen Cartoonists Guild. Walt was convinced, and stated publicly, that the strike was the result of Communist agitators infiltrating Hollywood. Settled after five weeks, the Guild won on all counts, and the "Disney family" became cynically known as the "Mouse Factory."

## An Even Darker Side

Disney was suspected of being a Nazi sympathizer; he often attended American Nazi Party meetings before the beginning of World War II. When prominent German filmmaker Leni Riefenstahl tried to screen her films for Hollywood studios, only Disney agreed to meet her. Yet, when World War II began, Disney projected a strictly all-American image and became closely allied with J. Edgar Hoover and the FBI.

According to more than 500 pages of FBI files, Disney was recruited by Hoover in late 1940 to be an informant, flagging potential Communist sympathizers among Hollywood stars and executives. In September 1947, Disney was called by the House Un-American Activities Committee to testify on

Communist influence in the motion picture industry. He fingered several of his former artists as Reds, again blaming much of the 1941 labor strike on their efforts. He also identified the League of Women Voters as a Communist-fronted organization. Later that evening, his wife pointed out that he meant the League of Women Shoppers, a consumer group that had supported the Guild strike. Disney's testimony contributed to the "Hollywood Blacklist," which included anyone in the industry even remotely suspected of Communist affiliation. The list resulted in many damaged or lost careers, as well as a number of suicides in the cinematic community. Included in the turmoil was Charlie Chaplin, whom Disney referred to as "the little Commie."

The FBI rewarded Walt Disney for his efforts by naming him "SAC—Special Agent in Charge" in 1954, just as he was about to open his first magical amusement park, Disneyland. Disney and Hoover continued to be pen pals into the 1960s; the FBI made script "suggestions" for *Moon Pilot*, a Disney comedy that initially spoofed the abilities of the Bureau. The bumbling FBI agents in the screenplay became generic government agents before the film's release.

After a lifetime of chain-smoking, Disney developed lung cancer and died in December 1966. His plans for Disney World in Florida had just begun—the park didn't open until 1971. Upon his passing, many remembered the man as kindly "Uncle Walt," while others saw him as the perfect father for a mouse—since he had always seemed to be a bit of a rat.

# Chapter 3

# How Is That Possible?

## Picture Perfect: Making Wax Sculptures

*Making a wax likeness of a person may be a centuries-old art, but this sort of portraiture is still a complicated process.*

✳   ✳   ✳   ✳

### The First Stages

AH, THE WAX sculpture—perhaps the most obvious sign that someone has made it as a cultural icon. The art of wax sculpting has been around since the 1700s, when the now well-known Madame Tussaud made her first figures. These days, before the statue slides its way into a museum, it has to make a long journey that begins with weeks of research.

Once a museum decides to commission a particular person's model, a team of artists begins to collect piles of photographs and measurements of the soon-to-be-immortalized person. But before they even think about building the separate parts and putting the pieces together, the museum must decide exactly how the end product should appear.

Curators consider every detail, ranging from the facial expression and posture to wardrobe and setting. They'll even go as far as interviewing barbers and dentists to get a better feel for the person's physical details. Once those decisions have been made and the data has been collected, it's time to start sculpting.

## Building the Face

Using a combination of photos and measurements and sometimes even a real-life impression, the artists create a plaster mold of the head using regular clay. Next, they pour hot wax into this mold. Beeswax is often used along with manufactured petroleum-based waxes, mixed together with artificial coloring and chemicals to help the goo stay strong and resist heat. After everything is in place, it's time to let the magic happen.

## The Fine Details

Once the mold has cooled, the wax is removed and the assembly begins. Prosthetic eyes are selected to best match the person's gaze. Porcelain teeth, similar to dentures, are used to fill the kisser. And real human hair is brought in to be inserted, one strand at a time, into every spot where it's needed: the head, the eyebrows and eyelashes, and even the arms and chest. Specially trained workers use a tiny needle to painstakingly place every last hair perfectly. This process alone takes up to 60 hours. One can imagine that, in the case of hirsute comedian Robin Williams's model, it could take 60 days.

Next, painters use translucent paint to even out the skin tone and add in any blemishes or distinguishing features. The paint is put on in thin layers, allowing the wax to shine through and look more lifelike. The crew then puts all the pieces together and passes the final figure off to the next team.

## The Big Picture

Now that the model is done, the rest of the work begins. Seamstresses and costuming consultants come in to create the figure's wardrobe and fit it onto the body. Designers then assemble the full set, including backgrounds, props, and furnishings to match the moment frozen in time. At long last, the model is ready to be placed into the scene. After final touch-ups, engineers are hired to design lighting that will play up the sculpture's features. Finally, the journey is done, and the show is ready to open.

All together, the entire process usually takes a minimum of six months. Some cases have been more extreme: Royal London Wax Museum's model of former U.S. President Bill Clinton took eight months, and its sculpture of former Canadian Prime Minister Jean Chretien took just over a year. Museums say the creations can cost anywhere from $10,000 to $25,000, not including the various furnishings. Kind of makes the salon's $25 wax special seem a little more reasonable, doesn't it?

# How to Shrink a Head

*As you might expect, the recipe for making a tiny noggin is just a tad gruesome.*

✳   ✳   ✳   ✳

## Those Wacky Jivaro

**W**ELL INTO THE 20th century, the Amazonian Jivaro tribe made a point of returning from battle toting the shrunken heads of its enemies. Talk about unique souvenirs.

These heads, or *tsantsa*, were a central element of the Jivaro practice of blood revenge. If someone from a neighboring tribe—or even a different group within the Jivaro tribe—wronged your family, it was essential that you exact revenge on his kin. The result was a cycle of murder, head collection, and hurt feelings.

Not only was *tsantsa* the best revenge, but it was also the best way to prevent supernatural harassment from your victim. The Jivaro believed that shrinking the victim's head captured his soul, keeping him from moving on to the afterlife, where he could torment you and your dead ancestors.

## The Process

The Jivaro decapitated the offending party—or one of his relatives—and looped a band through the head's mouth and neck hole, making a sort of handle. Then they high-tailed it to a secluded camp by a river, where they sliced open the back of the head, carefully peeled away the skin, and tossed the skull into the river as an offering to a spirit they believed lived in the anaconda snake.

Next, they sewed the eyes shut, fastened the mouth closed with wooden skewers, and placed the head in boiling water for up to two hours. The boiling process shrank the head to about a third of its normal size. After boiling, the Jivaro began the trip back home, continuing to work on the *tsantsa* along the way.

They turned the skin inside out and scraped away any remaining flesh before turning it right-side out and sewing up the back of the head. The Jivaro then put scorching rocks inside the head and filled and refilled it with hot sand, drying the skin and shrinking it further. Next, they removed the skewers from the lips and tied them shut with long lengths of string. The head then was hung over a fire for hardening and blackening and was covered in charcoal to seal in the spirit of the dead individual. Finally, the Jivaro cut a hole in the top of the head and inserted a stick with a loop of sturdy string tied to it. And there it was: a perfect shrunken head to wear around the neck.

## From Trophies to Toys

Back home, the *tsantsa* were the centerpieces of feasts. The shrinking process and the feasts were essential requirements for exacting revenge. After that purpose was served, the heads no longer were important and often ended up as toys for kids.

The tribe even set up a profitable side business, trading the heads to foreigners for guns and other goods, but the Peruvian and Ecuadorian governments cracked down on the practice in the 1930s and 1940s.

# Sound Secrets

*Take a Hollywood movie scene: A leather-jacketed hero scuffles with a bad guy and then walks through the snow before driving into the night. Sounds good, right? But what you really heard was a Foley artist punching a roasted chicken with a rubber kitchen glove and squeezing two balloons together while walking in a sandbox filled with cornstarch.*

✳   ✳   ✳   ✳

## Things Are Not What They Seem

WHETHER YOU NOTICE it or not, the sound of a movie can be as entertaining as the visual experience. But unbeknownst to many viewers, many of the sounds are not captured at the time of filming. Instead, they're either recorded in the studio by Foley artists or pulled from a library of sound bites that are not used until the sound is mixed for the movie.

The term "Foley artist" was used as early as 1927 when Al Jolson's movie *The Jazz Singer* became the first movie recorded with sound. In those days, recording the actors' dialogue superseded virtually all other sound or music recorded for the film. It wasn't until the early 1950s that producers discovered they could enhance the overall quality of the moviegoers' experience by adding specialized sounds that were purposely stripped away during filming in favor of an actor's spoken lines.

The profession's namesake, Jack Foley, was asked by his sound engineer to improve the quality of the audio by introducing a series of "studio clips." Foley discovered that in order to enhance the sound, three categories of sound were required, starting with "footsteps." Each actor executing a scene in a movie walks or runs with their own gait, on a variety of surfaces. By watching raw footage of the film, a Foley artist attempts to replicate and record the actor's pace and sound by walking on the most suitable surface, for instance, cement, gravel, or sand.

The second sound category that must be captured is the "moves." Moves accompany footsteps and include the sounds of skirts swishing, pants rustling, or leather jackets squeaking. Finally, all of the other sounds required to make the experience more believable must be either pulled from thousands of computer-generated archives or shot especially for the film.

## The Life of a Foley Artist

Foley artists are natural-born scavengers. When they're not actively involved in producing sound effects for films and television, you'll often find them scrounging around garage sales and piles of trash looking for anything that will generate a particular sound. A fertile imagination is key: What may sound like a couple passionately kissing in a movie may actually be a Foley artist sucking on his or her own forearm.

When Foley artist Marko Costanzo began freelancing for C5, Inc., he needed to come up with a variety of new sounds to use on his projects. Since most clips weren't available, he invented the following ingenious additions to his audio library:

✳ For a two-minute sequence of a dragonfly in *Men in Black*, Costanzo clipped off the ends of the blades of a simple plastic fan and replaced them with duct tape. When the fan was turned on, he could control the quality of the resulting flapping sound by brushing his fingers against the duct tape.

✳ For a knifing scene in the crime drama *Goodfellas*, Costanzo tried stabbing raw chickens, beef, and pork roasts with the bones intact.

✳ To achieve the sound of walking on freshly fallen snow, he walked on kosher sea salt covered with a thick layer of cornstarch.

✳ To emulate the sound of a dog walking across a hardwood surface, Costanzo glued press-on nails onto work gloves and clickity-clacked the nails on wood. The size of the dog could be indicated by the thickness of the nails used.

The motion picture industry thrives on creating fantasies. From the moment that the actor steps onto the soundstage, nothing is what it seems. Without Foley artists, our movie-going experience would be a lackluster one.

# Magnetic Hill Phenomenon

*It has taken researchers hundreds of years to finally solve the mystery of magnetic hills, or spook hills, as they're often called. This phenomenon, found all over the world, describes places where objects—including cars in neutral gear—move uphill on a slightly sloping road, seemingly defying gravity.*

✳   ✳   ✳   ✳

MONCTON, IN NEW Brunswick, Canada, lays claim to one of the more famous magnetic hills, called, appropriately, Magnetic Hill. Over the years, it has also been called Fool's Hill and Magic Hill. Since the location made headlines in 1931, hundreds of thousands of tourists have flocked there to witness this phenomenon for themselves.

## Go Figure

Much to the disdain of paranormal believers, people in science once assumed that a magnetic anomaly caused this event. But advanced physics has concluded this phenomenon is due "to the visual anchoring of the sloping surface to a gravity-relative eye level whose perceived direction is biased by sloping surroundings." In nonscientific jargon, it's an optical illusion.

Papers published in the journal of the Association of Psychological Science supported this conclusion based on a series of experiments done with models. They found that if the horizon cannot be seen or is not level then people may be fooled by objects that they expect to be vertical but aren't. False perspective is also a culprit; think, for example, of a line of poles on the horizon that seem to get larger or smaller depending on distance.

Engineers with plumb lines, one made of iron and one made of stone, demonstrated that a slope appearing to go uphill might in reality be going downhill. A good topographical map may also be sufficient to show which way the land is really sloping.

### I Know a Place

Other notable magnetic hills can be found in Wisconsin, Pennsylvania, California, Florida, Barbados, Scotland, Australia, Italy, Greece, and South Korea.

# How Do People Swallow Swords?

*And how long has this craziness existed?*

✻ ✻ ✻ ✻

VERRRY CAREFULLY. THERE are ways to fake it—such as using a trick sword with a plastic blade that collapses into the hilt—but authentic sword swallowing is no optical illusion. The blade isn't as sharp as that of a normal sword, but that doesn't change the fact that the swallower is pushing a hard metal shaft deep into his or her body.

Ironically, one of the essential skills of sword swallowing is not swallowing. When you stand and face upward, your upper gastrointestinal tract—the passageway that's made up of your throat, pharynx, esophagus, and stomach—is straight and flexible enough that a sword can pass through it. When you swallow, muscles contract and expand along the passageway in order to move food down to your stomach. Two sphincters along this tract—the upper esophageal sphincter between your pharynx and esophagus and the lower esophageal sphincter between your esophagus and stomach—are normally closed; they open involuntarily as food moves past. To keep the passageway clear, the swallower must learn deep relaxation techniques to resist the urge to swallow.

Sword swallowers also have to suppress their gag reflex, an automatic muscle contraction triggered when nerve endings in the back of the throat sense a foreign object. To deactivate the gag reflex, a sword swallower crams progressively larger objects into the back of the throat while trying not to gag. After hours of disgusting noises and vomiting, the gag reflex is suitably numbed and the aspiring swallower can get down to business.

As the sword slides down the gastrointestinal tract all the way into the stomach, it straightens the various curves of the tract. Some swallowers coat their swords with a lubricant, such as olive oil, to help them along.

This mind-over-matter feat is one of the oldest stunts there is. Historians believe that the practice originated in India around 2000 BC, as a part of rituals designed to demonstrate powerful connections to the gods. The ancient Romans, Greeks, and Chinese picked up the practice, but generally viewed it as entertainment rather than religious observance. Sword swallowers at the 1893 World's Fair in Chicago sparked America's interest in the spectacle, and it soon became a staple of traveling sideshows.

Did we mention that you shouldn't try this trick at home? It goes without saying that sword swallowing is a dangerous and generally ill-advised endeavor. Even master swallowers sustain injuries—cram a sword, even a dull one, down your throat enough times, and you're likely to nick something important. If you must impress your friends, stick with more manageable sharp objects, such as Doritos.

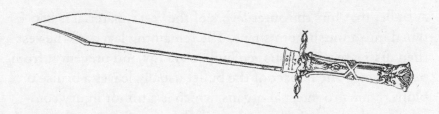

# How Does a Flak Jacket Stop a Bullet?

*"Flak" is an abbreviated form of the silly German word,
Fliegerabwehrkanone. There's nothing silly, however, about its
meaning: anti-aircraft cannon.*

✳   ✳   ✳   ✳

SERIOUS DEVELOPMENT OF flak jackets began during World
War II, when Air Force gunners wore nylon vests with steel
plates sewn into them as protection against shrapnel. After
the war, manufacturers discovered that they could remove the
steel plates and instead make the vests out of multiple layers of
dense, heavily woven nylon.

Without the steel plates, the vests became a viable option for
ground troops to wear during combat. Anywhere from sixteen
to twenty-four layers of this nylon fabric were stitched together
into a thick quilt. In the 1960s, DuPont developed Kevlar, a
lightweight fiber that is five times stronger than a piece of steel
of the same weight. Kevlar was added to flak jackets in 1975.

It seems inconceivable that any cloth could withstand the
force of a bullet. The key, however, is in the construction of the
fabric. In a flak jacket, the fibers are interlaced to form a super
strong net. The fibers are twisted as they are woven, which adds
to their density. Modern flak jackets also incorporate a coat-
ing of resin on the fibers and layers of plastic film between the
layers of fabric. The result is a series of nets that are designed to
bend but not break.

A bullet that hits the outer layers of the vest's material is flattened into a mushroom shape. The remaining layers of the vest
then dissipate the misshapen bullet's energy and prevent it from
penetrating. The impact of the bullet usually leaves a bruise or
blunt trauma to internal organs, which is a minor injury compared to the type of devastation a bullet is meant to inflict.

While no body armor is 100 percent impenetrable, flak jackets offer different levels of protection depending on the construction and materials involved. At the higher levels of protection, plates of lightweight steel or special ceramic are still used. But all flak jackets incorporate this netlike fabric as a first line of defense. *Fliegerabwehrkanone*, indeed.

# Why You Buy

*Supermarkets have gone to great lengths to make you think that "impulse" buy really was an impulse.*

✳   ✳   ✳   ✳

## End Caps

THE "END CAPS" are the shelves at the outer ends of each aisle, and they are the equivalent of beachfront property. Studies have shown that placing items on end caps can boost their sales by as much as a third. By giving items their own little plot of land, supermarkets convey the impression that they are special or that they are a good deal. Not necessarily. Just because something is on the end cap doesn't mean it's on sale. Worse, supermarkets sometimes use the end caps to move product that hasn't been selling that well—meaning those Little Debbie snack cakes you just threw into your cart might be expiring any day now.

## Ambience

Mood lighting. Sample counters. Espresso bars. These days, high-end grocery stores like Whole Foods more closely resemble Macy's than a traditional supermarket. That's because retailers know that the more welcoming you make an environment—and the longer people spend there—the more people will buy (this is also the theory behind Wal-Mart's greeters).

It's not just lighting and music. Supermarkets also use aromas to get you in the mood to shop. That's why you'll find the rotisserie chicken roasting near the entrance to many grocery stores.

## Changing Locations of Items

For many people, the grocery store becomes routine—they purchase the same staples each week, and after a while, shoppers on autopilot begin to ignore the other items in the store. To combat this, grocery stores will constantly rotate stock. By shifting items—even within the same aisle—supermarkets can force shoppers to consider new—and hopefully more expensive—items.

## Product Placement on Shelves

It's one of the fundamentals of marketing: People are lazy. But just how lazy is surprising. Study after study has shown that the average grocery shopper can't even be bothered to look at anything beyond eye level. Some supermarkets take advantage of this by putting the most expensive items on eye-level shelves in the aisles, while others charge suppliers a hefty fee for a spot there. Consumer experts suggest better deals can be found by simply checking out the items on the bottom or top shelves.

## Putting Promotional Displays or Nonfood Items at the Entrance

When's the last time you walked into a grocery story and saw what you needed at the entrance? Probably never. Consumer psychologists have found that shoppers need a little time to get into the shopping mind-set. As a result, the entrance of grocery stores are known as something of a dead zone, sales-wise. That's why you'll often find magazines, books, and the flower department near the front of the store—anything to get the shopper into a more relaxed state of mind.

## Advertising Nonsale Items in the Sale Flyers

Savvy grocery shoppers in search of the best deal head straight for the flyer rack when they enter a supermarket. Little do they know that those "sale flyers" are littered with nonsale items. Advertising items at their regular price alongside items that are actually on sale creates the illusion that the regularly priced items are a great buy.

# If Bats Are Blind, How Do They Know Where They're Going?

*We've all heard the expression "blind as a bat"—but the fact is, bats can see. All bat species have eyes, and some have pretty good vision.*

✳   ✳   ✳   ✳

TAKE THE MEGACHIROPTERA bat (more commonly known as the Old World fruit bat or flying fox). Members of this tropical suborder are known for their large eyes and excellent nighttime eyesight. Studies have shown that they're able to see things at lower light levels than even humans can. Most Megachiroptera bats rely completely on their vision to find the fruits and flower nectar they like to munch while flying around at night.

Smaller Microchiroptera bats count on their eyesight, too. These insect-eating bats can see obstacles and motion while navigating speedy, long-distance trips. However, like many bat species, mouselike Microchiroptera also receive some extra guidance from a remarkable physiological process known as echolocation. When flying in the dark, these bats emit high-frequency sounds and then use the echoes to determine distance and direction, as well as the size and movement of anything in front of them.

This "biological sonar system" is so refined that it can track the wing beats of a moth or something as fine as a human hair. Neuroethologists (people who study how nervous systems generate natural animal behavior) will tell you that our military doesn't even have sonar that sophisticated.

Bats have been the subject of myth, mystery, and misconception for centuries. Until recently, traditional thinking was that nocturnal bats could see at night but were blind by day. Now scientists at the Max Planck Institute for Brain Research in

Frankfurt, Germany, and at The Field Museum of Natural History in Chicago have discovered that Megachiroptera bats have daylight vision, too. Apparently, this vision comes in handy for locating predators and even for socializing. Flying foxes don't sleep all day—they bounce from treetop to treetop for daytime confabs with their batty neighbors.

So there you have it: Bats can see, and they definitely know where they are going. The next time you want to use a creative—though rather impolite—idiom to describe Aunt Millie's nearsightedness, you'd be more accurate to say she's "blind as a mole." That small, burrowing mammal has very small eyes and, indeed, very poor vision.

## How Can Celebrity Tabloids Get Away with Publishing Obviously Untrue Stories?

*Supermarket tabloids thrive on publishing outlandish celebrity rumors and innuendo. You'd think that the subjects of their articles would be suing them all the time.*

✳ ✳ ✳ ✳

How in the world could the tabloids survive the legal fees and multi-million-dollar judgments? The truth is, if tabloids are good at one thing, it's surviving.

There are two kinds of tabloids: the ridiculous ones that publish stories nobody really believes ("Bigfoot Cured My Arthritis!") and those that focus on celebrity gossip.

The ridiculous stories are easy to get away with. They're mostly fabricated or based on slender truths. As long as they contain nothing damaging about a real person, there's no one to file a lawsuit. Bigfoot isn't litigious.

Celebrity gossip is trickier. To understand how tabloids avoid legal problems, we need to learn a little bit about the legal definition of "libel." To be found guilty of libel, you must have published something about another person that is provably false.

Moreover, the falsehood has to have caused that person some kind of damage, even if only his or her reputation is harmed. If the subject of the story is a notable person, such as a politician or a movie star, libel legally occurs only if publication of the falsehood is malicious. This means that the publisher knows the information is false, had access to the truth but ignored it, and published the information anyway.

Tabloids generally have lawyers on staff or on retainer who are experts in media law and libel. By consulting with their lawyers, tabloid editors can publish stories that get dangerously close to libel but don't quite cross the line.

A defense against libel is publication of the truth: You can't sue someone for saying something about you that's true, no matter how embarrassing. Tabloids know that if they print something close to the truth, a celebrity is unlikely to sue because a trial could reveal a skeleton in the closet that's more embarrassing.

Libel lawyers also know that a tabloid is in the clear if it publishes a story based on an informant's opinion. Opinions can't be disproved, so they don't meet the criteria for libel. This explains headlines such as this: "Former Housekeeper Says Movie Star Joe Smith Is a Raving Lunatic!" As long as the tabloid makes a token effort to corroborate the story—or even includes a rebuttal of the housekeeper's claims within the article—it is fairly safe from a legal standpoint.

Of course, legal tricks don't always work. Some movie stars, musicians, and other celebrities have successfully sued tabloids for tens of millions of dollars. That tabloids continue to thrive despite such judgments shows just how much money there is to be made in the rumors-and-innuendo business.

# Castrati: Going Under the Knife to Hit the High Notes

*"Mutilated for their art" is how one period writer praised the castrati, male sopranos and alto-sopranos whose manhood was intentionally removed before puberty to keep their voices "sweet."*

✳ ✳ ✳ ✳

PUTTING YOUNG BOYS under the knife to create a corps of eunuchs had been done since antiquity in many cultures. While the practice was applied by the Byzantine, Ottoman, and Chinese to create castes of priests, civil servants, and harem guards, the Italians of the 16th century used it to populate their church choirs.

Young boys can hit the high notes for only so long before their hormones kick in and thicken the vocal cords, turning altos into tenors and sopranos into baritones, bass-baritones, or big men who sing bass. Italians of the late Renaissance, with the blessing of a Papal Bull from 1589, preempted this natural progression. Italian priests and choirmasters recruited boys, and parents sold or even volunteered their sons—often as young as eight years old—to undergo castration. The removal of their testicles ensured that the boys would maintain their sweet, high, angelic voices—voices which, as they grew into men would become stronger and louder and more powerful without dropping in tone and timbre. A castrati had the "chest of a man and the voice of a woman," as one enthusiastic supporter of the practice observed.

The Italians were not the first to introduce prepubescent emasculation in the name of art. Byzantine Empress Eudoxia first sanctioned this practice in AD 400 at the urging of her choirmaster, Brison, but the practice soon fell out of favor. Even so, as the Renaissance and the golden age of church music dawned, the castration of young boys began to occur with regularity throughout Europe, particularly in Germany. It was in Italy, however, where it became something of a mania and where it continued for the longest amount of time.

By the late 18th century, as many as 4,000 boys a year were inducted into the ranks of the castrati in Italy alone—an especially staggering statistic considering the almost complete lack of anesthesia and the crude medical practices of the era. All of this was done "in the name of divine service" and was meant as a way to praise the Lord.

Castrati also appeared in plays, taking female roles at a time when women were still banned from performing in public. Although most castrati never left the choir, the popularization and proliferation of opera in the 17th, 18th, and 19th centuries gave them a new stage on which to showcase their talents. Opera castrati were the superstars of their era; noted composers wrote lead roles for them. Prized for the power and pitch of their angelic voices, the best of them were the toast of Europe, courted by kings, praised by artists, and sought after by rich women, partly as ornaments, partly as sexual curiosities.

The French, Industrial, and other revolutions that rocked Europe eventually turned public opinion against this practice. At first only frowned upon, it was soon banned by law. Italy, in 1870, was the last of the European countries to enact such legislation. The Catholic Church, however, continued to welcome castrati into church choirs until 1902, and it was not until the following year that Pope Leo XIII revoked the Papal Bull of 1589.

Even as their ranks thinned, cries of *eviva il coltello* or "long live the knife" continued to resound for these aging stars when they performed. Castrati hit the high notes right up until the eve of the First World War. Alessandro Moreschi, who retired in 1913, was the last, and by some accounts, the greatest of these physically flawed artists. His angelic falsetto has been preserved in a rare recording made in 1902.

# It's Better Than a Sixth Sense: Squish Sense

*With some natural aptitude and years of training in an Eastern monastery, you may acquire certain fighting skills that let you drop a grown man to his knees in an instant—but even the most agile martial arts master struggles when it's time to swat a fly.*

✳ ✳ ✳ ✳

## A Bug's Life

INSECTS MAY BE tiny and powerless, but they have adaptations that give them an edge against the many larger forms of life that want to do them in. For starters, the bugs that you most want to squish—flies, cockroaches, and the like—are equipped with compound eyes. A compound eye is a collection of structures called ommatidia. A fly, for example, has four thousand ommatidia in each eye; each ommatidium has its own light-sensing cells and a focusing lens that's positioned for a unique field of view.

Collectively, the elements of its compound eyes produce a panoramic vision of the bug's surroundings. The resolution of the resulting image isn't so hot, but it does the trick for detecting sudden movements from almost any direction.

Even when their supercharged vision fails them, insects have other ways to escape your wrath. Many bugs can actually feel the flyswatter approaching thanks to special sensory hairs called setae. When you start your bug-smashing motion, you push air between you and your target. This shift in air pressure stimulates the bug's setae, which signal the brain that something is coming. The movement of the setae gives the bug an idea of where the threat is coming from, and the bug reacts by scurrying in the opposite direction.

## Planning Ahead

It also helps that some bugs are thinking about their get-aways before it even seems necessary. In 2008, biologists at the California Institute of Technology used high-speed cameras to observe a group of flies. They found that it takes less than a tenth of a second for a fly to identify a potential threat, plan an escape route, and position its legs for optimal takeoff. In other words, when you're sneaking up on a fly and getting ready to strike, that fly has probably already spotted you and is prepared to zip away. This little bit of extra preparation helps pave the way for a Houdini-like escape.

Will the valuable information gleaned from this research enable us to finally gain the upper hand—quite literally—in our ongoing chess match against bugs? Don't count on it.

# How Do Fireworks Form Different Shapes?

*Fireworks have been delighting people (and on the negative side, blowing off fingers) for more than seven hundred years, and the design hasn't changed much in that time. Getting those fireworks to form complex shapes is a tricky challenge, but the basic idea is still fairly old-school.*

✳  ✳  ✳  ✳

To UNDERSTAND WHAT's involved, it helps to know some fireworks basics. A fireworks shell is a heavy paper container that holds three sections of explosives. The first section is the "lift charge," a packet of black powder (a mixture of potassium nitrate, sulphur, and charcoal) at the bottom of the shell. To prepare the shell for launch, a pyrotechnician places the shell in a mortar (a tube that has the same diameter as the shell), with the lift charge facing downward. A quick-burning fuse runs from the lift charge to the top of the mortar. To fire the shell, an electric trigger lights the quick fuse. It burns down to ignite the black powder at the bottom of the shell, and the resulting explosion propels the shell out of the mortar and high into the air.

The second explosive section is the "bursting charge," a packet of black powder in the middle of the shell. When the electric trigger lights the quick-burning fuse, it also lights a time-delay fuse that runs to the bursting charge. As the shell is hurtling through the air, the time-delay fuse is burning down. Around the time the shell reaches its highest point, the fuse burns down to the bursting charge, and the black powder explodes.

Expanding black powder isn't exactly breathtaking to watch. The vibrant colors you see come from the third section of explosives, known as the "stars." Stars are simply solid clumps of explosive metals that emit colored light when they burn. For example, burning copper salts emit blue light and burning barium nitrate emits green light. The expanding black powder ignites the stars and propels them outward, creating colored streaks in the sky.

The shape of the explosion depends on how the manufacturer positions the stars in the shell. To make a simple ring, it places the stars in a ring around the bursting charge; to make a heart, it positions the stars in a heart shape. Manufacturers can make more complex fireworks patterns, such as a smiley face, by combining multiple compartments with separate bursting charges and stars in a single shell. As the fuse burns, these different "breaks" go off in sequence. In a smiley face shell, the first break that explodes makes a ring, the second creates two dots for the eyes, and the third forms a crescent shape for the mouth.

It's hard to produce designs that are much more complex than that, since only a few breaks can be set off in quick succession. So if you're hoping to see a fireworks tribute to origami, you're out of luck.

# Food Science: How They Salt Peanuts in the Shell

*No, bioengineers haven't created a super breed of naturally salty peanut plants (yet). The method isn't nearly that complicated.*

\* \* \* \*

To salt peanuts while they're still in the shell, food manufacturers soak them in brine (salty water). In one typical approach, the first step is to treat the peanuts with a wetting agent—a chemical compound that reduces surface tension in water, making it penetrate the shell more readily. Next, the peanuts are placed into an enclosed metal basket and immersed in an airtight pressure vessel that is filled with brine. The pressure vessel is then depressurized to drive air out of the peanut shells and suck in saltwater.

Peanuts may go through several rounds of pressurization and depressurization. Once the peanuts are suitably salty, they are rinsed with clean water and spun on a centrifuge in order to get rid of the bulk of the water. Finally, they are popped into an oven so that the drying process can be completed.

Now, if they could just figure out how to cram some chocolate into those peanuts.

# The Bermuda Dry-angle

*What happens to those socks that get lost in the dryer?*

\* \* \* \*

Dogs eat them. Aliens abduct them. Sock puppets kidnap them. The heat and rapid spinning motions of the dryer transport them to an alternate space-time continuum. Or maybe they wind up in the Bermuda Triangle or on a giant sock dune on the planet Saturn.

Of course, there's always the possibility that they've simply departed this physical world for the great big sock drawer in the sky. May 9 is officially Lost Sock Memorial Day. Come to think of it, one of those TV news magazine shows should really investigate the possibility of a sock suicide pact. Hey, if you spent your days warming the sweaty toes of some smelly teenager, wouldn't you consider checking out early?

Short of sending Geraldo Rivera undercover as a 100 percent stretch nylon Gold Toe (we could spin him around in a Maytag to see what happens), is there any way to know where all the lost socks go? There's got to be a logical explanation, right?

Well, conspiracy theorists maintain it all has to do with a long-time clandestine concordat between America's sock weavers and the major appliance makers. Have they created some sort of top-secret sock material and patented tumbling action that makes our anklets, crews, and knee-highs disintegrate into thin air?

Strange how socks seem to go missing without leaving a single thread of evidence behind. You can sweep that laundry room with the precision of a forensic scientist at a crime scene. The only clue you'll uncover in this case: U.S. sock sales amount to about $4.9 billion annually. Hmm…

Of course, reps from both sides adamantly deny any wrongdoing in the disappearance of perhaps millions of American socks over the years. In fact, executives at Michigan-based Whirlpool say it's not them, it's you. According to Whirlpool, your dirty socks often don't even make it to the machine. They fall out of the laundry basket in a trail behind you on the way to the washer. Or your kids shoot them around like basketballs so they end up under the bed. Research by Whirlpool's Institute of Fabric Science also reveals that static cling is a culprit. When socks do make it to the dryer, static can send one up a pant leg and another into the corner pocket of a fitted sheet.

What's the solution? Whirlpool recommends placing socks in mesh laundry bags, while Linda Cobb, a DIY Network host and the author of *Talking Dirty Laundry*, advocates the use of sock clips. These are designed to keep single pairs of socks together as they wash and dry.

Of course, clipping each and every pair of socks in the family hamper is going to be time-consuming—and who knows if it'll even work? It would be a whole lot easier to just accept that all those lost socks were taken by the "little people." You do know that gnomes, leprechauns, and pixies turn stolen socks into cozy blankets for their wee offspring, right?

# Shoichi Yokoi: Lost Soldier, Found

*Shoichi Yokoi fled from the Americans invading Guam in 1944 and was not captured until 1972. Repatriated to Japan, he quickly became a sensation—for better or worse.*

✳   ✳   ✳   ✳

O N THE NIGHT of July 21, 1944, Sergeant Shoichi Yokoi of the Japanese Imperial Army was engaged in a desperate fight with advancing Americans whose tanks were ripping apart his regiment. As the situation became increasingly dire, Yokoi chose to flee rather than be killed, or worse, captured alive. He was not alone: More than 1,000 Japanese soldiers were hiding in the jungles of Guam when Americans secured the island; nearly all were killed or captured soon afterward. Only Yokoi and eight other soldiers remained undiscovered in the dense depths of the jungle.

By 1964, his companions had either surrendered or died, and Yokoi was alone. He knew the war was over but he chose to remain hidden. "We Japanese soldiers were told to prefer death to the disgrace of getting captured alive," he later said. Certainly, Yokoi had another strong motive for remaining hidden. The Japanese army had been cruel to the native Guam population and Yokoi feared that he would be killed in reparation. So he hid and survived alone for another eight years—a remarkable 28 years total.

## How Did He Do It?

**Clothing:** Before the war, Yokoi had been a tailor's apprentice. Though his skills with fabric were of no help against American tanks, they proved very useful in the jungle. By pounding tree bark, Yokoi was able to make fiber that he used to fashion three suits of clothes. He reworked a piece of brass to make a sewing needle and repurposed plastic to make buttons.

**Food:** While hiding in the jungles of Guam, Yokoi ate snails, rats, eels, pigeons, mangoes, nuts, crabs, and prawns. Occasionally he'd have wild hog. Although he boiled all the water he drank, and cooked the meat thoroughly, he once became ill for a month after eating a cow.

**Shelter:** Surviving in the jungle for 28 years is one thing. Surviving *undetected* in the jungle is quite another. Yokoi went to great lengths to disguise his shelters. His most permanent dwelling was a tunnel-like cave, hand-dug using a piece of artillery shell. At one end of the three-foot-high shelter, a latrine emptied down an embankment into a river; at the other end a small kitchen contained some shelves, a cooking pot, and a coconut shell lantern.

## "It is with much embarrassment that I have returned alive"

The Japanese word *ganbaru* refers to the positive character traits associated with sticking to one's task during tough times. For many Japanese who survived the war, Yokoi was the living embodiment of ganbaru. However, for the young people of Japan's increasingly Western culture, Yokoi was an embarrassing reminder of the previous generations' blind fealty to the Emperor that had caused Japan's disgrace. Though he longed to see the Emperor and wrote a letter to apologize for having survived the war, Yokoi was never granted an audience.

## Reassimilation

Millions of television viewers across Japan watched Yokoi's return trip to his native village where a gravestone listed his death as September 1944. From those who considered him a hero, Yokoi received gifts of money totaling more than $80,000 and many marriage offers.

He purchased a modest home and married Mihoko Hatashin, who he described as a "nice, old-fashioned" girl, unlike the modern Japanese girls whom he described as "monsters whose virtue is all but gone from them, and who screech like apes."

Though horrified by the Westernization of his homeland, Yokoi prospered as a lecturer on survival techniques. He unsuccessfully ran for Parliament on a platform that stressed simplicity and discipline and included such measures as enforced composting and converting golf courses into bean fields. On September 22, 1997, Yokoi died of heart failure at age 82.

# How to Beat a Lie Detector Test

*If you've been told that you will need to take a polygraph test before accepting a job or to be cleared of a crime, watch out—you're about to be duped. The polygraph or "lie detector" test is one of the most misunderstood tests used in law enforcement and industry.*

✳   ✳   ✳   ✳

MANY EXPERTS WILL tell you that lie detector tests are based on fallible data—regardless of how scientific the equipment appears, there's no sure way a person can tell whether or not someone is lying. Since the test is so imperfect, be suspicious of anyone who makes your fate contingent upon the results. Still, here are a few suggestions on how to beat one:

1. Unless you're applying for a job, refuse to take the polygraph test. There are no laws that can compel anyone to take it.

2. Keep your answers short. Most questions asked of you can be answered with a "yes" or "no." Keep it simple.

3. During the polygraph test, you'll be asked three types of questions: irrelevant, relevant, and control questions. Irrelevant questions generally take the form of, "Is the color of this room white?" Relevant questions are the areas that get you into trouble. Control questions are designed to "calibrate" your responses during the test. See the next point.

4. Control questions are asked so that the technician can compare the responses to questions against a known entity. The easiest way to beat a lie detector test is to invalidate the control questions. Try these simple techniques when you are asked a control question:

♦ Change your breathing rate and depth from the normal 15 to 30 breaths per minute to anything faster or slower.

♦ Solve a math problem in your head, or count backward from 100 by 7.

♦ Bite the sides of your tongue until it begins to hurt.

# How Do Carrier Pigeons Know Where to Go?

*No family vacation would be complete without at least one episode of Dad grimly staring straight ahead, gripping the steering wheel, and declaring that he is not lost as Mom insists on stopping for directions. Meanwhile, the kids are tired, night is falling, and nobody's eaten anything except a handful of Cheetos for the past six hours. But Dad is not lost. He will not stop.*

❊    ❊    ❊    ❊

IT'S WELL KNOWN that men believe they have some sort of innate directional ability—and why not? If a creature as dull and dim-witted as a carrier pigeon can find its way home without any maps or directions from gas-station attendants, a healthy human male should certainly be able to do the same.

Little does Dad know that the carrier pigeon has a secret weapon. It's called magnetite, and its recent discovery in the beaks of carrier pigeons may help solve the centuries-old mystery of just how carrier pigeons know their way home.

Since the fifth century BC, when they were used for communication between Syria and Persia, carrier pigeons have been prized for their ability to find their way home, sometimes over distances of more than five hundred miles. In World War I and World War II, Allied forces made frequent use of carrier pigeons, sending messages with them from base to base to avoid having radio signals intercepted or if the terrain prevented a clear signal. In fact, several carrier pigeons were honored with war medals.

For a long time, there was no solid evidence to explain how these birds were able to find their way anywhere, despite theories that ranged from an uncanny astronomical sense to a heightened olfactory ability to an exceptional sense of hearing. Recently, though, scientists made an important discovery: bits of magnetic crystal, called magnetite, embedded in the beaks of carrier pigeons. This has led some researchers to believe that carrier pigeons have magneto reception—the ability to detect changes in the earth's magnetic fields—which is a sort of built-in compass that guides these birds to their destinations.

Scientists verified the important role of magnetite through a study that examined the effects of magnetic fields on the birds' homing ability. When the scientists blocked the birds' magnetic ability by attaching small magnets to their beaks, the pigeons' ability to orient themselves plummeted by almost 50 percent. There was no report, however, on whether this handicap stopped male pigeons from plunging blindly forward. We'd guess not.

# How to Break a Concrete Block with Your Hand

*It's an act that's synonymous with martial arts, and we reveal some of the tricks of the concrete-busting trade.*

✳ ✳ ✳ ✳

## Hand vs. Block

IN A FACE-OFF between hand and block, the hand has a surprising advantage: Bone is significantly stronger than concrete. In fact, bone can withstand about 40 times more stress than concrete before reaching its breaking point. What's more, the surrounding muscles and ligaments in your hands are good stress absorbers, making the hand and arm one tough weapon. So if you position your hand correctly, you're not going to break it by hitting concrete.

The trick to smashing a block is thrusting this sturdy mass into the concrete with enough force to bend the block beyond its breaking point. The force of any impact is determined by the momentum of the two objects in the collision. Momentum is a multiple of the mass and velocity of an object.

## Velocity Is the Key

When striking an object, the speed of your blow is critical. You also have to hit the block with a relatively small area of your hand, so that the force of the impact is focused in one spot on the block—this concentrates the stress on the concrete. As in golf, the only way for a martial arts student to hit accurately with greater speed is practice, practice, practice.

But there is a basic mental trick involved: You have to overcome your natural instinct to slow your strike as your hand approaches the block. Martial arts masters concentrate on an impact spot beyond the block, so that the hand is still at maximum speed when it makes contact with the concrete.

## Body Mass Counts, Too

You also need to put as much body mass as you can into the strike; this can be achieved by twisting your body and lowering your torso as you make contact. A black belt in karate can throw a chop at about 46 feet per second, which results in a force of about 2,800 newtons. (A newton is the unit of force needed to accelerate a mass.)

That's more than enough power to break the standard one-and-a-half-inch concrete slabs that are commonly used in demonstrations and typically can withstand only 1,900 newtons. Nonetheless, while hands are dandy in a block-breaking exhibition, you'll find that for sidewalk demolition and other large projects, jackhammers are really the way to go.

# Psychic Detectives

*When the corpse just can't be found, the murderer remains unknown, and the weapon has been stashed in some secret corner, criminal investigations hit a stalemate and law enforcement agencies may tap their secret weapons—individuals who find things through some unconventional methods.*

✳   ✳   ✳   ✳

### "Reading" the Ripper: Robert James Lees

WHEN THE PSYCHOTIC murderer known as Jack the Ripper terrorized London in the 1880s, the detectives of Scotland Yard consulted a psychic named Robert James Lees who said he had glimpsed the killer's face in several visions. Lees also claimed he had correctly forecasted at least three of the well-publicized murders of women. The Ripper wrote a sarcastic note to detectives stating that they would still never catch him. Indeed, the killer proved right in this prediction.

### Feeling Their Vibes: Florence Sternfels

As a psychometrist—a psychic who gathers impressions by handling material objects—Florence Sternfels was successful enough to charge a dollar for readings in Edgewater, New Jersey, in the early 20th century. Born in 1891, Sternfels believed that her gift was a natural ability rather than a supernatural one, so she never billed police for her help in solving crimes. Some of her best "hits" included preventing a man from blowing up an army base with dynamite, finding two missing boys alive in Philadelphia, and leading police to the body of a murdered young woman. She worked with police as far away as Europe to solve tough cases but lived quietly in New Jersey until her death in 1965.

## The Dutch Grocer's Gift: Gerard Croiset

Born in the Netherlands in 1909, Gerard Croiset nurtured a psychic ability from age six. In 1935, he joined a Spiritualist group, began to hone his talents, and within two years had set up shop as a psychic and healer. After a touring lecturer discovered his abilities in 1945, Croiset began assisting law enforcement agencies around the world, traveling as far as Japan and Australia. He specialized in finding missing children but also helped authorities locate lost papers and artifacts. At the same time, Croiset ran a popular clinic for psychic healing that treated both humans and animals. His son, Gerard Croiset, Jr., was also a professional psychic and parapsychologist.

## Accidental Psychic: Peter Hurkos

As one of the most famous psychic detectives of the 20th century, Peter Hurkos did his best work by picking up vibes from victims' clothing. Born in the Netherlands in 1911, Hurkos lived an ordinary life as a house painter until a fall required him to undergo brain surgery at age 30. The operation seemed to trigger his latent psychic powers, and he was almost immediately able to mentally retrieve information about people and "read" the history of objects by handling them.

Hurkos assisted in the Boston Strangler investigation in the early 1960s, and in 1969, he was brought in to help solve the grisly murders executed by Charles Manson. He gave police many accurate details including the name Charlie, a description of Manson, and that the murders were ritual slayings.

## The TV Screen Mind of Dorothy Allison

New Jersey housewife Dorothy Allison broke into the world of clairvoyant crime solving when she dreamed about a missing local boy as if seeing it on television. In her dream, the five-year-old boy was stuck in some kind of pipe. When she called police, she also described the child's clothing, including the odd fact that he was wearing his shoes on the opposite feet. When Allison underwent hypnosis to learn more details, she added that the boy's surroundings involved a fenced school and a factory. She was proven correct on all accounts when the boy's body was found about two months after he went missing, floating close to a pipe in a pond near a school and a factory with his little shoes still tied onto the wrong feet.

Allison, who began having psychic experiences as a child, considered her gift a blessing and never asked for pay. One of her more famous cases was that of missing heiress Patty Hearst in 1974. Although Allison was unable to find her, every prediction she made about the young woman came true, including the fact that she had dyed her hair red.

## Like a Bolt Out of the Blue: John Catchings

While at a Texas barbeque on an overcast July 4, 1969, a bolt of lightning hit 22-year-old John Catchings. He survived but said the electric blast opened him to his life's calling as a psychic. He then followed in the footsteps of his mother, Bertie, who earned her living giving "readings."

Catchings often helped police solve odd cases but became famous after helping police find a missing, 32-year-old Houston nurse named Gail Lorke. She vanished in October 1982, after her husband, Steven, claimed she had stayed home from work because she was sick. Because Catchings worked by holding objects that belonged to victims, Lorke's sister, who was suspicious of Steven, went to Catchings with a photo of Gail and her belt. Allegedly, Catchings saw that Lorke had indeed been murdered by her husband and left under a heap of refuse that included parts of an old, wooden fence. He also gave police several other key details. Detectives were able to use the information to get Steven Lorke to confess his crime.

Among many other successes, Catchings also helped police find the body of Mike Dickens in 1980 after telling them the young man would be found buried in a creek bed near a shoe and other rubbish, including old tires and boards. Police discovered the body there just as Catchings had described it.

## Fame from Fortunes: Irene Hughes

By 2008, famed investigative psychic Irene Hughes claimed a tally of more than 2,000 police cases on her website. Born around 1920 in rural Tennessee, Hughes shocked her church congregation at age four when she shouted out that the minister would soon leave them. She was right and kept on making predictions, advised by a "spirit guide" named Kaygee. After World War II, Hughes moved to Chicago to take a job as a reporter. She financed her trip by betting on a few horse races using her psychic abilities! She gained fame in 1967 when she correctly prophesied Chicago's terrible blizzard and that the Cardinals would win the World Series. By 1968, she was advising Howard Hughes and correctly predicted his death in 1976.

Hughes's more famous predictions included the death of North Vietnamese premiere Ho Chi Minh in 1969 (although she was off by a week), the circumstances of Ted Kennedy's Chappaquiddick fiasco, and that Jacqueline Kennedy would marry someone with the characteristics of her eventual second husband, Aristotle Onassis. Hughes operated out of a luxurious office on Chicago's Michigan Avenue and commanded as much as $500 an hour from her many clients. She hosted radio and TV shows, wrote three books, and in the 1980s and '90s, wrote a much-read column of New Year's predictions for the *National Enquirer*.

# Chapter 4

# Unsolved Mysteries

## Vanished: The Lost Colony of Roanoke Island

*Twenty years before England established its first successful colony in the New World, an entire village of English colonists disappeared in what would later be known as North Carolina. Did these pioneers all perish? Did Native Americans capture them? Did they join a friendly tribe? Could they have left descendants who live among us today?*

✳   ✳   ✳   ✳

### Timing Is Everything

Talk about bad timing. As far as John White was concerned, England couldn't have picked a worse time to go to war. It was November 1587, and White had just arrived in England from the New World. He intended to gather relief supplies and immediately sail back to Roanoke Island, where he had left more than 100 colonists who were running short of food. Unfortunately, the English were gearing up to fight Spain. Every seaworthy ship, including White's, was pressed into naval service. Not a one could be spared for his return voyage.

### Nobody Home

When White returned three years later, he was dismayed to find that the colonists were nowhere to be found. Instead, he stumbled upon a mystery—one that has never been solved.

The village that White and company had founded in 1587 on Roanoke Island lay completely deserted. Houses had been dismantled (as if someone planned to move them), but the pieces lay in the long grass along with iron tools and farming equipment. A stout stockade made of logs stood empty.

White found no sign of his daughter Eleanor, her husband Ananias, or their daughter Virginia Dare—the first English child born in America. None of the 87 men, 17 women, and 11 children remained. No bodies or gravesites offered clues to their fate. The only clues—if they were clues—that White could find were the letters CRO carved into a tree and the word CROATOAN carved into a log of the abandoned fort.

## No Forwarding Address

All White could do was hope that the colonists had been taken in by friendly natives.

Croatoan—also spelled "Croatan"—was the name of a barrier island to the south and also the name of a tribe of Native Americans that lived on that island. Unlike other area tribes, the Croatoans had been friendly to English newcomers, and one of them, Manteo, had traveled to England with earlier explorers and returned to act as interpreter for the Roanoke colony. Had the colonists, with Manteo's help, moved to Croatoan? Were they safe among friends?

White tried to find out, but his timing was rotten once again. He had arrived on the Carolina coast as a hurricane bore down on the region. The storm hit before he could mount a search. His ship was blown past Croatoan Island and out to sea. Although the ship and crew survived the storm and made it back to England, White was stuck again. He tried repeatedly but failed to raise money for another search party.

No one has ever learned the fate of the Roanoke Island colonists, but there is no shortage of theories as to what happened to them. A small sailing vessel and other boats that White had left with them were gone when he returned. It's possible that the colonists used the vessels to travel to another island or to the mainland. White had talked with others before he left about possibly moving the settlement to a more secure location inland. It's even possible that the colonists tired of waiting for White's return and tried to sail back to England. If so, they would have perished at sea. Yet there are at least a few shreds of hearsay evidence that the colonists survived in America.

## Rumors of Survivors

In 1607, Captain John Smith and company established the first successful English settlement in North America at Jamestown, Virginia. The colony's secretary, William Strachey, wrote four years later about hearing a report of four English men, two boys, and one young woman who had been sighted south of Jamestown at a settlement of the Eno tribe, where they were being used as slaves. If the report was true, who else could these English have been but Roanoke survivors?

For a century after the disappearance, stories emerged of gray-eyed Native Americans and English-speaking villages in North Carolina and Virginia. In 1709, an English surveyor said members of the Hatteras tribe living on North Carolina's Outer Banks—some of them with light-colored eyes—claimed to be descendants of white people. It's possible that the Hatteras were the same people that the 1587 colonists called Croatoan.

In the intervening centuries, many of the individual tribes of the region have disappeared. Some died out. Others were absorbed into larger groups such as the Tuscarora. One surviving group, the Lumbee, has also been called Croatoan. The Lumbee, who still live in North Carolina, often have Caucasian features. Could they be descendants of Roanoke colonists? Many among the Lumbee dismiss the notion as fanciful, but the tribe has long been thought to be of mixed heritage and has been speaking English so long that none among them know what language preceded it.

# Who Downed the Red Baron? The Mystery of Manfred von Richthofen

*He was the most successful flying ace of World War I—the conflict that introduced the airplane as a weapon of war. Yet his demise has been credited to a number of likely opponents, both in the sky and on the ground.*

✳  ✳  ✳  ✳

## Precious Little Prussian

**M**ANFRED VON RICHTHOFEN was born in Silesia, Prussia (now part of Poland), in May 1892. Coming from a family steeped in nobility, the young von Richthofen decided he would follow in his father's footsteps and become a career soldier. At 11 years old, he enrolled in the cadet corps and, upon completion, became a member of a Prussian cavalry unit.

## Up, Up, and Away

The Germans were at the forefront in using aircraft as offensive weapons against the British, French, and Russians during World War I. Von Richthofen was recruited into a flying unit as an "observer"—the second occupant of a two-seat plane who would direct the pilot over areas to gather intelligence. By 1915, von Richthofen decided to become a pilot himself, having already downed an enemy aircraft as an observer.

The young and green pilot joined a prestigious flying squad, one of the premier German *jagdstaffeln*—literally "hunting squadrons." In late 1916, von Richthofen's aggressive style brought him face-to-face with Britain's greatest fighter pilot, Major Lanoe Hawker. After a spirited battle in the sky, the German brought Hawker down in a tailspin, killing him. Von Richthofen called Hawker "a brave man and a sportsman." He later mounted the machine gun from the British plane over the door of his family home as a tribute to Hawker. The bold flying ace often showed a great deal of respect and affinity for his foes, once referring to his English dogfight opponents as "waltzing partners." Yet, he remained ruthless, even carrying with him a photograph of an Allied pilot he had viciously blown apart.

## Creating an Identity

Von Richthofen quickly became the most feared, and respected, pilot in the skies. As he sought faster and more nimble aircraft, he decided he needed to be instantly recognizable. He ordered his plane to be painted bright red, with the German Iron Cross emblazoned on the fuselage. The "Red Baron" was born.

## The End—But at Whose Hands?

By the spring of 1918, the Red Baron had shot down an amazing 80 Allied airplanes. This feat earned him the distinguished "Blue Max" award, and he assembled his own squadron of crack-shot pilots known as "the Flying Circus." But the celebrated pilot was not without his failures.

Von Richthofen suffered a head wound during an air battle in July 1917, which may have left an open wound exposing a small portion of his skull until his death. There are theories that this injury resulted in brain damage—if so, it would have caused the Red Baron to make some serious errors in judgment that may have led to his death on April 21, 1918.

On that day, von Richthofen was embroiled in a deadly dogfight with British Royal Air Force Sopwith Camels. As the Red Baron trained his machine-gun sights on a young pilot, enemy fire came seemingly from nowhere, striking his red Fokker. Von Richthofen crashed in an area of France occupied by Australian and Canadian allies. He was buried with full military honors by a respectful British Royal Air Force (RAF).

However, questions remain to this day as to who exactly killed von Richthofen. He suffered a fatal bullet wound through his chest. The RAF credited one of their pilots, but another story tells of Canadian soldiers who pounced on the plane crash and literally murdered the Red Baron. Still other tales claim von Richthofen was shot from the ground by rifle or machine-gun fire as he flew overhead.

The answer remains lost, perhaps forever. But there is no question as to the identity of the greatest flying ace of the First World War. That honor belongs to the Red Baron.

# Curse of the Little Rascals

*Beginning in 1922, the cast of the Our Gang comedies, more commonly referred to as The Little Rascals, filmed a staggering 221 episodes over several decades. After the series ended, many of the cast members met strange or untimely deaths.*

✳ ✳ ✳ ✳

## Alfalfa

AFTER LEAVING THE Little Rascals gang, Carl "Alfalfa" Switzer was never able to find steady acting work, but he did seem to find a lot of trouble. In late 1958, Switzer was shot and wounded while getting into his car, by an unknown assailant. On January 21, 1959, 32-year-old Switzer was shot and killed during an argument with another man over a $50 debt. The shooter was acquitted when it was ruled he acted in self-defense.

## Chubby

His unnatural girth may have brought lots of belly laughs, but off-camera, Norman "Chubby" Chaney's weight was the cause of some concern. When he first joined the series in 1929, he was an 11-year-old who wasn't quite 4 feet tall and weighed more than 110 pounds. In 1935, in bad health and with his weight at around 300 pounds, Chaney underwent an operation to correct a glandular problem. After the operation, Chaney quickly lost more than 135 pounds, but his health continued to deteriorate. Chaney passed away on May 29, 1936, at age 18.

## Froggy

Forever known for his bizarre, croaking voice, Billy "Froggy" Laughlin will also be remembered as the youngest Rascal to die. On August 31, 1948, the 16 year old was riding a scooter in La Puente, California, when a bus or truck struck him. He died instantly.

## Mickey

Mickey Daniels had the unique opportunity of having been a child on the series and then returning as an adult, playing a truant officer and even providing the laugh of the gang's donkey, Algebra. After the series ended, however, Daniels sank into alcohol-induced obscurity. On August 20, 1970, Daniels's body was discovered in a San Diego hotel room. The official cause of death was complications from cirrhosis of the liver.

## Jay

Freckly Jay R. Smith replaced Mickey in 1925. Although he lived to age 87, far longer than many of the other Rascals, Smith still suffered one of the most violent deaths. After he was reported missing from his Las Vegas home in October 2002, a massive search was launched. Several days later, Smith's body, riddled with stab wounds, was found dumped in the desert. An investigation found that Smith had been murdered by a homeless man that he had recently tried to befriend and help.

## Scotty

Forever by Spanky's side, Scott "Scotty" Beckett was one of the most-loved members of the cast. After leaving the series, Beckett enjoyed a successful acting career that was cut short by a series of run-ins with the police, including a shootout. On May 8, 1968, Beckett checked himself into a Hollywood nursing home, needing attention for what appeared to be wounds from a fistfight. Two days later, the 38 year old was found dead in his bed. Despite the fact that a suicide note and a bottle of pills were said to have been found on his nightstand, the coroner claimed he was unable to determine the cause of death.

## Wheezer

Born March 29, 1925, Robert "Wheezer" Hutchins was only two years old when he appeared in his first *Our Gang* episode. Over the next six years, Hutchins would star in nearly 60 shorts. After graduating high school, Hutchins joined the Army Air Corps during World War II (though he didn't see overseas combat). After the war, Hutchins decided to become an air cadet. On May 17, 1945, Hutchins was killed when his plane collided with another aircraft during training exercises at Merced Army Air Corps Field in California. He was only 20 years old.

# Who Built the Pyramids?

*The Great Pyramids of Egypt have maintained their mystery through the eons, and there's still a lot we don't know about them. But we do know this: Slaves, particularly the ancient Hebrew slaves, did not build these grand structures.*

❋    ❋    ❋    ❋

IT'S EASY TO see why people think slaves built the pyramids. Most ancient societies kept slaves, and the Egyptians were no exception. And Hebrew slaves did build other Egyptian monuments during their 400 years of captivity, according to the Old Testament. Even ancient scholars such as the Greek historian Herodotus (fifth century BC) and the Jewish historian Josephus (first century AD) believed that the Egyptians used slave labor in the construction of the pyramids.

Based on the lifestyles of these builders, however, researchers have discredited the notion that they were slaves (Nubians, Assyrians, or Hebrews, among others) who were forced to work. They had more likely willingly labored, both for grain (or other foodstuffs) and to ensure their place in the afterlife. What's more, we now know that the Great Pyramids were built more than a thousand years before the era of the Hebrews (who actually became enslaved during Egypt's New Kingdom).

Archaeologists have determined that many of the people who built the pyramids were conscripted farmers and peasants who lived in the countryside during the Old Kingdom. Archaeologist Mark Lehner of the Semitic Museum at Harvard University has spent more than a decade studying the workers' villages that existed close to the Giza plateau, where the pyramids were built. He has confirmed that the people who built the pyramids were not slaves—rather, they were skilled laborers and "ordinary men and women."

# The Dyatlov Pass Incident

*Nine experienced hikers and skiers trek into the Russian wilderness and promptly disappear. Weeks later, their mangled bodies are found among the ruins of the campsite, with no trace of evidence as to how they died. Read on for a closer look at one of the greatest, creepiest, unsolved mysteries of modern times.*

✳   ✳   ✳   ✳

## Off to the Otorten Mountain

IN EARLY 1959, a group of outdoor enthusiasts formed a skiing and hiking expedition to Otorten Mountain, which is part of the northern Ural range. The group, led by Igor Dyatlov, consisted of eight men and two women: Yury Doroshenko, Georgy Krivonischenko, Alexander Kolevatov, Rustem Slobodin, Nicolas Thibeaux-Brignolle, Yuri Yudin, Alexander Zolotaryov, Lyudmila Dubinina, and Zinaida Kolmogorova.

The journey began on January 27. The following day, Yudin became ill and returned home. It would be the last time he would see his friends. Using personal photographs and journals belonging to the members of the ski trip to piece together the chain of events, it appeared as though on February 1, the group got disoriented making their way to Otorten Mountain and ended up heading too far to the west. Once they realized they were heading in the wrong direction, the decision was made to simply camp for the night. What happened next is a mystery.

## Mountain of the Dead

When no word had been heard from the group by February 20, eight days after their planned return, a group of volunteers organized a search. On February 26, they found the group's abandoned campsite on the east side of the mountain Kholat Syakhl. (As if the story were written by a horror novelist, *Kholat Syakhl* happens to mean "Mountain of the Dead" in the Mansi language.) The search team found a badly damaged tent that appeared to have been ripped open from the inside. They also found several sets of footprints. Following the trail of footprints, searchers discovered the bodies of Krivonischenko and Doroshenko, shoeless and dressed only in their underwear. Three more bodies—those belonging to Dyatlov, Kolmogorova and Slobodin—were found nearby. It was later determined that all five had died from hypothermia.

On May 4, the bodies of the four other hikers were recovered in the woods near where the bodies of Krivonischenko and Doroshenko had been found. The discovery of these four raised even more questions. To begin with, Thibeaux-Brignolle's skull had been crushed and both Dubunina and Zolotaryov had major chest fractures. The force needed to cause these wounds was compared to that of a high-speed car crash. Oddly, Dubinina's tongue appeared to have been ripped out.

Looking at the evidence, it seemed as though all nine members had settled in for the night, only to be woken up by something so frightening that they all left the tent and ran into the freezing night. One by one, they either froze to death or succumbed to their injuries, the cause of which was never determined.

## Remains a Mystery

Things got even stranger at the funerals for the nine individuals. Family members would later remark that some of the deceased's skin had become orange and their hair had turned grey. Medical tests and a Geiger counter brought to the site showed some of the bodies had high levels of radiation.

So what happened to the hikers? Authorities eventually concluded that "an unknown compelling force" caused the deaths. The case would be officially closed in the spring of 1959 due to the "absence of a guilty party." Stories and theories still abound, pointing to everything from the Russian government covering up secret military exercises in the area to violent UFO encounters. Today, the area where the nine hikers met their untimely demise is known as Dyatlov Pass, after the leader of the ill-fated group.

# The Tunguska Event

*What created an explosion 1,000 times greater than the atomic bomb at Hiroshima, destroyed 80 million trees, but left no hole in the ground?*

✳ ✳ ✳ ✳

## The Event

O N THE MORNING of June 30, 1908, a powerful explosion ripped through the remote Siberian wilderness near the Tunguska River. Witnesses, from nomadic herdsmen and passengers on a train to a group of people at the nearest trading post, reported seeing a bright object streak through the sky and explode into an enormous fireball. The resulting shockwave flattened approximately 830 square miles of forest. Seismographs in England recorded the event twice, once as the initial shockwave passed and then again after it had circled the planet. A huge cloud of ash reflected sunlight from over the horizon across Asia and Europe. People reported there being enough light in the night sky to facilitate reading.

## A Wrathful God

Incredibly, nearly 20 years passed before anyone visited the site. Everyone had a theory of what happened, and none of it good. Outside Russia, however, the event itself was largely unknown. The English scientists who recorded the tremor, for instance, thought that it was simply an earthquake. Inside Russia, the unstable political climate of the time was not conducive to mounting an expedition. Subsequently, the economic and social upheaval created by World War I and the Russian Revolution made scientific expeditions impossible.

## Looking for a Hole in the Ground

In 1921, mineralogist Leonid A. Kulik was charged by the Mineralogical Museum of St. Petersburg with locating meteorites that had fallen inside the Soviet Union. Having read old newspapers and eyewitness testimony from the Tunguska region, Kulik convinced the Academy of Sciences in 1927 to fund an expedition to locate the crater and meteorite he was certain existed.

The expedition was not going to be easy, as spring thaws turned the region into a morass. And when the team finally reached the area of destruction, their superstitious guides refused to go any further. Kulik, however, was encouraged by the sight of millions of trees splayed to the ground in a radial pattern pointing outward from an apparent impact point. Returning again, the team finally reached the epicenter where, to their surprise, they found neither a meteor nor a crater. Instead, they found a forest of what looked like telephone poles—trees stripped of their branches and reduced to vertical shafts. Scientists would not witness a similar sight until 1945 in the area below the Hiroshima blast.

## Theories Abound

Here are some of the many theories of what happened at Tunguska.

**Stony Asteroid:** Traveling at a speed of about 33,500 miles per hour, a large space rock heated the air around it to about 44,500 degrees Fahrenheit and exploded at an altitude of nearly 28,000 feet. This produced a fireball that utterly annihilated the asteroid.

**Kimberlite Eruption:** Formed nearly 2,000 miles below the Earth's surface, a shaft of heavy kimberlite rock carried a huge quantity of methane gas to the Earth's surface where it exploded with great force.

**Black Holes & Antimatter:** As early as 1941, some scientists believed that a small antimatter asteroid exploded when it encountered the upper atmosphere. In 1973, several theorists proposed that the Tunguska event was the result of a tiny black hole passing through the Earth's surface.

**Alien Shipwreck:** Noting the similarities between the Hiroshima atomic bomb blast and the Tunguska event, Russian novelist Alexander Kazantsev was the first to suggest that an atomic-powered UFO exploded over Siberia in 1908.

**Tesla's Death Ray:** Scientist Nikola Tesla is rumored to have test-fired a "death ray" on June 30, 1908, but he believed the experiment to be unsuccessful—until he learned of the Tunguska Event.

## Okay, What Really Happened?

In June 2008, scientists from around the world marked the 100-year anniversary of the Tunguska event with conferences in Moscow. Yet scientists still cannot reach a consensus as to what caused the event. In fact, the anniversary gathering was split into two opposing factions—extraterrestrial versus terrestrial—who met at different sites in the city.

# What Really Killed John Wayne?

*The Conqueror (1956) wasn't exactly John Wayne's masterpiece. According to "The Duke" himself, the film was actually written with Marlon Brando in mind for the lead role, and this historical drama has been criticized for miscasting Wayne in the part. However,* The Conqueror *has been connected to far worse things than box office failure: Some say the movie is to blame for Wayne's death from stomach cancer two decades after its debut. What's more, Wayne isn't the only person believed to have died as a result of the project. Was a nearby nuclear testing site to blame?*

✳ ✳ ✳ ✳

## Radiation Exposure

THE QUESTIONS SURROUNDING *The Conqueror* come as a result of its filming location: It was shot near St. George and Snow Canyon, Utah, an area close to a nuclear testing site. In the early 1950s, the U.S. military set off nearly a dozen atomic bombs just miles from the location, sending clouds of radioactive dust into St. George and Snow Canyon. Work on *The Conqueror* began two years later, even though the film company knew about the radiation. To make matters worse, after the location work had wrapped, the film's crew transported dirt from the area back to Hollywood to help re-create the setting for in-studio shooting. (At the time, the effects of radiation exposure were not as well documented as they are now.)

In the years following the filming of *The Conqueror*, numerous members of the cast and crew developed cancer. Aside from Wayne, at least 45 people from the group died from causes related to the disease, including actress Agnes Moorehead, who died in 1974 from uterine cancer; actress Susan Hayward, who died from brain and skin cancer at age 57 in 1975; and director Dick Powell, who, in 1963, passed away at age 58 from lymphatic cancer. Actors Pedro Armendariz and John Hoyt both took their own lives after learning of their diagnoses.

An article published in *People* magazine in 1980 stated that 41 percent of those who worked on the movie—91 out of 220 people—later developed cancer. That figure reportedly didn't include the hundreds of Utah-based actors who worked as extras. Still, the numbers far exceeded any statistical normality for a given group of individuals. A scientist with the Pentagon's Defense Nuclear Agency was quoted in the article as saying: "Please, God, don't let us have killed John Wayne."

## Broader Findings

While many of the actors were heavy smokers—Wayne included—the strange circumstances surrounding the filming of *The Conqueror* have turned into an underground scandal of sorts. And the general findings from the city of St. George certainly don't help quell the concerns.

In 1997, a study by the National Cancer Institute found that children who lived in the St. George area during the 1950s were exposed to as much as 70 times the amount of radiation than was originally reported because of contaminated milk taken from exposed animals. Consequently, the study reported that the children had elevated risks for cancer development. The report further stated that the government "knew from the beginning that a Western test site would spread contamination across most of the country" and that the exposure could have easily been avoided.

The government eventually passed an act called the Radiation Exposure Compensation Act, which provided $50,000 to people who lived downwind of the nuclear testing site near St. George and had been exposed to radiation. At least 40,000 people are thought to have been exposed in Utah alone. While John Wayne is the most famous of them, the true cause of his cancer may never be definitively known.

# Shroud of Turin: Real or Fake?

*Measuring roughly 14 feet long by 3 feet wide, the Shroud of Turin features the front and back image of a man who was 5 feet, 9 inches tall. The man was bearded and had shoulder-length hair parted down the middle. Dark stains on the Shroud are consistent with blood from a crucifixion.*

❋   ❋   ❋   ❋

FIRST PUBLICLY DISPLAYED in 1357, the Shroud of Turin has apparent ties to the Knights of Templar. At the time of its first showing, the Shroud was in the hands of of the family of Geoffrey de Charney, a Templar who had been burned at the stake in 1314 along with Jacques de Molay. Some accounts say it was the Knights who removed the cloth from Constantinople, where it was kept in the 13th century.

Some believe the Shroud of Turin is the cloth that Jesus was wrapped in after his death. All four gospels mention that the body of Jesus was covered in a linen cloth prior to the resurrection. Others assert that the cloth shrouded Jacques de Molay after he was tortured by being nailed to a door.

Still others contend that the Shroud was the early photographic experiments of Leonardo da Vinci. He mentioned working with "optics" in some of his diaries and wrote his notes in a sort of mirrored handwriting style, some say, to keep his experiments secret from the church.

Is the Shroud of Turin authentic? In 1988, scientists using carbon-dating concluded that the material in the Shroud was from around 1260 to 1390, which seems to exclude the possibility that the Shroud bears the image of Jesus.

# The Champion of American Lake Monsters

*In 1609, French explorer Samuel de Champlain was astonished to see a thick, eight- to ten-foot-tall creature in the waters between present-day Vermont and New York. His subsequent report set in motion the legend of Champ, the "monster" in Lake Champlain.*

✳ ✳ ✳ ✳

## Eerie Encounters

EVEN BEFORE CHAMPLAIN'S visit, Champ was known to Native Americans as Chaousarou. Over time, Champ has become one of North America's most famous lake monsters. News stories of its existence were frequent enough that in 1873, showman P. T. Barnum offered $50,000 for the creature, dead or alive. That same year, Champ almost sank a steamboat, and in the 1880s, a number of people, including a sober sheriff, were treated to glimpses of it splashing playfully offshore. It is generally described as dark in color (olive green, gray, or brown) with a serpentlike body.

Sightings have continued into modern times, and witnesses have compiled some film evidence that is difficult to ignore. In 1977, a woman named Sandra Mansi photographed a long-necked creature poking its head out of the water near St. Albans, Vermont, close to the Canadian border. She estimated the animal was 10 to 15 feet long and told an investigator that its skin looked "slimy" and similar to that of an eel. Mansi presented her photo and story at a 1981 conference held at Lake Champlain. Although she had misplaced the negative by then, subsequent analyses of the photo have generally failed to find any evidence that it was manipulated.

In September 2002, a researcher named Dennis Hall, who headed a lake monster investigation group known as Champ Quest, videotaped what looked like three creatures undulating through the water near Ferrisburgh, Vermont. Hall claimed that he saw unidentifiable animals in Lake Champlain on 19 separate occasions.

In 2006, two fishermen captured digital video footage of what appeared to be parts of a very large animal swimming in the lake. The images were thoroughly examined under the direction of ABC News technicians, and though the creature on the video could not be proved to be Champ, the team could find nothing to disprove it, either.

## Champ or Chump?

As the sixth-largest freshwater lake in the United States (and stretching about six miles into Quebec, Canada), Lake Champlain provides ample habitat and nourishment for a good-size water cryptic, or unknown animal. The lake plunges as deep as 400 feet in spots and covers 490 square miles.

Skeptics offer the usual explanations for Champ sightings: large sturgeons, floating logs or water plants, otters, or an optical illusion caused by sunlight and shadow. Others think Champ could be a remnant of a species of primitive whale called a zeuglodon or an ancient marine reptile known as a plesiosaur, both believed by biologists to be long extinct. But until uncontestable images of the creature's entire body are produced, this argument will undoubtedly continue.

Champ does claim one rare, official nod to the probability of its existence: Legislation by both the states of New York and Vermont proclaim that Champ is a protected—though unknown—species and make it illegal to harm the creature in any way.

# The Guy Who Killed the Guy Who Killed Abraham Lincoln

*What's it take to bring down an assassin? Sharp-shooting skills and a story of your own.*

✱ ✱ ✱ ✱

## The Mad Hatter

**Y**OU MIGHT FIGURE that a guy who takes down a presidential assassin is a stand-up sort of fellow. But according to legend, Thomas "Boston" Corbett, the man who shot Lincoln's assassin, John Wilkes Booth, was just a few bullets shy of a full round.

Born in London in 1832, Thomas Corbett moved with his parents to Troy, New York, in 1839. As a young man, he became a hat maker and was exposed to the dangerous chemicals involved, included mercurious nitrate, which was used in curing felt. Long-term exposure would more than likely turn him into a certified "mad" hatter. After losing his first wife and child during childbirth, Corbett turned to the bottle. Later, however, he turned to Jesus Christ and moved to Boston. It was here that he rechristened himself as "Boston."

Described as a religious fanatic, an account from a hospital in Massachusetts states that Corbett cut off his own testes after reading from the Bible the book of Matthew chapters 18 and 19 (which discuss removing offending body parts) and being approached by prostitutes on the city streets. After removing his offending body part, he apparently attended church and ate dinner at home before calling the doctor.

## A Bullet for Booth

In 1861, Corbett enlisted as a private in Company I, 12th New York Militia. After several years in service, he found himself with a group on the hunt for the infamous assassin John Wilkes Booth. And though the cavalry was instructed to bring Booth in alive, it's generally accepted that Corbett shot him while Booth was surrounded in a burning barn. Given the chaos, the distance, and the smoke, it's surprising that the bullet even hit Booth.

## Fifteen Minutes of Fame

Corbett wasn't punished for shooting Booth. In fact, he received a share of the reward money, totaling $1,653.85. For a short period of time, Corbett was considered a hero and even signed autographs for his fans.

Afterward, Corbett moved around for a few years and eventually settled in Concordia, Kansas, where, in 1887, he was elected as the assistant doorkeeper to the Kansas House of Representatives. He lived as a bit of a hermit, but he preached at the Methodist Episcopal Church and became known as something of a loudmouth evangelist. People still came from other towns to see the famed gunman who took down Booth. Then one day in the winter of 1887, Corbett threatened to shoot people over an argument on the floor of the House of Representatives. He was arrested, determined to be unstable, and booked for a permanent vacation to a psych hospital.

## Loose Ends

That wasn't the last America would hear from Boston Corbett. He escaped from the hospital on his second attempt in May 1888, stole a pony that was tied up in front of the hospital, and high-tailed it out of there. He reappeared one week later in Neodesha, Kansas, and was said to have later headed down to Mexico.

Corbett seemed to have disappeared, though sightings were reported far and wide. As with everything surrounding the Lincoln assassination, there are plenty of conspiracy theories regarding Corbett: There are some who say that Corbett wasn't the one who shot Booth. Others say that it was not actually Booth who Corbett shot, and that Corbett later traveled to Enid, Kansas, to meet a man claiming to be Booth.

What is known about Corbett is that before he disappeared, he made a dugout home near Concordia, Kansas. Today, a stone marker between two trees in the middle of a pasture stands as a monument to the guy who killed the guy who killed the 16th president of the United States.

# 9 of History's Coldest Cases

*They were gruesome crimes that shocked us with their brutality. But as time passed, we heard less and less about them until we forgot about the crime, not even realizing that the perpetrator remained among us. Yet the files remain open, and the families of the victims live on in a state of semi-paralysis. Here are some of the world's most famous cold cases.*

✳   ✳   ✳   ✳

1. **Elizabeth Short:** Elizabeth Short, also known as the Black Dahlia, was murdered in 1947. Like thousands of others, Elizabeth wanted to be a star. Unlike the bevy of blondes who trekked to Hollywood, this 22-year-old beauty from Massachusetts was dark and mysterious. She was last seen alive outside the Biltmore Hotel in Los Angeles on the evening of January 9, 1947.

   Short's body was found on a vacant lot in Los Angeles. It had been cut in half at the waist and both parts had been drained of blood and then cleaned. Her body parts appeared to be surgically dissected, and her remains were suggestively posed. Despite receiving a number of false confessions and taunting letters that admonished police to "catch me if you can," the crime remains unsolved.

2. **The Zodiac Killer:** The Zodiac Killer was responsible for several murders in the San Francisco area in the 1960s and 1970s. His victims were shot, stabbed, and bludgeoned to death. After the first few kills, he began sending letters to the press in which he taunted police and made public

threats, such as planning to blow up a school bus. In a letter sent to the *San Francisco Chronicle* two days after the murder of cabbie Paul Stine in October 1969, the killer, who called himself "The Zodiac," included in the package pieces of Stine's blood-soaked shirt. In the letters, which continued until 1978, he claimed a tally of 37 murders.

3. **Swedish Prime Minister Olof Palme:** On February 28, 1986, Swedish Prime Minister Olof Palme was gunned down on a Stockholm street as he and his wife strolled home from the movies unprotected around midnight. The prime minister was fatally shot in the back. His wife was seriously wounded but survived.

   In 1988, a petty thief and drug addict named Christer Petterson was convicted of the murder because he was picked out of a lineup by Palme's widow. The conviction was later overturned on appeal when doubts were raised as to the reliability of Mrs. Palme's evidence. Despite many theories, the assassin remains at large.

4. **The Torso Killer:** In Cleveland, Ohio, during the 1930s, more than a dozen limbless torsos were found. Despite the efforts of famed crime fighter Eliot Ness, the torso killer was never found. The first two bodies, found in September 1935, were missing heads and had been horribly mutilated. Similar murders occurred during the next three years. Desperate to stop the killings, Ness ordered a raid on a run-down area known as Kingsbury's Run, where most of the victims were from. The place was torched, and hundreds of vagrants were taken into custody. After that, there were no more killings.

   The key suspect in the murders was Frank Dolezal, a vagrant who lived in the area. He was a known bully with a fiery temper. Dolezal was arrested and subsequently confessed, but his confession was full of inaccuracies. He died shortly thereafter under suspicious circumstances.

5. **Bob Crane:** In 1978, Bob Crane, star of TV's *Hogan's Heroes*, was clubbed to death in his apartment. Crane shared a close friendship with John Carpenter, a pioneer in the development of video technology. The two shared an affinity for debauchery and sexual excesses, which were recorded on videotape. But by late 1978, Crane was tiring of Carpenter's dependence on him and had let him know that the friendship was over.

The following day, June 29, 1978, Crane was bludgeoned to death with a camera tripod in his Scottsdale, Arizona, apartment. Suspicion immediately fell on Carpenter, and a small spattering of blood was found in Carpenter's rental car, but police were unable to connect it to the crime. Examiners also found a tiny piece of human tissue in the car. Sixteen years after the killing, Carpenter finally went to trial, but he was acquitted due to lack of evidence.

6. **Tupac Shakur:** On September 7, 1996, successful rap artist Tupac Shakur was shot four times in a drive-by shooting in Las Vegas. He died six days later. Two years prior to that, Shakur had been shot five times in the lobby of a Manhattan recording studio the day before he was found guilty of sexual assault. He survived that attack, only to spend the next 11 months in jail. The 1994 shooting was a major catalyst for an East Coast-West Coast feud that would envelop the hip-hop industry and culminate in the deaths of both Shakur and Notorious B.I.G. (Christopher Wallace).

On the night of the fatal shooting, Shakur attended the Mike Tyson-Bruce Seldon fight at the MGM Grand in Las Vegas. After the fight, Shakur and his entourage got into a scuffle with a gang member. Shakur then headed for a nightclub, but he never made it. No one was ever arrested for the killing.

7. **Jack the Ripper:** In London in the late 1880s, a brutal killer known as Jack the Ripper preyed on local prostitutes. His first victim was 43-year-old Mary Ann Nichols, who was nearly decapitated during a savage knife attack. Days later, 47-year-old Annie Chapman had her organs removed from her abdomen before being left for dead. The press stirred up a wave of panic reporting that a serial killer was at large. Three weeks later, the killer was interrupted as he tore apart Swedish prostitute Elizabeth Stride. He managed to get away, only to strike again later that same night. This time the victim was Kate Eddowes. The killer, by now dubbed Jack the Ripper, removed a kidney in the process of hacking up Eddowes's body. His final kill was the most gruesome. On the night of November 9, 1888, Mary Kelly was methodically cut into pieces in an onslaught that must have lasted for several hours.

   Dozens of potential Jacks have been implicated in the killings, including failed lawyer Montague John Druitt, whose body was fished out of the Thames River days after the last murder was committed. The nature of the bodily dissections has led many to conclude that Jack was a skilled physician with an advanced knowledge of anatomy. But more than a century after the savage attacks, the identity of Jack the Ripper remains a mystery.

8. **Jimmy Hoffa:** In 1975, labor leader Jimmy Hoffa disappeared on his way to a Detroit-area restaurant. Hoffa was the president of the Teamsters Union during the 1950s and 1960s. In 1964, he went to jail for bribing a grand juror investigating corruption in the union. In 1971, he was released on the condition that he not participate in any further union activity. Hoffa was preparing a legal challenge to that injunction when he disappeared on July 30, 1975. He was last seen in the parking lot of the Machus Red Fox Restaurant.

Hoffa had strong connections to the Mafia, and several mobsters have claimed that he met a grisly end on their say so. Although his body has never been found, authorities officially declared him dead on July 30, 1982. As recently as November 2006, the FBI dug up farmland in Michigan hoping to turn up a corpse. So far, no luck.

9. **JonBenét Ramsey:** In the early hours of December 26, 1996, Patsy Ramsey reported that her six-year-old daughter, JonBenét, had been abducted from her Boulder, Colorado, home. Police rushed to the Ramsey home where, hours later, John Ramsey found his little girl dead in the basement. She had been battered, sexually assaulted, and strangled.

Police found several tantalizing bits of evidence—a number of footprints, a rope that did not belong on the premises, marks on the body that suggested the use of a stun gun, and DNA samples on the girl's body. The ransom note was also suspicious. Police found that it was written with a pen and pad of paper belonging to the Ramseys. The amount demanded, $118,000, was a surprisingly small amount, considering that John Ramsey was worth more than $6 million. It is also interesting to note that Mr. Ramsey had just received a year-end bonus of $118,117.50.

A number of suspects were considered, but one by one they were all cleared. Finally, the police zeroed in on the parents. For years, the Ramseys were put under intense pressure by authorities and the public alike to confess to Ramsey's murder. However, a grand jury investigation ended with no indictments. In 2003, a judge ruled that an intruder had killed JonBenét. Then, in August 2006, John Mark Karr confessed, claiming that he was with the girl when she died. However, Karr's DNA did not match that found on JonBenét. He was not charged, and the case has remained unsolved.

# William Desmond Taylor

*The murder of actor/director William Desmond Taylor was like something out of an Agatha Christie novel, complete with a handsome, debonair victim and multiple suspects, each with a motive. But unlike Christie's novels, in which the murderer was always unmasked, Taylor's death remains unsolved nearly 90 years later.*

✳  ✳  ✳  ✳

ON THE EVENING of February 1, 1922, Taylor was shot in the back by an unknown assailant; his body was discovered the next morning by a servant, Henry Peavey. News of Taylor's demise spread quickly, and several individuals, including officials from Paramount Studios, where Taylor was employed, raced to the dead man's home to clear it of anything incriminating, such as illegal liquor, evidence of drug use, illicit correspondence, and signs of sexual indiscretion. However, no one called the police until later in the morning.

## Numerous Suspects

Soon an eclectic array of potential suspects came to light, including Taylor's criminally inclined former butler, Edward F. Sands, who had gone missing just before the murder; popular movie comedienne Mabel Normand, whom Taylor had entertained the evening of his death; actress Mary Miles Minter, who had a passionate crush on the handsome director who was 28 years her senior; and Charlotte Shelby, Minter's mother, who often wielded a loaded gun to protect her daughter's tarnished honor.

Taylor's murder was the last thing Hollywood needed at the time, coming as it did on the heels of rape allegations against popular film comedian Fatty Arbuckle. Scandals brought undue attention on Hollywood, and the Arbuckle story had taken its toll. Officials at Paramount tried to keep a lid on the Taylor story, but the tabloid press had a field day. A variety of personal foibles were made public in the weeks that followed, and both Normand and Minter saw their careers come to a screeching halt as a result. Taylor's own indiscretions were also revealed, such as the fact that he kept a special souvenir, usually lingerie, from every woman he bedded.

## Little Evidence

Police interviewed many of Taylor's friends and colleagues, including all potential suspects. However, there was no evidence to incriminate anyone specifically, and no one was formally charged.

Investigators and amateur sleuths pursued the case for years. Sands was long a prime suspect, based on his criminal past and his estrangement from the victim. But it was later revealed that on the day of the murder, Sands had signed in for work at a lumberyard in Oakland, California—some 400 miles away—and thus could not have committed the crime. Coming in second was Shelby, whose temper and threats were legendary. Shelby's own acting career had fizzled out early, and all of her hopes for stardom were pinned on her daughter. She threatened many men who tried to woo Mary.

In the mid-1990s, another possible suspect surfaced—a long-forgotten silent-film actress named Margaret Gibson. According to Bruce Long, author of *William Desmond Taylor: A Dossier*, Gibson confessed to a friend on her deathbed in 1964 that years before she had killed a man named William Desmond Taylor. However, the woman to whom Gibson cleared her conscience didn't know who Taylor was and thought nothing more about it.

## The Mystery Continues

Could Margaret Gibson (aka Pat Lewis) be Taylor's murderer? She had acted with Taylor in Hollywood in the early 1910s, and she may even have been one of his many sexual conquests. She also had a criminal past, including charges of blackmail, drug use, and prostitution, so it's entirely conceivable that she was a member of a group trying to extort money from the director, a popular theory among investigators. But according to an earlier book, *A Cast of Killers* by Sidney D. Kirkpatrick, veteran Hollywood director King Vidor had investigated the murder as material for a film script and through his research believed Shelby was the murderer. But out of respect for Minter, he never did anything about it.

Ultimately, however, we may never know for certain who killed William Desmond Taylor, or why. The case has long grown cold, and anyone with specific knowledge of the murder is likely dead. Unlike a Hollywood thriller, in which the killer is revealed at the end, Taylor's death is a macabre puzzle that likely will never be solved.

# Dream Weaver

*As an aeronautical engineer and author of books about paranormal phenomena, John William Dunne (1875–1949) questioned much in life, but nothing more keenly than human dreams and their meanings. His obsession with the twilight world was sparked by an odd event that he couldn't explain. How had Dunne been able to "see" one of the world's greatest tragedies while he was sleeping? And how could this have occurred before the event took place?*

✳  ✳  ✳  ✳

J. W. DUNNE is best known for the invention of the first practical and stable tailless airplane. But in addition to his aeronautic accomplishments, Dunne offered compelling theories about the very structure of time in his book *An Experiment with Time*. Dunne's interest in this area was prompted by his uncanny knack for forecasting events through his dreams. Of these, one proved particularly mind-boggling.

On the chance that there might be something to his nocturnal visions, Dunne recorded each dream in writing. In early May

1902, while working as an engineer for the British military in South Africa, Dunne had a dream in which he found himself on the island of Martinique. In his vision, the French territory exploded and some 30,000 people perished as a result. Waking up in a cold sweat, Dunne weighed his options. Should he warn the French authorities? Or would his amazing claim fall upon deaf ears? Dunne chose to alert the powers that be, but he was unable to persuade what he later called "incredulous French authorities" to evacuate the island.

A few days after he had his vision, Dunne received a newspaper at his outpost. To his absolute horror, he discovered that his chilling dream had become a reality: Mount Pelée, located on the island of Martinique, had erupted with unbelievable force. In its wake, around 30,000 people lay dead. Had Dunne foreseen the future, or are the past, present, and future simply illusive human perceptions? The question would preoccupy Dunne for the rest of his waking days—and many of his sleep-filled nights, too.

# Who Betrayed Anne Frank?

*Anne Frank and her family thwarted Nazis for two years, hiding in Amsterdam. They might have remained hidden and waited out the war, but someone blew their cover.*

✳   ✳   ✳   ✳

ANNELIES MARIE FRANK was born in Frankfurt am Main, Germany, on June 12, 1929. Perhaps the most well-known victim of the Holocaust, she was one of approximately 1.5 million Jewish children killed by the Nazis. Her diary chronicling her experience in Amsterdam was discovered in the Franks' secret hiding place by friends of the family and first published in 1947. Translated into more than 60 languages, *Anne Frank: The Diary of a Young Girl* has sold 30 million copies and is one of the most read books in the world.

The diary was given to Anne on her 13th birthday, just weeks before she went into hiding. Her father, Otto Frank, moved his family and four friends into a secret annex of rooms above his office at 263 Prinsengracht, near a canal in central Amsterdam, on July 6, 1942. They relied on trustworthy business associates, employees, and friends, who risked their own lives to help them. Anne poignantly wrote her thoughts, yearnings, and descriptions of life in the secret annex in her diary, revealing a vibrant, intelligent young woman struggling to retain her ideals in the most dire of circumstances.

On August 4, 1944, four or five Dutch Nazi collaborators under the command of an Austrian Nazi police investigator entered the building and arrested the Franks and their friends. The family was deported to Auschwitz, where they were separated and sent to different camps. Anne and her sister, Margot, were sent to Bergen-Belsen, where they both died of typhus a few weeks before liberation. Anne was 15 years old. Otto Frank was the only member of the group to survive the war.

Dutch police, Nazi hunters, and historians have attempted to identify the person who betrayed the Franks. Searching for clues, the Netherlands Institute for War Documentation (NIWD) has examined records on Dutch collaboration with the Nazis, the letters of Otto Frank, and police transcripts dating from the 1940s. The arresting Nazi officer was also questioned after the war by Nazi hunter Simon Wiesenthal, but he could not identify who informed on the Franks. For decades suspicion centered on Willem Van Maaren, who worked in the warehouse attached to the Franks' hiding place, but two police investigations found no evidence against him.

Two recent theories have been offered about who betrayed the Franks. British author Carol Anne Lee believes it was Anton Ahlers, a business associate of Otto's who was a petty thief and member of the Dutch Nazi movement. Lee argues that Ahlers informed the Nazis to collect the bounty paid to Dutch civilians who exposed Jews. She suggests he may have split the reward with Maarten Kuiper, a friend of Ahlers who was one of the Dutch Nazi collaborators who raided the secret annex. Ahlers was jailed for collaboration with the Nazis after the war, and members of his own family, including his son, have said they believe he was guilty of informing on the Franks.

Austrian writer Melissa Müller believes that a cleaning lady, Lena Hartog, who also worked in the warehouse, reported the Franks because she feared that if they were discovered, her husband, an employee of Otto Frank, would be deported for aiding Jews.

The NIWD has studied the arguments of both writers and examined the evidence supporting their theories. Noting that all the principals involved in the case are no longer living, it concluded that neither theory could be proved.

# Whatever Happened to D. B. Cooper?

*On the day before Thanksgiving, 1971, in Portland, Oregon, a man in his mid-forties who called himself Dan Cooper (news reports would later misidentify him as "D. B.") boarded a Northwest Orient Airlines 727 that was bound for Seattle. Dressed in a suit and tie and carrying a briefcase, Cooper was calm and polite when he handed a note to a flight attendant.*

✳   ✳   ✳   ✳

THE NOTE SAID that his briefcase contained a bomb; he was hijacking the plane. Cooper told the crew that upon landing in Seattle, he wanted four parachutes and two hundred thousand dollars in twenty-dollar bills.

His demands were met, and Cooper released the other passengers. He ordered the pilots to fly to Mexico, but he gave specific instructions to keep the plane under ten thousand feet with the wing flaps at fifteen degrees, restricting the aircraft's speed. That night, in a cold rainstorm somewhere over southwest Washington, Cooper donned the parachutes, and with the money packed in knapsacks that were tied to his body, he jumped from the 727's rear stairs.

For several months afterward, the FBI conducted an extensive manhunt of the rugged forest terrain, but the agents were unable to find even a shred of evidence. In 1972, a copycat hijacker named Richard McCoy successfully jumped from a flight over Utah with five hundred thousand dollars and was arrested days later. At first the FBI thought McCoy was Cooper, but he didn't match the description provided by the crew of Cooper's flight. Other suspects surfaced over the years, including a Florida antiques dealer with a shady past who confessed to his wife on his deathbed that he was Cooper—though he was later discredited by DNA testing.

Cooper hadn't hurt anybody, and he had no apparent political agenda. He became a folk hero of sorts—he was immortalized in books, in song, in television documentaries, and in a movie, *The Pursuit of D.B. Cooper*. In 1980, solid evidence surfaced: An eight-year-old boy found $5,800 in rotting twenty-dollar bills along the Columbia River, and the serial numbers matched those on the cash that was given to Cooper. But while thousands of leads have been investigated over the years, the case remains the only unsolved hijacking in U.S. history. Late in 2007, the FBI's Seattle field office kick-started the investigation, providing pictures on its website of some key evidence, including the money and Cooper's black clip-on tie.

Agent Larry Carr, who continued to work the case, thought he knew what happened to Cooper, who jumped into a wind of two hundred miles per hour in total darkness on a cold and rainy night. "Diving into the wilderness without a plan, without the right equipment, in such terrible conditions," Carr says, "he probably never even got his chute open."

# Who Cracked the Liberty Bell?

*Aside from the Statue of Liberty, the Liberty Bell might be the most enduring symbol of America. It draws millions of tourists to its home in Philadelphia each year. Yet for all of its historical resonance, anybody who has been to Independence Hall will attest that it's not the most attractive bell in existence.*

✳   ✳   ✳   ✳

IN FACT, IT looks kind of cruddy, due mostly to the enormous crack that runs down its side. Whom can we blame for the destruction of this national treasure? No one has come forth to take responsibility, though there is no shortage of theories regarding the crack's origin.

A quick survey of the Liberty Bell's rich history shows that it has been fraught with problems since it was struck. The original bell, which was constructed by British bell-founder Lester & Pack (which is still in business today as Whitechapel Bell Foundry), arrived in Philadelphia in 1752. Unfortunately, it cracked upon its very first tolling—an inauspicious beginning for a future national monument. (On its website, Whitechapel Bell Foundry repeatedly assures readers that good bell metal is "fragile.") Disgruntled Philadelphians called upon two local foundry workers, John Pass and John Stow, to recast the bell, with firm instructions to make it less brittle. The artisans did as they were told, but the new bell was so thick and heavy that the sound of it tolling resembled that of an axe hitting a tree. Pass and Stow were told to try again, and finally, in June 1753, the bell that we see today was hung in the State House.

Of course, in those days, it wasn't known as the Liberty Bell. It got that nickname much later, when abolitionists adopted its inscription—PROCLAIM LIBERTY THROUGHOUT ALL THE LAND UNTO ALL THE INHABITANTS THEREOF—as a rallying cry for the anti-slavery movement. By that time, the bell was already an important part of the

American mythos, having been rung in alarm to announce the onset of the Revolutionary War after the skirmishes at Lexington and Concord, and in celebration when independence was proclaimed in 1776.

Exactly when the crack happened is a matter of debate amongst historians, though experts have been able to narrow it down to between 1817 and 1846. There are several possible dates that are offered by the National Park Service, which is charged with caring for the bell (though it obviously wasn't charged with this task soon enough). The bell may have been cracked:

* in 1824, when it tolled to celebrate French Revolutionary War hero Marquis de Lafayette's visit to Philadelphia,

* in 1828, while ringing to honor the passage of the Catholic Emancipation Act in England, or

* in 1835, while ringing during the funeral procession of statesman and justice John Marshall.

All of these theories, however, are discounted by numerous contemporary documents—such as newspaper reports and town-hall meeting minutes—that discuss the bell without mentioning the crack. In fact, the first actual reference to the Liberty Bell being cracked occurred in 1846, when the Philadelphia newspaper *Public Ledger* noted that in order for the bell to be rung in honor of George Washington's birthday that year, a crack had to first be repaired. The newspaper states that the bell had cracked "long before," though in an article published several years later, "long before" is specified as having been during the autumn of 1845, a matter of a few months.

Unfortunately, the paper gives no explanation as to how the bell cracked or who did it. Nor does it explain something that, when confronted by the crack in the bell, many viewers ignore: Not only were the bell-makers fairly shoddy craftsmen, they were also terrible spellers. In the inscription, the name of the state in which the bell resides is spelled "Pensylvania."

# An Open Secret

*Was Amelia Earhart the victim of some kind of conspiracy? Her choice not to keep up with technological knowhow is more likely to blame for her disappearance.*

✳ ✳ ✳ ✳

PIONEERING AVIATOR AMELIA Earhart set records and made headlines because of her talent, courage, tireless work ethic, and willingness to craft her own image. But no one is perfect, of course. Earhart failed to keep up with the technologies that helped other pilots to call for help and made flying a much less dangerous job.

## Opening the Books

After Orville and Wilbur Wright made the first powered airplane flight in 1903, an ugly patent war began among inventors in the United States. A huge number of researchers from all kinds of backgrounds—the Wrights themselves were bicycle mechanics, publishers, and journalists—had made incremental improvements on one another's work, brainstormed similar ideas, and generally squabbled over who was making the best progress. Think of it as a grade-school classroom where all the students are grown men, and they've propped up folders and textbooks to hide their tests from their classmates.

These aviation pioneers were out-pettying today's worst startup companies in Silicon Valley. They went to court over fine details of one aircraft versus another, citing their own notes and evidence that had largely been kept secret. But after a decade of brutal lawsuits and public fighting over who was first, who invented what, and where the credit was due, the United States entered World War I. Aviation companies were de facto forced to pour their proprietary research and patents into a large pool shared by all of America's aircraft industry.

Making their technology "open source" was part of the war effort, but as with software and other inventions today, the open industry led to better and more rapid developments. After World War I ended, pilots began to set records left and right using ingenious inventions like the artificial horizon—something pilots still use in cockpits today, in a modernized form of course. And some pilots made their livings in traveling airshows as airplanes became more and more familiar, but no less mesmerizing, to the American people. Amelia Earhart was one of these pilots, traveling to build buzz for her own career.

## The Morse the Merrier

Earhart was a gifted and remarkable pilot, the first woman to *ride* in a plane (as a passenger) across the Atlantic and then to fly across it as the pilot. She started a professional organization for women pilots and took a faculty position at Purdue University. She and fellow groundbreaking pilot Charles Lindbergh were like movie stars by the 1930s, and Earhart was witty and engaging when she spoke with the press or members of the public. Her career was at a perfect point for her to make an outsize gesture in the form of a trip around the world. She wasn't the first, but she was definitely the most famous.

Technology leapt ahead during her career, and Morse code was in wide use by the time Earhart began her trip around the world. The world's leading navigation instructor offered to teach Earhart radio operation, Morse code, and cutting-edge navigation, but she didn't have time before her trip, which had already been delayed by a failed first attempt. The navigator she chose also didn't know Morse code. When they grew disoriented in poor weather over the Pacific Ocean, they could not call for help in Morse code, and their radio reception was too poor to send or receive verbal messages from the Navy ships assigned to support the open water sections of their flight.

The "what ifs" of Earhart's failed final journey stoke pop culture across the decades, and who can say what could have happened if she and her navigator were able to get help? Without specific coordinates or landmarks, which Earhart likely could have relayed to her support team, even modern rescuers can't cover large swaths of open ocean with success. Morse code might have made the critical difference.

# Gone Without a Trace

*While we all watch in amazement as magicians make everything from small coins to giant buildings disappear, in our hearts, we all know it's a trick. Things don't just disappear, especially not people. Or do they?*

\* \* \* \*

## Louis Le Prince

THE NAME LOUIS Aimé Augustin Le Prince doesn't mean much to most people, but some believe he was the first person to record moving images on film, a good seven years before Thomas Edison. Whether or not he did so is open to debate, as is what happened to him on September 16, 1890. On that day, Le Prince's brother accompanied him to the train station in Dijon, France, where he was scheduled to take the express train to Paris. When the train reached Paris, however, Le Prince and his luggage were nowhere to be found. The train was searched, as were the tracks between Dijon and Paris, but no sign of Le Prince or his luggage was ever found. Theories about his disappearance range from his being murdered for trying to fight Edison over the patent of the first motion picture to his family forcing him to go into hiding to keep him safe from people who wanted his patents for themselves. Others believe that Le Prince took his own life because he was nearly bankrupt.

## Dorothy Arnold

After spending most of December 12, 1910, shopping in Manhattan, American socialite Dorothy Arnold told a friend she was planning to walk home through Central Park. She never made it. Fearing that their daughter had eloped with her

one-time boyfriend George Griscom, Jr., the Arnolds immediately hired the Pinkerton Detective Agency, although they
did not report her missing to police until almost a month later.
Once the press heard the news, theories spread like wildfire,
most of them pointing the finger at Griscom. Some believed
he had murdered Arnold, but others thought she had died as
the result of a botched abortion. Still others felt her family had
banished her to Switzerland and then used her disappearance
as a cover-up. No evidence was ever found to formally charge
Griscom, and Arnold's disappearance remains unsolved.

## Frederick Valentich

To vanish without a trace is rather unusual. But to vanish in an
airplane while chasing a UFO—now that's unique. Yet that's
exactly what happened to 20-year-old pilot Frederick Valentich
on the night of October 21, 1978. Shortly after 7:00 p.m.,
while flying a Cessna 182L to King Island, Australia, Valentich
radioed that an "unidentified craft" was hovering over his plane.
For the next several minutes, he attempted to describe the
object, which had blinking lights and was "not an aircraft." At
approximately 7:12 p.m., Valentich stated that he was having
engine trouble. Immediately after that, the flight tower picked
up 17 seconds of "metallic, scraping sounds." Then all was
silent. A search began immediately, but no trace of Valentich
or his plane was ever found. Strangely enough, the evening
Valentich disappeared, there were numerous reports of UFOs
seen all over the skies of Australia.

## Frank Morris, John Anglin, and Clarence Anglin

Officially, records show that there was never a successful escape
from Alcatraz Prison while it was in operation. Of course,
those records leave out the part that three men *might* have
made it, but they disappeared in the process.

After spending two years planning their escape, inmates Frank
Morris and brothers Clarence and John Anglin placed homemade dummies in their bunks, crawled through hand-dug

tunnels, and made their way to the prison roof. Then they apparently climbed down, hopped aboard homemade rafts, and made their way out into San Francisco Bay.

The next day, one of the largest manhunts in history began. Pieces of a raft and a life preserver were found floating in the bay, as well as a bag containing personal items from the escapees, but that was all. The official report stated that in all likelihood, the men drowned. However, a 2003 episode of *Mythbusters* determined that the men may have survived.

# The Mystery of the Missing Comma

*Legend implies that a punctuation error sparked one of history's greatest unsolved mysteries: Did Queen Isabella give the order for her husband's death, or was it a misunderstanding?*

✳   ✳   ✳   ✳

KING EDWARD II of England is primarily remembered for his weakness for certain men and the way he died. He spent most of his life in submission to his alleged lovers, Piers Gaveston and, later, Hugh le Despenser, granting their every wish. When Edward married 12-year-old Princess Isabella of France in 1308, he politely greeted her upon her arrival in England—and then gave her wedding jewelry to Gaveston.

Isabella grew up as a queen accustomed to being pushed aside in favor of her husband's preferred companions. Even after Gaveston was murdered for being a bad influence on the king, Edward did not change, turning his affections to the greedy Despenser, whom the queen loathed and feared. When the opportunity arose for her to negotiate a treaty with her brother, the King of France, she took it, traveling to Paris and refusing to return.

## The Queen's Revenge

After nearly 20 years in an unhappy marriage, Isabella had had enough. Along with her lover, Roger Mortimer, she raised an army and led it into England in order to depose her husband. Once the king was in custody, the queen forced him to abdicate the throne to their 14-year-old son, Edward III, and proceeded to send a letter giving orders on how the deposed Edward should be treated in captivity.

## Conspiracy or Miscommunication?

Something very important was missing from Isabella's orders. In the letter, she wrote, "Edwardum occidere nolite timere bonum est." Many historians think she intended this to mean, "Do not kill Edward, it is good to fear." However, she neglected to write in a necessary comma. If the comma is inserted in a different place, the letter means "Do not be afraid to kill Edward; it is good." It's clear how Edward's jailers construed the message: Shortly after it was received, several men allegedly murdered Edward in his jail cell. Who knew that forgetting something as small as a comma could result in the murder of a king?

# Giant Frogman Spotted in Ohio!

*For the most part, frogs are rather unintimidating—unless they're more than four feet tall and standing along a dark road in the middle of the night.*

✳   ✳   ✳   ✳

## The First Encounter

ON MARCH 3, 1972, police officer Ray Shockey was driving his patrol car along Riverside Road toward the small town of Loveland, Ohio. At approximately 1:00 a.m., Shockey saw what he thought was a dog lying alongside the road, but as he got closer, the creature suddenly stood up on two feet. Amazed, Shockey stopped his car and watched the creature climb over a guardrail and scamper down the ditch toward the Little Miami

River. Shockey drove back to the police station and described what he'd seen to fellow officer Mark Matthews. Shockey said the creature was approximately four feet tall and weighed between 50 to 75 pounds. It stood on two legs and had webbed feet, clawed hands, and the head of a frog.

After hearing his story, Matthews accompanied Shockey back to the site of the encounter. The pair could not locate the frogman, but they did find strange scratch marks along the section of guardrail the creature had climbed over.

## Frogman Returns

On the night of March 17, Matthews was on the outskirts of town when he saw an animal lying in the middle of the road. Thinking that the animal had been hit by a car, Matthews stopped his squad car. But when the animal suddenly stood up on two legs, Matthews realized that it was the same creature that Shockey had encountered. Just as before, the creature walked to the side of the road and climbed over a guardrail. Matthews simply watched, although some reports say he shot at the animal. Either way, the creature moved down the embankment toward the river and vanished.

## The Aftermath

When news spread of a second Frogman sighting, the town of Loveland was inundated with calls from reporters across the country. Obviously, reports of four-foot-tall froglike creatures are rarely considered newsworthy, but two witnesses had seen the creature on different nights, and both were police officers.

In the beginning, Shockey and Matthews stuck to their stories and even had sketches made of the creature they'd encountered. But over time, the public turned on the officers, accusing them of fabricating the whole thing. In recent years, the officers now claim that what they encountered was merely an iguana. Most seem happy with that explanation. But it doesn't explain how an iguana stood up on two legs and walked across the road. Or why their sketches looked nothing like an iguana.

## So Where Is the Frog Today?

A local farmer also claimed he saw the Frogman lumbering through his field one evening, but there have been no other sightings since the 1970s. Those who believe in the Loveland Frogman claim that after Matthews allegedly shot at it, it became frightened and moved to a more isolated area. Others think that Matthews's shot killed the creature. Of course, there are some who believe that the Loveland Frogman is still out there and has merely become more elusive. Just something to consider should you ever find yourself driving alongside the Little Miami River near Loveland on a dark, moonless night.

# A Superior Tragedy: The Edmund Fitzgerald

*Many ships have been lost to storms on the Great Lakes, but few incidents have fascinated the world like the sinking of the* Edmund Fitzgerald *off the shores of northern Michigan on November 10, 1975. The mysterious circumstances of the tragedy, which took 29 lives—all memorialized in a 1976 song by Gordon Lightfoot—have kept the story fresh to this day. The fateful journey began in Wisconsin.*

✳   ✳   ✳   ✳

## Least Likely to Sink

THE 729-FOOT-LONG EDMUND *Fitzgerald* was considered as unsinkable as any steamer. At its christening in June 1958, it was the Great Lakes' largest and most expensive freighter. Its name honored Edmund Fitzgerald, the president of Northwestern Mutual Insurance Company of Milwaukee, who commissioned the boat.

During the christening, a few incidents occurred that some saw as bad omens. As a crowd of more than 10,000 watched, it took Mrs. Fitzgerald three tries to shatter the bottle of champagne. Then, when the ship was released into the water, it hit the surface at the wrong angle, causing a wave that splattered the entire ceremonial area with lake water and knocking the ship into a nearby dock. One spectator died on the spot of a heart attack.

## The Last Launch

The weather was unseasonably pleasant the morning of November 9, 1975, so much so that the crew of 29 men who set sail from Superior, Wisconsin, that day were unlikely to have been concerned about their routine trip to Zug Island on the Detroit River. But the captain, Ernest McSorley, knew a storm was in the forecast.

McSorley, a 44-year veteran of the lakes, had captained the *Fitzgerald* since 1972. He paid close attention to the gale warnings issued that afternoon, but no one suspected they would yield a "once-in-a-lifetime storm." However, when the weather report was upgraded to a full storm warning, McSorley changed the ship's course to follow a safer route closer to the Canadian shore.

Following the *Fitzgerald* was another freighter, the *Arthur Anderson*. The two captains stayed in touch as they traveled through winds measuring up to 50 knots (about 58 miles per hour) with waves 12 feet or higher. On November 10, around 1:00 p.m., McSorley told Captain Cooper of the *Anderson* that the *Fitzgerald* was "rolling." By about 2:45 p.m., as the *Anderson* moved to avoid a dangerous shoal near Caribou Island, a crewman sighted the *Fitzgerald* about 16 miles ahead, closer to the shoal than Cooper thought safe.

About 3:30 p.m., McSorley reported to Cooper that the *Fitzgerald* had sustained some minor damage and was beginning to roll to one side. The ships were still 16 to 17 miles apart. At 4:10 p.m., with waves now 18 feet high, McSorley radioed that his ship had lost radar. The two ships stayed in radio contact until about 7:00 p.m. when the *Fitzgerald* crew told the *Anderson* they were "holding [their] own." After that, radio contact was lost, and the *Fitzgerald* dropped off the radar. Around 8:30 p.m., Cooper told the Coast Guard at Sault Ste. Marie that the *Fitzgerald* seemed to be missing.

Evidently, the *Fitzgerald* sank sometime after 7:10 p.m, just 17 miles from the shore of Whitefish Point, Michigan. Despite a massive search effort, it wasn't until November 14 that a navy flyer detected a magnetic anomaly that turned out to be the wreck. The only other evidence of the disaster to surface was a handful of lifeboats, life jackets, and some oars, tools, and propane tanks. A robotic vehicle was used to thoroughly photograph the wreck in May 1976.

## One Mysterious Body

One odd aspect of the tragedy was that no bodies were found. In most temperate waters, corpses rise to the surface as decomposition forms gas. But the Great Lakes are so cold that decomposition is inhibited, causing bodies to stay on the bottom.

In 1994, a Michigan businessman named Frederick Shannon took a submarine equipped with a full array of modern surveillance equipment to the site, hoping to film a documentary about the ship. His crew discovered a body on the lake bottom near the bow of the wreck, covered by cork sections of a decayed canvas life vest. However, this body may not be associated with the *Fitzgerald*. Two French vessels were lost nearby in 1918, and none of those bodies had been recovered either. A sailor from one of them could have been preserved by the lake's frigid water and heavy pressure.

## What Sank the Mighty Fitz?

One theory is that the *Fitzgerald* got too close to the dangerous Six-Fathom Shoal near Caribou Island and scraped over it, damaging the hull. Another is that the ship's hatch covers were either faulty or improperly clamped, which allowed water in. Wave height may also have played a part, with the storm producing a series of huge swells known as the "Three Sisters"—a trio of lightning-fast waves that pound a vessel—the first washes over the deck, the second hits the deck again so fast that the first has not had time to clear itself, and the third quickly adds another heavy wash, piling thousands of gallons of water on the ship. Few ships can withstand this.

### For Whom the Bell Tolls

On July 4, 1995, the bell of the *Edmund Fitzgerald* was retrieved and laid to rest in the Great Lakes Shipwreck Historical Museum in Whitefish Bay, Michigan. A replica bell, symbolizing the ship's "spirit," was left with the wreckage. Every year on November 10, during a memorial service, the original, 200-pound bronze bell is rung 29 times—once for each crewmember who perished.

# The Anasazi

*Across the deserts and mesas of the region known as the Four Corners, where Arizona, New Mexico, Colorado, and Utah meet, backcountry hikers and motoring tourists can easily spot reminders of an ancient people.*

✳ ✳ ✳ ✳

FROM THE TOWERING stone structures at Chaco Culture National Historical Park to cliff dwellings at Mesa Verde National Park to the ubiquitous scatters of broken pottery and stone tools, these remains tell the story of a culture that spread out across the arid Southwest during ancient times. The Anasazi are believed to have lived in the region from about AD 1 through AD 1300 (though the exact beginning of the culture is difficult to determine because there is no particular defining event). In their everyday lives, they created black-on-white pottery styles that distinguish subregions within the culture, traded with neighboring cultures (including those to the south in Central America), and built ceremonial structures called kivas, which were used for religious or communal purposes.

## The Exodus Explained

Spanish conquistadors exploring the Southwest noted the abandoned cliff dwellings and ruined plazas, and archaeologists today still try to understand what might have caused the Anasazi to move from their homes and villages throughout the region. Over time, researchers have posed a number of theories, including the idea that the Anasazi were driven from their villages by hostile nomads, such as those from the Apache or Ute tribes. Others believe that the Anasazi fought among themselves, causing a drastic reduction in their populations, and a few extraterrestrial-minded theorists have suggested that the Anasazi were destroyed by aliens. Today, the prevalent hypothesis among scientists is that a long-term drought affected the area, destroying agricultural fields and forcing people to abandon their largest villages. Scientists and archaeologists have worked together to reconstruct the region's climate data and compare it with material that has been excavated. Based on their findings, many agree that some combination of environmental and cultural factors caused the dispersal of the Anasazi from the large-scale ruins seen throughout the landscape today.

## Their Journey

Although many writers romanticize the Anasazi as a people who mysteriously disappeared from the region, they did not actually disappear. Those living in large ancient villages and cultural centers did indeed disperse, but the people themselves did not simply disappear. Today, descendants of the Anasazi can be found living throughout New Mexico and Arizona. The Hopi tribe in northern Arizona, as well as those living in approximately 20 pueblos in New Mexico, are the modern-day descendants of the Anasazi. The Pueblos in New Mexico whose modern inhabitants consider the Anasazi their ancestors include: Acoma, Cochiti, Isleta, Jemez, Laguna, Nambe, Picuris, Pojoaque, San Felipe, San Ildefonso, Ohkay Owingeh (formerly referred to as San Juan), Sandia, Santa Ana, Santa Clara, Santo Domingo, Taos, Tesuque, Zia, and Zuni.

# Chapter 5

# Things You Probably Didn't Know

## The Hidden History of the Jockstrap

*On November 28, 2005, the Bike Athletic Company celebrated the production of its 350 millionth jockstrap, which was promptly framed and flown to the company's headquarters. Let's take a closer look at some landmarks in the long history of this piece of men's protective underwear.*

※　※　※　※

### The Birth of a Legend

THE ORIGIN OF the jockstrap begins in 1874, thanks to Charles Bennett, who worked for the Chicago-based sporting goods company Sharp & Smith. Originally, Bennett designed his garment to be used by bicyclists in Boston. In 1897, Bennett and his newly formed BIKE Web Company (as Bike Athletic was known then) officially patented his invention.

At the time, a bicycle craze was sweeping the nation. These bikes weren't like today's average cruisers; instead, the bicycles of yore were high-wheeled and quite precarious. Folks raced these bikes around steeply banked velodrome tracks as well as through Boston's bumpy cobblestone streets. The daredevils on the velodromes were known as "bike jockeys," which led to

Bennett naming his invention the "BIKE Jockey Strap," later shortened to "jockstrap." Two decades later, the U.S. Army issued jockstraps to World War I soldiers in order to reduce "scrotal fatigue." When the troops came home, the bicycle craze had been replaced by the rough and tumble sport of football; the jockstrap found a new home on the gridiron.

*Manly Fact:* There is some conjecture that the word "jock" is derived from a slang term for the penis.

## Entering Manhood Via the Locker Room

To most men of a certain age, the jockstrap is a rite of passage that signals the arrival of puberty and a need to protect the male reproductive organs during vigorous exercise. To the uninitiated, the jockstrap might contain some mystery, but its construction is rather simple. A jockstrap (or athletic supporter) consists of an elastic waistband and leg straps connected to a pouch that holds the testicles and penis close to the body, sometimes with the added plastic cup (ostensibly to avoid injury). The original design, with the addition of the cup, hasn't changed much since the early 1900s.

*Manly Fact:* Jockstrap size refers to waist size. In this case, bigger isn't necessarily better.

## A Milestone Missed

In 1974, the jockstrap turned 100 years old, but the anniversary was a quiet one—alas, no national magazine covers commemorating the garment, no ticker-tape parade. Perhaps it was due to a national feeling of modesty, yet 15 years later, as a journalist writing for the *Orlando Sentinel* remarked, a certain women's undergarment—the bra—received plenty of press for its centennial. In fact, when the bra turned 100, *LIFE* magazine issued six pages to celebrate, along with a pictorial, and a headline shouting "Hurrah for the bra." Ten years later, as the jockstrap turned 125, a *Houston Chronicle* writer wondered why we'd forgotten about the forsaken jockstrap. Perhaps we'd been too distracted by Y2K in 1999, he wrote, or maybe "the jock just isn't in the same league [as the bra] . . . A bra suggests female mystery; a jock suggests male vulnerability."

*Manly Fact:* In the early 1900s, the jockstrap influenced the invention of the Heidelberg Alternating Current Electric Belt, which claimed to cure nervous diseases in men and women.

### The Decline of the Jock?

In the past few decades, there has been some run on jockstrap territory by the likes of the more free-flowing boxer shorts, jockey shorts, and, for athletic types, "compression shorts." Slowing numbers can be pointed to increased competition, or perhaps men are acting out against years of ridicule by class-mates and less-than-tactful gym teachers. Still, after more than 130 years on the market, the jockstrap probably isn't going anywhere just yet.

# What Is the "7" in 7-Up?

*We'll never know for sure. The soft drink's creator, Charles Leiper Grigg, went to the grave without revealing where he got the name. But there are several interesting rumors regarding its origin.*

W HEN GRIGG INTRODUCED his drink in October 1929, it had neither a "7" nor an "Up" in its name. He called it "Bib-Label Lithiated Lemon-Lime Soda." (Imagine trying to order that bad boy at the Taco Bell drive-thru.) "Bib-Label" referred to the use of paper labels that were placed on plain bottles, and "Lithiated" related to the mood-altering substance lithium.

Despite having a bizarre name, hitting store shelves two weeks before the stock market crashed, and facing competition from about six hundred other lemon-lime sodas, the new drink sold pretty well. (Chalk it up to the cool, refreshing taste of lithium.) But even with this success, Grigg soon realized that

"Bib-Label Lithiated Lemon-Lime Soda" was a little tricky to remember, so he changed the name to 7-Up.

Here's the most pervasive (and logical) explanation for the name: The "7" refers to the drink's seven ingredients, and the "Up" has to do with the soda's rising bubbles. This version is supported by an early 7-Up tagline: "Seven natural flavors blended into a savory, flavory drink with a real wallop." The seven ingredients were carbonated water, sugar, citric acid, lithium citrate, sodium citrate, and essences of lemon and lime oils (technically two ingredients). Of course, it's entirely possible that ad executives devised the ingredients angle to fit the name rather than vice versa.

There are other possible origins, but these theories range from the unlikely to the preposterous. It's quite possible that the "7" refers to nothing at all—Grigg may have simply devised an enigmatic name to pique people's interest. In any case, the moniker worked out okay. By 1940, 7-Up was the third-best-selling soft drink in the world. And even after delicious lithium was dropped from the recipe in 1950, the drink remained a hit.

# How Did I Get My Birthmark?

*In the old days, you would have gone to your mother with some questions. While pregnant with you, did she: Spill wine on herself? Get an X-ray? Suffer a terrible fright? Eat excessive amounts of beets, watermelons, or strawberries?*

✳   ✳   ✳   ✳

SHE DID? WELL, that sure is interesting. But spilled wine, an X-ray, a scary incident, or an excessive consumption of beets, watermelons, or strawberries is not the reason for your birthmark, although many people—including a few doctors—used to think it was. Truth is, the causes of most birthmarks are unknown. We do, however, know how the two major types of birthmarks—vascular and pigmented—physically form.

Vascular birthmarks—such as macular stains, port-wine stains, and hemangiomas—happen when blood vessels get bunched together, tangled, or just don't grow normally. Pigmented birthmarks—such as café-au-lait spots, Mongolian spots, and congenital moles—form when an overgrowth of cells creates extra pigment on the skin.

Like we said, the experts insist that birthmarks are not caused by what your mother did, craved, ate, or wished for during her pregnancy. Furthermore, they can't be prevented. This earth-shaking news affects a whole lot of people: Up to a third of newborns have some kind of colorful spot, mark, mole, blemish, or blotch. Think of them as nature's tattoos.

Whether brown, red, pink, black, blue, or purple, most birthmarks are harmless. Some will shrink on their own over time. Others can be removed with surgery or the zap of a laser. The rest are permanent fixtures.

If you have a birthmark, don't waste time worrying about it. Instead, you should consider yourself special. Depending on the old wife with whom you consult, it could well be the sign of an angel's kiss or even a battle wound from a previous life. How's that for a mark of honor?

## How Do Dogs Remember Where They Bury Their Bones?

*Ever watched your dog bury a bone? After covering its treasure with dirt, it'll press its nose into the ground as if it's literally tamping the soil down with its snout. You can always tell when a dog's been digging: Its dirty nose is a dead giveaway.*

✳ ✳ ✳ ✳

So how does a dog find its treasure weeks or maybe months later? It follows its nose. The enzymes that are released by decomposing bones, especially raw ones, give off a special odor. We can't smell it, but a dog certainly can—dogs can smell one thousand to ten thousand times better than we can. A dog that's looking for its buried bone will sniff around, keeping its nose to the ground until it finds the exact spot.

And incidentally, this ability to detect decomposing bones is what enables dogs to help law enforcement officials find corpses. According to California's Institute for Canine Forensics, dogs are even used at archaeological digs to locate ancient burial grounds.

A dog's propensity for burying bones is what zoologists call cache behavior. It's also found among wolves, wild dogs, and foxes. When a kill is too large to be devoured at a single sitting, these animals bury what they can't eat in safe places. Canines are highly territorial. Your dog will never bury its bones in another dog's yard, though it may try to sneak in and dig up its neighbor's cache on the sly. Wild canines also bury food in areas that they have marked as their own, which they defend fiercely. During lean times, they will dig up their hidden food stores—it's sort of like having something set aside for the proverbial rainy day.

Do dogs always retrieve the bones they bury? Not necessarily. Cache behavior is an important survival technique for canines in the wild, but well-fed domestic pets may simply have no need for their buried leftovers. Furthermore, cooked bones don't hold the same allure as raw ones—they disintegrate faster, and their scent is sometimes masked by the odors of the surrounding soil.

If your yard is full of holes, you're probably wondering how you can stop your dog from burying bones. Well, the cache instinct is so powerful that there isn't much you can do to deter it. As any experienced dog owner can tell you, a dog will always bury something. If Fido doesn't have a bone, a favorite toy or even an old shoe will do. Indoor dogs often hide their toys under beds or behind sofa cushions. Some veterinarians recommend giving a dog its own sandbox or a pile of pillows where it can "play" at hiding and seeking. These vets add that encouraging cache behavior can be a great interactive way of getting to know your pet better.

So join the fun. Instead of punishing your dog for doing what comes naturally, roll up your sleeves, grab that tattered old stinky sneaker, and dig in.

# Top-Secret Locations You Can Visit

*There are plenty of stories of secret government facilities hidden in plain sight. Places where all sorts of strange tests take place, far away from the general public. Many of the North American top-secret government places have been (at least partially) declassified, allowing average Joes to visit. We've listed some locations where you can play Men in Black.*

✳   ✳   ✳   ✳

## Titan Missile Silo

JUST A LITTLE south of Tucson, Arizona, lies the Sonoran Desert, a barren, desolate area where nothing seems to be happening. That's exactly why, during the Cold War, the U.S. government hid an underground Titan Missile silo there.

Inside the missile silo, one of dozens that once littered the area, a Titan 2 Missile could be armed and launched in just under 90 seconds. Until it was finally abandoned in the 1990s, the government manned the silo 24 hours a day, with every member being trained to "turn the key" and launch the missile at a moment's notice. Today, the silo is open to the public as the Titan Missile Museum. Visitors can take a look at one of the few remaining Titan 2 missiles in existence, still sitting on the launch pad (relax, it's been disarmed). Folks with extra dough can also spend the night inside the silo and play the role of one of the crew members assigned to prepare to launch the missile at a moment's notice.

## Peanut Island

You wouldn't think a sunny place called Peanut Island, located near Palm Beach, Florida, could hold many secrets. Yet in December 1961, the U.S. Navy came to the island on a secret mission to create a fallout shelter for President John F. Kennedy and his family. The shelter was completed, but it was never used and was all but forgotten when the Cold War ended. Today, it is maintained by the Palm Beach Maritime Museum, which conducts weekend tours of the space.

## Wright-Patterson Air Force Base

If you believe that aliens crash-landed in Roswell, New Mexico, in the summer of 1947, then you need to make a trip out to Ohio's Wright-Patterson Air Force Base. That's because, according to legend, the UFO crash debris and possibly the aliens (both alive and dead) were shipped to the base as part of a government cover-up. Some say all that debris is still there, hidden away in an underground bunker beneath the mysterious Hanger 18.

While most of the Air Force Base is off-limits to the general public, you can go on a portion of the base to visit the National Museum of the U.S. Air Force, filled with amazing artifacts tracing the history of flight. But don't bother to ask any of the museum personnel how to get to Hanger 18—the official word is that the hanger does not exist.

## Los Alamos National Laboratory

Until recently, the U.S. government refused to acknowledge the Los Alamos National Laboratory's existence. But in the early 1940s, the lab was created near Los Alamos, New Mexico, to develop the first nuclear weapons in what would become known as the Manhattan Project.

Back then, the facility was so top secret it didn't even have a name. It was simply referred to as Site Y. No matter what it was called, the lab produced two nuclear bombs, nicknamed Little Boy and Fat Man—bombs that would be dropped on

Hiroshima and Nagasaki, effectively ending World War II. Today, tours of portions of the facility can be arranged through the Lab's Public Affairs Department.

## Fort Knox

It is the stuff that legends are made of: A mythical building filled with over 4,700 tons of gold, stacked up and piled high to the ceiling. But this is no fairytale—the gold really does exist, and it resides inside Fort Knox.

Since 1937, the U.S. Department of the Treasury's Bullion Depository has been storing the gold inside Fort Knox on a massive military campus that stretches across three counties in north-central Kentucky. Parts of the campus are open for tours, including the General George Patton Museum. But don't think you're going to catch a glimpse of that shiny stuff—visitors are not permitted to go through the gate or enter the building.

## Nevada Test Site

If you've ever seen one of those old black-and-white educational films of nuclear bombs being tested, chances are it was filmed at the Nevada Test Site, often referred to as the Most Bombed Place in the World.

Located about an hour north of Las Vegas, the Nevada Test Site was created in 1951 as a secret place for the government to conduct nuclear experiments and tests in an outdoor laboratory that is actually larger than Rhode Island. Out there, scientists blew everything up from mannequins to entire buildings.

Those curious to take a peek inside the facility can sign up for a daylong tour. Of course, before they let you set foot on the base, visitors must submit to a background check and sign paperwork promising not to attempt to photograph, videotape, or take soil samples from the site.

# America's Only King

*Few people would believe that a separate empire with its own full-fledged king once existed within the borders of the United States of America. But James Jesse Strang was indeed crowned ruler of a Lake Michigan island kingdom in the mid-1800s. His bizarre road to royalty, though, began in southeastern Wisconsin.*

✳  ✳  ✳  ✳

## Growing the Garden

STRANG WAS BORN in 1813 in Scipio, New York. He moved to Wisconsin in 1843 with his wife, Mary, to a large parcel of land just west of what would become the city of Burlington.

The red-haired Strang set up a law practice and, thanks to family connections, met the Mormon prophet Joseph Smith on a trip to Nauvoo, Illinois. Strang's rise to fame began, as Smith immediately appointed him an elder in the faith and authorized him to start a Mormon "stake" in Wisconsin named Voree, which meant "Garden of Peace."

Mormons from around the country flocked to Voree to build homes on the rolling, forested tract along the White River. A few months after Strang became a Mormon, Joseph Smith was killed. To everyone's amazement, Strang produced a letter that appeared to have been written and signed by Joseph Smith, which named Strang as the church's next Prophet.

Another leader named Brigham Young, whom you may have heard of, also claimed that title, and Young eventually won the subsequent power struggle. As a result, Strang broke away to form his own branch of Mormonism.

## Secrets from the Soil

In September 1845, Strang made a stunning announcement. He said that a divine revelation had instructed him to dig beneath an oak tree in Voree located on a low rise known as the "Hill of Promise." Four followers armed with shovels dug under the tree and unearthed a box containing some small brass plates, each only a few inches tall.

The plates were covered with hieroglyphics, crude drawings of the White River settlement area, and a vaguely Native American human figure holding what appeared to be a scepter. Strang said he was able to translate them using special stones, like the ones Joseph Smith had used to translate similar buried plates in New York. The writing, Strang said, was from a lost tribe of Israel that had somehow made it to North America. He managed to show the plates to hundreds of people before they mysteriously disappeared.

As his number of followers grew, he created sub-groups among them. There was the commune-style Order of Enoch, and the secretive Illuminati, who pledged their allegiance to Strang as "sovereign Lord and King on earth." Infighting developed within the ranks, and area non-Mormons also raised objections to the community. Some Burlington residents even went so far as to try to persuade wagonloads of Voree-bound emigrants not to join Strang.

In 1849, Strang received a second set of divine messages, called the Plates of Laban. He said they had originally been carried in the Ark of the Covenant. They contained instructions called *The Book of the Law of the Lord*, which he again translated with his stones. The plates were not shown to the group at that time, but they did eventually yield support, some would say rather conveniently, for the controversial practice of polygamy.

## Polygamy Problems

Strang had personal reasons for getting divine approval to have multiple wives. In July 1849, a 19-year-old woman named Elvira Field secretly became Strang's second wife. Just one problem—he hadn't divorced his first one. Soon, Field traveled with him posing as a young man named Charlie Douglas, with her hair cut short and wearing a man's black suit. Yet, the "clever" disguise did little to hide Field's ample figure.

At about that time, Strang claimed another angel visited to tell him it was time to get out of Voree. Strang was to lead his people to a land surrounded by water and covered in timber. This land, according to Strang, was Beaver Island, the largest of a group of islands in the Beaver Archipelago north of Charlevoix, Michigan. It had recently been opened to settlement, and the Strangites moved there in the late 1840s.

## The Promised Island

On July 8, 1950, Strang donned a crown and red cape as his followers officially dubbed him King of Beaver Island. Falling short of becoming King of the United States, he was later elected to Michigan's state legislature, thanks to strong voter turnout among his followers. Perhaps reveling in his new power, eventually, he took three more young wives, for a total of five.

On the island, Strang's divine revelations dictated every aspect of his followers' daily lives. He mandated that women wear bloomers and that their skirts measure a certain length, required severe lashings for adultery, and forbade cigarettes and alcohol. Under this strict rule, some followers began to rebel. In addition, relations with local fishermen soured as the colony's businesses prospered.

On June 16, 1856, a colony member named Thomas Bedford, who had previously been publicly whipped, recruited an accomplice and then shot Strang. The king survived for several weeks and was taken back to Voree by his young wives. He died in his parents' stone house—which still stands near Mormon Road on State Highway 11. At the time, all four of his young wives were pregnant. And back in Michigan, it wasn't long before local enemies and mobs of vigilantes from the mainland forcibly removed his followers from Beaver Island.

James Jesse Strang was buried in Voree, but his remains were later moved to a cemetery in Burlington. A marker, which has a map of the old community, stands just south of Highway

11 where it crosses the White River, and several of the old cobblestone houses used by group members are preserved and bear historical markers. Strang's memory also lives on in a religious group formed by several of his followers, the Reorganized Church of Jesus Christ of Latter-Day Saints.

# Who Says Dinosaurs Are Extinct?

*Dinosaurs vanished from Earth 65 million years ago . . . or did they? Don't get nervous—you won't see a Tyrannosaurus rex stomping down your street.*

✳   ✳   ✳   ✳

RECENT FINDINGS HAVE turned the field of paleontology on its head. Scientists now believe that there is a group of dinosaurs that are not extinct. In fact, they could be flapping around your neighborhood right now!

## Look . . . Up in the Sky!

The dinosaurs that exist today are descendants of theropod dinosaurs, a group that includes such popularly known creatures as velociraptor and T. rex, as well as myriad smaller dinosaurs. These living relics are avian dinosaurs—also known as birds.

For hundreds of years, scientists had observed similarities between birds and the fossils of theropod dinosaurs—features such as hollow bones and birdlike feet. The conceptual leap from "birdlike" to "bird" was cemented in 1996, when an extraordinary finding was reported from China's Liaoning Province. Paleontologist Chen Pei Ji presented a fossilized skeleton of a small theropod surrounded by impressions of fuzzy down on the perimeter of its body. Turns out, these were feathers. Since then, hundreds more of these feathered dinosaur specimens have been found all over the world.

### Jurassic Zoo

Our understanding of dinosaurs has always been limited by what we can glean from dusty fossilized remains. If you want to learn about how theropod dinosaurs moved, how their bodies were shaped, and even how they cared for their young, you can skip the trip to a natural history museum and go to the zoo instead. An afternoon with an emu could be your day with a dinosaur.

# The Mystery of the Lost Dauphin of France

*History is rife with conspiracy theories. More than 200 years later, the fate of the Lost Dauphin of France still baffles historians.*

✳   ✳   ✳   ✳

### Little Boy Lost

BORN IN 1785, Louis XVII, son of King Louis XVI and Queen Marie Antoinette, was the heir apparent to the throne (giving him the title of *le Dauphin*). The young boy's destiny was unfortunately timed, however, coinciding with the French Revolution's anti-royalist frenzy that swept away the monarchy. His father met his end on the guillotine in January 1793; as next in the line of succession, little eight-year-old Louis XVII was a dead boy walking.

The family was imprisoned and stripped of their regalia. A few months later, on the night of July 3, 1793, guards came for Louis. Realizing that she would never see her son again, Marie Antoinette clung to Louis, and for the next two hours she pleaded for his life. She finally relented after the commissioners threatened to kill both her son and daughter. The boy was dragged crying and screaming from his mother.

To keep the monarchy from being reestablished, Louis was imprisoned in solitary confinement in a windowless room.

Some reports state that the young boy was horribly starved and abused by his jailers. Less than two years later, on June 8, 1795, the ten-year-old Dauphin of France died. The official cause of death was tuberculosis.

But instead of ending the matter, the mystery of the true fate of Louis XVII had just begun.

## Pretenders to the Throne

Rumors grew like wildfire that the body of Louis XVII was actually someone else. Like any good mystery, there were plenty of stories to fuel the flames of conspiracy:

* Louis's jailers were a husband and wife. Later, the aged wife told the nuns who were nursing her that she and her husband had once smuggled out the Dauphin. "My little prince is not dead," she reportedly said.

* A doctor who had treated the Dauphin died "mysteriously" just before the boy did. The doctor's widow suggested he had refused to participate in some strange practices concerning his patient.

* The Dauphin's sister was never asked to identify his body.

* In 1814, the historian of the restored French monarchy claimed that Louis was alive.

* In 1846, the mass grave where the Dauphin had been buried was exhumed. Only one corpse, that of an older boy, showed evidence of tuberculosis.

## Contenders (or Pretenders?) to the Throne

With all of these doubts about what really happened to Louis, it's amazing that only about 100 people came forward throughout the years claiming to be the lost Dauphin and rightful heir to the throne. Among them were:

John James Audubon—Many people thought the famous naturalist Audubon was Louis because he was adopted, was the same age as the Dauphin would have been, and spoke with a French accent. Audubon liked a good story and sometimes implied that he was indeed the Dauphin. In 1828, while visiting France, he wrote a letter to his wife that said, ". . . dressed as a common man, I walk the streets! I who should command all!"

Eleazer Williams—Although his father was a member of the Mohawk tribe, this missionary from Wisconsin somehow convinced people that he was the Lost Dauphin and became a minor celebrity for a few years.

Karl Wilhelm Naundorff—Perhaps the most successful of all, this German clockmaker convinced both the Dauphin's nurse and the minister of justice under Louis XVI that he was indeed the lost heir. He was even recognized as such by the government of the Netherlands. Tests in the 1950s disproved his claim. Finally, in 2000, DNA tests confirmed that the boy who died in prison was indeed Louis XVII. Even so, as with many conspiracy theories, many people dispute the test's finding.

# Who Reads All Those Letters to Santa?

*This question is kind of confusing. Who else but Santa would read those letters? It's almost like saying that there isn't a Santa Claus. And that, of course, is preposterous. Isn't it? Please tell us it's preposterous.*

✳  ✳  ✳  ✳

OKAY, LET'S JUST say that Santa is too busy to read all of the letters that are sent to him each year—thank goodness there are plenty of helpers out there. They read the letters to Santa and sometimes even help Jolly Old Saint Nick fulfill some of the requests. These helpers range from high-tech to purely traditional.

Some websites give youngsters a place to send messages to Santa electronically, and Santa will even send a reply. While they're there, kids can play a trivia game, and fill out a "naughty or nice" list to gauge the likeliness that they'll be receiving coal on December 25.

The post office in New York City runs a more traditional project called "Operation Santa Claus" every December. (Other postal locations around the country promote similar programs.) To participate, volunteers can drop in to the office, pick up letters addressed to Santa—which are often heartbreaking missives by some of the area's neediest children—and see to it that the letter-writers' Christmas wishes are fulfilled.

Since the 1920s, residents of Santa Claus, Indiana, have been reading letters to Santa and responding to them. The town of about 2,200—which is located near the Kentucky border—is home to the Santa Claus Museum. In years past, Santa Clausians responded to as many as three million letters per year, but now the volume is closer to fifteen thousand. The responses are framed by one of three form letters—even people in Santa Claus, Indiana, have real jobs and personal lives to attend to—but the letters are personalized, and the postmark is obviously quite distinctive.

# Undiscovered Animals

*Since about 1.3 million animal species around the planet have been identified and named, you might think that we're down to the last few unknown critters by now. But according to many biologists, we're probably not even 10 percent of the way there.*

✳   ✳   ✳   ✳

## The Mysteries of the Oceans and Rain Forests

EXPERTS ESTIMATE THAT the planet holds ten million to 100 million undiscovered plant and animal species, excluding single-celled organisms like bacteria and algae. This whopping estimate is based on the number of species found in examined environments and on the sizes of the areas we have yet to fully investigate.

The broad span of the estimate shows just how little we know about life on Earth. At the heart of the mystery are the oceans and tropical rain forests. More than 70 percent of the planet is underwater. We know that the oceans teem with life, but we've explored only a small fraction of them. The watery realm is like an entire planet unto itself. Biologists haven't examined much of the tropical rain forests, either, but the regions that they have explored have turned up a truly dizzying variety of life. It's hard to say exactly how many life forms have yet to be discovered, but the majority probably are small invertebrates (animals without backbones).

## It's All about Insects

Insects make up the vast majority of the animal kingdom. There are about 900,000 known varieties, and this number will probably increase significantly as we further explore the rain forests. Terry Erwin is an influential coleopterist—in other words, a beetle guy—who estimated that the tropics alone could contain 30 million separate insect and arthropod species. This number is based on his examination of forest canopies in South America and Central America, and it suggests that you're on the wrong planet if you hate bugs.

Cataloging all of these critters is slowgoing. It requires special knowledge to distinguish between similar insect species and to identify different ocean species. It also takes real expertise to know which animals are already on the books and which are not. Qualified experts are in short supply, and they have a lot on their plates.

In some respects, time is of the essence. Deforestation and climate change are killing off animal and plant species even before they've been discovered. You may not particularly care about wildlife, but these are big losses. The knowledge gained from some of these undiscovered creatures that are on death row could help to cure a variety of human ailments and, thus, make the world a better place.

# Waiter, There's Meat in My Mincemeat

*Is mincemeat made of meat? Not anymore—at least not usually.*

✳ ✳ ✳ ✳

INCEMEAT PIE, AMERICAN style, is a common wintertime and Christmas treat alongside pumpkin pie and fruitcake. Recipes combine what we think of as "pumpkin pie spice," dried fruits soaked in alcohol, and vegetable or animal fat to make a rich, hearty pie filling. The original mincemeat often included minced meat, hence the name, and was made using animal fat called suet in both the pastry crust and the filling.

Both spices and sugar were cherished luxuries for most of human history, which led to their addition to savory dishes that sound a bit unsettling to us today. But in today's era of added sugar, even ketchup is very sweet. Maybe our ancestors' cooking wouldn't seem strange after all. Mincemeat's carnivore-friendly reputation endures: in 2015's season of *The Great Australian Bake Off*, the hosts referred to a modern fruit mincemeat as "vegetarian mincemeat."

# The "Moon Illusion"

*The moon looks bigger when it's near the horizon, a phenomenon that has flummoxed brilliant minds for thousands of years. Aristotle attempted an explanation around 350 BC, and today's scientists still don't know for sure what's going on.*

✳   ✳   ✳   ✳

## Here's What We Do Know

WE MAY NOT know exactly why the moon looks bigger when it's near the horizon—something that's known as the "moon illusion"—but great thinkers have at least ruled out several possible explanations. Hey, that's progress.

First, the moon is not closer to Earth when it's at the horizon. In fact, it's closer when it's directly overhead.

Second, your eye does not physically detect that the moon is bigger when it's near the horizon. The moon creates a .15-millimeter image on the retina, no matter where it is. You can test this yourself: Next time you see a big moon looming low behind the trees, hold a pencil at arm's length and note the relative size of the moon and the eraser. Then wait a few hours and try it again when the moon is higher in the sky. You'll see that the moon is exactly the same size relative to the eraser. The .15-millimeter phenomenon rules out atmospheric distortion as an explanation for the moon's apparent change in size.

Third, a moon on the horizon doesn't look larger just because we're comparing it to trees, buildings, and the like. Airline pilots experience the same big-moon illusion when none of these visual cues are present. Also, consider the fact that when the moon is higher in the sky and we look at it through the same trees or with the same buildings in the foreground, it doesn't look as large as it does when it's on the horizon.

## A Matter of Perception

What's going on? Scientists quibble over the details, but the common opinion is that the "moon illusion" must be the result of the brain automatically interpreting visual information based on its own unconscious expectations. We instinctively take distance information into account when deciding how large something is. When you see faraway building, for example, you interpret it as big because you factor in the visual effect of distance.

But this phenomenon confuses us when we attempt to visually compute the size of the moon. According to the most popular theory, this is because we naturally perceive the sky as a flattened dome when, in reality, it's a spherical hemisphere. This perception might be based on our understanding that the ground is relatively flat. As a result, we compute distance differently, depending on whether something is at the horizon or directly overhead.

According to this flattened-dome theory, when the moon is near the horizon, we have a fairly accurate sense of its distance and size. But when the moon is overhead, we unconsciously make an inaccurate estimate of its distance. As a result of this error, we automatically estimate its size incorrectly.

In other words, based on a faulty understanding of the shape of the sky, the brain perceives reality incorrectly and interprets the moon as being smaller when it's overhead than when it's on the horizon. That's right—your brain is tricking you. So what are you going to believe—science or your lying eyes?

# The Doubleday Myth

*It's a great story that's been passed from one generation to the next. It's also a work of fiction.*

✳  ✳  ✳  ✳

**❚❚** THE FIRST SCHEME for playing Baseball, according to the best evidence available to date, was devised by Abner Doubleday at Cooperstown, N.Y. in 1839."

That finding, announced after a three-year study by the Mills Commission in 1907, is the main reason the tiny central New York hamlet was chosen to be the home of the National Baseball Hall of Fame and Museum. This "creation myth" has since been debunked from so many angles it seems positively ridiculous now, but it was accepted as truth back then.

Had Abner Doubleday truly invented baseball in 1839 in Cooperstown, New York, as so many generations of children have been told over the years, pundits could answer the question "Why Cooperstown?" in far fewer words. As it stands, the response requires a little more explanation.

So why Cooperstown? "The answer involves a commission, a tattered baseball, a philanthropist, and a centennial celebration," describes the Hall of Fame in its official statement. The commission was the brainchild of sporting goods magnate Albert G. Spalding in 1905, in response to a story that baseball had evolved from the British game of rounders. The baseball in question was an old, tattered, homemade ball discovered in a dusty attic trunk in a farmhouse near Cooperstown in 1934. It became known as the "Doubleday Ball," and it served to support the commission's 1907 findings. Singer sewing machine magnate Stephen C. Clark purchased the "Doubleday ball" for $5 in 1935 and pushed for the formation of the Hall of Fame.

The museum's opening was planned to coincide with a "century of baseball" celebration set to take place in Cooperstown in 1939. Thanks largely to Clark and his family, the Hall of Fame opened its doors in June of that year.

Even before the Hall of Fame opened, many people questioned the findings of the Mills Commission, which said that Doubleday, a West Point cadet and Union general in the Civil War, had set down rules for a game of "town ball" for a group of Cooperstown boys to take on those from a neighboring town. The tale was based largely on the testimony of Abner Graves, a retired mining engineer who claimed to have witnessed the event. But historians later learned that Graves's testimony was questionable at best (he spent his final years in an insane asylum) and that baseball's presumed "founding father" was likely not in or even near Cooperstown in 1839.

Abner Doubleday's credibility as the inventor of baseball wasn't helped by the dozens of diaries he wrote after retiring from the U.S. Army in 1873. Neither the diaries nor the Doubleday obituary that appeared in *The New York Times* 20 years later include any mention of baseball.

In fact, the Hall of Fame plaque of Alexander Cartwright credits him as the "Father of Modern Base Ball." Cartwright, a New York bank teller and talented draftsman, organized the first regular team, which he called the New York Knickerbockers. Rather than play "town ball," where scores could top 100, Cartwright devised rules for a game that would feature bases 90 feet apart on a diamond-shape infield, nine players per side, a three-strikes-and-you're-out policy, and "force outs" at first base if the ball got to the infielder before the runner—all rules that have stood the test of time. The first game under Cartwright's rules was played at the Elysian Fields in Hoboken, New Jersey, on June 19, 1846.

# How Did Houdini Die?

*Ehrich Weiss, better remembered as Harry Houdini, was the master escape artist and illusionist of his time—perhaps of all time. Contrary to rumor, though, he did not die at the hands of angry spiritualists.*

✳ ✳ ✳ ✳

SEVERAL OF HOUDINI'S stunts almost did him in, especially if sabotage or malfunction affected the gear. He finished numerous escapes bleeding and bruised. But he was always a "show must go on" performer, and that's ultimately what caused his death.

Houdini was a consummate showman, but he was also a trifle odd. He developed the macho habit of encouraging people to test his stony abs by slugging him in the gut. In 1926, while visiting Houdini backstage before a performance in Montreal, a college student asked to give the famous abs the punch test. The eager recruit hit him before the magician could brace himself for the repeated blows, and a terrible pain shot through Houdini's side. Despite his agony, that night's performance went on.

Later that evening, in severe pain, Houdini was reading a newspaper while waiting for a train to Detroit. A burly "fan" approached him and drove a fist straight through the paper and into the performer's stomach, worsening matters considerably. In Detroit, Houdini finished his show by sheer will before finally checking into a hospital. Doctors found that he had an abnormally long appendix that spanned his pelvis, and as a result of the blows, it had ruptured. Rumors began to swirl that the student who had punched Houdini was actually an offended member of a group of spiritualists whom Houdini often spoke against. The truth isn't quite so sensational. Houdini died of peritonitis six days after he was hospitalized—quite fittingly, on Halloween.

# Pressing Ye Issue

*Ye Olde Pretend Old English has planted "ye" in the public imagination, but this was never meant to be pronounced "yee"— it's "the." Blame the confusion on the printing press.*

✳   ✳   ✳   ✳

## A Curious Inventor

A SPECIAL SET OF circumstances helped Johannes Gutenberg to invent the movable type printing press in 1440. He was a metalworker with a curious, entrepreneurial spirit that led him to experiment and learn at least a little bit about many different fields. He adapted the technology used in the wine press, which had evolved over thousands of years, to build his printing press. For the type itself, he made individual letter stamps from a strong, durable alloy of his own devising. As a goldsmith, he had learned firsthand how soft metals like gold could warp and distort with wear.

## Character vs. Character

Movable type was originally developed in China, with its own set of fortunate circumstances. Mandarin and other dialects of Chinese use characters arranged in columns, reading top to bottom, and the characters are designed to be the same width. Artisans could make consistent square "blanks" with characters on them and slide them into fixed columns that were the same from job to job. The cost of labor was high but different artisans could work in parallel to the same specs.

English used an alphabet of letter characters with different widths, mostly from the Latin alphabet but with a handful from the Norse runic alphabet. Crafting letter stamps that were all the same width would make awkward type and be an inefficient use of space on costly paper or parchment pages, especially compared with the fine, thoughtful work done by hand in monasteries or by scribes.

## Ye Olde Printing Mix-Up

Space-saving Middle English signpainters and calligraphers shortened the word "the" using a runic thorn, but typesetters didn't have access to thorns and used "y" instead—it looked very similar in the typefaces of the time. So all those Ye Olde Pubberies are just the old pubs after all. The pronoun ye, as in "We hardly knew ye," is separate and pronounced phonetically.

The letter switch may seem foreign to us, but modern life is filled with the same misapprehensions. Surely you or someone you know writes "would of" instead of "would have," or "all intensive purposes"? Let they who are without syntax cast the first stone.

# Who Really Discovered the 'Way to a Man's Heart'?

*Fanny Fern has been credited with coining the phrase that lets women know—conventionally speaking, of course—the way to a man's heart. However, the saying may have originated in Great Britain a few years earlier.*

✳   ✳   ✳   ✳

YEARS BEFORE MEDICAL science developed alternate ways to access the human body's blood-pumping mechanism, it was determined—quite probably by a woman—that the best way to reach a man's heart is through his stomach. Independent research over many decades has been unable to verify this with 100% certainty, although there is empirical evidence suggesting its truth.

Fanny Fern, a 19th-century American children's author, humor writer, and columnist, is most widely credited with proclaiming that the way to a man's heart is through his stomach. However, instances of the reference, or at least very close approximations, have been uncovered in literature that predates Fern.

The *Oxford Dictionary of Proverbs*, for example, cites John Adams as the author of an 1814 letter that proclaimed, "The shortest road to men's hearts is down their throats." Fern was not quite 3 years old at the time, so presumably had no impact on Adams' observation.

Dinah Mulock, on the other hand, was a contemporary of Fern's when she authored the quote, "The way to an Englishman's heart is through his stomach," although clearly men from other nations also react well to a delicious, home-cooked meal.

## Fern Made a Name

Whether or not she first penned the famous saying, Fern enjoyed many significant accomplishments through her writing career. She was born Sara Payson Willis in Portland, Maine. Her father was a newspaper owner and two of her siblings also went on to achieve fame. Older brother Nathaniel Parker Willis grew up to be a renowned journalist and magazine owner (*Home Journal*), while her younger brother Richard Storrs Willis became a musician and wrote the melody for "It Came Upon the Midnight Clear."

Sara chose the pen name Fanny Fern because it conjured the childhood memory of her mother picking ferns. She eventually stuck with it outside of her writing endeavors as well. Fern was a skilled and prolific writer who first made her name writing magazine articles and later authored books. Her first, *Fern Leaves*, was published in 1853 and became a bestseller. It sold 46,000 copies in its first four months on bookshelves, giving her enough wealth to purchase a home in Brooklyn.

By 1855, she was a *New York Ledger* columnist making $100 a week—an unheard-of sum for a journalist, particularly a female one. Her column ran every week from January 1856 until two days after her death in October 1872. During her great career, she also co-founded an organization for women writers and artists and was an ardent suffrage advocate.

Whether or not Fern first coined the phrase, she certainly used it at least once in her volumes of copy. And by the mid-1800s, it had become an oft-cited maxim, appearing in New Hampshire and Virginia newspapers in the 1830s, in multiple books in the 1840s, and in countless written and spoken tales from those days forward.

It can be argued that Fern either mastered the art of reaching a man's heart in this manner, or colossally failed at it. She was married three times.

# The Boston Tea Party

*We've all learned that our colonial forebears helped touch off the American Revolution by turning Boston Harbor into a big tea caddy to protest "taxation without representation." In fact, wealthy smugglers set the whole thing up.*

✳   ✳   ✳   ✳

IS THE ORIGINAL not a great tale of democracy in action? Angry patriots, righteously fed up with burdensome taxes imposed by the British oppressors, seize a British ship and destroy the cargo! In reality, there's a lot more to the story.

### The Backdrop

This tale begins with the 1765 Stamp Act, eight years before the start of the Revolution. Because it cost Britain money to defend the colonies, the king wanted help paying the bill. This would happen through tax stamps, similar to modern post-age stamps, required on various documents, printed materials, goods, etc. For the same reason that proclaiming "I will raise taxes" is the same as saying "Don't elect me" 12 generations later, this caused an outcry. Then, as now, most Americans would rather part with their lifeblood than pay an extra dime in taxes.

The colonists resorted to various forms of terrorism. Mobs tarred and feathered government officials, burned them in effigy, and torched their homes and possessions. Within months, the horrified British gave up on the Stamp Act fiasco.

## What's the Price of Tea?

Next the British tried the Townshend Act (1767), imposing customs duties and hoping the average citizen wouldn't notice. Tea, much loved in the colonies, was among the taxed imports. Of course, Britain lacked the resources to patrol the entire colonial coastline against enterprising Dutch smugglers, who snuck shiploads of tea past customs officials. Seeing opportunity, clever colonial businessmen bought and distributed smuggled tea; like teen-clothing branders two centuries later, they marketed their product by associating it with defiant rebellion. It worked: Colonials boycotted legally imported tea, often refusing to let it be unloaded from ships.

The Boston Massacre of 1770 (a shooting incident that escalated from heckling and a snowball fight) didn't help. The British realized that the Townshend Act wasn't working, but they maintained the tea tax as a symbol of authority. The British East India Company (aka John Company), which monopolized the importation of Indian tea to America, was losing a lot of money. In response, Parliament passed the 1773 Tea Act, which relaxed customs duties and allowed John Company to bypass costly London middlemen. It was a brilliant idea: John Company could unload ruinously vast inventories of tea while pacifying the tax-hating, bargain-hunting colonial ingrates.

## Tea and Cakes in the Harbor

In November 1773, three British merchant ships anchored in Boston Harbor with the first loads of tea. Amid much social brouhaha, the smugglers roused mobs that prevented the tea from being unloaded. But by December 16, it was clear that the ships would land their tea the next day.

One group of protesters fortified itself with lots of liquor, dressed up in "Indian" costumes, and staggered toward the wharf in an outrage. Those who didn't fall into the water along the way boarded the British ships and began dragging the cargo up from the holds, cracking open designated cases and heaving tea leaves into the water. By the end of the night, approximately 45 tons of tea had been dumped overboard, and tea leaves washed up on Boston shores for weeks.

Afterward, the Sons of Liberty wandered home, proud of their patriotic accomplishment. Similar tea "parties" occurred in other colonial ports. The colonies had successfully impugned King George III and maintained a healthy business climate for smugglers.

# Illinois's Little-Known Black Codes

*Did Illinois ban the immigration of black people into the state in 1862?*

✳   ✳   ✳   ✳

Not only did it ban black immigration—Illinois remained a slave state until the Emancipation Proclamation. In fact, the biggest myth of all in terms of Illinois's relationship to slavery is that it was a true-blue northern state. In reality, Illinois clung to severe laws that limited any free black traffic through the state, instead treating even casual travelers as though they must be someone's slaves by the very fact that they were black. It was actually illegal to free slaves in Illinois.

This kind of policy, and the length of time for which Illinois clung to it, puts the state in line more with Georgia than New York. So the rest of the nation was not surprised when Illinois residents easily voted to codify its anti-black laws in 1862, and the state kept these laws in place even as it ratified the thirteenth amendment in 1865.

# Washington's Tab

*Some people believe that as commander in chief of the Continental Army, General George Washington "selflessly" refused a salary in favor of an expense account. Talk about shrewd moves.*

✳ ✳ ✳ ✳

WHEN WASHINGTON TOOK over leadership of the Continental Army in 1775, he refused to accept a salary. Perhaps he did so to demonstrate sacrifice and to forge solidarity with the "have-nots," a group that included soldiers under his command. Many applauded Washington for his noble gesture without knowing that the general had just been granted carte blanche to use and perhaps even abuse government funds.

From September 1775 to March 1776, Washington spent more than $6,000 on alcohol alone. And during the harsh Valley Forge winter of 1777–78, when his weary troops were perishing from hunger and exposure, Washington indulged his appetite for extravagant foods. An expense-account entry included "geese, mutton, fowls, turkey, veal, butter, turnips, potatoes, carrots, and cabbage."

By 1783, Washington had spent almost $450,000 on food, saddles, clothing, accommodations, and sundries. In today's dollars, that's nearly $5 million. When he became president, Washington again gallantly offered to waive his salary in favor of an expense account. The offer was politely refused, and he was paid a $25,000 stipend. It seems America could no longer afford the general's brand of sacrifice.

# Tale of a Fateful Trip

Robinson Crusoe, *that classic tale of shipwreck and survival on a deserted island, is widely thought to be purely fictional. In fact, the story is based on the real-life adventures of Scotsman Alexander Selkirk.*

✳ ✳ ✳ ✳

ANIEL DEFOE'S *ROBINSON Crusoe*, frequently cited as the first novel published in English (1719), remains one of the world's most enduring adventure stories, having spawned books, TV shows, and movies that include *The Swiss Family Robinson*, *Gilligan's Island*, and *Castaway*. The book is a fictional autobiography of an Englishman who is stranded on a remote tropical island for 28 years. The real-life Scottish sailor who inspired the classic tale was born in 1676 as Alexander Selcraig, later to become Alexander Selkirk.

In 1704, Selkirk was part of an English pirate expedition that set out to plunder Spanish vessels in the Pacific Ocean. Before returning to England, Selkirk quarreled with his captain, insisting that the ship be repaired before they attempted to sail around the treacherous Cape Horn. The captain refused to delay the trip, so Selkirk deserted the ship and wound up marooned on the most western of the Juan Fernandez Islands, approximately 400 miles off the coast of Chile.

It turns out that Selkirk's desertion was wise, because the ship soon sank and most of those onboard died. At the time, though, he had no way of knowing this, as he had been stranded on the island for nearly four and a half years before being picked up by a passing ship captained by English privateer Woodes Rogers.

Some claim that Defoe actually met Selkirk in person, heard his tales firsthand, and even gained access to his personal papers. Others believe that Defoe simply read Rogers's published account of Selkirk's adventures. Either way, the link between the two was cemented in 1966 when the Chilean government changed the name of Selkirk's island home to "Robinson Crusoe Island."

# Show Me the Money

*If a police officer can't prove I was speeding, I can't get a ticket.*

✳   ✳   ✳   ✳

THIS MYTH IS redolent of wishful thinking, right? We can smell the hopeless cause. Police officers use radar guns to clock the speed of passing cars, but there are many other ways in which they can ticket you for speeding.

If you're a driver, consider a time you were on the interstate going at or near the speed limit when a reckless vehicle blew past you. You likely thought or even said aloud, "They must be going a hundred miles an hour." Cops are no less aggrieved by this kind of driving, and at high speeds they can simply ticket for reckless driving. Cars that are climbing rapidly in speed may not give a clear radar gun reading, and it's nonsensical to believe that exempts them from speeding tickets—"80 miles per hour and climbing" is the accepted parlance for someone with a lead foot in progress.

Obstructing traffic by driving too slowly or disrupting it by driving too fast are both easily spottable by police, as is going at or above the speed limit during inclement weather that should cause you to slow down. Some states even allow a regular old speeding ticket for a cop's impression of your speed. And the radar gun works better than you think, so the times at which you can in fact be clocked at speed are more frequent than you'd guess.

# On the Autobahn

*Owners of high-performance cars dream of pushing their vehicles to maximum speeds, and the road of their dreams is the autobahn. But this expressway isn't entirely a pedal-pusher's playground.*

✳ ✳ ✳ ✳

## Go, Speed Racer!

**M**OST PEOPLE AGREE that if you like to speed, Germany is the place to be. The autobahn has long stretches where you can legally drive as fast as you want, and it is not uncommon for cars to top 150 miles per hour. But driver, beware: The autobahn does have speed limits. In fact, almost half of the system is under some sort of speed control. As you approach major interchanges, cities, or difficult terrain, you'll start to see speed-limit signs. And even though you will rarely encounter any autobahnpolizei (highway patrols), if you speed and get caught, it will be expensive. Radar-linked cameras positioned over interchanges photograph the license plates of all speeders, who then receive considerable traffic fines in the mail.

## Green Concerns

The era of high-speed driving in Germany may actually be coming to an end. Concerns about fuel consumption and global warming have increased pressure to bring Germany's laws in line with the rest of Europe—that is to say, a maximum speed limit of 130 kilometers (81 miles) per hour. Studies have shown that $CO_2$ emissions would be cut by 15 percent in the long term once more fuel-efficient cars are on the roads. But German car companies are trying to keep this from happening, arguing that high-speed driving is a part of the "German brand." The Germans themselves are passionate about driving—and driving fast—and it is doubtful they will give up their speedy ways without a fight.

# Milk for Cats

*It's an image straight out of a Norman Rockwell painting: a kitty lapping up a saucer of milk as happy children look on. But now we know better—cats and milk don't mix.*

✳   ✳   ✳   ✳

✳ Cats may like milk—chances are they even crave it. But just as people should avoid certain things that we enjoy, cats are better off without milk (especially cow's milk).

✳ The notion that Fluffy favors dairy products could have originated on farms, where cats roam freely and help themselves to a quick lap out of the pails when cows are being milked. The question is, are the cats coveting a special source of moo juice or just quenching their thirst when water isn't readily available? Hard to say. But because it's a common behavior, people assume that cats prefer, and perhaps even need, milk.

✳ Once kittens are weaned, they no longer need milk in their diets. What's more, most grown cats are lactose intolerant. In the same way humans do, cats can experience stomach pain and diarrhea when they drink milk. Because cats don't know to stop drinking something that actually tastes good, they can have continuous diarrhea, which leads to a loss of fluids and nutrients and can endanger their health.

✳ Can you ever give your cat milk? As always, your veterinarian can tell you what's best for your particular pet. To be on the safe side, consider one of the latest products at pet-supply stores: milk-free milk—for cats! At the same time, though, remember that milk and milk substitutes are really a form of food rather than a beverage. The best way to quench your cat's thirst is with a handy source of fresh, cool water.

# Brains and Brawn

*The Olympic Games haven't always featured athletics alone. Relive the era when pens carried as much weight as the pentathlon and a gold-medal performance was measured in both breaststrokes and brushstrokes.*

✳  ✳  ✳  ✳

Today's olympic games feature sports exclusively, but there was a time when artists competed for gold medals alongside runners, swimmers, and discus throwers. Cultural events ran side-by-side with athletics during both the ancient and modern Olympics. But because the most recent edition of these "brain" games took place just prior to the television era, knowledge of them is limited.

## Herodotus the Hurtler?

Records are scarce, but it appears that the first competitor in this artistic free-for-all was the writer Herodotus. Competing in 444 BC at Olympia, Greece, the athlete participated in both writing and sporting contests. His pairing of brains and brawn would represent the ideal throughout much of the ancient era.

After a 1,500-plus-year hiatus, the Olympics made a comeback in 1896. International Olympic Committee founder Pierre de Coubertin lobbied to reinstate the cultural element into the modern games. His wish became reality at the Stockholm Olympics in 1912.

## A Slow Start

The roster of events at that meet included architecture, painting, sculpture, music, and literature. Despite its historic nature, turnout was disappointing—only 35 artists actually entered the competition.

The 1928 Amsterdam Olympics represented the height of artistic participation. More than 1,000 works of art were entered, and organizers permitted artists to sell them at the competition's end. This move, though well intended, violated the IOC's stance on amateurism. Following the 1948 games, an IOC report concluded that most artistic contestants were receiving money for their works and recommended that such competition be abolished.

# Bible Translations You've Probably Never Heard of

*From historical to hip, they don't get read much today.*

✳  ✳  ✳  ✳

1. **The Great Bible (1539)** This was the first authorized edition of the Bible in English. Though William Tyndale and John Wycliffe had already been flouting church law by translating scripture for the common folk, it was King Henry VIII who approved this version for his new Anglican church. It was prepared by a Tyndale crony, Miles Coverdale, commissioned by Thomas Cromwell. This was sometimes called the "Chained Bible," because churches would make it available to parishioners (as ordered by Cromwell), but chain it down for safekeeping.

2. **The Geneva Bible (1560)** For a half-century before the King James Version, this was the standard; it was mass-produced and widely used. When Milton or Shakespeare quoted scripture, it was from this version. The language was vigorous, edgy for its day, a clear improvement over previous translations. Amazingly, this was what modern publishers would call a "study Bible," with an assortment of study guides, introductions, maps, and woodcut illustrations.

3. **The Primitive New Testament (1745)** Bible translators have always tried to work from the best Hebrew and Greek originals, but archaeologists keep finding new manuscripts, which continually shed new light on the text. Eighteenth-century scholar William Whiston sought to improve on

the King James Version by working from some very early ("primitive") Greek manuscripts. A mathematician and scientist, Whiston suggested that Noah's flood had been caused by a comet.

4. **A Liberal Translation of the New Testament (1768)** A prolific writer and creative thinker, Edward Harwood brought the flowery language of 18th-century English prose to his free (liberal) paraphrase of the New Testament—as we can see in his 77-word subtitle (something about "the True Signification and Force of the Original . . . transfused into our Language"). His rendering of "Thy kingdom come"? "May the glory of thy moral government be advanced, and the great laws of it be more generally obeyed."

5. **The Twentieth Century New Testament (1898–1901)** A flood of new Bible translations came along in the 20th century, and this was the first, published in three parts, with a final collection offered in 1904. A team of about 20 Britons composed this version, but they weren't professional scholars—they were teachers, home-makers, ministers, and even railroad workers who had studied ancient Greek and wanted to bring the Bible to life in the modern age.

6. **Fenton's Bible (1903)** In 1853, a young London businessman began work on a personal project, translating the Bible into modern English. Fifty years later he published the complete work: The Holy Bible in Modern English. Farrar Fenton was trying to capture the essence of the original, so he treated the psalms as the songs they were. Painstakingly, he fit other poetic books (including Job) into poetic meter. He also tried to put the books of the Bible into chronological order.

7. **The Bible in Basic English (1941, 1949)** For people just learning to read English, how can they understand the Bible, with its big concepts and massive vocabulary? That

was the challenge taken by Samuel Henry Hooke, a British scholar. Using only 850 basic English words (defined by literacy experts), adding 100 words necessary for poetry and 50 distinctly Bible words, Hooke composed this easy-to-read version.

8. **The Amplified Bible (1958, 1962)** Where the BBE (see above) used fewer words, the Amplified Bible used more. Hebrew and Greek words seldom have direct parallels with English words. Instead, there might be multiple possible translations, nuances, or cultural associations. The Amplified Bible provides alternate readings and explanatory phrases in parentheses and brackets, just to make sure the full sense of the original is honored. It's hard to read out loud, but great for study. This was the first Bible project of the Lockman Foundation, which later sponsored the New American Standard Bible.

9. **The Berkeley Bible (1945, 1959, 1969)** English wasn't the native language of Dutch-born Gerrit Verkuyl, but as an undergrad in the United States, he began to see the need for a modern translation to supersede the KJV. He didn't have much time to work on it for the 40 years after he made the decision, though. As a retiree, he tackled the project, naming it after his new hometown, Berkeley, California. His New Testament, published in 1945, met such critical acclaim that many wanted a complete Bible. Since Old Testament Hebrew was not Verkuyl's specialty, his publisher assembled an all-star team of scholars to finish The Berkeley Version of the Bible in Modern English in 1959. (This was revised in 1969 as The Modern Language Bible.)

10. **The New Testament in the Language of Today (1963)** As a pastor in Iowa during the 1930s and '40s, William F. Beck found that even his Sunday school teachers were having trouble understanding the stately KJV language. He began translating New Testament passages from the original

Greek into language that made sense to them. After getting a doctorate in New Testament studies, he completed his translation of the NT, stating in his introduction that he wanted to "let God speak the language of today," the kind of language people use over "coffee and doughnuts."

# Point Me to the Welsh Rabbits

*It's not rabbit, and it's likely not Welsh.*

✳ ✳ ✳ ✳

Cheese on toast (an open-faced grilled cheese sandwich, to translate it into American) is a mainstay of British comfort food, and Welsh rabbit is a variation where a cheese sauce is poured over toast. Think of it as an extremely British version of nachos. The dish dates back hundreds of years and even has its own later adulterated name: Welsh rarebit.

The American term "grilled cheese" is probably British in origin as well, involving a musical chairs of cooking implements. What we call the broiler, Britons call the grill. What we call the grill, Britons call the barbecue. So our grilled cheese originates under a British oven grill rather than in the frying pan we use today. But if we called our sandwich a "fried cheese," we'd step on the toes of many other international delights, like queso frito or fried halloumi.

# No Cats Were Harmed

*What's the story with so-called "catgut," the material used in tennis and musical-instrument strings? It is really made of guts, but the guts don't come from cats.*

✳ ✳ ✳ ✳

### Intestinal Fortitude

The intestines of cattle and other livestock are cleaned, stripped of fat, and prepared with chemicals before they can be made into catgut string. Historically, preparation of string from animal tissue dates back thousands of years in recorded history and likely much longer ago in reality. Intestines are uniquely suited because of their combination of strength and elasticity, even in comparison to other pretty robust naturally occurring strings like horse hair or silk. This makes sense intuitively because of the role our intestines play in our bodies, but let's not think too hard about that. One downside is that the prepared gut fibers are still very absorbent— enough so that even atmospheric humidity can warp them out of shape.

## In Stitches

Historical humans realized surprisingly early that gut string was a good way to sew up wounds, and in this case the absorbency is a bonus. These humans weren't aware of issues like infection, so their ingenuity with gut string was a matter of simple craftsmanship: you should sew with the strongest material you can find, whether for clothing or shelter or for a wound. Thousands of years later, scientists experimented and realized that gut string could dissolve in the human body. With the eventual rise of germ theory, doctors were able to create and use sterilized dissolving sutures that would be recognizable to the ancient Egyptians who first documented their sewing of wounds. In fact, most dissolvable stitches are still made with prepared animal fibers or with synthetics that were designed to mimic animal fibers in the body.

## High Strung

For musical instruments, gut strings also date back thousands of years. In both Latin and Greek, the terms for strings and bowstrings (and our modern words chord and cord) were from the original Greek term meaning guts. Musicians found that gut strings made the best sound, but the strings warped, frayed, and broke quite quickly because of the effects of moisture in the air and from musicians' touch. Modern musicians can use strings with a core of gut that's surrounded by a snug winding of very fine metal. In a fine example of art imitating nature, this structure mimics the way our flexible gut fibers are arranged in our intestines, with both lengthwise fibers and circular bands.

### The Gut Racket

Gut strings are still considered the gold standard by many high-level tennis players and manufacturers. In tennis, the absorbency of gut strings is counteracted with topical wax that seals the strings. Choosing and making gut strings for tennis rackets is still an artisan craft, and some cattle—most if not all tennis gut strings come from cattle—apparently produce finer quality gut strings than others, creating a Wagyu-beef-like hierarchy among cattle ranchers.

### Digesting the Information

Humans have shown remarkable ingenuity since we first diverged from our most recent ancestor, but even by human standards, it's unusual to have a found material that works as both a durable tool and a nourishing food—depending on how you prepare it. Whether you're preparing for your Wimbledon debut or a period-correct Baroque chamber orchestra, consider the millennia-old tradition of the gut string.

# The Cat Toss

*Cats are curious creatures: Many people believe that a dropped kitty will right itself and land safely on it feet, only to step away aloof and unaffected.*

✳ ✳ ✳ ✳

A BELGIAN LEGEND HAS it that in AD 962, Baldwin III, Count of Ypres, threw several cats from a tower. It must have been a slow news year, because the residents of Ypres named the last day of their annual town fair "Cat Wednesday" and commemorated it by having the village jester throw live cats from a belfry tower—a height of almost 230 feet. But there's no need to call PETA: The last time live cats were used for this ceremony was in 1817, and since then stuffed animals have been thrown in their place.

As cruel as this custom was, it is unclear whether the cat toss was meant to kill cats or to demonstrate their resilience. After that last live toss in 1817, the village record keeper wrote the following: "In spite of the height of the fall, the animal ran off quickly so that it might never be caught again in a similar ceremony." How could the cat have survived such a tumble?

## Twist and Meow

Cats have an uncanny knack for righting themselves in midair. Even if a cat starts falling head first, it almost always hits the ground on its paws. The people of Ypres weren't the only ones amazed and amused by this feline feat. In 1894, French physiologist Etienne-Jules Marey decided to get to the bottom of the mechanics of cat-righting by taking a series of rapid photographs of a cat in midfall. Marey held a cat upside down by its paws and then dropped it several feet onto a cushion.

The resulting 60 sequential photos demonstrated that as the cat fell, it initiated a complex maneuver, rotating the front of its body clockwise and then the rear part counterclockwise. This motion conserved energy and prevented the cat from spinning in the air. It then pulled in its legs, reversed the twist again, and extended its legs slightly to land with minimal impact.

## High-Rise Syndrome

The story gets even more interesting. In 1987, two New York City veterinarians examined 132 cases involving cats that had fallen out of the windows of high-rise buildings (the average fall was five and a half stories). Ninety percent of the cats survived, though some sustained serious injuries. When the vets analyzed the data, they found that, predictably, the cats suffered progressively greater injuries as the height from which they fell increased. But this pattern continued only up to seven stories; above that, the farther the cat fell, the greater chance it had of surviving relatively unharmed.

The researchers named this peculiar phenomenon High-Rise Syndrome and explained it this way: A cat that fell about five stories reached its terminal velocity—that is, maximum downward speed—of 60 miles per hour. If it fell any distance beyond that, it had the time not only to right itself in midair but also to relax and spread itself out to slow down its fall, much like a flying squirrel or a parachute.

# Stealing the President

*While he was alive, President Abraham Lincoln was loved and admired by many. Perhaps his popularity was the reason why in 1876, a group of men decided that people would be willing to pay a lot of money to see the 16th president of the United States— even if he was dead.*

✳    ✳    ✳    ✳

## Breaking Out Boyd

THE PLOT WAS hatched in 1876, 11 years after President Lincoln's assassination by John Wilkes Booth. Illinois engraver Benjamin Boyd had been arrested on charges of creating engraving plates to make counterfeit bills. Boyd's boss, James "Big Jim" Kinealy, a man known around Chicago as the King of the Counterfeiters, was determined to get Boyd out of prison in order to continue his counterfeiting operation.

Kinealy's plan was to kidnap Lincoln's corpse from his mausoleum at the Oak Ridge Cemetery in Springfield, Illinois, and hold it for ransom—$200,000 in cash and a full pardon for Boyd. Not wanting to do the dirty work himself, Kinealy turned to two men: John "Jack" Hughes and Terrence Mullen, a bartender at The Hub, a Madison Street bar frequented by Kinealy and his associates.

Kinealy told Hughes and Mullen that they were to steal Lincoln's body on Election Night, November 7, load it onto a cart, and take it roughly 200 miles north to the shores of Lake

Michigan. They were to bury the body in the sand, to stow it until the ransom was paid. The plan seemed foolproof until Hughes and Mullen decided they needed a third person to help steal the body—a fellow named Lewis Swegles. It was a decision Hughes and Mullen would come to regret.

## The Plan Backfires

The man directly responsible for bringing Boyd in was Patrick D. Tyrrell, a member of the Secret Service in Chicago. Long before their current role of protecting the president of the United States, one of the main jobs for members of the Secret Service was to track down and arrest counterfeiters. One of Tyrrell's informants was a small-time crook by the name of Lewis Swegles. Yes, the same guy who agreed to help Hughes and Mullen steal the president's body. Thanks to the stool pigeon, everything the duo was planning was being reported back to the Secret Service.

On the evening of November 7, 1876, Hughes, Mullen, and Swegles entered the Lincoln Mausoleum, unaware of the Secret Service lying in wait. The hoods broke open Lincoln's sarcophagus and removed the casket, and Swegles was sent to get the wagon. Swegles gave the signal to make the arrest, but once the Secret Service men reached the mausoleum, they found it to be empty. In all the confusion, Hughes and Mullen had slipped away, leaving Lincoln's body behind.

Unsure what to do next, Tyrrell ordered Swegles back to Chicago to see if he could pick up the kidnappers' trail. Swegles eventually found them in a local Chicago tavern, and on November 16 or 17 (sources vary), Hughes and Mullen were arrested without incident.

## Lincoln Is Laid to Rest (Again)

With no laws on the books at the time pertaining to the stealing of a body, Hughes and Mullen were only charged with attempted larceny of Lincoln's coffin and a count each of conspiracy. After a brief trial, both men were found guilty. Their sentence for attempting to steal the body of President Abraham Lincoln: One year in the Illinois state penitentiary in Joliet.

As for Lincoln's coffin, it remains at its home in Oak Ridge Cemetery; it has been moved an estimated 17 times and opened 6 times. On September 26, 1901, the Lincoln family took steps to ensure Abe's body could never be stolen again: It was buried 10 feet under the floor of the mausoleum, inside a metal cage, and under thousands of pounds of concrete.

# Tracking Tektite Truths

*The origin of strangely shaped bits of glass called tektites has been debated for decades—do they come from the moon? From somewhere else in outer space? It seems the answer is more down-to-earth.*

✳   ✳   ✳   ✳

THE FIRST TEKTITES were found in 1787 in the Moldau River in the Czech Republic, giving them their original name, "Moldavites." They come in many shapes (button, teardrop, dumbbell, and blobs), have little or no water content, and range from dark green to black to colorless.

Originally, many geologists believed tektites were extraterrestrial in origin, specifically from the moon. They theorized that impacts from comets and asteroids—or even volcanic eruptions—on the moon ejected huge amounts of material. As the moon circled in its orbit around our planet, the material eventually worked its way to Earth, through the atmosphere, and onto the surface.

One of the first scientists to debate the tektite-lunar origin idea was Texas geologist Virgil Barnes, who contended that tektites were actually created from Earth-bound soil and rock. Many scientists now agree with Barnes, theorizing that when a comet or asteroid collided with the earth, it sent massive amounts of material high into the atmosphere at hypervelocities. The energy from such a strike easily melted the terrestrial rock and burned off much of the material's water. And because of the earth's gravitational pull, what goes up must come down—causing the melted material to rain down on the planet in specific locations. Most of the resulting tektites have been exposed to the elements for millions of years, causing many to be etched and/or eroded over time.

Unlike most extraterrestrial rocks—such as meteorites and micrometeorites, which are found everywhere on Earth—tektites are generally found in four major regions of the world called *strewn* (or *splash*) fields. The almost 15-million-year-old Moldavites are mainly found in the Czech Republic, but the strewn field extends into Austria; these tektites are derived from the Nordlinger Ries impact crater in southern Germany. The *Australites, Indochinites,* and *Chinites* of the huge Australasian strewn field extend around Australia, Indochina, and the Philippines; so far, no one has agreed on its source crater. The *Georgiaites* (Georgia) and *Bediasites* (Texas) are North American tektites formed by the asteroid impact that created the Chesapeake Crater around 35 million years ago. And finally, the 1.3-million-year-old *Ivorites* of the Ivory Coast strewn field originate from the Bosumtwi crater in neighboring Ghana. Other tektites have been discovered in various places around the world but in very limited quantities compared to the major strewn fields.

# Baby Ruth's Truth?

*Many people believe that the Baby Ruth candy bar was named for baseball great Babe Ruth. Others contend that the honor belongs to President Grover Cleveland's daughter Ruth.*

✳   ✳   ✳   ✳

GERMAN IMMIGRANT OTTO Schnering founded the Curtiss Candy Company in Chicago in 1916. With World War I raging in Europe, Schnering decided to avoid using his

Germanic surname and chose his mother's maiden name for the business. His first product was a snack called Kandy Kake, a pastry center covered with peanuts and chocolate. But the candy bar was only a marginal success, and to boost sales, it was renamed Baby Ruth in 1921. Five years later the company was selling millions of dollars worth of the bars every day. Whenever pressed for details on the confection's name, Curtiss explained the appellation honored Ruth Cleveland, the late and beloved daughter of President Grover Cleveland. But the company may have been trying to sneak a fastball past everybody.

Cleveland's daughter had died of diphtheria in 1904—a dozen years before the candy company was even started. One questions the logic in naming a candy bar after someone who had passed away so many years earlier. The gesture may have been appropriate for a president, but a president's relatively unknown daughter?

The more plausible origin of the name might be tied to the biggest sports star in the world at the time—George Herman "Babe" Ruth. Originally a star pitcher for the Boston Red Sox, Ruth became a fearsome hitter for the New York Yankees, slamming 59 home runs in the same year the candy bar was renamed Baby Ruth. Curtiss may have found a way to cash in on the slugger's fame—and name—without paying a dime in royalties. In fact, when Ruth gave the okay to use his name on a competitor's candy—the clunky Babe Ruth Home Run Bar— Curtiss successfully blocked it, claiming infringement on his own "baby."

# Civil War Myths

*There's a certain romance to the tales that have circulated in the almost 150 years since the Civil War. Many are true, but many others are laced with falsehoods.*

✳   ✳   ✳   ✳

A T THE RISK of bursting some American history bubbles, here is a sampling of the myths swirling around the Civil War.

## Myth: The Civil War was America's first disagreement over slavery.

The founders of the United States had been concerned with the ownership of slaves, particularly as it played out in the issue of states' rights, since the Articles of Confederation were ratified in 1781. A confederation, by definition, is a loose alignment of states, each with the power to self-regulate. The Southern states favored slavery, and every time the issue of states' rights emerged on the national front, the South would threaten to secede.

Other landmark Congressional acts and court judgments that influenced slavery in America before the Civil War include the Three-Fifths Compromise in the Constitution, the Missouri Compromise of 1820, the Compromise of 1850, the Kansas-Nebraska Act, and the Dred Scott Decision.

## Myth: The Emancipation Proclamation freed all the slaves in America.

Lincoln wrote the edict in September 1862, and it went into effect on January 1, 1863. The language of the document was clear: Any slave that was still held in the states that had seceded from the Union was "forever free" as of January 1, 1863.

Significantly, this edict did not include border states in which slaves were still held, such as Kentucky or Missouri, because Lincoln didn't want to stoke rebellion there. As one might expect, the Southern states paid hardly any attention to the announcement by the Union president. They'd already turned their backs on him and his nation, and as far as they were concerned, the Union president held no power over them.

## Myth: The Union soldiers firmly believed in the cause of freeing the slaves.

For the most part, soldiers had little, if any, opinion on slavery. At first, many men enlisted in the Union army as a romantic adventure. Early opinion estimated that the war would end within a few months, and many decided they could afford that much time away from their work, school, or home life.

## Myth: The South's secession was the first time in American history a state tried to leave the Union.

During the War of 1812, New England almost seceded in order to protect its trade with Great Britain. In the 1850s, President James Buchanan, who held office immediately before Abraham Lincoln, stated the federal government would not resort to force in order to prevent secession. In 1869, four years after the end of the war, the Supreme Court declared the act of state secession to be unconstitutional.

## Myth: The Confederate attack on Fort Sumter was the first act of Southern aggression against Northern targets.

The attack on Fort Sumter was preceded by attacks on other forts and military installations in Confederate territory. On January 9, 1861, Mississippi followed South Carolina to become the second state to secede from the Union. Within a week, Mississippi's governor ordered an armed battery placed on the bluff above the wharf at Vicksburg. His declared intention was to force Union vessels to stop to be searched—after all, it was rumored that a cannon had been sent to a Baton Rouge arsenal. Intentions aside, the fact is the battery actually fired on a number of vessels in order to make them come about, including the *Gladiator*, the *Imperial*, and the *A. O. Tyler*.

Prior to this incident, the Confederate Congress had approved the creation of a volunteer army of 100,000 soldiers—far larger than any military force that was intended strictly for keeping the peace would presumably need to be.

## Myth: Abraham Lincoln wrote his Gettysburg Address on the back of an envelope while riding the train on his way to make the speech.

Lincoln would never have waited until the last minute to write such an important oration, which was part of the consecration of the Gettysburg Cemetery in November 1863. But even if he had, the train ride itself would have prevented legible writing. The 1860s-period train cars bounced, swayed, and made horseback riding seem smooth by comparison. Several drafts of the Gettysburg Address (including what is referred to as the "reading draft") have been archived at the Library of Congress and other academic institutions. They are written—very legibly—on lined paper and Executive Mansion stationery.

## Myth: The "Taps" bugle call was first used by Union Captain Robert Ellicombe after Ellicombe discovered his son dead on the battlefield wearing a Confederate uniform. The son had been a music student, and the music for "Taps" was found in the boy's pocket. Captain Ellicombe had it played as tribute during his son's funeral.

There is no proof that Captain Robert Ellicombe even existed at all, and certainly there is no record of any captain by that name in the Union army during the Civil War. "Taps" actually came from Union General Daniel Butterfield, although it is not certain whether Butterfield composed the tune or adapted it from an earlier piece of music. Not happy with the existing bugle call for lights out, which the general thought was too formal, he presented his bugler, Oliver Norton, with the replacement during the summer of 1862. Although it was soon used by both Union and Confederate armies as a funeral call, it did not become an official bugle call until after the war.

# Some Registered Tax-Exempt Religions You've Never Heard of

*Perhaps you've read about Pastafarians who worship the Flying Spaghetti Monster. This so-called faith may inspire a few chuckles, but it's not a bona fide religion in the eyes of the U.S. government. But there are some surprising faith-based organizations that do qualify for federal tax-exempt status.*

✳ ✳ ✳ ✳

TAKE THE ORDO **Templi Orientis** (OTO), aka Order of Oriental Templars, for instance. Founded in 1904 by British mystic Aleister Crowley, the group currently has 44 lodges in 26 states, including the Leaping Laughter Lodge of Minneapolis and the Subtlety of Force Encampment of Albuquerque. Based on a system of beliefs called Thelema, the OTO claims to promote the acquisition of "light, wisdom, understanding, knowledge, and power through beauty, courage, and wit." A fairly tall order for any faith.

Speaking of tall orders, **Eckankar** teaches that people can connect with other realities through out-of-body experiences. This faith has its roots in the Age of Aquarius and was founded in 1965 by American spiritualist Paul Twitchel. Followers call themselves Eckists, and their leaders are referred to as Living Eck Masters.

The **Raelians,** by contrast, focus their attention on the future. Founded by French race-car enthusiast Claude Vorilhon in 1974, the Raelian Movement believes humans were created by extraterrestrials called Elohim who will one day return to Earth as foretold in Vorilhon's book *Let's Welcome Our Fathers from Outer Space.*

And finally, the **Monks of New Skete,** an offshoot of Eastern Orthodox Christianity, engage in a highly unorthodox practice. They train dogs, both as a source of income and as a spiritual pursuit. The monks have authored several popular books, including *How to Be Your Dog's Best Friend* and *I & Dog*. They even manufacture their own dog biscuits—a sure way to make a believer out of your pooch, if not out of you.

## Oh the Calamity!

*You probably know her from the HBO series* Deadwood. *But what's the real story behind Wild Bill Hickok's gal pal? And how did she get that nickname?*

✳   ✳   ✳   ✳

SHE CUSSED. SHE drank. She was an expert rider and was handy with a gun. She scouted for the army. She mined for gold. She wore men's pants. She did just about everything that 19th-century American women were not supposed to do. But Calamity Jane got away with all of it—and became a Wild West legend.

As with most of the legendary figures of the Wild West, it's hard to separate fact from fiction when it comes to Calamity Jane. We don't even know her real birthdate. What we do know is that she was born Martha Jane Canary (or Cannary) in Missouri, probably in 1852. Orphaned not long after her family left Missouri for the Montana Territory, teenage Martha turned to prostitution—a trade she'd ply occasionally throughout her life. Over the next decade or so, Martha drifted through the mining camps and army posts of the West, where she earned the respect of her masculine peers by showing that she could do anything a man could do—and in some cases, do it better. A heavy drinker, Calamity was thrown into various frontier jails for disturbing the peace.

She first started wearing men's clothes while scouting and carrying messages for the army during the Indian campaigns of the early 1870s. She won the name "Calamity Jane" when she rode to the rescue of an officer caught in an ambush—he declared that she'd saved him from "a calamity." (Though some say her moniker came from her threat that if any man messed with her, "it would be a calamity" for him.)

## Welcome to Deadwood

Around 1876, Calamity landed in Deadwood, South Dakota, where she developed a serious crush on the handsome gunslinger Wild Bill Hickok. Later in life, she claimed they'd been married and had a child together, but they were probably just "friends." She stayed in Deadwood after Hickok caught a bullet during a poker game. A couple of years later, tough Calamity showed her tender side by nursing victims of a smallpox epidemic that swept the town.

By then, word of this crossdressing hell-raiser had reached the publishers back East who were busy churning out "dime novels" to satisfy the public's taste for tales of Western derring-do. Calamity Jane quickly became a recurring character in these outlandish fictions. She was usually described as a beautiful woman; in illustrations, her baggy trousers mysteriously turned into skin-tight leggings. Photographs of Calamity don't exactly bear out this image.

It was all downhill from there for Calamity. She resumed drifting around the West, got married briefly, and in the 1890s she toured across the country with Buffalo Bill's famous Wild West Show. She got fired for drinking and ultimately died in poverty in Terry, South Dakota, in 1903. But she gets to spend eternity with Wild Bill; as per her deathbed request, she's buried next to him in Deadwood's cemetery.

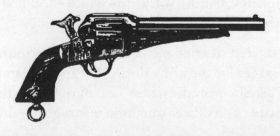

# Chapter 6

# History's Little Secrets

## The Day King Tut's Tomb Was Opened

*There was a time when archaeology was commissioned privately by wealthy individuals. Some of these benefactors desired to advance historical knowledge, while others simply hoped to enhance their personal collections of antiquities. The much-heralded opening of the tomb of the Pharaoh Tutankhamun, better known today as "King Tut," represented one of the last hurrahs for these old days of archaeology.*

✳ ✳ ✳ ✳

### Who Was King Tut, Anyway?

KING TUT WAS an ancient Egyptian ruler, or pharaoh. His full name, Tutankhamun, meant to say that he was the living image of the sun god, Amun. Tut ruled Egypt from 1333–1324 BC, during what is referred to as the New Kingdom period. Sometimes called "The Boy King," he became pharaoh when he was 9 years old and died at age 19. Researchers believe Tut died from an infection caused by a broken leg.

### How Was His Tomb Located?

Finding the tomb required scholarship, persistence, patience, and lots of digging. A wealthy Englishman, Lord Carnarvon, sponsored one of the day's brightest archaeologists, Howard Carter. With Carnarvon's backing, Carter poked around in Egypt between 1917 and 1922 with little luck. Then, in November 1922, just as Lord Carnarvon was ready to give up, Carter uncovered steps leading down to a tomb marked with Tut's royal seals. Carter dashed off a communiqué to Carnarvon, telling him to get to Egypt, and fast.

## What Happened Next?

Carnarvon wasted no time, and once the sponsor reached the scene, Carter was ready to cut his way into the tomb. Workers soon exposed a sealed doorway bearing Tut's name. Those present would witness the unveiling of history as Carter peered into the tomb. However, thanks to the meticulous nature of archaeology, work on Tut's tomb could only happen at a slow pace. The entire process stretched across ten years.

## What Was in There?

The contents of the tomb were incredible. It was clear that ancient plunderers had twice raided the tomb for some smaller items. Although they did leave the place a mess, many amazing treasures remained. Carter and company catalogued piles of priceless artifacts, including gold statues and everything from sandals to chariots. Tut's mummified body had been placed in an ornate coffin, and canopic jars held his internal organs. In addition, two mummified premature babies, thought to be Tut's children, were found. Tut was also buried with everything he would need to be stylish in the afterlife, including ornate bows and gloves fit for a pharaoh. Scholars would spend years preserving and studying the artifacts in the tomb.

King Tut's tomb was the archaeological find of that decade—perhaps even the find of the 20th century.

# Millions of Mummies

*It sounds like the premise of a horror movie—millions of excess mummies just piling up. But for the Egyptians, this was simply an excuse to get a little creative.*

✳   ✳   ✳   ✳

T HE ANCIENT EGYPTIANS took death seriously. Their culture believed that the afterlife was a dark and tumultuous place where departed souls (ka) needed protection throughout eternity. By preserving their bodies as mummies, Egyptians provided their souls with a resting place—without which they would wander the afterlife forever.

Starting roughly around 3000 BC, Egyptian morticians began making a healthy business on the mummy trade. On receiving a corpse, they would first remove the brain and internal organs and store them in canopic jars. Next, they would stuff the body with straw to maintain its shape, cover it in salt and oils to preserve it from rotting, and then wrap it in linens—a process that could take up to 70 days. Finally, the finished mummies would be sealed into a decorated sarcophagus, now ready to face eternity.

Mummies have always been a source of great mystery and fascination. The tales of mummy curses were wildly popular in their time, and people still flock to horror movies involving vengeful mummies. Museum displays, especially King Tut or Ramses II, remain a sure-fire draw, allowing patrons the chance for a remarkably preserved glimpse of ancient Egypt.

At first, mummification was so costly it remained the exclusive domain of the wealthy, usually royalty. However, when the middle class began adopting the procedure, the mummy population exploded.

Soon people were mummifying everything—even crocodiles. The practice of mummifying the family cat was also common; the owners saw it as an offering to the cat goddess Bast.

Even those who could not afford to properly mummify their loved ones unknowingly contributed to the growing number of mummies. These folks buried their deceased in the Egyptian desert, where the hot, arid conditions dried out the bodies, creating natural mummies. When you consider that this burial art was in use for more than 3,000 years, it's not surprising that over time the bodies began piling up—literally.

So, with millions of mummies lying around, local entrepreneurs began looking for ways to cash in on these buried treasures. To them, mummies were a natural resource, not unlike oil, which could be extracted from the ground and sold at a heavy profit to eager buyers around the world.

## Mummy Medicine

In medieval times, Egyptians began touting mummies for their secret medicinal qualities. European doctors began importing mummies, boiling off their oils and prescribing it to patients. The oil was used to treat a variety of disorders, including sore throats, coughs, epilepsy, poisoning, and skin disorders. Contemporary apothecaries also got into the act, marketing pulverized mummies to noblemen as a cure for nausea.

The medical establishment wasn't completely sold on the beneficial aspects of mummy medicine, however. Several doctors voiced their opinions against the practice, one writing that: "It ought to be rejected as loathsome and offensive," and another claiming: "This wicked kind of drugge doth nothing to help the diseased." A cholera epidemic, which broke out in Europe, was blamed on mummy bandages, and the use of mummy medicine was soon abandoned.

## Mummy Merchants

Grave robbers, a common feature of 19th-century Egypt, made a huge profit from mummies. Arab traders would raid ancient tombs, sometimes making off with hundreds of bodies. These would be sold to visiting English merchants who, on returning to England, could resell them to the wealthy. Victorian socialites would buy mummies and hold fashionable parties, inviting friends over to view the unwrapping of their Egyptian prize.

## Mummies in Museums

By the mid-19th century, museums were becoming common in Europe, and mummies were prized exhibits. Curators, hoping to make a name for their museums, would travel to Egypt and purchase a mummy to display back home. This provided a steady stream of revenue for the unscrupulous mummy merchants. In the 1850s, the Egyptian government finally stopped the looting of their priceless heritage. Laws were passed allowing only certified archaeologists access to mummy tombs, effectively putting the grave robbers out of business.

## Mummy Myths

There are so many stories regarding the uses of mummies that it's often hard to separate fact from fiction. Some historians suggest the linens that comprised mummy wrappings were used by 19th-century American and Canadian industrialists to manufacture paper. At the time, there was a huge demand for paper, and suppliers often ran short of cotton rags—a key ingredient in the paper-making process. Although there's no concrete proof, some historians claim that when manufacturers ran out of rags, they imported mummies to use in their place.

Another curious claim comes courtesy of Mark Twain. In his popular 1869 travelogue *The Innocents Abroad*, Twain wrote: "The fuel [Egyptian train operators] use for the locomotive is composed of mummies three thousand years old, purchased by the ton or by the graveyard for that purpose." This item, almost assuredly meant as satire, was taken as fact by readers and survives to this day. However, there is no historical record of Egyptian trains running on burnt mummies. Besides, the mischievous Twain was never one to let a few facts get in the way of a good story. Perhaps those who believe the humorist's outlandish claim might offset it with another of his famous quotes: "A lie can travel halfway around the world while the truth is putting on its shoes."

# The Mystery of the 700-Year-Old Piper

*It's an intriguing story about a mysterious piper and more than 100 missing children. Made famous by the eponymous Brothers Grimm, this popular fairy tale has captivated generations of boys and girls. But is it actually more fact than fiction?*

✳   ✳   ✳   ✳

THE LEGEND OF The Pied Piper of Hameln documents the story of a mysterious musician who rid a town of rats by enchanting the rodents with music from his flute. The musician led the mesmerized rats to a nearby river, where they drowned. When the townsfolk refused to settle their debt, the rat catcher returned several weeks later, charmed a group of 130 children with the same flute, and led them out of town. They disappeared—never to be seen again.

It's a story that dates back to approximately AD 1300 and has its roots in a small German town called Hameln. Several accounts written between the 14th and 17th centuries tell of a stained-glass window in the town's main church. The window pictured the Pied Piper with hands clasped, standing over a group of youngsters. Encircling the window was the following verse (this is a rough translation): "In the year 1284, on John's and Paul's day was the 26th of June. By a piper, dressed in all kinds of colors, 130 children born in Hameln were seduced and lost at the calvarie near the koppen."

The verse is quite specific: precise month and year, exact number of children involved in the incident, and detailed place names. Because of this, some scholars believe this window, which was removed in 1660 and either accidentally destroyed or lost, was created in memory of an actual event. Yet, the verse makes no mention of the circumstances regarding the departure of the children or their specific fate. What exactly happened in Hameln, Germany, in 1284? The truth is, no one actually knows—at least not for certain.

## Theories Abound

Gernot Hüsam, the current chairman of the Coppenbrügge Castle Museum, believes the word "koppen" in the inscription may reference a rocky outcrop on a hill in nearby Coppenbrügge, a small town previously known as Koppanberg. Hüsam also believes the use of the word "calvarie" is in reference to either the medieval connotation of the gates of hell—or since the Crusades—a place of execution.

One theory put forward is that Coppenbrügge resident Nikolaus von Spiegelberg recruited Hameln youth to emigrate to areas in Pomerania near the Baltic Sea. This theory suggests the youngsters were either murdered, because they took part in summertime pagan rituals, or drowned in a tragic accident while in transit to the new colonies.

But this is not the only theory. In fact, theories concerning the fate of the children abound. Here are some ideas about what really happened:

* They suffered from the Black Plague or a similar disease and were led from the town to spare the rest of the population.

* They were part of a crusade to the Holy Land.

* They were lost in the 1260 Battle of Sedemünder.

* They died in a bridge collapse over the Weser River or a landslide on Ith Mountain.

* They emigrated to settle in other parts of Europe, including Maehren, Oelmutz, Transylvania, or Uckermark.

* They were actually young adults who were led away and murdered for performing pagan rituals on a local mountain.

Historians believe that emigration, bridge collapse/natural disaster, disease, or murder are the most plausible explanations.

## Tracing the Piper's Path

Regardless of what actually happened in Hameln hundreds of years ago, the legend of the Pied Piper has endured. First accounts of the Piper had roots to the actual incident, but as time passed, the story took on a life of its own.

Early accounts of the legend date back to 1384, at which time a Hameln church leader was said to be in possession of a chorus book with a Latin verse related to the legend written on the front cover by his grandmother. The book was misplaced in the late 17th century and has never been found.

The oldest surviving account—according to amateur Pied Piper historian Jonas Kuhn—appears as an addition to a 14th-century manuscript from Luneburg. Written in Latin, the note is almost identical to the verse on the stained-glass window and translates roughly to:

"In the year of 1284, on the day of Saints John and Paul on the 26th of June 130 children born in Hamelin were seduced By a piper, dressed in all kinds of colors, and lost at the place of execution near the koppen."

Physician and philosopher Jobus Fincelius believed the Pied Piper was the devil. In his 1556 book, *Concerning the Wonders of His Times*, Fincelius wrote: "It came about in Hameln in Saxony on the River Weser . . . the Devil visibly in human form walked the lanes of Hameln and by playing a pipe lured after him many children t o a mountain. Once there, he with the children . . . could no longer be found."

In 1557, Count Froben Christoph von Zimmern wrote a chronicle detailing his family's lineage. Sprinkled throughout the book were folklore tales including one that referenced the Pied Piper. For some unknown reason, the count introduced rats into his version of the story: "He passed through the streets of the town with his small pipe . . . immediately all the rats . . . collected outside the houses and followed his footsteps." This first insertion of rodents into the legend led other writers to follow suit.

In 1802, Johan Wolfgang Goethe wrote "Der Rattenfanger," a poem based loosely on the legend. The monologue was told in the first person through the eyes of the rat catcher. Goethe's poem made no direct reference to the town of Hameln, and in Goethe's version the Piper played a stringed instrument instead of a pipe. The Piper also made an appearance in Goethe's literary work Faust.

Jacob and Wilhelm Grimm began collecting European folktales in the early 1800s. Best known for a series of books that documented 211 fairy tales, the brothers also published two volumes between 1816 and 1818 detailing almost 600 German folklore legends. One of the volumes contained the story of Der Rattenfanger von Hameln.

The Grimm brothers' research for The Pied Piper drew on 11 different sources, from which they deduced two children were left behind (a blind child and a mute child); the piper led the children through a cave to Transylvania; and a street in Hameln was named after the event.

## No End in Sight

While the details of the historical event surrounding the legend of The Pied Piper have been lost to time, the mystique of the story endures. Different versions of the legend have even appeared in literature outside of Germany: A rat catcher from Vienna helped rid the nearby town of Korneuburg of rats. When he wasn't paid, he stole off with the town's children and sold them as slaves in Constantinople. A vagabond rid the English town of Newton on the Isle of Wight of their rats, and when he wasn't paid, led the town's children into an ancient oak forest where they were never seen again. A Chinese version had a Hangchow district official use magic to convince the rats to leave his city.

The legend's plot has been adapted over time to fit whichever media is currently popular and has been used as a story line in children's books, ballet, theatre, and even a radio drama. The intriguing mystery of the piper will continue to interest us as long as there is mystery surrounding the original event.

# The Catacombs of Paris

*Six million souls are buried beneath the "City of Lights." According to reports, some aren't happy with the arrangement.*

✳  ✳  ✳  ✳

## For the Poor No More

INDIGENCE AND INDIGNITY seem to go hand in hand. In Paris during the 12th century, financially-strapped souls were buried in mass burial grounds, an unenviable fate worlds removed from the dignified private plots and ceremonies available to the rich.

During the late eighteenth century, however, the poor would have the last ghoulish laugh, when Parisian cemeteries were filled to overflowing and all deceased people, regardless of their station in life, were committed to a common grave. *Touché!*

An abandoned network of underground stone quarries beneath Paris was chosen for this macabre purpose. The Catacombs of Paris offered a way to sidestep the problem of decaying flesh leaching into the ground, a bona fide health concern for a society that drew its drinking water from underground wells. Over time, more than six million people were committed to the 'combs. Here, they would sleep away eternity. Or would they?

## Rest in Pieces

Piled up in a 180-mile stretch of tunnels, the dead bodies of the Catacombs are anything but ordinary. The remaining skulls and bones have been stacked in orderly if bizarre fashion to create grisly monuments and walls, and the dank, dark setting is conducive to frights both real and imagined.

This spooky underground netherworld currently operates as the Catacombs Museum. For a fee, visitors can walk through a section of the tunnels and commune with the dead.

Contrary to popular belief, visits to this no-man's-land of death and decay is anything but new. Tours of the Catacombs have taken place since 1867. Members of the French Resistance used the network of tunnels to hide out from the Germans during World War II, and the Germans used a portion of the Catacombs as a bunker during the same world-shaping conflict.

## Rude Awakenings

If visitors to the Catacombs should forget where they are, a sign reading "Arrête! C'est ici l'empire de la mort" (Stop! This is the Empire of Death) gives fair warning about what they will encounter. When six million corpses are crammed together, there are bound to be a few restless spirits. The Catacombs are deemed one of the most haunted places on earth by travel journals, and reports of ghostly sightings and other paranormal encounters seem as numerous as the bodies themselves.

## *Un*friendly Ghosts

Based on the accounts of startled witnesses, those who expect to find friendly ghosts in the Catacombs will be terrified by the ones that they do encounter. Some visitors claim that they were "touched by unseen hands." Others tell of an uncanny feeling of being watched as they walked through the underground labyrinth. Several people tell of an ominous group of shadows that followed them step for step as they moved through the tunnels. Photos of apparitions snapped by visitors are plentiful and varied. Creepy cold spots and inexplicable photographic orbs have also been detected. Some even claim to have been choked with great might by a frightening invisible force.

## Frightful Fun

Tours have occasionally been cut short when visitors grew hysterical due to such ghostly pranks, but the popularity of the Catacombs as a haven for visitors has remained strong throughout the years. In fact, more than one million visitors make the subterranean journey each year.

# Sandstone Gateway to Heaven

*For hundreds of years, rumors of the lost city of Angkor spread among Cambodian peasants. On a stifling day in 1860, Henri Mahout and his porters discovered that the ancient city was more than mere legend.*

✳    ✳    ✳    ✳

FRENCH BOTANIST AND explorer Henri Mahout wiped his spectacles as he pushed into the Cambodian jungle clearing. Gasping for breath in the rain forest's mists, he gazed down weed-ridden avenues at massive towers and stone temples wreathed with carvings of gods, kings, and battles. The ruins before him were none other than the temples of Angkor Wat.

Although often credited with the discovery of Angkor Wat, Mahout was not the first Westerner to encounter the site. He did, however, bring the "lost" city to the attention of the European public when his travel journals were published in 1868. He wrote: "One of these temples—a rival to that of Solomon, and erected by some ancient Michelangelo—might take an honorable place beside our most beautiful buildings."

Mahout's descriptions of this "new," massive, unexplored Hindu temple sent a jolt of lightning through Western academic circles. Explorers from Europe combed the jungles of northern Cambodia in an attempt to explain the meaning and origin of the mysterious lost shrine.

## The Rise of the Khmer

Scholars first theorized that Angkor Wat and other ancient temples in present-day Cambodia were about 2,000 years old. However, as they began to decipher the Sanskrit inscriptions, they found that the temples had been erected during the 9th through 12th centuries. While Europe languished in the Dark Ages, the Khmer Empire of Indochina was reaching its zenith.

The earliest records of the Khmer people date back to the middle of the 6th century. They migrated from southern China and Tibet of China and settled in what is now Cambodia. The early Khmer retained many Indian influences from the West—they were Hindus, and their architecture evolved from Indian methods of building.

In the early 9th century, King Jayavarman II laid claim to an independent kingdom called Kambuja. He established his capital in the Angkor area some 190 miles north of the modern Cambodian capital of Phnom Penh. Jayavarman II also introduced the cult of devaraja, which claimed that the Khmer king was a representative of Shiva, the Hindu god of chaos, destruction, and rebirth. As such, in addition to the temples built to honor the Hindu gods, temples were also constructed to serve as tombs when kings died.

The Khmer Empire built more than 100 stone temples spread out over about 40 miles. The temples were built from laterite (a material similar to clay that forms in tropical climates) and sandstone. The sandstone provided an open canvas for the statues and reliefs celebrating the Hindu pantheon that decorates the temples.

## Home of the Gods

During the first half of the 12th century, Kambuja's King Suryavarman II decided to raise an enormous temple dedicated to the Hindu god Vishnu, a religious monument that would subdue the surrounding jungle and dramatically illustrate the power of the Khmer king. His masterpiece—the largest temple complex in the world—would be known to history by its Sanskrit name, "Angkor Wat," or "City of Temple."

Pilgrims visiting Angkor Wat in the 12th century would enter the temple complex by crossing a square, 600-foot-wide moat that ran some four miles in perimeter around the temple grounds. Approaching from the west, visitors would tread the moat's causeway to the main gateway. From there, they would follow a spiritual journey representing the path from the outside world through the Hindu universe and into Mount Meru, the home of the gods. They would pass a giant statue of an eight-armed Vishnu as they entered the western gopura, or gatehouse, known as the "Entrance of the Elephants." They would then follow a stone walkway decorated with nagas (mythical serpents) past sunken pools and column-studded buildings once believed to house sacred temple documents.

At the end of the stone walkway, a pilgrim would step up to a rectangular platform surrounded with galleries featuring six-foot-high bas-reliefs of gods and kings. One depicts the Churning of the Ocean of Milk, a Hindu story in which gods and demons churn a serpent in an ocean of milk to extract the elixir of life. Another illustrates the epic battle of monkey warriors against demons whose sovereign had kidnapped Sita, Rama's beautiful wife. Others depict the gruesome fates awaiting the wicked in the afterlife.

A visitor to King Suryavarman's kingdom would next ascend the dangerously steep steps to the temple's second level, an enclosed area boasting a courtyard decorated with hundreds of dancing apsaras, female images ornamented with jewelry and elaborately dressed hair.

For kings and high priests, the journey would continue with a climb up more steep steps to a 126-foot-high central temple, the pinnacle of Khmer society. Spreading out some 145 feet on each side, the square temple includes a courtyard cornered by four high conical towers shaped to look like lotus buds. The center of the temple is dominated by a fifth conical tower soaring 180 feet above the main causeway; inside it holds a golden statue of the Khmer patron, Vishnu, riding a half-man, half-bird creature in the image of King Suryavarman.

### Disuse and Destruction

With the decline of the Khmer Empire and the resurgence of Buddhism, Angkor Wat was occupied by Buddhist monks, who claimed it as their own for many years. A cruciform gallery leading to the temple's second level was decorated with 1,000 Buddhas; the Vishnu statue in the central tower was replaced by an image of Buddha. The temple fell into various states of disrepair over the centuries and is now the focus of international restoration efforts.

# The Mound Builders: Mythmaking in Early America

*The search for an improbable past, or, how to make a mountain out of a molehill.*

✳  ✳  ✳  ✳

IN THE EARLY 1840s, the fledgling United States was gripped by a controversy that spilled from the parlors of the educated men in Boston and Philadelphia—the core of the nation's intellectual elite—onto the pages of the newspapers printed for mass edification. In the tiny farming village of Grave Creek, Virginia (now West Virginia), on the banks of the Ohio River stood one of the largest earthen mounds discovered during white man's progress westward. The existence of these mounds, spread liberally throughout the Mississippi Valley, Ohio River Valley, and much of the southeast, was commonly known and had caused a great deal of speculative excitement since Europeans had first arrived on the continent. Hernando de Soto, for one, had mentioned the mounds of the Southeast during his wandering in that region.

## Money Well Spent

The colonists who settled the East Coast noticed that the mounds, which came in a variety of sizes and shapes, were typically placed near excellent sites for villages and farms. The Grave Creek mound was among the first of the major earthworks discovered by white men in their westward expansion. By 1838, the property was owned and farmed by the Tomlinson family. Abelard B. Tomlinson took an interest in the mound on his family's land and decided to open a vertical shaft from its summit, 70 feet high, to the center. He discovered skeletal remains at various levels and a timbered vault at the base containing the remains of two individuals. More importantly, he discovered a sandstone tablet inscribed with three lines of characters of unknown origin.

## Who Were the Mound Builders?

Owing to the general belief that the aborigines were lazy and incapable of such large, earth-moving operations and the fact that none of the tribes who dwelt near the mounds claimed any knowledge of who had built them, many 19th-century Americans believed that the mound builders could not have been the ancestors of the Native American tribes they encountered.

Wild and fantastic stories arose, and by the early 19th century, the average American assumed that the mound builders had been a pre-Columbian expedition from the Old World—Vikings, Israelites, refugees from Atlantis—all these and more had their champions. Most agreed, however, that the New World had once hosted and given rise to a civilization as advanced as that of the Aztecs and Incas who had then fallen into disarray or been conquered by the savage barbarians that now inhabited the land. Speculation on the history of the mound builders led many, including Thomas Jefferson, to visit mounds and conduct their own studies.

## Mormons and the Mounds

Meanwhile, the Grave Creek tablet fanned the flames of a controversy that was roaring over the newly established, and widely despised, Church of Jesus Christ of Latter Day Saints, founded by Joseph Smith.

The Mormon religion is based upon the belief that the American continent was once inhabited by lost tribes of Israel who divided into warring factions and fought each other to near extinction. The last surviving prophet of these people, Mormon, inscribed his people's history upon gold tablets, which were interred in a mound near present-day Palmyra, New York, until they were revealed to fifteen-year-old Joseph Smith in 1823. Though many Americans were ready to believe that the mounds represented the remains of a non-aboriginal culture, they were less ready to believe in Smith's new religion.

Smith and his adherents were persecuted horribly, and Smith was killed by an angry mob while leading his followers west. Critics of the Saints (as the Mormons prefer to be called) point to the early 19th-century publication of several popular books purporting that the earthen mounds of North America were the remains of the lost tribes of Israel. These texts claimed that evidence would eventually be discovered to support their author's assertions. That the young Smith should have his revelation so soon after these fanciful studies were published struck many observers as entirely too coincidental. Thus, Abelard Tomlinson's excavation of the sandstone tablet with its strange figures ignited the passions of both Smith's followers and his detractors.

## Enter the Scholar

Into this theological, and ultimately anthropological, maelstrom strode Henry Rowe Schoolcraft, a mineralogist whose keen interest in Native American history had led to his appointment as head of Indian affairs. While working in Sault Ste. Marie, Schoolcraft married a native woman and mastered the Ojibwa language. Schoolcraft traveled to Grave Creek to examine Tomlinson's tablet and concluded that the figures were indeed a language but deferred to more learned scholars to determine just which language they represented.

The opinions were many and varied—from Celtic runes to early Greek; experts the world over weighed in with their opinions. Nevertheless, Schoolcraft was more concerned with physical evidence and close study of the mounds themselves, and he remained convinced that the mounds and the artifacts they carried were the products of ancestors of the Native Americans.

Schoolcraft's theory flew in the face of both those who sought to defend and those who sought to debunk the Mormon belief, and it would be more than three decades until serious scholarship and the emergence of true archeological techniques began to shift opinion on the subject.

## Answers Proposed, but Questions Still Abound

History has vindicated Schoolcraft's careful and thoughtful study of the mounds. Today, we know that the mound builders were not descendents of Israel, nor were they the offspring of Vikings. They were simply the ancient and more numerous predecessors of the Native Americans, who constructed the mounds for protection from floods and as burial sites, temples, and defense strongholds.

As for the Grave Creek tablet: Many scholars have concluded that the figures are not a written language but simply a fanciful design whose meaning, if ever there was one, has been lost to the ages. Still others believe the figures represent a language we have yet to positively identify. Though the Smithsonian Institute has several etchings of the tablet in its collection, the whereabouts of the actual tablet have been lost to the ages.

# The Library of the Muses

*By far the most famous library in history, the Library of Alexandria held an untold number of ancient works. Its fiery destruction meant the irrecoverable loss of a substantial part of the world's intellectual history.*

✳ ✳ ✳ ✳

## The Library's Beginnings

THE CITIES OF ancient Mesopotamia (e.g., Uruk, Nineveh, Babylon) and Egypt (e.g., Thebes, Memphis) had cultivated archives and libraries since the Bronze Age, but the idea for a library as grand as Alexandria did not occur in Greek culture until the Hellenistic Age, when Alexander the Great's conquests brought both Greece and these former civilizations under Macedonian rule. Previous Greek libraries were owned by individuals; the largest belonged to Aristotle (384–322 BC), whose work and school (the Lyceum) in Athens were supported by Alexander.

When Alexander died suddenly in 323 BC, his generals carved his empire into regional dynasties. The Hellenistic dynasties competed with each other for three centuries (until each was in turn conquered by either Rome or Parthia). Each dynasty desired cultural dominance, so they invited famous artists, authors, and intellectuals to live and work in their capital cities. Alexander's general Ptolemy, who controlled Egypt, decided to develop a collection of the world's learning (the Library) and a research center, the Mouseion (the Museum, or "Temple of the Muses"), where scholars on subsidy could study and add their research to the collection. This idea may well have come from Demetrius of Phaleron (350–280 BC), Ptolemy's advisor and the former governor of Athens, who had been a pupil at the Lyceum, but the grand project became one of the hallmarks of the Ptolemaic dynasty. Under the first three Ptolemies, the Museum, a royal library, and a smaller "daughter" library at the Temple of Serapis (the Serapeum) were built and grew as Alexandria became the intellectual, as well as commercial, capital of the Hellenistic world.

Egypt and Alexandria offered the Ptolemies distinct advantages for accomplishing their goals. Egypt was not only immensely rich, which gave it the wealth to purchase materials and to bring scholars to Alexandria, but it was the major producer of papyrus, a marsh reed that was beaten into a flat surface and made into scrolls for writing and copying. Alexandria was also the commercial hub of the Mediterranean, and goods and information from all over the world passed through its port.

## Bibliomania: So Many Scrolls, So Little Time

Acquiring materials for the libraries and Museum became somewhat of an obsession for the Ptolemies. Although primarily focused on Greek and Egyptian works, their interests included translating other traditions into Greek. Among the most important of these efforts was the production of the Septuagint, a Greek version of the Jewish scriptures. Besides employing agents to scour major book markets and to search out copies of works not yet in the library, boats coming into Alexandria were required to declare any scrolls on board. If they were of interest, the scrolls were confiscated and copied, and the owners were given the copies and some compensation. Ptolemy III (285–222 BC) may have acquired Athens' official state collection of the plays of Aeschylus, Sophocles, and Euripides in a similar way—putting up 15 talents of silver as a guarantee while he had the plays copied, then foregoing the treasure in favor of keeping the originals. Whether or not this is true, it speaks to the value he placed on getting important works and the resources he had at his disposal to do so.

Alexandria's efforts were fueled by a competition with the Hellenistic kingdom of Pergamum (modern Bergamo, Turkey), which created its own library. Each library sought to claim new finds and to produce new editions, leading at times to the acquisition of forgeries and occasional embarrassment. Alexandria tried to undercut its rival by cutting off papyrus exports, but Pergamum perfected a method for making writing material out of animal skins (now called "parchment" from the Latin *pergamina*). Eventually, however, Alexandria got the upper hand when the Roman general Marcus Antonius (Mark Antony) conquered Pergamum and made a present of its library to his lover, the Ptolemaic Queen Cleopatra.

Estimates as to the number of volumes in the Alexandrian library ranged wildly even in antiquity, generally between 200,000 and 700,000. Estimates are complicated by the fact that it isn't clear whether the numbers originate from works or scrolls: Some scrolls contained one work, some multiple works, and long works like the Iliad took multiple scrolls. Over time, a complex cataloguing system evolved, which culminated in a bibliographic survey of the library's holdings called the Pinakes. The survey was put together by the great Hellenistic scholar and poet Callimachus of Cyrene (305–240 BC). Unfortunately, this important work only exists in fragments today.

## Burning Down the House

The Royal Library and its holdings were accidentally set aflame in 48 BC when Caesar (who had taken Cleopatra's side in her claim to the throne against her brother) tried to burn his way out of being trapped in the port by opposing forces. Further losses probably occurred in AD 271 when Emperor Aurelian destroyed part of the Museum while recapturing Alexandria from Queen Zenobia's forces. The "daughter" library of the Serapeum was finally destroyed by Christians under Emperor Theodosius. But by then, much of the contents (like the contents of other great civic libraries of antiquity) had decayed or found their way into other hands, leaving the classical heritage scattered and fragmented for centuries. Much later, Christians dramatically blamed the burning of the library holdings on Muslim conquerors. Although this made for a good story, the legendary contents of the library were already long gone.

# Identities Lost: The Druids and the Picts

*What do you know about the Druids? How about the Picts? Chances are, what you know (or think you know) is wrong. These two "lost" peoples are saddled with serious cases of mistaken identity.*

✳ ✳ ✳ ✳

**M**OST CONTEMPORARY PERCEPTIONS of the Druids and Picts tend to be derived from legend and lore. As such, our conceptions of these peoples range from erroneous and unlikely to just plain foolish.

Let's start with the Druids. They are often credited with the building of Stonehenge, the great stone megalith believed to be their sacred temple, as well as their arena for savage human sacrifice rituals. True or False?

False. First off, Stonehenge was built around 2000 BC—about 1,400 years before the Druids emerged. Second, though we know admittedly little of Druidic practice, it seemed to be traditional and conservative. The Druids did have specific divinity-related beliefs, but it is not known whether they actually carried out human sacrifices.

What about the Picts? Although often reduced to a mythical race of magical fairies, the Picts actually ruled Scotland before the Scots.

So who were the Druids and the Picts?

## The Druids—The Priestly Class

As the priestly class of Celtic society, the Druids served as the Celts' spiritual leaders—repositories of knowledge about the world and the universe, as well as authorities on Celtic history, law, religion, and culture. In short, they were the preservers of the Celtic way of life.

The Druids provided the Celts with a connection to their gods, the universe, and the natural order. They preached of the power and authority of the deities and taught the immortality of the soul and reincarnation. They were experts in astronomy and the natural world. They also had an innate connection to all things living: They preferred holding great rituals among natural shrines provided by the forests, springs, and groves.

To become a Druid, one had to survive extensive training. Druid wannabes and Druid-trained minstrels and bards had to endure as many as 20 years of oral education and memorization.

## More Powerful than Celtic Chieftains

In terms of power, the Druids took a backseat to no one. Even the Celtic chieftains, well-versed in power politics, recognized the overarching authority of the Druids. Celtic society had well-defined power and social structures and territories and property rights. The Druids were deemed the ultimate arbiters in all matters relating to such. If there was a legal or financial dispute between two parties, it was unequivocally settled in special Druid-presided courts. Armed conflicts were immediately ended by Druid rulings. Their word was final.

In the end, however, there were two forces to which even the Druids had to succumb—the Romans and Christianity. With the Roman invasion of Britain in AD 43, Emperor Claudius mandated that the practice of Druidism throughout the Roman Empire was to be outlawed. The Romans destroyed the last vestiges of official Druidism in Britain with the annihilation of the Druid stronghold of Anglesey in AD 61. Surviving Druids fled to unconquered Ireland and Scotland, only to become completely marginalized by the influence of Christianity within a few centuries.

Stripped of power and status, the Druids of ancient Celtic society disappeared. They morphed into wandering poets and storytellers with no connection to their once illustrious past.

## The Picts—The Painted People

The Picts were, in simplest terms, the people who inhabited ancient Scotland before the Scots. Their origins are unknown, but some scholars believe that the Picts were descendants of the Caledonians or other Iron Age tribes who invaded Britain.

No one knows what the Picts called themselves; the origin of their name comes from other sources and probably derives from the Pictish custom of tattooing or painting their bodies. The Irish called them Cruithni, meaning "the people of the designs." The Romans called them Picti, which is Latin for "painted people"; however, the Romans probably used the term as a general moniker for all the untamed peoples living north of Hadrian's Wall.

## A Second-Hand History

The Picts themselves left no written records. All descriptions of their history and culture come from second-hand accounts. The earliest of these is a Roman account from AD 297 stating that the Picti and the Hiberni (Irish) were already well-established enemies of the Britons to the south.

The Picts were also well-established enemies of each other. Before the arrival of the Romans, the Picts spent most of their time fighting amongst themselves. The threat posed by the Roman conquest of Britain forced the squabbling Pict kingdoms to come together and eventually evolve into the nation-state of Pictland. The united Picts were strong enough not only to resist conquest by the Romans, but also to launch periodic raids on Roman-occupied Britain.

Having defied the Romans, the Picts later succumbed to a more peaceful invasion launched by Irish missionaries. Arriving in Pictland in the late 6th century, they succeeded in converting the polytheistic Pict elite within two decades. Much of the known history of the Picts comes from the Irish Christian annals. If not for the writings of the Romans and the Irish missionaries, we might not have knowledge of the Picts today.

Despite the existence of an established Pict state, Pictland disappeared with the changing of its name to the Kingdom of Alba in AD 843, a move signifying the rise of the Gaels as the dominant people in Scotland. By the 11th century, virtually all vestiges of them had vanished.

# Are You Related to Genghis Khan?

*Your DNA may carry the stuff you need to conquer the world.*

✳ ✳ ✳ ✳

## From Riches To Rags To Riches

GENGHIS KHAN WAS one of the first self-made men in history. He was born to a tribal chief in 1162, probably at Dadal Sum, in the Hentii region of what is now Mongolia. At age 9, Genghis was sent packing after a rival tribe poisoned his father. For three years, Genghis and the remainder of his family wandered the land living from hand to mouth.

Genghis was down, but not out. After convincing some of his tribesmen to follow him, he eventually became one of the most successful political and military leaders in history, uniting the nomadic Mongol tribes into a vast sphere of influence. The Mongol Empire lasted from 1206 to 1368 and was the largest contiguous dominion in world history, stretching from the Caspian Sea to the Sea of Japan. At the empire's peak, it encompassed more than 700 tribes and cities.

## A Uniter, Not A Divider

Genghis gave his people more than just land. He introduced a writing system, wrote the first laws to govern all Mongols, regulated hunting, and created a judicial system for fair trials. His determination to create unity swept old rivalries aside and made everyone feel like a single Mongol people. Today, Genghis Khan is seen as a founding father of Mongolia. However, he is not so fondly remembered in the Middle East and Europe, where he is regarded as a ruthless and bloodthirsty conqueror.

## Who's Your Daddy?

It seems that Genghis was father of more than the Mongol nation. Recently, an international team of geneticists determined that one in every 200 men now living is a relative of the great Mongol ruler. More than 16 million men in central Asia have been identified as carrying the same Y chromosome as Genghis Khan.

A key reason is this: Genghis's sons and other male descendants had many children by many women; one son, Tushi, may have had 40 sons of his own, and one of Genghis's grandsons, Chinese dynastic ruler Kublai Khan, fathered 22 sons with recognized wives and an unknown number with the scores of women he kept as concubines.

Genetically speaking, Genghis continues to "live on" because the male chromosome is passed directly from father to son, with no change other than random mutations (which are typically insignificant). When geneticists identify those mutations, called "markers," they can chart the course of male descendants through centuries. Is the world large enough for 16 million personal empires? Time—and genetics—will reveal the answer.

# Treasures Lost and Found

*Millions of dollars worth of treasure was pillaged, buried, sunken—you name it—during the riotous days of the Civil War.*

✳  ✳  ✳  ✳

TREASURES OF COIN, bullion, and other valuables had already been traveling along America's waters, rails, and roads before the Civil War began. Once that conflict erupted, these stores of wealth became targets for pirates, outlaws, and soldiers to intercept either for personal gain or to hit the enemy in the pocketbook—or both. The paths this loot took on the high seas, on the tracks, and in the backwoods of the country became more and more treacherous as the war developed.

## The Sources of Treasure

As early as January 1861, the Union's secretary of the Navy sent word to his commanders stationed along the water route from New York to California to "be vigilant and if necessary be prompt to use all the means at your command for the protection of the California steamers and their treasure." Commodore Cornelius Vanderbilt recommended adding guns on passenger ships because "our steamers may be seized or robbed on their voyage." Treasury Secretary Salmon Chase and other officials also begged for strong cannons to be mounted on merchant boats to protect them from Confederate bandits. One group of merchants petitioning for such assistance estimated that $40 million in gold traveled from San Francisco to New York every year.

The Confederate navy simply didn't match up to that of the Union, so the South hired private raiders to attack Northern merchant ships in an effort to stop general trade and the transport of items that assisted the Union war effort. In the first half of the war, Confederate-sponsored raiders captured 40 Northern ships. The South eventually commissioned about 200 warships that had been built in England. Many carried British sailors driven by the promise of reward. One daring raider, the Tallahassee, had a field day sinking ships off the coast of New Jersey and New York. It sank six ships in six hours before moving northward to attack coastal and transatlantic trading vessels.

## Weather Woes

Other Union merchant ships were subject to damage from the weather. The SS *Republic*, a twin-paddlewheel steamer reportedly carrying $400,000 in coins, sailed from New York to New Orleans in 1865 and was pounded not by a Confederate attack but by a powerful hurricane. The *Republic* disappeared beneath the waves many miles off the coast of Georgia.

After more than a decade of failing deep-sea hunts and haggling with the government over proper rights and authorization, two modern undersea explorers, John Morris and Greg Stemm of Odyssey Marine Exploration, hit the jackpot in 2003 when they discovered more than 50,000 coins and 13,000 artifacts totaling $75 million. Such excavations and treasure hunts are expensive, though, leaving much underwater Civil War loot out there waiting to be discovered.

## Bury the Loot

Money and assets on land during the war were also precious and subject to looting. Notorious Confederate General John Hunt Morgan pillaged Union towns in Kentucky and throughout the Ohio River Valley. This harsh Southerner rode with his raiders up to wealthy homes and threatened to burn them down unless the owner could pay the ransom. With a command of more than 2,000 troops, Morgan ravaged towns, stole from businesses, and even took collection plates from churches.

After Morgan's force conducted a tour of robberies in central Kentucky, which included a hit on a bank for $80,000, Union cavalry came upon the raiders. The cavalry dispersed Morgan's troops but their plunder was never found—was it buried in the Kentucky hills? The total wealth Morgan looted on his infamous raids will never be known, but it is likely that much of it was dispersed and hidden throughout the area along the trails and roads his forces traveled. One estimate is that Morgan accumulated as much as $1 million in gold and silver bullion.

## The Treasury's Depleting Treasure

Perhaps the largest stash that traveled through Confederate hands was the Confederate Treasury after Union soldiers encroached on the Southern capital of Richmond, Virginia. Nearing the point of surrender, President Jefferson Davis ordered the area evacuated and assigned the Treasury to Captain William Parker. Parker and his soldiers loaded the sum, which totaled upward of $1 million, onto boxcars and sent it as far as Danville, Virginia. Already on the run and trying to evade capture, several Southern leaders chose to distance themselves from the loot in favor of their own safety.

After the money bounced from town to town, it landed in Washington, Georgia. Here, Confederate troops charged with protecting the wealth feared for their safety and demanded payment on the spot. The military escort dwindled, as did the Treasury itself. As the loot traveled from farmhouse to farmhouse, it shrunk to $288,022.90 by the time it reached President Davis and what was left of the acting government. Some believe Davis took a large chunk of the money himself and buried it in several locations before he was captured.

On May 14, 1865, two Virginia bankers arrived in Washington with a federal order to commandeer the money, and Clark gave it up. The party carrying the money back to Richmond pulled over for the night 12 miles outside of the city only to be robbed. The outlaws, understanding that both law enforcement and Confederate soldiers were on their trail, buried their take before Confederates shot and killed them. Some believe the loot was buried on the south bank of the Savannah River.

## Secret Society

According to legend, documented history, and some modern-day discoveries, rebels buried much more wealth than this. The mysterious Knights of the Golden Circle likely left behind millions in coin and precious metals. This secret society, explains historian and Knights of the Golden Circle detective Bob Brewer, grew out of anti-Union, proslavery sentiment and had several chapters by 1855. Famous politicians and rank-and-file composed the secret membership society, helping foster the ideas behind nullification and secession. Through a complex system of Masonic codes, secret signals, handshakes, and other rites, the organization buried much of the South's wealth in the hopes of financing a later uprising to reassert and complete the goals of the temporarily defeated South.

Some of this loot has been found. Brewer discovered a jar with coins and gold pieces—now worth about $28,000—at a location 65 miles from Oklahoma City called Buzzard's Roost. Treasure hunters report that four caches of booty have been unearthed over the years near this location, totaling more than $1 million. Those who study the Knights predict a lot more is out there. The organization likely developed some type of grid system marked with tree and rock carvings directing fellow Knights to the wealth. While little or no known record of the alleged postwar scheme fully defines its scope, it is believed that information to locate the money and the group's cause has been handed down by word of mouth, from father to son, in the hopes that one day the South will rise again.

# The Tomb in Washington Square Park

*What exactly lies beneath the surface of a popular New York City park?*

✳ ✳ ✳ ✳

WHEN YOU WALK through an old public park in a large city, there's a chance you're really walking over an old graveyard. Many cities had to use parks to bury the dead during times of plague, and some major parks, like Chicago's Lincoln Park, actually served as the town's official burial ground before being converted into a normal public park as the city grew up around it.

Graveyard is only one of many functions that New York City's Washington Square Park has served over the years. It's been a friendly public gathering place for generations, but in earlier times it served as the town's site for public executions. A common urban legend states that the large elm tree at the northwest corner once served as the "hangman's elm," from which convicts were hanged by the neck until dead. Only one actual hanging is known to have taken place in the park, and eyewitness descriptions vary as to where, exactly, that hanging took place. But at more than 300 years old, the tree was certainly standing at the time when the execution occurred. It's the oldest tree in Manhattan.

## Lost Plot(s)

In the early days of the 19th century, the park served not only as a place of execution, but also as the city's "potter's field," a patch of ground where unmarked bodies were buried. But as New York grew from a market town into a modern metropolis, the city outgrew the small space, and it was closed for use as a cemetery in 1825. Records vary, but sources indicate that between 2,000 and 20,000 bodies were interred there. A 2005 archaeological survey suggested that 20,000 was a fairly low estimate, and found no evidence that any effort at all had been made to move the bodies when the space was converted into a "military parade ground" and park.

But apparently it wasn't only the poor and friendless who were buried in the park, and not all of the graves were anonymous or unmarked. As recently as 2009, an intact tombstone was found buried two feet under the ground, featuring an inscription stating, "Here lies the body of James Jackson who departed this life the 22nd Day of September 1799 aged 28 years native of the county of Kildare Ireland."

## A Tomb of One's Own

Mr. Jackson's body itself was not found, but perhaps his was among the many that had already been dug up inadvertently over the years. Since most people known to be interred in the old park were buried in unmarked graves, finding a tombstone was completely unexpected—but not as big a shock as the one that came in 1965. In that year, workers from the Consolidated Edison company were digging in the park to install a new electrical transformer when they came across something unexpected—a concrete dome buried four or five feet underground.

Workers assumed it to be one of the countless abandoned tunnels that lie beneath the ground in Manhattan, but upon breaking through the concrete, they found another dome made of brick and mortar. Breaking through that dome led them to a staircase, one that led downward to a wooden door. And when they opened the wooden door, they found that it led to a brick-walled underground room full of skeletons.

A spokesman for Consolidated Edison said that "The room was whitewashed, dry, and odorless . . . There were the outlines of coffins—the wood had disintegrated—and one of the skeletons lying in or near the outline of a coffin. Other skeletons were piled in a corner." Another spokesman said that he personally had never uncovered so much as a thigh bone before, but couldn't resist making a crack about the hippies who populated the park in those days: "I have," he told *The New York Times* with a wink, "seen some skeletons walking around that park with sandals on."

Finding skeletons in the park was hardly unusual for workers in the area—in fact, students of the nearby New York University once lined a fence with skulls that had ben dug up by workers digging out underground pipes and mains. Still, finding a full tomb in the park was completely unexpected. No one had any record of such a thing being built, and archaeologists could only guess about when it was constructed—and why.

The prevailing opinion was that the tomb had been hastily built to house victims who had been killed off by one of the many "plagues" that swept through the city in the late 1700s, such as a yellow fever epidemic from 1798. However, some records indicate that the "northeast quadrant" had once been a church cemetery, and that the vault was built for members of a Scottish Presbyterian church.

Even as late as 2005, when archaeologists released a study on the park, they were not entirely sure what the vault was, or how long it had been there—or even whether it was the only underground vault in the northeast quadrant. Workers in 1965 simply covered it back up, so the mysterious tomb is still lying beneath a seating plaza and a playground today. Those particular skeletons seem to be there to stay—but others continue to be found in the park regularly.

# Prehistoric Hollywood

*If a stroll along Rodeo Drive lined with Beverly Hills housewives isn't enough to convince you, Hollywood was once home to a vast array of Pleistocene ice age creatures. The La Brea Tar Pits, located near the Miracle Mile district of Los Angeles, have yielded the largest repository of fossils from the last ice age, including plants, insects, and mammals.*

✻　✻　✻　✻

DESPITE THE NAME, the La Brea Tar Pits are actually a series of asphalt deposits that bubble up from the ground. Over the centuries, oil has oozed to the surface to form sticky bogs that have trapped all manner of animals, condemning them to premature deaths but preserving their skeletons. Since paleontologists began excavating the tar pits in 1908, remains have been discovered that date back as far as 40,000 years. These include saber-toothed cats, short-faced bears, dire wolves, and even an American lion. In early 2009, as workers began excavating an underground parking garage next to the tar pits, they found a stunning collection of fossils, including a nearly intact mammoth dating back to the last ice age.

Curators from the George C. Page Museum, which houses fossils collected from the site, estimate that the mammoth—whom they named Zed—stood ten feet tall at the hip and was between 47 and 49 years old, which is young for a mammoth. Zed's three broken ribs indicate that he'd likely been injured fighting with other male mammoths, a precursor to the back-biting that is so common in Hollywood these days.

The La Brea Tar Pits are no stranger to the limelight, having been featured in several movies, including *Last Action Hero* (1993), Steven Spielberg's *1941* (1979), and the disaster movie, *Volcano* (1997), in which a volcanic eruption originates from the largest tar pit and spews lava on the streets of Hollywood.

# Why Didn't the Vikings Stay in North America?

*According to ancient Norse sagas that were written in the thirteenth century, Leif Eriksson was the first Viking to set foot in North America. After wintering at the place we now call Newfoundland in the year 1000, Leif went home. In 1004, his brother Thorvald led the next expedition, composed of thirty men, and met the natives for the first time. The Vikings attacked and killed eight of the nine native men they encountered. A greater force retaliated, and Thorvald was killed. His men then returned home.*

✳ ✳ ✳ ✳

SIX YEARS LATER, a larger expedition of Viking men, women, and various livestock set up shop in North America. They lasted two years, according to the sagas. The Vikings traded with the locals initially, but they soon started fighting with them and were driven off. There may have been one further attempt at a Newfoundland settlement by Leif and Thorvald's sister, Freydis.

In 1960, Norse ruins of the appropriate age were found in L'Anse aux Meadows, Newfoundland, by Norwegian couple Helge and Anne Stine Ingstad. The Vikings had been there, all right.

Excavations over the next seven years uncovered large houses and ironworks where nails and rivets were made, as well as woodworking areas. Also found were spindlewhorls, weights that were used when spinning thread; this implies that women were present, which suggests the settlement was more than a vacation camp. The ruins don't reveal why the Vikings left, but they do confirm what the old sagas claimed: The Vikings were in North America.

The sagas say that the settlers fought with the local *Skraelings*, a Norse word meaning "natives," until the *Skraelings* came at them in large enough numbers to force the Vikings out.

This sounds plausible, given the reputation of the Vikings—they'd been raiding Europe for centuries—and the Eriksson family's history of violence. Erik the Red, the father of Leif, founded a Greenland colony because he'd been thrown out of Iceland for murder, and Erik's father had been expelled from Norway for the same reason. Would you want people like that as your neighbors?

# Sorry, Mates, but Aussies Didn't Invent the Boomerang

*Contrary to popular myth, lore, and Australian drinking songs, boomerangs, or "The Throwing Wood," as proponents prefer to call them, did not originate down under.*

✳   ✳   ✳   ✳

THE COLONISTS, ADVENTURERS, prisoners, and explorers who ventured into the heart of the Australian wilderness may be excused for believing that the local aborigines created these little aerodynamic marvels, considering the proficiency with which they used the wooden devices to bring down wild game and wilder colonials. The gyroscopic precision with which boomerangs were (and still are) crafted by primitive peoples continues to intrigue and astonish those who come in contact with the lightweight, spinning missiles, which—if thrown correctly—actually will return to their throwers.

## Many Returns

As a weapon of war and especially as a tool for hunting small game, the boomerang has been around for nearly 10,000 years. In fact, evidence of boomerangs has been discovered in almost every nook and cranny in the world. Pictures of boomerangs can be found in Neolithic-era cave drawings in France, Spain, and Poland. The "lagobolon," or "hare club," as it was called, was commonly used by nobles in Crete around 2000 BC. And King Tut, ruler of Egypt around 1350 BC, had a large collection of boomerangs—several of which were found when his tomb was discovered in the 1920s.

The Greek mythological hero Hercules is depicted tossing about a curved "clava" or "throwing stick" on pottery made during the Homeric era. Carthaginian invaders in the 2nd century BC were bombarded by Gallic warriors who rained "catela" or "throwing clubs." The Roman historian Horace describes a flexible wooden "caia" used by German tribes, saying "if thrown by a master, it returns to the one who threw it." Roman Emperor Caesar Augustus's favorite contemporary author, Virgil, also describes a similar curved missile weapon in use by natives of the province of Hispania.

However, Europeans can no more claim the invention of the boomerang than their Australian cousins can. Archaeologists have found evidence of boomerang use throughout Neolithic-era Africa, from Sudan to Niger, and from Cameroon to Morocco. Tribes in southern India, the American southwest, Mexico, and Java all used the boomerang, or something very similar, and for the same purposes.

Australians, however, can be credited with bringing the boomerang to the fresh attention of the modern world. They helped popularize it both as a child's toy and as an item for sport. A World Cup is held every other year, and enthusiasts and scientists still compete to design, construct, and throw the perfect boomerang.

Though the tool, weapon, or toy known today as a boomerang did not originate in Australia—or at least did not originate exclusively in Australia—the word itself is Australian. *Boomerang* is a blending of the words, woomerang and bumarin, terms used by different groups of Australian aborigines to describe their little wooden wonders.

# Nostradamus: Seer of Visions

*Nostradamus was born in December 1503 in Saint-Rémy-de-Provence, a small town in southern France. Little is known about his childhood except that he came from a very large family and that he may have been educated by his maternal great-grandfather. In his teens, Nostradamus entered the University of Avignon but was only there for about a year before the school was forced to close its doors due to an outbreak of the plague. He later became a successful apothecary and even created a pill that could supposedly protect against the plague.*

✳  ✳  ✳  ✳

## Looking to the Future

IT IS BELIEVED that some time in the 1540s, Nostradamus began taking an interest in the occult, particularly in ways to predict the future. His preferred method was scrying: gazing into a bowl of water or a mirror and waiting for visions to appear.

Nostradamus published a highly successful almanac for the year 1550, which included some of his prophecies and predictions. This almanac was so successful that Nostradamus wrote more, perhaps even several a year, until his death in 1566. Even so, it was a single book that caused the most controversy, both when it was released and even today.

## Les Prophéties

In addition to creating his almanacs, Nostradamus also began compiling his previously unpublished prophecies into one massive volume. Released in 1555, *Les Prophéties* (*The Prophecies*) would become one of the most controversial and perplexing books ever written. The book contained hundreds of quatrains (four-line stanzas or poems), but Nostradamus worried that some might see his prophecies as demonic, so he encoded them to obscure their true meanings. To do this, Nostradamus did everything from playing with the syntax of the quatrains to switching between French, Greek, Latin, and other languages.

When first released, some people did think that Nostradamus was in league with the devil. Others simply thought he was insane and that his quatrains were nothing more than the ramblings of a delusional man. As time went on, though, people started looking to Nostradamus's prophecies to see if they were coming true. It became a common practice that after a major event in history, people would pull out a copy of *Les Prophéties* to see if they could find a hidden reference to it buried in one of Nostradamus's quatrains. It is a practice that has continued to this day and only gets more and more common as the years go by.

## Lost in Translation

One of the interesting and frustrating things about *Les Prophéties* is that due to the printing procedures in his time, no two editions of his book were ever alike. Not only were there differences in spelling or punctuation, but entire words and phrases were often changed, especially when translated from French to English. Presently, there are more than 200 editions of *Les Prophéties* in print, all of which have subtle differences in the text. So it's not surprising that people from all over the world have looked into their version and found references to the French Revolution, Napoleon, the rise of Hitler, the JFK assassination, even the Apollo moon landings. After the terrorist attacks of September 11, 2001, speculation again erupted. Did Nostradamus's quatrains contain secret predictions of these events?

Soon after the Twin Towers fell, an email started making the rounds, which claimed that Nostradamus had predicted the events and quoted the following quatrain as proof:

*In the City of God there will be a great thunder,*

*Two Brothers torn apart by Chaos,*

*While the fortress endures,*

*The great leader will succumb,*

*The third big war will begin when the big city is burning*

Anyone reading the above can clearly see that Nostradamus is describing September 11, the Twin Towers ("Two Brothers") falling, and the start of World War III. Pretty chilling, except Nostradamus never wrote it. It's nothing more than an online hoax that spread like wildfire.

It's a pretty bad hoax, too. First, Nostradamus wrote quatrains, which have four lines. This one has five. Also, consider that the date Nostradamus supposedly penned this—1654—was almost 90 years after he died. Nostradamus might have been able to see the future, but there's no mention of him being able to write from beyond the grave.

However, others believe Nostradamus did indeed pen a quatrain that predicted September 11. It is quatrain I 87, which when translated reads:

*Volcanic fire from the center of the earth*

*Will cause tremors around the new city;*

*Two great rocks will make war for a long time*

*Then Arethusa will redden a new river.*

Those who believe that this quatrain predicted the September 11 attacks believe that the "new city" is a thinly-veiled reference to New York City. They further state that Nostradamus would often use rocks to refer to religious beliefs and that the third stanza refers to the religious differences between the United States and the terrorists. Skeptic James Randi, however, believes that the "new city" referred to is Naples, not New York. So who's right? No one is really sure, so for now, the debate continues—at least until the next major catastrophe hits and people go scrambling to the bookshelves to see what Nostradamus had to say about it.

# A Discovery of Biblical Proportions

*While rounding up a stray animal near Qumran, Israel, in early 1947, Bedouin shepherd Mohammed el-Hamed stumbled across several pottery jars containing scrolls written in Hebrew. It turned out to be the find of a lifetime.*

✳ ✳ ✳ ✳

NEWS OF THE exciting discovery of ancient artifacts spurred archaeologists to scour the area of the original find for additional material. Over a period of nine years, the remains of approximately 900 documents were recovered from 11 caves near the ruins of Qumran, a plateau community on the northwest shore of the Dead Sea. The documents have come to be known as the Dead Sea Scrolls.

Tests indicate that all but one of the documents were created between the 2nd century BC and the 1st century AD. Nearly all were written in one of three Hebrew dialects. Most were written on animal hide. The scrolls represent the earliest surviving copies of Biblical documents. Approximately 30 percent of the material is from the Hebrew Bible. Every book of the Old Testament is represented with the exception of the Book of Esther and the Book of Nehemiah. Another 30 percent of the scrolls contain essays on subjects including blessings, war, community rule, and the membership requirements of a Jewish sect. About 25 percent of the material refers to Israelite religious texts not contained in the Hebrew Bible.

Since their discovery, debate about the meaning of the scrolls has been intense. One widely held theory subscribes to the belief that the scrolls were created at the village of Qumran and then hidden by the inhabitants. According to this theory, a Jewish sect known as the Essenes wrote the scrolls. Those subscribing to this theory have concluded that the Essenes hid the scrolls in nearby caves during the Jewish Revolt in AD 66, shortly before they were massacred by Roman troops.

A second major theory, put forward by Norman Golb, Professor of Jewish History at the University of Chicago, speculates that the scrolls were originally housed in various Jerusalem-area libraries and were spirited out of the city when the Romans besieged the capital in AD 68–70. Golb believes that the treasures documented on the so-called Copper Scroll could only have been held in Jerusalem. Golb also alleges that the variety of conflicting ideas found in the scrolls indicates that the documents are facsimiles of literary texts.

The documents were catalogued according to which cave they were found in and have been categorized into Biblical and non-Biblical works. Of the eleven caves, numbers 1 and 11 yielded the most intact documents, while number 4 held the most material—an astounding 15,000 fragments representing 40 percent of the total material found. Multiple copies of the Hebrew Bible have been identified, including 19 copies of the Book of Isaiah, 30 copies of Psalms, and 25 copies of Deuteronomy. Also found were previously unknown psalms attributed to King David, and even some stories about Abraham and Noah.

Most of the fragments appeared in print between 1950 and 1965, with the exception of the material from Cave 4. Publication of the manuscripts was entrusted to an international group led by Father Roland de Vaux of the Dominican Order in Jerusalem.

Access to the material was governed by a "secrecy rule"—only members of the international team were allowed to see them. In late 1971, 17 documents were published, followed by the release of a complete set of images of all the Cave 4 material. The secrecy rule was eventually lifted, and copies of all documents were in print by 1995.

Many of the documents are now housed in the Shrine of the Book, a wing of the Israel Museum located in Western Jerusalem. The scrolls on display are rotated every three to six months.

# The News Is What the President Says It Is

*When it comes to Lincoln's repression of newspapers, rumors battle with the truth.*

✳ ✳ ✳ ✳

POLITICIANS OFTEN CITE the actions of their historical forebears to justify their own indiscretions. Abraham Lincoln, for example, is said to have suppressed civil rights during the Civil War, so he occasionally gets referenced when a modern politician wants to do the same thing. Today's official might say, "Lincoln suppressed newspapers during the Civil War, so I should be able to meddle with a few civil liberties, too." But did Lincoln really work to curtail freedom of the press? It's not quite so clear cut.

## Freedom of the Press?

A handful of cases are frequently cited to demonstrate that Lincoln was opposed to a free press. In June 1863, the editor of the *Chicago Times* wrote inflammatory antiwar articles that attacked the efforts of Lincoln and the Republicans. Union General Ambrose Burnside, who was in command of the Department of the Ohio at the time, was alarmed at what he considered the *Times's* "repeated expression of disloyal and incendiary sentiments." The general had the editor arrested and the paper shut down. Although Lincoln had suspended habeas corpus in areas where he feared physical unrest, he was troubled by Burnside's actions and consulted his Cabinet for a response. They agreed that the editor's arrest had been improper, so Lincoln freed him and allowed the *Chicago Times* to return to press. When people asked Lincoln why he hadn't supported the closure of the newspaper that had been so critical of him, he wrote that those with such a question did "not fully comprehend the dangers of abridging the liberties of the people." That doesn't sound like something a hater of the press would write!

## Lies Instead of News

The President wasn't completely above shutting down a printing press if he thought it was necessary. On May 18, 1864, the *New York World* and the *Journal and Commerce* each published a forged presidential proclamation calling for a new draft of 400,000 troops. Once these papers were on the street, the administration wasted no time in going after them. Lincoln himself ordered General John A. Dix to arrest the publishers and editors and to seize their presses. When further investigation determined that the journalists had been taken in by the forgery themselves and had never intended to convey false information, the journalists were released and allowed to resume publication.

In his telegram to Dix releasing the journalists, Secretary of War Edwin Stanton wrote of the President, "He directs me to say that while, in his opinion, the editors, proprietors, and publishers of *The World* and *Journal of Commerce* are responsible for what appears in their papers injurious to the public service, and have no right to shield themselves behind a plea of ignorance or want of criminal intent, yet he is not disposed to visit them with vindictive punishment."

## The People Have Spoken

Official action from the government wasn't the only sort of suppression that affected newspapers. In March 1863, the 2nd Ohio Cavalry was camped outside of Columbus, Ohio. After the local newspaper, *The Crisis*, printed anti-army stories—including the wish that no member of the 2nd Ohio return from the war alive—the soldiers ransacked its offices. *The Crisis* continued publication, however. The next year, its editor was indicted by a federal grand jury and arrested for conspiracy. He died in November before he could go on trial.

Although Lincoln wasn't afraid to take action when he felt it necessary, he was keenly aware of the danger in restricting civil rights and did so only after careful consideration. Those wishing to use him as a role model for their actions against free speech should perhaps take a closer look.

# The Truth and the Myth of the Ninja

*Ninjas were the special forces of feudal Japan. Trained in assassination, espionage, and guerilla warfare, ninjas inspired fear in both rulers and commoners alike.*

✳ ✳ ✳ ✳

OVER THE YEARS, the ninja has taken on a mythical status. But like most myths, the story is filled with both fact and fiction.

## Humble Beginnings

Ninjas got their start as priests living in the mountains of Japan. Harassed by the central government and local samurai, they resorted to using *nonuse* (the art of stealth)—what we would call guerilla warfare. Their use of secrecy and stealth didn't win them many friends, but it secured them a role in the civil wars to come.

From roughly 794 to 1192, local rulers fought to gain control of Japan. While the Samurai fought the wars, it was left to the mountain priests to do those things that the Samurai considered cowardly—namely spying, sneaking around to gather information, and trying to assassinate their rivals. This is when the ninja (*nin*, meaning "concealment" and *sha*, meaning "person") was born.

## From Priests to Ninjas

These mountain priests made their reputation during the Japanese civil wars. They worked for anybody—often for both sides at the same time. In addition to being scouts, a favorite ninja job was to sneak into a castle under siege and cause as much chaos as possible. Dressed like the enemy, they made their way into enemy camps to set fires, start rebellions in the ranks, steal flags, and generally stir up confusion and keep the pressure on their opponents so that when the army outside stormed the gates, the defenders would already be demoralized and give up without a fight.

Ninjas used weapons uniquely suited to them. They wore claws on their gloves that helped them fight and climb. Because the ownership of weapons was forbidden to all but the samurai, ninjas used a common farming tool called a sickle for much of their fighting. And, of course, they used the throwing stars that everybody sees in the movies, though the real ninjas weren't nearly as accurate as their Hollywood counterparts. They also used "invisibility" weapons, usually an eggshell filled with an eye irritant or a bit of gunpowder with a fuse in case they had to make a quick getaway.

Eventually the Japanese civil wars came to an end, and the ninjas found themselves out of a job. The ninjas were gone but certainly not forgotten. The exploits of the ninja made their way into popular literature and eventually into legend.

## Ninja Fact and Fiction

The ninja were feared for their ability to assassinate their rivals, but there was never a documented case of any ruler being killed by a ninja. They tried, of course, but they were never successful.

Although ninjas are typically thought to be male, there were female ninjas as well. Whether male or female, one thing is certain: Ninjas didn't run around in black pajamas as Hollywood would have you believe.

This misconception originated in Kabuki Theater. During shows, the prop movers wore all black to shift things around while the play was going on. Everybody was supposed to ignore the people in black, pretending they were invisible. So when it became time for ninjas to be played in the theater, they simply wore the same black dress as the prop movers to symbolize their gift of invisibility. The crowds were delighted and bought in, and the black ninja suit was born.

The exploits of the ninja came to the West mainly after World War II. Like the Japanese theater, Hollywood's version of the ninja portrayed them either as an almost unbeatable mystical foe or as a clumsy fighter that the hero of the movie could take on singlehandedly.

Although there are martial arts schools that teach ninja techniques, the ninja have faded into history and legend.

# Sacajawea's Story

*There aren't many tour guides as famous as Sacajawea, but in truth, she wasn't a guide at all—she had no idea where she was going, and she didn't even speak English!*

✳  ✳  ✳  ✳

## Hooking Up with Lewis and Clark

MERIWETHER LEWIS (A soldier) and William Clark (a naturalist) were recruited by President Thomas Jefferson to explore the upper reaches of the Missouri River. Their job was to find the most direct route to the Pacific Ocean—the legendary Northwest Passage. Setting out in 1803, they worked their way up the Missouri River and then stopped for the winter to build a fort near a trading post in present-day North Dakota. This is where they met the pregnant Shoshone teenager known as Sacajawea.

Actually, they met her through her husband, Toussaint Charbonneau. He was a French fur trader who lived with the Shoshone (he is said to have purchased Sacajawea from members of another group who had captured her, so it may be inaccurate to call her his "wife"). Although Sacajawea is credited with guiding Lewis and Clark's expedition to the Pacific, the only reason she (and her newborn baby) went along at all was that her husband had been hired as a translator.

## Pop Culture Icon

The myth of Sacajawea as the Native American princess who pointed the way to the Pacific was created and perpetuated by the many books and movies that romanticized her story. For example, the 1955 movie *The Far Horizons*, which starred Donna Reed in "yellow-face" makeup, introduced the fictional plotline of a romance between Sacajawea and William Clark. Over time, she has evolved to serve as a symbol of friendly relations between the U.S. government and Native Americans. In 2000, she was given the U.S. Mint's ultimate honor when it released the Sacajawea Golden Dollar. At the same time, though, the Mint's website incorrectly states that she "guided the adventurers from the Northern Great Plains to the Pacific Ocean and back."

## The Real Sacajawea

The only facts known about Sacajawea come from the journals of Lewis and Clark's expedition team. According to these, we know that she did not translate for the group—with the exception of a few occasions when they encountered other Shoshone. But because she did not speak English, she served as more of a go-between for her husband, the explorers, and members of other tribes they encountered in their travels. Concerning her knowledge of a route to the Pacific, Lewis and Clark knew far more about the land than she did. Only when they reached the area occupied by her own people was she able to point out a few landmarks, but they were not of any great help.

This isn't to say that she did not make important contributions to the journey's success. Journals note that Sacajawea was a great help to the team when she took it upon herself to rescue essential medicines and supplies that had been washed into a river. Her knowledge of edible roots and plants was invaluable when game and other sources of food were hard to come by. Most important, Sacajawea served as a sort of human peace symbol. Her presence reassured the various Native American groups who encountered Lewis and Clark that the explorers' intentions were peaceful. No Native American woman, especially one with a baby on her back, would have been part of a war party.

There are two very different accounts of Sacajawea's death. Although some historical documents say she died in South Dakota in 1812, Shoshone oral tradition claims she lived until 1884 and died in Wyoming. Regardless of differing interpretaions of her life and death, Sacajawea will always be a heroine of American history.

# The Earl of Sandwich's Favorite Snack

*The famed English statesman John Montagu named, but did not invent, the sandwich.*

✳ ✳ ✳ ✳

LEGEND HOLDS THAT Montagu, the Fourth Earl of Sandwich, invented the tasty foodstuff that is his namesake. Montagu was a popular member of England's peerage in the 18th century, and it seems he had a knack for converting nouns into homage to his rank. The Hawaiian Islands were once known as the Sandwich Islands, thanks to explorer James Cook's admiration for the earl, who was the acting First Lord of Admirality at the time. And although it does seem likely that Montagu is responsible for dubbing the popular food item a "sandwich," he certainly was not the first to squash some grub between slices of bread.

## A Sandwich by Any Other Name

It seems likely that sandwiches of one sort or another were eaten whenever and wherever bread was made. When utensils weren't available, bread was often used to scoop up other foods. Arabs stuffed pita bread with meats, and medieval European peasants lunched on bread and cheese while working in the fields. The first officially recorded sandwich inventor was Rabbi Hillel the Elder of the first century BC. The rabbi sandwiched chopped nuts, apples, spices, and wine between two pieces of matzoh, creating the popular Passover food known as charoset.

In medieval times, food piled on bread was the norm—prior to the fork, it was common to scoop meat and other food onto pieces of bread and spread it around with a knife. The leftover pieces of bread, called "trenchers," were often fed to pets when the meal was complete.

Primary sources from the 16th and 17th centuries refer to handheld snacks as "bread and meat" or "bread and cheese." People often ate sandwiches; they simply didn't call them that.

## It Is Named—Therefore It Is?

Regardless of the sandwichlike foods that were eaten prior to the 18th century, it appears that the Fourth Earl of Sandwich is responsible for the emergence of the sandwich as a distinct food category—but how this happened is unclear. The most popular story relates to Montagu's fondness for eating salted beef between pieces of toasted bread. Montagu was also known for his gambling habit and would apparently eat this proto-sandwich one-handed during his endless hours at a famous London gambling club. His comrades began to request "the same as Sandwich," and eventually the snack acquired its name.

The source that supports this story is *Tour to London*, a travel book that was popular at the time among the upper echelons of society. In one passage, the author of the book, Pierre Jean Grosley, claimed that in 1765, "a minister of state passed four and twenty hours at a public gaming-table, so absorpt in play that, during the whole time, he had no subsistence but a bit of beef between two slices of toasted bread. This new dish grew highly in vogue . . . it was called by the name of the minister who invented it." According to this scenario, "sandwich" initially referred to Montagu's preferred beef-and-bread meal and was subsequently used as an umbrella phrase for any variety of sandwich types.

## Hard Work and Hunger

John Montagu's biographer, N. A. M. Rodger, offers an alternate explanation for the rise of the sandwich. He argues that during the 1760s, when the sandwich was first called a sandwich, the earl was actually very busy with government responsibilities and didn't have time to gamble much. He did, however, spend many late evenings working at his desk, during which time he liked to sustain himself with beef and bread. It is possible, Rodger argues, that the sandwich came to be as a reference to the earl's tireless work ethic and general fondness for late-night snacking.

# Ahead of His Time

*It's long been claimed that Dr. Joseph-Ignace Guillotin, the presumed creator of the guillotine, was put to death during the French Revolution by the decapitating contraption that bears his name. It would be the ultimate irony—if the story were true.*

✳ ✳ ✳ ✳

**B**EFORE WE TAKE a closer look at this long-lived myth, we should probably clear up an even larger misconception: Joseph Guillotin did not invent the guillotine. Mechanical beheading devices had long been used in Germany, Italy, Scotland, and elsewhere, though it was the French who made them (in)famous.

## The Good Doctor

Guillotin, a respected physician and member of the French National Assembly, opposed the death penalty. However, he realized that public executions weren't about to go out of style anytime soon, so he sought a more "humane" alternative to being drawn and quartered, which was the usual way that impoverished criminals were put to death.

A quick beheading, Guillotin argued, was far more merciful than being hacked apart by an ax. And it had the added benefit of making executions socially equal, since beheading had been, until that time, the method of execution only for aristocratic convicts who could buy themselves a quicker, kinder death.

Guillotin teamed with German engineer and harpsichord maker Tobias Schmidt, who built a prototype of the guillotine as we know it today. For a smoother cut, Schmidt suggested a diagonal blade rather than the traditional round blade.

## Heads Will Roll

The guillotine's heyday followed the French Revolution in 1789. After King Louis XVI had been imprisoned, the new civilian assembly rewrote the penal code to make beheading by guillotine the official method of execution for all convicted criminals—and there were a lot of them.

The first person to lose his head was Nicolas Jacques Pelletie, who was guillotined at Place de Greve on April 25, 1792. King Louis XVI felt the blade a year later, and thousands more followed. The last person to be publicly guillotined was convicted murderer Hamida Djandoubi, who died on September 10, 1977, in Marseilles.

Joseph Guillotin survived the French Revolution with his head attached, though he was forever stigmatized by his connection with the notorious killing machine. He died in 1814 from an infected carbuncle on his shoulder, and his children later petitioned the government for the right to change their last name, not wanting to be associated with their father's grisly past.

A common belief often associated with the guillotine is that people who are beheaded remain conscious for several agonizing seconds—and even respond to stimulus. Whether or not this is true remains open to debate. Many scientists believe that death is almost instantaneous, while others cite anecdotal evidence that suggests the deceased are well aware of what has happened to them.

Indeed, stories abound of "experiments" during the height of the guillotine boom in which doctors and others made agreements with condemned prisoners to determine once and for all if the head "lived" on for moments after being severed.

One story claims that Charlotte Corday, who was guillotined for killing Jean-Paul Marat, looked indignant when the executioner held her severed head aloft and slapped her across the face. However, it was also claimed that her cheeks reddened as a result of the slap, which seems unlikely given the loss of blood. It's been said that other severed heads have blinked or moved their eyes when spoken to, and some have allegedly bitten their executioners.

Most doctors agree that the brain may remain active for as long as 15 seconds after a beheading. Whether the individual is actually aware of what has transpired remains a medical mystery that likely will never be answered.

# History's Little Mystery

*Where's Napoleon's, uh, "little Napoleon"?*

✳  ✳  ✳  ✳

### *Au Revoir,* Napoleon

AFTER HIS MILITARY defeat, French general Napoleon Bonaparte died in exile on the remote island of St. Helena in 1821. Seventeen people attended his autopsy, including Bonaparte's doctor, several of his aides, and a priest.

As one version of the story goes, at some point during the autopsy, Napoleon's penis was removed and put aside to keep for posterity. While there are some historians who find this implausible, the fact remains that about 30 years later, one of Napoleon's aides published a memoir in which he claims to have helped remove several of Bonaparte's body parts.

### The Fate of the Relic

In 1924, a collector from Philadelphia named A. S. W. Rosenbach purchased a collection of Napoleon artifacts for about $2,000. Among the items he purchased was a "mummified tendon taken from Napoleon's body during the postmortem." Upon further inspection and research, Rosenbach declared the tendon was definitely the leader's penis.

Three years later, Rosenbach put the item on display in New York, and thousands of people viewed the penis under a glass case. The descriptions weren't kind; some likened the relic to "a shriveled seahorse" or "beef jerky." All the accounts have one thing in common: The item was a bit on the small side.

Oddly, the French government was wholly uninterested in the collection. And to this day, it refuses to even acknowledge the possibility of the object's authenticity, further casting doubt on whether or not the object is actually Napoleon's "little general."

In the late 1970s, a urologist and professor from Columbia University purchased the penis for about $3,000 at an auction. Whether or not it's actually the genuine article is still up for debate. Until scientists get their, er, hands on it, the public will just have to speculate about this odd collectible.

# Reward: One Lost Island

*Did the legendary island of Atlantis ever really exist? Or did Plato make the whole thing up?*

✳    ✳    ✳    ✳

IT'S HARD TO believe that Plato, an early Greek philosopher, was the type to start rumors. But in two of his dialogues, *Timaeus* and *Critias*, he refers to what has become one of the most famous legends of all time: the doomed island of Atlantis.

In *Timaeus*, Plato uses a story told by Critias to describe where Atlantis existed, explaining that it "came forth out of the Atlantic Ocean, for in those days the Atlantic was navigable; and there was an island situated in front of the straits which are by you called the Pillars of Heracles; the island was larger than Libya and Asia put together, and was the way to other islands ." Not only that, but Plato also divulges the details of its fate: "afterwards there occurred violent earthquakes and floods; and in a single day and night of misfortune all your warlike men in a body sank into the earth, and the island of Atlantis in like manner disappeared in the depths of the sea. For which reason the sea in those parts is impassable and impenetrable, because there is a shoal of mud in the way; and this was caused by the subsidence of the island." In *Critias*, the story revolves around Poseidon, the mythical god of the sea, and how the kingdom of Atlantis attempted to conquer Athens.

Although many ascribe Plato's myth to his desire for a way to emphasize his own political theories, historians and writers perpetuated the idea of the mythical island for centuries, both in fiction and nonfiction. After the Middle Ages, the story of the doomed civilization was revisited by such writers as Francis Bacon, who published *The New Atlantis* in 1627. In 1870, Jules Verne published his classic *Twenty Thousand Leagues Under the Sea*, which includes a visit to sunken Atlantis aboard Captain Nemo's submarine *Nautilus*. And in 1882, *Atlantis: The Antediluvian World* by Ignatius Donnelly was written to prove that Atlantis did exist—initiating much of the Atlantis mania that has occurred since that time. The legendary Atlantis continues to surface in today's science fiction, romantic fantasy, and even mystery stories.

More recently, historians and geologists have attempted to link Atlantis to the island of Santorini (also called Thera) in the Aegean Sea. About 3,600 years ago, one of the largest eruptions ever witnessed by humans occurred at the site of Santorini: the Minoa, or Thera, eruption. This caused the volcano to collapse, creating a huge caldera or "hole" at the top of the volcanic mountain. Historians believe the eruption caused the end of the Minoan civilization on Thera and the nearby island of Crete, most likely because a tsunami resulted from the massive explosion. Since that time, most of the islands, which are actually a complex of overlapping shield volcanoes, grew from subsequent volcanic eruptions around the caldera, creating what is now the volcanic archipelago of islands called the Cycladic group.

Could this tourist hot spot truly be the site of the mythological island Atlantis? Some say that Plato's description of the palace and surroundings at Atlantis were similar to those at Knossos, the central ceremonial and cultural center of the Minoan civilization. On the scientific end, geologists know that eruptions such as the one at Santorini can pump huge volumes of material into the air and slump other parts of a volcanic island into the oceans. To the ancient peoples, such an event could literally be translated as an island quickly sinking into the ocean. But even after centuries of study, excavation, and speculation, the mystery of Atlantis remains unsolved.

Dan Brown's blockbuster novel *The Da Vinci Code* reignited public interest in Atlantis in a roundabout way. Brown's story referenced the Knights Templar, an early Christian military order with a dramatic history that involved bloodshed, exile, and secrets—one of which was that they were carriers of ancient wisdom from the lost city of Atlantis.

# Aztalan: A Prehistoric Puzzle

*A millennium ago, a vanished people ruled Wisconsin.*

✳ ✳ ✳ ✳

## A Mysterious Site

AZTALAN IS A fortified settlement of mysterious outsiders who worshiped the sun. The Middle Mississippian culture erected stepped pyramids, may have practiced cannibalism, and enjoyed coast-to-coast trade. Some have linked the Mississippians to the Aztecs and even to the legendary city of Atlantis. All that is truly certain is that they lived at Aztalan for 150 years. Then they disappeared.

Aztalan, near present-day Lake Mills, is now a state park and, in fact, a National Historic Landmark. Still, what happened at Aztalan and the truth about the people who lived there are among the greatest archaeological puzzles in the world.

Aztalan is ancient. During the period when it was settled, sometime between AD 1050 and 1100, gunpowder was invented in China. Macbeth ruled Scotland. The Orthodox and Roman Catholic churches split. In America, across the Mississippi from St. Louis in what is now Illinois, there was a strange, 2,000-acre city of earthen pyramids later dubbed "Cahokia." Its population was roughly 20,000—more than London at that time.

Aztalan appears to be the northern outpost of the Cahokia peoples. Because of location, archaeologists call their civilization Middle Mississippian. They are distinct from the Woodland peoples, who were there first and remained afterward. The Mississippians were quite enamored with the sun, and at Cahokia, residents erected wooden solar observatories, similar to Britain's Stonehenge.

Like Cahokia, Aztalan was a truly mystifying place: 22 acres surrounded by a stockade with 32 watch towers, all made from heavy timbers and then covered with hard clay. Inside, pyramidal mounds stood as high as 16 feet. Outside the fortifications, crops were planted. According to experts, the Mississippians are responsible for bringing corn to North America.

Today, Aztalan looks much different than it did at its peak. The mounds remain, and part of the stockade has been rebuilt. Also, the Friends of Aztalan group is trying to recreate antique agriculture with a small garden of gourds, squash, sunflowers, and an early type of corn, all planted just as the Mississippians would have.

In addition to vegetables, the Mississippian diet may have included some more interesting dishes—namely human flesh. At Cahokia there's evidence of human sacrifice, and since the time of Aztalan's discovery by whites in 1836, it has been thought that its residents practiced at least some sort of cannibalism. But science and interpretations change with time. There is speculation that the so-called "cannibalism" could have simply been a ceremonial or funerary practice that had nothing to do with eating human flesh.

## Gone with No Trace

Another puzzle is why the Mississippians suddenly vanished from the Midwest sometime between AD 1200 and 1300. Answers both mundane and cataclysmic have been suggested. Author Frank Joseph has taken the folklore of three continents and concocted a fanciful theory that links Atlantis, Aztalan, and the Aztecs in his books, *The Lost Pyramids of Rock Lake* and *Atlantis in Wisconsin*. Joseph's contention is that the people of Atlantis founded Cahokia and Aztalan, mined copper, cast it into ingots, and shipped it back, fueling Europe's Bronze Age. After a cataclysm destroyed their Mediterranean island empire, the leaderless survivors in the Wisconsin settlement migrated south. They eventually created a new Aztalan in Mexico and became the Aztecs.

The Aztecs themselves referred to their far-away, long-ago homeland—wherever it was—as "Aztlan." However, scholars deny that residents of Aztalan ever used that name. It was merely a fanciful label applied by European settlers.

Joseph's evidence is circumstantial but admittedly fascinating. One of the great mysteries of Europe's Bronze Age is where all the necessary copper came from (bronze is made of copper and tin). Known low-grade deposits in Great Britain and Spain would have been quickly exhausted. Yet Lake Superior's shores have, and had, the only known workable virgin, native copper deposits in the world.

The Mississippians certainly knew that—they mined Michigan's Upper Peninsula. Meanwhile, according to legend, Atlantis was reigning supreme, enjoying great wealth derived from its trade throughout the known world of precious metals, especially copper. The Lake Superior mines closed precisely when Europe's Bronze Age ended. Coincidentally, or perhaps not, it was at this time that Atlantis supposedly sank and disappeared forever.

Many more answers about the Mississippian culture are yet be found. According to the Cahokia Mounds Museum Society, archaeologists have explored only a fraction of the sprawling site. Could it be that the decisive link to Atlantis or the Aztecs is still buried beneath the grounds of Cahokia or Aztalan? Only time will tell.

* As the name suggests, Mississippian culture spanned the length of the Mississippi River, including areas in what are now the states of Mississippi, Georgia, Alabama, Missouri, Arkansas, Illinois, Indiana, Kentucky, Ohio, Wisconsin, and Minnesota.

* It must have been desirable real estate! While Aztalan is usually considered to be a Mississippian settlement, there are many artifacts at the site from other groups of people that predate their arrival.

* For many years before it was studied and preserved, the area of Aztalan was plowed for farming; pottery and other artifacts were carted away by souvenir hunters.

* Aztalan became a National Historic Landmark in 1964 and was added to the National Register of Historic Places in 1966.

* There is speculation that some of the mounds at Aztalan could have been used for astronomical purposes.

* It is believed that Aztalan was a planned community with spaces for the general public, ceremonial locations, residential areas, and sections designated for elite individuals.

* Based on the artifacts unearthed at Aztalan, it appears that the people living there were skilled at farming, hunting, and fishing.

# The Mystery of Easter Island

*On Easter Sunday in 1722, a Dutch ship landed on a small island 2,300 miles from the coast of South America. Polynesian explorers had preceded them by a thousand years or more, and the Europeans found the descendants of those early visitors still living on the island. They also found a strange collection of almost 900 enormous stone heads, or moai, standing with their backs to the sea, gazing across the island with eyes hewn out of coral. The image of those faces haunts visitors to this day.*

✳   ✳   ✳   ✳

## Ancestors at the End of the Land

EASTER ISLAND LEGEND tells of the great Chief Hotu Matu'a, the Great Parent, striking out from Polynesia in a canoe, taking his family on a voyage across the trackless ocean in search of a new home. He made landfall on Te-Pito-te-Henua, the End of the Land, sometime between AD 400 and 700. Finding the island well-suited to habitation, his descendants spread out to cover much of the island, living off the natural bounty of the land and sea.

With their survival assured, they built *ahu*—ceremonial sites featuring a large stone mound—and on them erected moai, which were representations of notable chieftains who led the island over the centuries. The moai weren't literal depictions of their ancestors, but rather embodied their spirit, or mana, and conferred blessings and protection on the islanders.

The construction of these moai was quite a project. A hereditary class of sculptors oversaw the main quarry, located near one of the volcanic mountains on the island. Groups of people would request a moai for their local ahu, and the sculptors would go to work, their efforts supported by gifts of food and other goods. Over time, they created 887 of the stone moai, averaging just over 13 feet tall and weighing around 14 tons, but ranging from one extreme of just under four feet tall to a behemoth that towered 71 feet. The moai were then transported across the island by a mechanism that still remains in doubt, but that may have involved rolling them on the trunks of palm trees felled for that purpose—a technique that was to have terrible repercussions for the islanders.

When Europeans first made landfall on Easter Island, they found an island full of standing moai. Fifty-two years later, James Cook reported that many of the statues had been toppled, and by the 1830s none were left standing. What's more, the statues hadn't just been knocked over; many of them had boulders placed at strategic locations, with the intention of decapitating the moai when they were pulled down. What was going on?

## A Culture on the Brink

It turns out the original Dutch explorers had encountered a culture on the rebound. At the time of their arrival, they found two or three thousand living on the island, but some estimates put the population as high as fifteen thousand a century before. The story of the islanders' decline is one in which many authors find a cautionary tale: The people simply consumed natural resources to the point where their land could no longer support them. For a millennium, the islanders simply took what they needed: They fished, collected bird eggs, and chopped down trees to pursue their obsession with building moai. By the 1600s, life had changed: The last forests on the island disappeared, and the islanders' traditional foodstuffs disappeared from the archaeological record. Local tradition tells of a time of famine and even rumored cannibalism, and it is from this time that island history reveals the appearance of the spear. Tellingly, the Polynesian words for "wood" begin to take on a connotation of wealth, a meaning found nowhere else that shares the language. Perhaps worst of all, with their forests gone, the islanders had no material to make the canoes that would have allowed them to leave their island in search of resources. They were trapped, and they turned on one another.

The Europeans found a reduced society that had just emerged from this time of terror. The respite was short-lived, however. The arrival of the foreigners seems to have come at a critical moment in the history of Easter Island. Either coincidentally or spurred on by the strangers, a warrior class seized power across the island, and different groups vied for power. Villages were burned, their resources taken by the victors, and the defeated left to starve. The warfare also led to the toppling of an enemy's moai—whether to capture their mana or simply prevent it from being used against the opposing faction. In the end, none of the moai remained standing.

## Downfall and Rebound

The troubles of Easter Island weren't limited to self-inflicted chaos. The arrival of the white man also introduced smallpox and syphilis; the islanders, with little natural immunity to the exotic diseases, fared no better than native populations elsewhere. As if that weren't enough, other ships arrived, collecting slaves for work in South America. The internal fighting and external pressure combined to reduce the number of native islanders to little more than a hundred by 1877—the last survivors of a people who once enjoyed a tropical paradise.

Easter Island, or Rapa Nui, was annexed by Chile in 1888. As of 2009, there are 4,781 people living on the island. There are projects underway to raise the fallen moai. As of today, approximately 50 have been returned to their former glory.

# The Fast-Draw Myth

*A deeply ingrained image of the Wild West is that of two men approaching each other with hands on their gun butts, determined to prove who can draw and fire faster. Exciting stuff, but it seldom happened that way.*

✳   ✳   ✳   ✳

I N THIS CLASSIC showdown, usually outside the town saloon, the two scowling scoundrels stand motionless. After a blur of movement and two nearly simultaneous gunshots, one man drops, hit by the first bullet. Variations of this scenario include one gunman shooting his adversary in the hand or, with even greater sportsmanship, letting his opponent draw first.

In 1865, Wild Bill Hickok and Dave Tutt met in front of an expectant crowd for a prearranged pistol duel in Springfield, Missouri. At a distance of 75 yards, Tutt fired and missed. Hickok steadied his revolver with his left hand and triggered a slug into Tutt's heart. It's a stereotypical depiction, but this sort of face-off was actually uncommon.

In Western gunfights, the primary consideration was accuracy, not speed. Gunfighters usually didn't even carry their weapons in holsters. Pistols were shoved into hip pockets or waistbands, and a rifle or shotgun was usually preferred over a handgun. A study of almost 600 shootouts indicates that in one gunfight after another, men emptied their weapons at their adversaries without hitting anyone (except, perhaps, for a luckless bystander) or inflicting only minor wounds.

During the first decade of the 20th century, Westerns became a staple of the burgeoning film industry. Hollywood pounced on the handful of duels such as Hickok versus Tutt, and soon the fast-draw contest became an integral part of the genre. Like modern detective films without car chases, Westerns were incomplete without fast-draw duels.

# Labor of Love: The Taj Mahal

*Known as one of the Wonders of the World, the Taj Mahal was a shrine to love and one man's obsession. Today an average of three million tourists a year travel to see what the United Nations has declared a World Heritage site.*

✳  ✳  ✳  ✳

## Taj Mahal: Foundations

THE MUGHAL (OR "Mogul") Empire occupied India from the mid-1500s to the early 1800s. At the height of its success, this imperial power controlled most of the Indian subcontinent and much of what is now Afghanistan, containing a population of around 150 million people.

During this era, a young prince named Khurram took the throne in 1628, succeeding his father. Six years prior, after a military victory Khurram was given the title Shah Jahan by his emperor father. Now, with much of the subcontinent at his feet, the title was apt: *Shah Jahan* is Persian for "King of the World."

## When Khurram Met Arjumand

Being shah had a lot of fringe benefits—banquets, treasures, and multiple wives, among other things. Shah Jahan did have several wives, but one woman stood out from the rest. When he was age 15, he was betrothed to 14-year-old Arjumand Banu Begam. Her beauty and compassion knocked the emperor-to-be off his feet; five years later, they were married. The bride took the title of *Mumtaz Mahal,* which means, according to various translations, "Chosen One of the Palace," "Exalted One of the Palace," or "Beloved Ornament of the Palace."

Court historians recorded the couple's close friendship and intimate relationship. They traveled extensively together, Mumtaz often accompanying her husband on his military jaunts. But tragedy struck in 1631, when on one of these trips, Mumtaz died giving birth to what would have been their 14th child.

## Breaking Ground

Devastated, Shah Jahan began work that year on what would become the Taj Mahal, a monument to his wife and their ever-lasting love. While there were surely many hands on deck for the planning of the Taj, the architect who is most often credited is Ustad Ahmad Lahori. The project took until 1648 to complete and enlisted the labor of 20,000 workers and 1,000 elephants. The structure and surrounding grounds covers 42 acres. Here are the basic parts of Mumtaz's giant mausoleum.

**The Gardens:** To get to the structural parts of the Taj Mahal, one must cross the enormous gardens surrounding it. Following classic Persian garden design, the grounds to the south of the buildings are made up of four sections divided by marble canals (reflecting pools) with adjacent pathways. The gardens stretch from the main gateway to the foot of the Taj.

**The Main Gateway:** Made of red sandstone and standing 100 feet high and 150 feet wide, it is composed of a central arch with towers attached to each of its corners. The walls are richly adorned with calligraphy and arabesques inlaid with gemstones.

**The Tomb:** Unlike most Mughal mausoleums, Mumtaz's tomb is placed at the north end of the Taj Mahal, above the river and in between the mosque and the guesthouse. The tomb is entirely sheathed in white marble with an exterior dome that is almost 250 feet above ground level. The effect is impressive: Depending on the light at various times of the day, the tomb can appear pink, white, or brilliant gold.

**The Mosque and the Jawab:** On either side of the great tomb lie two smaller buildings. One is a mosque, and the other is called the *jawab*, or "answer." The mosque was used as a place of worship; the jawab was often used as a guesthouse. Both buildings are made of red sandstone so as not to take away too much from the grandeur of the tomb. The shah's monument to the love of his life still stands, and still awes, more than 360 years later.

# Chapter 7

# Fringeworthy: Not-So-Secret Societies

## Hey, It's the Freemasons!

*For many, talk of "Freemasonry" conjures up images of intricate handshakes, strange rituals, and harsh punishment for revealing secrets about either. In actuality, the roots of the order are brotherhood and generosity. Throughout the ages, Masons have been known to fiercely protect their members and the unique features of their society.*

✳   ✳   ✳   ✳

THE FANTASTICALLY NAMED Most Ancient and Honorable Society of Free and Accepted Masons began like other guilds; it was a collection of artisans brought together by their common trade, in this case, stone cutting and crafting. (There are many speculations as to when the society first began. Some believe it dates back to when King Solomon's temple was built. Others believe the guild first formed in Scotland in the 16th century.) The Freemasons made the welfare of their members a priority. Group elders devised strict work regulations for masons, whose skills were always in demand and were sometimes taken advantage of.

Organized Freemasonry emerged in Great Britain in the mid-17th century with the firm establishment of Grand Lodges and smaller, local Lodges. (No one overarching body governs

Freemasonry as a whole, though lodges worldwide are usually linked either to England or France.) In 1730, transplanted Englishmen established the first American Lodge in Virginia, followed in 1733 by the continent's first chartered and opened Grand Lodge in Massachusetts. Boasting early American members including George Washington, Benjamin Franklin, and John Hancock, Freemasonry played a part in the growth of the young nation in ways that gradually attracted curiosity, speculation, and concern.

The source of the organization's mysterious reputation lay partly in its secrecy: Masons were prohibited from revealing secrets (some believed Masons would be violently punished if they revealed secrets, though the Masons deny such rumors). The Masonic bond also emphasized a commitment to one another. Outsiders feared the exclusivity smacked of conspiracy and compromised the motives of Masons appointed to juries or elected to public office. And nonmembers wondered about the meanings of the Freemasons' peculiar traditions (such as code words and other secretive forms of recognition between members) and symbolism (often geometric shapes or tools, such as the square and compass). Design elements of the one-dollar bill, including the Great Seal and the "all-seeing eye," have been credited to founding fathers such as Charles Thomson and other Masons.

Freemasonry in the United States suffered a serious blow in September 1826 when New York Masons abducted a former "brother" named William Morgan. Morgan was about to publish a book of Masonic secrets, but before he could, he was instead ushered north to the Canadian border and, in all likelihood, thrown into the Niagara River.

His disappearance led to the arrest and conviction of three men on kidnapping charges (Morgan's body was never found)—scant penalties, locals said, for crimes that surely included murder.

The affair increased suspicion of the brotherhood, spawning an American Anti-Mason movement and even a political party dedicated to keeping Freemasons out of national office.

In the decades following the Civil War, men were again drawn to brotherhood and fellowship as they searched for answers in a turbulent age, and Freemasonry slowly regained popularity. Today, Freemasonry remains an order solidly devoted to its own members, charitable causes, and the betterment of society. It has a worldwide membership of at least five million. Its members are traditionally male, though certain associations now permit women.

Despite the name, most members are not stonemasons. They are, however, required to have faith in a supreme being, but not necessarily the Christian god (Mohammed, Buddha, and so forth are all acceptable).

# Now They Have to Kill Us: The Bavarian Illuminati

*Before delving into the intricacies of the Illuminati's origin, we'd recommend donning a tinfoil hat and cape. It will protect you against the New World Order conspiracy.*

**Q: What does Illuminati actually mean?**

A: "The Enlightened." Like many religious faiths and secret societies, the original Bavarian Illuminati were founded in search of enlightenment. Prior groups with similar ideas used similar names.

**Q: Did earlier Illuminati groups evolve into the Bavarian Illuminati?**

A: Well, let's examine some earlier groups. Spain's Alumbrados ("enlightened") dated to the time of Columbus (1490s), suffered from the Inquisition, and developed a following in France (as the Illuminés) that endured until the late 1700s, when the

French Revolution sat on them. The Rosicrucians started in Germany in the early 1600s, claiming lineage from the Knights Templar; by the late 1770s, their theme was becoming increasingly Egyptian. Many Rosicrucians were also Freemasons, a group with unbroken lineage to the present day.

They all had ideas in common with the Bavarian Illuminati; however, the Bavarian Illuminati sprang from the fertile mind of an iconoclastic law professor, not from a previous group. At most, the Bavarian group experienced some cross-pollination with other similar groups (notably Freemasonry), but that doesn't equal ancestral continuity.

**Q: How'd the Bavarian group get going?**

A: It began in Ingolstadt, Bavaria, with a German 20-something named Adam Weishaupt. In 1775, Weishaupt accepted a natural and canon law professorship at the University of Ingolstadt that had recently been vacated by an ejected Jesuit.

Weishaupt was a maverick prone to anticlerical utterances: the anti-Jesuit, if you will. He soon managed to convince himself, without irony, that he was destined to lead humanity out of superstition toward enlightenment. Unsurprisingly, the Jesuits hated his guts.

Evidently, Weishaupt couldn't afford the Masons' fees, so he launched the Perfectibilists (later the Bavarian Illuminati) on May 1, 1776 (this would later fuel plentiful conspiracy theories about May Day celebrations). Fascinated with Egyptian stuff, he assigned his society a pyramid as its symbol.

**Q: Did this group extend tentacles into business, government, and church?**

A: To extend tentacles, one must first possess some. The Illuminati concerned themselves mostly with secret degrees and titles, plus absolute obedience to the chain of command with Weishaupt at the top. There is no evidence the group ever controlled anything. Illuminati were supposed to spurn superstition and strive toward rationalism to help perfect each other's mentalities. The meta-goal was clearing the earth of inhumanity and stupidity, or, as Weishaupt put it, "to create a state of liberty and moral equality, freed from the obstacles which subordination, rank, and riches, continually throw in our way." It actually sounds more than a little like modern Scientology, at least in terms of stated goals (as opposed to reality).

**Q: That sounds like the vision of a new world order.**

A: It is. The modern conspiracy question rests not in the nature of the original Bavarian Illuminati, which is well documented, but rather to what degree it has survived to exert control over modern affairs. As any nightly news broadcast will show, their work didn't make a lasting dent in either inhumanity or stupidity.

**Q: Why not?**

A: Could it be because inhumanity and stupidity are so very human? Think of the Illuminati as a crucible intended to mint enlightened persons. This crucible possessed one fundamental crack: Its concept of enlightenment categorically discouraged questioning the autocratic leader. That's no way to run a freethinkers' group. In such groups, true freethinkers drift away, leaving only quasi-freethinkers who don't argue with the Maximum Leader.

**Q: But the organization still grew. Why?**

A: It only grew for a brief time, and that had much to do with the work of Baron Adolph Knigge, who joined in the 1780s. Knigge was both well-known and a capable administrator who gave the Illuminati a great deal of practical Masonic wisdom, helping sort out Weishaupt's rather rinky-dink organization. By its peak in 1784, it had several thousand members.

**Q: What sent it downhill?**

A: First there was the inevitable squabble between Weishaupt and Knigge, which ended with Knigge telling Weishaupt where to shove his little fiefdom. It's tempting to blame the whole thing on Weishaupt, but the evidence indicates that Knigge had an ego to match Weishaupt's and could be just as great a horse's posterior. The deathblow came when Duke Karl Theodor of Bavaria banned all unauthorized secret societies.

**Q: Did that simply shatter the organism into many pieces that grew independently?**

A: Evidence suggests that the ban, plus police raids, shattered the Illuminati into dying pieces rather than living ones. Sacked from teaching, Weishaupt fled to a neighboring state and died in obscurity.

Others tried to keep Illuminati islets alive, without apparent success. Like witchcraft of an earlier age, the actual practice became far rarer than the accusation—and official paranoia over dangerous secret societies and sedition kept the term Illuminati cropping up.

**Q: So, why does the intrigue linger?**

A: Perhaps for the same reason the Freemasons, Knights Templar, and so forth keep showing up in conspiracy theories: When someone wants to point to a potential conspiracy, he or she can usually find some bit of circumstantial evidence hinting a connection to one of the above. Those who disagree, of course, must be toadies of the conspiracy! It's an argument that can't end.

But insofar as we are guided by actual evidence, the Bavarian Illuminati did end. Whatever world conspiracies there might be today, it's doubtful any descend directly from Weishaupt's ideological treehouse club.

# Wicca: That Good Ol' Time Religion?

*Until Wicca grew more popular in the 1990s, many people had never even heard of it. Even among Wiccans the debate continues to percolate: How old is this, really?*

✴  ✴  ✴  ✴

## Definitions

To study the genesis of the religious and magical practice of Wicca, one must be sure not to confuse "Wicca" with "witchcraft." Not all witches are Wiccan; Wicca is a nature religion that can involve the practice of witchcraft.

## Antiquity

Throughout human existence, most cultures have had populations that might be considered "witches": esoteric specialists, such as midwives or herbalists, or people claiming spiritual contacts or divinatory skill. To believe someone a witch is to believe that person is able to foresee or change outcomes. Some cultures fear and hate witches; others embrace them. We might call them folk practitioners, shamans, or witch doctors. Wicca cannot demonstrate descent from such folk practitioners, but it draws much inspiration from old Celtic and English folk practice and religion.

During the worst medieval persecutions, Christian leaders slew thousands of Europeans over witchcraft accusations. Many of that era's popular definitions of witchcraft were hardly credible because the persecutors themselves wrote them. They equated witchcraft with diabolism simply because if it wasn't Christian, it had to be Satanic.

Evidence suggests that the persecutions had little to do with witchcraft but much to do with vendettas, estate seizures (especially of affluent widows), and the governmental need for a group enemy on which to focus public anger. Some Wiccans claim that Wicca endured in secret among the most skilled survivors of these persecutions. Unfortunately, there's no evidence that recognizable Wicca existed during "the Burning Times" in the first place, so survival is moot.

## Victorian Renaissance

Interest in secret societies and the occult grew in Europe in the 19th century. With admiration of ancient Greco-Roman philosophy grew admiration of ancient divinity concepts—including a feminine divine presence or, more bluntly, the idea of God as a woman. While that notion revolted many Judeo-Christian traditionalists, others found it appealing.

By the early 1900s, several British occult organizations and movements drew upon and combined pre-Christian religious ideas and magical theory. Some groups were simply excuses to party, whereas others were stuffy study groups. Others blurred the distinctions or went back and forth. While none were visibly Wiccan, they would later help to inspire Wicca.

## Gardner

During the 1930s, an English civil servant named Gerald B. Gardner developed a strong interest in the occult. Some sources claim that socialite Dorothy Clutterbuck had initiated him into a witches' coven, but that's doubtful because Mrs. Clutterbuck was widely known as a devout Anglican. More likely, his initiation came from a woman known only as "Dafo," who later distanced herself from occultism.

Wherever Gardner learned his witching, he definitely ran with it. In the early 1950s, Gardner began popularizing a duotheistic (the god/the goddess) synthesis of religion and magic that he inititally called "Wica." Why then? Well, in 1951, Parliament repealed the 1735 Witchcraft Act, so it was now legal. Wicca borrowed all over the place, creating a tradition of eclecticism that thrives today.

## Buckland

When Wicca came to America with Gardner's student Raymond Buckland in 1964, its timing was impeccable. For Wicca, the 1960s counterculture was rich soil worthy of a fertility goddess. Today, self-described "eclectic Wiccans"— Wiccans who essentially define their own Wicca to suit themselves—probably outnumber Gardnerians, a group one might fairly call "orthodox Wiccans."

Rough estimates place the number of Wiccans in the United States today between 200,000 and 500,000.

# The IRA and Sinn Féin

*The Irish Republican Army (IRA) and its political body, Sinn Féin, are two of the most controversial institutions in Ireland. Deciphering their history is like trying to trace the lineages of the old European monarchies—there are countless crossbreedings, divergences, and circuitously snaking twists along the way.*

✳   ✳   ✳   ✳

## Back to the Beginning

THE ENGLISH INFILTRATION of Ireland began in AD 1170, when the Normans, who had already colonized England, decided to make Ireland a part of their kingdom. In the following centuries, the Irish increasingly adopted the customs, system of government, and language of their English neighbors. For the Irish clans that continued to rule and practice their customs, English dominion was a constant threat.

Since the northern tip of Ireland is the farthest from England, the population there retained a culture distinct from the southern areas of the island. But in the early 1600s, Queen Elizabeth I established the Plantation of Ulster in Northern Ireland, and colonists from England, Scotland, and Wales flooded the land. The native Irish Catholics in Ulster were forced to the margins of society.

Thus began the sectarian struggle in Northern Ireland that continued for centuries. The largely Protestant descendants of the colonization of Ulster fought—militarily, culturally, ideologically—with the largely Catholic descendants of the area's original inhabitants. It was within this inflammatory context that the IRA and Sinn Féin emerged.

## The Early Days of Sinn Féin and the IRA

According to Irish political lingo, those who seek a united Ireland free from English rule are called *nationalists*, while those who desire continued political allegiance with England are called *unionists*. Sinn Féin was founded as a political party in 1905 by a nationalist who wanted Ireland to establish its own monarchy. During this period, a group of young revolutionary nationalists sought to establish a socialist democracy in Ireland. They built up an army and staged the famous Easter Rising of 1916. Although the rebellion was quickly suppressed, supporters of the nationalist movement formed the Irish Republican Army in the following years. The political party Sinn Féin had been mistakenly credited with the Easter Rising, so from that point on, it was considered the political arm of the IRA.

The Irish War of Independence, which consisted of bloody guerrilla warfare between England and the IRA, was fought between 1919 and 1921. The Anglo-Irish treaty of 1922 officially liberated the southern 26 counties of Ireland from English rule but kept the 6 counties of Northern Ireland under English control. Sinn Féin negotiated the treaty, but some party members were none too happy with the decision to divide Ireland. When the agreement was ratified, many members of Sinn Féin defected, taking with them the anti-treaty contingent of the IRA.

Civil war ensued. The pro-treaty forces in Ireland, assisted by the English, won the war. The Irish Free State (now the Republic of Ireland) gained its independence, while Northern Ireland remained part of the United Kingdom.

## Schism in the Party

After the end of the civil war, Sinn Féin split. Some members founded the new Free State's political parties, while those opposing the government became a radical political party that would not participate in the parliament. The IRA became a fringe paramilitary group, also consisting of those who refused to accept the existence of the Free State or acknowledge that Northern Ireland was part of the United Kingdom. During the 1940s, '50s, and '60s, the IRA carried out attacks on police stations in Northern Ireland and staged political assassinations and intermittent bombings.

During the 1960s, many members of Sinn Féin adopted a more Marxist outlook. They began to denounce the bloody tactics of the IRA. At the same time, violence and rioting continued in Northern Ireland, where nationalists and Catholics protested the civil rights abuses that were practiced against them by Protestants and unionists.

In an attempt to abstain from violence, the IRA failed to protect the Catholic communities of Northern Ireland and the group splintered. The Official IRA and the Official Sinn Féin favored a peaceful approach to securing a united Ireland. The Provisional IRA and Provisional Sinn Féin, however, believed that violence was the answer. They also continued to abstain from parliamentary politics. The Official Sinn Féin has since morphed into other Irish leftist parties, such as the Labour Party and the Workers Party. The IRA and Sinn Féin of today are descendants of the Provisional IRA and Sinn Féin.

## The Troubled Pathway to Peace

In 1972, British paratroopers killed 14 unarmed demonstrators in what became known as the Bloody Sunday massacre. In the aftermath of this event, IRA membership dramatically increased. The IRA became a clandestine operation with a complex and ambiguous network of terrorist cells, while Sinn Féin sought to establish itself as a legitimate political party. The

British government suppressed the IRA and its sympathizers: During the '70s and '80s, thousands of political prisoners were arrested. Meanwhile, the IRA terrorized communities in Northern Ireland, murdering or torturing civilians suspected of being informants. They also started bombing England.

The popularity of Sinn Féin was jeopardized by the unpopularity of the IRA. Most nationalists in Northern Ireland, while sympathetic to the IRA, preferred a peaceful approach to negotiations with England. In 1986, Sinn Féin leader Gerry Adams sought to bring the party into mainstream politics, while a group led by Ruairí Ó Brádaigh refused to do so until a united, free Ireland was established. The latter group broke off to form the radical Republican Sinn Féin.

## Progress at Last

Adams's Sinn Féin is now a major player in Irish politics. In 1997, an IRA cease-fire was declared. In 1998, the monumental Belfast Agreement paved the way for self-determination for Northern Ireland. Yet the implementation of the agreement remains troubled. One provision was that the IRA decommission all of its weapons, and indeed this qualification has been met. Sinn Féin denies any connection with violence instigated by those claiming affiliation with the IRA, but allegations have been made against top Sinn Féin officials regarding their continued involvement. Moreover, some Sinn Féin officials have been accused of being double agents for the UK.

As for the IRA, violence continues under the auspices of newly created fringe groups such as the "Real IRA." Sinn Féin's connection with the IRA remains ambiguous, yet its popularity has grown substantially due to its involvement in the peace process and its support of reforms in areas such as health care and minority rights. Sinn Féin is now the largest nationalist party in Ireland.

# In Your Eostre Bonnet

*Easter, which celebrates Jesus Christ's resurrection from the dead, is thought by some to be nothing more than a pagan holiday. Despite all the bunnies and bonnets, though, its religious roots hold firm.*

✳   ✳   ✳   ✳

SOME PEOPLE THINK Easter has its origins in paganism because it falls roughly at the time of the spring equinox, when the earth comes back to life from the dead of winter. However, Easter's roots are Judaic. It was first associated with Passover, the Jewish holiday that celebrates the Hebrews' release from bondage in Egypt. Jesus and his disciples were in Jerusalem to celebrate Passover when he was arrested, tried, and crucified. Following his resurrection, the disciples understood Jesus to be the sacrificial lamb that took away the sins of the world, a fulfillment of the Passover lambs that were sacrificed each year. Hence the original name for Easter was *Pasch*, from the Hebrew word for Passover, *Pesach*.

So where does the word *Easter* come from? It derives from *Eostre*, the Old English name for the month of April. According to the ancient historian Bede (writing in the eighth century), the month of Eostre was named after a goddess of the same name. Much later, Jacob Grimm (of the Brothers Grimm) speculated that Eostre was named for the ancient German goddess Ostara. The reference could also come from the word *east*—the direction of the sunrise—or from the old Germanic word for "dawn."

As for the date of Easter, which varies from year to year, it's calculated based on the lunar calendar and complex ecclesiastical rules. These calculations include the spring equinox, when the sun is directly above Earth's equator. But whether the equinox and Easter fall close together is purely a matter of chance.

# The Moles of NYC

*It's no secret that New York City includes a reasonably sizable homeless population. Thousands of homeless people sleep in municipal shelters every night. Thousands more are forced to sleep outdoors in parks, on the streets, and in the subway system.*

\* \* \* \*

**W**AIT A MINUTE—THE subway system? That's right. The labyrinthine tunnels of the subway system contain an awful lot of empty space. Sure, it's dark, dirty, and dangerous, but settlers in the area generally don't have their turf invaded. And some tunnels even have free electricity.

The homeless population inhabiting the subway tunnels is sometimes referred to as "the mole people," and years of study and a lot of speculation have yielded few facts about them. For starters, no one is sure how many homeless people live underground. Some say hundreds; others, thousands. The lore surrounding the mole people can get quite bizarre. Some of the more creative urban legends purport that underground dwellers have evolved webbed feet to navigate the mucky terrain and are cannibals preying on unobservant commuters.

Back in 1993, journalist Jennifer Toth published *The Mole People: Life in the Tunnels Beneath New York City*, a controversial book in which she claimed to have visited mole people in the tunnels. The book described a complex underground society with a justice system and official governing powers. But many people, including public transportation experts, smelled a rat. Details didn't all add up, especially Toth's architectural descriptions of the tunnel networks.

Here's what we do know: For many decades, *some* homeless people have lived underground in the subway tunnels, especially around the transportation hubs of Penn Station and Grand Central Station. It can't be confirmed whether these people are living independently or if they've established hierarchical underground cities. But don't worry—if you doze off on the train, you're far more likely to miss your stop or get your wallet stolen than you are to be eaten.

# Shhh! It's a Secret Society

*Though documentation proves this secret organization to preserve the Southern cause did indeed exist, many mysteries remain about the Knights of the Golden Circle.*

✳   ✳   ✳   ✳

THE KNIGHTS OF the Golden Circle was a pro-South organization that operated out of the Deep South, the border states, the Midwest, and even parts of the North both before and during the Civil War. Much of its history is unknown due to its underground nature, but it is known that this secret society, bound by passwords, rituals, and handshakes, intended to preserve Southern culture and states' rights.

Its precise origin, membership, and purpose are documented in a handful of primary sources, including the club's handbook, an exposé published in 1861, and a wartime government report that revealed the K.G.C. to be a serious threat to the federal government and its effort to quash the rebellion and maintain the Union.

Some historians trace the organization of the Knights of the Golden Circle back to the 1830s, though the name did not surface publicly until 1855. According to a report by the U.S. government in 1864, the organization included as many as 500,000 members in the North alone and had "castles," or local chapters, spread across the country. Members included everyone from notable politicians to the rank and file, all prepared to rise up against federal coercion as they saw their rights to slavery slipping away.

## What's in a Name?

The group's name referred to a geographic "Golden Circle" that surrounded the Deep South. Its boundaries were the border states on the north, America's western territories, Mexico, Central America, and even Cuba. Southern leaders and organization members hoped to gain control of these lands to create a strong agrarian economy dependent on slavery and plantations. This would either balance the numbers of slave states to free states in the federal government or provide a distinct nation that could separate from the Union. The proslavery leader John C. Calhoun of South Carolina was the group's intellectual mentor, although the K.G.C. didn't likely achieve great numbers before his death in 1850. The 1864 government report cited that members initially used nuohlac, Calhoun spelled backward, as a password.

## Adding Fuel to the Fire

Once the Civil War began, the K.G.C. became a concern for both state and federal governments. The most obvious public figure associated with the K.G.C. was Dr. George Bickley, an eccentric pamphleteer of questionable character. He is credited with organizing the first castle of the Knights of the Golden Circle in his hometown of Cincinnati. He also sent an open letter to the Kentucky legislature declaring that his organization had 8,000 members in the state, with representatives in every county. The legislature called for a committee to investigate the organization, which had begun to menace that state's effort to remain neutral by importing arms and ammunition for the secession cause. Federal officers arrested Bickley in New Albany, Indiana, in 1863 with a copy of the society's Rules, Regulations, and Principles of the K.G.C. and other regalia on his person. He was held in the Ohio state prison until late 1865. Bickley died two years later, never having been formally charged with a crime.

## Methods and Tactics

The underground group used subversive tactics to thwart the Lincoln administration's effort once the war began. A telegram between a Union colonel and Secretary of War Edwin Stanton states how the "Holy Brotherhood" sought to encourage Union soldiers to desert and to paint the conflict as a war in favor of abolition. Some of the government's more questionable wartime tactics, such as the suspension of habeas corpus and the quelling of some aspects of a free press, were rallying points in the Midwest, and they were issues that surely connected northern dissidents such as Copperheads with the Knights in spirit if not in reality. When antiwar sentiment and Peace Democrats influenced populations in Indiana, a U.S. court subpoenaed witnesses for a grand jury to learn more about the organization. The grand jury claimed the secret organization had recruited 15,000 members in Indiana alone and indicted 60 people in August 1862. The Union army attempted to infiltrate the organization and expose its subversive operations by sending new recruits back home to join the K.G.C.

## Political Ties

Nationally known political leaders were also allegedly tied to the group. The 1861 exposé referred to a certain "Mr. V—of Ohio" as one of the few reliable members among prominent Northern politicians. It would likely have been assumed that this referred to leading Copperhead and Ohio Representative Clement Vallandigham, who decried abolition before the war and criticized Republicans in Congress and the administration. Union officers arrested Vallandigham, and a military court sent him to exile in the South. Another possible member might have been John C. Breckenridge, vice president under James Buchanan and a presidential candidate in 1860. Even former President Franklin Pierce was accused of having an affiliation with the organization.

## Assassination Conspiracy

Some also believe that the K.G.C. had a hand in the assassination of Abraham Lincoln. The contemporary exposé stated, "Some one of them is to distinguish himself for—if he can, that is—the assassination of the 'Abolition' President." According to a later anonymous account, Lincoln's assassin, John Wilkes Booth, took the oath of the society in a Baltimore castle in the fall of 1860.

The organization had several counterparts during the war, including the Knights of the Golden Square, the Union Relief Society, the Order of American Knights, and the Order of the Sons of Liberty, to name a few.

# Who Founded the Mafia?

*To be honest, we really didn't want to answer this question. But then our editors made us an offer we couldn't refuse.*

✳   ✳   ✳   ✳

THIS IS LIKE asking, "Who founded England?" or "Who founded capitalism?" The Mafia is more of a phenomenon than an organization—it's a movement that rose from a complicated interaction of many factors, including history, economics, and politics. Thousands of pages have been written by historians, novelists, screenwriters, and criminologists who have attempted to chart the history of the Mafia, so it's doubtful that we'll be able to provide any real revelations in a few hundred words. But we're a hardy bunch, and we'll do our best.

By all accounts, the Mafia came to prominence in Sicily during the mid-1800s. Given Sicily's history, this makes sense—the island has repeatedly been invaded and occupied, and has a long history of dire poverty. The abolition of feudalism and the lack of a central government simply made things worse than they usually were.

As sociologists will confirm, people who live in areas that fall victim to such upheaval tend to rely on various forms of self-government. In Sicily, this took the form of what has become known as the Mafia. The fellowship, which originated in the rural areas of the Mediterranean island, is based on a complicated system of respect, violence, distrust of government, and the code of *omertà*—a word that is synonymous with the group's code of silence and refers to an unspoken agreement to never cooperate with authorities, under penalty of death. Just as there is no one person who founded the Mafia, there is no one person who runs it. The term "Mafia" refers to any group of organized criminals that follows the traditional Sicilian system of bosses, *capos* ("chiefs"), and soldiers. These groups are referred to as "families."

Although the Mafia evolved in Sicily during the nineteenth century, most Americans equate it to the crime families that dominated the headlines in Chicago and New York for much of the twentieth century. The American Mafia developed as a result of the huge wave of Sicilian immigrants that arrived in the United States in the late nineteenth and early twentieth centuries. These newcomers brought with them the Mafia structure and the code of *omertà*.

These Sicilian immigrants often clustered together in poor urban areas, such as Park Slope in Brooklyn and the south side of Chicago. There, far from the eyes of authorities, disputes were handled by locals. By the 1920s, crime families had sprung up all over the United States and gang wars were prevalent. In the 1930s, Lucky Luciano—who is sometimes called the father of the American Mafia—organized "The Commission," a faux-judiciary system that oversaw the activities of the Mafia in the United States.

Though Mafia families have been involved in murder, kidnapping, extortion, racketeering, gambling, prostitution, drug dealing, weapons dealing, and other crimes over the years, the phenomenon still maintains the appeal that it had when gangsters like Al Capone held the nation's attention. Part of it, of course, is the result of the enormous success of the *Godfather* films, but it is also due, one presumes, to the allure of the principles that the Mafia supposedly was founded upon: self-reliance, loyalty, and *omertà*.

So there you have it: a summary of the founding of the Mafia. Of course, we could tell you more, but then we'd have to . . . well, you know.

# Valachi Speaks

*On June 22, 1962, in the federal penitentiary in Atlanta, Georgia, a man serving a sentence of 15 to 20 years for heroin trafficking picked up a steel pipe and murdered another convict. The killer was Joseph "Joe Cargo" Valachi; the intended victim was Joseph DiPalermo—but Valachi got the wrong man and killed another inmate, Joe Saupp. This mistake touched off one of the greatest criminal revelations in history.*

✳   ✳   ✳   ✳

JOE VALACHI, A 59-year-old Mafia "soldier," was the first member of the Mafia to publicly acknowledge the reality of that criminal organization—making La Cosa Nostra (which means "this thing of ours") a household name. He opened the doors to expose an all-pervasive, wide-ranging conglomerate of crime families, the existence of which was repeatedly denied by J. Edgar Hoover and the FBI. By testifying against his own organization, Valachi violated the code of silence.

## The Boss's Orders

Vito Genovese was the boss of New York's mighty Genovese crime family. Valachi had worked for the family most of his life—mostly as a driver, but also as a hit man, enforcer, numbers runner, and drug pusher. When Valachi went to prison after having been found guilty of some of these activities,

Genovese believed the small-time operator had betrayed him to obtain a lighter sentence for himself. So Genovese put a $100,000 bounty on Valachi's head. He and Valachi were actually serving sentences in the same prison when Valachi killed Joe Saupp—mistaking him for Joseph DiPalermo, whom he thought had been assigned by Genovese to murder him. Whether or not Valachi had broken the code of silence and betrayed Genovese before the bounty was placed on his head, he certainly did it with a vengeance afterward.

But why did Valachi turn informer? The answer to that question isn't entirely clear. Most speculate that Valachi was afraid of a death sentence for killing Saupp and agreed to talk to the Feds in exchange for a lighter sentence.

## The Cat Is out of the Bag

Valachi was a barely literate, street-level miscreant whose knowledge of the workings of the organization was limited. However, when he was brought before John L. McClellan's Senate Permanent Investigations Subcommittee in October 1963, he began talking beyond his personal experience, relaying urban legends as truth, and painting a picture of the Mafia that was both fascinating and chilling.

All in all, Joe Valachi helped identify 317 members of the Mafia. His assistance gave Attorney General Robert Kennedy "a significant addition to the broad picture of organized crime." Unlike Hoover, Bobby Kennedy had no problem acknowledging the Mafia. (One theory about Hoover's denials is that they were a result of long-term Mafia blackmail regarding his homosexuality.)

Valachi's revelations ran the gamut from minor accuracies to babbling exaggerations, as well as from true to false, but the cat was out of the bag. Americans became fascinated with crime families, codes of honor, gang wars, hit killings, and how widely the Mafia calamari had stretched its tentacles. Very private criminals suddenly found their names splashed across headlines and blaring from televisions. During the next three years in the New York-New Jersey-Connecticut metropolitan area, more organized criminals were arrested and jailed than in the previous 30 years. Whatever safe conduct pass the Mafia may have held had expired.

### On the Screen and in Print

When journalist Peter Maas interviewed Valachi and came out with *The Valachi Papers*, the U.S. Department of Justice first encouraged but then tried to block its publication. Regardless, the book was released in 1968. This work soon became the basis of a movie that starred Charles Bronson as Joe Valachi. The novel *The Godfather* was published in 1969, and in the film *The Godfather: Part II*, the characters of Willie Cicci and Frank Pentangeli were reportedly inspired by Valachi.

The $100,000 bounty on the life of Joseph Valachi was never claimed. In 1966, Valachi unsuccessfully attempted to hang himself in his prison cell using an electrical cord. Five years later, he died of a heart attack at La Tuna Federal Correctional Institution in Texas. He had outlived his chief nemesis, Genovese, by two years.

# The Underground Railroad

*The very mention of the Underground Railroad reaches deep into the American psyche, invoking images of daring midnight escapes, secret tunnels, and concealed doors, as well as the exploits of thousands of daring men and women.*

✳ ✳ ✳ ✳

### "... That all men are created equal"

THE STORY OF American slaves seeking escape from their masters long predates the invention of the railroad and its associated terms. The reasons for escape are easily understood and existed equally across slaves of all levels of privilege, from field hands to highly skilled laborers. Even before the

Underground Railroad, escapees were often aided by individuals or organizations opposed to the institution of slavery. In fact, one prominent slaveholder—George Washington—complained in a letter that some of his fellow citizens were more concerned with helping one of his runaway slaves than in protecting his property rights as a slaveholder.

As the United States careened toward civil war, the arguments between supporters of slavery and those opposed to it became increasingly heated. Northern states began abolishing slavery on an individual basis—and became instant magnets for those fleeing servitude. In response, Congress passed Fugitive Slave Acts in 1793 and 1850, rendering escaped slaves fugitives for life, eligible for return to bondage on nothing more than the word of a white man. Any constable who refused to apprehend runaway slaves was fined. With the Northern states thus a less attractive final destination, runaways headed to Canada, where slavery had been outlawed in 1834. Meanwhile, abolitionist societies began to spring up, though a surprising number of them supported the return of escaped slaves to their masters, believing they could end the practice through moral persuasion rather than by violating the law.

## All Aboard

Despite hesitation on the part of some abolitionist societies, however, there were always individuals and groups who were sympathetic to the cause of the runaway slave and willing to place themselves at risk to help slaves find freedom. These benefactors ranged from white citizens to free blacks to other slaves willing to risk being beaten or sold for giving aid to runaways. Often, these protectors acted alone with little more than a vague idea of where to send a fugitive slave other than in the general direction of north. When a sympathetic individual discovered a runaway, he or she would often simply do what seemed best at the moment, whether that meant providing food and clothing, throwing pursuers off the track, or giving the slave a wagon ride to the next town.

By the 1840s, the expansion of the railroad was having a major impact on society, and abolitionist activists quickly adopted its terminology. Conductors were those who helped their passengers—runaway slaves—onto the next station, or town, where they made contact with a stationmaster—the person in charge of the local organization. The most famous conductor, Harriet Tubman, was herself an escaped slave who risked no less than 19 trips back to guide out family members and others. Despite her kindheartedness, she could be as ruthless as the life or death stakes the game demanded; she dosed infants with sedatives to keep them quiet during the trip and once threatened to shoot one of her passengers for having a change of heart rather than let him leave and threaten the freedom of the party.

In some areas, small cells sprang up in which each person knew only about a contact on the next farm or in the next town, perhaps with the goal of somehow sending escapees into the care of well-known abolitionist societies in far-off Philadelphia or Boston. The image of one overriding organization guiding the effort is largely a misleading one, but it was one encouraged by both abolitionists and slaveholders.

The abolitionists were not hesitant to play up the romantic railroad imagery in an effort to bolster their efforts. Likewise, Southern plantation owners were quick to play up the reports as proof that there was a vast abolitionist conspiracy bent on robbing them of their legal investment in slaves. As a result, some slave owners in border states converted their slaves to cash—selling them to the deep south rather than risking their escape, a fate many slaves considered nothing less than a death sentence.

## "Devils and good people, walking in the road at the same time"

Despite the presence—even the widespread prevalence, in some locations—of Underground Railroad workers, the experience of a runaway slave was never anything other than harsh.

On striking out for freedom, even successful escapees faced an ordeal that could last months. During their journey, they rarely had food, shelter, or appropriate clothing. Every white face was a potential enemy, as were some of their fellow black people, who were sometimes employed as decoys to help catch runaways. A false Underground Railroad even existed. Participants would take a runaway in and promise him safe passage only to deliver him to the local slave market. Often the escapees had no idea where they were going or the distance to be covered.

Although estimates vary, one widely reported figure is that approximately 100,000 slaves found freedom either through their own initiative or with the aid of the Underground Railroad. The history of the Railroad was largely written decades after the fact, and it is occasionally hard to separate reliable facts from the aged recollections of those justifiably proud of their efforts at securing liberty for their fellow man.

## Famous Revolutionary Organizations: Where There's a Will, There's a Warrior

*Since time began, people have formed organizations that espouse their political, social, cultural, or nationalistic ideas. These groups come from every walk of life, every continent, and every era. The only commonality they share is their passion for what they believe—ideas for which they will give anything, including their lives.*

✳ ✳ ✳ ✳

### Carbonari

WHILE IT IS unknown whether the group originally developed in France or Italy, the Carbonari, or "charcoal burners," derived their philosophy from the ideals of the French Revolution and the Enlightenment. Primarily a political organization, the Carbonari opposed absolutism and desired the establishment of a republic or, second-best, a constitutional monarchy in Italy. The society had a clearly delineated, hierarchical structure, not unlike that of the Freemasons. Like many other revolutionary organizations, the Carbonari were not averse to using violence to achieve their goals.

## Black Hand

While this underground sect, whose more official name is Unification or Death, is sometimes grouped with secret societies, it is more often defined as a terrorist organization. Established in 1911 in Serbia from the remnants of the more mainstream pan-slavic organization National Defense, the Black Hand was dedicated to forming a greater Serbia. Violence was the group's primary tool. A member of the Black Hand assassinated Archduke Franz Ferdinand in 1914. The fallout from this act resulted in World War I.

## The Fenians

Even before the Norman Conquest, the Irish were fighting for independence from English influence. In the 1850s, a more organized resistance to English rule developed in the form of the Fenian Brotherhood. Their name came from *Fianna*, legendary Irish soldiers. Although the term *Fenian* applies to the broader movement, most Fenians belonged to the Irish Republican Brotherhood—which originated in the United States in 1858. The revolutionary group saw armed conflict as the main tool for achieving independence from England.

## Satyagraha

Indian independence leader Mohandas Gandhi originated a philosophy of social action called *satyagraha*. It was derived, in part, from the Hindu concept of *ahimsa*, a principle of noninjury. Satyagraha further developed into a campaign of civil disobedience and non-violent resistance as the people of India agitated for freedom from British rule.

The Indian National Congress, the oldest political organization in India and a major force in the crusade to free India, adopted satyagraha under Gandhi's leadership in the 1920s. Satyagraha helped lead to the eventual independence of India in 1947 and influenced numerous other nonviolent struggles throughout the world, including the American civil rights movement of the 1960s.

## Tongmenghui

Founded in Tokyo in 1905, Tongmenghui was also called the Chinese United League or the Chinese Revolutionary Alliance. Led by Sun Yat-Sen and Song Jiaoren, the secret organization was designed to unify the disparate antimonarchy forces within China. It encompassed republicans, nationalists, and socialists. In addition to governmental change, Tongmenghui also sought social revolution with the reestablishment of Chinese culture and agricultural revolution in the form of land redistribution.

## The Bolsheviks

Their name derived from the Russian word for "majority," the Bolsheviks were a splinter group from the more mainstream Social Democratic Labor party. With Vladimir Lenin as their leader, the Bolshevik faction argued that the agrarian class should be the power base for the impending Marxist revolution, while their opponents (later called the *Menshevik*, or "minority," by Lenin) believed that anyone committed to Marxist ideals should be included. The more extreme view of the Bolsheviks eventually won the day; they became the ruling Communist party of Russia in March 1918.

# The Ku Klux Klan:
# A Southern Phenomenon?

*Since the first Ku Klux Klan formed in Tennessee in 1865, the white sheet and hood have symbolized intimidation and ethnic hatred. Although the Klan was born in Dixie, many of its power bases have been—and remain— far outside the former Confederacy.*

✳   ✳   ✳   ✳

## The First Klan: Politics by Other Means

To understand the first Ku Klux Klan, one must understand the times. The same year that Robert E. Lee surrendered to Ulysses S. Grant, numerous former Confederates decided that if they couldn't have their old status quo on paper, they'd have it in practice. This meant keeping the Democratic Party in state and local power, which would occur only if Republican-sympathizing African Americans didn't vote. The Ku Klux Klan's primary aim was to suppress black voting.

The first KKK was less a centralized organization than a handy label adopted by ad hoc local political terrorists and racists. Those types also existed in non-Southern states but were less likely to call themselves Klansmen. General public revulsion at Klan tactics led to the Ku Klux Klan Act of 1871, which started sending members to jail for civil-rights violations. Membership waned to a few die-hards.

## The Second Klan: Loyal Order of Hoodlums in Hoods

This Klan, born from the general hoopla over the 1915 film sensation *Birth of a Nation*, soon went mainstream and national. Its focus was anti-Catholic, anti-Communist, anti-immigrant, anti-Semitic, and anti–African American. Some KKK members lynched and burned, but for most it was a social pastime much like a fraternal lodge. This Klan boasted millions of members.

Politically and numerically, the Klan was strongest in Illinois, Indiana, and Michigan, with lesser power bases in California, Oregon, and the South. Woodrow Wilson praised it, and evidence indicates that Warren G. Harding joined it. Its downfall began with a 1925 violent-assault scandal, then accelerated with the onset of the Depression and the rise of Hitler in Germany. This was the deepest KKK penetration of government and society, but it was more Midwestern than Southern; by World War II, it had subsided to just a few thousand hardcore bigots.

## The Klan of the Civil Rights Era: White Supremacy

The 1950s brought a national movement toward any good Klansman's worst nightmare: African Americans as equal participants in society. Again the Klan rose, though in nothing resembling the numbers of the 1920s. This version was much like the first Klan—mostly Southern, with tentacles in other regions, balkanized into numerous groups competing for the sympathies of militant racists.

This time the atrocities occurred in the light of modern mass media, as the nation watched Klan violence on the nightly news. Anyone trying to excuse the Ku Klux Klan as a harmless social club looked delusional, and in the mainstream American psyche, the Klan bedsheet came to emblemize terrorism. After losing the war against the civil-rights movement, the Klan once again receded to several thousand members.

## The Modern Klan: Stolen Thunder

By the 1980s, the Klan had become a minor player in racist subculture. Christian identity, neo-Nazism, and the skinhead movement attracted many who would have raided their linen closets in another era. In the past, police had at least attempted to protect civil-rights demonstrators from Klan violence; now angry crowds rained scorn on KKK rallies. Only police protection shielded Klansmen from the brand of violence their ideological forebears used to dish out.

By 2006, the Ku Klux Klan consisted of scattered islets dotting the map from Maine to Louisiana to California. Thus, the Klan does have Southern roots and a Southern presence, but it has often taken on a decidedly Northern and Western character.

# The Rise and Fall of the Knights Templar

*The Crusades, Christendom's quest to recover and hold the Holy Land, saw the rise of several influential military orders. Of these, the Knights Templar had perhaps the greatest lasting influence—and took the hardest fall.*

✳ ✳ ✳ ✳

JULY 15, 1099: On that day, the First Crusade came storming into Jerusalem and began a wholesale slaughter of everyone in sight—Jews, Muslims, Christians—didn't matter. This unleashed a wave of pilgrimage, as European Christians flocked to now-accessible Palestine and its holy sites. Though Jerusalem's loss was a blow to Islam, it was a bonanza for the region's thieves, from Saracens to lapsed Crusaders: a steady stream of naive pilgrims to rob.

## Defending the Faithful

French knight Hugues de Payen, with eight chivalrous comrades, swore to guard the travelers. In 1119, they gathered at the Church of the Holy Sepulchre and pledged their lives to poverty, chastity, and obedience before King Baldwin II of Jerusalem. The Order of Poor Knights of the Temple of Solomon took up headquarters in said Temple.

## Going Mainstream

The Templars did their work competently, and in 1127 Baldwin sent a Templar embassy to Europe to secure a marriage that would ensure a peaceable royal succession in Jerusalem. Not only did the embassy succeed, they became rock stars of sorts. Influential nobles showered the Order with money and real estate, the foundation of its future wealth. With this growth came a formal code of rules. Some highlights include:

* Templars could not desert the battlefield or leave a castle by stealth.

* They had to wear white habits, except for sergeants and squires who could wear black.

* They had to tonsure (shave) their crowns and wear beards.

* They had to dine in communal silence, broken only by Scriptural readings.

* They had to be chaste, except for married men joining with their wives' consent.

## Never Mind That Pesky "Poverty" Part

Now with offices in Europe to manage the Order's growing assets, the Templars returned to Palestine to join in the Kingdom's ongoing defense. In 1139, Pope Innocent II decreed the Order answerable only to the Holy See. Now exempt from the tithe, the Order was entitled to accept tithes! The Knights Templar had come far.

By the mid-1100s, the Templars had become a church within a church, a nation within a nation, and a major banking concern. Templar keeps were well-defended depositories, and the Order became financiers to the crowned heads of Europe—even to the Papacy. Their reputation for meticulous bookkeeping and secure transactions underpinned Europe's financial markets, even as their soldiers continued fighting for the faith in the Holy Land.

## Downfall

Templar prowess notwithstanding, the Crusaders couldn't hold the Holy Land. In 1187, Saladin the Kurd retook Jerusalem, martyring 230 captured Templars. Factional fighting between Christians sped the collapse as the 1200s wore on. In 1291, the last Crusader outpost at Acre fell to the Mamelukes of Egypt.

Though the Templars had taken a hosing along with the other Christian forces, their troubles had just begun. King Philip IV of France owed the Order a lot of money, and they made him more nervous at home than they did fighting in Palestine. In 1307, Philip ordered the arrest of all Templars in France. They stood accused of apostasy, devil worship, sodomy, desecration, and greed. Hideous torture produced piles of confessions, much like those of the later Inquisition. The Order was looted, shattered, and officially dissolved. In March 1314, Jacques de Molay, the last Grand Master of the Knights Templar, was burned at the stake.

## Whither the Templars?

Many Templar assets passed to the Knights Hospitallers. The Order survived in Portugal as the Order of Christ, where it exists to this day in form similar to British knightly orders. A Templar fleet escaped from La Rochelle and vanished; it may have reached Scotland. Swiss folktales suggest that some Templars took their loot and expertise to Switzerland, possibly laying the groundwork for what would one day become the Swiss banking industry.

# What Is Mensa?

*Almost everybody, it seems, has heard about Mensa—the club for really, really smart people—but nobody is sure exactly what it is. Or how to get in. Or what the standards are for membership.*

✳   ✳   ✳   ✳

MORE THAN 50,000 AMERICANS are part of the international society called Mensa. They're just people who have scored in the top 2 percent in one of more than 200 acceptable standardized tests. (Although spokespeople won't say exactly what the magic number happens to be, the standard measurement for "very superior" intelligence is an IQ of 130 or above.) About one in 50 Americans—six million in total—qualify for Mensa membership, whether they realize it or not (you can see for yourself at www.us.mensa.org/join/testscores/qualifying-test-scores). Mensa boasts over 130 local chapters that offer a variety of activities, including movie nights at a member's home and dinners out with others. The group's name, which is related to three Latin words meaning "mind," "table," and "month," would seem to suggest meeting and eating every four weeks.

### Brilliant Origins

The group was originally founded in Great Britain in 1946, with the American branch beginning in 1960 in Brooklyn, New York. There don't appear to be any scary, arcane rituals involved, or any need to keep proving oneself once "inside." One of the organization's main tenets is to provide intellectual company for like-minded individuals (in America, the membership is 65 percent male, the remainder female). While the club protects members' privacy, there are some notable folks who are or were willing to be identified, including actors Geena Davis and Alan Rachins, sci-fi writer Isaac Asimov, and NASA astronaut Bill McArthur.

# The Intergalactic Journey of Scientology

*There are few who don't know about the aura of mystery and scandal that surrounds the Church of Scientology, which boasts a small membership and a seismic pocketbook. Scientology frequently graces the headlines, with stories ranging from accounts of Tom Cruise tomfoolery to an endless stream of lawsuits and accusations of bribery and abuse.*

✳ ✳ ✳ ✳

THE FANTASTICAL ELEMENTS to the saga of Scientology were perhaps written into the religion from its beginning, given that Scientology sprang from the fertile mind of its late creator, fiction writer turned religious messiah, L. Ron Hubbard. Hubbard, born in 1911, began his writing career in the 1930s after flunking out of college. Hubbard had always preferred imagination to reality: Accounts of his past reveal hallucinogenic drug use and an obsession with black magic and Satanism. In between prolific bouts of writing, Hubbard served in the Navy during World War II, became involved in various start-up ventures, and, of course, dabbled in black magic ceremonies. Allegation has it that Hubbard and wealthy scientist friend John Parsons performed a ritual in which they attempted to impregnate a woman with the antichrist. The woman was Parsons's girlfriend, but she soon became Hubbard's second wife—though he was still married to his first wife.

## Down to a Science

In 1949, Hubbard developed a self-help process that he called Dianetics. All of humanity's problems, according to Dianetics, stem from the traumas of past lives. These traumas are called *engrams,* and Hubbard's own e-meter (a machine using simple lie detector technology) can identify and help eliminate these engrams. Getting rid of engrams can have amazing results—from increasing intelligence to curing blindness. The first Dianetics article appeared in a sci-fi publication called *Astounding Science Fiction.* In 1950, Hubbard opened the Hubbard Dianetic Research Foundation in New Jersey, and in that same year *Dianetics: The Modern Science of Mental Health* was published and sold well.

Hubbard and his followers attempted to establish Dianetics as an official science. But the medical profession didn't appreciate Dianetics masquerading as science. The Dianetic Research Foundation came under investigation by the IRS and the American Medical Association. Hubbard closed his clinics and fled New Jersey.

## Actually, It's a Religion

Dianetics wasn't making the cut as a scientific theory, so Hubbard played another card. Years before, Hubbard is reputed to have told a friend "writing for a penny a word is ridiculous. If a man really wants to make a million dollars, the best way would be to start his own religion." After fleeing Jersey, Hubbard moved to Phoenix, Arizona, declared Dianetics an "applied religious philosophy," and, in 1954, Hubbard's organization was recognized as a religion by the IRS and granted tax-exempt status.

Thus the Church of Scientology was born. Hubbard added new stories to the original Dianetics creation, and by the 1960s, humans were spiritual descendants of the alien Thetans, who were banished to live on Earth by the intergalactic terrorist dictator Xenu 75 million years ago. Scientologist disciples must not only expel the traumas of past lives but of past lives on different planets. Discovering these traumas is an expensive process, so the Church actively recruits wealthy devotees. As for Hubbard, he died in 1986, soon after the IRS accused him of stealing $200 million from the Church. Today, Scientology and its various offshoot nonprofit groups and private business ventures continue to hold a vast fortune, and Scientology's ongoing litigation with the IRS, the press, and ex-devotees (hundreds of lawsuits are pending) are so bizarre, they seem almost out of this world.

# A Man's Bedroom Can Be His Kingdom

*The micronation of Talossa began with a 14-year-old kid in Milwaukee, long before the Internet. Now its global membership produces its own heraldry.*

✳ ✳ ✳ ✳

O N DECEMBER 26, 1979, Talossa was born when Robert Ben Madison, a boy of 14, held a ceremony in his family home. Crowning himself with an old fire department dress uniform cap, he announced his bedroom's secession from the United States. Madison had made a flag for the occasion and even chosen a national anthem (Fleetwood Mac's "Tusk"). With most people at the helm, Talossa would have lasted about a week. Ben Madison wasn't most people.

His family humored the eccentric young monarch. A linguistic prodigy, Madison borrowed Talossa (rhymes with mimosa) from the Finnish for "in the house." A selected motto translated to "A Man's Room is His Kingdom" from rough Finnish. The Kingdom of Talossa had become a micronation of one. Since the U.S. government offered no comment, Madison inferred that Uncle Sam didn't mind.

Madison began publishing newsletters, adopting and changing political alignments, switching the national language, rebelling against Talossa's (his own) "oppressive" regime, and living an active "national" fantasy life. He soon began involving his friends. Talossa's first "war" involved another teenage micronationalist vandalizing the Madison family's garage and tripping the king's sister after church.

Madison dissolved Talossa in July 1981, having encountered insurmountable difficulty in explaining his "kingdom" to girls. However, when ending Talossa didn't end his dating problem, Madison decided to reactivate his micronation. In large part due to his charisma, will, and abundant spare time, Talossa struggled along. For the next 15 years, it normally consisted of a dozen or so Milwaukeean "citizens," some active and others simply humoring Madison (who lived at home into adulthood). Talossa claimed a chunk of Milwaukee's East Side as its territory, as well as a slice of Antarctica and a French island. The political system became a parliamentary monarchy.

Talossa's political development peaked and valleyed, featuring parties like PUNK (People United for No King), the Bob Fights Ticket, and STOMP (Schneider's Talossan Marxist Party). Madison designed Talossan as a Romance language, authoring a dictionary and rules of grammar. *El Glhe* ("the tongue") used every single accent mark, circumflex, and other foreign character Madison could locate. Talossa adopted Gloria Estefan as National Entertainer (whether she realized this or not) and Taco Bell as its ethnic cuisine. Its citizens gathered for meals, political events, and board-gaming sessions. Talossans published newsletters, ranging from the mature to the angry to the bizarre; in one infamous episode, a dissident citizen began publishing detailed records of his bathroom visits.

The pre-internet Regipäts Talossan ("Kingdom of Talossa") eventually grew to about 30 citizens, mostly Milwaukeeans. Madison remained its primary sustaining force.

## Going Online—and Worldwide

In January 1996, Madison published Talossa's first web page. Its whimsical, inviting tone attracted notice. Few "bathtub kingdoms" had their own languages, let alone 16 years of history and personality. Madison was bombarded with online inquiries, and a few people were even willing to jump through all the naturalization hoops. Thereafter, the diversifying citizenry would increasingly define Talossa in terms beyond face-to-face friendship with Ben Madison. Some "Old Growth" Talossans spurned the internet entirely; most "cybercits" were unlikely to make pilgrimages to Milwaukee. Madison bridged the space between the two groups. By this time, numerous online micronations had sprung up, but Talossa remained the most successful and mature (at least, in a cultural development sense). Talossa denied citizenship to citizens of "bug nations"— Madison's scornful term for other micronations.

From 1996 to 2004, Madison's control over the Regipäts gradually declined. Various groups continued the long-term political role-playing game begun in 1979: ranting, resigning ministries, starting and disbanding parties, renouncing and regaining citizenship, amending its 1997 constitution, developing the language, and growing to roughly 75 citizens located in over half a dozen countries. The Milwaukee core was anything but unified, and had become a decided minority to boot.

## A Crumbling Kingdom

On June 1, 2004, while Madison was touring Africa, his brainchild kingdom schismed out of his grasp. Citing grave exception to Madison's mistreatment of some citizens, 11 of the more active Talossans seceded to form the "Republic of Talossa," taking with them administration rights to the "Wittenberg" discussion group where most of Talossa happened. Madison and his loyalists fought back by relaxing citizenship requirements, quickly growing the Regipäts back to its former size. After an early burst of activity, and some new faces in the form of former kingdom citizens and rejected hopefuls, the republic stagnated.

The kingdom thrived—but away from Madison. Barely a year later, the new influx of Talossa citizens had his loyalist faction politically outgunned. On August 15, 2005, Madison renounced his Talossan citizenship: It was the end of an era that had spanned a quarter-century. Except for a short-lived rump kingdom, which gathered no steam, Ben Madison was done with Talossa.

## Post-Madisonian Talossa

The loss of its king, which might have killed Talossa in 1985, barely dented it in 2005. The citizenry chose a Coloradoan as its new king, and the kingdom continued to grow. Women finally began joining in numbers. Relations with the republic remained chilly for years, until its citizenry rejoined the royal fold in 2012. In true Talossan fashion, the ex-republicans promptly formed an anti-monarchical political party.

# Chapter 8

# Conspiratorially Speaking

## Mysterious Marilyn

*Marilyn Monroe's life story has been exposed and analyzed countless times. The problem is that each version seems to contradict the others, making it difficult to sort out even the simplest details of her complicated life.*

✳　✳　✳　✳

THE ICONIC FILM star whose work includes classics such as *How to Marry a Millionaire* and *Some Like it Hot* continues to be the subject of intense scrutiny. But despite all of the books and movies made about Marilyn Monroe, misconceptions about her life abound, including the following:

**Myth:** Marilyn was illegitimate.

**Fact:** According to Marilyn's birth certificate, her mother's estranged husband, Martin Edward Mortensen, was her father, but Marilyn never believed this. Her mother, Gladys, abandoned Mortensen after several months of marriage and proceeded to have a series of affairs, most notably with Stanley Gifford, an employee at the film lab where she worked. Mortensen, who had never met Marilyn, always claimed that he was her real father. After his death in 1981, a copy of Marilyn's birth certificate was found in his effects, and it is now widely believed that he was telling the truth.

**Myth:** Marilyn was born blonde.

**Fact:** Marilyn Monroe's natural hair color was brown. In 1946, she was offered a job modeling for a series of Lustre Cream shampoo ads on the condition that she trade her flowing brunette curls for a straightened blonde hairstyle. It is said that she strongly resisted coloring her hair but ultimately relented under pressure. She was 20 years old at the time and would remain a blonde for the rest of her life.

**Myth:** Marilyn personified the dumb blonde.

**Fact:** Marilyn Monroe rose to stardom playing the "dumb blonde" and was considered a master of this Hollywood archetype. But was she actually featherbrained? She definitely played up that image for the public, but her private pursuits were surprisingly intellectual. She wasn't interested in vapid romance novels; instead, she was often observed on her movie sets absorbed in classic works such as Thomas Paine's *The Rights of Man*. Her library was filled with titles by Willa Cather, Dorothy Parker, and Carson McCullers, among many other notable authors. In one famous photograph, she is sitting in front of her book collection reading a copy of *Poetry and Prose: Heinrich Heine*.

Marilyn also took her work as an actress very seriously and insisted that every take be perfect, which often resulted in her being perceived as difficult to work with. Her 1955 departure from Hollywood to study with Lee Strasberg at the Actors Studio in New York City was a bold attempt to take control of her career. She even went so far as to start her own production company, which enabled her to reject any director or script of which she did not approve.

**Myth:** Marilyn committed suicide.

**Fact:** On August 5, 1962, Marilyn was found deceased in her home in Brentwood, California. The Los Angeles County coroner's office classified her death as "probable suicide," but many people, especially those closest to her, never believed it. During the summer of 1962, things were looking up for Marilyn. She had just achieved a major publicity coup with a cover story in *Life* magazine. Her contract with 20th Century Fox studios had been successfully renegotiated, and several projects were in the pipeline, including a film version of the Broadway musical *A Tree Grows in Brooklyn*. She was busy planning renovations of her new house, the first she had ever purchased (albeit with a little help from her ex-husband Joe DiMaggio). To those who knew her well, it did not make sense that she would take her own life, and there are even conspiracy theorists who claim that President John F. Kennedy had a hand in her death. But given the fact that her long-term addiction to sleeping pills had led to near-over-doses in the past, the most logical explanation is that her death was an accident.

# The Men on the Moon

*On July 20, 1969, millions of people worldwide watched in awe as U.S. astronauts became the first humans to step on the moon. However, a considerable number of conspiracy theorists contend that the men were just actors performing on a soundstage.*

✳  ✳  ✳  ✳

THE NATIONAL AERONAUTICS and Space Administration (NASA) has been dealing with this myth for nearly 40 years. In fact, it has a page on its official website that scientifically explains the pieces of "proof" that supposedly expose the fraud. These are the most common questions raised.

**If the astronauts really did take photographs on the moon, why aren't the stars visible in them?** The stars are there but are too faint to be seen in the photos. The reason for this has to do with the fact that the lunar surface is so brightly lit by the sun. The astronauts had to adjust their camera settings to accommodate the brightness, which then rendered the stars in the background difficult to see.

**Why was there no blast crater under the lunar module?**
The astronauts had slowed their descent, bringing the rocket on the lander from a maximum of 10,000 pounds of thrust to just 3,000 pounds. In addition, the lack of atmosphere on the moon spread the exhaust fairly wide, lowering the pressure and diminishing the scope of a blast crater.

**If there is no air on the moon, why does the flag planted by the astronauts appear to be waving?** The flag appears to wave because the astronauts were rotating the pole on which it was mounted as they tried to get it to stand upright.

**When the lunar module took off from the moon back into orbit, why was there no visible flame from the rocket?** The composition of the fuel used for the takeoff from the surface of the moon was different in that it produced no flame.

Conspiracy theorists present dozens of "examples" that supposedly prove that the moon landing never happened, and all of them are easily explained. But that hasn't kept naysayers from perpetuating the myth.

Twenty-three years after the moon landing, on February 15, 2001, Fox TV stirred the pot yet again with a program titled *Conspiracy Theory: Did We Land on the Moon?* The show trotted out the usual array of conspiracy theorists, who in turn dusted off the usual spurious "proof." And once again, NASA found itself having to answer to a skeptical but persistent few.

Many people theorize that the landing was faked because the United States didn't have the technology to safely send a crew to the moon. Instead, it pretended it did as a way to win the final leg of the space race against the Soviet Union. But consider the situation: Thousands of men and women worked for almost a decade (and three astronauts died) to make the Apollo mission successful. With so many people involved, a hoax of that magnitude would be virtually impossible to contain, especially after almost four decades.

For additional proof that the moon landing really happened, consider the hundreds of pounds of moon rocks brought back by the six missions that were able to retrieve them. Moon rocks are unique and aren't easily manufactured, so if they didn't come from the moon, what is their source? Finally, there's no denying the fact that the astronauts left behind a two-foot reflecting panel equipped with dozens of tiny mirrors. Scientists are able to bounce laser pulses off the mirrors to pinpoint the moon's distance from Earth.

The myth of the faked moon landing will probably never go away. But the proof of its reality is irrefutable. In the words of astronaut Charles Duke, who walked on the moon in 1972 as part of *Apollo 16*: "We've been to the moon nine times. Why would we fake it nine times, if we faked it?"

# Thomas Ince: A Boating Excursion Turns Deadly

*Film mogul Thomas Ince joins other Hollywood notables for a weekend celebration in 1924 and ends up dead. Was it natural causes or one of the biggest cover-ups in Hollywood history?*

✳ ✳ ✳ ✳

THE MOVIE INDUSTRY has been rocked by scandal throughout its history, but few incidents have matched the controversy and secrecy surrounding the death of Thomas Ince, a high-profile producer and director of many successful silent films. During the 1910s, he set up his own studio in California where he built a sprawling complex of small homes, sweeping mansions, and other buildings that were used as sets for his movies. Known as Inceville, the studio covered several thousand acres, and it was there that Ince perfected the idea of the studio system—a factory-style setup that used a division of labor amongst large teams of costumers, carpenters, electricians, and other film professionals who moved from project to project as needed. This system, which allowed for the mass production of movies with the producer in creative and financial control, would later be adopted by all major Hollywood film companies.

Down on his luck by the 1920s, Ince still had many influential friends and associates. In November 1924, newspaper magnate William Randolph Hearst offered to host a weekend birthday celebration for the struggling producer aboard his luxury yacht the *Oneida*. Several Hollywood luminaries attended, including Charlie Chaplin and Marion Davies, as well Louella Parsons, then a junior writer for one of Hearst's East Coast newspapers. But at the end of the cruise, Ince was carried off the ship on a medical gurney and rushed home, where he died two days later. A hastily scribbled death certificate blamed heart failure.

## The Rumors Fly

Almost immediately, the rumor mill churned out shocking and sordid versions of the incident. The stories were sensational, and very different from the official line. A Chaplin employee, who was waiting at the docks when the boat returned, reportedly claimed that Ince was suffering from a gunshot wound to the head when he was taken off the *Oneida*. Could he have been the victim of a careless accident at the hands of a partying Hollywood celeb? Perhaps, but film industry insiders knew of complex and passionate relationships among those on board, and a convoluted and bizarre scenario soon emerged and has persisted to this day. As it turns out, Davies was Hearst's longtime mistress, despite being almost 34 years his junior. She was also a close friend of the notorious womanizer Chaplin. Many speculate that Hearst, enraged over the attention that Chaplin was paying to the young ingenue, set out to kill him but shot the hapless Ince by mistake.

Certain events after Ince's death helped the rumors gain traction. Ince's body was cremated, so no autopsy could be performed. And his grieving widow was whisked off to Europe for several months courtesy of Hearst—conveniently away from the reach of the American press. Louella Parsons was also elevated within the Hearst organization, gaining a lifetime contract and the plum assignment as his number-one celebrity gossip columnist, which she parlayed into a notoriously self-serving enterprise. Conspiracy theorists believe that she wrangled the deal with Hearst to buy her silence about the true cause of Ince's death.

## Lingering Mystery

Was Ince the victim of an errant gunshot and subsequent cover-up? If anyone in 1920s California had the power to hush witnesses and bend officials to his will in order to get away with murder, it was the super rich and powerful Hearst. But no clear evidence of foul play has emerged after all these decades. Still, the story has persisted and even served as the subject for *The Cat's Meow*, a 2002 film directed by Peter Bogdanovich, which starred Kirsten Dunst as Davies and Cary Elwes as the doomed Ince.

# The Franklin Syndicate

*What does it take to fleece the public? Confidence, a believable lie, and something everybody wants: money. Take a closer look at the first big American pyramid scheme.*

✳   ✳   ✳   ✳

I N 1898, A low-wage clerk named William F. Miller was working at a New York brokerage firm, desperately trying to support his family on meager earnings. At only 19 years old, Miller was tantalizingly close to the world of financial success but lacked the funds to participate. One evening while leading his Bible study class, Miller hit upon the idea of inviting the men in his group to invest $10 each in return for a 10 percent return every week. Though skeptical at first, but knowing that their friend had some sort of job on Wall Street, the men were eventually won over.

## Robbing Peter to Pay Paul

Although Miller originally conceived his scheme as a means to raise quick money to speculate in the stock market, he quickly realized that it was far easier to simply find new investors and pocket the profits. These investors, convinced by the returns being paid to the current investors, gladly contributed money and most often chose to reinvest their dividends. Miller named his new enterprise "The Franklin Syndicate" and set up a Brooklyn office. Because he promised a 10 percent return every week (520 percent per year), he quickly became known as "520% Miller."

## 144 Floyd Street

All of the syndicate's advertising featured the visage of Benjamin Franklin and his quotation: "The way to wealth is as plain as the road to the market." Indeed, many were beguiled into believing that the road to wealth lay in Miller's office located in a house at 144 Floyd Street. Miller soon began hiring clerks to accommodate the crush of eager investors.

At the peak of the syndicate's popularity, the house was a beehive of financial activity with 50 clerks working into the night. Miller, sitting at the top of the front porch stoop, received the cash, distributed receipts, and seemed to hardly notice as the money piled up behind him. His clerks opened correspondence, distributed dividends, and mailed advertisements. It was reputed that investors could receive or drop off money in any of the rooms, including the kitchen, parlor, or laundry.

People from as far away as Louisiana and Manitoba, Canada, sent money. The activity and evidence of so much money easily enticed even the delivery men and postal carriers to deposit their cash as well. The press of people eager to hand over their hard-earned wages was so great on one particular Friday that the stoop collapsed. At the end of each day, Miller and his clerks literally waded through knee-high mounds of cash.

Overwhelmed, Miller added Edward Schlessinger as a partner. Schlessinger helped open the Franklin Syndicate's second office in Boston. In return, he took a third of the profits away in a money-filled bag every evening.

## Enter the Colonel

When the newspapers, particularly the *Boston Post* and a New York financial paper edited by E. L. Blake, began to cast doubts about the syndicate's legitimacy, Miller's advertising agent introduced him to an attorney named Colonel Robert A. Ammon. Charismatic, compelling, and utterly corrupt, Ammon incorporated the company, did battle with the press, and increasingly became the syndicate's chief behind-the-scenes operator.

When the *Post* alleged that the Franklin Syndicate was a swindle, Ammon and Miller took $50,000 in a bag to the paper's office to prove their liquidity. When a police chief referred to the Franklin Syndicate as a "green goods business" the two men repeated the display, whereupon the police chief apologized.

## The Swindler Is Swindled

Miller, Ammon, and Schlessinger knew that the end was near, but only Ammon knew just how close it really was. Having fully duped Miller into believing he was acting in his best interest, Ammon prodded the young man to squeeze every last dollar from the enterprise before it collapsed.

On November 21, 1899, Miller placed $30,500 in a satchel and went to Ammon's office. Ammon advised his client to give him the money to protect it from the investors. Ammon also convinced Miller to surrender securities, bonds, and a certificate of deposit, all of which totaled more than $250,000. On Ammon's advice, Miller opened the Floyd Street office the following day, a Friday and the last best chance to gather additional funds.

After work, Miller was pursued by a detective but eluded his pursuer by ducking through a Chinese laundry and fleeing to Ammon's office. Upon learning that Miller had been indicted in

Kings County for conspiracy to defraud, the lawyer convinced his client to flee to Canada.

## Die in Prison or Let Your Family Suffer?

It's unclear whether Miller returned two weeks later because he missed his wife and baby or because Ammon, nervous about scrutiny being cast on his own role in the syndicate, convinced him to come back. What is certain is that, with Ammon acting as his counsel, Miller was sentenced to the maximum ten years in Sing Sing prison. Knowing that Miller was the only man capable of implicating him, Ammon gave his client's family $5 a week and reminded Miller that without the allowance his family would starve. After three years, the District Attorney finally convinced Miller, sick from his years in prison and tempted by the possibility of a pardon, to turn evidence against Ammon.

## Just Desserts?

Ammon served five years—the maximum penalty for receiving stolen goods. Schlessinger fled with $175,000 in cash to Europe where he gambled and lived well until his premature death in 1903.

Miller was released after five years in prison. He moved his family to Long Island where he operated a grocery until his death. When a man named Charles Ponzi was being tried for running a pyramid scheme 20 years later, a reporter from the *Boston Post* located Miller and asked him to compare his scheme to Ponzi's. Though there is no record that Ponzi knew of "520% Miller," the reporter concluded that the two men's schemes were remarkably similar.

# The Mysterious Death of Christopher Marlowe

*Who exactly is responsible for the death of Christopher Marlowe?*

✳  ✳  ✳  ✳

IN 1593, CHRISTOPHER Marlowe, the most famous playwright in London, was killed when he accidentally stabbed himself during a tavern brawl. His premature death is one of the greatest tragedies in English literature, snuffing out a career that may have still been in its infancy—Shakespeare, who was Marlowe's same age, was just coming into his own as a writer at the time. But some people continue to doubt the official story (i.e., that Marlowe accidentally stabbed himself while fighting over the bill). After all, Marlowe and some of the others in the room with him had ties to the Elizabethan underworld. Was his really an accidental death—or could it have been murder?

## Rise of a Shoemaker's Son

Born to a shoemaker the same year that Shakespeare was born to a glove maker, Marlowe attended Cambridge University, where he posed for a portrait that showed him in a black velvet shirt, smirking beside his Latin motto, *Quod met nutrit me destruit* ("What nourishes me destroys me.") He was a distinguished enough scholar that he seems to have been recruited, as many Cambridge scholars of the day were, to work as an undercover agent. Letters from the government excusing him from missing classes seem to back up the widely held theory that he went on spy missions in Spain. When he returned to London, he found fame as a playwright, churning out "blood and thunder" shockers such as *Doctor Faustus* that helped pioneer the use of blank verse, and were some of the first great pieces of secular theatrical entertainment produced in the English language.

But to say that Marlowe had a wild side is to put things mildly. He was imprisoned twice, once for his role in a fight that left a tavern keeper dead (he was acquitted when a jury determined that he'd acted in self-defense), and ran with an underground group of atheists who called themselves "The School of Night." They hung around in graveyards, reading poetry and having the sort of blasphemous debates that were illegal in Elizabethan England, where everyone was required to be a member of the Church of England. Breaking somewhat from her predecessors, Queen Elizabeth generally didn't care too much if people doubted religion in their minds, as long as they kept their mouths shut and kept attending church services. But for someone as famous as Marlowe, to be an open heretic was potentially dangerous.

Richard Baines, a professional snitch, wrote a letter to the government containing a bunch of blasphemous things that he claimed to have heard Marlowe say, such as that Moses was really just a juggler, that people in the New World had stories and histories dating back 10,000 years (which went against the "official" view that the Adam and Eve had lived "within six thousand years,"), and that the Virgin Mary was "dishonest." Around the same time, the government arrested Thomas Kyd, Marlowe's former roommate, for possessing atheist literature, and Kyd said under torture that it was Marlowe who had turned him on to atheism in the first place.

And so, at the height of his fame, Marlowe was arrested for blasphemy. He was released on parole and ordered to check in every day until he was brought to trial, at which he faced a possible sentence of death. If lucky, he would just get his nose chopped off.

Marlowe never once checked in with authorities, so far as is known, and he was killed in Deptford only a couple of weeks later, while awaiting trial.

## An Accident?

The exact circumstances of his death are still not quite agreed upon, though a detailed coroner's report exists. Official documents state that Marlowe and a few other men had spent the day in an establishment owned by "The Widow Bull," but what sort of business this was is a matter of some mystery—it's been variously described as a tavern, a brothel, or a sort of bed and breakfast. The fact that the investigations into what happened that day mention a "reckoning" (bill) is about the only evidence we have that it was any sort of business at all, not just a house owned by Ms. Eleanor Bull.

However, according to official reports, a bill of some sort was presented to Marlowe and his friends. A fight broke out over who should pay it, and in the scuffle, Marlowe somehow accidentally stabbed himself just below the eye and "then and there instantly died."

Now, most fights over bills ("I shouldn't have to pay an equal share, because I just had water and appetizers, not steak and beer . . .") don't end in knife fights, but this explanation seems sensible enough on the surface: The theatres were closed at the time due to a plague outbreak, and Marlowe was probably hard up for money. Perhaps he had taken up an offer of going to dinner thinking that his meal was being paid for, and when he was asked to kick in for the bill, his hot temper got the best of him. He reached for the dagger of one of the other men present— one Ingram Frizer—and stabbed himself while the other men tried to stop him from attacking.

The death was officially determined to be the result of an accidental, self-inflicted wound, but more and more scholars now believe that Marlowe was murdered to make sure he didn't reveal sensitive information at his upcoming trial. It does seem that a lot of people may have had a reason to want Marlowe to be killed before he could go to trial. Frizer, for example, had been working for Thomas Walsingham, a relative of Queen

Elizabeth's secretary of state, and had Marlowe been convicted of atheism, Walsingham himself would have been disgraced, and financially ruined, for having once been Marlowe's patron. Perhaps Frizer was acting on his boss's orders and killed Marlowe to ensure his own future.

But others believe that the "political murder" theory doesn't go far enough, and that the body on the coroner's slab wasn't Marlowe at all, but the body of a man named John Penry who had been hastily hanged. According to this theory, Marlowe wasn't killed at all, but instead escaped to the continent, where he kept on writing. Some of the wildest theories in this vein hold that he was the true author of Shakespeare's plays.

It seems far-fetched at first glance, but if anyone could have pulled off faking his own death, it was Christopher Marlowe. And while conspiracy theorists have tried to claim several people as the "true" author of Shakespeare's works, Marlowe is the only one who was a good enough author that he could have rivaled Shakespeare for the title of greatest dramatist of the English language.

# The Death of John Dillinger or Someone Who Looked Like Him

*On July 22, 1934, outside the Biograph Theater on Chicago's north side, John Dillinger, America's first Public Enemy Number One, passed from this world into the next in a hail of bullets. Or did he? Conspiracy theorists believe that FBI agents shot and killed the wrong man and covered it all up when they realized their mistake. So what really happened that night? Let's first take a look at the main players in this gangland soap opera.*

✳  ✳  ✳  ✳

## Hoover Wants His Man

BORN JUNE 22, 1903, John Dillinger was in his early thirties when he first caught the FBI's eye. They thought they were through with him in January 1934, when he was arrested after shooting a police officer during a bank robbery in East Chicago, Indiana. However, Dillinger managed to stage a daring escape from his Indiana jail cell using a wooden gun painted with black shoe polish.

Once Dillinger left Indiana in a stolen vehicle and crossed into Illinois, he was officially a federal fugitive. J. Edgar Hoover, then director of the FBI, promised a quick apprehension, but Dillinger had other plans. He seemed to enjoy the fact that the FBI was tracking him—rather than go into hiding, he continued robbing banks. Annoyed, Hoover assigned FBI Agent Melvin Purvis to ambush Dillinger. Purvis's plan backfired, though, and Dillinger escaped, shooting and killing two innocent men in the process. After the botched trap, the public was in an uproar and the FBI was under close scrutiny. To everyone at the FBI, the message was clear: Hoover wanted Dillinger, and he wanted him ASAP.

## The Woman in Red

The FBI's big break came in July 1934 with a phone call from a woman named Anna Sage. Sage was a Romanian immigrant who ran a Chicago-area brothel. Fearing that she might be deported, Sage wanted to strike a bargain with the feds. Her proposal was simple: In exchange for not being deported, Sage was willing to give the FBI John Dillinger. According to Sage, Dillinger was dating Polly Hamilton, one of her former employees. Melvin Purvis personally met with Sage and told her he couldn't make any promises but he would do what he could about her pending deportation.

Several days later, on July 22, Sage called the FBI office in Chicago and said that she was going to the movies that night with Dillinger and Hamilton. Sage quickly hung up but not before saying she would wear something bright so that agents could pick out the threesome in a crowd. Not knowing which movie theater they were planning to go to, Purvis dispatched several agents to the Marbro Theater, while he and another group of agents went to the Biograph. At approximately 8:30 p.m., Purvis believed he saw Dillinger, Sage, and Hamilton enter the Biograph. As she had promised, Sage indeed wore something bright—an orange blouse. However, under the marquee lights, the blouse's color appeared to be red, which is why Sage was forever dubbed "The Woman in Red."

Purvis tried to apprehend Dillinger right after he purchased tickets, but he slipped past Purvis and into the darkened theater. Purvis went into the theater but was unable to locate Dillinger in the dark. At that point, Purvis left the theater, gathered his men, and made the decision to apprehend Dillinger as he was exiting the theater. Purvis positioned himself in the theater's vestibule, instructed his men to hide outside, and told them that he would signal them by lighting a cigar when he spotted Dillinger. That was their cue to move in and arrest Dillinger.

### "Stick 'em up, Johnny!"

At approximately 10:30 p.m., the doors to the Biograph opened and people started to exit. All of the agents' eyes were on Purvis. When a man wearing a straw hat, accompanied by two women, walked past Purvis, the agent quickly placed a cigar in his mouth and lit a match. Perhaps sensing something was wrong, the man turned and looked at Purvis, at which point Purvis drew his pistol and said, "Stick 'em up, Johnny!" In response, the man turned as if he was going to run away, while at the same time reaching for what appeared to be a gun. Seeing the movement, the other agents opened fire. As the man ran away, attempting to flee down the alleyway alongside the theater, he was shot four times on his left side and once in the back of the neck before crumpling on the pavement. When Purvis reached him and checked for vitals, there were none. Minutes later, after being driven to a local hospital, John Dillinger was pronounced DOA. But as soon as it was announced that Dillinger was dead, the controversy began.

## Dillinger Disputed

Much of the basis for the conspiracy stems from the fact that Hoover, both publicly and privately, made it clear that no matter what, he wanted Dillinger caught. On top of that, Agent Purvis was under a lot of pressure to capture Dillinger, especially since he'd failed with a previous attempt. Keeping that in mind, it would be easy to conclude that Purvis, in his haste to capture Dillinger, might have overlooked a few things.

First, it was Purvis alone who pointed out the man he thought to be Dillinger to the waiting agents. Conspiracy theorists contend that Purvis fingered the wrong man that night, and an innocent man ended up getting killed as a result. As evidence, they point to Purvis's own statement: While they were standing at close range, the man tried to pull a gun, which is why the agents had to open fire. But even though agents stated they recovered a .38-caliber Colt automatic from the victim's body (and even had it on display for many years), author Jay Robert Nash discovered that that particular model was not even available until a good five months after Dillinger's alleged death! Theorists believe that when agents realized they had not only shot the wrong man, but an unarmed one at that, they planted the gun as part of a cover-up.

Another interesting fact that could have resulted in Purvis's misidentification was that Dillinger had recently undergone plastic surgery in an attempt to disguise himself. In addition to work on his face, Dillinger had attempted to obliterate his fingerprints by dipping his fingers into an acid solution.

On top of that, the man who Purvis claimed was Dillinger was wearing a straw hat the entire time Purvis saw him. It is certainly possible that Purvis did not actually recognize Dillinger but instead picked out someone who merely looked like him. If you remember, the only tip Purvis had was Sage telling him that she was going to the movies with Dillinger and his girlfriend.

Did Purvis see Sage leaving the theater in her orange blouse and finger the wrong man simply because he was standing next to Sage and resembled Dillinger? Or was the whole thing a setup orchestrated by Sage and Dillinger to trick the FBI into executing an innocent man?

## So Who Was It?

If the man shot and killed outside the theater wasn't John Dillinger, who was it? There are several conflicting accounts, but one speculation is that it was a man named Jimmy Lawrence, who was dating Polly Hamilton.

If you believe in the conspiracy, Lawrence was simply in the wrong place at the wrong time. Or possibly, Dillinger purposely sent Lawrence to the theater hoping FBI agents would shoot him, allowing Dillinger to fade into obscurity.

Of course, those who don't believe in the conspiracy say the reason Lawrence looked so much like Dillinger is because he was Dillinger using an alias. Further, Dillinger's sister, Audrey Hancock, identified his body. Finally, they say it all boils down to the FBI losing or misplacing the gun Dillinger had the night he was killed and inadvertently replacing it with the wrong one. Case closed.

Not really, though. It seems that whenever someone comes up with a piece of evidence to fuel the conspiracy theory, someone else has something to refute it. Some have asked that Dillinger's body be exhumed and DNA tests be performed, but nothing has come of it yet. Until that happens, we'll probably never know for sure what really happened on that hot July night back in 1934. But that's okay, because real or imagined, everyone loves a good mystery.

# Thelma Todd: Suicide or Murder?

*During her nine-year film career, Thelma Todd appeared in dozens of classic comedies with the likes of Harry Langdon, Laurel and Hardy, and the Marx Brothers. Today, however, the "Ice Cream Blonde," as she was known, is best remembered for her bizarre death, which remains one of Hollywood's most enduring mysteries. Let's explore what could have happened.*

✳ ✳ ✳ ✳

## Sins Indulged

TODD WAS BORN in Lawrence, Massachusetts, in 1906 and arrived in Hollywood at age 20 via the beauty pageant circuit. Pretty and vivacious, she quickly became a hot commodity and fell headlong into Tinseltown's anything-goes party scene. In 1932, she married Pasquale "Pat" DiCicco, an agent of sorts who was also associated with gangster Charles "Lucky" Luciano. Their marriage was plagued by drunken fights, and they divorced two years later.

For solace, Todd turned to director Roland West, who didn't approve of her drinking and drug use, but was apparently unable to stop her. With his help, Todd opened a roadhouse called Thelma Todd's Sidewalk Café, located on the Pacific Coast Highway, and the actress moved into a spacious apartment above the restaurant. Shortly after, Todd began a relationship with gangster "Lucky" Luciano, who tried to get her to let him use a room at the Sidewalk Café for illegal gambling. Todd repeatedly refused.

On the morning of December 16, 1935, Todd was found dead in the front seat of her 1934 Lincoln Phaeton convertible, which was parked in the two-car garage she shared with West. The apparent cause of death was carbon monoxide poisoning, though whether Todd was the victim of an accident, suicide, or murder remains a mystery.

Little evidence supports the suicide theory, outside the mode of death and the fact that Todd led a fast-paced lifestyle that sometimes got the better of her. Indeed, her career was going remarkably well, and she had purchased Christmas presents and was looking forward to a New Year's Eve party. So suicide does not seem a viable cause, though it is still mentioned as a probable one in many accounts.

## The Accident Theory

However, an accidental death is also a possibility. The key to her car was in the "on" position, and the motor was dead when Todd was discovered by her maid. West suggested to investigators that the actress turned on the car to get warm, passed out because she was drunk, and then succumbed to carbon monoxide poisoning. Todd also had a heart condition, according to West, and this may have contributed to her death.

Nonetheless, the notion of foul play is suggested by several incongruities found at the scene. Spots of blood were discovered on and in Todd's car and on her mouth, and her nose was broken, leading some to believe she was knocked out then placed in the car to make it look like a suicide. (Police attributed the injuries to Todd falling unconscious and striking her head on the steering wheel.)

In addition, Todd's blood-alcohol level was extremely high—high enough to stupefy her so that someone could carry her without her fighting back—and her high-heeled shoes were clean and unscuffed, even though she would have had to ascend a flight of outdoor, concrete stairs to reach the garage, which was a 271-step climb behind the restaurant. Investigators also found an unidentified smudged handprint on the left side of the vehicle.

## Two with Motive

If Todd was murdered, as some have suggested, who had motive? Because of her wild and reckless lifestyle, there are several potential suspects, most notably Pasquale DiCicco, who was known to have a violent temper, and "Lucky" Luciano, who was angry at Todd for refusing to let him use her restaurant for illegal activities.

Despite the many questions raised by the evidence found at the scene, a grand jury ruled Todd's death accidental. The investigation had been hampered by altered and destroyed evidence, threats to witnesses, and cover-ups, making it impossible to ever learn what really happened.

An open-casket service was held at Forest Lawn Memorial Park, where the public viewed the actress bedecked in yellow roses. After the service, Todd was cremated, eliminating the possibility of a second autopsy. Later, when her mother, Alice Todd, died, the actress's ashes were placed in her mother's casket so they could be buried together in Massachusetts.

# Anything but Splendor: Natalie Wood

*The official account of Natalie Wood's tragic death is riddled with holes. For this reason, cover-up theorists continue to run hog-wild with conjecture. Here's a sampling of the questions, facts, and assertions surrounding the case.*

✳   ✳   ✳   ✳

## A Life in Pictures

THERE ARE THOSE who will forever recall Natalie Wood as the adorable child actress from *Miracle on 34th Street* (1947) and those who remember her as the sexy but wholesome grown-up star of movies such as *West Side Story* (1961), *Splendor in the Grass* (1961), and *Bob & Carol & Ted & Alice* (1969). Both groups generally agree that Wood had uncommon beauty and talent. At the time of her death, Natalie Wood's future was bright.

Wood appeared in her very first film, *Happy Land* (1943), in a bit part alongside other people from her hometown of Santa Rosa, California, where the film was shot. She stood out to the director, who remembered her later when he needed to cast a child in another film. Wood was uncommonly mature and professional for a child actress, which helped her make a relatively smooth transition to ingenue roles.

Although Wood befriended James Dean and Sal Mineo—her troubled young costars from *Rebel Without a Cause* (1955)—and she briefly dated Elvis Presley, she preferred to move in established Hollywood circles. By the time she was 20, she was married to Robert Wagner and was costarring with Frank Sinatra in *Kings Go Forth* (1958), which firmly ensconced her in the Hollywood establishment. The early 1960s represent the high point of Wood's career, and she specialized in playing high-spirited characters with determination and spunk.

She added a couple more Oscar nominations to the one she received for *Rebel* and racked up five Golden Globe nominations for Best Actress. This period would also prove to be personally turbulent for Wood, as she suffered through a failed marriage to Wagner and another to Richard Gregson. After taking time off to raise her children, she remarried Wagner and returned to her acting career.

## Shocking News

And so, on November 29, 1981, the headline hit the newswires much like an out-of-control car hits a brick wall. Natalie Wood, the beautiful, vivacious 43-year-old star of stage and screen, had drowned after falling from her yacht the *Splendour*, which was anchored off California's Santa Catalina Island. Wood had been on the boat during a break from her latest film, *Brainstorm*, and was accompanied by Wagner and *Brainstorm* costar Christopher Walken. Skipper Dennis Davern was at the helm. Foul play was not suspected.

## In My Esteemed Opinion

After a short investigation, Chief Medical Examiner Dr. Thomas Noguchi listed Wood's death as an accidental drowning. Tests revealed that she had consumed "seven or eight" glasses of wine, and the coroner contended that in her intoxicated state Wood had probably stumbled and fallen overboard while attempting to untie the yacht's rubber dinghy. He also stated that cuts and bruises on her body could have occurred when she fell from the boat.

## Doubting Thomases

To this day, many people question Wood's mysterious demise and believe that the accidental drowning theory sounds a bit too convenient. Pointed questions have led to many rumors: Does someone know more about Wood's final moments than they're letting on?

Was her drowning really an accident, or did someone intentionally or accidentally *help* her overboard? Could this be why she sustained substantial bruising on her face and the back of her legs? Why was Wagner so reluctant to publicly discuss the incident? Were Christopher Walken and Wood an item as had been rumored? With this possibility in mind, could a booze-fueled fight have erupted between the two men? Could Wood have then tried to intervene, only to be knocked overboard for her efforts? And why did authorities declare Wood's death accidental so quickly? Would such a hasty ruling have been issued had the principals not been famous, wealthy, and influential?

## Ripples

At the time of Wood's death, she and Wagner were seven years into their second marriage to each other. Whether Wood was carrying on an affair with Walken, as was alleged, may be immaterial, even if it made for interesting tabloid fodder. But Wagner's perception of their relationship could certainly be a factor. If nothing else, it might better explain the argument that ensued between Wagner and Walken that fateful night.

## Case Closed?

Further information about Wood's death is sparse because no eyewitnesses have come forward. However, a businesswoman whose boat was anchored nearby testified that she heard a woman shouting for help, and then a voice responding, "We'll be over to get you," so the woman went back to bed. Just after dawn, Wood's body was found floating a mile away from the *Splendour*, approximately 200 yards offshore. The dinghy was found nearby; its only cargo was a stack of lifejackets.

In 2008, after 27 years of silence, Robert Wagner recalled in his autobiography, *Pieces of My Heart: A Life*, that he and Walken had engaged in a heated argument during supper after Walken had suggested that Wood star in more films, effectively keeping her away from their children. Wagner and Walken then headed topside to cool down.

Sometime around midnight, Wagner said he returned to his cabin and discovered that his wife was missing. He soon realized that the yacht's dinghy was gone as well. In his book, he surmised that Wood may have gone to secure the dinghy that had been noisily slapping against the boat. Then, tipsy from the wine, she probably fell into the ocean and drowned. Walken notified the authorities.

Was Natalie Wood's demise the result of a deadly mix of wine and saltwater as the coroner's report suggests? This certainly could be the case. But why would she leave her warm cabin to tend to a loose rubber dinghy in the dark of night? Could an errant rubber boat really make such a commotion?

Perhaps we'll never know what happened that fateful night, but an interview conducted shortly before Wood's death proved prophetic: "I'm frightened to death of the water," said Wood about a long-held fear. "I can swim a little bit, but I'm afraid of water that is dark."

# It's a Bird! It's a Plane! It's ... Avrocar?!?

*Not all UFOs are alien spaceships. One top-secret program was contracted out by the U.S. military to an aircraft company in Canada.*

✳  ✳  ✳  ✳

O H, THE 1950S—A time of sock hops, drive-in movies, and the Cold War between America and the Soviet Union, when each superpower waged war against the other in the arenas of scientific technology, astronomy, and politics. It was also a time when discussion of life on other planets was rampant, fueled by the alleged crash of an alien spaceship near Roswell, New Mexico, in 1947.

## Watch the Skies

Speculation abounded about the unidentified flying objects (UFOs) spotted nearly every week by everyone from farmers to airplane pilots. As time passed, government authorities began to wonder if the flying saucers were, in fact, part of a secret Russian program to create a new type of air force. Fearful that such a craft would upset the existing balance of power, the U.S. Air Force decided to produce its own saucer-shape ship.

In 1953, the military contacted Avro Aircraft Limited of Canada, an aircraft manufacturing company that operated in Malton, Ontario, between 1945 and 1962. Project Silverbug was initially proposed simply because the government wanted to find out if UFOs could be manufactured by humans. But before long, both the military and the scientific community were speculating about its potential. Intrigued by the idea, designers at Avro—led by British aeronautical engineer John Frost—began working on the VZ-9-AV Avrocar. The round craft would have been right at home in a scene from the classic science fiction film *The Day the Earth Stood Still*. Security for the project was so tight that it probably generated rumors that America was actually testing a captured alien spacecraft—speculation that remains alive and well even today.

## Of This Earth

By 1958, the company had produced two prototypes, which were 18 feet in diameter and 3.5 feet tall. Constructed around a large triangle, the Avrocar was shaped like a disk, with a curved upper surface. It included an enclosed 124-blade turbo-rotor at the center of the triangle, which provided lifting power through an opening in the bottom of the craft. The turbo also powered the craft's controls. Although conceived as being able to carry two passengers, in reality a single pilot could barely fit inside the cramped space. The Avrocar was operated with a single control stick, which activated different panels around the ship. Airflow issued from a large center ring, which was controlled by the pilot to guide the craft either vertically or horizontally.

The military envisioned using the craft as "flying Jeeps" that would hover close to the ground and move at a maximum speed of 40 miles per hour. But that, apparently, was only going to be the beginning of the hovering age. Avro had its own grand plans, which included not just commercial Avrocars, but also a family-size Avrowagon, an Avrotruck for larger loads, Avroangel to rush people to the hospital, and a military Avropelican, which, like a pelican hunting for fish, would conduct surveillance for submarines.

## But Does It Fly?

The prototypes impressed the U.S. Army enough to award Avro a $2 million contract. Unfortunately, the Avrocar project was canceled when an economic downturn forced the company to temporarily close and restructure. When Avro Aircraft reopened, the original team of designers had dispersed. Further efforts to revive the project were unsuccessful, and repeated testing proved that the craft was inherently unstable.

It soon became apparent that whatever UFOs were spotted overhead, it was unlikely they came from this planet. Project Silverbug was abandoned when funding ran out in March 1961, but one of the two Avrocar prototypes is housed at the U.S. Army Transportation Museum in Fort Eustis, Virginia.

# The Philadelphia Experiment

*In 1943, the Navy destroyer USS Eldridge reportedly vanished, teleported from a dock in Pennsylvania to one in Virginia, and then rematerialized—all as part of a top-secret military experiment. Is there any fact to this fiction?*

✳ ✳ ✳ ✳

### The Genesis of a Myth

THE STORY OF the Philadelphia Experiment began with the scribbled annotations of a crazed genius, Carlos Allende, who in 1956 read *The Case for the UFO*, by science enthusiast Morris K. Jessup. Allende wrote chaotic annotations in his copy of the book, claiming, among other things, to know the answers to all the scientific and mathematical questions that Jessup's book touched upon. Jessup's interests included the possible military applications of electromagnetism, antigravity, and Einstein's Unified Field Theory.

Allende wrote two letters to Jessup, warning him that the government had already put Einstein's ideas to dangerous use. According to Allende, at some unspecified date in October 1943, he was serving aboard a merchant ship when he witnessed a disturbing naval experiment. The USS *Eldridge* disappeared, teleported from Philadelphia, Pennsylvania, to Norfolk, Virginia, and then reappeared in a matter of minutes. The men onboard the ship allegedly phased in and out of visibility or lost their minds and jumped overboard, and a few of them disappeared forever. This strange activity was part of an apparently successful military experiment to render ships invisible.

## The Navy Gets Involved

Allende could not provide Jessup with any evidence for these claims, so Jessup stopped the correspondence. But in 1956, Jessup was summoned to Washington, D.C., by the Office of Naval Research, which had received Allende's annotated copy of Jessup's book and wanted to know about Allende's claims and his written comments.

Shortly thereafter, Varo Corporation, a private group that does research for the military, published the annotated book, along with the letters Allende had sent to Jessup. The Navy has consistently denied Allende's claims about teleporting ships, and the impetus for publishing Allende's annotations is unclear. Morris Jessup committed suicide in 1959, leading some conspiracy theorists to claim that the government had him murdered for knowing too much about the experiments.

## The Facts in the Fiction

It is not certain when Allende's story came to be termed the "Philadelphia Experiment," but over time, sensationalist books and movies have touted it as such. The date of the ship's disappearance is usually cited as October 28, though Allende himself did not verify the date or identify any other witnesses. However, the inspiration behind Allende's claims is not a complete mystery.

In 1943, the Navy was in fact conducting experiments, some of which were surely top secret, and sometimes they involved research into the applications of some of Einstein's theories. The Navy had no idea how to make ships invisible, but it *did* want to make ships "invisible"—i.e., undetectable—to enemy magnetic torpedoes. Experiments such as these involved wrapping large cables around Navy vessels and pumping them with electricity in order to descramble their magnetic signatures.

# The Mystery of Montauk

*Montauk, a beach community at the eastern tip of Long Island in the state of New York, has been deigned the Miami Beach of the mid-Atlantic. Conspiracy theorists, however, tell another tale. Has the U.S. government been hiding a secret at the former Camp Hero military base there?*

✳  ✳  ✳  ✳

IN THE LATE 1950s, Montauk was not the paradise-style resort it is today. It was an isolated seaside community boasting a lighthouse commissioned by George Washington in 1792, an abandoned military base called Camp Hero, and a huge radar tower. This tower, still standing, is the last semiautomatic ground environment radar tower still in existence and features an antenna called AN/FPS-35. During its time of air force use, the AN/FPS-35 was capable of detecting airborne objects at a distance of more than 200 miles. One of its uses was detecting potential Soviet long-distance bombers, as the Cold War was in full swing. According to conspiracy theorists, however, the antenna and Camp Hero itself had a few other tricks lurking around the premises, namely human mind control and electromagnetic field manipulation.

## Vanishing Act

As detailed in the previous article, the USS *Eldridge* was allegedly made invisible to human sight for a brief moment as it sat in a naval shipyard in Philadelphia in 1943. The event, which has been sworn as true by eyewitnesses and other believers for decades, is said to have been part of a U.S. military endeavor called Project Rainbow.

Studies in electromagnetic radiation had evidenced that manipulating energy fields and bending light around objects in certain ways could render them invisible. Since the benefits to the armed forces would be incredible, the Navy supposedly forged ahead with the first experiment.

There are many offshoots to the conspiracy theory surrounding the alleged event. The crew onboard the USS *Eldridge* at the time in question are said to have suffered various mental illnesses, physical ailments, and, most notably, schizophrenia, which has been medically linked to exposure to electromagnetic radiation. Some of them supposedly disappeared along with the ship and relocated through teleportation to the naval base in Norfolk, Virginia, for a moment. Despite severely conflicting eyewitness reports and the navy's assertion that the *Eldridge* wasn't even in Philadelphia that day, many websites, books, a video game, and a 1984 science fiction film detail the event.

But what does this have to do with Montauk right now?

## What's in the Basement?

Camp Hero was closed as an official U.S. Army base in November 1957, although the Air Force continued to use the radar facilities. After the Air Force left in 1980, the surrounding grounds were ultimately turned into a state park, which opened to the public in September 2002. Yet the camp's vast underground facility remains under tight government jurisdiction, and the AN/FPS-35 radar tower still stands. Many say there is a government lab on the site that continues the alleged teleportation, magnetic field manipulation, and mind-control experiments that originated with Project Rainbow. One reason for this belief is that two of the sailors onboard the *Eldridge* on October 24, 1943—Al Bielek and Duncan Cameron—claimed to have jumped from the ship while it was in "hyperspace" between Philadelphia and Norfolk, and landed at Camp Hero, severely disoriented.

Though Project Rainbow was branded a hoax, an urban legend continues to surround its "legacy," which is commonly known as the Montauk Project. Theorists cite experiments in electromagnetic radiation designed to produce mass schizophrenia over time and reduce a populace's resistance to governmental control, which, they say, would explain the continual presence of the antenna. According to these suspicions, a large number of orphans, loners, and homeless people are subjected to testing in Camp Hero's basement; most supposedly die as a result. Interestingly, some conspiracy theorists believe that one outcropping of the experiments is the emergence and rapid popularity of the cell phone, which uses and produces electromagnetic and radio waves. Who knew that easier communication was really an evil government plot to turn people into mindless robots?

# Welcome to Hell Town

*Looking for a scary adventure in Ohio? Then dare to travel to Hell Town in Summit County. According to local legend, it's a sinister place where a host of nefarious characters partner with the U.S. government to protect dark secrets.*

✳   ✳   ✳   ✳

STANFORD ROAD, THE only road into the once prosperous town of Boston Mills, is chained off at both ends. Throughout the town, conspicuous "U.S. PROPERTY—NO TRESPASSING" signs are affixed on abandoned houses. At night, local law enforcement officials curtly order loiterers to move on during regular patrols.

This is a place known throughout large parts of Ohio as Hell Town. According to local legend, it's an evil and foreboding place that holds dark secrets—and though it may seem quiet, danger is all around.

From all the signs posted, conspiracy theorists have jumped to the conclusion that the government doesn't want people hanging around. Supposedly, it's all part of an elaborate scheme to cover up a disastrous chemical spill that turned town residents into disfigured mutants. The urban myth goes on to say that most were evacuated and never seen again, but some still lurk about, snatching those who unwittingly wander into the town.

## Cults, Ghosts, and Lunatics

The legend maintains that the government cover-up is only part of the story. A lot of weird stuff is said to happen in Hell Town, all of which is perpetrated by a host of dark, sinister characters. In short, it's not just chemically altered mutants out to get you in Hell Town:

**A Satanic cult now calls Boston Mills home!** Satanists have chained Stanford Road to keep people out and their devilish activities a secret. Devil-worshipping congregations hold candlelit black masses at the old Mother of Sorrows church, which is marked by Satanic symbols of upside-down crosses, and practice other nefarious rituals in the abandoned funeral home (also called the old slaughterhouse) near the Boston Cemetery.

**The Highway to Hell!** An evil paranormal force compels cars to crash or veer off of Stanford Road, dubbed the "Highway to Hell." Passengers then fall prey to swarms of cult members who suddenly emerge from the woods—or the ruthless axe murderer who lives in the woods and continues to elude capture by the police.

**The marauding hearse!** If they somehow manage to dodge the cult members and axe murderer on Stanford Road, visitors who reach town should beware a creepy man driving an old funeral hearse with one working headlight. If they try chasing him down, he and his ghoulish wheels will simply vanish.

**The haunted cemetery!** The grounds of the old Boston Cemetery are haunted by a specter that sits on a bench and stares into the distance, and they are also guarded by Satanists who mystically maneuver the trees from one spot to another to scare people away.

**Get on the bus of death!** An old abandoned school bus sits in the town, a reminder of a grisly incident in which the last children to ride on it were slaughtered in the woods by an escaped mental patient (or a serial killer or the Satanists again) after the bus ran out of gas on a secluded road. There are no seats in the bus, but at night, the kids can be seen sitting on the bus in their spots—sometimes they're calm, other times they're crying and screaming. Sitting in the back of the bus is an eerie ghostlike man smoking a cigarette. All attempts to remove the bus have ended in tragic misfortune, so now it's left to sit.

**The church cellar dweller!** An evil old man dwells in the basement of the Boston Community Church. Once a respected member of the community, he now hides his face when spotted through the basement windows, ashamed of his secretive past as the leader of a clandestine Satanic cult.

## And Now, the Real Story:

The federal government did force residents to leave Boston Mills, but not because of a disfiguring chemical spill. In the mid-1970s, the National Park Service appropriated hundreds of properties in the area to create national parkland—and most homeowners were compelled to sell and move from the area. It was all done rather quickly, thus making it seem as if the locals had vanished overnight. The government slapped its signs on the houses; some were demolished, some were boarded up and left untouched, and a few were used for firefighting training.

Abandoned and burned-out houses, closed roads, government signs, police patrols—and not a soul for miles. It's all given rise to rumors of sinister happenings at Boston Mills. For the record, there never was a chemical spill at Boston Mills; the local municipality closed Stanford Road because it's in a state of disrepair. The cops on patrol are merely there to ward off the increased numbers of vandals and trespassers as the town grows in infamy. While they make for a great story, the legends surrounding the town—and the attention they generate—are of serious detriment to the few residents who elected to stay.

# Who Shot JFK?
# Conspiracy Theories

*Conspiracy theories are a favorite American pastime, right up there with alien abductions and Elvis sightings. Perhaps no conspiracy theories are more popular than the ones involving that afternoon in Dallas—November 22, 1963—when the United States lost a president. John F. Kennedy's life and death have reached out to encompass everyone from Marilyn Monroe to Fidel Castro, Sam Giancana to J. Edgar Hoover.*

✳ **The single-shooter theory:** This is the one the Warren Commission settled on—that Lee Harvey Oswald (and only Lee Harvey Oswald), firing his Mannlicher-Carcano rifle from the window of the Texas Book Depository, killed the president in Dealey Plaza. But this is the official finding, and where's the excitement in that?

✳ **The two-shooter theory:** A second shooter on the nearby grassy knoll fired at the same time as Oswald. His bullets hit Texas Governor John Connally and struck President Kennedy from the front. This theory arose after U.S. Marine sharpshooters at Quantico tried to duplicate the single-shooter theory but found it was impossible for all the shots to have come from the Book Depository.

✳ **The LBJ theory:** Lyndon Johnson's mistress, Madeleine Brown, said that the vice president met with powerful Texans the night before the killing. She claimed he told her, "After tomorrow those goddamn Kennedys will never embarrass me again—that's no threat—that's a promise." Jack Ruby also implicated LBJ, as did E. Howard Hunt, just before his death.

✳ **The CIA theory:** After Kennedy forced Allen Dulles to resign as head of the CIA following the Bay of Pigs fiasco, the CIA, resenting Kennedy's interference, took its revenge on the president. They'd had plenty of practice helping plotters take out Patrice Lumumba of the Congo, Rafael Trujillo of the Dominican Republic, and President Ngo Dinh Diem of Vietnam.

* **The Cuban exiles theory:** Reflecting more bitterness over the Bay of Pigs, the powerful Cuban exile community in the United States was eager to see Kennedy dead and said so. However, this probably played no part in the assassination.

* **The J. Edgar Hoover and the Mafia theory:** The Mafia was said to have been blackmailing Hoover about his homosexuality for ages. The theory goes that when Attorney General Robert Kennedy began to legally pursue Jimmy Hoffa and Mafia bosses in Chicago, Tampa, and New Orleans, they sent Hoover after JFK as payback.

* **The organized crime theory:** Chicago Mafia boss Sam Giancana, who supposedly shared the affections of Marilyn Monroe with both JFK and RFK—using Frank Sinatra as a go-between—felt betrayed when RFK went after the mob. After all, hadn't they fixed JFK's 1960 election? This theory is a tabloid favorite.

* **The Soviet theory:** High-ranking Soviet defector Ion Pacepa said that Soviet intelligence chiefs believed that the KGB had orchestrated the Dallas killing. But they were probably just bragging.

* **The Roscoe White theory:** According to White's son, this Dallas police officer was part of a three-man assassination team. The junior White, however, gives no indication of the reasons behind the plot.

* **The Saul theory:** A professional hit man was paid $50,000 to kill Kennedy by a group of very powerful, unknown men. He was also supposed to kill Oswald. Clearly, this theory isn't thick with details.

* **The Castro theory:** Supposedly the Cuban government contracted Oswald to kill Kennedy, telling him that there was an escape plan. There wasn't.

* **The Israeli theory:** Angry with JFK for pressuring them not to develop nuclear weapons and/or for employing ex-Nazis in the space program, the Israelis supposedly conspired in his assassination.

* **The Federal Reserve theory:** Kennedy issued Executive Order 11110, enabling the U.S. Treasury to print silver certificates in an attempt to drain the silver reserves. It is theorized that such a development would severely limit the economic power of the Federal Reserve. Could this have played into his assassination?

People will probably still be spinning these theories in a hundred years. But then, everyone needs a hobby.

# Manhattan Decoded

*When rumors emerged that Nazi Germany was developing an atomic bomb during World War II, the United States quickly initiated its own program, the Manhattan Project. Where did this name come from?*

✻   ✻   ✻   ✻

THE VENTURE CULMINATED in the detonation of the first atomic weapon in the New Mexico desert on July 16, 1945, and then the strikes on Hiroshima and Nagasaki that ended the war. Many people assume that the top-secret plan was given the cover name the Manhattan Project simply to confuse the enemy. In fact, the New York borough played a key part in the development of the bomb.

In 1942, General Leslie R. Groves, deputy chief of construction for the U.S. Army Corps of Engineers, was appointed to direct the top-secret project. The United States needed to build an atomic weapon before Germany or Japan did. Groves established three large engineering and production centers at remote U.S. sites in Oak Ridge, Tennessee; Hanford, Washington; and Los Alamos, New Mexico. The project's headquarters, however, was situated at 270 Broadway, New York City, home to the Army Corps of Engineers' North Atlantic division.

## Standard Operating Procedure

The first proposed cover name for the project was the Laboratory for the Development of Substitute Materials. That hardly rolls off the tongue, and Groves also felt that it would draw unwanted attention to the operation. Instead, he opted to follow Corps procedure and name the unit after its geographical area. The initial cover name of Manhattan Engineer District soon was shortened to the Manhattan Project. In 1943, the headquarters moved to Oak Ridge, Tennessee, and while much of Manhattan's early role in the project has been forgotten, there is a poignant reminder on Riverside Drive outside the New York Buddhist Church: It's the statue of a monk that survived the atomic bombing of Hiroshima.

# Space Ghosts

*Shortly after the Soviet Union successfully launched Sputnik 1 on October 4, 1957, rumors swirled that several cosmonauts had died during missions gone horribly wrong, and that their spacecraft had drifted out of Earth's orbit and into the vast reaches of the universe.*

❋   ❋   ❋   ❋

IT WAS EASY to believe such stories at the time. After all, the United States was facing off against the Soviet Union in the Cold War, and the thought that the ruthless Russians would do anything to win the space race—including sending cosmonauts to their doom—seemed plausible.

However, numerous researchers have investigated the stories and concluded that, though the Soviet space program was far from perfect and some cosmonauts had in fact died, there are no dead cosmonauts floating in space.

According to authors Hal Morgan and Kerry Tucker, the earliest rumors of deceased cosmonauts even mentioned their names and the dates of their doomed missions: Aleksei Ledovsky in 1957, Serenti Shiborin in 1958, and Mirya Gromova in 1959. In fact, by the time Yuri Gagarin became the first human in space in April 1961, the alleged body count exceeded a dozen.

## Space Spies

So prevalent were these stories that no less an "authority" than *Reader's Digest* reported on them in its April 1965 issue. Key to the mystery were two brothers in Italy, Achille and Giovanni Battista Judica-Cordiglia, who operated a homemade listening post with a huge dish antenna. Over a seven-month period, the brothers claimed to have overheard radio signals from three troubled Soviet spacecraft:

+ On November 28, 1960, a Soviet spacecraft supposedly radioed three times, in Morse code and in English, "SOS to the entire world."

+ In early February 1961, the brothers are alleged to have picked up the sound of a rapidly beating heart and labored breathing, which they interpreted to be the final throes of a dying cosmonaut.

+ On May 17, 1961, two men and a woman were allegedly overheard saying, in Russian, "Conditions growing worse. Why don't you answer? We are going slower . . . the world will never know about us."

## The Black Hole of Soviet PR

One reason rumors of dead cosmonauts were so believable was the extremely secretive nature of the early Soviet space program. Whereas the United States touted its program as a major advance in science and its astronauts as public heroes, the Soviet Union revealed little about its program or the people involved in it.

It's not surprising, then, that the Soviet Union did not report to the world the death of Valentin Bondarenko, a cosmonaut who died tragically in a fire after he tossed an alcohol-soaked cotton ball on a hot plate and ignited the oxygen-rich chamber in which he was training. He died in 1961, but it wasn't revealed publicly until 1986.

Adding to the rumors was the fact that other cosmonauts had been mysteriously airbrushed out of official government photographs. However, most had been removed because they had been dropped from the space program for academic, disciplinary, or medical reasons—not because they had died during a mission. One cosmonaut, Grigoriy Nelyubov, was booted from the program in 1961 for engaging in a drunken brawl at a rail station (he died five years later when he stepped in front of a train). Nelyubov's story, like so many others, was not made public until the mid-1980s.

Only one Soviet cosmonaut is known to have died during an actual space mission. In 1967, Vladimir Komarov was killed when the parachute on his *Soyuz 1* spacecraft failed to open properly during reentry. A Russian engineer later acknowledged that Komarov's mission had been ordered before the spacecraft had been fully debugged, likely for political reasons.

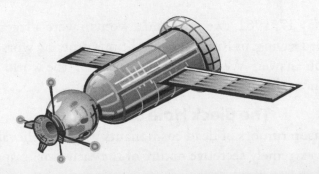

# The Real Manchurian Candidates

*From the mid-1950s through at least the early 1970s, thousands of unwitting Americans and Canadians became part of a bizarre CIA research project codenamed MKULTRA. Participants were secretly "brainwashed"—drugged with LSD and other hallucinogens, subjected to electro-convulsive shock therapy, and manipulated with abusive mind-control techniques.*

✳  ✳  ✳  ✳

MKULTRA BEGAN IN 1953 under the orders of CIA director Allen Dulles. The program, which was in direct violation of the human rights provisions of the Nuremberg Code that the United States helped establish after WWII, was developed in response to reports that U.S. prisoners of war in Korea were being subjected to Communist mind-control techniques.

CIA researchers hoped to find a "truth drug" that could be used on Soviet agents, as well as drugs that could be used against foreign leaders (one documented scheme involved an attempt in 1960 to dose Fidel Castro with LSD). They also aimed to develop means of mind control that would benefit U.S. intelligence, perhaps including the creation of so-called "Manchurian Candidates" to carry out assassinations. As part of MKULTRA, the CIA investigated parapsychology and such phenomena as hypnosis, telepathy, precognition, photokinesis, and "remote viewing."

MKULTRA was headed by Dr. Sidney Gottlieb, a military psychiatrist and chemist known as the "Black Sorcerer," who specialized in concocting deadly poisons. More than 30 universities and scientific institutes took part in MKULTRA. LSD and other mind-altering drugs including heroin, mescaline, psilocybin, scopolamine, marijuana, and sodium pentothal were given to CIA employees, military personnel, and other government workers, often without the subjects' knowledge or prior consent. To broaden their subject pool, researchers targeted unsuspecting civilians, often those in vulnerable or socially compromising situations. Prison inmates, prostitutes, and mentally ill hospital patients were often used. In a project code-named Operation Midnight Climax, the CIA set up brothels in several U.S. cities to lure men as unwitting test subjects. Rooms were equipped with cameras that filmed the experiments behind one-way mirrors. Some civilian subjects who consented to participation were used for more extreme experimentation. One group of volunteers in Kentucky was given LSD for more than 70 straight days.

In the 1960s, Dr. Gottlieb also traveled to Vietnam and conducted mind-control experiments on Viet Cong prisoners of war being held by U.S. forces. During the same time period, an unknown number of Soviet agents died in U.S. custody in Europe after being given dual intravenous injections of barbiturates and amphetamine in the CIA's search for a truth serum.

MKULTRA experiments were also carried out in Montreal, Canada, between 1957 and 1964 by Dr. Donald Ewen Cameron, a researcher in Albany, New York, who also served as president of the World Psychiatric Association and the American and Canadian psychiatric associations. The CIA appears to have given him potentially deadly experiments to carry out at Canadian mental health institutes so U.S. citizens would not be involved. Cameron also experimented with paralytic drugs—in some cases inducing a coma in subjects for up to three months—as well as using electro-convulsive therapy at 30 times the normal voltage. The subjects were often women being treated for anxiety disorders and postpartum depression. Many suffered permanent damage. A lawsuit by victims of the experiments later uncovered that the Canadian government had also funded the project.

At least one American subject died in the experiments. Frank Olson, a U.S. army biological weapons researcher, was secretly given LSD in 1953. A week later, he fell from a hotel window in New York City following a severe psychotic episode. A CIA doctor assigned to monitor Olson claimed he jumped from the window, but an autopsy performed on Olson's exhumed remains in 1994 found that he had been knocked unconscious before the fall.

The U.S. army also conducted experiments with psychoactive drugs. A later investigation determined that nearly all army experiments involved soldiers and civilians who had given their informed consent, and that army researchers had largely followed scientific and safety protocols. Ken Kesey, who would later write *One Flew over the Cuckoo's Nest* and become one of the originators of the hippie movement, volunteered for LSD studies at an army research center in San Francisco in 1960. LSD stolen from the army lab by test subjects was some of the first in the world used "recreationally" by civilians. The army's high ethical standards, however, seem to have been absent in at least one case. Harold Blauer, a professional tennis player in New York City who was hospitalized for depression following his divorce, died from apparent cardiac arrest during an army experiment in 1952. Blauer had been secretly injected with massive doses of mescaline.

CIA researchers eventually concluded that the effects of LSD were too unpredictable to be useful, and the agency later acknowledged that their experiments made little scientific sense. Records on 150 MKULTRA research projects were destroyed in 1973 by order of CIA Director Richard Helms. A year later, the *New York Times* first reported about CIA experiments on U.S. citizens. In 1975, congressional hearings and a report by the Rockefeller Commission revealed details of the program. In 1976, President Gerald Ford issued an executive order prohibiting experimentation with drugs on human subjects without their informed consent. Ford and CIA Director William Colby also publicly apologized to Frank Olson's family, who received $750,000 by a special act of Congress.

Though no evidence exists that the CIA succeeded in its quest to find mind-control techniques, some conspiracy theories claim that the MKULTRA project was linked to the assassination of Robert F. Kennedy. Some have argued that Kennedy's assassin, Sirhan B. Sirhan, had been subjected to mind control. Sirhan claims that he has no recollection of shooting Kennedy, despite attempts by both government prosecutors and his defense lawyers to use hypnosis to recover his memories.

# Murder in the Vatican

*As head of the Catholic Church, they serve as the Vicar of Christ and are among the world's most respected leaders. Yet over the centuries, this hasn't always been the case for the popes of Rome. Dozens have met untimely fates at the hands of pagan oppressors, rivals to their papal throne, scheming cardinals, plotting aristocrats, and outraged husbands.*

✳ ✳ ✳ ✳

MANY OF THE first 25 popes are believed to have been martyred by the Romans. Pontian (230–235) is the first pope recorded by history as having been murdered for his beliefs. Arrested under the orders of the emperor, Pontian was exiled to Sardinia—then known as the "island of death"— where he is believed to have died from starvation and exposure. Sixtus II (257–258) was another early martyr, killed in the persecutions of Emperor Valerian, who condemned all Christian priests, bishops, and deacons to death. Sixtus was arrested by soldiers while giving a sermon and may have been beheaded on the spot. Martin I (649–653) began his papacy on bad terms with Emperor Constans II, who refused to recognize his election. Martin made matters worse by condemning the doctrines of the Monothelite heretics, whose tenets were followed by many powerful Roman officials, including Constans II. Ordered to Constantinople, Martin I was sentenced to death and exiled to the Crimea, where he died of starvation.

The martyrdom of popes passed into history with the fall of the Roman Empire, but the ascendancy of the Church was accompanied by endless intrigues. From the 9th to the 20th centuries—when popes served not only as head of the church but as rulers of the Papal State, a substantial kingdom in central Italy—rumors abounded that many had been murdered.

Most documented murders occurred during the Middle Ages, particularly between 867 and 964, the so-called Iron Age of the Papacy, when the politically powerful families of Rome had pontiffs elected, deposed, and killed to advance their own ambitions. Seven popes died by violence during this period.

The first to receive this dubious honor was Pope John VIII (872–882), who was so concerned about plots swirling around him that he had several powerful bishops and cardinals excommunicated. Unknown conspirators convinced a relative to poison his drink. When the poison failed to kill him, he was clubbed to death by his own aides. According to some accounts, however, Pope John was actually Pope Joan—a female pope who was erased from the historical record when her true identity was uncovered. Though some historians believe Pope Joan is a myth, others point to a supposed Church ritual that began in the late 9th century, in which a papal candidate sat in an elevated chair with his genitals exposed, prompting passing cardinals to exclaim in Latin, "He has testicles, and they hang well!" Lacking a similar endowment, Pope Joan may have paid with her life.

Stephen VI (896–897) was the "mad pope" who placed his rival, the late Pope Formosus, on trial nine months after his death. The dead pope had enraged Stephen by crowning one of the illegitimate heirs of Charlemagne as emperor, after having performed the same rite for Stephen's favorite candidate. Formosus's corpse was disinterred, placed on a throne in the council chambers, and provided with legal council. When Stephen VI had finished hurling abuse at the corpse, it was thrown from a balcony to a waiting mob and dumped into the Tiber River. All ordinations performed by Formosus were annulled. In the tumult that followed among the Roman aristocracy, Stephen was imprisoned and ultimately strangled to death, making way for a saner pontiff.

The carnage continued over the next few hundred years. Adrian III (884–885) was allegedly poisoned. Leo V (903) was allegedly strangled. John X (914–928) may have been smothered with a pillow. Both Stephen VII (928–931) and Stephen VIII (939–942) met similar untimely ends due to palace intrigues.

John XII (955–964) was only 18 years old when elected pope. A notorious womanizer, he turned the papal palace into something resembling a brothel. He either suffered a heart attack while with a mistress or was murdered by a cuckolded husband. Pope Benedict V (964–966) raped a young girl and fled to Constantinople with the papal treasury, only to return to Rome when his coffers were empty. He was killed by a jealous husband, his corpse bearing a hundred dagger wounds as it was dragged through the streets.

Benedict VI (973–974) and John XIV (983–984) had strangely parallel fates. Intriguers rebelled against Benedict VI after the death of his protector, Emperor Otto the Great. Benedict VI was strangled by a priest on the orders of Crescentius, brother of the late Pope John XIII. Boniface Franco, a deacon who supported Crescentius, became Pope Boniface VII but fled Rome due to the people's outrage over Benedict's murder, becoming Antipope Boniface. John XIV was chosen as a replacement by Emperor Otto II without consultation of the Church. When Otto suddenly died, another new pope was left without allies. Antipope Boniface returned and had John XIV thrown in prison, where he starved to death.

Popes Gregory V (996–999), Sergius IV (1009–1012), Clement II (1046–1047), and Damasus II (1048) were all allegedly poisoned or met otherwise convenient ends. Boniface

VIII (1294–1303) died from beatings by his French captors while held prisoner in Anagni. Benedict XI (1304–1305) may have also been poisoned.

Officially, no pope has been murdered in the modern age, though rumors held that Pope Clement XIV was poisoned in 1771, following his disbandment of the Jesuits. Two hundred years passed before such allegations arose again in 1978 with the sudden death of Pope John Paul I, who had planned such reforms as ordaining women as priests and welcoming gays into the church. In both cases, coroners and investigators found no evidence of foul play. John Paul's successor, John Paul II, was nearly murdered in St. Peter's Square in 1981 by Mehmet Ali Agca, a Turkish gunman who was part of a conspiracy involving the KGB and Bulgarian secret police.

# The Explosion of the *Sultana*

*A mysterious ship explosion took the lives of hundreds on board, including many Union soldiers on their way back home after the South had surrendered.*

✳ ✳ ✳ ✳

IT SHOULD HAVE been a voyage of joy for many of the Union soldiers on the steamship *Sultana*. On April 27, 1865, the war was over, and they had finally been released from Andersonville and other prison camps. They were hungry and fatigued, and they simply wanted to go home. Passing the time on the two-day voyage north up the Mississippi, they played cards, slept, and told stories of the war recently concluded. They didn't know that, although the war was over, their ordeal was not.

## Heavy Load

The *Sultana* had only been in service for two years. A side-wheel steamboat of 1,700 tons, it was overcrowded as it left the port of Memphis at around midnight on its way to Cairo, Illinois. At least 2,300 people crowded the decks, far more than the boat's capacity of at least 400. In addition to its soldiers, refugees, and civilians, the boat had also taken on more than 1,500 horses, cows, pigs, and other animals.

## Boiling Point

Nate Wintringer, the *Sultana*'s chief engineer, had been dealing with a leak in the ship's boiler since the start of the voyage in Vicksburg, Mississippi. Wintringer and his crew were doing the best they could to patch the boiler with plugs and iron straps. He knew the boiler needed major work, but his experience told him the machine would hold out until they reached their final destination.

At about 2:00 a.m., as the ship was passing Paddy's Old Hen and Chickens islands just north of Memphis, a huge explosion shook the vessel. Passengers scrambled to escape the flaming wreckage, but the disaster claimed about 1,700 lives—because the precise number of passengers is unknown, so is the number who died, but it was more than died on the *Titanic*. Many of the hundreds who did make it off later died from the wounds they had sustained. Only one woman escaped: Anna Annis. Her husband—Union Lieutenant Harvey Annis—her child, and her sister all perished in the tragedy.

## Conspiracy Theory

An official inquiry blamed the explosion on the leaking boiler, although leaking equipment such as that was not known to explode. Theories abounded that it was a guerrilla attack, which would not have been unheard of at the time. Confederate sympathizers continued to harass Union ships and troops, even after the official surrender had been signed. In fact, just before the *Sultana* sailed, a communications ship named the *Greyhound* had been sabotaged when explosives were placed in the coal bunkers.

The belief that the explosion was not an accident was given new life in 1888 when William Streetor, formerly a Union prison clerk, claimed that Robert Lowden, a known Confederate operative, had destroyed the *Sultana*. Streetor said that Lowden had told him how he smuggled a bomb disguised as a lump of coal onto the ship and placed it in the coal pile. When it was shoveled into the furnace, the theory goes, the ship exploded.

### Sunken Treasure

Following the explosion, the charred hulk of the ship would remain in the Mississippi mud. When the river was low, bones, skulls, and personal articles could be seen on the ship. Some of the items would occasionally wash to shore to be grabbed by morbid souvenir hunters. A rumor also surfaced that $18,000 in gold was on the ship, launching a number of dives, but no such treasure was ever discovered.

# Indestructible Fidel: Assassination Plots Against Castro

*American intelligence agencies were active and successful during the Cold War. But how come no one could kill the leader of Cuba?*

✳   ✳   ✳   ✳

PERHAPS NO HUMAN being in history has survived more assassination attempts than Fidel Castro. A popular leader who overthrew the hated Cuban dictator Fulgencio Batista in 1959, Castro had first attempted to organize the people of Cuba directly into revolution, but he was thrown into prison in 1953. He had his first brush with assassination there: Batista ordered the guards to poison Castro, but none of them would do it. In 1955, after Batista made an election promise to free political prisoners, he ordered Castro's release. But the dictator was not about to let bygones be bygones. He sent an assassin named Eutimio Guerra to get close to Castro, but the revolutionary leader was suspicious of Guerra and gave him the slip. Castro seemed to lead a charmed life, and his revolutionary army moved from town to town fighting for Cuba until it was free of Batista.

After overthrowing Fulgencio Batista and liberating the island nation, Castro became wildly popular with the majority of Cubans, although he was looked on with suspicion by almost everyone else abroad. And because he did not receive support from Cuba's traditional allies (including the United States) Castro had little or no choice but to ally Cuba with the Soviet Union. After all, he was just following the age-old maxim—"The enemy of my enemy is my friend." And what an enemy he made!

## Before the Bay of Pigs

Most people think that the halfhearted backing of the Bay of Pigs invasion was the starting gun for hostility between Castro and John F. Kennedy, but it was Dwight Eisenhower who set the "Kill Fidel Contest" in motion in 1960 with what ultimately became Operation Mongoose—400 CIA agents working full-time to remove the Cuban dictator.

At first, they decided to train paramilitary guerrillas to eliminate Castro in a traditional commando operation, but his immense popularity among the Cuban people made that impossible. The CIA did all the preliminary work on the Bay of Pigs. Then Eisenhower left office, and Kennedy came upon the scene.

The Bay of Pigs invasion turned out to be a fiasco, and a year and a half later the Cuban Missile Crisis almost triggered a full-scale nuclear war. America's only answer seemed to be to get rid of Fidel and try to turn Cuba back into a pliant banana republic (or in this case, sugarcane republic). But who would do it—and how?

## Up to the Job?

The problem was that everyone wanted to get in on the act. The U.S. government hated having a Soviet base 90 miles from Florida. Batista Cubans, who'd lost their big-moneyed businesses, wanted their privileged lives back. Anticommunists such as FBI boss J. Edgar Hoover viewed a plot to assassinate

Castro as a struggle against elemental evil. American businesses that relied on sugar felt the loss of their cheap supply. The Mafia, which had owned lucrative casinos and brothels in Havana, wanted revenge. As it turned out, the Mafia had the best shot—and they had help.

The CIA, not being able to handle the job themselves, hired Mafia members to terminate Castro with extreme prejudice. In exchange, the CIA pressured the FBI to offer the Mafia a certain amount of immunity in the United States. But the Mafia got used to the new leniency, which would end if Castro were killed, so they strung the Agency along with false promises to kill Castro if the CIA would continue to protect them from the FBI.

Meanwhile, President Kennedy grew impatient. Changing the name of Operation Mongoose to Operation Freedom, he sent the American intelligence community in a full-time rush to whack Fidel. But after the Bay of Pigs, intelligence planners believed that conventional measures wouldn't work, so the attempts became more strange:

❋ During a United Nations meeting at which Castro was present, an agent working for the CIA managed to slip a poisoned cigar into Fidel's cigar case, but someone figured it out before Castro could light up.

❋ Another idea was to send Castro on an acid trip by dosing his cigars with LSD. He would appear psychotic, and his sanity would be questioned. When this story finally came out, it merely gave a lot of hippies a few laughs.

❋ Castro was an avid scuba diver, so the CIA sprayed the inside of a wet suit with tuberculosis germs and a fungal skin disease called Madura foot. Then they gave it to a lawyer heading to Havana to negotiate the release of Bay of Pigs prisoners. He was supposed to give the suit to Castro, but at the last minute the lawyer decided that the plot was too obvious and was an embarrassment to the United States, so he didn't take the suit with him.

* Perhaps the most famous dumb idea of all was to find out where Fidel's favorite diving spot was and prepare an exploding conch shell to kill him, but for many obvious reasons this plan was dropped as being unfeasible.

* Traditional assassination methods were also tried. Cuban exiles were sent to Havana with high-powered rifles and telescopic sights to take care of the problem with good old-fashioned lead, but none of them could get close enough to shoot Castro.

* One of Castro's guards was given a poison pen that worked like a hypodermic needle, but he was discovered before he could get close enough to inject the leader.

* Not all the plots involved killing the Cuban leader. In another instance, a Castro aide was bribed to put special powder inside the dictator's boots—it contained a poison that would make his beard fall out. This never happened.

Starting in the 1970s, the CIA seemed to lose interest in these plans, and thereafter most attempts to kill the leader were carried out by Cuban exiles (with CIA funding, of course), who had made hating Castro almost a religion. Fabian Escalante, Castro's head of security, claimed that there have been 638 plots to kill Castro.

Before Fidel led a revolution, he came to the United States to try out for major league baseball. By all accounts, he was actually a terrific pitcher. If he had made the majors, recent history might have been very different. For one thing, a lot of amateur assassins would have had to find something better to do with their time.

# Sitting on the Laps of Power

*Former Secretary of State Henry Kissinger called power "the ultimate aphrodisiac." For centuries, influential—and married—men have been attracting women drawn by power.*

✳ ✳ ✳ ✳

## Presidential Follies

AMERICAN PRESIDENTIAL DALLIANCES seemed almost commonplace in the 20th century. Bill Clinton had Monica Lewinsky. Franklin D. Roosevelt had a decades-long affair with Lucy Mercer (later Rutherfurd). In fact, it was she, and not his wife Eleanor, who was with him when he died at Warm Springs, Georgia, in 1945. John Kennedy allegedly had Angie Dickinson, Marilyn Monroe, Jayne Mansfield, and Judith Campbell Exner, among others.

Warren G. Harding worked as a genial former newspaper editor and U.S. senator from Ohio before he decided to capitalize on America's war-weariness by running for president. He became the nation's 29th president in 1920, and he promised America a "return to normalcy." However, despite being married to a woman he called "Duchess," Harding had previously carried on a 15-year-long affair with Carrie Phillips, the wife of a good friend. When that affair ended, he took up with Nan Britton, a much younger woman who was rumored to still be a virgin when she began seeing Harding.

## Amorous Also-Rans

Sometimes a man lusting after both the presidency and other women finds the two desires don't mix well. Such was the case in July 1791, when U.S. Treasury Secretary Alexander Hamilton began an affair with Maria Reynolds, a pretty 23-year-old woman who tearfully implored him for help as her husband had left her.

A few months later Reynolds's husband James, a professional con man, mysteriously returned, and blackmailed Hamilton. Although he paid $1,750 to keep the affair quiet, Hamilton learned the sad truth that blackmailers are never satisfied. In 1797, the affair came to light, creating one of the first sex scandals in American politics. Although Hamilton apologized, many historians believe the damage to his reputation cost him the presidency he so coveted.

Another man who saw his presidential chances wrecked on the rocks of infidelity was Gary Hart. The odds-on favorite to win the 1988 Democratic presidential nomination, the married senator from Colorado was caught by the press in April 1987, in the company of Donna Rice, a blonde 29-year-old actress and model. One of the places they had allegedly been together was on a yacht called, appropriately enough, *Monkey Business*. After several days of feverish headlines, Hart withdrew from the presidential race. Although he reentered the race later that year, Hart's monkey business had finished him as a force in national politics.

Political cost was likely not on the mind of Thomas Jefferson if, and when, he began an affair with Sally Hemings, a slave at Monticello. Although he was a powerful political figure, Jefferson was also a lonely widower who had promised his dying wife in 1782 that he would never remarry. At the time, scholars hypothesize, that he began the affair with Hemings, the presidency must have seemed a distant dream. However, in 1800, Jefferson became president. Two years later, a newspaper editor named James Callendar first published the charge that Jefferson and Hemings were an item, thus igniting a historical controversy that still rages today.

## Foreign Affairs

Of course, it is not only American political figures that have had a roving eye. Charles Stewart Parnell was a leader of Ireland's Independence Movement in the 1880s. It seemed as if British Prime Minister William Gladstone was about to support Parnell and finally give Ireland its freedom, but in November 1890, it was revealed that Parnell had long been involved with Kitty O'Shea, the wife of William Henry O'Shea. The disclosure rocked prim-and-proper England, causing Gladstone to distance himself from Parnell and pull back from endorsing Irish independence. Thus not just a political career, but also the fate of an entire nation was affected by one man's indiscretion.

Of course, there's much more at stake than a failed political career. Claretta Pettachi was a beautiful young Italian girl who became Italian dictator Benito Mussolini's lover. To her credit (or discredit), she stayed loyal to him to the end. In April 1945, she and Mussolini were captured as they tried to flee Italy. According to legend, Pettachi was offered her freedom but refused, and she threw her body in front of Mussolini's in a vain attempt to shield him from a firing squad's bullets. Photos show their bodies, which were subsequently hung upside down in a public square.

Pettachi's devotion to her fascist lover is perhaps only topped by that of Prince Pedro of Portugal. Pedro began an affair with one of his wife's maids, Inês de Castro, who bore him two children. His wife died in 1349, and de Castro was put to death in 1355. When Pedro became king in 1357, he had his mistress' body exhumed, married the corpse, and forced his entire court to honor her remains.

History is filled with many more examples of famous men and the women they attracted. However, the attraction doesn't seem to work in the opposite direction—stories of powerful women and the men they attracted are much less common. Perhaps it is as Eleanor Roosevelt once observed: "[How] men despise women who have real power."

# A Bodyguard of Lies: The Allied D-Day Deception

*Germany had more than enough muscle behind the guns and forts of the Atlantic Wall to blast any seaborne invasion to rags-—but only if that muscle were all brought to bear swiftly in the right place. The Allies planned to make that task as challenging as possible.*

✳   ✳   ✳   ✳

THE GERMANS EXPECTED the Allies to attempt to invade France, but they weren't sure when or how the attack would happen. They knew the risk of a seaborne invasion increased with the distance sailed. Therefore, Allies would most likely invade as near as possible to British ports to avoid aero-naval interception, remain in range of air cover, and lessen the impact of weather. RAF fighters had enough range to cover Normandy and the Pas de Calais region just opposite Dover. As the Allies saw it, Calais was the quickest sail, but also the Atlantic Wall's sharpest teeth. Instead, they planned to endure the longer ride to Normandy, where the defenses were less formidable.

Of course, any invasion could fail if the Germans guessed its location in advance. To throw them off, the Allies contrived Operation Bodyguard, a key part of which was Operation Fortitude, a deception plan divided into North and South. Fortitude North's goal was to tie German troops up in Norway to repel a phantom invasion. Fortitude South would try to mislead the Germans about the real invasion's location—and hide that the Allies were planning multiple landings.

Fortitude North faked radio traffic to make the small northern UK garrison sound like a full army preparing to invade Norway. Thanks to achievements in broadcasting and recording, a single radio truck could simulate the chatter of a divisional headquarters; a signals battalion could simulate an army.

Fortitude South's first job was to convince the Germans that the blow would land near Calais, with possible feints elsewhere. After the troops landed in Normandy, the second phase of Fortitude South would be to maintain the impression that a second, heavier blow was still to come at the Pas de Calais. The planners invented a fictitious army under General Patton: the 1st U.S. Army Group (FUSAG), complete with nonexistent infantry divisions.

Germany depended upon its spies to confirm or contradict what the Allies were really planning. But its intelligence turned out to be unreliable—every German spy reporting from Britain was actually working for the British.

General Dwight D. Eisenhower assumed that if at any point the Germans figured out the plans for the true D-Day invasion, Field Marshal Erwin Rommel would hurl every tank toward the Normandy beaches while the invasion was at sea—perhaps disobeying even Hitler—to prepare a lethal reception. Eisenhower took the possibility seriously enough to prepare two speeches before the invasion: one praising its success, and one taking all blame if it failed.

As it was, D-Day achieved tactical surprise. The Germans had indeed expected the Allies to storm the Pas de Calais sector. Noting that "known" FUSAG elements had not yet been sent into battle, they committed only a portion of the panzer reserve to holding off the Allied forces at Normandy. The rest were withheld to oppose FUSAG's expected second invasion. This gave the Allies those few crucial days needed to reinforce and consolidate the Normandy beachhead. The second invasion came not in June at the Pas de Calais, but on August 15, 1944, in southern France.

FUSAG never fired a rifle shot, yet it helped defeat Germany. The Allies' D-Day deception effort went down as one of the best-executed ruses in military history.

# Warren G. Harding

*Few presidents have had a reputation such as that of Warren G. Harding, the publisher-turned-politician who, after a landslide presidential victory, wrought havoc upon the United States for two years before dying while in office.*

✳   ✳   ✳   ✳

A BUSINESSMAN, FREEMASON, AND consummate Republican, Warren G. Harding was born not far from Marion in 1865. He remained there for much of his adult life, becoming a prominent member of the business community before entering political life in 1898. He served two terms as a state senator and briefly held the post of lieutenant governor before running an unsuccessful gubernatorial campaign. But after introducing fellow Ohioan and then-nominee for the presidency William Howard Taft at the 1912 Republican National Convention, Harding, who was by all accounts a captivating but hollow orator, quickly rose to political stardom.

He was elected to the U.S. Senate two years later and by 1920 was campaigning for the White House. Harding became the Republican candidate for president only as the result of a deadlock between the other candidates, but he nevertheless defeated James M. Cox, the Democratic governor of Harding's native Ohio, in a landslide victory with a little more than 60 percent of the popular vote.

## The Ohio Gang

Harding's presidency is not usually revered for its policy, which sought to overturn major legislation from the Wilson administration, deregulate large businesses, and limit American involvement in international affairs. Most historians agree that Harding's policies contributed greatly to the economic collapse at the end of the 1920s. Still, Harding performed the ceremonial functions that officially brought World War I to a close, supported both the railroads and domestic agriculture, and created the federal budget. Though he died in the middle of his first term, many of his policy goals were carried out by his successors: Calvin Coolidge, his vice president, and Herbert Hoover, his secretary of commerce.

However destructive they may have been, Harding's failed policies have been largely overshadowed by the magnitude of his administration's corruption, which included fraud, bribery, embezzlement, and drug and alcohol trafficking. The most serious offense was the Teapot Dome scandal, when Secretary of the Interior Albert B. Hall illegally leased government land (the Teapot Dome oil field in Wyoming) to oil companies in exchange for bribes and under-the-table private loans. Hall and other members of the administration—known as the Ohio Gang, though none actually hailed from the Buckeye State—were forced to resign amidst a sea of public outrage; Hall went to prison, and his colleague Jess Smith committed suicide.

## And That's Not All

Though the Teapot Dome affair went on under Harding's watch, many historians question whether he was even aware of the corruption in his cabinet. The only offense attributed directly to Harding is his rumored alcoholism. Despite his unwavering support for Prohibition, Harding was, by all accounts, a drunkard, regularly consuming contraband liquor in the White House even when it was against federal law to do so. For good measure, he was also accused of fathering a child out of wedlock with an admirer named Nan Britton. Britton made the accusations public when she published a lurid account of their relationship, *The President's Daughter*, in 1927.

Harding died of a heart attack in 1923 after less than two and a half years in office. He is regularly ranked among the worst presidents in U.S. history, both for the rampant corruption in his administration and his support of policies that discouraged regulation and indirectly led to the Great Depression.

# Blacklisted!

*During the Red Scare, hundreds of film and television careers were destroyed by a vindictive hunt for communists in Hollywood.*

✳  ✳  ✳  ✳

IN SEPTEMBER 1947, Dalton Trumbo was at the height of his career as a screenwriter. He was highly acclaimed, well paid, and still basking in the accolades he received for his work on two patriotic war films: *A Guy Named Joe* (1943) and *Thirty Seconds Over Tokyo* (1944). That month, an FBI agent delivered Trumbo a subpoena from the House Un-American Activities Committee (HUAC), a special investigative committee of the U.S. House of Representatives. Trumbo, along with 42 other film industry professionals—actors, directors, producers, and writers—were named as key witnesses in HUAC's probe into Communist subversion in Hollywood. The good times were about to end for Dalton Trumbo.

## The Hunt for Reds in October

HUAC was created in 1937 to "investigate disloyal or subversive activities in America," such as the Ku Klux Klan and organizations sympathetic to Nazi Germany. HUAC also worked diligently to ferret out American Communist Party (ACP) members and supporters in the U.S. government and media. HUAC cooled its heels during World War II, when the Soviet Union was an ally, but ramped up its pursuits with the postwar onset of the Second Red Scare, which later gave rise to a similar but totally unrelated Red-baiting phenomenon: Joseph McCarthy and the notorious Senate Committee hearings of the 1950s. But in 1947, HUAC had turned its attention to Hollywood.

Citing Soviet-sympathetic war films such as *Mission to Moscow* (1943) and *Song of Russia* (1944), HUAC announced formal hearings to determine if Hollywood filmmakers were undermining U.S. security and freedom by covertly planting

Communist propaganda in American films. Those subpoenaed by HUAC were expected to provide details of Communist activity in Hollywood and, more importantly, name names.

On October 20, 1947, the hearings opened with testimony from several "friendly" witnesses. One of them was Walt Disney, who readily fingered several individuals as Communists, claiming that they were agitators inciting labor unrest in Hollywood. Ronald Reagan, then-president of the Screen Actors Guild, also testified and claimed that Communist intrigue was rampant in Tinseltown.

## The Hollywood Ten

Disney and Reagan were followed by ten individuals (including Trumbo, Samuel Ornitz, and John Howard Lawson—screenwriters who were also members of the Writers Guild of America, which Lawson founded) who refused to cooperate with the investigation, which they considered a modern-day witch hunt. These "unfriendly" witnesses condemned the hearings as unconstitutional and invoked their Fifth Amendment rights when asked about their relationship with Communist organizations.

For their defiance, the Hollywood Ten, as they were dubbed, were cited for contempt of Congress on November 24. They were also fired by their respective studios and the Motion Picture Producers and Distributors of America barred them from working in Hollywood until they were acquitted or purged of contempt and declared under oath that they were not Communists.

The ten remained unrepentant, and in early 1948, they were convicted of contempt. In 1950, after failed appeals, they began serving six-month to one-year prison sentences. Trumbo and his cohorts also became charter members of the now-notorious Hollywood blacklist.

## The List That Ate Hollywood

During the next several years, the blacklist grew into a monster that devoured Hollywood careers—a monster that was willingly fed by numerous anticommunist organizations. In 1949, the American Legion presented Hollywood execs with a list of 300 film industry members that they suspected of Communist affiliation. Fearing Legion-organized film boycotts, the studios adopted it as their de facto blacklist. In 1950, a pamphlet known as *Red Channels* pegged 151 TV and radio professionals as Communist sympathizers. Those named were blacklisted from their respective industries to avoid boycotts of products sponsored by the shows.

From 1951 to 1952, HUAC launched more hearings in which witnesses sold out others in an effort to save their own careers. Among them was director Edward Dmytryk, a guilt-ridden member of the Hollywood Ten, who betrayed 26 colleagues in exchange for an early jail release and the resumption of his directing career.

HUAC reports produced another blacklist of 212 Hollywood professionals who soon lost their jobs. Most were writers who were relatively unknown outside Hollywood. But several prominent actors, producers, and directors landed on the list, including Charlie Chaplin, Lee Grant, Zero Mostel, Orson Bean, and Larry Parks.

Many on the list also had earlier screen credits omitted. Unable to earn a living, dozens of blacklisted professionals left Hollywood (and even America) to continue their careers elsewhere. Approximately 90 percent of those blacklisted never worked in Hollywood again.

## Breaking the Blacklist

Open resistance to the blacklist began to emerge in 1956, when TV and radio personality John Henry Faulk sued the group Aware Inc. after its erroneous labeling of him as a Communist supporter kept him from getting a job at a radio station. Faulk's court victory in 1962 put an end to the blacklist altogether. Soon afterward, several television productions began hiring and crediting blacklisted artists.

Even before then, there were signs that the blacklist was losing strength. In 1960, director Otto Preminger named Dalton Trumbo as the screenwriter for his upcoming film *Exodus*. That same year, Universal Pictures announced that Trumbo would be similarly credited on *Spartacus*, having been hired two years before by the film's executive producer and star, Kirk Douglas. Dalton Trumbo's 13-year nightmare was coming to an end.

Few knew it then, but Trumbo had already trumped the blacklist. During the 1950s, some blacklisted artists, including Trumbo, worked under different names. Trumbo wrote *Roman Holiday* (1953) under the alias Ian McLellan Hunter. He also penned *The Brave One* (1956) using the name Robert Rich as his "front." Both efforts earned Oscars for Best Writing, which meant golden redemption for Dalton Trumbo.

# Delay by Quaker Guns

*A clever Confederate ruse spelled humiliation for General George McClellan.*

✻   ✻   ✻   ✻

IN DECIDING HOW best to attack the Confederate capital of Richmond, Virginia, Union General George B. McClellan decided to transport his army by ship to Fort Monroe near Norfolk. From there, they would rapidly march up the Virginia Peninsula and capture Richmond before the Confederates could construct strong defenses. This plan collapsed in part due to a clever ruse: McClellan had been tricked by a small Confederate force using Quaker guns.

On April 4, 1862, McClellan advanced the 24 miles up the peninsula from Fort Monroe to Yorktown, flanked by approximately 50,000 soldiers. Meanwhile, Confederate General John B. Magruder's small force was ordered to hold off the federal army as long as possible while the bulk of the Confederate army, commanded by General Joseph E. Johnston, strengthened the Richmond defenses. Magruder used a series of deceptions to give McClellan the impression that he faced a force twice as large as was really there. It looked as though the area was heavily fortified with plenty of cannons and artillery. In fact, only 17,000 Southern soldiers held the 13 miles of the Yorktown defenses along the Warwick River.

McClellan decided to use siege operations to avoid a direct assault on the "heavily defended" positions. Union engineers constructed field works along the federal line, but it was a month before McClellan felt that he had enough artillery to begin action of any sort.

McClellan finally fired on Yorktown at midnight on May 5. Federals met no resistance in entering the Confederate works. Magruder had fallen back that evening, leaving behind a number of Quaker guns—logs painted black and mounted on wheels to look like cannons. McClellan had easily been deceived, which marked a poor beginning to what would be a disastrous Peninsula Campaign.

# Chapter 9

# UFOs and Strange Encounters

## Fireball in the Sky

*While playing football on the afternoon of September 12, 1952, a group of boys in Flatwoods, West Virginia, saw a large fireball fly over their heads. The object seemed to stop near the hillside property of Bailey Fisher. Some thought the object was a UFO, but others said it was just a meteor. They decided to investigate.*

❋   ❋   ❋   ❋

DARKNESS WAS FALLING as the boys made their way toward the hill, so they stopped at the home of Kathleen May to borrow a flashlight. Seeing how excited the boys were, May, her two sons, and their friend, Eugene Lemon, decided to join them. The group set off to find out exactly what had landed on the hill.

### Walking into Darkness

As they neared the top of the hill, the group smelled a strange odor that reminded them of burning metal. Continuing on, some members of the group thought they saw an object that resembled a spaceship. Shining their flashlights in front of them, the group was startled when something not of this world moved out from behind a nearby tree.

## The Encounter

The description of what is now known as the Flatwoods Monster is almost beyond belief. It stood around 12 feet tall and had a round, reddish face from which two large holes were visible. Looming up from behind the creature's head was a large pointed hood. The creature, which appeared to be made of a dark metal, had no arms or legs and seemed to float through the air. Looking back, the witnesses believe what they saw was a protective suit or perhaps a robot rather than a monster.

When a flashlight beam hit the creature, its "eyes" lit up and it began floating toward the group while making a strange hissing noise. The horrible stench was now overpowering and some in the group immediately felt nauseous. Because she was at the head of the group, Kathleen May had the best view of the monster. She later stated that as the creature was moving toward her, it squirted or dripped a strange fluid on her that resembled oil but had an unusual odor to it.

Terrified beyond belief, the group fled down the hillside and back to the May house, where they telephoned Sheriff Robert Carr, who responded with his deputy, Burnell Long. After talking with the group, they gathered some men and went to the Fisher property to investigate. But they only found a gummy residue and what appeared to be skid marks on the ground. There was no monster and no spaceship. However, the group did report that the heavy stench of what smelled like burning metal was still in the air.

## The Aftermath

A. Lee Stewart, a member of the of the search party and also copublisher of the *Braxton Democrat*, knew a good story when he saw one, so he sent the tale over the news wire, and almost immediately, people were asking Kathleen May for interviews. On September 19, 1952, May and Stewart discussed the Flatwoods Monster on national TV. For the show, an artist made a sketch of the creature based on May's description, but he took some liberties, and the resulting sketch was so outrageous that people started saying the whole thing was a hoax.

Slowly, though, others came forward to admit that they too had seen a strange craft flying through the sky near Flatwoods on September 12. One witness described it as roughly the size of a single-car garage. He said that he lost sight of the craft when it appeared to land on a nearby hill.

Since that night in 1952, the Flatwoods Monster has never been seen again, leaving many people to wonder what exactly those people encountered. A monster? An alien from another world? Or perhaps nothing more than a giant owl? One thing is for sure: There were far too many witnesses to deny that they stumbled upon something strange that night.

## The Nazca Lines—Pictures Aimed at an Eye in the Sky?

*Ancient works of art etched into a desert floor in South America have inspired wild theories about who created them and why. Did space aliens leave them on long-ago visits? Decades of scientific research reject the popular notion, showing that the lines were the work of mere Earthlings.*

✳   ✳   ✳   ✳

FLYING ABOVE THE rocky plains northwest of Nazca, Peru, in 1927, aviator Toribio Mejía Xesspe was surprised to see gigantic eyes looking up at him. Then the pilot noticed that the orbs stared out of a bulbous head upon a cartoonish line drawing of a man, etched over hundreds of square feet of the landscape below.

The huge drawing—later called "owl man" for its staring eyes—turned out to be just one of scores of huge, 2,000-year-old images scratched into the earth over almost 200 square miles of the parched Peruvian landscape.

There is a 360-foot-long monkey with a whimsically spiraled tail, along with a 150-foot-long spider, and a 935-foot pelican. Other figures range from hummingbird to killer whale. Unless the viewer knows what to look for, they're almost invisible from ground level. There are also geometric shapes and straight lines that stretch for miles across the stony ground.

## The Theory of Ancient Astronauts

The drawings have been dated to a time between 200 BC and AD 600. Obviously, there were no airplanes from which to view them then. So why were they made? For whose benefit?

In his 1968 book *Chariots of the Gods?*, Swiss author Erich Von Däniken popularized the idea that the drawings and lines were landing signals and runways for starships that visited southern Peru long before our era. In his interpretation, the owl man is instead an astronaut in a helmet. Von Däniken's theory caught on among UFO enthusiasts. Many science-fiction novels and films make reference to this desert in Peru's Pampa Colorado region as a site with special significance to space travelers.

## Coming Down to Earth

Examined up close, the drawings consist of cleared paths—areas where someone removed reddish surface rocks to expose the soft soil beneath. In the stable desert climate—averaging less than an inch of rain per year—the paths have survived through many centuries largely intact.

Scientists believe the Nazca culture—a civilization that came before the Incas—drew the lines. The style of the artwork is similar to that featured on Nazca pottery. German-born researcher Maria Reiche (1903–1998) showed how the Nazca could have laid out the figures using simple surveying tools such as ropes and posts. In the 1980s, American researcher Joe Nickell duplicated one of the drawings, a condor, show-ing that the Nazca could have rendered parts of the figures "freehand"—that is, without special tools or even scale models. Nickell also demonstrated that despite their great size, the figures can be identified as drawings even from ground level. No alien technology would have been required to make them.

### Still Mysterious

As for why the Nazca doodled in the desert, no one is sure. Reiche noted that some of the lines have astronomical relevance. For example, one points to where the sun sets at the winter solstice. Some lines may also have pointed toward underground water sources.

Most scholars think that the marks were part of the Nazca religion. They may have been footpaths followed during ritual processions. And although it's extremely unlikely that they were intended for extraterrestrials, many experts think it likely that the lines were oriented toward Nazca gods—perhaps a monkey god, a spider god, and so on, who could be imagined gazing down from the heavens upon likenesses of themselves.

# Red Eyes over Point Pleasant: The Mysterious Mothman

*In 1942, the U.S. government took control of several thousand acres of land just north of Point Pleasant, West Virginia. The purpose was to build a secret facility capable of creating and storing TNT that could be used during World War II. For the next three years, the facility cranked out massive amounts of TNT, shipping it out or storing it in one of the numerous concrete "igloo" structures that dotted the area. In 1945, the facility was shut down and eventually abandoned, but it was here that a flying creature with glowing red eyes made its home years later.*

✳   ✳   ✳   ✳

### "Red Eyes on the Right"

ON THE EVENING of November 15, 1966, Linda and Roger Scarberry were out driving with another couple, Mary and Steve Mallette. As they drove, they decided to take a detour that took them past the abandoned TNT factory.

As they neared the gate of the old factory, they noticed two red lights up ahead. When Roger stopped the car, the couples were horrified to find that the red lights appeared to be two glowing red eyes. What's more, those eyes belonged to a creature standing more than seven feet tall with giant wings folded behind it. That was all Roger needed to see before he hit the gas pedal and sped off. In response, the creature calmly unfolded its wings and flew toward the car. Incredibly, even though Roger raced along at speeds close to 100 miles per hour, the red-eyed creature was able to keep up with them without much effort.

Upon reaching Point Pleasant, the two couples ran from their car to the Mason County Courthouse and alerted Deputy Millard Halstead of their terrifying encounter. Halstead couldn't be sure exactly what the two couples had seen, but whatever it was, it had clearly frightened them. In an attempt to calm them down, Halstead agreed to accompany them to the TNT factory. As his patrol car neared the entrance, the police radio suddenly emitted a strange, whining noise. Other than that, despite a thorough search of the area, nothing out of the ordinary was found.

## More Encounters

Needless to say, once word got around Point Pleasant that a giant winged creature with glowing red eyes was roaming around the area, everyone had to see it for themselves. The creature didn't disappoint. Dubbed Mothman by the local press, the creature was spotted flying overhead, hiding, and even lurking on front porches. In fact, in the last few weeks of November, dozens of witnesses encountered the winged beast. But Mothman wasn't the only game in town. It seems that around the same time that he showed up, local residents started noticing strange lights in the evening sky, some of which hovered silently over the abandoned TNT factory. Of course, this led some to believe that Mothman and the UFOs were somehow connected. One such person was Mary Hyre of *The Athens Messenger*, who had been reporting on the strange activities in Point Pleasant since they started. Perhaps that's why she became the first target.

## Beware the Men in Black

One day, while Mary Hyre was at work, several strange men visited her office and began asking questions about the lights in the sky. Normally, she didn't mind talking to people about the UFO sightings and Mothman. But there was something peculiar about these guys. For instance, they all dressed exactly the same: black suits, black ties, black hats, and dark sunglasses. They also spoke in a strange monotone and seemed confused by ordinary objects such as ballpoint pens. As the men left, Hyre wondered whether they had been from another planet. Either way, she had an up-close-and-personal encounter with the legendary Men in Black.

Mary Hyre was not the only person to have a run-in with the Men in Black. As the summer of 1967 rolled around, dozens of people were interrogated by them. In most cases, the men showed up unannounced at the homes of people who had recently witnessed a Mothman or UFO sighting. For the most part, the men simply wanted to know what the witnesses had seen. But sometimes, the men went to great lengths to convince the witnesses that they were mistaken and had not seen anything out of the ordinary. Other times, the men threatened witnesses. Each time the Men in Black left a witness's house, they drove away in a black, unmarked sedan. Despite numerous attempts to determine who these men were and where they came from, their identity remained a secret. And all the while, the Mothman sightings continued throughout Point Pleasant and the surrounding area.

## The Silver Bridge Tragedy

Erected in 1928, the Silver Bridge was a gorgeous chain suspension bridge that spanned the Ohio River, connecting Point Pleasant with Ohio. On December 15, 1967, the bridge was busy with holiday shoppers bustling back and forth between

West Virginia and Ohio. As the day wore on, more and more cars started filling the bridge until shortly before 5:00 p.m., when traffic on the bridge came to a standstill. For several minutes, none of the cars budged. Suddenly, there was a loud popping noise and then the unthinkable happened: The Silver Bridge collapsed, sending dozens of cars and their passengers into the freezing water below.

Over the next few days, local authorities and residents searched the river hoping to find survivors, but in the end, 46 people lost their lives in the bridge collapse. A thorough investigation determined that a manufacturing flaw in one of the bridge's supporting bars caused the collapse. But there are others who claim that in the days and weeks leading up to the collapse, they saw Mothman and even the Men in Black around, on, and even under the bridge. Further witnesses state that while most of Point Pleasant was watching the Silver Bridge collapse, bright lights and strange objects were flying out of the area and disappearing into the winter sky. Perhaps that had nothing to do with the collapse of the Silver Bridge, but the Mothman has not been seen since. Or has he?

## Mothman Lives!

There are reports that the Mothman is still alive and well and has moved on to other areas of the United States. There are even those who claim that he was spotted flying near the Twin Towers on September 11, 2001, leading to speculation that Mothman is a portent of doom and only appears when disasters are imminent. Some believe Mothman was a visitor from another planet who returned home shortly after the Silver Bridge fell. Still others think the creature was the result of the toxic chemicals eventually discovered in the area near the TNT factory. And then there are skeptics who say that the initial sighting was nothing more than a giant sand crane and that mass hysteria took care of the rest. Whichever theory you choose to believe, the Mothman Lives website compiles all sightings of the creature from the 1960s to the present.

# Unidentified Submerged Objects

*Much like their flying brethren, unidentified submerged objects captivate and mystify. But instead of vanishing into the skies, USOs, such as the following, plunge underwater.*

❋   ❋   ❋   ❋

## Sighting at Puerto Rico Trench

IN 1963, WHILE conducting exercises off the coast of Puerto Rico, U.S. Navy submarines encountered something extraordinary. The incident began when a sonar operator aboard an accompanying destroyer reported a strange occurrence. According to the seaman, one of the subs traveling with the armada broke free from the pack to chase a USO. This quarry would be unlike anything the submariners had ever pursued.

Underwater technology in the early 1960s was advancing rapidly. Still, vessels had their limitations. The U.S.S. *Nautilus*, though faster than any submarine that preceded it, was still limited to about 20 knots (23 miles per hour). The bathyscaphe *Trieste*, a deep-sea submersible, could exceed 30,000 feet in depth, but the descent took as long as five hours. Once there, the vessel could not be maneuvered side to side.

Knowing this, the submariners were stunned by what they witnessed. The USO was moving at 150 knots (170 miles per hour) and hitting depths greater than 20,000 feet! No underwater vehicles on Earth were capable of such fantastic numbers. Even today, modern nuclear subs have top speeds of about 25 knots (29 miles per hour) and can operate at around 800-plus feet below the surface.

Thirteen separate crafts witnessed the USO as it criss-crossed the Atlantic Ocean over a four-day period. At its deepest, the mystery vehicle reached 27,000 feet. To this day, there's been no earthly explanation offered for the occurrence.

## USO with a Bus Pass

In 1964, London bus driver Bob Fall witnessed one of the strangest USO sightings. While transporting a full contingent of passengers, the driver and his fares reported seeing a silver, cigar-shape object dive into the nearby waters of the River Lea. The police attributed the phenomenon to a flight of ducks, despite the obvious incongruence. Severed telephone lines and a large gouge on the river's embankment suggested something far different.

## Shag Harbour Incident

The fishing village of Shag Harbour lies on Canada's East Coast. This unassuming hamlet is to USOs what Roswell, New Mexico, is to UFOs. Simply put, it played host to the most famous occurrence of a USO ever recorded.

On the evening of October 4, 1967, the Royal Canadian Mounted Police (RCMP) were barraged by reports of a UFO that had crashed into the bay at Shag Harbour. Laurie Wickens and four friends witnessed a large object (approximately 60 feet in diameter) falling into the water just after 11:00 p.m. Floating approximately 1,000 feet off the coast they could clearly detect a yellow light on top of the object.

The RCMP promptly contacted the Rescue Coordination Center in Halifax to ask if any aircraft were missing. None were. Shortly thereafter, the object sank into the depths of the water and disappeared from view.

When local fishing boats went to the USO crash site, they encountered yellow foam on the water's surface and detected an odd sulfuric smell. No survivors or bodies were ever found. The Royal Canadian Air Force officially labeled the occurrence a UFO, but because the object was last seen under water, such events are now described as USOs.

## Pascagoula Incident

On November 6, 1973, at approximately 8:00 p.m., a USO was sighted by at least nine fishermen anchored off the coast of Pascagoula, Mississippi. The fishermen witnessed an underwater object an estimated five feet in diameter that emitted a strange amber light.

First to spot the USO was Rayme Ryan. He repeatedly poked at the light-emitting object with an oar. Each time he made contact with the strange object, its light would dim and it would move a few feet away, then brighten once again.

Fascinated by the ethereal quality of this submerged question mark, Ryan summoned the others. For the next half hour, the cat-and-mouse game played out in front of the fishermen until Ryan struck the object with a particularly forceful blow. With this action, the USO disappeared from view.

The anglers moved about a half mile away and continued fishing. After about 30 minutes, they returned to their earlier location and were astounded to find that the USO had returned. At this point, they decided to alert the Coast Guard.

After interviewing the witnesses, investigators from the Naval Ship Research and Development Laboratory in Panama City, Florida, submitted their findings: At least nine persons had witnessed an undetermined light source whose characteristics and actions were inconsistent with those of known marine organisms or with an uncontrolled human-made object. Their final report was inconclusive, stating that the object could not be positively identified.

# The Kecksburg Incident

*Did visitors from outer space once land in a western Pennsylvania thicket?*

✳  ✳  ✳  ✳

## Dropping in for a Visit

O<small>N DECEMBER</small> 9, 1965, an unidentified flying object streaked through the late-afternoon sky and landed in Kecksburg—a rural Pennsylvania community about 40 miles southeast of Pittsburgh. This much is not disputed. However, specific accounts vary widely from person to person. Even after closely examining the facts, many people remain undecided about exactly what happened. "Roswell" type incidents—ultramysterious in nature and reeking of a governmental cover-up—have an uncanny way of causing confusion.

## Trajectory-Interruptus

A meteor on a collision course with Earth will generally "bounce" as it enters the atmosphere. This occurs due to friction, which forcefully slows the average space rock from 6 to 45 miles per second to a few hundred miles per hour, the speed at which it strikes Earth and officially becomes a meteorite. According to the official explanation offered by the U.S. Air Force, it was a meteorite that landed in Kecksburg. However, witnesses reported that the object completed back and forth maneuvers before landing at a very low speed—moves that an un-powered chunk of earthbound rock simply cannot perform. Strike one against the meteor theory.

## An Acorn-Shape Meteorite?

When a meteor manages to pierce Earth's atmosphere, it has the physical properties of exactly what it is: a space rock. That is to say, it will generally be unevenly shaped, rough, and darkish in color, much like rocks found on Earth. But at Kecksburg, eyewitnesses reported seeing something far, far different. The unusual object they described was bronze to golden in color, acorn-shape, and as large as a Volkswagen Beetle automobile. Unless the universe has started to produce uniformly shaped and colored meteorites, the official explanation seems highly unlikely. Strike two for the meteor theory.

## Markedly Different

Then there's the baffling issue of markings. A meteorite can be chock-full of holes, cracks, and other such surface imperfections. It can also vary somewhat in color. But it should never, ever have markings that seem intelligently designed. Witnesses at Kecksburg describe intricate writings similar to Egyptian hicroglyphics located near the base of the object. A cursory examination of space rocks at any natural history museum reveals that such a thing doesn't occur naturally. Strike three for the meteor theory. Logically following such a trail, could an unnatural force have been responsible for the item witnessed at Kecksburg? At least one man thought so.

## Reportis Rigor Mortis

Just after the Kecksburg UFO landed, reporter John Murphy arrived at the scene. Like any seasoned pro, the newsman immediately snapped photos and gathered eyewitness accounts of the event. Strangely, FBI agents arrived, cordoned off the area, and confiscated all but one roll of his film. Undaunted, Murphy assembled a radio documentary entitled *Object in the Woods* to describe his experience. Just before the special was to air, the reporter received an unexpected visit by two men. According to a fellow employee, a dark-suited pair identified themselves as government agents and subsequently confiscated a portion of Murphy's audiotapes. A week later, a clearly perturbed Murphy aired a watered-down version of his documentary. In it, he claimed that certain interviewees requested their accounts be removed for fear of retribution at the hands of police, military, and government officials. In 1969, John Murphy was struck dead by an unidentified car while crossing the street.

## Resurrected by Robert Stack

In all likelihood the Kecksburg incident would have remained dormant and under-explored had it not been for the television show *Unsolved Mysteries*. In a 1990 segment, narrator Robert Stack took an in-depth look at what occurred in Kecksburg, feeding a firestorm of interest that eventually brought forth two new witnesses. The first, a U.S. Air Force officer stationed at Lockbourne AFB (near Columbus, Ohio), claimed to have seen a flatbed truck carrying a mysterious object as it arrived on base on December 10, 1965. The military man told of a tarpaulin-covered conical object that he couldn't identify and a "shoot to kill" order given to him for anyone who ventured too close. He was told that the truck was bound for Wright–Patterson AFB in Dayton, Ohio, an installation that's alleged to contain downed flying saucers. The other witness was a building contractor who claimed to have delivered 6,500 special bricks to a hanger inside Wright–Patterson AFB on December 12, 1965. Curious, he peeked inside the hanger and saw a "bell-shaped" device, 12-feet high, surrounded by several men wearing anti-radiation style suits. Upon leaving, he was told that he had just witnessed an object that would become "common knowledge" in the next 20 years.

## Will We Ever Know the Truth?

Like Roswell before it, we will probably never know what occurred in western Pennsylvania back in 1965. The more that's learned about the case, the more confusing it becomes. For instance, the official 1965 meteorite explanation contains more holes than Bonnie and Clyde's death car, and other explanations, such as orbiting space debris (from past U.S. and Russian missions) reentering Earth's atmosphere, seem equally preposterous. In 2005, as the result of a new investigation launched by the Sci-Fi Television Network, NASA asserted that the object was a Russian satellite. According to a NASA spokesperson, documents of this investigation were somehow misplaced in the 1990s. Mysteriously, this finding directly contradicts the official Air Force version that nothing at all was found at the Kecksburg site. It also runs counter to a 2003 report made by NASA's own Nicholas L. Johnson, Chief Scientist for Orbital Debris. That document shows no missing satellites at the time of the incident. This includes a missing Russian Venus probe (since accounted for)—the very item that was once considered a prime crash candidate.

### Brave New World

These days, visitors to Kecksburg will be hard-pressed to find any trace of the encounter—perhaps that's how it should be. Since speculation comes to an abrupt halt whenever a concrete answer is provided, Kecksburg's reputation as "Roswell of the East" looks secure, at least for the foreseeable future. But if one longs for proof that something mysterious occurred there, they need look no further than the backyard of the Kecksburg Volunteer Fire Department. There, in all of its acorn-shape glory, stands an full-scale mock-up of the spacecraft reportedly found in this peaceful town on December 9, 1965. There too rests the mystery, intrigue, and romance that have accompanied this alleged space traveler for more than 40 years.

# An Underground Mystery

*For centuries, people have believed that Earth is hollow. They claim that civilizations may live inside Earth's core or that it might be a landing base for alien spaceships. This sounds like fantasy, but believers point to startling evidence, including explorers' reports and modern photos taken from space.*

✳ ✳ ✳ ✳

### A Prize Inside?

HOLLOW EARTH BELIEVERS agree that our planet is a shell between 500 and 800 miles thick, and inside that shell is another world. It may be a gaseous realm, an alien outpost, or home to a utopian society.

Some believers add a spiritual spin. Calling the interior world Agartha or Shambhala, they use concepts from Eastern religions and point to ancient legends supporting these ideas.

Many Hollow Earth enthusiasts are certain that people from the outer and inner worlds can visit each other by traveling through openings in the outer shell. One such entrance is a hole in the ocean near the North Pole. A November 1968 photo by the ESSA-7 satellite showed a dark, circular area at the North Pole that was surrounded by ice fields.

Another hole supposedly exists in Antarctica. Some Hollow Earth enthusiasts say Hitler believed that Antarctica held the true opening to Earth's core. Leading Hollow Earth researchers such as Dennis Crenshaw suggest that President Roosevelt ordered the 1939 South Pole expedition to find the entrance before the Germans did.

The poles may not hold the only entrances to a world hidden deep beneath our feet. Jules Verne's famous novel *Journey to the Center of the Earth* supported yet another theory about passage between the worlds. In his story, there were many access points, including waterfalls and inactive volcanoes. Edgar Allan Poe and Edgar Rice Burroughs also wrote about worlds inside Earth. Their ideas were based on science as well as fantasy.

## Scientists Take Note

Many scientists have taken the Hollow Earth theory seriously. One of the most noted was English astronomer Edmund Halley, of Halley's Comet fame. In 1692, he declared that our planet is hollow, and as evidence, he pointed to global shifts in Earth's magnetic fields, which frequently cause compass anomalies. According to Halley, those shifts could be explained by the movement of rotating worlds inside Earth. In addition, he claimed that the source of gravity—still debated in the 21st century—could be an interior world.

In Halley's opinion, Earth is made of three separate layers or shells, each rotating independently around a solid core. We live on the outer shell, but the inner worlds might be inhabited, too. Halley also suggested that Earth's interior atmospheres are luminous. We supposedly see them as gas leaking out of Earth's fissures. At the poles, that gas creates the *aurora borealis*.

## Scientists Look Deeper

Hollow Earth researchers claim that the groundwork for their theories was laid by some of the most notable scientific minds of the 17th and 18th centuries. Although their beliefs remain controversial and largely unsubstantiated, they are still widely discussed and have a network of enthusiasts.

Some researchers claim that Leonhard Euler (1707–1783), one of the greatest mathematicians of all time, believed that Earth's interior includes a glowing core that illuminates life for a well-developed civilization, much like the sun lights our world. Another mathematician, Sir John Leslie (1766–1832), suggested that Earth has a thin crust and also believed the interior cavity was filled with light.

In 1818, a popular lecturer named John Cleves Symmes, Jr., proposed an expedition to prove the Hollow Earth theory. He believed that he could sail to the North Pole, and upon reaching the opening to Earth's core, he could steer his ship over the lip of the entrance, which he believed resembled a waterfall. Then he would continue sailing on waters inside the planet. In 1822 and 1823, Symmes petitioned Congress to fund the expedition, but he was turned down. He died in 1829, and his gravestone in Hamilton, Ohio, is decorated with his model of the Hollow Earth.

## Proof Gets Woolly and Weird

In 1846, a remarkably well-preserved—and long extinct— woolly mammoth was found frozen in Siberia. Most woolly mammoths died out about 12,000 years ago, so researchers were baffled by its pristine condition.

Hollow Earth enthusiasts say there is only one explanation: The mammoth lived inside Earth, where those beasts are not extinct. The beast had probably become lost, emerged into our world, and froze to death shortly before the 1846 discovery.

## Eyewitnesses at the North Pole

Several respected scientists and explorers have visited the poles and returned with stories that suggest a hollow Earth. At the start of the 20th century, Arctic explorers Dr. Frederick A. Cook and Rear Admiral Robert E. Peary sighted land—not just an icy wasteland—at the North Pole. Peary first described it as "the white summits of a distant land." A 1913 Arctic expedition also reported seeing "hills, valleys, and snow-capped peaks." All of these claims were dismissed as mirages but would later be echoed by the research of Admiral Richard E. Byrd, the first man to fly over the North Pole. Hollow Earth believers suggest that Byrd actually flew into the interior world and then out again, without realizing it. They cite Byrd's notes as evidence, as he describes his navigational instruments and compasses spinning out of control.

## Unidentified Submerged Objects

Support for the Hollow Earth theory has also come from UFO enthusiasts. People who study UFOs have also been documenting USOs, or unidentified submerged objects. These mysterious vehicles have been spotted—mostly at sea—since the 19th century.

USOs look like "flying saucers," but instead of vanishing into the skies, they plunge beneath the surface of the ocean. Some are luminous and fly upward from the sea at a fantastic speed—and without making a sound.

UFO enthusiasts believe that these spaceships are visiting worlds beneath the sea. Some are certain that these are actually underwater alien bases. Other UFO researchers think that the ocean conceals entries to a hollow Earth, where the aliens maintain outposts.

## The Search Continues

Some scientists have determined that the most likely location for a northern opening to Earth's interior is at 84.4 N Latitude, 141 E Longitude. It's a spot near Siberia, about 600 miles from the North Pole. Photos taken by *Apollo 8* in 1968 and *Apollo 16* in 1972 showed dark, circular areas confirming the location. Some scientists are studying seismic tomography, which uses natural and human-made explosions as well as earthquakes and other seismic waves to chart Earth's interior masses. So far, scientists confirm that Earth is comprised of three separate layers. Strangely, some images could suggest a mountain range at Earth's core. Could what seems like a fantasy from a Jules Verne novel turn out to be an astonishing reality? Hollow Earth societies around the world continue to look for proof of this centuries-old legend. Who knows what they might find?

# The "Roswell" Incident

*Whether or not you believe that space aliens landed in Roswell, New Mexico, you are at least entitled to know where the real crash site was.*

✳   ✳   ✳   ✳

ON JULY 7, 1947, something strange touched ground in New Mexico. The two most popular theories are (1) that aliens crash-landed in the desert—and the military covered up recovery of the aircraft—and (2) that the wreckage consisted of the remnants of a military research balloon launched from a nearby airfield.

That morning, rancher Mac Brazel, foreman of the Foster Ranch near Corona, New Mexico, found strange metal debris and a gouged-out trench across a portion of the property. After the mysterious material was discovered, Brazel reported that the sheep he was herding refused to cross the debris field, and from there, reports of alien crash sites started springing up around the region.

Oddly, not one of the sites was actually in Roswell. On a detailed map of the southeastern corner of New Mexico, amid the names of mesas, canyons, and draws, one can find three "alleged UFO debris sites": the Corona Site, the Jim Ragsdale Site, and a third one on the Hub Corn Ranch. The third site is the closest to Roswell, but even that is a good 30 miles north of town, down an isolated dirt road. In a book about the incident, *Crash at Corona*, the authors note, "Nothing crashed at Roswell, despite the titles of the books; it was just the largest city within 75 miles of the crash site."

# Ohio's Mysterious Hangar 18

*An otherwordly legend makes its way from New Mexico to Ohio when the wreckage from Roswell ends up in the Midwest.*

✳ ✳ ✳ ✳

EVEN THOSE WHO aren't UFO buffs have overheard a little about the infamous Roswell Incident. But what most people don't know is that according to legend, the mysterious aircraft was recovered (along with some alien bodies), secreted out of the area, and came to rest just outside of Dayton, Ohio.

## Something Crashed in the Desert

While the exact date is unclear, sometime during the first week of July 1947, Mac Brazel decided to go out and check his property for fallen trees and other damage after a night of heavy storms and lightning. Brazel came across an area of his property littered with strange debris unlike anything he had ever seen before—some of the debris even had strange writing on it.

Brazel showed some of the debris to a few neighbors and then took it to the office of Roswell sheriff George Wilcox, who called authorities at Roswell Army Air Field. After speaking with Wilcox, intelligence officer Major Jesse Marcel drove out to the Brazel ranch and collected as much debris as he could. He then returned to the airfield and showed the debris to his commanding officer, Colonel William Blanchard, commander of the 509th Bomb Group that was stationed at the Roswell Air Field. Upon seeing the debris, Blanchard dispatched military vehicles and personnel back out to the Brazel ranch to see if they could recover anything else.

## "Flying Saucer Captured!"

On July 8, 1947, Colonel Blanchard issued a press release stating that the wreckage of a "crashed disk" had been recovered. The bold headline of the July 8 edition of the *Roswell Daily Record* read: "RAAF Captures Flying Saucer on Ranch in Roswell Region." Newspapers around the world ran similar headlines. But then, within hours of the Blanchard release, General Roger M. Ramey, commander of the Eighth Air Force in Fort Worth, Texas, retracted Blanchard's release for him and issued another statement saying there was no UFO. Blanchard's men had simply recovered a fallen weather balloon.

Before long, the headlines that had earlier touted the capture of a UFO read: "It's a Weather Balloon" and "'Flying Disc' Turns Up as Just Hot Air." Later editions even ran a staged photograph of Major Jesse Marcel, who was first sent to investigate the incident, kneeling in front of weather balloon debris. Most of the general public seemed content with the explanation, but there were skeptics.

## Whisked Away to Hangar 18?

Those who believe that aliens crash-landed near Roswell claim that, under cover of darkness, large portions of the alien spacecraft were brought out to the Roswell Air Field and loaded onto B-29 and C-54 aircrafts. Those planes were then supposedly flown to Wright-Patterson Air Force Base, just outside of Dayton. Once the planes landed, they were taxied over to Hangar 18 and unloaded. According to legend, it's all still there.

There are some problems with the story, though. For one, none of the hangars on Wright-Patterson Air Force Base are officially known as "Hangar 18." There are no buildings designated with the number 18 either. Rather, the hangars are labeled 1A, 1B, 1C, and so on. And there's also the fact that none of the hangars seem large enough to house and conceal an alien spacecraft. But just because there's nothing listed as Hangar 18 on a Wright-Patterson map doesn't mean it's not there. Conspiracy theorists believe that hangars 4A, 4B, and 4C might be the infamous Hangar 18. As for the overall size of the hangars, it's believed that most of the wreckage has been stored down in giant underground tunnels and chambers deep under the hangar, both to protect the debris and to keep it safe from prying eyes. It is said that Wright-Patterson is currently conducting experiments on the wreckage to see if scientists can reverse-engineer the technology.

## So What's the Deal?

The story of Hangar 18 only got stranger as the years went on, starting with the government's Project Blue Book, a program designed to investigate reported UFO sightings across the United States. Between 1947 and 1969, Project Blue Book investigated more than 12,000 UFO sightings before being disbanded. And where was Project Blue Book headquartered? Wright-Patterson Air Force Base.

Then in the early 1960s, Arizona senator Barry Goldwater, himself a retired major general in the U.S. Army Air Corps (and a friend of Colonel Blanchard), became interested in what, if anything, had crashed in Roswell. When Goldwater discovered Hangar 18, he first wrote directly to Wright-Patterson and asked for permission to tour the facility but was quickly denied. He then approached another friend, General Curtis LeMay, and asked if he could see the "Green Room" where the UFO secret was being held. Goldwater claimed that LeMay gave him "holy hell" and screamed at Goldwater, "Not only can't you get into it, but don't you ever mention it to me again."

Most recently, in 1982, retired pilot Oliver "Pappy" Henderson attended a reunion and announced that he was one of the men who had flown alien bodies out of Roswell in a C-54 cargo plane. His destination? Hangar 18 at Wright-Patterson. Although no one is closer to a definitive answer, it seems that the legend of Hangar 18 will never die.

*"I certainly believe in aliens in space. They may not look like us, but I have very strong feelings that they have advanced beyond our mental capabilities . . . I think some highly secret government UFO investigations are going on that we don't know about—and probably never will unless the Air Force discloses them."*

—Barry Goldwater

# The Mysterious Orb

*If Texas were a dartboard, the city of Brownwood would be at the center of the bull's-eye. Maybe that's how aliens saw it, too.*

✳ ✳ ✳ ✳

BROWNWOOD IS A peaceful little city with about 20,000 residents and a popular train museum. A frontier town at one time, it became the trade center of Texas when the railroad arrived in 1885. Since then, the city has maintained a peaceful lifestyle. Even the massive tornado that struck Brownwood in 1976 left no fatalities. The place just has that "small town" kind of feeling.

## An Invader from the Sky

In July 2002, however, the city's peace was broken. Brownwood made international headlines when a strange metal orb fell from space, landed in the Colorado River, and washed up just south of town. The orb looked like a battered metal soccer ball—it was about a foot across, and it weighed just under ten pounds. Experts described it as a titanium sphere. When it was X-rayed, it revealed a second, inner sphere with tubes and wires wrapped inside.

That's all that anybody knows (or claims to know). No one is sure what the object is, and no one has claimed responsibility for it. The leading theory is that it's a cryogenic tank from some kind of spacecraft from Earth, used to store a small amount of liquid hydrogen or helium for cooling purposes. Others have speculated that it's a bomb, a spying device, or even a weapon used to combat UFOs.

### It's Not Alone

The Brownwood sphere isn't unique. A similar object landed in Kingsbury, Texas, in 1997, and was quickly confiscated by the Air Force for "tests and analysis." So far, no further announcements have been made.

Of course, the Air Force probably has a lot to keep it busy. About 200 UFOs are reported each month, and Texas is among the top three states where UFOs are seen. But until anything is known for sure, those in Texas at night should keep an eye on the skies.

# The Great Texas Airship Mystery

*Roswell, New Mexico, may be the most famous potential UFO crash site, but did Texas experience a similar event in the 19th century?*

✳   ✳   ✳   ✳

ONE SUNNY APRIL morning in 1897, a UFO crashed in Aurora, Texas.

Six years before the Wright Brothers' first flight and 50 years before Roswell, a huge, cigar-shape UFO was seen in the skies. It was first noted on November 17, 1896, about a thousand feet above rooftops in Sacramento, California. From there, the spaceship traveled to San Francisco, where it was seen by hundreds of people.

## A National Tour

Next, the craft crossed the United States, where it was observed by thousands. Near Omaha, Nebraska, a farmer reported the ship on the ground, making repairs. When it returned to the skies, it headed toward Chicago, where it was photographed on April 11, 1897, the first UFO photo on record. On April 15, near Kalamazoo, Michigan, residents reported loud noises "like that of heavy ordnance" coming from the spaceship.

Two days later, the UFO attempted a landing in Aurora, Texas, which should have been a good place. The town was almost deserted, and its broad, empty fields could have been an ideal landing strip.

## No Smooth Sailing

However, at about 6 a.m. on April 17, the huge, cigar-shape airship "sailed over the public square and, when it reached the north part of town, collided with the tower of Judge Proctor's windmill and went to pieces with a terrific explosion, scattering debris over several acres of ground, wrecking the windmill and water tank and destroying the judge's flower garden."

That's how Aurora resident and cotton buyer S. E. Haydon described the events for *The Dallas Morning News*. The remains of the ship seemed to be strips and shards of a silver-colored metal. Just one body was recovered. The newspaper reported, "while his remains are badly disfigured, enough of the original has been picked up to show that he was not an inhabitant of this world."

On April 18, reportedly, that body was given a good, Christian burial in the Aurora cemetery, where it may remain to this day. A 1973 effort to exhume the body and examine it was successfully blocked by the Aurora Cemetery Association.

## A Firsthand Account

Although many people have claimed the Aurora incident was a hoax, an elderly woman was interviewed in 1973 and clearly recalled the crash from her childhood. She said that her parents wouldn't let her near the debris from the spacecraft, in case it contained something dangerous. However, she described the alien as "a small man."

Aurora continues to attract people interested in UFOs. They wonder why modern Aurora appears to be laid out like a military base. Nearby, Fort Worth seems to be home to the U.S. government's experts in alien technology. Immediately after the Roswell UFO crash in 1947, debris from that spaceship was sent to Fort Worth for analysis.

## Is There Any Trace Left?

*The Aurora Encounter*, a 1986 movie, documents the events that began when people saw the spacecraft attempt a landing at Judge Proctor's farm. Today, the Oates gas station marks the area where the UFO crashed.

Metal debris was collected from the site in the 1970s and studied by North Texas State University. That study called one fragment "most intriguing": It appeared to be iron but wasn't magnetic; it was shiny and malleable rather than brittle, as iron should be.

As recently as 2008, UFOs have appeared in the north central Texas skies. In Stephenville, a freight company owner and pilot described a low-flying object in the sky, "a mile long and half a mile wide." Others who saw the ship several times during January 2008 said that its lights changed configuration, so it wasn't an airplane. The government declined to comment.

Today, a plaque at the Aurora cemetery mentions the spaceship, but the alien's tombstone—which, if it actually existed, is said to have featured a carved image of a spaceship—was stolen many years ago.

# Strange Lights in Marfa

*According to a 2007 poll, approximately 14 percent of Americans claim that they've seen a UFO. How many of them have been in Marfa?*

✳   ✳   ✳   ✳

**I**F ANYONE IS near Marfa at night, they should watch for odd, vivid lights over nearby Mitchell Flat. Many people believe that the lights from UFOs or even alien entities can be seen. The famous Marfa Lights are about the size of basketballs and are usually white, orange, red, or yellow. These unexplained lights only appear at night and usually hover above the ground at about shoulder height. Some of the lights—alone or in pairs—drift and fly around the landscape.

From cowboys to truck drivers, people traveling in Texas near the intersection of U.S. Route 90 and U.S. Route 67 in southwest Texas have reported the lights. And these baffling lights don't just appear on the ground. Pilots and airline passengers claim to have seen the Marfa Lights from the skies. So far, no one has proved a natural explanation for the floating orbs.

## Eyewitness Information

Two 1988 reports were especially graphic. Pilot R. Weidig was about 8,000 feet above Marfa when he saw the lights and estimated them rising several hundred feet above the ground. Passenger E. Halsell described the lights as larger than the plane and noted that they were pulsating. In 2002, pilot B. Eubanks provided a similar report.

In addition to what can be seen, the Marfa Lights may also trigger low-frequency electromagnetic waves—which can be heard on special receivers—similar to the "whistlers" caused by lightning. However, unlike waves from power lines and electrical storms, the Marfa whistlers are extremely loud. They can be heard as the orbs appear, and then they fade when the lights do.

## A Little Bit about Marfa

Marfa is about 60 miles north of the Mexican border and about 190 miles southeast of El Paso. This small, friendly Texas town is 4,800 feet above sea level and covers 1.6 square miles.

In 1883, Marfa was a railroad water stop. It received its name from the wife of the president of the Texas and New Orleans Railroad, who chose the name from a Russian novel that she was reading. A strong argument can be made that this was Dostoyevsky's *The Brothers Karamazov*. The town grew slowly, reaching its peak during World War II when the U.S. government located a prisoner of war camp, the Marfa Army Airfield, and a chemical warfare brigade nearby. (Some skeptics suggest that discarded chemicals may be causing the Marfa Lights, but searchers have found no evidence of such.)

Today, Marfa is home to about 2,500 people. The small town is an emerging arts center with more than a dozen artists' studios and art galleries. However, Marfa remains most famous for its light display. The annual Marfa Lights Festival is one of the town's biggest events, but the mysterious lights attract visitors year-round. The Marfa Lights are seen almost every clear night, but they never manifest during the daytime. The lights appear between Marfa and nearby Paisano Pass, with the Chinati Mountains as a backdrop.

## Widespread Sightings

The first documented sighting was by 16-year-old cowhand Robert Reed Ellison during an 1883 cattle drive. Seeing an odd light in the area, Ellison thought he'd seen an Apache campfire. When he told his story in town, however, settlers told him that they'd seen lights in the area, too, and they'd never found evidence of campfires.

Two years later, 38-year-old Joe Humphreys and his wife, Sally, also reported lights at Marfa. In 1919, cowboys on a cattle drive paused to search the area for the origin of the lights. Like the others, they found no explanation for what they had seen.

In 1943, the Marfa Lights came to national attention when Fritz Kahl, an airman at the Marfa Army Base, reported that airmen were seeing lights that they couldn't explain. Four years later, he attempted to fly after them in a plane but came up empty again.

## Explanations?

Some skeptics claim that the lights are headlights from U.S. 67, dismissing the many reports from before cars were in the Marfa area. Others insist that the lights are swamp gas, ball lightning, reflections off mica deposits, or a nightly mirage.

At the other extreme, a contingent of people believe that the floating orbs are friendly observers of life on Earth. For example, Mrs. W. T. Giddings described her father's early 20th-century encounter with the Marfa Lights. He'd become lost during a blizzard, and according to his daughter, the lights "spoke" to him and led him to a cave where he found shelter.

Most studies of the phenomenon, however, conclude that the lights are indeed real but cannot be explained. The 1989 TV show *Unsolved Mysteries* set up equipment to find an explanation. Scientists on the scene could only comment that the lights were not made by people.

## Share the Wealth

Marfa is the most famous location for "ghost lights" and "mystery lights," but it's not the only place to see them. Here are just a few of the legendary unexplained lights that attract visitors to dark roads in Texas on murky nights.

* In southeast Texas, a single orb appears regularly near Saratoga on Bragg Road.

* The Anson Light appears near Mt. Hope Cemetery in Anson, by U.S. Highway 180.

* Since 1850, "Brit Bailey's Light" glows five miles west of Angleton near Highway 35 in Brazoria County.

* In January 2008, Stephenville attracted international attention when unexplained lights—and perhaps a metallic spaceship—flew fast and low over the town.

The Marfa Lights appear over Mitchell Flat, which is entirely private property. However, the curious can view the lights from a Texas Highway Department roadside parking area about nine miles east of Marfa on U.S. Highway 90. Seekers should arrive before dusk for the best location, especially during bluebonnet season (mid-April through late May), because this is a popular tourist stop.

The Marfa Lights Festival takes place during Labor Day weekend each year. This annual celebration of Marfa's mystery includes a parade, arts and crafts booths, great food, and a street dance.

# E. T. Phone Canada?

*Do extraterrestrials prefer Canada? The nation ranks first in UFO sightings per capita, with a record high of 1,004 reported in 2008 and about 10 percent of Canadians claiming to have encountered one.*

* * * *

## What's That?

THOUGH RECORDED INSTANCES of UFO sightings on Canadian soil date back to the 1950s, extraterrestrial encounters emerged most prominently on the global radar in 1967 with two startling occurrences. The first happened when a quartz prospector near a mine at Falcon Lake in Manitoba was allegedly burned by a UFO.

The second followed in October of that year at Shag Harbour, Nova Scotia, when several witnesses—including residents, the Royal Canadian Mounted Police, and an Air Canada pilot—reported strange lights hovering above the water and then submerging. A search of the site revealed only odd yellow foam, suggesting something had indeed gone underwater, but whether it was a UFO remains a mystery.

### A Growing Phenomenon

Since then, the number of sightings in Canada has increased nearly every year. Most take place in sparsely populated regions—the rationale being that "urban glow" obscures the lights of spaceships and that country folk spend more time outdoors and thus have better opportunities to glimpse UFOs. It may also be that rural areas are simply more conducive to extraterrestrial activity. (We've heard of crop circles, but parking garage circles? Not so much.)

Most sightings reported are of the "strange light" and "weird flying vessel" variety, and indeed most have rather banal explanations (stars, airplanes, towers). Still, each year between 1 and 10 percent of sightings remain a mystery.

# To the Moon!

*Television and film star Jackie Gleason was fascinated with the paranormal and UFOs. But he had no idea that an innocent game with an influential friend would lead him face to face with his obsession.*

✳  ✳  ✳  ✳

JACKIE GLEASON WAS a star of the highest order. The rotund actor kept television audiences in stitches with his portrayal of hardheaded but ultimately lovable family man Ralph Kramden in the 1955 sitcom *The Honeymooners*. He made history with his regularly aimed, but never delivered, threats to TV wife Alice, played by Audrey Meadows: "One of these days Alice, one of these days, pow, right in the kisser," and "Bang, zoom! To the moon, Alice!"

But many fans didn't know that Gleason was obsessed with the supernatural, and he owned a massive collection of memorabilia on the subject. It was so large and impressive that the

University of Miami, Florida, put it on permanent exhibit after his death in 1987. He even had a house built in the shape of a UFO, which he christened, "The Mothership." The obsession was legendary, and it climaxed in an unimaginable way.

## A High Stakes Game

An avid golfer, Gleason also kept a home close to Inverrary Golf and Country Club in Lauderhill, Florida. A famous golfing buddy lived nearby—U.S. President Richard M. Nixon, who had a compound on nearby Biscayne Bay. The Hollywood star and the controversial politician shared a love of the links, politics, and much more.

The odyssey began when Gleason and Nixon met for a golf tournament at Inverrary in February 1973. Late in the day their conversation turned to a topic close to Gleason's heart—UFOs. To the funnyman's surprise, the president revealed his own fascination with the subject, touting a large collection of books that rivaled Gleason's. They talked shop through the rest of the game, but Gleason noticed reservation in Nixon's tone, as if the aides and security within earshot kept the president from speaking his mind. He would soon learn why.

Later that evening around midnight, an unexpected guest visited the Gleason home. It was Nixon, alone. The customary secret service detail assigned to him was nowhere to be seen. Confused, Gleason asked Nixon the reason for such a late call. He replied only that he had to show Gleason something. They climbed into Nixon's private car and sped off. The drive brought them to Homestead Air Force Base in South Miami-Dade County. Nixon took them to a large, heavily guarded building. Guards parted as the pair headed inside the structure, Gleason following Nixon past labs before arriving at a series of large cases. The cases held wreckage from a downed UFO, Nixon told his friend. Seeing all of this, Gleason had his doubts and imagined himself the target of an elaborately constructed hoax.

Leaving the wreckage, the pair entered a chamber holding six (some reports say eight) freezers topped with thick glass. Peering into the hulls, Gleason later said he saw dead bodies—but not of the human variety. The remains were small, almost childlike in stature, but withered in appearance and possessing only three or four digits per hand. They were also severely mangled, as if they had been in a devastating accident.

Returning home, Gleason was giddy. His obsession had come full circle. The enthusiasm changed in the weeks that followed, however, shifting to intense fear and worry. A patriotic American, Gleason couldn't reconcile his government's secrecy about the UFO wreckage. Traumatized, he began drinking heavily and suffered from severe insomnia.

### The "Truth" Comes Out

Gleason kept details of his wild night with Nixon under wraps. Unfortunately, his soon-to-be-ex-wife didn't follow his lead. Beverly Gleason spilled the beans in *Esquire* magazine and again in an unpublished memoir on her marriage to Gleason. Supermarket tabloids ate the story up.

Gleason only opened up about his night with Nixon in the last weeks of his life. Speaking to Larry Warren, a former Air Force pilot with his own UFO close encounter, a slightly boozy Gleason let his secret loose with a phrase reminiscent of his *Honeymooners* days: "We've got 'em — Aliens!"

# John Lennon Sees a UFO

*Lucy in the sky with warp drive.*

✳ ✳ ✳ ✳

IN MAY 1974, former Beatle John Lennon and his assistant/mistress May Pang returned to New York City after almost a year's stay in Los Angeles, a period to which Lennon would later refer as his "Lost Weekend." The pair moved into Penthouse Tower B at 434 East 52nd Street. As Lennon watched television on a hot summer night, he noticed flashing lights reflected in the glass of an open door that led onto a patio. At first dismissing it as a neon sign, Lennon suddenly realized that since the apartment was on the roof, the glass *couldn't* be reflecting light from the street. So—sans clothing—he ventured onto the terrace to investigate. What he witnessed has never been satisfactorily explained.

## Speechless

As Pang recollected, Lennon excitedly called for her to come outside. Pang did so. "I looked up and stopped mid-sentence," she said later. "I couldn't even speak because I saw this thing up there . . . it was silvery, and it was flying very slowly. There was a white light shining around the rim and a red light on the top . . . [it] was silent. We started to watch it drift down, tilt slightly, and it was flying below rooftops. It was the most amazing sight." She quickly ran back into the apartment, grabbed her camera, and returned to the patio, clicking away.

Lennon friend and rock photography legend Bob Gruen picked up the story: "In those days, you didn't have answering machines, but a service [staffed by people], and I had received a call from 'Dr. Winston.'" (Lennon's original middle name was Winston, and he often used the alias "Dr. Winston O'Boogie.") When Gruen returned the call, Lennon explained his incredible sighting and insisted that the photographer come round to pick up and develop the film personally. "He was serious," Gruen said. "He wouldn't call me in the middle of the night to joke around." Gruen noted that although Lennon had been known to partake in mind-altering substances in the past, during this period he was totally straight. So was Pang, a non-drinker who never took drugs and whom Gruen characterized as "a clear-headed young woman."

The film in Pang's camera was a unique type supplied by Gruen, "four times as fast as the highest speed then [commercially] available." Gruen had been using this specialty film, usually employed for military reconnaissance, in low-light situations such as recording studios. The same roll already had photos of Lennon and former bandmate Ringo Starr, taken by Pang in Las Vegas during a recording session.

Gruen asked Lennon if he'd reported his sighting to the authorities. "Yeah, like I'm going to call the police and say I'm John Lennon and I've seen a flying saucer," the musician scoffed. Gruen picked up the couple's phone and contacted the police, *The Daily News*, and the *New York Times*. The photographer claims that the cops and the *News* admitted that they'd heard similar reports, while the *Times* just hung up on him.

## It Would Have Been the Ultimate Trip

Gruen's most amusing recollection of Lennon, who had been hollering "UFO!" and "Take me with you!" was that none of his NYC neighbors either saw or heard the naked, ex-Beatle screaming from his penthouse terrace. And disappointingly, no one who might have piloted the craft seemed to acknowledge Lennon's pleas.

Gruen took the exposed film home to process, keeping it between two rolls of his own. Gruen's negatives came out perfectly, but Pang's film was "like a clear plastic strip," Gruen says. "We were all baffled that it was completely blank."

Lennon remained convinced of what he'd seen. In several shots from a subsequent photo session with Gruen that produced the iconic shot of the musician wearing a New York City T-shirt (a gift from the photographer), John points to where he'd spotted the craft. And on his *Walls and Bridges* album, Lennon wrote in the liner notes: "On the 23rd Aug. 1974 at 9 o'clock I saw a U.F.O.—J.L."

Who's to say he and May Pang didn't? Certainly not Gruen, who still declares—more than 35 years after the fact—"I believed them."

And so the mystery remains.

# One Reptile to Rule Them All

*Some people are ruled by their pets; others are ruled by their work. Conspiracy theorist David Icke believes that we're all being ruled by reptilian humanoids.*

✳ ✳ ✳ ✳

## Worldwide Domination

**D**AVID ICKE HAS worn many hats: journalist, news anchor for the BBC, spokesman for the British Green Party, and professional soccer player. But after an experience in Peru in 1991, he took on another role: famed conspiracy theorist.

Like many other conspiracy theorists, Icke believes that a group called the Illuminati, or "global elite," controls the world. According to these theorists, the group manipulates the economy and uses mind control to usher humanity into a submissive state. Icke also believes that the group is responsible for organizing such tragedies as the Holocaust and the Oklahoma City bombings.

Some of the most powerful people in the world are members, claims Icke, including ex-British Prime Minister Tony Blair and former U.S. President George H. W. Bush, as well as leaders of financial institutions and major media outlets. However, not all members are human. According to Icke, those at the top of the Illuminati bloodlines are vehicles for a reptilian entity from the constellation Draco. These shape-shifters can change from human to reptile and back again, and they are essentially controlling humanity.

## Is Icke Onto Something?

In the documentary *David Icke: Was He Right?*, Icke claims that many of his earlier predictions, including a hurricane in New Orleans and a "major attack on a large city" between the years 2000 and 2002, have come true. But are we really being ruled by reptilian humanoids or is Icke's theory a bunch of snake oil? Icke was nearly laughed off the stage in a 1991 appearance on a BBC talk show. But with 16 published books, thousands attending his speaking engagements, and thousands of weekly hits to his website, perhaps it's Icke who's laughing.

# Alleged Celebrity UFO Sightings

*It's not just moonshine-swilling farmers in rural areas who claim to have seen UFOs hovering in the night sky. Plenty of celebrities have also reportedly witnessed unidentified flying objects and have been happy to talk about their experiences afterward.*

✳ ✳ ✳ ✳

## Jimmy Carter

**N**OT EVEN PRESIDENTS are immune from UFO sightings. During Jimmy Carter's presidential campaign of 1976, he told reporters that in 1969, before he was governor of Georgia, he saw what could have been a UFO. "It was the darndest thing I've ever seen," he said of the incident. He claimed that the object that he and a group of others had watched for ten minutes was as bright as the moon. Carter was often referred to as "the UFO president" after being elected because he filed a report on the matter.

## David Duchovny

In 1982, long before he starred as a believer in the supernatural on the hit sci-fi series *The X-Files*, David Duchovny thought he saw a UFO. Although, by his own admission, he's reluctant to say with any certainty that it wasn't something he simply imagined as a result of stress and overwork. "There was something in the air and it was gone," he later told reporters. "I thought: 'You've got to get some rest, David.'"

## Ronald Reagan

Former actor and U.S. president Ronald Reagan witnessed UFOs on two occasions. Once during his term as California governor (1967–1975), Reagan and his wife Nancy arrived late to a party hosted by actor William Holden. Guests including Steve Allen and Lucille Ball reported that the couple excitedly described how they had just witnessed a UFO while driving along the Pacific Coast Highway. They had stopped to watch the event, which made them late to the party.

Reagan also confessed to a *Wall Street Journal* reporter that in 1974, when the gubernatorial jet was preparing to land in Bakersfield, California, he noticed a strange bright light in the sky. The pilot followed the light for a short time before it suddenly shot up vertically at a high rate of speed and disappeared from sight. Reagan stopped short of labeling the light a UFO, of course. As actress Lucille Ball said in reference to Reagan's first alleged UFO sighting, "After he was elected president, I kept thinking about that event and wondered if he still would have won if he told everyone that he saw a flying saucer."

## William Shatner

For decades, the man who played Captain Kirk in the original *Star Trek* series claimed that an alien saved his life. When the actor and a group of friends were riding their motorbikes through the desert in the late 1960s, Shatner was inadvertently left behind when his bike wouldn't restart after driving into a giant pothole. Shatner said that he spotted an alien in a silver suit standing on a ridge and that it led him to a gas station and safety. Shatner later stated in his autobiography, *Up Till Now*, that he made up the part about the alien during a television interview.

# Circle Marks the Spot: The Mystery of Crop Circles

*The result of cyclonic winds? Attempted alien communication? Evidence of hungry cows with serious OCD? There are many theories as to how crop circles, or grain stalks flattened in recognizable patterns, have come to exist. Most people dismiss them as pranks, but there are more than a few who believe there's something otherworldly going on.*

✳   ✳   ✳   ✳

## Ye Olde Crop Circle

SOME EXPERTS BELIEVE the first crop circles date back to the late 1600s, but there isn't much evidence to support them. Other experts cite evidence of more than 400 simple circles 6 to 20 feet in diameter that appeared worldwide hundreds of years ago. The kinds of circles they refer to are still being found today, usually after huge, cyclonic thunderstorms pass over a large expanse of agricultural land. These circles are much smaller and not nearly as precise as the geometric, mathematically complex circles that started cropping up in the second half of the 20th century. Still, drawings and writings about these smaller circles lend weight to the claims of believers that the crop circle phenomenon isn't a new thing.

The International Crop Circle Database reports stories of "UFO nests" in British papers during the 1960s. About a decade or so later, crop circles fully captured the attention (and the imagination) of the masses.

## No, Virginia, There Aren't Any Aliens

In 1991, two men from Southampton, England, came forward with a confession. Doug Bower and Dave Chorley admitted that they were responsible for the majority of the crop circles found in England during the preceding two decades.

Inspired by stories of "UFO nests" in the 1960s, the two decided to add a little excitement to their sleepy town. With boards, string, and a few simple navigational tools, the men worked through the night to create complex patterns in fields that could be seen from the road. It worked, and before long, much of the Western world was caught up in crop circle fever. Some claimed it was irrefutable proof that UFOs were landing on Earth. Others said God was trying to communicate with humans "through the language of mathematics."

For believers, there was no doubt that supernatural or extra-terrestrial forces were at work. But skeptics were thrilled to hear the confession from Bower and Chorley, since they never believed the circles to be anything but a prank in the first place.

Before the men came forward, more crop circles appeared throughout the 1980s and '90s, many of them not made by Bower and Chorley. Circles "mysteriously" occurred in Australia, Canada, the United States, Argentina, India, and even Afghanistan. In 1995, more than 200 cases of crop circles were reported worldwide. In 2001, a formation that appeared in Wiltshire, England, contained 409 circles and covered more than 12 acres.

Many were baffled that anyone could believe these large and admittedly rather intricate motifs were anything but human-made. Plus, the more media coverage crop circles garnered, the more new crop circles appeared. Other people came forward, admitting that they were the "strange and unexplained power" behind the circles. Even then, die-hard believers dismissed the hoaxers, vehemently suggesting that they were either players in a government cover-up, captives of aliens forced to throw everyone off track, or just average Joes looking for 15 minutes of fame by claiming to have made something that was clearly the work of nonhumans.

Scientists were deployed to ascertain the facts. In 1999, a well-funded team of experts was assembled to examine numerous crop circles in the UK. The verdict? At least 80 percent of the circles were, beyond a shadow of a doubt, created by humans. Footprints, abandoned tools, and video of a group of hoaxers caught in the act all debunked the theory that crop circles were created by aliens.

## But Still . . .

So if crop circles are nothing more than hoaxers having fun or artists playing with a unique medium, why are we still so interested? Movies such as *Signs* in 2002 capitalized on the public's fascination with the phenomenon, and crop circles still capture headlines. Skeptics will scoff, but from time to time, there is a circle that doesn't quite fit the profile of a human-made prank.

There have been claims that fully functional cell phones cease to work once the caller steps inside certain crop circles. Could it be caused by some funky ion-scramble emitted by an extra-terrestrial force? Some researchers have tried to re-create the circles and succeeded, but only with the use of high-tech tools and equipment that wouldn't be available to the average prankster. If all of these circles were made by humans, why are so few people busted for trespassing in the middle of the night? And where are all the footprints?

Eyewitness accounts of UFOs rising from fields can hardly be considered irrefutable evidence, but there are several reports from folks who swear they saw ships, lights, and movement in the sky just before crop circles were discovered.

# Chapter 10

# Haunting Enigmas

## The Philip Phenomenon: Creating a Ghost out of Thin Air

*Which came first: the ghost or the séance? That's the million-dollar question regarding the Philip Phenomenon—an astonishing experiment that successfully conjured up a spirit. The only problem is that this ghost never really lived. Or did it?*

✳ ✳ ✳ ✳

I T ALL BEGAN in 1972, when members of the Toronto Society for Psychical Research (TSPR) conducted an experiment to determine if they could "create" a ghost and study how the power of suggestion affected the results. They wanted to know if they could work with a totally fictitious character—a man they invented from scratch—and somehow make contact with its spirit. And they did.

Dr. A.R.G. Owen, the organization's chief parapsychology researcher, gathered a group of eight people who were interested in the paranormal but had no psychic abilities of their own. The Owen Group, as it was called, was made up of people from all walks of life, including Owen's wife, an accountant, an industrial designer, a former MENSA chairwoman, a housewife, a student, and a bookkeeper. Dr. Joel Whitton, a psychologist, was also present at many of the meetings as an observer.

## The Making of a Ghost

The first order of business was to create the ghost, giving it physical characteristics and a complete background story. According to Dr. Owen, it was important to the study that the spirit be totally made-up, with no strong ties to any specific historical figure.

The group named the ghost Philip and proceeded to bring him to life—on paper, that is. A sketch artist even drew a picture of Philip as the group imagined him. Here is his story:

Philip Aylesford was an aristocratic Englishman who was born in 1624. As a supporter of the King, he was knighted at age 16 and went on to make a name for himself in the military. He married Dorothea, the beautiful daughter of a nobleman who lived nearby. Unfortunately, Dorothea's appearance was deceiving, as her personality was cold and unyielding. As a Catholic, Philip wouldn't divorce his wife, so he found escape by riding around the grounds of his estate. One day, he came across a gypsy camp. There, he found true love in the arms of the raven-haired Margo, whose dark eyes seemed to look into his soul. He brought her to Diddington Manor, his family home, and hid her in the gatehouse near the stable. But it wasn't meant to be: Dorothea soon discovered her husband's secret affair and retaliated by accusing the gypsy woman of stealing and practicing witchcraft. Afraid of damaging his own reputation, Philip did not step forward in Margo's defense, and she was burned at the stake. After the death of his beloved, Philip was tormented with guilt and loneliness; he killed himself in 1654 at age 30.

## Focus, Focus, Focus

In September 1972, after the tale was written, the group began meeting regularly. Reports of these meetings vary. Some accounts describe them as mere gatherings in which group members would discuss Philip and meditate on the details of his life. With no results after about a year, the group moved on to a more traditional method of communing with ghosts:

holding séances in a darkened room, sitting around a table with appropriate music and objects that might have been used by Philip or his family. Another version has the group beginning with séances and switching to the more casual setting later.

The setting itself is ultimately secondary to the results: Through the focus and concentration of the group, Philip soon began to make his presence known. He answered questions by tapping on the table for "yes" or "no." Just to be sure, a "yes" tap confirmed that he was, indeed, Philip.

## A Physical Presence

After communication was established, the Philip Phenomenon took on a life of its own. Through the tapping, Philip was able to answer questions about the details of his life. He was also able to correctly answer questions about people and places of that historical time period, although these were all facts that were familiar to at least one member of the group.

Philip even seemed to develop a personality, exuding emotions that changed the atmosphere of the entire room. But most amazingly, he was able to exhibit some remarkable physical manifestations, such as making objects move, turning lights on and off at the group's request, and performing incredible feats with the table: It shifted, it danced on one leg, and it even moved across the room.

In order to demonstrate the results of this experiment, the group held a séance in front of an audience of 50 people; the session was also videotaped. Philip rose to the occasion—and so did the table. In addition to tapping on the table and manipulating the lights, Philip made the entire table levitate half an inch off the ground!

The experiment was deemed a success, as there was little doubt that something paranormal was occurring during the sessions. However, the Owen Group never actually realized its original goal of getting the ghost of Philip to materialize. But the TSPR did go on to re-create the experiment successfully on several other occasions with a new group and a new fictional "ghost."

### Real, Random, or What?

So what can be concluded from all this? No one knows for sure, but several schools of thought have developed regarding the matter. Some believe that Philip was a real ghost and that he had once been a living, breathing person. Perhaps he had a few of the characteristics of the fictional Philip and simply responded to the group's summons. Some who believe in the ghost theory say that it may have been a playful spirit (or a demonic one) that just pretended to be Philip as a prank.

A less-popular theory suggests that someone close to the group was aware of the background information as well as the times and places of the meetings. He or she might have planned an elaborate hoax to make it appear as though the ghost was real.

But it is also possible that after creating Philip, the Owen Group put forth enough energy, focus, and concentration to bring him to life, in a manner of speaking. Ghosts may well be products of our imaginations, existing only in our minds, but this study does prove one thing: When people put those minds together, anything is possible—even an apparent visit from the Other Side.

# The Dark Side of the White House

*From the East Wing to the West Wing, our presidential palace is reportedly one of the most haunted government buildings anywhere, which is hardly surprising given the uniquely rich history that has transpired within its walls.*

✳ ✳ ✳ ✳

### The White House's First Ghost

THE GHOST OF David Burns may be the first unearthly spirit that haunted the White House. While still alive, Burns donated the acreage on which the original structure was built.

One day, Franklin Roosevelt heard his name being called, and when he replied, the voice said that it was "Mr. Burns." FDR's valet, Cesar Carrera, told a similar story: Carrera was in the Yellow Oval Room when he heard a soft, distant voice say, "I'm Mr. Burns." When Carrera looked around, no one was there.

Later, during the Truman years, a guard at the White House also heard a soft voice announce itself as Mr. Burns. The guard naturally assumed it was James Byrnes, Truman's secretary of state, but no one appeared. What's more, the guard checked the roster and learned that Byrnes hadn't been in the building at all that day.

### William Henry Harrison Feels a Little Blue

William Henry Harrison was the first American president to die in office. While giving his inauguration address in icy, windy weather on March 4, 1841, Harrison caught a cold that quickly turned into pneumonia.

Stories abound about Harrison wandering the corridors of the White House, half-conscious with fever, looking for a quiet room in which to rest. Unfortunately, there was no escape from the doctors whose treatments may have killed him. While Harrison's lungs filled with fluid and fever wracked his body, his doctors bled him and then treated him with mustard, laxatives, ipecac, rhubarb, and mercury. It is speculated that the president died not from the "ordinary winter cold" that he'd contracted, but from the care of his doctors. Harrison passed away on April 4, 1841, just one month after taking office.

Harrison's translucent ghost is seen throughout the White House, but it is most often spotted in the residential areas. His skin is pale blue and his breathing makes an ominous rattling noise. He appears to be looking for something and walks through closed doors. Some believe that he's looking for rest or a cure for his illness; others say he's searching for his office so that he can complete his term as president.

## Andrew Jackson Likes the Ladies

If you'd prefer to see a happier ghost, look for the specter of Andrew Jackson; he's often seen in the Queen's Bedroom, where his bed is on display. But Jackson may not necessarily be looking for his old bed; in life, "Old Hickory" was quite the ladies' man, and today, the Queen's Bedroom is reserved for female guests of honor.

Visitors sometimes simply sense Jackson's presence in the Queen's Bedroom or feel a bone-chilling breeze when they're around his bed. Some have reported that Jackson's ghost climbs under the covers, sending guests shrieking out of the room.

Mary Todd Lincoln frequently complained about the ghost of Andrew Jackson cursing and stomping in the corridors of the White House. After she left the presidential estate, Jackson stopped fussing.

## Oh Séance Can You See

Séances at the White House have been nearly as numerous as the phantoms that inhabit its hallways. It has been well documented that in the early 1860s, President Lincoln and his wife contacted the spirit of Daniel Webster while attempting to reach their dearly departed son Willie during a séance. According to witnesses, the former secretary of state implored the president to continue his efforts to end slavery. Some years later, relatives of President Ulysses S. Grant held another séance at the White House, during which they reputedly spoke with young Willie Lincoln.

In 1995—with the help of medium Jean Houston—First Lady Hillary Rodham Clinton reportedly established contact with Eleanor Roosevelt and Mahatma Gandhi. It seems some séances yield better results than others. Describing her fascination with White House spirits, Clinton said, "There is something about the house at night that you just feel like you are summoning up the spirits of all the people who have lived there and worked there and walked through the halls there."

## Ghosts of Presidents' Families and Foes

Abigail Adams used to hang laundry on clotheslines in the White House's East Room; her ghost appears there regularly in a cap and wrapped in a shawl. She's usually carrying laundry or checking to see if her laundry is dry.

The spirit of Dorothea "Dolley" Madison defends the Rose Garden that she designed and planted. When Woodrow Wilson's wife Edith ordered staff members to dig up the garden to plant new flowers, Dolley's apparition appeared and allegedly insisted that no one was going to touch her roses. The landscaping ceased, and to this day, Dolley's roses remain exactly as they were when the Madisons lived in the White House in the early 1800s.

After Abraham Lincoln's son Willie died in February 1862 following a brief illness, the president became obsessed with his son's death and had his coffin reopened at least twice, just to look at him. Willie's apparition has been seen at the White House regularly since his death, most often manifesting in the bedrooms on the second floor, where his ghost was once witnessed by Lyndon Johnson's daughter Lynda.

Other spirits seemed to like that room: Harry Truman's mother died there and may have made her presence known afterward. Lynda used to report hearing unexplained footsteps in the bedroom. And sometimes, her phone would ring in the middle of the night; when she answered, no one was on the line. Also on the second floor, people have heard the ghost of Frances Cleveland crying, perhaps reliving the time when her husband, Grover, was diagnosed with cancer.

One very out-of-place spirit appears to be that of a British soldier from around 1814, when the White House was besieged and burned. The uniformed specter looks lost and holds a torch. When he realizes that he's been spotted, he becomes alarmed and vanishes.

# These Lighthouses Harbor Spirits

*There's something beautiful about the simplicity of lighthouses: They stand high above the water and shine their beacons to guide weary sailors home. But there's also something about lighthouses that seems to attract spirits. Ghosts of sailors and lighthouse keepers alike seem to find it hard to leave this earthly plane. Here are a few lighthouses that harbor phenomena that are a bit otherworldly.*

✳   ✳   ✳   ✳

### St. Augustine Light (St. Augustine, Florida)

VISITORS TO THE St. Augustine Light—one of the most haunted places in a very haunted city—have heard phantom footsteps on the tower stairs and observed a tall man who haunts the basement. Some have reportedly heard the laughter of two girls who drowned in 1873 while their father was working on the property. There's also a prankster ghost that likes to play tricks on staff members by relocating merchandise in the gift shop. And several times a week, someone reports the smell of cigar smoke wafting from the tower—even though no one else is around.

### Gibraltar Point Lighthouse (Toronto, Ontario)

Toronto's Gibraltar Point Lighthouse doesn't hide its ghostly secrets—it announces them outright: A plaque on the property warns visitors that the site is thought to be haunted. According to legend, in the early 1800s, two drunken soldiers killed the lighthouse's first caretaker, John Paul Rademuller, but his body was never found. (In the late 19th century, another caretaker unearthed some human bones, which gave credibility to the tale.) Today, unexplained lights appear in the windows, bloodstains have reportedly been found on the stairway, moaning can be heard, and the ghostly figure of a man is seen walking on the beach nearby.

## White River Light Station (Whitehall, Michigan)

Listen for the tap-tap-tapping of Captain William Robinson's cane as he continues to tend to his former home—the White River Light Station—even though he died in 1919, just two weeks after he was forced to retire at age 87. No scandal or tragedy occurred at this lighthouse; Robinson and his wife simply loved their home of 47 years so much that they have apparently found it impossible to leave. Mrs. Robinson has been known to lend assistance by doing some light housekeeping, leaving display cases cleaner than they were without the help of human hands.

## St. Simons Lighthouse (St. Simons, Georgia)

In 1880, an argument between lighthouse keeper Frederick Osborne and his assistant John Stevens ended with a fatal gunshot that killed Osborne. Stevens was arrested, but he was acquitted of the murder, and he subsequently took over tending the lighthouse. He later said that he could hear strange footfalls on the spiral staircase to the tower. Subsequent caretakers, their families, and visitors have also heard the same slow tread on the tower's 129 steps.

## Boston Light (Boston, Massachusetts)

The ghost that resides at the Boston Light is thought to be that of a sailor who was once guided by the beacon. Cold spots, phantom footsteps, empty rocking chairs that move back and forth on their own, and something eerie that makes cats hiss are all hallmarks of this haunted lighthouse. These are all typical behaviors for a ghost, but this one does have its quirks: Coast Guard members on the premises report that whenever they turn on a rock-and-roll radio station, the receiver suddenly switches to a classical music channel further down the dial.

## Heceta Head Lighthouse (Yachats, Oregon)

Home of Rue (aka "the Gray Lady"), this former lighthouse is now a bed-and-breakfast. It is believed that Rue was the mother of a baby who was found buried on the grounds.

Perhaps she feels the need to stay and protect her child, but if that's the case, she finds plenty of other ways to stay busy: Objects are moved, cupboard doors open and close by themselves, and a fire alarm was once mysteriously set off. Although Rue doesn't seem to mean any harm, she once frightened a workman so terribly that he accidentally broke a window and fled, leaving broken glass all over the floor. That night, workers heard a scraping noise coming from upstairs; in the morning, they found that the broken glass had been swept into a nice, neat pile.

## Barnegat Lighthouse (Barnegat, New Jersey)

If you travel with children, you may draw the attention of the ghosts at the Barnegat Lighthouse. According to legend, a couple was on a ship off the New Jersey coast when a severe storm struck. Feeling that the ship was safe, the man decided to stay aboard, and his wife stayed by his side. They did, however, send their baby ashore with one of the ship's mates. Although the ship survived the storm, the couple was not so lucky: They froze to death that winter night. Now, on cold, clear nights in January and February, their spirits approach other parents who are out for a stroll with their own infants. The friendly ghosts typically compliment the parents on their beautiful baby, and then they quickly disappear.

## Seguin Island Lighthouse (Seguin Island, Maine)

Lighthouses can often be lonely places; this was the case for the wife of one of the Seguin Island Lighthouse's early caretakers. At great expense, her husband had a piano brought to the lighthouse for her. But she had only one piece of music, which she played over and over, until one day, her husband went insane. He took an ax to the piano and then to his wife and then killed himself. Death may not be the escape he hoped for, however: People still report hearing faint strains of the tune that his wife played incessantly.

### Fairport Harbor Light (Fairport Harbor, Ohio)

Lake Erie's Fairport Harbor Light is home to an unusual spirit: a ghost cat. This old lighthouse was abandoned in 1925 and later became a museum; its curator was the first person to see the spectral kitty with golden eyes and gray fur. They became friendly, and the curator even threw socks for the cat to chase. In life, the animal most likely belonged to the last family who tended the lighthouse; when the caretaker's wife became ill, she was comforted by a small kitten that loved to chase a ball down the hall. In 2001, workers found a mummified cat in a crawl space; the little guy must have gotten trapped and was unable to get out.

# If These Walls Could Talk... Oh, Wait, They Do Talk!

*There are few haunted places featured in more publications and on more television shows than the Whispers Estate, which is considered one of the most haunted places in Indiana. This 3,700-square-foot Victorian mansion in the town of Mitchell has attracted tourists, ghost hunters, psychics, the media, and, of course, ghosts galore.*

✳   ✳   ✳   ✳

WHEN DR. JOHN Gibbons and his wife, Jessie, moved into their dream house in 1899, they had no idea that it would one day become famous for incredibly unusual reasons. The childless couple adopted three orphans, but tragedy surrounded the family. Their oldest daughter, Rachael, set a fire in the building's parlor, severely burning herself in the process. She died in an upstairs bedroom two days later, and soon after, her spirit began showing itself to the living. Her apparition is often seen roaming around the estate, and burn marks are still visible in the parlor.

The Gibbons family suffered another tragedy when adopted daughter Elizabeth died of unknown causes at age 10 months. She passed away in the master bedroom, and many guests who have stayed in this room have reportedly smelled baby powder lingering in the air. Some have also heard the soft sound of a baby crying.

Due to yet another misfortune that befell this family, the master bedroom has been the site of other ghostly activity. After the deaths of her two children, Mrs. Gibbons contracted pneumonia. Already run-down, she developed respiratory complications and succumbed to her illness two weeks later—in the master bedroom. In addition to the sound of a baby nearby, visitors to this room have heard noises that resemble ragged breathing and coughing. Some have even noticed the distinct feeling of pressure on their chests. Other odd occurrences have been observed there as well, including a closet door that opens suddenly and doorknobs that jiggle by themselves.

## A Gathering of Ghosts

Old houses often have rich histories, but the Whispers Estate has witnessed more sadness than most. In 1966, a man died of a heart attack in the house. In 1974, his nine-year-old son—who suffered from hydrocephalus (water on the brain)—fell down a flight of stairs and passed away before help could arrive. In the estate's early years, Dr. Gibbons ran his practice on the main level of the house, and it is quite likely that several of his patients died there as well.

In addition to the house, which seems to have produced quite a sizable ghost population of its own, four graves and an area called the "pit grave" are on the property. In the pit grave, the doctor disposed of the by-products of his medical practice, such as miscarried or aborted fetuses, amputated limbs, and even organs that he removed.

While there is no evidence of illegal activity on the property, psychics who have investigated the Whispers Estate without knowing its history sensed that sinister things happened there. They all felt that the doctor may have been involved in unethical practices, including performing abortions and unnecessary surgeries, taking liberties with his female patients, and keeping several mistresses at a time. There's nothing like a little dark energy to contribute to the paranormal activity at a house.

## It's Hard to Sleep with All That Whispering

In 2006, the building was turned into a bed-and-breakfast, but apparently, the spirits of those who once lived there objected to the idea, so they came out in full force. Guests at the B & B have reported hearing whispering throughout the entire mansion. It is difficult to pinpoint the source of these voices, but those hearing them—and there are many—all describe the same type of muffled noises. Thus, the place became known as the Whispers Estate; unfortunately, the building's reputation proved to be bad for business.

However, word about the house spread among those interested in the paranormal, and the Whispers Estate has since become a popular destination for ghost hunters and reporters who come to document the terrifying tales. One paranormal phenomenon at the inn that does not seem directly related to any one person or event is an apparition or shadow that has been dubbed "Big Black," which investigators agree is "not of this world." Big Black has been viewed most often in the doctor's quarters, but it has occasionally been seen in other areas of the building as well.

In addition, guests who've stayed at the bed-and-breakfast have reported feeling intense tremors while in the doctor's bathroom. And in the master bedroom, many have seen the beds shake. Women, especially, have felt the sensation that Dr. Gibbons is whispering in their ears, and some have reported feeling that his ghost actually touched or groped them.

## Sensory Scent-sations

Unexplained smells can occur in haunted places, and Whispers Estate is no exception. In addition to the smell of baby powder—which is strongest in the master bedroom but has been detected elsewhere—many visitors have caught whiffs of cologne, cigars, and the rancid odor of discarded bandages.

Paranormal investigators who have studied the Whispers Estate have experienced many unusual phenomena, but one that has been noted over and over is associated with the door in the servants' quarters. When investigators leave that area, the heavy wooden door often mysteriously slams shut behind them with tremendous force. This may be the ghostly version of the phrase, "Here's your hat; what's your hurry?" After all, the ghostly whispers never seem to say, "Please stay."

# Popping His Top: The Seaford Poltergeist

*Poltergeists are the publicity hounds of the spirit world. While other ghosts are content to appear in the shadows and then vanish so that nobody's ever exactly sure what they saw, poltergeist activities are always very flashy and conspicuous. Need furniture rearranged or doors opened or slammed shut? How about knickknacks moved around or plates smashed? If so, just call your neighborhood poltergeist; they love to perform such mischief. Poltergeists don't care—they aren't part of the ghostly union. They just enjoy annoying (and scaring) the living.*

✳  ✳  ✳  ✳

## Pop! Pop! Pop!

THE SCIENCE OF investigating poltergeist activity has come a long way since the days when people blamed it all on witchcraft. One of the cases that got folks thinking that there might be more to it was the story of the Seaford Poltergeist.

This entity first made itself known to the Herrmann family of Seaford, Long Island, in early February 1958. Mrs. Herrmann had just welcomed her children Lucille and Jimmy home from school when several bottles in various rooms of the house all popped their tops and spewed their contents all over. The family considered various explanations, such as excess humidity or pressure building up in the bottles, but the tops were all of the twist-off variety. Short of a miniature tornado yanking the tops off, there seemed to be no rational explanation.

After the same thing happened several more times, Mr. Herrmann began to suspect that his son Jimmy—who had an interest in science—was somehow pulling a fast one on the family. However, after carefully watching the child while the incident happened, Herrmann knew that unless his son was a future Einstein, there was no way that the boy could be responsible. With no "ghost busters" to consult, Mr. Herrmann did the next best thing he could in 1958: He called the police.

Dubious at first, they launched an investigation after witnessing some of the episodes firsthand. But answers were not forthcoming, and the incidents kept occurring. Even having a priest bless the house and sprinkle holy water in each of its rooms didn't help. An exorcism was considered but rejected because the incidents didn't resemble the work of a demon. Rather, they seemed to be the antics of a poltergeist (a noisy spirit).

## Explanation Unknown

Word of the events attracted the attention of the media as well as curiosity seekers. All explanations—from the scientifically sound (sonic booms, strong drafts, freakish magnetic waves) to the weird and wacky (Soviet satellite *Sputnik*)—were considered and dismissed. Although this was the Cold War era, it was unclear how tormenting a single American family fit into the Soviets' dastardly scheme of world domination.

What was far more worrisome was that the incidents seemed to be escalating in violence. Instead of just bottles popping open, objects such as a sugar bowl, a record player, and a heavy bookcase were tossed around. Fortunately, help soon arrived in the form of experts from Duke University's Parapsychology Laboratory. Their theory was that someone in the house was unwittingly moving objects via Recurrent Spontaneous Psychokinesis (RSPK). Children seemed to attract such activity, and the Duke team discovered that Jimmy had been at or near the scene of the incidents most of the time.

When one of the researchers spent time with the boy—playing cards, helping him with his homework, or just talking—the unusual activity declined. Two more incidents occurred in early March before the Seaford Poltergeist apparently packed its bags and moved on. After 67 recorded incidents in five weeks, the lives of the Herrmann family returned to normal. To this day, it is still unknown exactly what caused the strange events in the Herrmann household in early 1958.

# The Watseka Wonder: A Tale of Possession

*Spiritual possession—in which a person's body is taken over by the spirit of another—is easy to fake, and legitimate cases are incredibly rare. One of the most widely publicized possessions occurred in Watseka, Illinois, in the late 1870s, when the spirit of Mary Roff, a girl who had died 12 years earlier, inhabited the body of 13-year-old Lurancy Vennum. This astounding case became known as the "Watseka Wonder."*

✳   ✳   ✳   ✳

### A Troubled Life

IN 1865, MARY Roff was just 18 years old when she died in an insane asylum following a lifelong illness that had tormented her with frequent fits, seizures, and strange voices in her head. She had also developed an obsession with bloodletting and would apply leeches to her body, poke herself with pins, and cut herself with razors. Doctors thought that Mary was mentally ill, but others—including her own family—came to believe that her problems were supernatural in origin.

At the time of Mary Roff's death, Lurancy Vennum was barely a year old. Born on April 16, 1864, Lurancy moved with her family to Watseka a few years after Mary Roff's death and knew nothing of the girl or her family.

In July 1877, about 12 years after Mary passed away, Lurancy started to exhibit symptoms similar to Mary's, including uncontrollable seizures. Her speech became garbled, and she often spoke in a strange language. She sometimes fell into trances, assumed different personalities, and claimed to see spirits, many of which terrified her.

The townspeople of Watseka didn't know what to make of Lurancy. Many thought that she was insane and should be committed, as Mary had been. But the Roffs, who had become ardent Spiritualists as a result of their daughter's troubles, believed that unseen forces were tormenting Lurancy. They felt that she was not insane but rather was possessed by the spirits of the dead. With the permission of Lurancy's parents, Asa Roff—Mary's father—met with the young girl in the company of Dr. E. Winchester Stevens, who was also a Spiritualist. During their visit, a friendly spirit spoke to Lurancy and asked to take control of her body to protect her from sinister forces. That spirit was Mary Roff.

## Sent to Heaven

After Mary took possession of Lurancy's body, she explained that Lurancy was ill and needed to return to heaven to be cured. Mary said that she would remain in Lurancy's body until sometime in May.

Over the next few months, it seemed apparent that Mary's spirit was indeed in control of Lurancy's body. She looked the same, but she knew nothing about the Vennum family or her life as Lurancy. Instead, she had intimate knowledge of the Roffs, and she acted as though they were her family. Although she treated the Vennums politely, they were essentially strangers to her.

In February 1878, Lurancy/Mary asked to go live with her parents—the Roffs. The Vennums reluctantly consented. On the way to the Roff home, as they traveled past the house where they'd lived when Mary was alive, Lurancy wanted to know why they weren't stopping. The Roffs explained that they'd moved to a new home a few years back, which was something that Lurancy/Mary would not have known. Lurancy/Mary spent several months living in the Roff home, where she identified objects and people that Lurancy could not have known.

On one occasion, Lurancy sat down at the Roff's family piano and began to play, singing the same songs Mary had sung in her youth. One member of the Roff family commented, "As we stood listening, the familiar [songs] were hers, though emanating from another's lips."

Once word spread of Lurancy's spiritual possession, interested people started to visit. Lurancy/Mary typically met them in the Roffs' front parlor, where she frequently demonstrated knowledge of events that had transpired long before Lurancy was even born.

During one encounter with a Mrs. Sherman, Mary was asked about the people she had met in the afterlife. Immediately, Mary started listing the names of some of Mrs. Sherman's deceased family members, as well as several of Mrs. Sherman's neighbors who had died. Again, this was information that Lurancy could not possibly have known.

## Scene at a Séance

In April 1878, during a séance that was held in the Roff home and attended by several people (including Dr. Stevens), one member of the group became possessed by the spirit of another member's dead brother, who addressed the gathering. After the spirit had left the man's body, Mary removed herself from Lurancy's body (which immediately rolled over against the person next to her, as if dead) and possessed the body of a participant named Dr. Steel. Through him, Mary proved to everyone present that it was indeed her. She then abandoned Dr. Steel's body and reentered Lurancy's.

## Going Home

Mary permanently left Lurancy's body on May 21, 1878. When Lurancy awoke from her trance, she was no longer afflicted by the numerous problems that had previously plagued her, nor did she have any recollection of being spiritually possessed by Mary.

By all accounts, she came away from the experience a healthy young lady. Indeed, Lurancy grew to be a happy woman and exhibited no ill effects from the possession. She went on to marry and have 13 children.

But Mary didn't abandon Lurancy completely. According to some sources, Lurancy kept in touch with the Roff family, with whom she felt a strange closeness, although she had no idea why. She would visit with them once a year and allow Mary's spirit to possess her briefly, just like it did in the late 1870s.

The story of the Watseka Wonder still stands as one of the most authentic cases of spirit possession in history. It has been investigated, dissected, and ridiculed, but to this day, no clear scientific explanation has ever been offered.

*The boundaries which divide life from death are at best shadowy and vague. Who shall say where the one ends and the other begins.*

—EDGAR ALLAN POE, *THE PREMATURE BURIAL*

# Phantom Hitchhikers

*The tale of the vanishing hitchhiker is what's known as an urban legend—an account of something that usually happened to a "friend of a friend of a friend" (almost never to the person telling the story) that typically contains some kind of moral or surprise ending. According to Jan Harold Brunvand, who has written numerous books about urban legends, the story of the vanishing hitchhiker is one that has been reported in newspapers and elsewhere since at least the 1930s, and possibly earlier. Are any of these anecdotes true? That's for you to decide.*

✳ ✳ ✳ ✳

## The Hitchhiker's Tale

THE BASIC STORY goes like this: A motorist driving down a country road sees a young lady hitchhiking, so he stops to offer her a ride. The girl tells him that she lives in a house a few miles down the road, but she is otherwise uncommunicative, spending most of the drive staring out the window. When they arrive at the house, the driver turns to his passenger, only to find that she has disappeared. Curious, he knocks on the door of the house and tells the person who answers about his experience. The homeowner says that he or she had a daughter who fit the description of the hitchhiker, but that she disappeared (or died) several years earlier while hitchhiking on the road on which the driver found the girl. The parent tells the driver that, coincidentally, it's the daughter's birthday.

The specifics of this tale often vary. For example, sometimes a married couple picks up the ghostly hitchhiker, and sometimes the hitchhiker is a young man. However, the story's shocking ending is almost always the same.

## In the Early Days

One version of the vanishing hitchhiker story was first told sometime between 1935 and 1941. A traveling salesman from Spartanburg, South Carolina, stopped for a woman who was walking along the side of a road. The woman told the man that she was going to her brother's house, which was about three miles up the road. The man offered to give her a ride and encouraged her to sit next to him, but the woman would only sit in the backseat. They talked briefly, but soon the woman grew quiet.

Upon arriving at the home of the woman's brother, the driver turned to the backseat, only to find it empty. The driver told the woman's brother his story, but the brother didn't seem surprised: He said that the woman was his sister and that she had died two years earlier. Several drivers had picked her up on that road, but she had yet to reach the house.

Like all good stories, the tale of the vanishing hitchhiker often acquires some new and unique details with each retelling. In one example, the female hitchhiker suddenly pulled the car's emergency brake at a particular intersection, preventing a deadly collision; the driver was momentarily shaken, but when he finally remembered his passenger, she was gone—though she had left a book in the backseat. (In other accounts, the object is a purse, a sweater, or a scarf.) The driver assumed that she simply got out so that she could walk the rest of the way. Regardless, he drove to the intended destination, where the homeowner told him that the girl the driver had picked up was his daughter, who had died in a car accident at the same intersection where the collision had been averted. Taking the book from the driver, the father went to his library, where he found an empty space where the book should have been.

The story of the vanishing hitchhiker may only be an urban legend—a story designed to shock the listener—but when dealing with the paranormal, who can be sure? Keep that in mind the next time you spot a young lady hitchhiking along the side of a quiet back road.

# Griggs Mansion

*A notoriously haunted house in St. Paul, Minnesota, changes hands, and then all paranormal activity ceases. Was the house ever haunted? If so, what made the once-frisky ghosts decide to pack up and leave? It's a question that is difficult to answer. A house that's haunted to some seems completely benign to others. Who is right? Let's examine the evidence.*

✳ ✳ ✳ ✳

## First Frights

**B**UILT IN 1883 BY wholesale grocery tycoon Chauncey W. Griggs, the imposing 24-room Griggs Mansion features high ceilings, a dark interior, and a stone facade that looks decidedly menacing. Although the home bears his name, Griggs lived there for only a scant four years before moving to sunnier climes on the West Coast. After that, the house changed hands quite frequently, which some say is a sure sign that the place was haunted.

The first ghost sightings at the house date back to 1915, when a young maid—who was despondent over a breakup—hanged herself on the mansion's fourth floor. Soon after the woman's burial, her spirit was supposedly seen roaming the building's hallways. According to witnesses, the ghost of Charles Wade arrived next. In life, he was the mansion's gardener and caretaker; in death, he reportedly liked to cruise through the building's library.

## Unexplained Activity

Strange occurrences are the norm at the Griggs Mansion. Over the years, residents and visitors have reported hearing disembodied footsteps traveling up and down the staircases, seeing doors open and close by themselves, hearing voices coming from unoccupied rooms, and experiencing all manner of unexplainable incidents, which suggest that the Griggs Mansion is indeed haunted.

In 1939, the mansion was donated to the St. Paul Gallery and School of Art. During the 1950s, staffer Dr. Delmar Rolb claimed that he saw the apparition of a "tall thin man" in his apartment in the basement of the building. In 1964, Carl L. Weschcke—a publisher of books relating to the occult—acquired the house. He said that as soon as he would close a particular window, it would mysteriously reopen. Determined to stop this game, Weschcke nailed the window shut; however, when he returned home the next day, it was open once again.

## Ghost Investigators

In 1969, reporters from a local newspaper spent a night at the Griggs Mansion. The journalists—who were all initially skeptics—became believers after spending a harrowing night on the premises; unexplained footsteps and an unnerving feeling that a presence accompanied them were enough to do the trick. The frightened reporters fled the mansion in the wee hours of the morning and never returned.

## More Skeptics

In 1982, Tibor and Olga Zoltai purchased the mansion. "When we first moved in, there were people who would cross to the other side of the street to pass the house," Olga recalled in an interview with a local newspaper. "One even threw a piece of Christ's cross into the yard." However, in nearly three decades of living inside the reputedly haunted house, the couple has never experienced anything out of the ordinary. To show just how silly they found the ghost stories, the playful couple assembled an "emergency kit" that contained a clove of garlic, a bottle of holy water, a crucifix, and a stake. They figured that these items would provide ample protection against any restless spirits in the house.

## Yea or Nay

So are there ghosts at the Griggs Mansion or not? Those who claim to have witnessed paranormal activity there stand firmly behind their stories; those who have not offer other possible explanations. "If you go into a situation thinking something is going to happen, it probably will," reasons Chad Lewis, author of *Haunted St. Paul*, in reference to the terrifying night that the reporters spent at the mansion. That said, however, Lewis isn't convinced that the ghost stories surrounding the Griggs Mansion are mere figments of people's imaginations. "I think the stories are true. I don't think people are making them up or hallucinating or suffering from mental illness. I think something happened there, but what happened there, I don't know."

# The Weeping Woman in Gray

*If you ever find yourself at Camp Chase Confederate Cemetery in Columbus, Ohio, find the grave of Benjamin F. Allen and listen very closely. If you hear the faint sound of a woman weeping, you're in the presence of the cemetery's Lady in Gray.*

✳   ✳   ✳   ✳

ESTABLISHED IN MAY 1861, Camp Chase served as a prison for Confederate officers during the Civil War. However, as the number of Confederate POWs grew, the prison could not be quite so selective. As 1863 dawned, Camp Chase held approximately 8,000 men of every rank.

The sheer number of prisoners soon overwhelmed Camp Chase. Men were forced to share bunks, and shortages of food, clothing, medicine, and other necessities were common. Under those conditions, the prisoners were vulnerable to disease and malnutrition, which led to many deaths—500 in one particular month alone, due to an outbreak of smallpox. Eventually, a cemetery was established at the camp to handle the large number of bodies.

Although Camp Chase was closed shortly after the war, the cemetery remains. Today, it contains the graves of more than 2,100 Confederate soldiers. Although restless spirits are commonly found where miserable deaths occurred, just one ghost is known to call Camp Chase its "home haunt": the famous Lady in Gray. Dressed in a flowing gray dress with a veil covering her face, she is often seen standing and weeping silently over Allen's grave. At other times, she can be found sobbing at the grave of an unidentified soldier. Occasionally, she will leave flowers on the tombstones.

The Lady in Gray has also been spotted walking among the many gravestones in the cemetery; she's even been observed passing right through the locked cemetery gates. No one knows who she was in life, but some speculate that she was Allen's wife. However, her attention to the grave of the unknown soldier baffles researchers. One thing seems certain, though: As long as the Camp Chase Confederate Cemetery exists, the Lady in Gray will watch over it.

# The Greenbrier Ghost: Testimony from the Other Side

*The strange tale of the Greenbrier Ghost stands out in the annals of ghost lore. Not only is it part of supernatural history, it is also part of the history of the U.S. judicial system. To this day, it is the only case in which a crime was solved and a murderer convicted based on the testimony of a ghost.*

✳  ✳  ✳  ✳

### A Doomed Marriage

LITTLE IS KNOWN about her life, but it is believed that Zona Heaster was born in Greenbrier County, West Virginia, around 1873. In October 1896, she met Erasmus "Edward" Stribbling Trout Shue, a drifter who had recently moved to the area to work as a blacksmith. A short time later, the two were married, despite the animosity felt toward Shue by Zona's mother, Mary Jane Heaster, who had instantly disliked him.

Unfortunately, the marriage was short-lived. In January 1897, Zona's body was discovered at home by a young neighbor boy who had come to the house on an errand. After he found Zona lying on the floor at the bottom of the stairs, he ran to get the local doctor and coroner, Dr. George W. Knapp. By the time Dr. Knapp arrived, Shue had come home, found his wife, and carried her body upstairs where he laid her on the bed and dressed her in her best clothing—a high-necked, stiff-collared dress with a big scarf tied around her neck and a veil placed over her face.

While Dr. Knapp was examining Zona's body in an attempt to determine the cause of death, Shue allegedly stayed by his wife's side, cradling her head, sobbing, and clearly distressed over anyone touching her body. As a result, Knapp did not do a thorough examination. Although he did notice some bruising on Zona's neck, he initially listed her cause of death as "everlasting faint" and then as "childbirth." Whether or not Zona was pregnant is unknown, but Dr. Knapp had been treating her for some time prior to her death. When Mary Jane Heaster was informed of her daughter's death, her face grew dark as she uttered: "The devil has killed her!" Zona's body was taken to her parents' home where it was displayed for the wake.

Those who came to pay their respects whispered about Shue's erratic behavior—one minute he'd be expressing intense grief and sadness, then displaying frenetic outbursts the next. He would not allow anyone to get close to the coffin, especially when he placed a pillow and a rolled-up cloth around his wife's head to help her "rest easier." Still, when Zona's body was moved to the cemetery, several people noted a strange looseness to her head. Not surprisingly, people started to talk.

## Ghostly Messages from the Other Side

Mary Jane Heaster did not have to be convinced that Shue was acting suspiciously about Zona's death. She had always hated him and wished her daughter had never married him. She had a sneaking suspicion that something wasn't right, but she didn't know how to prove it.

After the funeral, as Heaster was folding the sheet from inside the coffin, she noticed that it had an unusual odor. When she placed it into the basin to wash it, the water turned red. Stranger still, the sheet turned pink and then the color in the water disappeared. Even after Heaster boiled the sheet, the stain remained. To her, the bizarre "bloodstains" were a sign that Zona had been murdered.

For the next four weeks, Heaster prayed fervently every night that Zona would come to her and explain the details of her death. Soon after, her prayers were answered. For four nights, Zona's spirit appeared at her mother's bedside, first as a bright light, but then the air in the room got cold and her apparition took form. She told her mother that Shue had been an abusive and cruel husband, and in a fit of rage, he'd attacked her because he thought she had not cooked any meat for supper. He'd broken her neck, and as evidence, Zona's ghost spun her head around until it was facing backward.

Heaster's suspicions were correct: Shue had killed Zona and she'd come back from beyond the grave to prove it.

## Opening the Grave

After Zona's ghostly visit, Heaster tried to convince the local prosecutor, John Alfred Preston, to reopen the investigation into her daughter's death. She pleaded that an injustice was taking place and, as evidence, she told him about her encounters with Zona's spirit. Although it seems unlikely that he would reexamine the case just because of the statement of a ghost, the investigation was, in fact, reopened. Preston agreed to question Dr. Knapp and a few others involved in the case. The local newspaper reported that a number of citizens were suspicious of Zona's death, and rumors were beginning to circulate throughout the community.

Dr. Knapp admitted to Preston that his examination of Zona's body was cursory at best, so it was agreed that an autopsy would be done to settle any outstanding questions. They could find out how Zona really died, and, if he was innocent, ease the suspicions surrounding Shue.

The local newspaper reported that Shue "vigorously complained" about the exhumation and autopsy of his wife's body, but he was required to attend. A jury of five men gathered together in the chilly building to watch the autopsy along with officers of the court, Shue, and other witnesses.

The autopsy findings were rather damning to Shue. When the doctors concluded that Zona's neck had been broken, Shue's head dropped, and a dark expression crossed his face. "They cannot prove that I did it," he said quietly.

A March 9 report stated: "The discovery was made that the neck was broken and the windpipe mashed. On the throat were the marks of fingers indicating that she had been choken [sic]. The neck was dislocated between the first and second vertebrae. The ligaments were torn and ruptured. The windpipe had been crushed at a point in front of the neck."

Despite the fact that—aside from Zona's ghost—the evidence against Shue was circumstantial at best, he was arrested, indicted, and formally arraigned for murder. All the while, he maintained his innocence and entered a plea of "not guilty." He repeatedly told reporters that his guilt in the matter could not be proven.

While awaiting trial, details about Shue's unsavory past came to light. Zona was actually his third wife. In 1889, while he was in prison for horse theft, he was divorced from his first wife, Allie Estelline Cutlip, who claimed that Shue had frequently beaten her during their marriage. In fact, at one point, Shue allegedly beat Cutlip so severely that a group of men had to pull him off of her and throw him into an icy river.

In 1894, Shue married his second wife, Lucy Ann Tritt. She died just eight months later under mysterious circumstances. Shue left the area in the autumn of 1896 and moved to

Greenbrier. When word got out that Shue was suspected of murdering Zona, stories began circulating about the circumstances behind Tritt's death. No wrongdoing was ever proven.

Despite the fact that he was in jail, Shue seemed in good spirits. Remarking that he was done grieving for Zona, he revealed that it was his life's dream to have seven wives. Because Zona was only wife number three and he was still fairly young, he felt confident that he could achieve his goal.

## Testimony from a Ghost

When Shue's trial began in June 1897, numerous members of the community testified against him. Of course, Heaster's testimony was the highlight of the trial. She testified as both the mother of the victim and as the first person to notice the unusual circumstances of Zona's death. Preston wanted her to come across as sane and reliable, so he did not mention the spirit encounter, which would make Heaster look irrational and was also inadmissible as evidence. Zona's testimony obviously could not be cross-examined by the defense and, therefore, was hearsay under the law.

Unfortunately for Shue, his attorney did ask Heaster about her ghostly visit. Certainly, he was trying to destroy her credibility, characterizing her "visions" as the overactive imagination of a grieving mother. He was tenacious in trying to get her to admit that she was mistaken about what she'd seen, but Heaster stuck to her story. When Shue's attorney realized that she was not going to budge from her story, he dismissed her.

But by then, the damage was done. Because the defense—not the prosecution—had brought up Zona's otherworldly testimony, the judge had a difficult time ordering the jury to ignore it. Clearly, the townspeople believed that Heaster had been visited by her daughter's ghost. Shue testified in his own defense, but the jury quickly found him guilty. Ten of the jury members voted for Shue to be hanged, but because they could not reach a unanimous decision, he was sentenced to life in prison.

Shue didn't carry out his sentence—he died in March 1900 at the West Virginia State Penitentiary in Moundsville. Until her death in 1916, Heaster told her tale to anyone who would listen, never recanting her story of her daughter's ghostly visit.

It seems that after visiting her mother to offer details of her murder, Zona was finally able to rest in peace. Although her ghost was never seen again, she did leave a historical mark on Greenbrier County, where a roadside marker still commemorates the case today. It reads:

"Interred in nearby cemetery is Zona Heaster Shue. Her death in 1897 was presumed natural until her spirit appeared to her mother to describe how she was killed by her husband Edward. Autopsy on the exhumed body verified the apparition's account. Edward, found guilty of murder, was sentenced to the state prison. Only known case in which testimony from ghost helped convict a murderer."

# The Unhealthy Mansion

*Violent, unexpected deaths are likely to produce ghosts, and shipwrecks are no exception. And when drowning deaths are combined with injustice, it's pretty much a given that there will be reports of a few restless spirits remaining earthbound. That was exactly the scenario for the haunting at the Mansion of Health.*

✳   ✳   ✳   ✳

BUILT IN 1822, on New Jersey's Long Beach Island, the Mansion of Health was the largest hotel on the Jersey Shore upon its completion. This sprawling three-story structure featured a sweeping top-floor balcony that ran the length of the building and provided an unencumbered view of the glistening ocean, which was just a few hundred feet away. However, on April 18, 1854, the sea was anything but sparkling.

On that day, a violent storm turned the water into a foaming cauldron of death. Into this maelstrom came the *Powhattan*, a ship that was filled with more than 300 German immigrants who were bound for new lives in America. Unfortunately, the ship never had a chance. As it approached the coast of Long Beach Island, the storm tossed the boat onto the shoals and ripped a hole in its side. Passengers tumbled overboard, and later, dozens of bodies washed up on the shore.

## Stealing from the Dead

Back in those days, a person known as a "wreck master" was responsible for salvaging cargo from shipwrecks and arranging the storage of those killed until the coroner took charge of their bodies. The wreck master for Long Beach Island was Edward Jennings, who was also the manager of the Mansion of Health. Accordingly, all of the bodies from the *Powhattan* that had come ashore were brought to the beach in front of the Mansion of Health.

When the coroner arrived hours later, he examined the bodies, although it didn't take a medical degree to determine that they had died from drowning. However, the coroner did find something peculiar: None of the dead had any money in their possession. It seemed unusual to him that immigrants who were coming to America to start new lives didn't carry any cash. Money belts were fashionable at the time, yet not a single victim was wearing one.

Suspicion immediately fell upon Jennings, who was the only person who'd had access to the bodies for many hours. However, no one had any proof of such a crime occurring, so the accusations died down.

## The Long Arm of the Ghostly Law

Four months later, another storm revealed a hole near the stump of an old tree on the beach near the Mansion of Health. In the hole, dozens of money belts were found; they were all cut open and empty.

When word of this discovery got out, Jennings took one look at the writing on the wall and hightailed it out of town, narrowly evading the long arm of the law. But there are some things that you can't escape, as Jennings found out the hard way. Supposedly, he became a broken man and was haunted by nightmares that destroyed his sleep and ruined his life. He died several years later in a barroom brawl in San Francisco.

However, the spirits of the *Powhattan* victims were not content to simply haunt Edward Jennings. Shortly after the accident, strange things began to happen at the Mansion of Health: Disembodied sobs were heard at night, and ghostly figures were seen walking across the hotel's expansive balcony. Guests also reported feeling uneasy, which is not exactly the best advertisement for a place that was supposed to be restful and encourage good health.

## The Haunted Mansion

Eventually, the Mansion of Health became known as the "Haunted Mansion," and the locals started to avoid it like the plague. Soon, the building was abandoned; the brooding hulk of a structure that towered over the beach slowly began to fall to ruin.

During the summer of 1861, five young men who had more bravado than brains decided to spend the night in the gloomy structure. After cavorting through the empty halls and dashing around the balcony without seeing a single spirit, the men decided to sleep on the allegedly haunted third floor. After most of the young men had drifted off to sleep, one who remained awake suddenly noticed the luminous figure of a woman bathed in moonlight standing on the balcony; she appeared to hold a baby in her arms. The apparition was gazing sadly out to sea, as if mourning the life that had been taken away from her so abruptly.

The startled young man quietly shook each of his companions awake, and all five gazed in disbelief at the figure. Each of them observed that the moonlight passed right through the woman. Then, suddenly and without warning, the woman vanished.

The young men quickly gathered their belongings and fled the building, and from then on, not even vandals dared to enter the Haunted Mansion.

In 1874, a fire destroyed the standing remains of the Mansion of Health. But the hotel's real end had come years earlier, when Edward Jennings made the unfortunate decision to tamper with the dead.

# Westover Plantation's Friendly Ghost

*She said that she wanted to return in a nice way, so as not to frighten anyone. And in the afterlife, Evelyn Byrd seems to have gotten her wish to become a friendly ghost.*

✳ ✳ ✳ ✳

## Love Byrd

EVELYN BYRD WAS born in 1707; her father was William Byrd II, who founded the city of Richmond, Virginia. When she was ten years old, Evelyn was sent to school in England. While she was away, she fell in love with someone whom her father disliked—as young girls sometimes do. And as fathers often do, William forced the lovebirds to end their relationship. A few years later, when a brokenhearted Evelyn returned to her father's Virginia estate—which was known as Westover Plantation—she simply withdrew from everyday life. She only maintained regular contact with a friend named Anne Carter Harrison; the two girls met almost daily in a nearby poplar grove.

This continued for several years until one day, Evelyn confided to Anne that she felt the approach of death. However, she urged her friend to continue going to the poplar grove; she said that after her death, they would still meet there. Evelyn insisted that she would return but not in a scary sort of way.

## The Genial Ghost

Evelyn's prophecy was correct: She died shortly thereafter at age 29. One day soon after, Anne was in the poplar grove when she saw Evelyn wearing a stunning white dress and strolling through the trees, just as she had in life. Evelyn smiled at Anne and then vanished. Thus began the sightings of Evelyn, both on the grounds of Westover and inside the house. What sets Evelyn apart from most ghosts is that she's often seen as a three-dimensional figure that's only identified as a ghost when she vanishes.

Once, when a workman walked into a bedroom at Westover to complete some repairs, he was startled to see a woman sitting in front of a mirror combing her hair. Surprised that the room was occupied, the workman told the homeowner about it. When they returned to the room, it was empty.

Clearly, Evelyn wants to be as unobtrusive as possible while still making her presence known. On another occasion, a little girl visiting Westover awoke to see Evelyn—resplendent in her white dress—staring benignly at her. Another visitor woke up in the middle of the night, casually gazed out the window, and spotted Evelyn standing on the front lawn. Evelyn motioned the woman away from the window, as if to say, "Go away. You've got all day. This is my time now." The guest obediently closed the drapes.

Sometimes, Evelyn just seems to want to be a part of the action at Westover, such as the time when she began following a person out of the house. Thinking that it was a friend, the person turned and gazed back to see a woman with black hair wearing a beautiful white dress. As soon as the two made eye contact, the woman in the white dress disappeared.

## Byrds of a Feather Haunt Together

Evelyn does not hold a ghostly monopoly at Westover. Her sister-in-law, Elizabeth Hill Carter Byrd, had an unhappy marriage and died tragically in her bedroom when the heavy chest of drawers that she was searching for evidence of her husband's infidelity fell on top of her and crushed her. Even today, people hear horrible disembodied screams coming from her old bedroom; it is believed that Elizabeth is doomed to forever reenact her agonizing death.

Still another Westover ghost is that of Evelyn's brother, William Byrd III, who committed suicide in his bedroom in 1777 after he lost the family fortune due to his gambling. Once, a person who was spending the night in that room felt an icy cold presence enter and then sensed it glide over to a chair. After that, the room was filled with an oppressive atmosphere, which the visitor suspected was caused by the anguished spirit of William Byrd III. But it's Evelyn Byrd, the friendly spirit, who holds the most sway at Westover, which proves that nice ghosts don't necessarily finish last.

# The Ubiquitous Lady in White

*"So there I was, sitting in the empty hallway, when all of a sudden I felt like a cold wind was blowing through me. I felt a chill down to my bones, and then I looked up and saw a woman in a long white dress walking down the staircase without touching the ground."*

✳   ✳   ✳   ✳

N° ONE KNOWS why so many ghostly women wear white dresses (or, for that matter, exactly why ghosts wear clothes at all), but stories of ladies in white go back hundreds of years. In fact, tales of some of the spectral women in white that supposedly wander the forests of New England were among the very first American ghost stories.

Today, when paranormal investigators interview witnesses who talk about seeing women in white, they tend to be instantly skeptical. But these stories didn't just come from out of nowhere. Some say it's an image of ghosts that was created by Hollywood or by Victorian-era novelist Wilkie Collins (whose hit novel *The Woman in White* wasn't even about a ghost). However, such stories have actually been common in supernatural lore for centuries, and these spectral women are reported—often by reputable witnesses—more and more every year. Ladies in white were following children in dark woods, stalking the lonely hallways of old buildings, and wandering the streets of small rural towns long before movies could have created such images.

## Forever Awaiting His Return

One of the more venerable ladies in white is the White Lady of the Bridgeport Inn, which was built in 1877 for Hiram Leavitt and his family in the mining town of Bridgeport, California. There, a woman in white has been seen in Room 19 so often that she's mentioned on the building's historical marker.

The most common story surrounding the origin of this ghost is that she was the fiancée of a young miner during the late 1800s. After a particularly good day of prospecting, the miner decided to walk from the room that he'd rented from Leavitt to the nearest bank—which was several miles away—to trade his gold for cash. His fiancée wanted to go with him, but they didn't call it "the Wild West" for nothing: The young miner knew that he risked being robbed while carrying so much gold, so he told her to wait in their room (Room 19) at the inn. And so she waited. And waited. And waited.

After several hours of listening for his footsteps and hearing nothing but the howling of the wind, she began to fear the worst. Finally, her fears were realized when she heard the news that her fiancé had been robbed and murdered by highwaymen.

In her grief, the poor woman hanged herself in Room 19, where her ghost has been seen ever since—often wearing a long white wedding gown.

## Connecticut's Lady in White

In Easton, Connecticut—on the other side of the country from Bridgeport—is Union Cemetery, a burial ground that dates back to New England's earliest settlers, who arrived nearly 400 years ago. Dressed in a long white dress and a bonnet, Easton's Lady in White is sometimes seen at the graveyard or on the road outside of it, which stretches between Union Cemetery and the nearby Stepney Cemetery.

Countless witnesses—including police officers and firefighters—have reported hitting a woman in white with their vehicles on the road that connects the graveyards. They slam on their brakes when she mysteriously appears in front of their cars, but it's too late: The terrified drivers hear the dreadful thud of the impact and watch her limp body fly away from their vehicles to the side of the road. They pull over, rush to the side of the road, and find nothing. The woman has vanished, leaving nothing but an imprint in the snow where her body landed. In 1993, a collision with the ghostly woman even left a dent in a firefighter's car. Roadside phantoms that vanish after being hit are not uncommon, but for them to leave behind such physical evidence is quite unusual.

So common were sightings of Easton's Lady in White that paranormal experts Ed and Lorraine Warren—founders of the New England Society for Psychic Research and one of the first couples to turn ghost hunting into a profession—used Union Cemetery as the subject of their 1992 book *Graveyard*.

During their research, the Warrens spoke with a man whose late wife had been buried in Union Cemetery. One evening, while he was visiting his wife's grave, he heard something rustling the leaves behind him. When he turned, he saw the Lady in White looking down at him.

"I wish," she said, as he knelt frozen in place, "that my husband had loved me as much as you loved your wife." Before he could reply, she disappeared.

Others have seen the Lady in White surrounded by darker forms, with whom she appears to be engaged in a heated argument. When she vanishes, the dark shadows disappear along with her.

No one is sure who this Lady in White was in life, but sightings of her were not reported before the late 1940s, despite the fact that the cemetery dates back to the 1600s. Ed Warren speculated that it is the spirit of a woman who was murdered shortly after World War II.

Ed also claimed to have captured video evidence of the Lady in White, but in 2008, his widow, Lorraine, told reporters from NBC that she keeps it under lock and key "because it's so valuable." He's hardly the only person to photograph her, though— several ghost hunters have taken photographs that feature strange phenomena at the cemetery.

The Lady in White may not be the only ghost at Union Cemetery. Many paranormal investigators have encountered an entity there known as "Red Eyes," which is exactly that: a pair of glowing red eyes that keep watch over the cemetery.

The fame of Connecticut's Lady in White has spread throughout the ghost-hunting community, so much so that the town of Easton has had to take steps to protect the cemetery from vandals: It is closed after dark, and the police vigilantly keep trespassers from entering it after hours. But it's not unheard of for officers to see a pale, glowing form behind the gates in the middle of the night.

# Spectral Ships and Phantom Crews

*Ghost ships seem to have the ability to slip back and forth between this world and the next, often making appearances that foretell of impending doom. Come with us as we set sail in search of some of the most famous ghost ships in maritime history.*

✳ ✳ ✳ ✳

## The *Mary Celeste*

THE AMAZON WAS cursed from the day she left port: During her maiden voyage, the ship's captain died. After being salvaged by an American company that renamed her *Mary Celeste*, the ship left New York on November 7, 1872, bound for Genoa, Italy. On board were Captain Benjamin Briggs, his family, and a crew of seven.

On December 4, the crew of the *Dei Gratia* found the *Mary Celeste* abandoned. There was plenty of food and water on the ship, but the only living soul on board was a cat. The crew and the captain's family were missing, and no clues suggested where they went. The last entry in the captain's log was dated almost two weeks prior to the ship's discovery, so the vessel had somehow piloted itself all that time.

What happened to the *Mary Celeste* and those on board remains a mystery. Many believe that a ghostly crew sailed the ship and kept her safe until she was found.

## The *Iron Mountain*

A ship disappearing on the high seas is one thing, but on a river? That's exactly what happened to the *Iron Mountain*. In June 1872, the 180-foot-long vessel left New Orleans on its way to Pittsburgh on the Mississippi River with a crew of more than 50 men. A day after stopping at Vicksburg, Mississippi, to pick up additional cargo, which was towed behind the ship on barges, the *Iron Mountain* steamed its way north and promptly vanished. Later that day, the barges were recovered, but the *Iron*

*Mountain* and its crew were never seen nor heard from again. For years after it disappeared, riverboat captains whispered about how the *Iron Mountain* was simply sucked into another dimension through a ghostly portal.

## The *Palatine*

According to legend, shortly after Christmas 1738, the *Princess Augusta* ran aground and broke into pieces on the coast of Block Island, Rhode Island. Roughly 130 years later, poet John Greenleaf Whittier renamed the European vessel and told his version of the shipwreck in his poem "The Palatine", which was published in *The Atlantic Monthly*. Today, strange lights are still reported in the waters around Block Island, especially on the Saturday between Christmas and New Year's Day; they are said to be the fiery ghost ship.

## The *Edmund Fitzgerald*

When it comes to ghost ships, the *Edmund Fitzgerald* is the biggest—literally. More than 720 feet long, the freighter shuttled iron ore across the Great Lakes beginning in the late 1950s. On November 10, 1975, the mammoth ship sank during a violent storm without ever issuing a distress signal. All 29 members of the crew were presumed dead, but their bodies were never found. Nearly ten years to the day after the "Fitz" sank, a strange dark ship was seen on Lake Superior. One look at the monstrous vessel was all that witnesses needed to recognize it as the *Edmund Fitzgerald*.

## The *Flying Dutchman*

Stories say that during the 1800s, Captain Hendrick Vanderdecken was attempting to sail the *Flying Dutchman* around the Cape of Good Hope when a violent storm blew up. Rather than pull into port, the stubborn captain claimed that he would navigate around the Cape even if it took him all of eternity to do so. The ship and its crew were lost in the storm, and, as promised by Vanderdecken, they were condemned to sail the high seas for all eternity.

Almost immediately thereafter, people all over the world began spotting the Dutch ship moving silently through the ocean, often cast in an eerie glow. Because of the legend associated with Captain Vanderdecken, sightings of the *Flying Dutchman* are now thought to be bad omens. Case in point: One of the most recent sightings of the spectral vessel occurred off the coast of North Carolina's Outer Banks just prior to Hurricane Isabel's arrival in 2003.

# Ghosts of the *Queen Mary*

*Once considered a grand jewel of the ocean, the decks of the Queen Mary played host to such rich and famous guests as Clark Gable, Charlie Chaplin, Laurel and Hardy, and Elizabeth Taylor. Today, the Queen Mary is permanently docked, but she still hosts some mysterious, ghostly passengers!*

❋ ❋ ❋ ❋

### The *Queen Mary* Goes to War

THE QUEEN MARY took her maiden voyage in May 1936, but a change came in 1940 when the British government pressed the ocean liner into military service. She was given a coat of gray paint and was turned into a troop transport vessel. The majestic dining salons became mess halls and the cocktail bars, cabins, and staterooms were filled with bunks. Even the swimming pools were boarded over and crowded with cots for the men. The ship was so useful to the Allies that Hitler offered a $250,000 reward and hero status to the naval commander who could sink her. None of them did.

Although the *Queen Mary* avoided enemy torpedoes during the war, she was unable to avoid tragedy. On October 2, 1942, escorted by the cruiser HMS *Curacoa* and several destroyers, the *Queen Mary* was sailing on the choppy North Atlantic near Ireland. She was carrying about 15,000 American soldiers.

Danger from German vessels was always present, but things were quiet until suddenly, before anyone could act, the *Queen Mary's* massive bow smashed into the *Curacoa*. There was no way to slow down, no time for warning, and no distress calls to the men onboard. They had only seconds to react before their ship was sliced in two. Within minutes, both sections of the ship plunged below the surface of the icy water, carrying the crew with them. Of the *Curacoa's* 439-man crew, 338 of them perished on that fateful day. The *Queen Mary* suffered only minor damage and there were no injuries to her crew.

After that, the *Queen Mary* served unscathed for the remainder of the war. Following the surrender of Germany, she was used to carry American troops and GI war brides to the United States and Canada, before returning to England for conversion back to a luxury liner.

## Last Days of an Ocean Liner

After the war, the *Queen Mary* and her sister ship, the *Queen Elizabeth*, were the preferred method of transatlantic travel for the rich and famous. But by the 1960s, airplane travel was faster and cheaper, and so, in late 1967, the *Queen Mary* steamed away from England for the last time. Her decks and staterooms were filled with curiosity seekers and wealthy patrons who wanted to be part of the ship's final voyage. She ended her 39-day journey in Long Beach, California, where she was permanently docked as a floating hotel, convention center, museum, and restaurant. She is now listed on the National Register of Historic Places and is open to visitors year-round.

## The Haunted *Queen Mary*

The *Queen Mary* has seen much tragedy and death, so it's no surprise that the ship plays host to a number of ghosts. Because of the sheer number of passengers who have walked her decks, accidents were bound to happen. One such mishap occurred on July 10, 1966, when John Pedder, an engine room worker, was crushed to death when an automatic door closed on him.

There have been other reported deaths onboard, as well. For instance, during the war, when the ship was used for troop transport, a brawl broke out in one of the galleys and a cook was allegedly shoved into a hot oven, where he burned to death. There are also reports of a woman drowning in the ship's swimming pool and stories of passengers falling overboard.

Another strange death onboard was that of Senior Second Officer William Stark, whose ghost has often been spotted on deck and in his former quarters. Stark died after drinking lime juice mixed with cleaning solution, which he mistook for gin. He realized his error, and while he joked about it, he called the ship's doctor. Unfortunately, though, Stark soon felt the effects of the poison. As the young officer's condition worsened, he lapsed into a coma and died on September 22, 1949.

Witnesses have also encountered a spectral man in gray overalls who has been seen below deck. He has dark hair and a long beard and is believed to be a mechanic or maintenance worker from the 1930s.

Another friendly spirit, dubbed "Miss Turner," is believed to have been a switchboard operator on the ship. A ghostly woman known as "Mrs. Kilburn" wears a gray uniform with starched white cuffs. She was once in charge of the stewardesses and bellboys, and she's still watching over the comings and goings on the ship. And although it is unknown who the ship's "Lady in White" might be, she haunts the *Queen*'s Salon and is normally seen wearing a white, backless evening gown. Witnesses say she dances alone near the grand piano as if listening to music only she can hear, then vanishes.

Security guards, staff members, and visitors have also reported doors unlocking, opening, and closing on their own, often triggering security alarms. Other unexplained occurrences include phantom voices and footsteps, banging and hammerings sounds, cold spots, inexplicable winds that blow through closed-off areas, and lights that turn on and off.

During a tour of the ship, one guest felt someone tugging on her purse and sweater and stroking her hair. Cold chills crept down her spine when she realized there was no one near her at the time!

In 1967, some 25 years after the tragic accident with the *Curacoa*, a marine engineer working inside the ship heard the terrible sound of two ships colliding. He even heard screams and shredding steel. Did the terrible events of 1942 somehow leave an impression on the atmosphere of this grand old ship? Or worse, is the crew of the *Curacoa* still doomed to relive that fateful October afternoon for eternity?

## Echoing the Present

The stories of mysterious encounters and strange events go on and on. It seems almost certain that the events of the past have left an indelible impression on the decks, corridors, and cabins of the *Queen Mary*, creating a haunting that is rivaled by few others in the annals of the supernatural.

# Europe's Most Haunted Hotels

*Many of Europe's haunted hotels are located in Britain and Ireland, where ghosts are often considered as friends or even members of the family, and are given the same respect as any living person—or even more. Other European cultures aren't as comfortable with ghosts—opting to tear down haunted hotels instead of coexisting with spirits—but there are still a few places in Europe where ghost hunters can explore.*

✳ ✳ ✳ ✳

## Comlongon Castle, Dumfries, Scotland

LADY MARION CARRUTHERS haunts Scotland's beautiful Comlongon Castle. On September 25, 1570, Lady Marion leaped to her death from the castle's lookout tower rather than submit to an arranged marriage. Visitors can easily find the exact spot where she landed; for more than 400 years, it's been difficult to grow grass there. Because Lady Marion's death was a suicide, she was denied a Christian burial, and it seems her spirit is unable to rest in peace. Dressed in green, her ghost wanders around the castle and its grounds.

### Ettington Park Hotel, Alderminister, England

You may feel chills when you see the Ettington Park Hotel, where the classic 1963 horror movie *The Haunting* was filmed. It was an apt choice for the movie locale because the hotel features several ghosts.

The Shirley family rebuilt this Victorian Gothic structure in the mid-1800s, and the ghost of the "Lady in Gray" has appeared on the staircase regularly since that time. Her identity is unknown, unlike the phantom "Lady in White," who was supposedly a former governess named Lady Emma. The voices of crying children are probably the two Shirley children who drowned nearby in the River Stour; they're buried by the church tower.

Watch out for poltergeists in the Library Bar, where books fly across the room. And don't be alarmed if you hear a late-night snooker game when no one is in the room—it's just the ghosts having fun.

### Ye Olde Black Bear, Tewkesbury, England

If you're looking for headless ghosts dragging clanking chains, Ye Olde Black Bear is just the place. Built in the early 1300s, the structure is the oldest inn in Gloucestershire. The hotel's headless ghost may be one individual or several—without a head, it's difficult to tell. However, the ghost's uniform suggests that he was a soldier killed in a battle around the 1470s. Those who've seen the figure at the hotel suspect he doesn't realize he's dead—Ye Olde Black Bear was supposedly a favorite hangout for soldiers during his era.

## Renvyle House Hotel, Galway, Ireland

Renvyle House Hotel is not old by haunted hotel standards. The site has been built on, destroyed, built again, destroyed again—once by a fire set by the IRA—and so on, until the current hotel was erected in the 1930s. But its ghosts have an impressive pedigree, dating back to a 16th-century Irish pirate queen, Gráinne O'Malley. A redheaded boy is a more recent spirit, possibly a son of the Blake family who owned the site in the 19th century. The hotel is haunted by so many spirits that it was regularly visited by celebrities, such as poet W. B. Yeats, who conducted séances there. Today, Renvyle House Hotel is still a favorite destination for ghost hunters, and it is included in many "haunted hotel" tours.

## Royal Lion Hotel, Lyme Regis, England

The Royal Lion Hotel was built in 1601 as a coaching inn, but some of its ghosts may be visiting from across the street, where executions allegedly took place. Other misty, ghostly figures around the hotel may be the spirits of pirates who sailed into the port, or they could be some of the rebels who were hung and quartered on the nearby beach after trying to overthrow King James II in 1685. Waterfront hotels are often haunted due to their association with pirates and wrecked ships. However, with several dozen different spirits, this site reports more ghosts than most.

## Dragsholm Slot Hotel, Nekselø Bay, Denmark

In Danish, the word slot means "castle," and the Dragsholm is one of the world's great haunted castle hotels. According to legend, Dragsholm's "Gray Lady"—a 12th-century maid who loved working at the hotel—visits on most nights. She silently checks on guests to be sure they are comfortable. The "White Lady" haunts the corridors nightly. She may be the young woman who was allegedly walled up inside the castle; her ancient corpse was found during 19th-century renovations.

James Hepburn, the Fourth Earl of Bothwell, is the castle's most famous ghost. Hepburn became the third husband of Mary, Queen of Scots, after he helped murder her previous spouse. For his role in that crime, Bothwell spent the last ten years of his life chained to a pillar in Dragsholm. If you think you've seen his ghostly apparition, you can compare it to his mummified body in a nearby church in Faarevejle.

## Hotel Scandinavia, Venice, Italy

The Hotel Scandinavia is in a building dating back to the year 1000, and it's surrounded by stories of ghosts and apparitions. In the 15th century, the apparition of a wealthy (and rather buxom) Madonna first appeared close to the hotel's palazzo. Witnesses report hearing sounds from the sorrowful ghosts of condemned prisoners who long ago crossed the nearby Bridge of Sighs. This famous bridge was where convicts caught a final glimpse of Venice before being imprisoned. These spirits apparently visit the hotel, and their voices are most often heard in the lobby. Because of the location's unique ghosts and how often they're heard, the Hotel Scandinavia is consistently ranked as one of the world's top five haunted hotels.

# Chapter 11

# Of Shady Provenance

## The Hitler Diaries Hoax

*Adolf Hitler was an ambitious politician, but when it came to writing, he could be pretty darn lazy. After the success of* Mein Kampf, *the first volume of which was published in 1925 and the second in 1926, he seemed content to rest on his laurels, even if those laurels were in a cozy cell in Landsberg prison. Surely such a significant figure would leave behind a greater written legacy than that. This literary lethargy would eventually make historians very cranky—and very gullible.*

※　※　※　※

### The Roots of the Hoax

THOUGH HITLER DID halfheartedly pen a 200-page sequel to *Mein Kampf* in 1928, he grew bored with the project and never bothered to have it published. In fact, only two copies existed, and those were kept under lock and key by Hitler's order. This manuscript was discovered by American troops in 1945, but though authenticated by several of Hitler's associates, it was considered to be both an inflammatory piece of Nazi propaganda and a dull rehash of *Mein Kampf*. For these reasons, the book was never published widely.

Hitler was literally a "dictator," relying on secretaries to take down his ideas and plans. Often, even Hitler's most grandiose and terrible commands—such as the one to destroy European Jewry—were given only verbally. Historians were also frustrated by the dearth of personal correspondence that could be linked to Hitler. His mistress, Eva Braun, was not the brightest woman to ever walk the face of the earth, and their letters have not been found.

## Fertile Ground for a Fake

This lack of primary-source material is what made the Hitler diaries hoax such a success at first. A staff reporter at West Germany's *Stern* magazine, Gerd Heidemann, fell for the ruse hook, line, and sinker, and saw the publication of the diaries as a way of advancing his stalled career in journalism.

He convinced his editors at *Stern* that the journals were real, and they paid 9.3 million marks (about 6 million U.S. dollars at that time) for the first serial rights. On April 25, 1983, *Stern* hit the streets with a sensational cover story: "Hitler's Diary Discovered." Media outlets around the world were more than happy to follow *Stern*'s lead, and the *New York Times*, *Newsweek*, and the *London Sunday Times* all immediately jumped on the huge story.

The editors at *Stern* certainly should have been more wary of Heidemann's incredible story, as he was already obsessed with all things Hitler and the Third Reich. He had a passion for acquiring Nazi collectibles of almost any sort, even emptying his bank account to buy Hermann Göring's dilapidated private yacht. However, Heidemann's enthusiasm was so contagious, and the demand for all things Hitler so great, that it seems his superiors simply couldn't resist. But from whom had Heidemann obtained the diaries? And where had they been all these decades?

## Fabricating the Führer

Konrad Kujau had started forging documents as a youth in East Germany, but he really hit his stride after defecting to West Germany and setting up an antiquities store in Stuttgart. Kujau was brazen and seemingly fearless in his work. He made and sold "genuine" Nazi items that sound ludicrous now and should have raised alarms for his clients then: Who could believe, for example, that Hitler had once written an opera? Yet his customers wanted to believe, and as long as Kujau shunned publicity, he was able to make a nice living off their ignorance and inexperience. After all, these were private collectors who wanted to hold onto their purchases as investments. But Kujau got greedy, and maybe just a little hungry for fame. Enter *Stern* reporter Heidemann, sniffing for a story.

In 1981, Kujau showed Heidemann 62 volumes of what he claimed were Hitler's diaries, dated from 1932 to 1945. Heidemann was astonished and asked Kujau about their history; how had such important documents remained hidden and unknown for so many years? Kujau was ready with a plausible-sounding (to Heidemann, at least) explanation: Nazi flunkies had tried to fly Hitler's personal belongings, including the diaries, out of Berlin, but the plane had been shot down and crashed in Dresden, its cargo surviving without any major damage. Conveniently for Kujau, Dresden was now behind the Iron Curtain, so his claim of obtaining the volumes one at a time from an East German general could not easily be confirmed or disproved. But if anyone longed to believe it was true, it was Heidemann.

## Media Circus

The publication of the diaries was an international bombshell, with historians, journalists, politicians, and antiquities dealers lining up to take sides in the media. Some historians immediately pointed out Hitler's aversion to writing in longhand, but others, such as the esteemed British World War II expert Hugh Trevor-Roper, declared the diaries to be authentic.

On the day the story was published, *Stern* held a press conference in which Trevor-Roper, along with German historians Eberhard Jackel and Gerhard Weinberg, vouched for the documents. It would be a mistake all three would grievously regret.

The media uproar only intensified when, less than two weeks later, it was revealed beyond any question that the Hitler diaries were forged. Not only were the paper and ink modern, but the volumes were full of events and times that did not jibe with Hitler's known activities and whereabouts.

Kujau was so careless in his fakery that he didn't even bother to get the monogram on the title page right: It read FH rather than AH. Some observers pointed out that the German letters F and A are quite similar, but surely as a German himself, Kujau would have known the difference. The best guess is that the diaries were sloppily prepared for his usual type of client—a dullish foreigner who wouldn't ask too many questions—and that Heidemann's arrival on the scene turned what might have been just another smooth and profitable transaction into a worldwide scandal.

## Off to the Clink

Heidemann was arrested and tried for fraud, and Kujau was arrested and tried for forgery. Both men wound up serving more than four years in prison. Kujau reveled in his celebrity after his release, appearing on talk shows and selling paintings as "genuine Kujau fakes." But although Kujau tried to treat his crime as a lighthearted joke, it should be noted that had he not been unmasked, the diaries could have done real damage. Perhaps most serious—the document claimed that Hitler had no knowledge of the Holocaust.

# The Enigma of the Crystal Skulls

*Once upon a time, a legendary set of crystal skulls was scattered across the globe. It was said that finding one of these skulls would bring the lucky person either wealth or death. The story also goes on to say that if all the skulls were located and placed together, they would begin to speak and reveal prophecies, including the end of the world. Could these skulls really exist?*

❋  ❋  ❋  ❋

## The History, Maybe

ADMITTEDLY, THE BACKGROUND of the crystal skulls is a little patchy. According to the legend, either the Aztecs or the Mayas hid 13 crystal human-size skulls around the world (though the number varies story to story). The skulls are said to possess supernatural powers, including the ability to speak as well as to heal, so perhaps they were hidden to prevent them from falling into the wrong hands.

Incredibly, several crystal skulls do exist—you can even see them in respected museums such as the British Museum and the Smithsonian. However, there is no documentation to support that any of the skulls were found during an excavation, or how they were found at all, for that matter. So where did they come from?

## Selling Skulls and Seeing Visions

In the late 1800s, Eugene Boban was enjoying a successful career as a world-traveling antiques dealer. Boban is believed to have owned at least three of the crystal skulls, although it is unclear where he acquired them. However, two of these Boban skulls would end up in museums—one in the British Museum and one in Paris' Musee de l'Homme.

But the most intriguing crystal skull is one that Boban did not own. This skull was discovered in 1924 by Anna Le Guillon Mitchell-Hedges, the adopted daughter of famed British adventurer F. A. Mitchell-Hedges. Anna claimed she found the skull in what is now Belize, inside a pyramid. Interestingly, her father wrote several books, but he never once mentions his daughter finding a crystal skull. Professional jealousy or did he regard the skull as a sham? Regardless, Anna claimed that the skull had magical powers and that she once stared into the skull's eye sockets and had a premonition of President John F. Kennedy's assassination.

## Putting the Skulls to the Test

Since the legends say that the skulls were handcarved, or a gift from the heavens (or aliens), scientists were eager to determine how they were formed. When the British Museum conducted tests on the two skulls they owned, they found marks that made it clear the skulls were carved using modern rotary tools. Likewise, Paris' Musee de l'Homme also found that their skull was created using modern tools. Both museums also discovered that the type of crystal used to form the skulls wasn't even available anywhere in the Aztec or Mayan empires.

At first, Anna Mitchell-Hedges was open to having the skull she found tested by the company Hewlett Packard (HP). They found that the skull was indeed crystal—and one solid block of crystal at that, which is incredibly difficult to carve, whether by hand or using modern machinery. Interestingly, Hewlett Packard also found that the quartz crystal is the same kind of crystal used in making computers.

## The Legend Continues

Skeptics dismiss the crystal skulls as nothing more than a silly story. And it is an entertaining theory: Even director Steven Spielberg jumped on the bandwagon with his 2008 movie, *Indiana Jones and the Kingdom of the Crystal Skull*. True believers, on the other hand, firmly believe that just because the current skulls may be fakes, it doesn't mean the real skulls aren't still out there waiting to be found. And, say the believers, once all 13 are placed together in a room, the skulls will begin to speak, first to each other and then to anyone else who might be present. But until then, the crystal skulls are keeping their mouths shut.

# Time Travelers

*Hold on to your hat—you're in for a wild, mind-blowing ride back and forth through the realms of time!*

✳  ✳  ✳  ✳

IN 2013, MANY people didn't believe President Obama when he claimed that he often fired guns on the skeet shooting range at Camp David. But others believed that Obama had actually come close to revealing the "real" truth: that he has been working for the CIA for more than 30 years, and that he had personally used the CIA's top secret "jump room" to visit Mars on several occasions as a young man. This is probably not the wildest conspiracy theory about a president that's ever circulated, but it's certainly in the top tier.

However, there's at least one witness who claims to have known the future president in his Mars-hopping days: a Seattle attorney named Andrew Basiago, who also only claims to have been to Mars himself as an Earth ambassador to a Martian civilization in the early 1980s.

But by then, Basiago says, he was an old hand with the CIA: some years before, when he was only 12, he was a participant in a top secret initiative called "Project Pegasus," an elite force that used "radiant energy" principles discovered in the papers of inventor Nikola Tesla to travel through time.

Basiago claims that he traveled through time using eight different technologies as a boy, but mainly using a teleporter that consisted of two "elliptical booms" that stood eight feet tall, positioned about ten feet apart and separated by a curtain of "radiant energy." Participants would jump through the curtain and enter a "vortal tunnel" that took them through time and space. By jumping though, Basiago claims to have attended Ford's Theatre on the night Abraham Lincoln was shot more than once—often enough that on a few occasions, he saw himself, on other trips, among the crowd. Oddly, though this would imply that each "jump" took him to the same "timeline," he says that every time he attended the theatre, the events of the night came off slightly differently, as though he were going to different "timelines" on each trip.

But Lincoln's assassination wasn't the only historic event Basiago claims to have attended. In 1972, he says, he used a "plasma confinement chamber" in East Hanover, New Jersey, to travel back to 1863 to see the Gettysburg Address. Basiago even claims that photographic evidence of this exists; In the foreground of the one photograph of Lincoln at Gettysburg that exists stands a young boy in oversized men's shoes, standing casually outside of the crowd in the background. Basiago says that the boy is him.

Basiago told his story over the course of several appearances on a radio program where conspiracies, UFOs, hauntings, and other strange phenomena are discussed during late night broadcasts. The online forums on which listeners discuss the topics spoken about on the show once brought forth the story of another alleged time traveler: the story of John Titor, who began posting on the forum in 2000 and claimed to be a time traveler from 2036. Physicists tried to drill him on the mathematics and theories behind time travel, and he seemed to pass every test.

Titor claimed that he was a soldier based in Tampa who was visiting year 2000 for personal reasons—perhaps to collect old family photos that had been destroyed by his time. He even posted schematics showing the devices he used to travel in time, and many at the time became convinced that he was telling the truth. However, the stories he told about the future of the United States failed to come to pass. In 2001, he claimed that unrest in America surrounding the 2004 presidential election would gradually build up until it became a full-on Civil War, broadly defined as a war between urban and rural parts of the country eventually splitting the United States into five regions. In 2011, he claimed, he was a young teenage soldier for a group called The Fighting Diamondbacks fighting for the rural armies. But the war, he said, would end in 2015 when Russia launched a nuclear assault destroying most American cities, killing as many as half of the people in the country and creating a "new" America in which Omaha, Nebraska served as the nation's capital. Titor said there was an upside to this: in many ways, he said, the world was better with half of the people gone.

Titor's odd story found a lot of supporters when it was first posted, and the events of September 11, 2001 convinced many people that World War III was, in fact, at hand. However, the 2004 election came and went without anything happening in the United States that could ever reasonably be called a civil war breaking out. There was still no such war going in 2008, either, by which time Titor claimed that the war would be fully raging and undeniable.

These are certainly not the only people who claim to have traveled through time. Some of the supposed time travelers have far more bona fide military credentials than Titor, who eventually disappeared from the forums. In 1935, Sir Victor Goddard, an air marshall in the Royal Air Force, claimed that he flew into a strange storm while flying his plane above an airfield in Scotland. The turbulence was so bad that he nearly crashed, and he emerged from the storm to find that the landscape beneath him now contained strange-looking aircraft in hangars that weren't there before, all attended by officers wearing blue uniforms instead of the brown ones the RAF normally used. Four years later, the RAF officially changed the uniforms from brown to blue and began using planes like the ones he had seen after the "storm."

This wasn't Goddard's only brush with the unknown. A decade later, he overheard an officer telling of a dream he'd had in which Air Marshall Goddard had died in a wreck when the plane he was flying in iced over and crashed on a beach. That night, Goddard's plane did, indeed, ice over, and an emergency landing was forced on a beach. Though the dream had ended with Goddard dead, Goddard, having had a sort of early warning, kept his cool and brought the plane safely down. The dream he overheard may very well have saved his life.

# P. T. Barnum's Giant Sucker

*P. T. Barnum, the consummate huckster, supposedly laughed at the audiences he tricked, saying, "There's a sucker born every minute." But have we misjudged America's Greatest Showman?*

✳  ✳  ✳  ✳

THE PHRASE—WHICH SUGGESTS that every scam, no matter how obvious, will find a gullible mark—has been attributed to several late-19th-century sources, including con man Joseph "Paper Collar Joe" Bessimer and humorist Mark Twain. Most often, it is attributed to P. T. Barnum.

## What a Circus!

Phineas Taylor Barnum (1810–91) both amused and appalled audiences with his collections of freaks, oddities, and wonders. Writer Herman Melville boldly declared him "sole heir to all lean men, fat women, dwarfs, two-headed cows, amphibious sea-maidens, large-eyed owls, small-eyed mice, rabbit-eating anacondas, bugs, monkies and mummies." In the name of entertainment, he promoted "humbugs"—obvious hoaxes designed to delight and entertain audiences, such as the "Feejee Mermaid" and a woman he claimed was George Washington's 161-year-old nanny.

Barnum insisted that people enjoyed being fooled so long as they got "several times their money's worth." Though it seems likely that such a showman would utter this phrase, Barnum's acquaintances denied it upon inquiry from his biographer, saying that Barnum treasured and respected his patrons.

## Start of the Punchline

The true story behind the phrase can be traced to George Hull, a businessman from Binghamton, New York. In 1868, Hull (a fervent atheist) argued with a fundamentalist preacher who insisted the Bible be taken literally, including Genesis 6:4 ("There were giants in the earth in those days"). Hull purchased an enormous slab of gypsum and hired a stonecutter to carve it into a ten-foot-tall statue of a giant with lifelike details such as toenails, fingernails, and pores. The statue was stained with sulfuric acid and ink and shipped to a farm near Cardiff, New York, where it was then buried.

A year later, Hull hired workers to dig a well near the spot where the statue was buried. As he intended, the workers discovered the statue and were excited by their find. (Six months earlier, fossils had been unearthed—with much publicity—at a nearby farm.) Hull had the workers excavate the statue, and then he charged people to see the Cardiff Giant, as it had become known.

Hull sold his statue for nearly $40,000 to a group of exhibitors headed by David Hannum. Barnum became interested in the find and offered to rent it for $50,000, but Hannum refused. Rather than make a higher offer, Barnum built his own Cardiff Giant, which he put on display, declaring that Hannum had sold him the giant after all and that Hannum's was the forgery. Newspapers widely publicized Barnum's story, causing audiences to flock to Barnum while Hannum bitterly declared, "There's a sucker born every minute," in reference to the duped crowds.

## Careful What You Sue For

Hannum sued Barnum for calling his giant a sham. At trial, Hull admitted that the original giant was a hoax. The judge ruled in Barnum's favor, saying that it is not a crime to call a fake a fake.

Later, one of Barnum's competitors, Adam Forepaugh, mistakenly attributed (or intentionally misattributed) Hannum's phrase to Barnum. The consummate showman didn't deny saying it; in fact, he thanked Forepaugh for the publicity.

# It's Not What You Think: Famous Faked Photos

*Some photographs are so iconic that it's nearly impossible to separate the image from the event: President John F. Kennedy's funeral, the* Eagle *spacecraft landing on the moon, the raising of the flag at Iwo Jima. But seeing is not always believing.*

✳    ✳    ✳    ✳

## A New Era

IN THE BRAVE new world of digital photography, photographers can manipulate images with ease while media mavens worry over the ethics of photographic alterations. But photographers were editing reality long before the computer: As early as the Civil War, photographers posed battlefield shots to get the best effect. Nineteenth-century photographers used double exposures and other darkroom sleight-of-hand to create photographs of spirits and the supernatural. In Stalinist Russia, discredited leaders were removed from the picture—in more ways than one. Check out these famous "faked" photographs from the days before Photoshop.

## The Loch Ness Monster

In 1934, London surgeon Robert Kenneth Wilson sold a photograph he had taken while on a birding expedition to the

*London Daily Mail.* In the photo, the long slender neck of an unknown animal rises from the water of Scotland's Loch Ness.

Wilson's story held for 60 years until 1994, when a Loch Ness Monster believer named Alastair Boyd uncovered evidence that the photograph was a hoax. It turned out that in 1933, the *Daily Mail* had hired big-game hunter Marmaduke Wetherell to investigate reported sightings at Loch Ness and find the monster. Instead of Nessie, however, Wetherell found tracks that had been faked with a dried hippo foot. Working with his son and stepson, Wetherell staged the Loch Ness photograph in revenge, attaching a head and neck crafted from plasticine to the conning tower of a toy submarine. A friend convinced Wilson to be the front man.

It was Wetherell's stepson who broke the story, admitting his part in the hoax to Boyd in 1994. However, Wetherell's son Ian had published his own version of the hoax in an obscure article in 1975.

## Raising the Flag at Iwo Jima

Associated Press photographer Joe Rosenthal won a Pulitzer Prize for his photograph of American servicemen raising the flag at the Battle of Iwo Jima during WWII. He spent the rest of his life fighting charges that the picture had been posed.

The charges were based on a misunderstanding. Rosenthal was halfway up Mount Suribachi when he learned he had missed the flag-raising. Told the view was worth the climb, he continued up the mountain where he found the Marine commanders had decided to replace the original flag with a larger one.

Trying to get a shot of the second flag going up, he stood on a pile of stones to get a better angle and almost missed the second flag-raising as well. When he saw the flag go up out of the corner of his eye, he swung his camera and shot. Knowing a single exposure taken on the fly was a gamble, and wanting to be sure he had something worth printing, Rosenthal took a picture of jubilant Marines gathered under the flag, a photo he called the "gung-ho" shot. He then sent his film to the military press center and left for his next assignment.

Rosenthal had no way of knowing his first, off-the-cuff shot had succeeded, and the congratulatory wire he received from the Associated Press didn't tell him which picture they were congratulating him for. When someone asked him a few days later if he had posed the picture, Rosenthal assumed they were talking about the "gung-ho" shot and said "Sure." A few days later, *TIME* magazine's radio program reported the picture had been posed. *TIME* retracted the story a few days later, but the misunderstanding haunted Rosenthal for the rest of his life.

## Makeshift Propaganda

When Soviet war photographer Yevgeny Khaldei entered Nazi Berlin with the Red Army in 1945, he was looking for one thing: his own "Iwo Jima shot." When he didn't find one, he created it.

Khaldei chose the Reichstag building as the site for his photograph, and then discovered he didn't have a Soviet flag to raise. He flew back to Moscow, took three red tablecloths his news agency used for official events, and spent the night sewing a Soviet flag to take back to Berlin.

But the Reichstag was heavily defended—it took two days of fighting before Russians gained control of the roof. On the morning of May 2, while the Germans surrendered the building, a team of soldiers chosen for their political significance stood on the roof and Khaldei posed his masterpiece of Soviet propaganda.

Manipulation of the image didn't end with the pose. Official censors noticed one of the soldiers was wearing two watches, presumably acquired while looting. Khaldei was ordered to edit out the evidence. He also added smoke to the background to heighten the drama.

Khaldei later justified posing his wartime photos by claiming that pictures should match the importance of the event.

## Kisses Both Real and Fake

Alfred Eisenstaedt's photograph of a sailor kissing a nurse in a white uniform in Times Square on V-J Day, August 14, 1945, was real enough, snapped on the fly as the seaman exuberantly kissed his way through the crowd.

French photographer Robert Doisneau, however, posed his seemingly spontaneous "Kiss by the Hotel De Ville" for a 1950 *LIFE* magazine photo spread on Parisian lovers, using theater student Françoise Bornet and her then-boyfriend Jacques Carteaud as models. The photo found new life as an icon of romantic love when a poster company rediscovered it in the '80s.

# The Great Piano Con

*Lauded late in life as a great piano virtuoso, British pianist Joyce Hatto produced the largest collection of recorded piano pieces in the history of music production. But were they hers?*

✳   ✳   ✳   ✳

JOYCE HATTO WAS known as an extraordinary pianist. Her recorded repertoire available in the UK grew to more than 100 CDs and included some of the most difficult piano pieces around. What was truly amazing is that she somehow managed to record this music while suffering the effects of cancer and dealing with the usual wear and tear of an aging body. How did she do it? Perhaps her penchant for plagiarism helped. As it turned out, the majority of her works were stolen from other artists' recordings and then reproduced as her own!

Having enjoyed a full, albeit rather insignificant, career as a concert pianist, Hatto abandoned her stage show in 1976 to focus on her advancing disease. On the cusp of 50, she had only a few recorded numbers under her belt. However, that soon changed, as she spent her remaining years prolifically, but as it turned out, falsely, adding to that collection.

## The CD Deluge Begins

That Hatto's husband, William Barrington-Coupe, ran the Concert Artists Recordings label under which her recordings were released undoubtedly helped to assist in the harmonious heist. His music-business acumen provided both the technological savvy to engineer the pieces that had been previously released by other pianists and the means to unleash the forged works on an unsuspecting public.

Of course, the scam couldn't last forever. Internet rumors began surfacing in 2005, but *Gramophone*, a monthly music magazine in London, wasn't able to definitively break the news of the deception until February 2007, about eight months after Hatto's death. In fact, her death at age 77 may have actually been an impetus for the discovery.

After Hatto's passing, her celebrity fire burned hotter than ever. Beloved by a small fan base during her life, Hatto-mania came out in full force upon her death. Some even deemed her one of the great pianists of modern times. But with that superstar status came a renewed flurry of suspicions surrounding the likelihood of a woman of her age and ailing health being able to produce such a copious collection. *Gramophone* issued a summons for anyone who knew of any fraudulence. Months passed with no evidence, until a reader finally contacted the magazine to reveal his strange findings. As it turned out, this man's computer actually discovered the deceit.

## The Con Revealed

Popping in a purported CD of Hatto hits, the reader's computer identified that a particular ditty was not a work of Hatto but one by little-known pianist Lazlo Simon. The reader immediately contacted *Gramophone* with his discovery. Based on his report, *Gramophone* sent the recordings to a sound engineer, who put music science to the test, comparing sound waves from

Hatto's ostensible recording of Liszt's *Transcendental Studies* to Simon's version. An identical match was uncovered! After that, more and more tested pieces attributed to Hatto were found to belong to other musicians.

Hatto and husband were able to manage the ruse by utilizing music technology to recycle others' recordings and reproduce them as Hatto's own; by that same technology, the deceptive duo was discovered. So, how could the pair not foresee that music science would reveal them, even as they used its wizardry themselves? Barrington-Coupe has not, as of yet, produced a viable answer.

Although he denied any wrongdoing at first, Barrington-Coupe eventually confessed to the fraud, defending his actions by insisting that Hatto knew nothing of the scheme and he had made very little money on it. He further claimed that the whole plot was inspired by nothing more than his love for his ailing wife and his attempt to make her feel appreciated by the music community during her final years. An assertion such as this can neither be proved nor disproved, but *Gramophone* pointed out that Barrington-Coupe continued to sell the false CDs after she had died.

## Hitler's Death, a Hoax?

*Rumors of Hitler's survival persisted for years. The charred corpse was a double; he had offspring; he was living in South America, keeping that old Nazi spirit alive. Some of the wilder tales were fueled by Soviet propaganda.*

✳   ✳   ✳   ✳

THEY WERE FALSE. In 1993 the Russian government opened the old Soviet files. We now know beyond any reasonable doubt what happened. The NKVD (Russian intelligence) investigation began the moment Soviet troops overran the Führerbunker. They exhumed the Hitler and Goebbels bodies, bringing in close acquaintances for positive identification; for example, Eva and Adolf's former dentist and his assistant both recognized their own professional handiwork. The original announcement had been correct: Adolf Hitler had died April 30, 1945. After sending Hitler's jaw back to Moscow for safekeeping, the NKVD secretly reburied the other remains at a military base near Magdeburg, German Democratic Republic (East Germany).

In 1970, the Soviet military prepared to hand over the Magdeburg base to the East Germans. The KGB (successor to the NKVD) dared not leave the Nazi remains. On April 4, 1970, the KGB exhumed the fragmentary remains of Adolf and Eva Hitler and the Goebbels family. Hitler's skull was identified, and the bullet-holed portion was sent to Moscow. The next day, the KGB incinerated the rest of the remains, crushed them to dust and dumped what was left in a nearby river.

Therefore, of Eva Braun and the Goebbels family nothing at all remains. Of Hitler, today only his jaw and a skull fragment exist in Russian custody.

# Leaping Lemmings

*A bit of fraudulent filmmaking and a popular video game have done much to uphold the long-standing misconception that lemmings commit mass suicide.*

✳   ✳   ✳   ✳

THE IMAGE OF lemmings hurtling over cliffs to certain doom is entrenched in our culture to the point where "lemming" has become a metaphor for any sort of collective self-destruction. But, come on: Lemmings don't commit suicide. No animal does, with the exception of human beings. Unlike people, lemmings do not mindlessly follow crowds at their own peril, but they do engage in one behavior en masse, and that is mating.

## Numbers Are Up, Numbers Are Down

These fuzzy Arctic rodents mate only a few weeks after being born and birth litters of as many as 13 pups three weeks after mating. Lemmings can give birth multiple times in one summer, leading to a classic exponential boom in population. Every four years, there is what is known as a "lemming year," when the critters' numbers reach a critical mass that can no longer be sustained by their surroundings. Violence among the animals increases, and they begin to disperse over large distances in search of food.

Contrary to popular belief, they do not move together as one single pack but instead go in all directions, following one another in randomly formed lines. They often end up at riverbanks or cliffs and will enter the water and swim as far as they can in an attempt to reach land or an ice patch. Of course, some end up drowning—but that's purely accidental.

Curiously, "lemming years" are followed by a crash in population numbers, with the next year's crowd dwindling to practically nothing. What happens to all of the lemmings after a boom year? Scientists have settled on increased predation as the explanation. When the lemming population surges, owls, foxes, and seabirds gorge themselves on the rodents, which in turn gives rise to a boom in their own populations. The next summer there are so many more predators that they bring the lemming population down to near extinction. That's where the furious mating comes in handy—in no time, the cycle starts all over again.

## Another Disney-Made Myth

So how did the popular theory about lemming mass suicides come to be? Most sources point to the 1958 Disney movie *White Wilderness*. This film depicts a collection of lemmings scurrying across a cliff until they reach the edge of a precipice overlooking the Arctic Ocean. The lemmings then leap over the cliff to sad and certain oblivion. But a bit of creative license was taken to create this shot—it was filmed in Alberta, Canada, which is landlocked. (Lemmings aren't even native to Canada. All of the creatures used in the film were imported.) In order to give the illusion that the lemmings were migrating in large groups, the filmmakers covered a turntable with snow and put a few lemmings on it, filming as the animals went around and around. To show the lemmings landing in the water, the film-makers herded a group over a riverbank. Once in the water, the little guys had just a short, safe swim to shore.

Those who missed the Disney nature film can witness (and manipulate) a version of a lemming mass suicide in a video game released in 1991. *Lemmings*, one of the most popular video games of all time, has players rescuing lemmings as they follow one another aimlessly off ledges and into a host of treacherous death traps, many involving lava or acid. Suddenly, a plunge into a cool pool of water doesn't look so bad.

# Outrageous Media Hoaxes

*Fair and balanced hasn't always been the mantra of the media. In fact, some newspapers used to pride themselves on the outlandish stories they could come up with. Here are a few of the most outrageous hoaxes in journalism.*

✳ ✳ ✳ ✳

### Man on the Moon

IN 1835, IN one of America's earliest media hoaxes, *The New York Sun* reported that a scientist had seen strange creatures on the moon through a telescope. The story described batlike people who inhabited Earth's neighbor. Readers couldn't get enough of the story, so other publishers scrambled to create their own version. When faced with criticism, *The Sun* defended itself, stating that the story couldn't be proven untrue, but eventually the stories were revealed as hoaxes.

## Hoaxer Ben Franklin

For nearly a decade, Ben Franklin perpetrated a hoax continually claiming that Titan Leeds, the publisher of the main
competitor to Franklin's *Poor Richard's Almanac*, was dead.
This greatly decreased Leeds's circulation, since no one wanted
to read the ramblings of a dead man. Leeds protested, but
year after year, Franklin published annual memorials to his
"deceased" competitor. When Leeds really did pass away,
Franklin praised the man's associates for finally admitting he
was dead.

## Anarchy in London

In 1926, a dozen years before *The War of the Worlds*, the BBC
staged a radio play about an anarchic uprising. The "newscast"
told of riots in the streets that led to the destruction of Big Ben
and government buildings. The population took the play so
seriously that the military was ready to put down the imaginary
rioters. The following day the network apologized and the government assured the public that the BBC would not be allowed
such free range in the future. The British were ridiculed worldwide, especially in the United States, where the public had not
yet been introduced to a young actor named Orson Welles.

## Wild Animals on the Loose in New York City

In 1874, the *New York Herald* published stories detailing
how animals at the city zoo had escaped and were rampaging
through the streets. The mayor ordered all citizens to remain in
their homes while the National Guard grappled with the situation. The problem was that the stories weren't true. In fact, the
final line of the article read, "Of course, the entire story given
above is pure fabrication." Apparently, no one read that far as
the city was thrown into a panic. When the smoke cleared, the
editor wasn't fired . . . he was given a bonus for raising the newspaper's circulation.

## Mr. Hearst's War

Media mogul William Randolph Hearst had no problem with manipulating the truth to sell newspapers. One of his most famous hoaxes was a series of misrepresentations of what was really occurring in Cuba during the lead-up to the Spanish–American War. He sent artist Frederic Remington to the island to capture the atrocities, but the artist found none. "You furnish the pictures, I'll furnish the war," Hearst replied. But Hearst's misuse of pictures was not limited to that event. Consumed with a passion to defeat the communists, he once ordered his editors to run pictures showing an imaginary Russian famine. However, on the same day, they unwittingly published truthful stories about the rich harvest Russia was enjoying.

## Poe's Prank

Though Edgar Allan Poe is best known for his macabre works of fiction, he had his hand in a few works of journalistic fiction as well. One of his best known was a piece that ran in *The New York Sun* in 1844, the same year he wrote his classic poem "The Raven." The article claimed that daring adventurer Monck Mason had crossed the Atlantic in a hot air balloon. Mason had only intended to cross the English Channel but had been blown off course and arrived 75 hours later in South Carolina. When readers investigated the claim, Poe and *The Sun* admitted they had not received confirmation of the story.

## Millard Fillmore's Bathtub Bunk

Everyone seems to know that Millard Fillmore was the first president to have a bathtub installed in the White House. The only problem is, it isn't true. The story, along with a detailed history of the bathtub, was a hoax perpetrated by writer H. L. Mencken when he worked for *The New York Evening Mail*. "The success of this idle hoax, done in time of war, when more serious writing was impossible, vastly astonished me," Mencken wrote. The excitement around his piece and the public's inability to accept the truth affected Mencken, and he began to wonder how much of the rest of history was, in his words, "bunk."

# The Cottingley Fairy Hoax

*It was a story so seemingly real that even the creator of the world's most intelligent literary detective was convinced that it was true.*

✳  ✳  ✳  ✳

## Pixie Party

**I**T WAS SUMMERTIME in the English village of Cottingley in 1917 when cousins Elsie Wright and Frances Griffiths borrowed Elsie's father's new camera. When he later developed the glass plate negatives, he saw a photo of Frances with a group of four tiny, winged fairies. A prank, he figured. Two months later, the girls took another photo. This one showed Elsie with a gnome. At that point, her father banned them from using the camera again.

But a few years later, Wright's wife mentioned her daughter's fairy photos within earshot of theosophist Edward Gardner, who was so taken with them that he showed them to a leading photographic expert. After studying them extensively, this man declared the photos genuine. They caught the attention of spiritual believer Sir Arthur Conan Doyle, author of the Sherlock Holmes series, who published a magazine article announcing the Cottingley fairies to the world.

## A Delusional Doyle

In 1922, Doyle published *The Coming of the Fairies*. The book argued for the existence of fairies and contained the original photos along with three new pictures that Elsie and Frances had produced. Both the article and book ignited a pitched battle between believers and doubters. Many thought Doyle's fertile imagination had finally gotten the better of him.

## Fairy Tale?

As years passed, people remained fascinated by the story. In 1981, Elsie admitted that the whole thing was a hoax taken too far, and that the fairies were actually paper cutouts held up by hatpins. Frances, however, maintained the fairies were authentic even up to her death.

# Bigfoot: The King of All Monsters

*Let's face it—if you had to pick one monster that stands head (and feet) above all others, it would be Bigfoot. Not only is it the stuff of legends, but its likeness has also been used to promote everything from pizza to beef jerky. Bigfoot has even had amusement park rides and monster trucks named after it.*

❋   ❋   ❋   ❋

## Early Sightings

FOLKTALES FROM NATIVE American tribes throughout the Northwest, the area that Bigfoot traditionally calls home, are filled with references to giant, apelike creatures roaming the woods. They described the beast as between seven and ten feet tall and covered in brown or dark hair. (Sasquatch, a common term used for the big-footed beast, is actually an anglicization of a Native American term for a giant supernatural creature.)

Walking on two legs, there was something humanlike about Sasquatch's appearance, although its facial features more closely resembled that of an ape, and it had almost no neck. With looks like that, it's not surprising that Native American folklore often described the creature as cannibalistic, supernatural, and dangerous. Other tales, however, said Sasquatch appeared to be frightened of humans and mostly kept to itself.

It wasn't until the 1900s, when more and more woodlands were being devoured in the name of progress, that Sasquatch sightings started to increase. It was believed that, though generally docile, the beast did have a vicious streak when feeling threatened. In July 1924, Fred Beck and several others were mining in a remote mountainous area of Washington State. One evening, the group spotted and shot at what appeared to be an apelike creature. After fleeing to their cabin, the group was startled when several more hairy giants began banging on the walls, windows, and doors. For several hours, the creatures pummeled the cabin and threw large rocks at it before disappearing shortly before dawn. After several such encounters in the same general vicinity, the area was renamed Ape Canyon.

## My, What Big Feet You Have!

In August 1958, Jerry Crew, a bulldozer operator, showed up for work at a wooded site in Bluff Creek, California. Walking up to his bulldozer, which had been left there overnight, Crew found giant footprints in the dirt. At first, they appeared to be the naked footprints of a man, but with one major difference— these feet were huge! After the tracks appeared on several occasions, Crew took a cast of one of them and brought it to *The Humboldt Times* in Eureka, California. The following day, the newspaper ran a front-page story, complete with photos of the footprint and a name for the creature: Bigfoot. The story and photographs hit the Associated Press, and the name stuck.

Even so, the event is still rife with controversy. Skeptics claim that it was Ray Wallace, not Bigfoot, who made the tracks as a practical joke on his brother Wilbur, who was Crew's supervisor. Apparently the joke backfired when Crew arrived at the site first and saw the prints before Wilbur. However, Ray Wallace never admitted to faking the tracks or having anything to do with perpetrating a hoax.

## Video Evidence?

In 1967, in response to numerous Bigfoot sightings in northern California, Roger Patterson rented a 16mm video camera in hopes of filming the elusive creature. Patterson and his friend, Robert Gimlin, spent several days on horseback traveling though the Six Rivers National Forest without coming across as much as a footprint.

Then, on October 20, the pair rounded a bend and noticed something dark and hairy crouched near the water. When the creature stood up on two legs and presented itself in all its hairy, seven-foot glory, that's when Patterson said he knew for sure he was looking at Bigfoot. Unfortunately, Patterson's horse saw the creature, too, and suddenly reared up. Because of this, it took Patterson several precious seconds to get off the horse and remove the video camera from his saddlebag. Once he did that, he ran toward the creature, filming as he went.

As the creature walked away, Patterson continued filming until his tape ran out. He quickly changed his film, and then both men retrieved their frightened horses and attempted to follow Bigfoot further before eventually losing sight of it.

When they arrived back in town, Patterson reviewed the film. Even though it was less than a minute long and extremely shaky in spots, the film appeared to show Bigfoot running away while occasionally looking toward the camera. For most Bigfoot enthusiasts, the Patterson–Gimlin film stands as the Holy Grail of Bigfoot sightings—physical proof captured on video. Skeptics, however, alleged that Patterson and Gimlin faked the entire incident and filmed a man in an expensive monkey suit. Nevertheless, more than 40 years after the event occurred, the Patterson–Gimlin film is still one of the most talked about pieces of Bigfoot evidence, mainly because neither man ever admitted to a hoax and the fact that no one has been able to figure out how they faked it.

## Gone Sasquatching

The fact that some people doubt the existence of Bigfoot hasn't stopped thousands of people from heading into the woods to try to find one. Even today, the hairy creature makes brief appearances here and there. Of course, websites like YouTube have given rise to dozens of "authentic" videos of Bigfoot, some of which are quite comical.

# Under City Sidewalks

*The myth that albino alligators sightlessly prowl the New York
City sewer system has its roots in an alleged decades-old fad.*

✳    ✳    ✳    ✳

**S**OME SAY VACATIONERS brought the infant gators home
from Florida, while others insist that New York pet shops
enjoyed a thriving trade in such babies (the reptiles sometimes
sold in stores today are actually caimans, crocodilians from
South America). When these gator tots grew too large for
apartment dwelling, they were supposedly dispatched by flush-
ing down the toilet—a trip these hardy creatures survived all
the way down to the sewers, where, it was claimed, they evolved
over the years, adapting to their new environment by becoming
blind and losing their pigmentation. The legend grew legs, as it
were, when an alleged eyewitness—a retired sewer official who
swore he'd seen a colony of the things back in the 1930s—was
quoted in a 1959 book entitled *The World Beneath the City*.
Thomas Pynchon also wrote of them in his 1963 novel *V*.

Reports of regular alligators in New York City might be a little
bit more believable. In 1932, "swarms" of alligators were reportedly spotted in the Bronx River, and on February 10, 1935, the
*New York Times* wrote that several urban teens had pulled a
seven-footer from an open manhole while clearing snow—and
had beaten the beast to death after it snapped at them. The
paper suggested that perhaps the animal had escaped from a
ship "from the mysterious Everglades." Even before this—a full
century earlier in 1831—a little-known paper called *The Planet*
noted a gator sighting in the East River.

However, any herpetologist worth his or her scales will tell
you that it's impossible for the tropical-thriving alligator to get
through a New York City winter, in polluted waters, no less.
One explained that alligators can't digest food when they're
cold. Plus, living without sun destroys their ability to utilize

calcium, which would result in too soft of a skeletal structure for the creature to survive. As one spokesperson for the city's Department of Environmental Protection, who has been denying the rumors for 30 years, wearily sighed: "Sewers simply are not a prime environment for alligators."

But—you're still going to check before you sit down though, right?

# I Know What It's Like to Be Dead: The "Paul Is Dead" Hoax

*Four lads from Liverpool were the biggest thing in pop culture for much of the 1960s. But by the end of the decade, were the Beatles really a trio?*

✳   ✳   ✳   ✳

THEY WERE BIGGER than Elvis . . . they were bigger than Sinatra . . . bigger than life. The Beatles had rewritten the book on stardom and fame, influencing not only the pop music world but also fashion, politics, and religion. Their slightest movements were reported by the media.

## He Blew His Mind Out in a Car

In the fall of 1969, a Detroit radio DJ reported that Paul McCartney, "the cute Beatle," had been killed in a car crash three years earlier and been replaced by a look-alike contest winner named William Campbell. The story, which had been floating around the rumor mill, was propelled by an Eastern Michigan University student writing a review of the Beatles' latest album, Abbey Road. The review claimed that many clues, collected from album covers and song lyrics, proved that McCartney was deceased (although the student admitted in a radio interview that most of his thesis was pure fabrication). Of course, the media had a field day. Radio and TV stations blared the "facts" nightly, and newspapers put their best investigative reporters on the story.

## And, in the End

*Life* magazine devoted the cover story of a November 1969 issue to revealing the truth—McCartney was very much alive. Calling the whole story "bloody stupid," Paul hinted at something more serious—while he was full of life, the Beatles were not—claiming "the Beatle thing is over." No one seemed to pick up on that clue—that the greatest band of the '60s would be DOA within six months.

# The Mysterious Blue Hole

*State Route 269 hides a roadside attraction of dubious depth and mysterious origin, a supposedly bottomless pool of water that locals simply call the "Blue Hole."*

❋ ❋ ❋ ❋

EVERY STATE HAS its tourist traps and bizarre little roadside attractions that are just intriguing enough to pull the car over to see. Back in the day, no roadside attraction brought in more Ohio travelers than a bottomless pond filled with blue water: the mysterious Blue Hole of Castalia.

## The Blue Hole's Origins

The Blue Hole is believed to have formed around 1820, when a dam burst and spilled water into a nearby hole. The ground surrounding Castalia is filled with limestone, which does not absorb groundwater well. The water quickly erodes the limestone, forming cave-ins and sinkholes. It wouldn't be until the late 1870s, however, that most people were made aware of the Blue Hole's existence; the hole was in a very isolated location in the woods. Once the Cold Creek Trout Club opened up nearby, however, its members began taking boat trips out to see the hole, and people all over the area were talking about the mysterious Blue Hole hiding out in Castalia. In 1914, a cave-in resulted in the Blue Hole growing to its current size of almost 75 feet in diameter.

## Stop and See the Mystery

The owners of the property where the Blue Hole is situated began promoting it as a tourist stop beginning in the 1920s. It didn't hurt that the entrance to the Blue Hole property was along State Route 269, the same road that people took to get to Cedar Point amusement park. It is estimated that, at the height of its popularity, close to 165,000 people a year came out to take a peek at the Blue Hole.

The Blue Hole was promoted as being bottomless. Other strange stories were often played up as well, including the fact that the water temperature remained at 48 degrees Fahrenheit year-round. Tour guides would point out that regardless of periods of extreme rainfall or even droughtlike conditions, the Blue Hole's water level remained the same throughout.

## So What's Going On?

Despite all the outlandish claims and theories surrounding the Blue Hole and its mysterious origins, the facts themselves are rather mundane. The Blue Hole is really nothing more than a freshwater pond. It isn't even bottomless. Sure, the bright blue surface of the water does indeed make the hole appear infinitely deep, but in fact, it's really only about 45 feet to the bottom at its deepest parts.

The blue color of the water is from an extremely high concentration of several elements, including lime, iron, and magnesium. That's the main reason there are no fish in the Blue Hole; they just can't survive with all that stuff in the water.

## One Hole or Two?

During the 1990s, the owners of the Blue Hole fell on hard times, forcing them to close the attraction. Families who would show up at the front entrance were forced to stare sadly through a locked gate at the small trail into the woods. That is until several years ago, when the nearby Castalia State Fish Hatchery began clearing land to expand its hatchery. Lo and behold, workers uncovered a second Blue Hole.

Just how this second Blue Hole came to be is still unknown, although the popular belief is that both holes are fed by the same underground water supply. None of that seems to matter to the Blue Hole faithful—they're just thankful to be able to take a gander at a Blue Hole again.

# No "Lightbulb" Moment for Edison

*Although Thomas Alva Edison was one of the most prolific inventors in history, the lightbulb was not one of his brainstorms.*

✳   ✳   ✳   ✳

EDISON REPORTEDLY CONDUCTED more than 3,000 experiments in an attempt to perfect the filament for a lightbulb, but his research was based on the work of diligent inventors before him. Historians cite at least 22 people who had presented various forms of the incandescent lamp prior to Edison. They include Englishman Humphry Davy, who in 1802 demonstrated the world's first incandescent light. In 1835, Scotsman James Lindsay demonstrated a constant electric light, and in 1841, Frederick de Moleyns of England was granted the first patent for an incandescent lamp. In 1845, American John W. Starr acquired a patent for an incandescent bulb that used carbon filaments.

These early inventors were followed by Joseph Wilson Swan, an English physicist who in 1850 demonstrated a workable, though short-lived, vacuum bulb. As Swan turned his attention to producing a better carbon filament, Edison began his own research. In 1879, he successfully demonstrated a carbon filament bulb that lasted 13 hours. When he began commercializing his invention in Great Britain, however, Swan sued him. Eventually, their two companies merged, as Ediswan. In America, Edison lost his patent in 1883 when the U.S. Patent Office ruled that his work was based on the prior research of inventor William Sawyer. After a number of court hearings, that ruling was overturned in 1889.

# Franklin Flies a Kite

*As it turns out, Benjamin Franklin did not discover electricity. What's more, the kite he famously flew in 1752 while conducting an experiment was not struck by lightning. If it had been, Franklin would be remembered as a colonial publisher and assemblyman killed by his own curiosity.*

✳ ✳ ✳ ✳

## Before Ben

B LESSED WITH ONE of the keenest minds in history, Benjamin Franklin was a scientific genius who made groundbreaking discoveries in the basic nature and properties of electricity. Electrical science, however, dates to 1600, when Dr. William Gilbert, physician to Queen Elizabeth, published a treatise about his research on electricity and magnetism. European inventors who later expanded on Gilbert's knowledge included Otto von Guericke of Germany, Charles Francois Du Fay of France, and Stephen Gray of England.

## The Science of Electricity

Franklin became fascinated with electricity after seeing a demonstration by showman/doctor Archibald Spencer in Boston in 1743. Two years later, he bought a Leyden jar—a contraption invented by a Dutch scientist that used a glass container wrapped in foil to create a crude battery. Other researchers had demonstrated the properties of the device, and Franklin set about to increase its capacity to generate electricity while testing his own scientific hypotheses. Among the principles he established was the conservation of charge, one of the most important laws of physics. In a paper published in 1750, he announced the discovery of the induced charge and broadly outlined the existence of the electron. His experiments led him to coin many of the terms currently used in the science of electricity, such as battery, conductor, condenser, charge, discharge, uncharged, negative, minus, plus, electric shock, and electrician.

As Franklin came to understand the nature of electricity, he began to theorize about the electrical nature of lightning. In 1751, he outlined in a British scientific journal his idea for an experiment that involved placing a long metal rod on a high tower or steeple to draw an electric charge from passing thunder clouds, which would throw off visible electric sparks. A year later, French scientist Georges-Louis Leclerc successfully conducted such an experiment.

## The Kite Runner

Franklin had not heard of Leclerc's success when he undertook his own experiment in June 1752. Instead of a church spire, he affixed his kite to a sharp, pointed wire. To the end of his kite string he tied a key, and to the key a ribbon made of silk (for insulation). While flying his kite on a cloudy day as a thunderstorm approached, Franklin noticed that loose threads on the kite string stood erect, as if they had been suspended from a common conductor. The key sparked when he touched it, showing it was charged with electricity. But had the kite actually been struck by lightning, Franklin would likely have been killed, as was Professor Georg Wilhelm Richmann of St. Petersburg, Russia, when he attempted the same experiment a few months later.

## The Lightning Rod

Although Franklin did not discover electricity, he did uncover many of its fundamental principles and proved that lightning is, in fact, electricity. He used his knowledge to create the lightning rod, an invention that today protects structures and ships at sea. He never patented the lightning rod but instead generously promoted it as a boon to humankind. In 21st-century classrooms, the lightning rod is still cited as a classic example of the way fundamental science can produce practical inventions.

# Big Signature. Big Talk. Tall Tale?

*As he put his oversize signature on the Declaration of Independence, did John Hancock really do some big talking to fire up the document's other signers?*

✳   ✳   ✳   ✳

TAKE A LOOK at the Declaration of Independence—specifically, the 56 signatures affixed on the document that formally kicked off the American Revolution. You'll notice that one name stands out from the rest. It's written in large, flamboyant script in the center of the page directly below the main body of text.

That signature, of course, belongs to John Hancock, and it is the most readily recognized autograph on one of the most revered pieces of paper in American history. Hancock's inscription is so well known that his name has become synonymous with the word signature, as in "put your John Hancock on the dotted line."

John Hancock's John Hancock is big, bold, and symbolic of the stout defiance of America's founders toward England's tyrannical King George III. Adding to the aura of Hancock's in-your-face signature was the verbal extemporizing that history says he used to impress his fellow signers. Some accounts say that Hancock brashly stated, "There, I guess King George will be able to read that!"

Hancock's audacious declaration is indeed rousing—too bad he never actually made it. Hancock was the first to sign the Declaration of Independence and, aside from a colleague named Charles Thomson, no one was around when he did (the other signatories didn't begin signing the document until August 1776). Thomson never attributed any such statement to Hancock, and unless Hancock was in the habit of making loud, bold assertions to himself, he very likely signed the document in silence.

# Based on a True Fake

*When movies try to depict fact, it's almost inevitable that a little bit (or a lot) of fiction will get in the way.*

\* \* \* \*

THE PROBLEM WITH movies that claim to be based on a true story is not the definition of true—it's the definition of based on. Movies tend to take some parts of a particular event or story and focus on them—thereby exaggerating their importance and relevance—while ignoring other circumstances completely. Here are a few examples.

### A Beautiful Mind

John Nash is a mathematician whose work in game theory earned him a 1994 Nobel Prize in Economics. He attended Princeton University and worked on his equilibrium theory. After earning a doctorate in 1950, he continued to work on his thesis, part of which became the Nash Equilibrium. In 1951, he was hired as a member of the MIT mathematics faculty. In 1957, he married Alicia Lopez-Harrison de Lardé, and shortly after that, he was admitted to a mental hospital for schizophrenia. The couple had a son in 1959 but divorced in 1963. They became friendly again in 1970, renewed their romantic relationship in 1994, and remarried in 2001.

But in the movie *A Beautiful Mind*, Nash is plagued by schizophrenia throughout his education at Princeton. He struggles to maintain relationships with his classmates but flourishes as he discovers various mathematical theories. He is also asked by the government to decode covert Soviet messages. He gets married and has a son but is slowly eaten up by his schizophrenia until he's hospitalized. Through the love of his wife and his own strength of will, however, he becomes an award-winning recluse who is happily accepted within the hallowed halls of higher education.

One catch is that Nash's true-life delusions were auditory, not visual. Also, while the movie portrayed John and Alicia's marriage as a tense one, it also portrayed it as continuous. There are at least two more important changes the movie made to Nash's life: The pen ceremony at Princeton never really happened, and Nash never gave a rousing yet humble speech when he received his Nobel Prize.

## Catch Me If You Can

Frank Abagnale was a con artist who passed bad checks during five years in the 1960s. He impersonated a pilot, a physician, an attorney, and a teacher. Once captured, Abagnale had the dubious distinction of having 26 countries with extradition orders against him. After serving in prison for his crimes, he founded Abagnale & Associates, a legitimate company that advises businesses on fraud.

In the movie, a lonely only child deals with his wacky dad and nervous mom, but in no time, he's on his way to New York, alone and fending for himself. This is where the story takes off into fraud and impersonations, with an FBI agent chasing Abagnale around the globe. In reality, no FBI agent chased Abagnale down. *Catch Me If You Can* follows Abagnale's life, which already seems pretty exaggerated, and exaggerates it even more. In the movie, Abagnale writes $10 million in bad checks; in reality the total was only $2.5 million. And Abagnale was never on the FBI's Ten Most Wanted list.

## Finding Neverland

Scottish novelist and dramatist J. M. Barrie created Peter Pan. Barrie's traumatic childhood included the death of his brother and the withdrawal of his mother, crushed by her son's death. As an adult, Barrie moved to London, where he became a journalist, then a novelist, then a playwright. He became friends with the Llewelyn Davies family, who provided the inspiration for his fictional work. Eventually, after the deaths of the boys' parents, Barrie ended up providing support for the sons of the family. Barrie died of pneumonia on June 19, 1937.

In the movie *Finding Neverland*, we're treated to the moment when Barrie meets and befriends the Llewelyn Davies children and their mother. The movie then weaves the lives of Barrie and the family together. It's a sweet story but it's only a sliver of the real events.

The real Barrie had many literary friends, famous ones at that, and a prolific outpouring of books and plays. When the real Barrie initially met and befriended the Llewelyn Davies children, their father was alive; in the movie, he's already dead. In the film, there are four children; in reality, there were five. Most importantly, Barrie suffered from psychogenic dwarfism—he was 4'0" tall. In the film, Barrie is played by Johnny Depp, who is significantly taller than that.

# Satanic Marketing

*What's behind the vicious rumor that put mega-corporation Procter & Gamble on many churches' hit lists?*

✳    ✳    ✳    ✳

PROCTER & GAMBLE, one of the largest corporations in the world, manufactures a plethora of products that range from pet food to potato chips. The company takes pride in its reputation as a business that can be trusted, so it came as a huge shock when, starting in the 1960s, Christian churches and individuals around the country spread the rumor that P&G was dedicated to the service of Satan.

## The Devil Is in the Details

How the rumor got started remains a mystery. According to one of the most popular versions of the story, the president of P&G appeared on *The Phil Donahue Show* in March 1994 and announced that, because of society's new openness, he finally felt comfortable revealing that he was a member of the Church of Satan and that much of his company's profits went toward the advancement of that organization. When Donahue supposedly asked him whether such an announcement would have a negative impact on P&G, the CEO replied, "There aren't enough Christians in the United States to make a difference."

There's one problem with this story—and with the variations that place the company president on *The Sally Jessy Raphael Show*, *The Merv Griffin Show*, and *60 Minutes*: It didn't happen.

## Lose the Logo

Adding fuel to the fable was the company's logo, which featured the image of a "man in the moon" and 13 stars. Many interpreted this rather innocuous design to be Satanic, and some even claimed that the curlicues in the man's beard looked like the number 666—the biblical "mark of the Beast" referred to in the Book of Revelation. By 1985, the company had become so frustrated by the allegations that it had no choice but to retire the logo, which had graced P&G products for more than 100 years.

## Speaking Out

Procter & Gamble did all it could to quell the rumors, which resulted in more than 200,000 phone calls and letters from concerned consumers. Company spokespeople vehemently denied the story, explaining in a press release: "The president of P&G has never discussed Satanism on any national televised talk show, nor has any other P&G executive. The moon-and-stars trademark dates back to the mid-1800s, when the "man in the moon" was simply a popular design. The 13 stars in the design honor the original 13 colonies."

In addition, the company turned to several prominent religious leaders, including evangelist Billy Graham, to help clear its name, and when that didn't work, it even sued a handful of clergy members who continued to spread the offending story.

Talk show host Sally Jessy Raphael also denied the allegations, noting, "The rumors going around that the president of Procter & Gamble appeared on [my] show and announced he was a member of the Church of Satan are not true. The president of Procter & Gamble has never appeared on *The Sally Jessy Raphael Show*."

### Senseless Allegations

Of course, like most urban legends, this story falls apart under scrutiny. Foremost, one must ask why the CEO of an international conglomerate (especially one that must answer to stockholders) would risk decades of consumer goodwill—not to mention billions of dollars in sales—to announce to the world that his company was run by Satanists. And even if that were the case, he needn't bother announcing it, since any deals made with the devil would be a matter of public record.

In 2007, a jury awarded Procter & Gamble $19.25 million in a civil lawsuit filed against four former Amway distributors accused of spreading false rumors about the company's ties to the Church of Satan. The distributors were found guilty of using a voicemail system to inform customers that P&G's profits were used to support Satanic cults.

# Everything Ventured, Nothing Gained (Yet)

*Some people consider Oak Island, a small island off the coast of Nova Scotia, Canada, the repository of one of the world's most fantastic treasures. Others, however, think that it's a natural monument to the gullibility of man.*

✳    ✳    ✳    ✳

### Stay Away

IT'S ONLY A short boat ride across the channel (and an even shorter walk across the causeway) between the Nova Scotia mainland and Oak Island. Aside from the oak trees that give the island its name, there's little to distinguish the 140-acre island from the nearly 400 others that dot Mahone Bay. Nevertheless, boats are not permitted to land here, and the causeway is fenced off with a "No Trespassing" sign.

If the casual visitor could set foot on the island, however, they would find its surface permeated by hundreds of mine shafts. Thanks to plenty of folklore and gossip, for over two centuries Oak Island has been the focus of spectacular digging operations, with excavators using everything from pick and spade to modern industrial boring equipment. To date, these exertions have consumed millions of dollars.

## Why All the Fuss?

Depending on the source (and there are many), Oak Island is the final resting place of any number of precious objects, including:

✳ Captain Kidd's pirate treasure

✳ Manuscripts proving that Sir Francis Bacon wrote Shakespeare's plays

✳ South American gold

✳ Marie Antoinette's jewels

✳ The Holy Grail

✳ The accumulated wealth of the Knights Templar and/or the Freemasons

## The Legend Begins

As the story goes, in 1795 a boy named Daniel McGinnis ventured onto the island and gleaned from marks on a tree that rope and tackle had been used to lower something into the ground. The next day, he returned with two companions and initiated the first attempt to recover treasure from what has since become known as the Money Pit—a vertical shaft that by 1897 had already been excavated by a series of individuals and companies. Depths ran to 111 feet with core samples drilled to over 170 feet deep.

## The Problem

Flooding in the shafts, which many believe to be caused by special tunnels built as booby traps to foil treasure seekers, has always thwarted digging operations on Oak Island. Attempts to block these subterranean channels have been unsuccessful and have only revealed that the water from the shafts flows outward to the sea at various locations.

Despite the difficulties, treasure seekers continue to labor on Oak Island because the Money Pit, its auxiliary shafts, and the various features on the island's surface have yielded tantalizing indications that something of value lies beneath. Among the evidence: a stone inscribed with strange markings, a primitive pair of scissors, large amounts of coconut husk, and a piece of sheepskin parchment bearing what appeared to be an inscribed Roman numeral.

## The Skeptics Have Their Say

Naysayers take plenty of issue with Oak Island's supposed treasure. They point out that while it may be likely that at one time pirates or even Freemasons landed on the island, that doesn't necessarily spell buried treasure. And there's nothing weird about sinkholes and subterranean chambers in limestone, they say. In fact, they're all over the region.

Moreover, skeptics note the lack of evidence of any digging on the island before the 1840s. They figure it's much more likely that a story about someone discovering a treasure cave got a few people excited. Legend built upon legend until, like the island itself, the story was muddied and mixed-up by the passage of time. Either way, perhaps Oak Island's greatest treasure is simply the human imagination.

# Chapter 12

# The Bible

## One God or Many?

*Every true Christian, Jew, and Muslim will insist that there is and has always been only one God. Many believe that this certainty goes back at least as far as Abraham and that, since then, only "pagans" have ever believed in more than one god. But the Bible actually says otherwise.*

✳ ✳ ✳ ✳

MONOTHEISM, OR BELIEF in one God, came slowly, in halting stages. Formal worship of the deity known as Yahweh probably started when the patriarch Abraham took Yahweh as his personal God upon moving to Canaan from Mesopotamia. But even though Abraham chose Yahweh as the chief deity of his clan, he probably believed that other gods existed. We know for sure that Laban, Abraham's close relative, had idols in his house because Laban's daughter Rachel stole them when she left home with her husband, Jacob (Genesis 31:19).

Some scholars hold that Moses, not Abraham, initiated the practice of worshipping only one god. As we read in Exodus, God appeared to Moses in a burning bush, commissioned him to free his people (the Israelites) from slavery in Egypt, and revealed his name as Yahweh. Moses soon succeeded in freeing his people with the help of Yahweh, who parted the waters of the Red Sea to let them escape the Egyptians. Moses then made a pact, or covenant, with Yahweh at Mount

Sinai. In return for following certain laws (notably, the Ten Commandments), Yahweh would give the Israelites both land and protection.

## First Commandment

In the very first commandment, God tells Moses that he shall have no other gods (Exodus 20:2–3). But the commandment does not explicitly claim that Yahweh is the *only* god; nor does it say that anyone would be a fool to worship other gods because they do not exist. On the contrary, even though the first commandment forbids the Israelites to worship them, it seems to accept the fact that there are other gods (or at least the fact that people will continue to believe that they exist).

As the God who freed them from slavery in Egypt, Yahweh demands that the Israelites worship him and him alone. Ironically, even while Moses is in the act of receiving this commandment, his people are breaking it by worshipping a calf made of gold.

Forty years later, as the Israelites are preparing to enter Canaan (the land God promised them), Moses begs his people to stay away from the Canaanites, who will lure them away from Yahweh and into idol worship. If they want Yahweh to support them in their new land, the Israelites must worship Yahweh alone. But the people ignore Moses' warnings, and in their new land they engage in a cycle of worshipping Yahweh, turning to other gods and goddesses, and returning to Yahweh when in trouble (Judges 2:11–22).

## Influence of Kings

When David established the kingdom of Israel, he vigorously promoted the exclusive worship of Yahweh. But Solomon, David's son, grew lax in his old age and personally built shrines to foreign deities himself. He also married many foreign women, who introduced the cults of their own deities into Jerusalem (1 Kings 11:5–8).

In the divided kingdom, after Solomon's time, most of the people worshipped both Yahweh and other deities. In the southern kingdom of Judah, the kings, who were descendants of David, continued to promote the worship of Yahweh for the most part, but many of the kings of the northern kingdom of Israel let idolatry spread everywhere.

## Yahweh Alone!

Several prophets rode herd, lambasting the people for idolatry and reminding them of the covenant they had with Yahweh. One of the first and most vigorous of these prophets was Elijah, who strove hard to abolish idolatry, taking especial aim at the cult of the god Baal, which was strongly promoted by Jezebel, the Phoenician wife of Israel's King Ahab. Some scholars believe that Elijah headed a small but enthusiastic Yahweh-alone movement that strenuously promoted the worship of Yahweh and only Yahweh. This group may even have been made up of the sons of the prophets—a kind of prophets' guild headed by Elijah that appears in 2 Kings. The Yahweh-alone movement continued with renewed force under Elijah's successor, Elisha, and may even have used terrorist activities to purify the religion of Israel. According to the Bible, God told Elijah to anoint Jehu as the next king of Israel and predicted that Jehu would overthrow the Ahab dynasty and kill all the Baal worshippers. Furthermore, whoever wasn't killed by Jehu would be killed by Elisha (1 Kings 19:17).

## Hosea and Jeremiah

The situation did not improve. Both the kings and the people kept violating the first commandment and even practiced child sacrifice (Jeremiah 19:13).

The prophets Isaiah and Jeremiah preached against these violations, holding that it was foolish to worship human-made idols that had eyes that could not see and ears that could not hear and had no power to save anyone. Jeremiah also warned the Israelites that the Babylonians would conquer Jerusalem if they did not turn back to Yahweh and ask his help. But no one listened, and the Babylonians did destroy Jerusalem and take most of its people to Babylon as exiles.

## At Last the Truth

In exile, some Jews believed that Jerusalem fell because Marduk, the Babylonian god, was more powerful than Yahweh. However, the prophets managed to convince most of them that Yahweh had simply used the Babylonians to punish his people for neglecting his worship. Isaiah then took the final step in establishing monotheism. He told his people that not only was Yahweh a powerful God who would continue to care for them once they returned home to the land he had given them, but that he is the only real God. Isaiah became the first to reveal that there is, in fact, only one God (Isaiah 45:14, 22).

After the return home from exile in Babylon, the Jews rebuilt Jerusalem. As the Bible does not report that Ezra and his followers were compelled to inveigh against the worship of idols, the Jews had probably come to fully accept the strict monotheism that all Jews, Christians, and Muslims hold dear today.

# Ezekiel's Wheel: What in the World? Vision? UFO?

*This scriptural passage is responsible for some of the most interesting speculation in the Bible's history. What was it that Ezekiel saw?*

✳   ✳   ✳   ✳

## Scriptural Description

GOING TO THE source (Ezekiel 1), first the prophet describes some extremely strange living creatures in a fiery cloud: humanoids with four faces (human, eagle, ox, lion), four wings, bronze bodies, surrounding something like fiery coals. He then relays that each creature is accompanied by a wheel. The wheels appear to be made of beryl, with each wheel having another wheel inside it. The rims of the outer wheels are full of living eyes. The wheels follow the creatures wherever they go.

Any lesser person than an Old Testament prophet of God might take a few aspirin and swear off hard liquor for life.

## Otherworldly Interpretations

Plenty of artists have tried to depict Ezekiel's wheel. Most efforts look like gyroscopes: two shining circles intersecting. Picture a globe with a steel-blue ring around the equator. Imagine another metallic ring at a right angle to the first, passing through the North and South Poles. Subtract the globe. Could this be an ancient spaceship? All we have going for us is our science-fiction ideas of alien spacecraft. Some very educated minds suggest that Ezekiel is indeed describing a credible alien spaceship. We can't prove either way.

One book that fueled much of the speculation was Erich von Däniken's *Chariots of the Gods*. Von Däniken's thesis—that many ancient writings about gods, including the Bible, refer to contact with aliens—is unacceptable to most believers. Therefore, his thesis hasn't gained lasting traction with Jews and Christians. Nevertheless, some suspect that, with regard to Ezekiel 1, von Däniken had gotten hold of a grain of the truth.

## Non-SF Views

Since we can only speculate, let's do so: The simplest explanation might be an angelic vision of the Lord's might. Ezekiel seems to have thought so (see Ezekiel 10) when he reflected on the matter. Perhaps the four forms represent archangels. They could also represent the four Gospels, identifying Matthew with the lion, Mark with the ox, Luke with the man, and John with the eagle.

Considering that Ezekiel's vision came from God, one might consider the rims full of eyes to mean that God sees everything in all directions. One supposes that Ezekiel, as a believer, wouldn't normally need a reminder of this—but perhaps the

Lord felt he did, or he wanted to dramatize it. That veers into trying to guess God's motives, which is problematic for the human mind.

One mainstream Jewish view, according to rabbinic wisdom and analysis, is that Ezekiel saw a heavenly chariot/throne bearing *Hashem* (God). It represented a vision of the Lord, a symbol of his ultimate generosity in showing his glory to his people. Given the location—near Babylon (modern Iraq)—it could foretell the equipment the region's main product (oil) would fuel someday.

We don't know. We can, however, compare the theories of the learned (and the imaginative) and determine for ourselves with the minds God gave us.

# Did the Ark of the Covenant Break God's Law?

*Fanciful winged figures, known as cherubim, were carved into the lid of the Ark of the Covenant. But the commandments seem to outlaw such images. Did the chest that contained God's commandments break one of them?*

✳   ✳   ✳   ✳

ON MOUNT SINAI, God instructed Moses to construct a chest, or ark, to hold the tablets of the Ten Commandments and to fashion its lid with two cherubim facing each other. The lid would represent God's throne, and the chest itself, God's footstool (Exodus 25:10–22). Now the second commandment (part of the first for Jews and Catholics) forbids making images of living things. What's going on here?

It seems the commandment originally applied only to idols, and because the cherubim were servants of God, their depiction was legitimate. As idolatry increased, however, religious leaders narrowed the prohibition against images. Trouble began as soon as Moses came down from Mount Sinai carrying the law tablets and erupted when he found people worshipping a calf made from melted gold.

The cherubim were positioned above the Ark, and later in Solomon's temple, two cherubs were placed over the Ark in the Holy of Holies, though they were not seen by the public. Still, the creation of idols continued to increase, compelling the prophets to preach against it.

## More Calves

Things reached a climax after Solomon's death, when his kingdom split in two and the king of the northern kingdom of Israel built shrines—adorned with golden calves—to serve as footstools for God. Unfortunately, these calves reminded the priests in Jerusalem, in the southern kingdom of Judah, of the idols of Moses' time. Although the calves followed the idea of the cherubim over the Ark, the priests of Jerusalem were outraged, calling the calves idols, and from then on the commandment against making any images of living things was strictly enforced. No more cherubim.

# Who Was the Queen of Heaven?

*Many Christians, particularly Catholics, believe that Mary, the mother of Jesus, is the queen of heaven. But as far as the Bible is concerned, she's not. Even though Christians later gave Mary this title, the Bible never refers to her as queen of anything. The only biblical queen of heaven is a Canaanite goddess.*

✳ ✳ ✳ ✳

THE QUEEN OF heaven appears in the Bible only as an object of scorn (in Jeremiah 7:18 and 44:17–25). Throughout his career, the prophet Jeremiah preached against idolatry, trying to drum it into his people's heads that if they continued to worship idols God would punish them and they would lose their land and go into exile. Unfortunately, Jeremiah's preaching was rarely effective, and idol worship flourished in Israel. In particular, women favored one special deity, the so-called queen of heaven, and they involved their entire families in her worship. In Jeremiah 7:17–18, God angrily points out these families and explains their idolatry in detail to Jeremiah.

## So Who Was She?

Although she is never named, the queen of heaven was probably Astarte, the Canaanite equivalent of Ishtar, the Assyrian-Babylonian goddess of the planet Venus. Ishtar was a fertility goddess who also oversaw childbirth. She was especially popular among women because sacrifices to her were said to assure safe and healthy children and her cult gave women a role in worship that they did not have at the Jerusalem temple. Offerings to the queen of heaven included wine and star-shaped or crescent-shaped cakes and figurines bearing the image of the goddess.

After Jeremiah had preached himself blue in the face against the worship of the queen of heaven, women seemed to have given it up, though this may not have been in response to the prophet. The cult may have been suppressed as part of King Josiah's religious reforms of 622 BC. Whatever the reason, we hear nothing about the queen of heaven for a while.

## Exile and Renewed Idolatry

After Josiah's death, the people of Israel again began worshipping various foreign idols and otherwise offending their one true God, Yahweh. In 586 BC, the Babylonians invaded and destroyed Jerusalem and sent most of the people of Israel to Babylon as exiles. However, Jeremiah and some other Jews avoided capture and relocated to Egypt for safety.

In Egypt, much to Jeremiah's horror, his people revived the cult of the queen of heaven. When Jeremiah again preached against the cult, the guilty parties defended themselves by claiming that it is because they had stopped worshipping the queen of heaven that Jerusalem had been destroyed and they were in exile (Jeremiah 44:15–28). As long as they had worshipped this goddess in Judah, they told Jeremiah, they had prospered and suffered no evil. In short, the Jews in Egypt truly believed that the queen of heaven had given them all they had, not Yahweh—the only God and Israel's true God and sole benefactor. With no way of countering this argument, Jeremiah simply tried to convince his people that things were actually the other way round. The queen of heaven did not punish them for terminating her worship in Judah. Yahweh punished them for worshipping the powerless queen of heaven.

### Ending with a Twist

Jeremiah probably died in exile in Egypt, agonizing over his failure to stop the people's idolatry, for he did fail. Not only did the cult of the queen of heaven survive him in Egypt, but it seems to have continued well into the Christian era. However, it is possible that leaders of the early Syrian church transformed the cult of the queen of heaven into veneration of Jesus' mother Mary. If this is so, we do have a connection with Mary after all. By diverting believers away from a false goddess, the Syrians may have initiated devotion to Jesus' mother.

# Original Raiders of the Not-Yet Lost Ark

*Harrison Ford wasn't the first to have adventures as a result of the Ark of the Covenant (the chest containing the Ten Commandments). During their 40 years in the wilderness, the Israelites carried it with them wherever they went—and one man even dropped dead from touching it. They also took it into battle to assure God's protection—but it was captured by the enemy!*

✳   ✳   ✳   ✳

AFTER MOSES RECEIVED the stone tablets inscribed with the Ten Commandments, he had skilled craftsmen build an elaborate chest in which to keep them. In the Bible, this chest is variously called the Ark of the Covenant, the Ark of God (or Yahweh), the Ark of Testimony, or simply the Ark. It is a chest that measured just over four feet long and a little under three feet wide and high. The chest had a solid gold lid over which were carvings of two cherubim that faced each other with their wings extended forward and meeting at the center of the Ark. Four rings attached to the sides of the chest accommodated two poles (made of gold-plated acacia wood like the chest). The poles were used for carrying the Ark. However, the Ark was considered sacred and could only be handled by priests or by Levites (other men of the priestly clan).

## The Presence of God

The Israelites took the Ark with them everywhere they went during their 40 years in the wilderness, carrying it in procession as the people moved from one location to another. For them it represented the presence of God himself, and the tablets of the law inside the Ark represented the covenant, or contract, that the Israelites had made with God. He would protect them and bring them into their own land in return for their undivided allegiance and their obedience to the laws enclosed in the Ark.

When the Israelites were in camp, they kept the Ark in a special tent, known as the tabernacle, and it was to that tent that Moses went to consult God, who spoke to him from between the gold cherubim that hovered over the Ark.

Although the Israelites by no means believed that God was physically contained within the Ark or its tent, they saw the chest as a representation of his presence among them, a symbol of his protection. In some fanciful way, they also envisioned the Ark as the footstool used by God as he sits enthroned in the heavens. As the Israelites moved toward the land that God had promised them, they marched behind the Ark itself, which was carried by Levites.

## Crossing Jordan

When the Israelites reached the Jordan River after 40 years in the wilderness, the Ark played a significant role. The priests led a grand procession, reverently carrying the Ark of the Covenant, and the people followed at a respectful distance. As the priests waded into the river, Joshua, following Yahweh's instructions, had them stand still. The powerful presence of God in the Ark caused the flow of the river to stop, and all the people of Israel crossed the river as though the river bottom were dry land (Joshua 3:17)—just as their parents and grandparents had passed through the Red Sea 40 years earlier. This clearly shows that God is with Joshua and with his people.

Once safely across the Jordan and in the Promised Land, the Israelites continued to carry the Ark when they went to war to oust the resident Canaanites. In their very first battle, the Ark played a significant role. During the siege of the city of Jericho, the Israelites paraded around the city walls for seven days, shouting and blowing trumpets. But the most significant part of the parade was the Ark of the Covenant, which was carried behind the priests who were blowing the trumpets (ram's horns). The Israelites never raised a weapon, and even though they blew trumpets and shouted, the mere noise was not enough to bring them victory. It was God, whose presence was proudly represented in the Ark, who caused the walls to come tumbling down. From that time on, the Israelites never went into battle without the Ark—or almost never.

## The Ark Narrative

Even after the Israelites had taken possession of their land, they had to fight off troublesome neighbors, particularly the Philistines, who had settled along the Mediterranean coast. During one battle with the Philistines, the Israelites failed to carry the Ark with them and they lost, suffering 4,000 casualties. Resolved to correct their grievous error, they again fought the Philistines, but this time they decided to carry the Ark with them. When the Ark was brought into the Israelite camp, the soldiers began shouting so loudly the earth shook (1 Samuel 4:5). When the Philistines heard the noise of the shouting, they began to express fear of this "god" (the Ark) and recalled how Yahweh had saved the Israelites in Egypt. Despite their fear, the Philistines fought hard and won the battle, killing 30,000 Israelite foot soldiers and capturing the Ark.

The Israelites were stunned. They felt that God had deserted them. Meanwhile, in the city of Ashdod, the Philistines placed the Ark of the Covenant in their temple beside a statue of their own god, Dagon, contemptuously offering this weak foreign god of the Israelites (as they saw the Ark) to their own more powerful god. However, when the Philistines returned to their temple in the morning, they found the Dagon idol lying face down before the Ark, assuming a penitential posture. They were shocked but tried to reason it away. Then, on another morning, they found their precious idol with its hands and head cut off. Later, the Philistines were stricken with boils that were attributed to the Ark.

Totally terrified, the Philistines realized that Yahweh wielded great power and that no one should mess with his Ark. They frantically looked for a way of returning the Ark safely. Finally, they packed the Ark into a cart, together with many rich peace offerings to placate Yahweh. Then they put the cart on a road and yoked it to two milk cows, hoping that the cows would pull the cart to the Israelites.

And indeed they did, lowing all the way. In a kind of reenactment of the Exodus, the Ark returned home. In this story, commonly known as the Ark Narrative (1 Samuel 4–6), God at first seemed powerless (enduring capture and mockery) but was soon shown as powerful again. After being defeated, Yahweh rose again much as Jesus would do later.

## What Happened to the Ark?

The Ark continued to be kept in its tent. When King David decided to bring it into Jerusalem, the Ark tipped over during transport and Uzzah, one of the oxcart drivers, reached up to steady it. But when he touched the sacred Ark, he was instantly struck dead. David was then afraid to bring the Ark into the city, and so he left it in the care of a man from Gath named Obed-edom. When David later discovered that Obed-edom and his entire family had been blessed because of the Ark, he decided to bring the Ark into the city after all, and he did so amid great rejoicing. When Solomon built his temple, he placed the Ark in its innermost room, known as the Holy of Holies, where only the high priest could enter.

Sometime just before the Babylonians destroyed the temple in 586 BC, the Ark disappeared—no one knows where. After the Babylonian Exile, the Holy of Holies remained empty. According to one early tradition, the prophet Jeremiah hid the Ark as the Babylonians were advancing on Jerusalem, meaning to rescue it at a later time. However, Jeremiah was soon taken off to Egypt (against his will) and never had the opportunity to let anyone in charge know where the Ark was hidden. According to the book of Revelation, however, the Ark of the Covenant will be seen again in the temple of the New Jerusalem at the end of time.

# Biblical Dragons (or Sea Serpents)

*Who says that there were never any dragons? The Bible talks about them, so they must have existed. In fact, the Bible gives two different names to dragons, or sea serpents: Leviathan, which means "twisting one," and Rahab, which means "boisterous one." There's also that dragon in the book of Revelation.*

✳ ✳ ✳ ✳

WHEN GOD CREATED the universe, he did not start from nothing but brought order out of a watery chaos

(Genesis 1:1–2). According to myths from Babylon and the Canaanite city of Ugarit, before creating the universe we know today, it was necessary to destroy a seven-headed dragon that represented chaos. Although there is no mention of this dragon in Genesis, Psalm 74, in addressing Yahweh, reminds him that at the Creation, he divided the sea, broke the heads of dragons, and crushed the heads of Leviathan (Psalm 74:13–14). The dragon, or sea serpent, Leviathan, is a monster from the past, present, and yet to come.

## Primeval Dragon of Chaos

The book of Job has the most to say about the primeval dragon of chaos. In responding to Job, God appears in a whirlwind and reminds him that he is insignificant in comparison with himself, the Almighty. Job was certainly not present at the Creation, when Yahweh formed all that is. It is God, not Job, who is all-powerful, the one who stilled the sea, the one who struck down Rahab (Job 26:12).

God gives some physical details about this beast, telling Job that it has a double coat of mail and its back is made of a row of shields. Most dragonlike of all are the flaming torches and sparks of fire that leap out of its mouth. Smoke pours out of its nose and its breath will start coals on fire (Job 41:19–21). No humanmade weapon can harm it. And finally, it can make the sea boil like a pot (Job 41:31).

God asks Job if he thinks he can capture such a monster. God further mocks and derides Job by asking him if he thinks he can play with it like a bird or put it on a leash (Job 41:5). This is probably a reference to Psalm 104, in which God seems to regard Leviathan as a kind of personal plaything.

## Dragons of Biblical Times

While Leviathan/Rahab does not appear in the historical accounts of the Israelites, the beast is sometimes summoned as a metaphor for Israel's enemies. Rahab is used as a name for Egypt in Isaiah 30:7, and the pharaoh is called a great dragon in Ezekiel 29:3–5 and 32:2–8. Jeremiah and Habakkuk also refer to the Babylonians as dragons and monsters. In the additions to the book of Daniel (part of the Protestant apocrypha but included in the Catholic Bible as chapter 14 of Daniel), the king of Babylon tells the prophet Daniel that a great dragon in the land (a giant reptile?) is an immortal god. With the king's permission, however, Daniel feeds the beast a mixture of pitch, fat, and hair boiled together. After consuming the mixture, the dragon bursts open, showing that it was no god after all.

### Dragons Yet to Come

As it was in the beginning, so will it be at the end of time, for the battle against Leviathan will be fought again: On that day, God is supposed to punish Leviathan with a mighty sword and also kill a dragon dwelling in the sea (Isaiah 27:1).

In chapter 12 of Revelation, the archangel Michael slays the red dragon with seven heads, which is equated with Satan. Finally, in Revelation 13:1–10, there is an echo of this same monster in the seven-headed beast from the sea, which represents Rome.

# The Antichrist Is Everywhere

*Who isn't the Antichrist? There are plenty of online raconteurs who accuse just about every celebrity and world leader—from David Hasselhoff to the Pope—of being the dark figure of Biblical prophecy. But the Bible itself doesn't say a lot on the subject.*

✳ ✳ ✳ ✳

### Biblical References

THE BIBLE CONTAINS only four mentions of the word "Antichrist," all of which appear in the letters of John, and they paint a murky picture. The passages say that the Antichrist comes at "the last hour" and denies the divinity of Jesus Christ. They also allude to multiple Antichrists who are said to have come already. (Some scholars believe that this refers to former followers of Christ who split with their congregation.)

Scriptural scholars have tried to get to the bottom of these ambiguous verses by connecting them with prophecies that are found elsewhere in the Bible. For example, there's a man known as "the little horn" in the Old Testament Book of Daniel; he is an evil figure who the prophet says will come to power over God's people and rule until God defeats him. Other Jewish texts mention a similar character called Beliar, an evil angel and agent of Satan who will be God's final adversary. Beliar also appears in the New Testament as a "man of lawlessness" who proclaims himself to be God and takes his seat in the temple in the final days. He also can be found in the Book of Revelation, as two beasts and a dragon that are defeated by Jesus in a climactic battle.

## The Modern Interpretation

As with most religious matters, there's no definitive interpretation of the Antichrist. But the prevailing view among contemporary believers is that the Antichrist is the opponent of God and Jesus Christ described in these prophecies. He is seen as an agent of Satan, in a relationship analogous to the one between Jesus and God. Many commentators expect that the Antichrist will be a charismatic leader who will draw people away from Christianity in the time immediately before Jesus Christ returns to Earth. Then, in the final battle between good and evil, Jesus will defeat the Antichrist, ushering in the era of the Kingdom of God on Earth.

This idea evolved through centuries of Biblical scholarship, involving a variety of theories about who or what the Antichrist is. Many prominent figures, beginning with the Roman emperor Nero, have been pegged as Antichrists. This continues today—just google "Antichrist" for a roundup of the usual suspects. While it's impossible to rule anyone out definitively, we'll go out on a limb and say that David Hasselhoff is probably innocent.

# Books You'll Never See

*There are many more books of the Bible than those found in the New and Old Testaments. Why are they missing?*

✳ ✳ ✳ ✳

To the faithful, the Bible is the literal word of God, perfect in every way. But all is not as it seems. There are 39 books in the Old Testament and 27 books in the New Testament yet many more books have been uncovered, including some mentioned in the Bible but not found there.

Before we examine this phenomenon, it is important to note that the Bible as we know it today is based on texts written many, many years after the events they chronicle. The books that compose the Old Testament canon, for example, are believed to have been written over several centuries beginning sometime in the 10th century BC, though certain parts, carried forward through oral tradition, may go as far back as the 18th century BC. Similarly, the books that compose the New Testament were compiled long after the life of Jesus. The oldest surviving complete text of the New Testament is the Codex Sinaiticus, which dates back to the 4th century AD.

## What's Not There

The books contained in the Old Testament mention several other books that, for reasons that remain unclear, are not part of the Bible. Joshua 10:13, for example, mentions the book of Jashar. So does 2 Samuel 1:18. And yet, the book of Jashar is nowhere to be found.

There are numerous other examples. 1 Kings 11:41 mentions the book of the Acts of Solomon, while 1 Chronicles 29:29 mentions the books of Nathan the Prophet and Gad the Seer. Additional books mentioned but not found in the Bible include the following:

* 2 Chronicles 12:15: The book of Shemaiah the Prophet.

* 2 Chronicles 20:34: The book of Jehu.

* 2 Chronicles 33:18–19: The book of the Kings of Israel.

* Jude 14: The Book of the Prophesies of Enoch.

## The Apocrypha

A discussion of the missing books of the Bible must also address the Apocrypha—dozens of books dating from both Old and New Testament eras that have been left out of the official Bible for various reasons. (Some editions of the Bible contain the Apocrypha, but not all of the associated books.) Certain elements of the early church considered many of these books to be inspired by God and the apostles, but in the end they simply didn't make the editorial cut, so to speak. Others, however, were and remain controversial, even heretical in the eyes of many.

The Infancy Gospel of Thomas is a good example. It supposedly describes Jesus' childhood and paints him as a show-off and, for lack of a better description, a vengeful bully. According to this book, which many biblical scholars consider a fraud, young Jesus performed a variety of bizarre miracles in his youth, such as returning to human form a man who had been transformed into a mule by a bewitching spell, bringing to life clay birds and animals, and lengthening a wood throne built by his father that was too short. It also alleges that Jesus killed some boys who had opposed him.

It is believed that the Infancy Gospel of Thomas originated in the mid-2nd century AD. It shares certain stories also found in the book of Luke, but apparently was never seriously considered for inclusion in the official Bible. Not surprisingly, many of the earliest Christian writers considered its contents heresy because of its bizarre portrayal of Jesus as a child.

Needless to say, the Infancy Gospel of Thomas and many other books that are a part of the Apocrypha have always been regarded as illegitimate by many mainstream churches. However, that didn't stop these missing books from finding an audience.

## Publication of the Apocrypha

In 1820, several books of the Apocrypha were collected into a volume called *The Apocryphal New Testament*, a sort of alternative to the mainstream Bible that was a collection two English translations originally published in 1736 and 1738. The book was reissued in 1926 as *The Lost Books of the Bible*, and it was reprinted in 1979. According to some experts, the earliest publications of these missing books were an effort to further biblical study. Subsequent editions, however, were less scholarly and put into print because they were considered so scandalous.

Though the Bible has been altered, edited, and updated through the centuries, its most basic canons have remained set and resolute from the very beginning. The issue of "missing" books is just one of the mysteries surrounding its history, but one shouldn't place too much emphasis on their importance. The books it does contain have served believers well since the earliest days of both Judaism and Christianity.

# In the Footsteps of Their Fathers

*Though Jesus would later be considered a dangerous radical, his professional choice was quite conventional.*

✳ ✳ ✳ ✳

EVERYONE KNOWS THAT Jesus began as a carpenter, just like his earthly father, Joseph (Matthew 13:55). Ancient Israel was a patriarchal society, and most sons went into the same business as their fathers, though it was not unheard of for a son to develop his own interest and be apprenticed out to another man in another field. But Jesus took the more conventional route and learned carpentry from his own dad. Long before he became a famous religious leader who was known throughout the entire country, he lived in obscurity with his family and worked hard at his humble yet respectable trade. What was his all-but-anonymous life like in those early years? What were his workdays like?

## Skills and Scarcity

Though carpenters were vital in ancient Israel and always in demand, the trade was not without its hardships. The work was intensely physical, and since there was a scarcity of timber in urban areas such as Jerusalem, much time could be eaten up in gathering and hauling. Because of this shortage of wood, Hebrew carpenters did less work on houses, which were constructed of stone by masons, than did carpenters in many other places in the world.

A carpenter would add the finishing touches, such as a wooden door, window shutters, or decorative latticework, but his handiwork was more likely to be seen inside. The Bible speaks many times of the tables and chairs made by carpenters, but furniture was mostly a luxury for the wealthy. Peasants simply sat on the floor when resting or eating.

Luckily for carpenters, there were a number of places in Israel that were full of trees. Oak, fir, olive, fig, cedar, acacia, cypress, and pomegranate—these are just some of the trees that provided lumber for the carpenter's work. Carpenters especially loved working with the cedar tree. The cedar was (and is) a beautiful red color, and the sap from its trunk and cones is tantalizingly fragrant.

Location was crucial to a carpenter's professional focus. If he lived in a coastal area, he might specialize in the construction and repair of boats, which were of great importance to the large fishing industry. If his neighbors were farmers, his specialty might be ploughs or ox carts for hauling produce. If he was well-connected in religious circles, he might concentrate on creating intricate and beautiful interior decorations for synagogues. In ancient Israel, as today, who you knew was as important as what you knew.

## Thinking Outside the Toolbox

Also just like today, it was necessary for skilled workers such as carpenters to adapt to changing times and trends. Archaeologists have discovered that during biblical times, improvements were made in the tools of carpentry: saws, hammers, awls, nails, chisels, bow drills, and adzes (the last is an instrument that looks like a combination ax/hoe and is used to shape and gouge wood). The successful carpenter would have made it his business to keep abreast of these improvements through communication with others in his trade.

In Old Testament times, a carpenter was likely to be paid in barter, for example with livestock, flour, wine, dry goods, or even land if the job was big enough. By the time of Jesus, however, coinage had become standardized in Israel, and it is likely that Jesus and Joseph were paid for their work in a mixture of coins and barter. In their neck of the woods—Nazareth—the most bartered items would probably have been pickled fish, wool, olive oil, and dried figs. Of course, however a carpenter in ancient Israel was paid, it would not be long until the taxman came looking for his cut. After leaving carpentry and devoting himself full time to spreading God's Word, Jesus would make one of those taxmen, Matthew, one of his beloved apostles (Matthew 9:9, 10:3).

# Philistines

*Today we call someone a "philistine" if she or he can't appreciate beauty and quality. The label is simply unfair, as any ancient Israelite who ever owned a fine Philistine iron sword could attest.*

✳  ✳  ✳  ✳

## Who Were They?

THE PHILISTINES CAME to Palestine (named for them) as the "sea peoples," fierce invaders who poured in from Crete and Asia Minor around 1200 BC. They crushed the Hittites and stormed southward, finally halted in the Holy Land by Egyptian arms. The Egyptians made them settle in a tiny strip of the modern Israeli coast just north of the Gaza strip, in five cities: Gaza, Ashkelon, Gath, Ekron, and Ashdod, all called Philistia. While history has painted them in barbarian colors (mainly for fighting regularly with the tribes of Israel), the Philistines were a sophisticated society of traders, ironsmiths, and warriors. As polytheists, they did not worship God.

## Where Are They Now?

Philistine independence was finished with their conquest by Assyrian forces in 732 BC, and with it they lost their cultural identity. By 400 BC, Philistia identified a region but not a people, and their cities had become mainly Jewish. Israelite culture absorbed them well before Jesus' day.

## Biblical Mentions

Abraham lived among the Philistines for a time. When the Israelites slipped into paganism, as described in Judges, God let the Philistines (among others) oppress his people until they repented. When the Israelites did the same thing again, God let the Philistines have at the Israelites for another 40 years.

Samson delivered the Israelites from Philistine domination by torching Philistine crops and killing a thousand Philistines with a donkey jawbone. Philistine Delilah was his downfall;

she cut his hair and he lost his power. The Philistines captured the holy Ark of the Covenant, but they sent it back after God dumped plagues on their cities. Goliath of Gath, slain by David, was a Philistine champion. Scripture characterizes the Philistines as Israel's archenemies.

# Why Is the Song of Songs in the Bible?

*The Song of Songs seems to be a love song that has nothing to do with religion. And its language is so erotic that many perplexed interpreters have endeavored to find more pious meanings in the book. Some have even questioned why it is in the Bible.*

✳ ✳ ✳ ✳

A BEAUTIFULLY POETIC BOOK, the Song of Songs celebrates the mutual, unwavering love of a man and a woman, now meeting, now parting, now seeking, and now finding each other. Although it seems entirely secular, never so much as mentioning God, it was accepted as part of the Hebrew Bible sometime before the time of Christ, presumably without offending anyone. By the end of the first century, however, rabbis began to react to the sexual nature of the text and question its place in the Bible. Eminent first-century Jewish scholar Rabbi Akiba defended it as "the holiest of the holy," but then went on to condemn those who profane it by singing it in banquet houses. He did not see the texts as profane songs of sexual love—but others did.

From then on, the jig was up. Both Jews and Christians went to great lengths to interpret the Song of Songs in any way they could to avoid admitting it was sexual (though by no means pornographic). Jews saw it as describing God's love for the Jews or even the marriage of God and Israel. The prophets Hosea and Jeremiah had described Israel as God's bride, but in their prophecies Israel is condemned as an adulterous wife, while there is no hint that the woman in the Song of Songs is unfaithful. Others saw the book as an allegory of the love between God and the Synagogue or Church or between God and the Christian soul, or even between Mary and her son Jesus, though this came shudderingly close to suggesting incest.

One offbeat interpretation insists that the Song of Songs was originally written in Egyptian hieroglyphics and is solely about Jesus' death and believers who long for Jesus' return.

## The Song as History

The Song of Songs was also often seen as a history of Israel or of the Christian Church, though ending in different eras. Jews saw it as ending with the Jews returning from exile in Babylon. One commentator sees the "city" the woman goes through in search of her lover in verse 3:2 as the desert the Jews crossed, noting that 600,000 Jews in the desert would constitute a city. For Christians, the history ended variously with the founding of the Church, the Reformation, or the Last Judgment.

## Some Verse Readings

Verse-by-verse readings also went far afield to avoid the erotic, and they often had little to do with the text. For example, the lovers' kiss has been interpreted as the oral law (Jewish laws passed down by word of mouth). The narrator's description of his lover's belly as a heap of wheat encircled with lilies (7:2) was said to refer to the book of Leviticus, for just as the belly is situated between the heart above and the legs below, so Leviticus has two books before it and two after it.

The woman's breasts are the tablets of the Ten Commandments or the Old and New Testaments, which produce the milk that nourishes Christians. Or, in one anti-Semitic view, the Jews have the two breasts of the she-goat (the tablets of the Ten Commandments), but Christians, like cows, have the four breasts of the Gospels—full of the sweet milk of wisdom.

## So What's It All About?

Today the Song of Songs is generally accepted as love poetry, but it is love poetry with a purpose—to teach what ideal love is all about. The relationship between lovers in the Song of Songs is unwavering, faithful, strong, and selfless. It dissolves the boundaries set between male and female by ancient Near Eastern society. The woman is seen as a whole character, an individual with her own opinions and desires—and with her own will. The man supplements the woman rather than dominating her. She in turn complements him. Together, they make a perfect whole. So there's no need to blush or toss the book out of the Bible. It's a beautiful lesson on how to love—and we can learn much from it.

# A Messianic Age? Why Jews Do Not Consider Jesus the Jewish Messiah

*Mainstream Judaism most fundamentally disagrees with Christian theology over the status of a certain Jewish guy from Nazareth. Here we summarize the primary Jewish arguments.*

❋  ❋  ❋  ❋

## What Constitutes a Jewish Messiah?

THE HEBREW WORD *Moshiach* means "Anointed One." Jews believe that *Hashem* ("The Name," second syllable accented, a reverent Jewish way to refer to God) will send this Messiah to forever change the nature of human existence. Christianity accepts Jesus of Nazareth as this Messiah. Judaism does not.

Judaism's messianic teaching is based on Old Testament prophecies, which a prospective messiah must fulfill. The Old Testament says that the messiah will be a prophet. He will be a normal man, not a worker of miracles, of King David's lineage through his father. He will embrace and observe the Torah.

## Problems

For Jews, the time of prophets ended around 300 BC, when the Jews migrating back to Israel from Babylon didn't achieve a majority. Jews believe that Hashem's prophets can only appear when the majority of the world's Jews live in Israel. Thus, Jews can't accept Jesus as a prophet.

If Jesus was born to a virgin, it follows that he didn't descend through his father's line from King David. The New Testament attributes numerous supernatural events to Jesus, inconsistent with messianic prophecy. In Judaism, the Torah has no statute of limitations; it remains unalterably binding on humanity forever and denounces as false anyone (including Jesus) who proposes changing Torah. Christianity teaches that some of the Torah's requirements have been amended or discarded; furthermore, according to the New Testament, Jesus did not fully abide by the Torah.

## Non-Achievements

Jews interpret Ezekiel 37 and Amos 9 to predict that the messiah will build the third temple. Isaiah 43 tells them that he will reunite all Jews in Israel. Isaiah 2 speaks of an end to all war—swords into ploughshares. In Zechariah 9, the prophet foretells that the faith of Hashem will unify humanity in its true faith. These messianic prophecies are central to the vision of a messianic age. An anointed king of Israel who brings them about will fulfill the prophecies.

No one argues that Jesus achieved them all, for no scriptural evidence indicates that he did. The temple isn't rebuilt, many Jews are scattered worldwide, Israel knows that all war has not ended, and Jews would laugh loudest at any claim that the world has adopted Judaism. Rather, Christianity teaches that Jesus will return to fulfill all of these, with the proviso that Christianity represents the new faith of Hashem to which all will gather. The Jewish rejoinder: Original prophecies do not speak of a Second Coming—just a single one.

## Translation Issues

Judaism begins biblical study from the Hebrew of the Old Testament, which means that any disagreement or misunderstanding of the original leads one astray.

Christians believe Jesus was born to a virgin, in accordance with Isaiah 7. In that passage, however, Hebrew scholars contend that the term Christian scholars translate as "virgin" meant simply "young woman" in ancient Hebrew. Much would seem to hinge on this. Christian scholars see in Psalms 22 a reference to the Crucifixion, specifically to gouging the hands and feet, whereas Jewish scholarship translates the same passage as "like a lion." In Isaiah 53, Christians see a reference to Jesus in the suffering servant of Hashem. Jewish belief debates the context of this reference, interpreting it as referring to the nation of Israel (that would be themselves).

## Shema

Perhaps the most fundamental disagreement has to do with the Trinity. The Shema, Judaism's basic expression of core faith, says: "Hear, O Israel: Hashem is our God, Hashem Alone." A triune deity—a Father, Son, and Holy Spirit—contradicts a tenet that Judaism specifies cannot be altered.

# Naked Man Running

*Mark's Gospel tells us that at the time of Jesus' arrest, soldiers grab a young man by his garment, but the man manages to disengage and run off naked. Who is this guy?*

✳   ✳   ✳   ✳

TWO PUZZLING VERSES in the Gospel of Mark present a person who is not otherwise mentioned in the Bible—or so it seems. When Jesus is arrested in the Garden of Gethsemane, his followers desert him. According to a brief passage in the Gospel of Mark, this includes an unidentified young man. The passage explains that this man, wearing nothing but a linen cloth, was accosted but managed to escape sans linen (Mark 14:51–52). Who is this young man and why is he in the garden wearing nothing but a linen cloth? It's an intriguing puzzle with intriguing possible solutions.

## What's It All About?

The first thing the situation brings to mind is how the patriarch Joseph, while a young slave, escaped the sexual advances of his master's wife by running from her and losing his garment in the process. But Joseph was acting heroically, while the young man in the garden was not. It is hard to see why Mark would have introduced the memory of Joseph here. Clearly the answer lies elsewhere. Some scholars see the incident as an allusion to an Old Testament end-time prophecy, while others speculate that the young man is either the Gospel's author or someone he knows, and he is adding a personal recollection here. Still others see the young man as a negative counterpart to the ideal disciple, who leaves everything to follow Jesus. But this seems unlikely, as Jesus' true disciples also leave Jesus at this time.

## A Secret Gospel

Possibly the most interesting theory about the young man involves an earlier edition of Mark's Gospel. There is good reason to believe that Mark's Gospel went through several editions before reaching the revered text now in the Bible.

In addition, one of the earlier editions was known as the Secret Gospel of Mark because it contained material that was meant only for mature Christians—material that may be misunderstood by spiritual neophytes. In order to make the Gospel safe for all Christians, this material was later excised and all of it was lost—well, maybe not all.

## Surviving Fragments

Some of the lost material appears in an 18th century copy of a letter from the Church Father Clement of Alexandria. In his letter, Clement defends the authenticity of both the canonical Gospel and the Secret Gospel against a falsified version.

When Mark died, the letter claims, he left the Secret Gospel to the church at Alexandria, Egypt, where it is "read only to those being initiated into the greater mysteries." In discussing the Secret Gospel, Clement reproduces passages about a rich young man from Bethany who brings to mind both the naked man in Gethsemane and Lazarus, whom Jesus had earlier raised from the dead. According to the cited passages, when the young man dies, Jesus raises him from the dead at the request of the man's sister. At his rising, the young man looks upon Jesus and loves him. Six days later, he comes to Jesus, wearing only a linen cloth on his naked body (possibly as a baptismal garment). Jesus then teaches him the mystery of the kingdom of God.

### Conclusions

Scholars who have studied the passages in Clement's letter believe they predate the Gospel we know. If this is so, they may preserve an early telling of the story of the raising of Lazarus, as later told in John's Gospel. In addition, the texts bring to mind the young man who runs off naked at Jesus' arrest. If the Secret Gospel passages are authentic, then the young man at Gethsemane may be a part of the story of the young man in the Secret Gospel. It is possible that the editor charged with deleting this story from the Gospel overlooked these two brief verses, which then remained in the final text of Mark's Gospel to mystify us.

# Mary Magdalene After the Gospels

*Little is said about Mary Magdalene in the New Testament, but Mary had an active life in the early Christian Church and even has her own gospel. Some go so far as to suggest that Mary and Jesus were married! Who was Mary really?*

✳ ✳ ✳ ✳

THE GOSPEL OF John repeatedly refers to the disciple whom Jesus loved. Most readers believe that disciple was John.

However, there was another disciple who was just as close, if not closer, to Jesus, and it was a woman: Mary Magdalene. From the time she first met Jesus, Mary remained close to him, followed him everywhere, listened to his teaching, and even helped support him financially. She stood at the foot of the cross as he died and was the first to see the risen Lord.

## Mary Magdalene and Jesus

Mary is introduced into the Gospels as one of three women whom Jesus had cured (Luke 8:2). Jesus had cast seven demons out of Mary, but this did not mean that she was sinful. The demons could just as well have been the causes of physical or mental illness. Although Mary is popularly represented as a prostitute, there is no reason to believe she was. The label was attached to her centuries later—perhaps because her hometown, Magdala, had a reputation for licentiousness. Nor did Mary Magdalene wash Jesus' feet, as sometimes alleged. The foot washing is done by an unnamed woman just before Mary is introduced, and there is no known connection between the two women.

According to the Gospels (free of unfair traditional associations), Mary Magdalene and the other women Jesus had healed were apparently wealthy, for they followed Jesus during his mission and helped support him financially out of their own means. No details are given of Mary's personal relationship with Jesus, but Mary was among the women who stood at the foot of the cross while Jesus breathed his last and she watched as he was buried. Her faith in Jesus never wavered, but even she did not expect his resurrection.

## Mary Magdalene at Jesus' Tomb

All four Gospels name Mary as one of the women who went to Jesus' tomb on Easter Sunday. In the Gospels of Matthew, Mark, and Luke, when the women arrive at the site around dawn they find the tomb empty and are informed by an angel that Jesus has risen. They then run off to tell the apostles.

The Gospel of John depicts the incident as a personal story about Mary Magdalene. Mary goes to the tomb just before dawn (the other women aren't mentioned) and sees that the stone blocking the tomb's entrance has been rolled back. In a panic, she then runs back to the city and tells Peter and a disciple "whom Jesus loved" (this was probably John), that someone has take Jesus from the tomb and disappeared with the body (John 20:2). The two disciples race to the tomb and find that Jesus' body is indeed missing but his burial cloths have been left in the tomb.

The disciples return home, and Mary remains near the tomb, weeping. Then two angels suddenly appear inside the tomb and ask Mary why she is weeping. Mary tells them, and then she turns and sees Jesus standing nearby, but she doesn't recognize him, mistaking him for the gardener. It is only when Jesus softly and affectionately speaks her name that Mary realizes she is seeing the risen Christ. Jesus instructs Mary to go tell the disciples all she has seen, and she faithfully does so.

## Gospel of Mary

During the early years of Christianity, Mary Magdalene emerged as an important figure, as well as the center of a controversy over the role of women in the church. Much of what we know of her comes from a book entitled the Gospel of Mary, which was probably written in the late first or early second century. Long lost, the Gospel of Mary now survives only in bits and pieces. The surviving text (about half the gospel) begins as Jesus is teaching his disciples, including Mary, that salvation comes from seeking the true spiritual nature of humanity within oneself. Jesus then instructs the disciples to go forth and preach the Gospel to others and leaves.

The disciples are left disconcerted. They have not understood what Jesus was teaching them—except for Mary and Levi (Matthew). Rather than seek peace within, most worry about Jesus' departure and their own deaths.

Mary quietly takes over and begins to comfort them and give them further instructions—acting as Jesus had done in the past and taking over his role. She tells them about a vision she has had in which Jesus had told her how to win the battle over the powers of the world that keep the soul ignorant of its own spiritual nature. But Andrew and Peter continue to deny Mary's teaching because they are so offended that Jesus preferred a woman over them.

As in the canonical Gospels, the disciples are slow to learn and misunderstand Jesus' teachings at first hearing. (After all, Jesus had predicted his death to them three times and they still did not believe it until it happened.) Levi then reminds Peter that he has an inclination to anger and should keep it in check, adding: "If the Savior considered her to be worthy, who are you to disregard her? For he knew her completely and loved her devotedly." He then advises all the disciples to go out and preach the Gospel as Jesus had instructed.

## Mary in Other Writings

Whereas the Gospel of Mary is the most important of the books about Mary Magdalene, many of the other extra-biblical works refer to her, and all speak of her closeness to Jesus. She is often referred to as the favorite of three female companions of Jesus, all called Mary.

The most provocative statement about Mary Magdalene is found in the Gospel of Philip. Although the only surviving copy of that book is dated around AD 350, it is obviously a copy of an older book, which, in turn, is a collection of sayings that go as far back as the time of Christ.

One of the brief entries in this so-called gospel states that the Lord loved Mary Magdalene more than all the disciples, and he used to kiss her on her mouth more than the other disciples. At least, we think he used to kiss her on the mouth, for the word "mouth" has been torn away. The missing word could conceivably be "cheek" or "head" or "hand," though this seems unlikely as these kisses seem to infuriate the male disciples, who accuse Jesus of loving Mary more than them. In fact, the male disciples seem to be suffering from a religious version of sibling rivalry, and the situation reflects that of the earlier Gospel of Mary in which the men resent that a woman is taking on the role of spiritual leader.

## Much Ado About Kissing

In his super-popular novel *The Da Vinci Code*, Dan Brown made a big thing about the passage in which Jesus kisses Mary, alleging that it proves that Jesus and Mary Magdalene were married. This is not only wildly imaginative, but counterintuitive. If the incident had anything to say about marriage at all, it wouldn't be that the two were man and wife, but just the opposite! A man kissing his wife would not be objectionable, while a man kissing a woman he was not married to (and a disciple at that) might indeed cause a stir.

But of course, *The Da Vinci Code* is fiction, so it needn't be true—or even reasonable. Brown could depict Mary as flying around on a broomstick if he wished. A more spiritual take on the kiss, though, is that it symbolized a transmission of knowledge, which the male disciples believed they were more entitled to receive than a woman.

Although some of the teachings in these extra-biblical books were later deemed heretical by a number of Christian thinkers, the writings seem to emphasize that Mary Magdalene was a major figure in the early Church, though her authority was resented by some of the men. In time, men completely took over the leadership of the Church and, deliberately or not, pushed the women into more subservient roles.

# Mystery Author

*Who wrote Hebrews? Bible scholars still don't know for sure, but they have some hunches.*

✳    ✳    ✳    ✳

**IDing Letters:** Most New Testament letter writers identify themselves. That's how we know Paul authored Romans through Philemon. Jesus' brother James wrote James. First and Second Peter are the apostle Peter's works (though there is some debate), while the apostle John wrote 1–3 John (as well as Revelation and the Gospel of John). Another brother of Jesus penned Jude.

**The Lone Anonymous Letter:** Only one New Testament letter—Hebrews—departs from this norm. Foregoing greetings, it dives right into teaching that's peppered throughout with Old Testament passages and written in impeccable Greek. Until recent years, copies of the King James Bible gave Paul credit for writing Hebrews. However, earlier manuscripts (found since the KJV's translation) don't name an author. That's why modern translations and newer copies of older translations tend to leave the byline blank.

**Whodunit?:** Paul remains the prime suspect as writer. Tertullian (AD 160–220)—who was alive when the original manuscripts were around—referred to Hebrews as the Epistle of Barnabas. Martin Luther guessed that Apollos wrote it. Other nominations are the apostle Philip or Priscilla. Clement of Alexandria (AD 150–215) surmised that Paul wrote it first in Hebrew and then, to account for the excellent Greek, Luke translated it. This might be the best guess of all.

**Wonderful Irony!:** Is it coincidence that the only unidentified New Testament author wrote the Bible's premier chapter on faith? Hebrews 11 begins, "Now faith is the assurance of things hoped for, the conviction of things not seen."

It does make you think!

# Phoenicians

*They were one of the most influential peoples of the ancient world, yet few today can identify them.*

✳   ✳   ✳   ✳

## Who Were They?

PHOENICIA WAS THE coastal land of modern Lebanon and southern Syria, home to a grouping of city-states occupied by the Semitic Canaanite people we call Phoenicians. While they were never an empire, from before 1200 BC until the Persian conquest, the Phoenicians operated one of the most famous seafaring and trading cultures in Western history. Sidon, Tyre, Byblos, Acre, and Tripoli were their most important Near Eastern cities, though their African colony of Carthage, founded in 814 BC (in modern Tunisia), arguably outshone any of the homeland city-states as a minor empire until the Romans eradicated it. Most importantly, the Phoenicians developed a phonetic alphabet that is the ancestor of all other Western alphabets. Phoenician religion was Canaanite polytheism.

## Where Are They Now?

Cyrus of Persia occupied Syrian Phoenicia in 539 BC. Soon after Alexander the Great conquered the region in 332 BC, Greek culture swamped the Phoenician homeland. Rome's destruction of Carthage in 143 BC dealt the death-stroke to Phoenician identity. Distant Phoenician descendants are found today all along the southern Mediterranean coast from Morocco to Asia Minor and in most major Mediterranean islands, notably Malta.

## Biblical Mentions

When one considers the Phoenicians as Canaanites, the biblical interest comes into clear focus. God promised the Israelites a chunk of Canaan—but they were not to intermarry with Canaanites. In general, the Jewish and Christian view of

Phoenicia was chilly; they saw it as a land of sin, idolaters, slippery merchants, and hedonists. Isaiah in particular railed about Tyre, characterizing it as a prostitute; Ezekiel prophesied its conquest. Christ visited Phoenicia, and the apostles preached there—as surely they must if they meant to evangelize far and wide; for even as Roman subject cities, Phoenician ports were gateways to the Mediterranean.

# Possible Authors of the Gospels

*Seems pretty simple at first glance; each Gospel was written by the book's namesake, as direct testament of that writer's experiences with Jesus Christ. Indeed, for most of the history of Christianity, this was the unquestioned interpretation. But in the past two centuries, biblical scholars have begun to question these assumptions.*

✳   ✳   ✳   ✳

PART OF THE problem in finding the authors is the phenomenon of "pseudoepigraphy"—falsely attributing a book to an author, often as a means to validate the work. Pseudoepigraphy is common throughout the world and throughout history, but it was especially common in ancient times. Another problem is that most biblical scholars agree that the original Gospels were written in Greek—unlikely if the authors were poor disciples of Jesus who spoke Hebrew or Aramaic. So who were the authors of these important works?

## Gospel of Matthew

Until the 18th century, the unquestioned author of the Gospel of Matthew was ... the apostle named Matthew. The Gospel of Matthew was also considered the first one written. By the 19th century, biblical scholars began to question this authorship. Today, the majority of scholars believe the Gospel of Matthew was written by an anonymous Jewish Christian toward the end of the first century.

**The case for Matthew:**

✳ Early Christian scholars claim it was Matthew. Papias of Hierapolis, an early Christian writer, states that Matthew wrote a Gospel in Hebrew. Though the Gospel of Matthew was written in Greek, some modern scholars believe the Hebrew book may have been a prototype. Unfortunately, Papias, who is one of the primary sources for much of what we know about early Christian writing, was considered "a man of meager intelligence" by his contemporaries.

✳ The writer was probably Jewish. Textual clues in the narrative, such as a familiarity with Jewish customs and local geography, as well as a familiarity with the Old Testament, indicate the writer was Jewish.

✳ The writer didn't like Pharisees. The Pharisees are depicted in a dim light in Matthew. The Pharisees were hard on tax collectors, and Matthew was a tax collector.

**The case against Matthew:**

✳ Matthew copied Mark. Though presented first in the New Testament, biblical scholars agree that Matthew was actually written after Mark, using Mark as a source. Evidence for this includes the fact that Matthew incorporates passages from Mark wholesale. Why would an apostle, who was an eyewitness, need to copy from Mark, who was writing everything down secondhand?

✳ The book was written in Greek. Not only was it written in Greek, but it was an eloquent Greek. Very few people could write at this time, much less in a nonnative language.

## Gospel of Mark

Traditionally, the Gospel of Mark was associated with John Mark the Evangelist. The Gospel was written not as an eyewitness account, but as a summary of what Mark had heard from Peter's preaching in Rome. Of all the Gospels, Mark's authorship of the Gospel bearing his name is the one that is most widely accepted.

**The case for Mark:**

* Church fathers didn't ascribe the Gospel to an apostle. It would make sense for the early church fathers to ascribe the most important accounts of Jesus' life to apostolic sources— as they did with Matthew and John—to provide added credibility to the text. There is no reason to give credit to Mark, who is a minor character in the New Testament.

* The book displays an ignorance of Palestine. An apostle of Jesus would be intimately familiar with Palestine, including its geography. Time and again the author of Mark bungles basic details, which shows that the author probably was not a Jew and was hearing it second-hand.

* The Gospel seems to be written for gentiles. The book is written for a gentile audience and seems to be designed to bolster the faith of those under threat of persecution—as Christians were in Rome during the time Mark was there.

**The case against Mark:**

* Persecution was widespread. Just because the Gospel seemed concerned about persecution doesn't mean it was written in Rome, a main contention of pro-Mark scholars. Skeptics suggest this indicates the writer *could* have been someone other than Mark.

## Gospel of Luke

The author of the Gospel of Luke was consistently assumed to be Luke the Evangelist, during the first century. Luke was a contemporary and companion of Paul, and so the Gospel is not an eyewitness account.

**The case for Luke:**

* All early writings attribute the Gospel to Luke. The oldest surviving manuscript referencing the Gospel, dating back to AD 200, attributes the book to Luke.

* Luke spoke fluent Greek. The Gospel of Luke was originally written in an eloquent Greek of the sort a highly educated physician might use.

* The Gospel of Luke and Acts of the Apostles is written by the same person. Both books exhibit the same writing style and are dedicated to the same patron, Theophilus.

* Textual clues indicate Luke wrote Acts, and therefore Luke. At several places in Acts the writer refers to Paul and his companions as "we." Scholars determined that the "we" passages correspond to times when Luke was in Paul's company.

**The case against Luke:**

* Contradictions between Acts and Paul's letters. Multiple contradictions occur in Acts. These contradictions cause skeptics to suggest Luke the physician did not write Acts, since the real Luke, a companion of Paul, would not have made such errors. And since he didn't write Acts, he could not have written the Gospel of Luke.

## Gospel of John

The authorship of John is the most hotly debated. Traditionally, the Gospel was ascribed to John the Apostle. The book was said to have been written to refute the heretical writings of the gnostic scholar Cerinthus, who taught that Jesus was separate from Christ. Today most scholars agree that John the Apostle was most likely not the author of the Gospel.

**The case for John:**

* Every existing manuscript attributes its origin to him. While this is not evidence that John wrote the Gospel, it is worth

noting that none of the manuscripts we have containing early versions of the Gospel suggest otherwise.

✳ The author claims to be an eyewitness. The manuscript indicates intimate familiarity with Jesus and the other disciples.

**The case against John:**

✳ The book was written well after John's death. Scholars' best estimates peg the writing of John as AD 70. This would be difficult for the apostle John, considering that some scholars believe he was martyred with his brother James several decades before.

✳ Contradictions with the other Gospels. John's Gospel is littered with details that are at odds with the synoptic (Matthew, Mark, and Luke) Gospels.

✳ John was probably illiterate. Most scholars now agree that John was illiterate.

So who *did* write the Gospel of John? Over the years, various scholars have put forth theories:

✳ Cerinthus: Cerinthus was a 1st-century gnostic writer who is the author of several important pieces of early Christian writing. The Alogi, a 2nd century Christian sect, attributed the Gospel to him.

✳ Mary Magdalene: Mary Magdalene was not one of the apostles, but she could be interpreted as the "beloved disciple" referred to in John. Additionally, Ephesus, where Mary Magdalene was from, is considered the likely place of origin for the Gospel.

✳ John the Elder: Papias of Hierapolis claims that the Gospel of John is written by "the elder John," leading some to believe that John the Elder is the actual author of the Gospel.

✳ Multiple authors: One of the most popular interpretations is that the Gospel of John was a composite work. The theory holds that the work originated with John's recollections, which were then expanded and formed by multiple authors over several years into the Gospel we have today.

### . . . and Q

Most might associate Q with James Bond, but the Q of the Gospels is more intriguing—a hypothetical, lost source book from which the authors of Matthew and Luke drew inspiration. The possibility of this book was first proffered in the early 19th century. The term Q, which stands for the German word *Quelle* ("source"), was first proffered by German theologian Johannes Weisse in the late 1800s and is theorized to have been a collection of Jesus' sayings.

# Lamech, History's Second Killer

*A descendant of Cain, the first murderer, Lamech becomes the second man on record to kill another human being—and the first polygamist.*

✳   ✳   ✳   ✳

**A**FTER CAIN MURDERS his brother, Abel, God tells him that he will no longer be able to farm the land, as he had been doing, for God was putting a curse on the land because it had absorbed the innocent blood of Abel. Instead of farming, Cain will lead a life of wandering. When Cain expresses fear that anyone he meets in the future will know him as a fratricide and kill him, God puts a mark on Cain. The mark implies that anyone who kills Cain will in turn suffer vengeance (Genesis 4:15). Cain eventually marries and has children. Genesis completes Cain's story with a brief genealogy, ending with the birth of Lamech, Cain's great-great-great-grandson—of the seventh generation of humankind.

Lamech distinguishes himself by being the first to take two wives, named Adah and Zillah, making him the first polygamist. Each wife has significant sons. Adah gives birth to Jabal, the first animal herder (aside from the murdered Abel, whose career was cut short). According to Genesis, Jabal and his descendants live in tents and care for their cattle. Adah's other son, Jubal, is the world's first musician. Zillah's son is Tubal-cain, the world's first metalworker. Zillah also bears a daughter, named Naamah.

## A Boast of Killing—in Verse!

Lamech's primary boast is not about his sons but about his heinous action. Apparently, he gets in a fight with a man and recieves a wound. The injury Lamech receives can't be severe, as it doesn't keep him from killing his opponent. This defensive action far exceeds the original offense. If this imbalance is not enough, Lamech then sings a song to his wives about the event. He recalls the seven-fold vengeance God granted his ancestor Cain and proclaims that anyone who takes action against him for his crime will in this case suffer vengeance ten times worse than that.

Lamech's song is one of the earliest surviving poems in Hebrew, but it already uses parallelism, the literary device found in much biblical verse. In parallelism, the second half of a line of verse repeats the first half in different words, contradicts it, or extends its meaning. Lamech's song itself seems to demonstrate the downward spiral morality has taken since the Fall. It will culminate in the flood and a subsequent renewal of life.

## Another Lamech—No Relation

Lamech, the bigamist and boastful killer, is not the only Lamech in Genesis. Another Lamech is named as a descendant of Adam and Eve's third son, Seth. This other Lamech's claim to fame is that he is the son of Methuselah, who reaches the ripe old age of 969, making him the oldest man in the Bible.

When Lamech is himself 182 years old, he gives Methuselah a grandson, Noah, and Lamech prophesies that Noah will bring relief from the curse God had put upon the earth when Cain killed Abel. Noah eventually fulfills that prophecy by rebooting civilization after the Great Flood. Lamech himself dies at the age of 777—a mere boy compared to his father.

Unlike the Lamech who was descended from Cain, the Lamech who was descended from Seth is peace-loving. Instead of bursting into song about his killing of a man who had only slightly injured him, he looks forward to the period of peace that his son Noah will initiate.

# Jericho: The Archaeological Record

*It's one of the greatest of ancient biblical cities—and what a story it has to tell!*

\* \* \* \*

## How We Know

SEVERAL MID-20TH-CENTURY DIGS revealed some of the murky history of Jericho, which lies just north of the Dead Sea and about a mile from its modern incarnation, the Arab town of Ariha. One method archaeologists use—and the one that revealed a great deal at Jericho—was the deep-trench technique, which enables scientists to study the layers of habitation. In the 1950s, Dame Kathleen Kenyon, one of Britain's most accomplished archaeologists, dug all the way to the most ancient human evidence at Jericho.

## Stone Age: 10,800–8500 BC

Jericho's earliest people were hunter-gatherers. To place this in context, the most ancient evidence of the rise of civilization in Sumer dates back before 5000 BC, and the last Ice Age was still winding down in 10,000 BC. The people at that time in Jericho were part of the Natufian culture, a rough grouping of humanity that left its markings all over what is now Israel.

For meat, they hunted gazelle, deer, wild cattle, wild pigs, and presumably whatever else they could bring down. They supplemented this food with wild-growing wheat, barley, and tree nuts. Natufians lived in half-sunken huts. They may have had dogs as pets or helpers; another Natufian site holds the oldest-known instance of a human buried with a puppy. Jericho had fertile soil and a steady water supply, which would prove central to its place in history.

## Late Stone Age: 8500–3100 BC

The first people to make Jericho a year-round permanent home lived like the Natufians, for the most part, but with a more sophisticated city and social structure. We infer this because in the early part of this period there is what appears to be a temple or religious shrine at Jericho—such a building requires and implies that the people are organized and are staying put. One of the most interesting bits from this period entails skulls, plastered and painted to look like people, with shells for eyes. Did descendants keep these in their huts to remember the deceased? Whatever the reason, this is one of the oldest known examples of portraiture.

Jericho also had walls (though not the ones Joshua knocked down) and a tower in this time frame. This tells us that not only were they organized, they felt the need for watchfulness and defense—probably against invaders or raiders. These walls were rebuilt multiple times, possibly after earthquake damage. As the Stone Age wound down, evidence gets sparser at Jericho, and at times the site seems to have been empty.

## Bronze Age: 3100–1400 BC

This was Jericho's glory era, when its people built major defensive walls connected by towers. It was also Jericho's biblical phase, in which it grew into a Canaanite city of great importance. Joshua was leading the Israelites to claim their Promised Land, and Jericho looked like a formidable obstacle. He didn't have to settle in for a long siege, though. The Israelite army marched around the walls for a week with the Ark of the Covenant, blowing *shofarim* (rams' horns). On day seven, down came the walls, and the Israelite army slaughtered almost the entire Canaanite population.

While archaeologists have debated evidence for the walls' fall, there is evidence for an assault some time between 1600–1400 BC, and it seems connected to Joshua's siege. The Israelites moved on their path of conquest.

## Shadows of Glory

The site of Jericho was reoccupied after 1000 BC, but the town never again mattered much. It became something of a resort town for bigwigs, especially Herod, who built a winter palace at Jericho shortly before Christ's time. For the next three millenia—indeed, until and including today—Jericho was a minor town taking orders from a series of overlords: Assyrian, Babylonian, Persian, Macedonian, Roman, Muslim, Christian, Ottoman, British, Jordanian, and Israeli.

Today, as you may imagine, in addition to agriculture, Ariha makes a living off Jericho's past.

# What Enoch Did After Leaving Earth

*According to the Bible, Enoch did not die but was simply taken up to heaven by God. This spurred questions about what Enoch did later. One answer is that he wrote books about what he saw and learned in heaven. We can still read them today.*

✳ ✳ ✳ ✳

LITTLE IS KNOWN about Enoch. After reporting his birth, Genesis devotes only a few verses to him. We are told that Enoch was the oldest son in the sixth generation. That's the sixth generation ever, as Enoch was directly descended from Adam's third son, Seth. In other words, Enoch was the great-great-great-great-grandson of Adam and Eve. (There was another Enoch, but he was the son of Cain and an entirely different person.)

## Walking with God into Heaven

In primordial times (just after the Creation), people lived long lives. Enoch's father, Jared, lived 962 years and Enoch's first son, Methuselah, lived to be 969, making him the oldest person in the Bible—or maybe not, because Enoch probably never died. Aside from genealogical information, all the Bible reports about Enoch is that he had a close relationship with God— that after Methuselah's birth, Enoch walked with God three hundred years (Genesis 5:22).

But the clincher is found in Genesis 5:24: After living 365 years, Enoch disappeared—because God "took" him. The implication is that Enoch didn't die but was taken into heaven to be with God. The New Testament's Letter to the Hebrews further explains that because Enoch had pleased God so much, Enoch missed out on the experience of death (Hebrews 11:5). The only other person to avoid death was the prophet Elijah, who was taken up to heaven in a fiery chariot.

Enoch's mysterious end led to lots of speculation about what happened to him after God took him. Ancient Jewish traditions hold that even before his final exit, Enoch had spent "hidden years" with the angels, who taught him things unknown to others. These traditions continued to grow, and then, sometime between the 2nd century BC and the early Christian era, three books appeared that claimed to record Enoch's special wisdom—and his warnings about the end times. These books of Enoch never made it into the Bible, but they became very influential. They even inspired two great epic poems: Dante's *Divine Comedy* and Milton's *Paradise Lost*.

## 1 Enoch

The First Book of Enoch, or 1 Enoch, falls into five parts in imitation of the Pentateuch—the first five books of the Bible, which are considered the Jewish Law, or Torah.

The first part, the Book of the Watchers, tells of the fall of the angels, a tale not in the Bible, though it is firmly rooted in

Christian lore as the origin of Satan. It also relates how angels took Enoch on two tours of the universe, showing him the cornerstone of the earth, the forbidden tree in the Garden of Eden, and the mountain that holds the spirits of the dead awaiting the Day of Judgment.

Part 2, the Book of Parables, tells of Enoch's journey through the cosmos to the heavenly throne, where God appoints an end-time judge who will reverse the fortunes of the oppressed and condemn their oppressors. Oddly enough, the judge—who is variously called the righteous one, chosen one, messiah, and son of man—turns out to be Enoch.

In the Astronomical Book, part 3, the angel Uriel explains to Enoch the structure of the universe and the movement of the stars and winds, all of which God controls.

In the Book of Dreams, part 4, Enoch experiences two visions. The first tells of the coming Flood. The second (the Animal Apocalypse) presents biblical history with animals in place of people! The patriarchs are bulls, the gentiles are wild beasts, and Israel is a flock of sheep. The history ends with the story of the Maccabean Revolt in the 2nd century BC, the probable time of the book's composition.

The Epistle of Enoch, part 5, includes a story about the birth of Noah, suggesting that just as God brought salvation after the Flood through Noah, so too will salvation follow the end of the world. A section called the Apocalypse of Weeks divides history into uneven units of time, called weeks. Enoch warns his people to repent, for they are already in the seventh week and the last judgment will begin in the eighth.

## 2 Enoch

In the Second Book of Enoch, probably written in the first century, two angels lead Enoch through seven so-called heavens—though some are more like hell. In the first heaven, Enoch sees angels tending the stars and the sources of the weather. In the second, he finds people who have turned away from God weeping. In the third, he sees the Garden of Eden, which is meant for the righteous, and a place of punishment for sinners. The fourth heaven contains the paths for the sun and moon. The fifth holds the fallen angels prisoner. In the sixth heaven, all the orders of angels, archangels, cherubim, and the like sing to the glory of God, and some keep records of the deeds and misdeeds of every human.

In the seventh heaven, Enoch meets God, who gives him an account of history from the Creation to the final judgment. Enoch returns to earth to impart his discoveries to his descendants, exhorting them to observe God's laws. He then returns to heaven for good.

## 3 Enoch

The final work associated with Enoch is a collection of writings in which Ishmael Ben Elisha, a renowned rabbi of the 2nd century AD, ascends to the seventh heaven and is greeted by the archangel Metatron, who turns out to be none other than Enoch—transformed into an angel.

Ishmael takes a tour of heaven, discovering its mysteries. However, these mysteries seem to reflect those explored by the Kabala, a Jewish mystical movement, in the 5th to the 6th centuries—the most likely time of the book's composition.

If Enoch wrote these books, he took a few thousand years to do so. But, in fact, he probably didn't write a word. Scholars agree that the books of Enoch belong to pseudepigraphia—books written under the pseudonym of an important person of the past. That means we still have no idea what Enoch did after leaving earth.

# In Mushrooms We Trust

*John Allegro: linguist, showman, and certifiable eccentric*

✳ ✳ ✳ ✳

IT'S NOT OFTEN that the academic world produces a character like John Marco Allegro. Born in 1923, Allegro first studied for the Methodist ministry but later became a brilliant scholar of Hebrew dialects. This latter course of study made him a perfect fit for the international team formed to decipher the Dead Sea Scrolls, the earliest surviving manuscripts of the Bible.

Because Allegro was part scholar and part showman, he became a star in the otherwise sober world of biblical scholarship. At the time, the historical importance of the scrolls was a cause for controversy, and Allegro gleefully submerged himself into the debate.

Suddenly, however, Allegro took the debate in an absurd direction with his infamous book: *The Sacred Mushroom and the Cross*. In it, he argued that Biblical figures like Moses and Christ were actually literary inventions. In fact, he contended that the Jewish and Christian scriptures were allegories, written to promote an ancient fertility cult. To Allegro, Jesus represented a hallucinogenic mushroom, which followers ingested to enhance their perception of God.

Allegro tried to prove that the Bible was actually a coded text written to preserve the secrets of this drug-worshipping cult. When the writers of these "folktales" died, he argued, their original meaning was lost. Subsequent followers—early Christians—began taking scripture literally and interpreted as factual what Allegro maintained was meant as fable.

This peculiar thesis was roundly panned by the academic community. Allegro's reputation was destroyed. Though he died in disrepute, Allegro did inspire a group of supporters who, even to this day, still try to defend the man and his zany thesis.

※ **Chapter 13**

# Sporting Anomalies

## How Did the Biathlon Become an Olympic Event?

*It's one thing to ski through the frozen countryside; it's quite another to interrupt that heart-pounding exertion and muster up the calm and concentration needed to hit a target that's a few centimeters wide with a .22-caliber bolt-action rifle.*

※　※　※　※

Yᴇs, ᴛʜᴇ ʙɪᴀᴛʜʟᴏɴ is an odd sport. Cross-country skiing combined with rifle marksmanship? Why not curling and long jump? Figure skating and weight lifting? In actuality, however, the two skills that make up the biathlon have a history of going hand in hand, so combining them as an Olympic event makes perfect sense.

It's no surprise that the inspiration for the biathlon came from the frigid expanses of northern Europe, where there's not much to do in the winter besides ski around and drink aquavit. Cross-country skiing provides a quick and efficient way to travel over the snowy ground, so northern cultures mastered the technique early—and it was especially useful when it came time to hunt for winter food. People on skis were killing deer with bows and arrows long before such an activity was considered a sport.

But skiing and shooting (with guns, eventually) evolved from an act of survival into a competition. The earliest biathlon competitions were held in 1767 as informal contests between Swedish and Norwegian border patrols. The sport spread through Scandinavia in the nineteenth century as sharpshooting skiers formed biathlon clubs. In 1924, it was included as a demonstration sport in the Winter Olympics in Chamonix, France, although it was called military patrol.

In 1948, the Union Internationale de Pentathlon Moderne et Biathlon—the first international governing body for the sport—was formed. The official rules for what would come to be the modern biathlon were hammered out over the next several years.

During the 1960 Olympics at Squaw Valley Ski Resort in California, a biathlon was contested as an official Olympic event for the first time. The sport has evolved over the decades—it now features smaller-caliber rifles, different distances, various types of relays, and the participation of women. (A women's biathlon was first staged as an Olympic event in 1992 in Albertville, France.)

Today, biathlon clubs and organizations are active all over the world, and there are versions of the sport for summer in which running replaces skiing. Still, the biathlon's popularity remains strongest in its European birthplace.

# How the Marathon Didn't Get Started

*The primary connection between the modern race and the ancient messenger lies in a 19th-century poem that gets the details wrong.*

✳ ✳ ✳ ✳

## The Basic Legend

ALMOST EVERYONE HAS heard it: The Athenians paddled the Persians in the Battle of Marathon (490 BC), saving Greece from becoming a Persian province. Afterward, Pheidippides the messenger ran all the way to Athens to announce the elating news, then fell dead. Thereafter, a distance-racing sport called the Pheidippidaion became popular.

Okay, that wasn't its name. Can you imagine the "Boston Pheidippidaion"? It sounds like a tongue twister. And "Pheidippi-de-doo-dah" would never have caught on.

Did the run happen? We can't know for sure; it isn't impossible. Did the run inspire an ancient sport? No. Evidently, distance running was already an ancient sport if we believe Herodotus, since he clearly calls Pheidippides a professional distance runner. The longest race at the ancient Olympics was the well-documented *dolichos*, which literally means "long race" and was anywhere from 7 to 24 stades, or 1,400 to 4,800 meters. Pheidippides probably ran this race.

## Ancient Sources

For those not steeped in the ancient world, Herodotus is revered as the "father of history"; antiquarians do not casually dismiss him. The story about Pheidippides usually gets pinned on Herodotus, but people garble what the great man actually wrote. Pheidippides (others name him "Philippides" or "Phidippides") was a professional runner sent to Sparta (which was also in for a stomping if Persia won) to ask for help.

Pheidippides returned, saying that the god Pan had waylaid him. "How come you ungrateful Athenians never worship Me? After all I do for you, too. I hear you have a battle coming up; planned to pitch in there as well. The least you could do is throw Me a decent bash now and then," whined the deity. (Herodotus digresses that the Athenians responded to this come-to-Pan meeting by initiating annual ceremonies and a torch-race honoring him, mindful of his help in the battle.)

As for Spartan aid, Pheidippides relayed their lame excuse: Spartan law forbade them to march until the moon was full. That's a heck of a note for someone who purportedly just ran 135 miles in two days, then returned at the same pace. Gods only knew how quickly Pheidippides might have arrived had he not stopped to listen to Pan complain.

Herodotus says nothing of a messenger to Athens after the battle. (One wonders just how the Athenians had managed to reach 490 BC without acquiring a horse.) A few later Greek sources refer to the event, but none ever met living witnesses to this Marathon. Herodotus may well have met some elderly survivors, writing nearly half a century after the events.

## More Recently

As with numerous popular legends, this one owes its modern currency to a poet. In 1879, Robert Browning published "Pheidippides," in which the runner makes the run to Sparta and back *á la* Herodotus' histories, then the run to Athens where he announces Athens' salvation before keeling over.

People believed this, as they are apt to believe nearly any legend embellished by a poet. What's more, a philhellenic era was about to revive the ancient Olympics in modern form, minus the prostitutes and blood sports. In 1896, the modern Olympics restarted and included a marathon for men. It took 88 more years to include one for women. Marathon lengths have varied over the years but not by much. The modern distance is 26.22 miles.

Today, of course, "marathon" has come to mean either an endur-ance footrace or any ultra-long event, such as an 18-inning baseball game or an office meeting that lasts until nearly every bladder present is about to rupture.

## A Grand Gesture

*In ancient Rome, gladiators fought each other in front of thousands of spectators, but the last thing the loser wanted to see from the crowd was a collective "thumbs-up."*

✳    ✳    ✳    ✳

IN THE ROMAN empire of the first centuries AD, gladiatorial games that pitted man against man or man against beast were the most popular form of public entertainment. With these games came an involved set of rules, including what a gladia-tor should do once he had his opponent defeated: go for the kill, or show mercy. Historians have argued that this decision was often left up to the crowd. According to popular belief, a thumbs-down gesture meant instant slaughter, while spectators' thumbs turned up meant the loser would live. In fact, it worked the opposite way.

It is almost certain that the Roman crowds used some sort of thumb gesture to indicate the fate they wished on the van-quished, but the assumption that a "thumbs-up" meant mercy is probably colored by the contemporary Western meaning of the signal. Some historians believe "thumbs-down" actually indicated that the triumphant gladiator should lay down his weapon and spare his foe, while "thumbs-up" indicated that the victor should slash open his opponent's throat. Another theory posits that a "thumbs-sideways" motion symbolized a slash to the neck.

# Why Isn't a Boxing Ring Round?

*Boxing has been around for ages because, when you get down to it, humans like to pummel each other. The ancient Greeks were the ones who decided to make it into a legitimate sport: Boxing was introduced as an Olympic event in 688 BC. The competitors wrapped pieces of soft leather around their hands and proceeded to fight.*

＊　＊　＊　＊

THE ROMANS TOOK it a little further, adding bits of metal to the leather. No wonder those guys ruled most of the known world for so long! Fast forward to England in the eighteenth century. Boxing was popular—and it was violent. The fighters battled each other inside a ring of rope that was lined with—and sometimes held up by—spectators. That's right, a *ring*. These spectators couldn't be counted on to be sober and often raucously crowded the boxers—the rope ring would get smaller and smaller until the onlookers were practically on top of the fighters. Often the spectators would have a go at it with the boxers themselves.

Naturally, the fighters got a bit testy about this. Jack Broughton, a heavyweight champion, came up with a set of rules to protect his fellow boxers in 1743. These included a chalked-off square inside which boxers would fight. Event organizers attached rope to stakes that were pounded into the ground, which prevented the fighting area from changing sizes and from being invaded. Why a square? Because it was easy to make.

Broughton's rules were eventually revised to formalize the square shape. By 1853, the rules stated that matches had to take place in a twenty-four-foot square "ring" that was enclosed by ropes. That, good reader, is the origin of what boxing aficionados call "the squared circle."

# The Sad Saga of Sonny Liston

*Climbing up from utter poverty, this world heavyweight champ found controversial success in the boxing ring but couldn't maintain his balance on the outside.*

✳ ✳ ✳ ✳

CHARLES "SONNY" LISTON was born the son of an impoverished sharecropper in rural Arkansas, probably on May 8, but the year of his birth is unknown. This is the first of many mysteries in the life of a complicated, impenetrable man. Though many who knew him said he was born in 1927, Liston himself claimed he was born in 1932, and contemporary documents seem to back him up. Emotionally and physically abused, young Liston was not unhappy when his miserable parents split up and his mother moved to St. Louis—in fact, he followed her there as soon as he could.

## The Hard Time

Liston was only in his early teens when he made his way north, and like everyone else in his family, he was illiterate. He had his imposing build going for him, however, and this led local organized crime to recruit him as a debt collector. As long as Liston stuck to breaking kneecaps, he was to some degree under the mob's protection from law enforcement. But when he struck out on his own, robbing two gas stations and a restaurant with other youths in 1950, the police caught up to him, and he was busted. Liston pleaded guilty to two counts of robbery and two counts of larceny—he was lucky to be sentenced to concurrent prison terms that ran only five years.

In the penitentiary, a Roman Catholic priest noticed Liston's remarkable physique and urged him to take up boxing. Liston followed that advice, and after serving only two years of his time, he was paroled to a team of "handlers" who worked for St. Louis mobster John Vitale. Vitale set Liston up in the boxing world and controlled his contract for six years before selling it to Frankie Carbo and Blinky Palermo, underworld figures on the East Coast. Eventually, Liston's criminal ties would lead him all the way to the U.S. Senate, where in 1960 he testified before a subcommittee investigating organized crime's control of boxing.

## The Big Time

Liston's first professional fight lasted only 33 seconds—he took out Don Smith with only one punch. His first five fights were in St. Louis, but his sixth was in Detroit. In that nationally televised bout, he won an eight-round decision against John Summerlin. The odds had been long, so the fight garnered the young upstart a lot of attention. He suffered his first professional defeat from his next opponent, when Marty Marshall broke his jaw. Nevertheless, Liston moved steadily up the ranks, and finally, at Chicago's Comiskey Park in 1962, he became the heavyweight champion of the world by knocking out Floyd Patterson in the first round.

Fighting success did not keep him out of trouble with the law, however. A total of 19 arrests and a second jail sentence made Liston an unpopular figure on the American sports scene. Many of his fights were thought to be fixed, and some considered him a puppet of the mob. Unfortunately for him, Liston's most famous moment was one of defeat: his knockout by Muhammad Ali on May 25, 1965. In one of the most famous sports photos ever taken, *Sports Illustrated* photographer Neil Leifer shot Liston sprawled on the mat with a menacing, screaming Ali towering over him. Some claim that Ali's punch was a "phantom punch" that never connected and that Liston had taken a dive because he feared the Nation of Islam.

## Strange Death

On January 5, 1971, he was found dead in his Las Vegas home by his wife, Geraldine, who had been out of town. Though the coroner ruled that he had died from heart failure and lung congestion, Liston's body was in a state of decomposition, and there was much speculation that Liston had been murdered by unsavory associates. The man who came into the world so anonymously that his birth year was not really known left it in fame, but with just as many unanswered questions.

## Fran's Father

*It is said that the death of Fran Tarkenton's father was caused by officiating miscues in the 1975 playoff game between Minnesota and Dallas. Tarkenton's father did die during the game, but it was before the referees made their blunders.*

✳ ✳ ✳ ✳

ONE MUST APPROACH such a macabre myth delicately, which is more than can be said for the perpetrators of this tall tale, who were probably the same lunatics who plunked an on-field official with a whiskey bottle during the tumultuous NFL contest that was played on December 28, 1975.

That year, the Minnesota Vikings had pillaged their way through the regular season, posting a 12–2 record. Bolstered by quarterback Fran Tarkenton, the Vikings were not expected to have any trouble subduing the Dallas Cowboys when they clashed in Minnesota on that solemn Sunday. Less than six minutes remained on the clock when the men in stripes began their football follies.

The first questionable call came when Dallas receiver Drew Pearson appeared to step out of bounds before snagging a do-or-die pass on a fourth-and-sixteen play. The officials ruled that Pearson had kept both feet in play. With only a handful of ticks left in the game and Dallas still trailing 14–10, Roger Staubach pitched a prayer toward the end zone before disappearing under a mound of Minnesota muscle. Pearson caught the ball, but he appeared to push Viking defender Nate Wright to the ground before grabbing the toss. Once again, the on-field zebras ignored the malfeasance and signaled a touchdown.

A shower of debris rained onto the field, including the well-flung bottle that bopped field judge Armen Terzian. After the contest, Tarkenton learned that his father had suffered a fatal heart attack during the third quarter of the game, long before the tables had turned. Staubach's miracle missile was later described as a "Hail Mary," the first time that divine designation was applied to a flying football.

# The Bad and the Ugly

*The integrity of the game is of utmost importance in baseball. Unfortunately, that honor has not always been upheld.*

✳   ✳   ✳   ✳

### Money to Be Made? You Bet

GAME-FIXING DIDN'T START with the 1919 White Sox, although the Black Sox scandal has come to define this crime. It actually began when the National League was barely a year old.

The first-place 1877 Louisville Grays made a number of suspicious errors during an Eastern road trip that caused them to lose seven games and tie one. This prompted speculation that players dumped games—and the pennant—intentionally. It turned out they did. Western Union telegrams linked players with a known gambler, and four men—Bill Craver, Jim Devlin, Al Nichols, and George Hall (who confessed)—were banned from baseball for life.

The first two decades of the 20th century were also filled with baseball corruption. First baseman Hal Chase served as its poster boy, having been linked to several "thrown" games before earning a ban for his role in the Black Sox scandal. There were attempts to bribe umpires (Bill Klem in 1908) and even official scorers (a 1910 attempt to get Cleveland's Nap Lajoie a batting title over the unpopular Ty Cobb). Suspicions that the 1914, 1917, and 1918 World Series were fixed were never proven, or perhaps the drama of 1919 would have been avoided. As it was, the eight White Sox players banned for life served notice that baseball was serious about keeping its games on the up-and-up.

## Charlie "Hustle"

If the 1919 White Sox are Exhibit A in the argument against game-fixing, Pete Rose holds the same distinction when it comes to the dangers of gambling. In 1989, the all-time major-league hits king was banned from baseball (and subsequently from becoming eligible for Hall of Fame election) for bets he made while managing the Cincinnati Reds.

Initially, Rose vehemently denied having bet on the game. In his 2003 book *My Prison Without Bars*, however, he admitted to placing wagers with bookmakers as many as five times per week on Reds games while serving as the team's manager. He insists he never bet against the Reds as he continues to plead his case for reinstatement, but thus far the commissioner's office has held its ground.

Rose wrote: "I've consistently heard the statement: 'If Pete Rose came clean, all would be forgiven.' Well, I've done what you've asked. The rest is up to the commissioner and the big umpire in the sky."

## Colluding with the "Enemy"

Collusion is defined as a secret agreement, particularly one used for treacherous purposes. Baseball fans learned the word in the 1980s, when owners apparently worked together to keep player salaries down at a time when the game was thriving financially.

From 1984 to 1987, baseball attendance soared, as did profits, yet free-agent salaries did not. For example, in 1985 more than half of all players who filed for free agency wound up signing with other clubs. The following year, however, only four of 33 signed deals with new teams. The rest re-signed with their old clubs—some for less money than they'd made before. Furthermore, most were only offered one-year contracts.

The players union filed a grievance in February 1986 called Collusion I, and 19 months later an arbitrator ruled in their favor. Team owners were forced to pay damages for their decision not to outbid one another for players, thus stifling salary growth. Collusion grievances were brought twice more against owners during this period. An arbitrator sided with players on those occasions, too. In all, owners were found to owe more than $100 million in the 1980s collusion cases.

## Cocaine Crackdown

Celebrating wins or drowning the sorrow of a loss into the early morning hours can be traced back to baseball's inception. And some of the game's greatest players were also among its legendary carousers. Somewhere along the line, however, instances of illegal and dangerous off-field behavior became no innocent matter.

Texas pitcher Fergie Jenkins was arrested in 1980 and charged with possession of marijuana, hashish, and cocaine. What followed was a rapid-fire succession of drug-related incidents. Padres rookie Alan Wiggins was arrested for cocaine possession in 1982. That year also marked the first of several rehab attempts by Dodgers pitcher Steve Howe, who was also repeatedly suspended. Kansas City teammates Willie Aikens, Vida Blue, Jerry Martin, and Willie Wilson pleaded guilty in 1983 to attempting to purchase cocaine.

In 1985, a federal grand jury in Pittsburgh heard testimony from 11 active big-leaguers. The result: An indictment of seven drug dealers who were linked to players between 1979 and '85. During the "Pittsburgh Drug Trials," Mets first baseman Keith Hernandez estimated that 40 percent of players had used cocaine by 1980. Soon after, some of his teammates—most notably Dwight Gooden and Darryl Strawberry—could be counted among that number.

## Steroid Scandals

During the last decade, the game's longstanding home run records have fallen in rapid succession as several players have made enormous gains in strength and stature. Few would argue that some of those gains have not been natural ones. In fact, in his 2004 State of the Union address, President George W. Bush called for "strong steps" to be taken to rid baseball of performance-enhancing drugs.

While the "steroid scandal" has been highlighted by far more speculation than fact, grand jury testimony in a highly publicized case against the San Francisco–area laboratory BALCO did produce some compelling testimony about the use of these drugs. As a result of the same case, Barry Bonds admitted to using two types of performance enhancers—the "clear" and the "cream"—but said it was without knowledge of what those substances contained.

As President Bush (a former part-owner of the Texas Rangers) said in his State of the Union address, "The use of performance-enhancing drugs like steroids in baseball, football, and other sports is dangerous and sends the wrong message—that there are shortcuts to accomplishment."

# When Bicycles Ruled the (Sporting) World

*What sport lasted a day longer than the ancient Olympics, broke the race barrier before baseball, and caused more injuries than modern football? Turn-of-the-century bicycle racing, of course.*

✳ ✳ ✳ ✳

## Blood, Guts, and Determination

IN 1900, THE most popular sport in North America was the grueling phenomenon known as the six-day bicycle race. Usually held on indoor velodromes with wooden tracks, teams of two would compete for 144 hours, taking turns accruing laps and competing in sprinting events. These six-day events were not a sport for the faint of heart. At a race, as many as 70,000 fans would thrill to the sight of these riders sustaining serious, often fatal, injuries and pushing themselves to the limits of endurance. Here are some of the sport's major players.

### Reggie McNamara (1887–1970)

Dubbed the "Iron Man" of cycling, Australian Reggie McNamara had a seemingly inhuman capacity for the punishment and exertion that defined the six-day events. On the fourth day of a competition in Melbourne, McNamara underwent an emergency trackside operation without anesthesia to remove a large abscess "from his side." Though he lost a considerable amount of blood, he rose from the dust and, ignoring the entreaties of his trainer and doctor, resumed the race. In fact, his injuries on the track put him in the hospital so often that he wound up marrying an American nurse after a 1913 competition in New York. He achieved several world records and defeated the French champions so soundly that they refused to ride against him.

### Bobby Walthour (1878–1949)

During his career, bicycling champion Bobby Walthour of Atlanta, Georgia, suffered nearly 50 collarbone fractures and was twice assumed to be dead on the track—only to rise and continue riding. By the time he was age 18, he was the undisputed champion of the South; soon he held the title of international champion and kept it for several years. In addition to making himself and cycling familiar to people all over the world, Walthour brought a great deal of prominence to his native Atlanta. Invigorated by his accomplishments, Atlanta built the Coliseum, one of the world's preeminent velodromes at the time.

## Marshall "Major" Taylor (1879–1932)

African American cyclist Major Taylor, the son of an Indianapolis coach driver, proved that endurance bicycling was a sport in which individual talent could not be denied. In an era of overt racism and discrimination, he rose through the cycling ranks to become one of the highest paid athletes of his time. After relocating to the somewhat more race-tolerant Worcester, Massachusetts, Taylor began to rack up a string of impressive victories in the six-day and sprinting competitions. Dubbed the "Worcester Whirlwind," Taylor toured the world, defeated Europe's best riders, and set several world records during his professional career.

## Enter the Machines

Like modern stock car racing, six-day cycling events used pacing vehicles. Originally, these were bicycles powered by two to five riders. But in 1895, English races began using primitive motorcycles. These new pace vehicles allowed the cyclists to travel faster, owing to the aerodynamic draft produced by the machines. Crowds thrilled to the speed and noise of these mechanical monsters, which weighed about 300 pounds each.

It took two men to operate the motorcycles, one to steer and one to control the engine. They were also quite dangerous: A tandem pacer forced off the track in Waltham, Massachusetts on May 30, 1900, killed both riders and injured several fans. The advent of motorcycles increased the popularity of the six-day races for a time, but it waned with the arrival of a new vehicle spectators preferred over bicycles: the automobile.

# A Royal Flush

*Every year at the end of January, rumors begin to swirl that the sewer systems in several major cities fail due to the number of toilets that are flushed during halftime of the Super Bowl.*

✳   ✳   ✳   ✳

## A Mad Dash

DURING SUPER BOWL XVIII in 1984, a water main in Salt Lake City ruptured, dampening the sporting spirit in that community. The next day, conversations around office water coolers were rife with rumors that toilet trauma, prompted by a flood of beverage-logged football fans all using the facilities at the same time, had caused the sewer systems of numerous cities to clog up. Such a myth would almost make sense if it were applied to the final of the World Cup of Soccer, where there is continuous action without stoppages of any kind until the halftime break. But anyone who has sat through the six-plus-hour spectacle known as the Super Bowl realizes that there is no merit to this tall tale. The North American brand of football—especially the game played on that particular Sunday—has numerous breaks, pauses, and lapses throughout. So to suggest there is a simultaneous dash to the latrine at any time during this all-day marathon is silly.

## Can't-Miss TV

The quality of Super Bowl TV commercials (which can cost millions of dollars for a mere 30-second spot) usually keeps even disinterested viewers glued to their seats. Although the ads aired on Super Bowl Sunday are among the most highly anticipated events in that day's lineup, most of them are shown during the pre-game, halftime, and post-game spectacles, leaving valuable lulls during football action for human nature's pause for the cause.

# Why Is a Football Shaped That Way?

*Would you rather call it a bladder? Because that's what footballs were made of before mass-produced rubber or leather balls became the norm.*

✳  ✳  ✳  ✳

**T**HE ORIGINS OF the ball and the game can be traced back to the ancient Greeks, who played something called *harpaston*. As in football, players scored by kicking, passing, or running over the opposition's goal line. The ball in harpaston was often made of a pig's bladder. This is because pigs' bladders were easy to find, roundish in shape, relatively simple to inflate and seal, and fairly durable. (If you think playing ball with an internal organ is gross, consider what the pig's bladder replaced: a human head.)

Harpaston evolved into European rugby, which evolved into American football. By the time the first "official" football game was played at Rutgers University in New Jersey in the fall of 1869, the ball had evolved, too. To make the ball more durable and consistently shaped, it was covered with a protective layer that was usually made of leather.

Still, the extra protection didn't help the pig's bladder stay permanently inflated, and there was a continuous need to reinflate the ball. Whenever play was stopped, the referee unlocked the ball—yes, there was a little lock on it to help keep it inflated—and a player would pump it up.

Footballs back then were meant to be round, but the sphere was imperfect for a couple reasons. First, the bladder lent itself more to an oval shape; even the most perfectly stitched leather covering couldn't force the bladder to remain circular. Second, as a game wore on, players got tired and were less enthused about reinflating the ball. As a result, the ball would flatten out and take on more of an oblong shape. The ball was easier to grip in that shape, and the form slowly gained popularity, particularly after the forward pass was introduced in 1906.

Through a series of rule changes relating to its shape, the football became slimmer and ultimately developed its current look. And although it's been many decades since pigs' bladders were relieved of their duties, the football's nickname—a "pigskin"—lives on.

# The Heisman Curse

*After being named best college football player in the nation, one's best position might be "fallback." Those who believe the Heisman Curse is just a sports myth should consider the following.*

✳ ✳ ✳ ✳

DURING A FOOTBALL game in 1934, University of Chicago running back Jay Berwanger collided with University of Michigan defender Gerald Ford, bloodying the tackler's left cheek. The resulting scar on the future U.S. president would be permanent—as would, some say, the so-called Heisman Curse it begat.

A year later, Berwanger was awarded the first Heisman Trophy, emblematic of the best player in college football. Although he also became the first man ever drafted by the NFL, the "Genius of the Gridiron" never played another snap. Surprisingly few of the over six dozen trophy recipients since have made more of an impact.

In recent years, the list of Heisman honorees has included several pro football busts, especially at the marquee quarterback position. Charlie Ward (1993), Eric Crouch (2001), and Jason White (2003) never played an NFL game. Danny Wuerffel (1996) earned just ten starts, and though Chris Weinke (2000) made 19, his team won just one of them.

Berwanger himself tacitly acknowledged that the Heisman wasn't worth the 25 pounds of bronze used to cast it. Until he eventually donated it to his alma mater, the trophy was displayed in his aunt's library—as a doorstop.

## The Phantom Punch

*When Sonny Liston hit the canvas less than two minutes into his second heavyweight-belt bout with Muhammad Ali, pundits immediately accused the former champ of taking a dive. Did the lumbering Liston really fake a fall?*

❋　❋　❋　❋

EVEN WITHOUT THE controversial conclusion to the widely publicized Sonny Liston-Muhammad Ali rematch on May 25, 1965, there was enough ink and intrigue to fill a John LeCarre spy novel. The bout against Ali—who had just joined the Nation of Islam and changed his name from Cassius Clay—was held in a 6,000-seat arena in Lewiston, Maine, after numerous states refused to sanction the fight because of militant behavior associated with the Muslim movement.

Robert Goulet, the velvet-voiced crooner entrusted with singing the national anthem, forgot the words to the song, and the third man in the ring, Jersey Joe Walcott, was a former heavyweight champion but a novice referee. One minute and 42 seconds into the fight, Ali threw a quick uppercut that seemed to connect with nothing but air. Liston tumbled to the tarmac, though no one seemed sure whether it was the breeze from the blow or the blow itself that put him there. Liston was ultimately counted out by the ringside timer, not the in-ring referee.

Since it was a largely invisible swing (dubbed the "phantom punch" by sports scribes) that floored Liston, he was accused of cashing it in just to cash in. Evidence proves otherwise. Film footage of the bout shows Liston caught flush with a quick, pistonlike "anchor" punch that Ali claimed was designed to be a surprise. Liston actually got back up and was trading body blows with the Louisville Lip when the referee stepped in, stopped the fight, and informed Liston that his bid to become the first boxer to regain the heavyweight title was over.

# Gambling

*Most people would cheat Las Vegas blind if they could get away with it—but few bother to try. We asked some questions about the fine art of betting, and its shady side.*

**Q: How would someone mark cards?**

A: You need two things: very sharp eyes and a deck with a repeating pattern on the back—Bicycles, Bees, and Aviators are great, but corporate logo decks are terrible. Ideally, use cards with backs printed in a color matching a fine-tip permanent marker. Then decide what mark will encode each suit and rank, and very carefully mark the cards. Since cards can be upside-down, and since most people fan them so as to view the upper left corners, mark both the upper left and lower right of each card. Wear prescription sunglasses so people can't see you staring at the backs of the cards they're holding.

**Q: Does card counting really work in blackjack?**

A: Depends how many decks there are, first of all. The more decks are used at once, the less fruit card counting can bear. There are two types of card counting: in your head and mechanically assisted. The casino can't stop you from counting cards in your head; it can only make it more difficult for you. Some states have laws against mechanical assistance, and if you're caught with it, expect a quick blackball from every casino in the region.

**Q: Is anyone getting away with counting cards?**

A: Have no doubt of that. You'll never hear of them, because they will never be caught. Pigs get fat; hogs get slaughtered, as tax accountants say. They make reasonable money, they go to different places, they lose sometimes, they act like your everyday gambling addict or hobbyist. They don't give the game away by placing suspicious bets; they know how to behave, be friendly, flirt with employees. They stay under the radar. When the numbers are in their favor, they bet more; when numbers aren't good, they bet less, but they don't overdo it.

**Q: How do casinos battle card counters?**

A: First of all, from the pit boss to the security office, people are watching. When gambling you should consider yourself under surveillance from head to toe. I wouldn't put it past casinos to have night-vision cameras underneath the tables. They have a lot of experience and know what to look for. Free drinks are another tool, because hardly anyone's counting skills improve with alcohol intake. If the boss thinks you're counting, he or she may "flat bet" you—ask you to make the same wager on every hand, which is the opposite of what a counter is trying to do. What they're looking for is your reaction to that request. If you don't follow it, they'll ask you to leave.

**Q: What are the best and worst games in terms of payout?**

A: Casino poker, blackjack card counting, and video poker generally pay best. Slot machines are terrible, as are live keno and Wheel of Fortune. House payouts tend to range from 85 to 95 percent overall, so on the whole, the game favors the casino. Do you think all those pyramids, sphinxes, complimentary buffets, and neon lights come from the money people have won?

# The Shotgun Offense

*Some college football coaches have armed state troopers with them on the sideline, a peculiar tradition that dates back more than 50 years.*

✳ ✳ ✳ ✳

## It Began with the "Bear"

**A** COUPLE OF STATE troopers are the ultimate accessories for a major-college football coach—especially in the pigskin-crazed South. No one is certain how the tradition started, but it's usually attributed to Paul "Bear" Bryant, who was a legendary coach at the University of Alabama. The story is that Bear got a trooper entourage for security in 1958 or 1959. Not to be outdone, Ralph "Shug" Jordan, coach at Auburn University, Alabama's bitter in-state rival, secured a larger posse of troopers soon after. Let the games begin.

The tradition is both ceremonial and practical. Ceremonially, the troopers represent state pride, whether at home or away. Troopers have no law enforcement authority in another state, but armed and dressed in their official garb, they can be an imposing presence on the sideline.

From a practical perspective, the troopers' chief responsibility is to provide protection. This rarely is an issue during the game, but the playing field can fill up quickly with excited and rambunctious fans once the final seconds have ticked away. It is the job of troopers to escort the coach through the ensuing chaos to midfield for the traditional handshake with the opposing coach (who also might be flanked by troopers) and then to the locker room.

## The Price of Packing Heat

This sort of security doesn't come cheap. In 2008, for example, ten schools in Alabama each paid the state police more than $38,000 for "football detail." However, some troopers in other states provide coach protection at no cost, as long as the college pays for meals and travel expenses.

The practice is nearly ubiquitous among NCAA Division I-A teams in the Southeastern Conference and has also caught on with some schools in the ACC, Big East, Big 12, and Big Ten conferences. Trooper detail hasn't taken root in the West, however—the Pacific-10 Conference is explicitly opposed to the practice. Teams that don't have trooper support generally rely on campus police for coach security.

For a trooper assigned to a coach, staying calm, cool, and collected might be the toughest part of the gig. Troopers typically are huge fans of their assigned teams, but they're expected to maintain stoic professionalism. And this is no small feat if they've just witnessed a game-winning touchdown.

# Whistle Stop!

*What do a police officer directing traffic, a football referee calling a foul, and a schoolteacher trying to keep students under control have in common? If they're using a whistle, it was probably manufactured by the American Whistle Corporation.*

✳ ✳ ✳ ✳

BASED IN COLUMBUS, Ohio, the American Whistle Corporation is the only metal whistle manufacturer based in the United States. And AWC takes its product seriously—in certain circumstances, a loud whistle can save lives. The company was founded in 1956 as Colsoff Manufacturing and was purchased by its current owner, Ray Giesse, in 1987. It currently manufactures more than a million chrome-plated brass whistles a year for clients that range from municipal police departments to the referees who officiate at major sporting events like the Super Bowl.

## The Loudest Around

Whistles from AWC have been found in some truly unique places, including the wedding of Giesse's daughter. To commemorate the event, Giesse produced 230 custom whistles, each stamped with a heart and the names of the bride and groom. Guests received their whistles at the reception, resulting in an almost deafening din.

A lot goes into the production of an AWC whistle. According to the company's website, the process begins with coiled brass, 30-ton presses, and state-of-the-art soldering tables; and continues with polishing and specialized plating. Lastly, a tiny ball made of synthetic cork is stuffed inside each whistle.

AWC whistles are the loudest commercial whistles available— at least four decibels higher than those of their competitors, according to company PR. Whistle lovers can join the thousands who have toured the company's manufacturing plant by calling AWC and reserving a spot.

# Oddities Surrounding the 1900 Olympics

*The second modern Olympic Games were held in 1900 in Paris and were billed as part of the Exposition Universelle Internationale, the world's fair that featured the unveiling of the Eiffel Tower. It was the first Olympiad to be held outside of Greece, and there were plenty of other firsts to it as well.*

✳ ✳ ✳ ✳

✳ Despite the fact that nearly a thousand athletes competed in the 1900 Olympics, spectator attendance was low. The press preferred to focus on the Paris Exposition and seldom referred to the games as actual Olympic events. Instead, they were reported variously as "International Championships," "Paris Championships," "World Championships," and even "Grand Prix of the Paris Exposition." The founder of the International Olympic Committee, Baron Pierre de Coubertin, later said: "It's a miracle that the Olympic movement survived that celebration."

\* The Olympic status of the athletes was equally downplayed, to the extent that many competitors never actually knew they were participating in the Olympics. Margaret Ives Abbott, a student from Chicago who won the nine-hole women's golf tournament, died in 1955 without realizing she was America's first female Olympic champion.

\* Because the Olympics were held in conjunction with the Paris Exhibition, the scheduling and locations of the sporting events were often absurd. The fencing competition, for instance, was held as a sort of sideshow in the exhibition's cutlery area, and swimmers were forced to battle the polluted waters and strong currents of the Seine.

\* After preliminary rounds, Myer Prinstein (from Syracuse University) had a clear lead in the long-jump competition and seemed poised to win. But when the final jump was scheduled on a Sunday, the official in charge of U.S. athletes disapproved of their competing on the Christian Sabbath. The athletes gave their word not to participate; Prinstein, who was Jewish, reluctantly agreed as well. On Sunday, however, Prinstein's main rival, Alvin Kraenzlein (University of Pennsylvania), broke his promise and competed, beating Prinstein's qualifying jump by a centimeter and winning the gold. Allegedly, Prinstein was so angry that he punched Kraenzlein in the face.

\* Alvin Kraenzlein also won the 110-meter hurdles, the 220-meter hurdles, and the 60-meter dash—and he did it in three days. He was the first track-and-field athlete to accomplish the feat of winning four gold medals in individual events at a single Olympics.

* Women made their first appearance in the 1900 Games, albeit in small numbers: Of the thousand or so athletes participating, only 22 were women. The first female Olympic champion was Charlotte Cooper of Great Britain, who won the tennis singles and the mixed doubles. Female athletes wore the ankle-length skirts and dresses typical of the time.

* Ray Ewry of Indiana won the gold in three championships—standing high jump, standing long jump, and standing triple jump—all on the same day. A remarkable feat for any man, these victories amounted to Olympic heroism for Ewry, who had spent his childhood confined to a wheelchair because of polio.

* After the French won both gold and silver medals in the marathon, three runners from the United States contested the results, accusing the winners of taking a short cut. As proof, they submitted their observation that the new champions were the only contestants not splattered with mud. Although the objection was not sustained, the celebratory spirit had been soured.

# The Game of Kings

*Chess is a game where protecting the king is key. So it should come as little surprise that it may once have been a favorite of royalty.*

\* \* \* \*

OFTEN CALLED THE "royal game," chess is one of the world's most popular games and is enjoyed by millions. It is played informally by friends, in clubs, in tournaments, and even in international tournaments. In its design and strategy, chess delightfully meshes simplicity with complexity and has attracted players the world over; by phone, by mail, and online, players carry on long, thoughtful games that can last years.

Chess has its roots in India and dates to the sixth century AD. It arrived in Europe in the tenth century, where it soon became a court favorite of the nobility. Europe is the likely origin of the modern pieces, which include a king and queen and other notable ranks of the Middle Ages—eight pawns, a pair of knights, a pair of bishops, and a pair of rooks. The latter pieces were called *chariots* in the Persian game before transforming to the castle pieces in the Westernized version.

The game is played on an eight-by-eight board of 64 squares. Players take alternating turns, and the game continues until one player is able to "checkmate" the opponent's king, a strategic move that prevents the king from escaping an attack on the next turn. The game can also end in a draw in certain scenarios. Each piece moves according to specific rules that dictate how many squares it can traverse and in what direction. The queen is generally considered the most powerful piece on the board—perhaps a nod to the power the queen wielded when the game arrived in Europe.

The first modern chess tournament was held in London in 1851 and was won by Adolf Anderssen, who would become a leading chess master. Since then, computer programmers have developed game strategy using artificial intelligence, and for years there were attempts to create a computer that could defeat the best human players. This finally happened in 1997 when a computer defeated world champion Garry Kasparov.

# The Art of Gurning

*An untold number of mothers have warned their children, "If you keep twisting your face, it will stay that way permanently!" Little did Mom know that making ugly faces could be viewed as training for a gurning competition.*

❋  ❋  ❋  ❋

GURNING IS A contest that pits challengers vying to contort their faces into unbelievable displays of anatomical distortions. The mother of all gurning contests is held each year at the Egremont Crab Fair in Cumbria, England. Contestants come from every corner of the globe to see who can pull the "world's ugliest face." But, unlike other natural advantages in life, being ugly to begin with doesn't necessarily mean that you'll win.

"Just because you're oogly doesn't mean to say that ya [gonna] win it," says gurning champion Peter Jackman in the book *True Brits*. "Because gurnin' means the art of pullin' faces, not oogliness." On the other hand, points are awarded to contestants who can accentuate what they do or don't naturally have to work with. "You get fellows like Peter," says Egremont organizer Alan Clements. "He's a good-lookin' guy, but he can make himself into a monster—that's what you're lookin' for."

Winning a gurning championship doesn't come easy. Champs like Gordon Mattinson practice day in and day out until they can accomplish with their faces what you can only imagine in your nightmares. The most successful gurners even come up with names for their faces. Mattinson perfected his "Quasimodo," while the late Ron Looney became famous for his "Popeye."

And, just in case you're thinking about stopping by Egremont on your next vacation to capture the prize, be advised that gurning is a sport for professionals. Amateurs rarely make it to the final round. "They don't really know what gurnin's about," says Jackman. The Egremont Gurning Championship is held every year during the third week of September.

# Danger on the Golf Course

*Most golfers have encountered some wildlife on the golf course. And many of us have heard stories about people being struck by lightning—or errant golf balls. But if these golf courses could talk, they'd have some really scary stories to tell. Players beware.*

✳ ✳ ✳ ✳

## Beachwood Golf Course, Natal, South Africa

AFTER HITTING HER way out of a bunker on this beautiful African course, Molly Whittaker didn't have time to revel in her success. A monkey scrambled out of some nearby bushes, jumped on the unsuspecting woman, and tried to strangle her. Fortunately, her caddie knew just which club would stop the monkeyshines.

## Crane's Landing Golf Course at the Marriott Resort, Lake Villa, Illinois

While the name alone evokes the image of large and graceful birds gliding in for a smooth landing, golfers on this course were not prepared for what they saw touch down on a spring day in 2008. Out of nowhere, a 1949 Piper Clipper airplane landed in the middle of the golf course. A man and his son hopped out, explaining to the surprised and worried golfers that this wasn't an emergency landing. The son was simply late for his tennis lesson across the street and this seemed the best way to get him there fast. Really?

## Merapi Golf Course, Indonesia

The scenery is nothing short of spectacular at this golf course in Indonesia. Surrounded by lush forests, rich farmland, and majestic mountains, it's positively breathtaking—until the mountain volcano comes to life. Yes, Mount Merapi is still an active volcano, having erupted three times since 1990. It's an exciting place to play—but if the emergency warning whistle goes off, don't ask questions. Just run.

### Singapore Island Country Club, Singapore

When pro golfer Jim Stewart played this course in 1982, he was horrified when he was confronted by a ten-foot cobra. He used his golf club to kill the interloper—and then watched in shocked disbelief as another snake slithered out of the dead cobra's mouth.

### Pelham Bay and Split Rock Golf Course, Bronx, New York

On *Law and Order* it seems like all the dead bodies turn up in dumpsters or the East River. But venture a little further, and you'll find another deadly dumping ground. Unfortunately, it's not where you'd want or expect a body to turn up—right in the middle of your Sunday golf game. Between 1986 and 1992 alone, more than 40 bodies were discovered on the grounds of Pelham Bay Park. Now there's an incentive to stay in the fairway.

### Cape Kidnapper's Golf Course, Hawke's Bay, New Zealand

Afraid of heights? This course will take that phobia to a new level. A 550-foot drop to the sea borders six holes. And you thought the rough was bad.

### Uummannaq Golf Course, Greenland

A golfer's paradise this course is not. It's more likely a destination for those interested in extreme sports or defying Mother Nature. Located in Greenland, the world's northernmost golf course is situated on the ice and snow of a glacier, making the play not only chilly, but dangerous.

Golfers shoot orange golf balls (the better to be seen in the snow) and dress in layers upon layers of thermal snow pants and insulated jackets. Oh yeah, and did we mention that golfers are required to sign a waiver relieving the owners of any liability in case of injuries or death caused by the extreme conditions?

### Lundin Links, Fife, Scotland

Most golf courses are on the quiet side. Lundin Links is no exception—except for the train tracks that run along the 5th green. Unfortunately for golfer Harold Wallace, even this area is quiet most of the time—until a train comes barreling down the tracks. Mr. Wallace had the misfortune of getting hit while crossing the tracks on his way to the green.

### Skukuza Golf Course, Kruger National Park, South Africa

Violent monkeys like the one that choked Molly Whittaker are probably scarce on this course due to the abundance of other wildlife—lions, elephants, buffaloes, rhinos, and leopards. Wild animals are truly common here, and dangerous. There have been numerous deaths over the years, of both humans and animals. But don't worry—according to management, most of the attacks have been against staff rather than paying guests.

### Prison View Golf Course, Angola, Louisiana

Called the bloodiest prison in the United States, Prison View decided to open a golf course on the premises to encourage employees to hang around on their days off. Now that it's open to the public, who wouldn't jump at the chance to play a round? Just remember these simple rules: You'll need to allow at least 48 hours between making your tee time and actually hitting the links so they can conduct a complete background check. When you arrive, be prepared to undergo an airport-style security check and vehicle search. In case you were wondering, no alcohol or weapons are allowed on the premises. And if a big burly guard—or anyone wearing handcuffs—catches up with your foursome, you might want to let them play through.

# Beefed Up

*You're probably familiar with the terms "juiced," "roid-raged," "hyped," and "pumped"—all used to describe the effects of anabolic steroids. For better or for worse, steroids have invaded the worlds of professional and amateur sports, and even show business.*

✳   ✳   ✳   ✳

## Better Living Through Chemistry

ANABOLIC STEROIDS (ALSO called anabolic-androgenic steroids or AAS) are a specific class of hormones that are related to the male hormone testosterone. Steroids have been used for thousands of years in traditional medicine to promote healing in diseases such as cancer and AIDS. French neurologist Charles-Édouard Brown-Séquard was one of the first physicians to report its healing properties after injecting himself with an extract of guinea pig testicles in 1889. In 1935, two German scientists applied for the first steroid-use patent and were offered the 1939 Nobel Prize for Chemistry, but they were forced to decline the honor by the Nazi government.

Interest in steroids continued during World War II. Third Reich scientists experimented on concentration camp inmates to treat symptoms of chronic wasting as well as to test its effects on heightened aggression in German soldiers. Even Adolf Hitler was injected with steroids to treat his endless list of maladies.

## Giving Athletes a Helping Hand

The first reference to steroid use for performance enhancement in sports dates back to a 1938 *Strength and Health* magazine letter to the editor, inquiring how steroids could improve performance in weightlifting and bodybuilding. During the 1940s, the Soviet Union and a number of Eastern Bloc countries built aggressive steroid programs designed to improve the performance of Olympic and amateur weight lifters. The program was so successful that U.S. Olympic team physicians worked with American chemists to design Dianabol, which they administered to U.S. athletes.

Since their early development, steroids have gradually crept into the world of professional and amateur sports. The use of steroids have become commonplace in baseball, football, cycling, track—even golf and cricket. In the 2006 *Monitor the Future* survey, steroid use was measured in eighth-, tenth-, and twelfth-grade students; a little more than 2 percent of male high school seniors admitted to using steroids during the past year, largely because of their steroid-using role models in professional sports.

## Bigger, Faster, Stronger—Kinda

Steroids have a number of performance enhancement perks for athletes such as promoting cell growth, protein synthesis from amino acids, increasing appetite, bone strengthening, and the stimulation of bone marrow and production of red blood cells. Of course, there are a few "minor" side effects to contend with as well: shrinking testicles, reduced sperm count, infertility, acne, high blood pressure, blood clotting, liver damage, headaches, aching joints, nausea, vomiting, diarrhea, loss of sleep, severe mood swings, paranoia, panic attacks, depression, male pattern baldness, the cessation of menstruation in women, and an increased risk of prostate cancer—small compromises in the name of athletic achievement, right?

While many countries have banned the sale of anabolic steroids for non-medical applications, they are still legal in Mexico and Thailand. In the United States, steroids are classified as a Schedule III controlled substance, which makes their possession a federal crime, punishable by prison time. But that hasn't deterred athletes from looking for that extra edge. And there are thousands of black-market vendors willing to sell more than 50 different varieties of steroids. Largely produced in countries where they are legal, steroids are smuggled across international borders. Their existence has spawned a new industry for creating counterfeit drugs that are often diluted, cut with fillers, or made from vegetable oil or toxic substances. They are sold through the mail, the internet, in gyms, and at competitions. Many of these drugs are sub-medical or veterinary grade steroids.

## Impact on Sports and Entertainment

Since invading the world of amateur and professional sports, steroid use has become a point of contention, gathering supporters both for and against their use. Arnold Schwarzenegger, the famous bodybuilder, actor, and politician, freely admits to using anabolic steroids while they were still legal. "Steroids were helpful to me in maintaining muscle size while on a strict diet in preparation for a contest," says Schwarzenegger, who held the Mr. Olympia bodybuilding title for seven years. "I did not use them for muscle growth, but rather for muscle maintenance when cutting up."

Lyle Alzado, the colorful, record-setting defensive tackle for the Los Angeles Raiders, Cleveland Browns, and Denver Broncos admitted to taking steroids to stay competitive but acknowledged their risks. "Ninety percent of the athletes I know are on the stuff. We're not born to be 300 lbs. or jump 30 ft. But all the time I was taking steroids, I knew they were making me play better," he said. "I became very violent on the field and off it. I did things only crazy people do. Now look at me. My hair's gone, I wobble when I walk and have to hold on to someone for support and I have trouble remembering things. My last wish? That no one else ever dies this way."

Recently, a few show business celebrities have come under scrutiny for their involvement with steroids and other banned substances. In 2008, 61-year-old *Rambo* star Sylvester Stallone paid $10,600 to settle a criminal drug possession charge for smuggling 48 vials of Human Growth Hormone (HGH) into the country. HGH is popularly used for its anti-aging benefits.

"Everyone over 40 years old would be wise to investigate it (HGH and testosterone use) because it increases the quality of your life," says Stallone.

"If you're an actor in Hollywood and you're over 40, you are doing HGH. Period," said one Hollywood cosmetic surgeon. "Why wouldn't you? It makes your skin look better, your hair, your fingernails. Everything."

# How Do Corked Bats Help Cheating Baseball Players Hit the Ball Farther?

*In this age of performance-enhancing drugs, it's almost refreshing when a hitter gets caught cheating the old-fashioned way. Corked bats somehow recall a more innocent time.*

\* \* \* \*

THERE ARE DIFFERENT ways to cork a wooden baseball bat, but the basic procedure goes like this: Drill a hole into the top of the bat, about an inch in diameter and twelve inches deep; fill the hole with cork—in rolled sheets or ground up—and close the top with a wooden plug that matches the bat; finally, carefully stain and finish the top of the bat so that the plug blends in.

The supposed benefits of a corked bat involve weight and bat speed. Cork is lighter than wood, which enables a player to generate more speed when swinging the bat. The quicker the swing, the greater the force upon contact with the ball—and the farther that ball flies. The lighter weight allows a batter more time to evaluate a pitch, since he can make up the difference with his quicker swing; this extra time amounts to only a fraction of a second, but it can be the difference between a hit and an out at the major league level.

Following the logic we've set forth, replacing the wood in the bat with nothing at all would make for an even lighter bat and, thus, provide more of an advantage. The problem here is that an empty core would increase the likelihood that the bat would break; at the very least, it would cause a suspicious, hollow sound upon contact with the ball. The cork fills in the hollow area, and does so in a lightweight way.

Not everyone believes that a corked bat provides an advantage; some tests have indicated that the decreased bat density actually diminishes the force applied to the ball. But Dr. Robert Watts, a mechanical engineer at Tulane University who studies sports science, sees things differently. He concluded that corking a bat increases the speed of the swing by about 2.5 percent; consequently, the ball might travel an extra fifteen to twenty feet, a distance that would add numerous home runs to a player's total over the course of his career.

# How Come Nobody Else Calls It Soccer?

*Millions of kids across the United States grow up playing a game that their parents hardly know, a game that virtually everyone else in the world calls football. It's soccer to us, of course, and although Americans might be ridiculed for calling it this, the corruption is actually British in origin.*

✳ ✳ ✳ ✳

SOCCER—FOOTBALL, AS THE Brits and others insist—has an ancient history. Evidence of games resembling soccer has been found in cultures that date to the third century BC. The Greeks had a version that they called *episkyro*. The Romans brought their version of the sport along when they colonized what is now England and Ireland. Over the next millennium, the game evolved into a freewheeling, roughneck competition—matches often involved kicking, shoving, and punching.

In England and Ireland, the sport was referred to as football; local and regional rules varied widely. Two different games—football and rugby—slowly emerged from this disorganized mess. The Football Association was formed in 1863 to standardize the rules of football and to separate it from rugby. The term "soccer" most likely is derived from the association's work.

During the late nineteenth century, the Brits developed the linguistic habit of shortening words and adding "-ers" or "-er." (We suffer this quirk to this day in expressions like "preggers." A red card to the Brits on this one.) One popular theory holds that given the trend, it was natural that those playing "Assoc." football were playing "assoccers" or "soccer." The term died out in England, but was revived in the United States in the early part of the twentieth century to separate the imported sport with the round white ball from the American sport with the oblong brown ball.

Soccer has long struggled to catch on as a major spectator sport in the United States. For most Americans, there just isn't enough scoring or action. In fact, many Yanks have their own word for soccer: boring.

# The Trampoline: A New Sport Springs to Life

*The trampoline has become a fixture in backyards and gymnasiums as a source of recreation. But can its origin really be traced to Alaska?*

✳ ✳ ✳ ✳

IF POSTCARDS SOLD in the Anchorage, Alaska, airport are to be believed, the genesis of the trampoline can be traced all the way to the Arctic Circle. The tourist tokens show Eskimos stretching a piece of walrus skin and using the taut tarp to toss each other in the air. It's a good story, but it's not true.

It was actually an athlete and coach from the University of Iowa who created the first manufactured version of the rebounding rig known as the trampoline.

During the winter of 1934, George Nissen, a tumbler on the college gymnastics team, and Larry Griswold, his assistant coach, were discussing ways to add some flair to their rather staid sport. The two men were intrigued by the possibilities presented by the buoyant nature of the safety nets used by trapeze artists. Griswold and Nissen constructed an iron frame and covered it with a large canvas, using springs to connect the cloth to the frame. The apparatus was an effective training device and a popular attraction among the kids who flocked to the local YMCA to watch Nissen perform his routines. The pair of cocreators eventually formed the Griswold-Nissen Trampoline & Tumbling Company and started producing the first commercially available and affordable trampolines.

Nissen can also claim fame for attaching a name to his pliant production. While on a tour of Mexico in the late 1930s, Nissen discovered the Spanish word for springboard was *el trampolin*. Intrigued by the sound of the word, he Anglicized the spelling, and the trampoline was born. In 2000, trampolining graduated from acrobatic activity to certified athletic achievement when it was officially recognized as a medal-worthy Olympic sport.

# If You Build It, They Will Play

*It's safe to say that the inventor of miniature golf hit a hole in one!*

✳    ✳    ✳    ✳

MINIATURE GOLF HAS been described as a novelty game, but it requires the same steady hands, analytical observation, and maneuvering as regular golf.

In their infancy, miniature golf courses were designed the same as full-size courses but were built at one-tenth the size, much like the popular par-3 courses of today. In 1916, James Barber of Pinehurst, North Carolina, created a miniature golf course that resembles the game played today. He dubbed his design "Thistle Dhu," supposedly a twist on the phrase "This'll do." Barber's course was an intricate maze of geometric shapes coupled with symmetric walkways, fountains, and planters. Until 1922, mini-golf courses used live grass—just like the real game—and were subject to the same grooming needs and growing woes. That all changed when a man named Thomas McCulloch Fairbairn prepared a mixture of cottonseed hull—or mulch, sand, oil, and green dye—and used the concoction to resurface the miniature golf course he was designing. The first artificial putting green was born.

The game boomed for the next few years, with hundreds of miniature golf outlets opening around the country, including 150 rooftop courses in New York City alone. The arrival of the Great Depression severed the popularity of the pastime, and its growth remained stagnant until 1938 when brothers Joseph and Robert R. Taylor Sr. revitalized the game. The Taylors redesigned the sport by adding complicated obstacles such as windmills, castles, and wishing wells to increase the competitive enjoyment. Today, international miniature golf tournaments are held around the world.

# Who's Too Old for the Olympics?

*Think of the average Olympic athlete, and the following images likely come to mind: physical perfection, drive, determination—and youth? Not necessarily. It could be just a matter of time before the AARP holds its own Olympic trials.*

✳　✳　✳　✳

**Hilde Pedersen.** When Norway's Pedersen took home the bronze in the ten-kilometer cross-country-skiing event at the 2006 Turin Winter Olympics, she became the oldest woman to win a Winter Games Olympic medal. It was an impressive achievement for the 41-year-old, but as she and other "older" competitors have proved in the past, age is no barrier to claiming an Olympic medal.

**Oscar Swahn.** Swedish shooter Swahn participated in three Olympic Games. At age 60, he won two gold medals and a bronze at his first Olympics, which took place in London in 1908. Four years later, at the Sweden Games, he won a gold in the single shot running deer team, making him the world's oldest gold medalist. Swahn returned to the Olympics in 1920 at age 72 and managed to win a silver medal in the double shot running deer competition.

**Anders Haugen.** Even at the ripe age of 72, Swahn is not the oldest person to have won an Olympic medal. At the first Winter Olympic Games in Chamonix, France (1924), U.S. ski jumper Anders Haugen placed fourth with a score of 17.916 points. Third-place winner, Norway's Thorlief Haug, received a score of 18.000 points. Fifty years later, a sports historian determined that Haug's score had been miscalculated and that he should have finished behind Haugen. At a special ceremony in Oslo, Haugen was finally awarded the bronze medal when he was 83 years old, making him the "eldest" recipient of an Olympic medal and the only American to ever win a medal in the ski-jump event.

# Dribbling Drivel

*There are numerous rules on how to properly dribble a basketball, but bouncing the ball with such force that it bounds over the head of the ball handler is not illegal.*

※　※　※　※

ALTHOUGH IT MIGHT fun-up the standard NBA game to see players drumming dribbles with the exaggerated effort of the Harlem Globetrotters, it wouldn't do anything to move the game along. And contrary to popular belief, there is no restriction on how high a player may bounce the ball, provided the ball does not come to rest in the player's hand.

Anyone who has dribbled a basketball can attest to the fact it takes a heave of some heft to give the globe enough momentum to lift itself even to eye-level height. Yet, the myth about dribbling does have some connection to reality. When Dr. James Naismith first drafted the rules for the game that eventually became known as basketball, the dribble wasn't an accepted method of moving the ball. In the game's infancy, the ball was advanced from teammate to teammate through passing. When a player was trapped by a defender, it was common practice for the ball carrier to slap the sphere over the head of his rival, cut around the befuddled opponent, reacquire possession of the ball, and then pass it up court. This innovation was known as the overhead dribble, and it was an accepted way to maneuver the ball until the early part of the 20th century. The art of "putting the ball on the floor" and bouncing it was used first as a defensive weapon to evade opposing players.

By the way, there is absolutely no credence to wry comments made by courtside pundits that the "above the head" rule was introduced because every dribble that former NBA point guard Muggsy Bogues took seemed to bounce beyond the upper reaches of his diminutive frame.

## Jeu de Paume, Anyone?

*Ever watch people playing handball and wonder, "Ow! Isn't that hell on their hands?" Well, it can be. That's why some players decided to take a different approach to handball, and used a racket instead. Here's more on the origins of tennis.*

✳   ✳   ✳   ✳

### Tennis: Sport of Monks

INTERESTINGLY, NO ONE is quite sure exactly when tennis was invented. Some folks believe it's an ancient sport, but there's no credible evidence that tennis existed before AD 1000. Whenever the time period, most people can agree that tennis descends from handball.

The first reliable accounts of tennis come from tales of 11th-century French monks who needed to add a little entertainment to their days spent praying, repenting, and working. They played a game called *jeu de paume* ("palm game," that is, handball) off the walls or over a stretched rope. The main item separating tennis from handball—a racket—evolved withinin these French monasteries. (The first rackets were actually used in ancient Greece, in a game called *sphairistike* and then in *tchigan*, played in Persia.) The monks had the time and means to develop these early forms of the tennis racquet: Initially, webbed gloves were used for hand protection, then paddles, and finally a paddle with webbing. The first balls were made from leather or cloth stuffed with hair, wool, or cork.

## Banned by the Pope

Once outside the cloister, the game's popularity spread across the country with the speed of an Amélie Mauresmo backhand. According to some sources, by the 13th century, France had more than 1,800 tennis courts. Most of the enthusiasts were from the upper classes. In fact, the sport became such a craze that some leaders, including kings and the pope, tried to discourage or ban the game as too distracting. Not to be torn from their beloved game, the people played on.

It didn't take long for tennis to reach merry olde England. There the game developed a similar following, counting kings Henry VII and Henry VIII among its fans. Even The Bard, William Shakespeare, refers to the game in his play *Henry V.* At England's Hampton Court Palace, research suggests that the first tennis court was built there between 1526 and 1529. Later, another court was built, The Royal Tennis Court, which was last refurbished in 1628 and is still in use.

## 15-Love!

Those who believe that tennis originated in ancient Egypt argue that the word "tennis" derives from the Egyptian town of Tinnis. It is also possible that the term comes from the French cry of *"Tenez!"* which in this context could mean, "take this!" or "here it comes!" using the formal address. A similar version would be *"Tiens!"* As with any living language, French pronunciation has evolved, so it's difficult to know precisely whether the word actually grew out of French monastery trash-talk—but it's quite plausible.

Ever wonder what's up with tennis's weird scoring system? And what does any of it mean, anyway? Here are a few tennis pointers.

The term "Love," meaning a score of zero, may descend from *L'Oeuf*, which means "the egg"—much like "goose egg" means zero in American sports slang.

Evidently, the scoring once went by 15s (0, 15, 30, 45, and Game). But for some reason, it was decided that the numbers should have the same number of syllables. Hence, the "5" got dropped from the French word *quarante-cinq* (45), leaving just *quarante* (40), which is in use today.

The term "Deuce" (when the game ties 40–40 and is reset to 30–30) likely comes from *"À Deux!"* which loosely translates as "two to win!" This is because in tennis, one must win by two.

# Why Do Golfers Wear Such Silly Clothes?

*In most of the major sports, athletes don't have much choice when it comes to what they wear. Basketball, football, baseball, and hockey teams all have uniforms. But other athletes aren't so lucky (and neither are their fans). Golfers, for example, are allowed to choose their own garb, leading to a parade of "uniforms" that sometimes look as if they were stitched together by a band of deranged clowns.*

✳ ✳ ✳ ✳

WHY BIG-TIME GOLFERS wear such hideous clothes is a source of bewilderment. Some apologists blame it on the Scots. Golf, after all, was supposedly invented by shepherds in Scotland back in the twelfth century, and it almost goes without saying that a sport born in a country where man-skirts are considered fashionable is doomed from the start. We'd like to point out that we are no longer in twelfth-century Scotland— let's move on, people.

But history may indeed play a role in golf's repeated fashion disasters. Kings and queens were reputed to have hit the links in the sixteenth and seventeenth centuries, and by the late nineteenth century, golf was a popular pastime amongst the nobility of England and Scotland.

The nobility, however, wasn't exactly known for its athletic prowess. The other "sports" many of these noblemen participated in were activities like steeplechase (which has its own awful fashion), and so most early golfers had no idea what types of clothes would be appropriate for an athletic endeavor. Early golfers simply took to the links wearing the fashionable attire of the day—attire that, unfortunately, included breeches and ruffled cravats (these were like neckties).

The tradition of wearing stuffy, silly attire continued into the twentieth century (as did the tradition of wealthy, paunchy white guys playing the sport), with awful sweaters, loud patterns, and polyester pants replacing the ruffled cravats and knee-length knickers. Yet, remarkably, modern golfers take umbrage at the stereotype that duffers have no sense of fashion. According to one golf wag, the knock on golfers for being the world's worst-dressed athletes is unfair because nowadays almost everybody wears Dockers and polo shirts. (We'll pause while that gem sinks in.)

To be fair, the dreadful golf fashions of the 1970s and 1980s have given way to a more benign blandness that is at least less offensive, if not remotely what anybody would call "stylish." Of course, all fashion is less offensive than it was in the 1970s and 1980s, so perhaps golf fashion is proportionally no better.

"Golf," Mark Twain once complained, "is a good walk spoiled." We love Mark Twain, but we have to say that spoiling a good walk is the least of golf's transgressions.

# Chapter 14

# Miscellaneous Secrets

## The Bordentown Bonaparte

*Not many people know that after the Battle of Waterloo in June 1815, Napoleon Bonaparte had the chance to flee to America. Though he didn't flee—at least not then—his older brother Joseph did, and wound up in . . . New Jersey.*

✳   ✳   ✳   ✳

### Born to Run?

**A**s all of Napoleon's dreams and ambitions were crashing down around him, in July 1815, the general and his brother Joseph met at Rochefort on the Atlantic coast of France. The men needed to make a big decision. Joseph urged his brother to flee to the United States, but Napoleon was unwilling to run like a common criminal. He remained behind, while Joseph set sail for America.

Joseph tried living in New York City and then Philadelphia, but found that he could not blend into the crowded city background without meeting someone who knew him. What he needed was an isolated country estate. What he found was Point Breeze in Bordentown, New Jersey.

### Peace and Quiet

Situated between Crosswicks Creek and the Delaware River, Point Breeze was a 211-acre estate that gave Joseph ample opportunity to indulge his passion for landscaping, gardening, and building. Joseph closed on the property in either 1816 or 1817 (sources differ), paying $17,500. The total property eventually included 1,000–1,800 acres.

Having ruled as both King of Naples and Sicily (1806–1808) and King of Spain (1808–1813), Joseph had developed a love of finery, and so he began building a house to be second only to the White House. He had hated the politics thrust upon him in Europe, and so he reveled in the peace of Point Breeze. "This country in which I live is very beautiful," he wrote. "Here one can enjoy perfect peace . . . the people's way of life is perfect."

Joseph spent hours roaming his estate and beautifying the grounds. He created artificial lakes and planted many trees and a great lawn in front of his house bordered with rhododendrons and magnolias. He covered the grounds with miles of winding lanes, placed sculpture, and built pastoral cabins.

He didn't neglect the magnificent house he was building either. He filled it with valuable furniture, fine works of art and sculpture, and thousands of books. When all was done, Joseph had a house that rivaled the finest in America.

Then, on January 4, 1820, the house burned to the ground.

Joseph, in New York at the time, hurried home to find that many of his treasures had been saved by the townspeople. Not used to this sort of kindness and honesty in his previous life of war and intrigue, he wrote a letter gratefully thanking the residents of Bordentown.

Joseph built an even more fabulous home, with great fireplaces, marble mantels, and winding staircases. He employed many locals, which endeared him to the residents. He filled the grounds on his property with pheasants, hares, and swans. Local children played on the deer and lion statues in the park and went ice-skating on his lakes in winter.

## Mystery Man

But much like Joseph, his estate was more than met the eye. He had also built a network of tunnels underneath the house. Ostensibly built to bring supplies into the house, and for the convenience of females to move between buildings in foul weather, later the tunnels gave rise to speculation that they were built so Joseph could escape from anti-Bonaparte forces.

In 1914, *The World Magazine* had a better theory: Perhaps Napoleon did not die at St. Helena in 1821, but escaped to America—and to Joseph.

"He could have been rowed from the Delaware River directly into his brother's house," postulated the writer. "And during the years that he was watching for a chance to return to power, he could have had the freedom, through a labyrinth of secret underground passages, of one of the most beautiful estates in America."

Eventually Joseph abandoned Point Breeze and returned to Europe, where he died in 1844. Did his brother live with him in New Jersey? Unfortunately, we may never know—though the idea of Napoleon prowling the streets of tiny Bordentown late at night is too intriguing to completely dismiss.

# The Mystery of the Fortune Cookie

*The fortune cookie may be the most famous symbol of Chinese food in America. But venture over to China and you won't find an advice-filled twist of dough anywhere in sight.*

✳   ✳   ✳   ✳

A FORTUNE COOKIE IS to Chinese food as a stomachache is to a greasy-spoon joint: There's no question it'll follow the meal. It turns out, though, that the former is far from common in China; in fact, you might be hard-pressed to find anyone there who's even heard of one. So where did this crunchy cookie come from? It seems no single proverb holds the answer.

## The Chinese Theories

Some theories trace the cookie's creation to the early Chinese immigrants in America as a means to carry on traditions from their homeland. One story says the cookie's roots originated as far back as 12th-century China, during the rule of the Yuan Dynasty. According to that tale, rebel monks started making a special kind of mooncake, into which they'd slip secret messages to their comrades without the invading Mongols finding out. Legend has it the men baked the cakes, messages and all, then sold them to Chinese families to spread their plans for upcoming rebellions.

Another theory traces the first fortune back to ancient Chinese parlor games. In these sessions, men would write proverbs on paper and then place them inside twisted pastries.

Yet another hypothesis puts the cookie credit in the hands of George Jung, founder of Los Angeles's Hong Kong Noodle Company. Jung is believed by many to have cooked up the first fortune cookies as a way to add some happiness in the dreary post–World War I era. However, some speculate the cookies may have also served as a simple distraction for Jung's guests while their food was being prepared.

## The Japanese Alternative

The other school of thought claims the Japanese actually invented the fortune cookie. Researchers have found family bakeries in the city of Kyoto that have been making similarly shaped fortune crackers since the late 1800s, long before the treat first surfaced in America around 1907.

Called *tsujiura senbei* (fortune crackers) or *omikuji senbei* (written fortune crackers), the Japanese cookies do have some differences: They are larger, darker in color, and have more of a sesame-miso flavor than the vanilla-butter combo of the Chinese variety. The fortunes are also presented within the fold rather than inside the cavity. Even so, fortune-cookie devotees insist the similarities are too great to ignore.

Some Japanese families theorize that the cookies first came to the United States around 1890, when a man named Makoto Hagiwara helped build the Japanese Tea Garden in San Francisco's Golden Gate Park. A nearby bakery called Benkyodo, Makoto's family claims, served the cookies to visitors. It was from here, they say, that other Asian restaurants in California got the idea, leading to its nationwide explosion.

## Unfortunate Resistance

Wherever it began, years later the fortune cookie still hasn't taken off within the nation of China. American importers have tried to change that, but it hasn't been easy. With added packaging requirements, translation costs, and international taxes, the cookies end up costing more than double their worth. Disdain aside, though, the beloved little cookie doesn't seem to be in any danger of disappearing from Chinese custom in America—and that's one fortune you can count on.

# Bunsen's Burner: Scientific Error

*A staple in chemistry classes for generations, this gas burner's hot blue flame has heated up the experiments of countless budding scientists. But the so-called "Bunsen burner" is actually a misnomer.*

✳   ✳   ✳   ✳

AMONG THE ACHIEVEMENTS of 19th-century scientist Robert Wilhelm Bunsen are the co-discovery of chemical spectroscopy—the use of an electromagnetic light spectrum to analyze the chemical composition of materials—and the discovery of two new elements, cesium and rubidium. Bunsen is best known, however, for his invention of several pieces of laboratory equipment, including the grease-spot thermometer, the ice calorimeter, and a gas burner that became the standard for chemical laboratories the world over.

In 1852, Bunsen was hired as a lecturer at the University of Heidelberg and insisted on a brand new state-of-the-art laboratory with built-in gas piping. Although already in use, gas burners at the time were excessively smoky and produced flickering flames of low heat intensity. Bunsen had the idea of improving a burner invented by Scottish scientist Michael Faraday by pre-mixing gas with air before combustion, giving the device a hotter-burning and non-luminous flame. He took his concept to the university mechanic, Peter Desaga, who then designed and built the burner according to Bunsen's specifications, adding a control valve that regulated the amount of oxygen mixed with gas.

Bunsen gave Desaga the right to manufacture and sell the burner, and Desaga's son, Carl, started a company to fill the orders that began arriving from around the world. Bunsen and Desaga, however, did not apply for a patent, and soon other manufacturers were selling their versions. Competitors applied for their own patents, and Bunsen and Desaga spent decades refuting these claims. The court of history seems to have judged Bunsen the winner.

## As Good as It Gets

*Jack Nicholson's sister was actually his mother. Who knew? Certainly not Jack.*

✳   ✳   ✳   ✳

IT HAPPENED WHEN the soon-to-be smash movie *Chinatown* was opening in theaters. The film's star, Hollywood powerhouse Jack Nicholson, was being interviewed for a cover story for *Time* magazine. Amidst a battery of standard questions, an offbeat query was tossed Nicholson's way. The *Time* reporter asked if his sister was really his mother. Befuddled by the bizarre question, Nicholson denied it emphatically—but his curiosity was piqued.

When the actor was born, his 18-year-old biological mother June made a pivotal decision. Rather than derail a promising dancing career by admitting that she had become pregnant out of wedlock, she decided with her mother Ethel May to disguise the truth. The ploy was simple. June would pose as Nicholson's sister while Ethel May would pretend that both June and Jack were her children. The plan worked. Many years passed with Jack and most everyone else believing the ruse.

When the *Time* interview concluded, however, a suspicious Nicholson contacted his brother-in-law, Shorty, the husband of his sister Lorraine. At first Shorty told him that the rumor wasn't true, but later that day Lorraine tearfully confirmed the story. In one fell swoop Nicholson came to learn that his presumed sister June was his mother; his sister Lorraine was his aunt; and the woman that he had believed to be his mother was his grandmother.

Nicholson took the news in stride. During a 2006 interview with director Peter Bogdanovich, the actor weighed in on the well-orchestrated story. "I understood it; I know exactly what my initial reaction was: gratitude . . . I've often said about them: Show me any women today who could keep a secret, confidence, or an intimacy to that degree, you got my kind of gal."

# Babysittin' Joe

*Did Joe DiMaggio really play a part in the discovery of the breast cancer gene? This delightfully strange but true fact is one of the most satisfying morsels in the public imagination.*

✳ ✳ ✳ ✳

CELEBRITIES DABBLE IN science and invention, like Abraham Lincoln's boat-safety patent or Danica McKellar's math books and activism. But Joltin' Joe happened to be in the right place at the right time to help someone out, and that someone made a world-changing discovery.

Genetic scientist Dr. Mary-Claire King told her story to *The Moth*: She had plans to meet with the National Institutes of Health about a careermaking grant when a series of obstacles nearly derailed her. Her husband left her, causing her aggrieved mother to refuse to babysit Dr. King's daughter. While trying to accommodate her mother's wishes to return home, Dr. King was forced to choose between making her own flight and helping her mother.

It was then, in line, that Joe DiMaggio appeared—retired for 30 years but still just 67 years old. He offered to watch Dr. King's daughter and they became fast friends. Dr. King was able to secure the grant that began her brilliant march toward the discovery of BRCA1, the breast cancer gene.

# The Bronzed Age

*Who decided suntans are attractive?*

\* \* \* \*

SUNTANS HAVE BEEN in and out of fashion throughout history. In many primitive societies, the sun was revered as the center of the spiritual universe, and a perpetual tan was a sign of religious fidelity. In our own slightly less primitive time, sun worship is still common, but the purpose isn't religious. We do it because, as Paris Hilton might put it, "it's hot."

How did it get that way? In the nineteenth century, debutantes and socialites—the Paris Hiltons of their day—would have been praised for their paleness. To compare a lady's skin to alabaster—a hard, white mineral used in sculpture—was to offer a high compliment indeed.

But toward the end of the nineteenth century, doctors began to realize that sunlight is necessary for good health, as it promotes vitamin formation in the body. This didn't make suntans attractive overnight, but it helped dissolve the stigma against them. In the twentieth century, tans grew more and more popular from aesthetic and social perspectives, even as evidence that linked sun exposure to skin cancer mounted.

If one person deserves credit for really sparking the current suntan rage, it's famed fashion designer Coco Chanel. She was sunburned while on vacation one summer in the 1920s, and her resulting tan became all the rage. "The 1929 girl must be tanned," she would later say. "A golden tan is the index of chic." A pronouncement of this kind of out-and-out shallowness is perfectly suited to today's world, too, though it might translate to the current youth vernacular as something more like, "OMG tans rule!!!!" Coco was clearly on to something: As a society, we do think that tans are attractive.

Experts say that a suntan nowadays suggests someone who is rugged, athletic, and unafraid of things. It also suggests wealth, leisure, and the freedom to be outside while others are slaving away indoors. This represents a dramatic change from the nineteenth century, when tanned skin was more likely to indicate a life of manual labor in the fields—a sign of someone at the bottom of the social ladder rather than the top.

That's the sociological explanation. There's also a theory that centers on evolutionary psychology—it has to do with the "attractiveness of averageness." Studies have shown that when there is a heterogeneity (or range) of genes present in a person, the resulting face is more average—it is free of unusual quirks of size or shape. Over the millennia, humans have come to innately understand that such a person is also more robust physically, without the genetic weaknesses or flaws inherent in inbreeding.

When a fair-skinned person's face is tan, it appears to be closer to the overall human average. If this seems far-fetched, consider that studies have shown that people of all skin colors tend to believe that the most attractive faces have hues that are between light and dark. In other words, the folks we find most alluring have suntans.

# Philo T. Farnsworth—The Teenager Who Invented Television

*Responsible for what may have been the most influential invention of the 20th century, this farm boy never received the recognition he was due.*

✳ ✳ ✳ ✳

**P**HILO T. FARNSWORTH's brilliance was obvious from an early age. In 1919, when he was only 12, he amazed his parents and older siblings by fixing a balky electrical generator on their Idaho farm. By age 14, he had built an electrical laboratory in the family attic and was setting his alarm early so he could get up and read science journals for an hour before doing the chores.

Farnsworth hated the drudgery of farming. He often day-dreamed solutions to scientific problems as he worked. During the summer of 1921, he was particularly preoccupied with the possibility of transmitting moving pictures through the air.

Around the same time, big corporations like RCA were spending millions of research dollars trying to find a practical way to do just that. As it turned out, most of their work was focused on a theoretical dead-end. Back in 1884, German scientist Paul Nipkow had patented a device called the Nipkow disc. By rotating the disc rapidly while passing light through tiny holes, an illusion of movement could be created. In essence, the Nipkow disc was a primitive way to scan images. Farnsworth doubted that this mechanical method of scanning could ever work fast enough to send images worth watching. He was determined to find a better way.

His "Eureka!" moment came as he plowed a field with a horse team. Swinging the horses around to start another row, Farnsworth glanced back at the furrows behind him. Suddenly, he realized that the scanning could be done electronically, line-by-line. Light could be converted into streams of electrons and then back again with such rapidity that the eye would be fooled. He immediately set about designing what would one day be called the cathode ray tube. Seven years would pass, however, before he was able to display a working model of his mental breakthrough.

Upon graduating from high school, Farnsworth enrolled at the University of Utah but dropped out after a year because he could no longer afford the tuition. Almost immediately, though, he found financial backers and moved to San Francisco to continue his research. The cathode ray tube he developed there became the basis for all television. In 1930, a researcher from RCA named Vladimir Zworykin visited Farnsworth's California laboratory and copied his invention. When Farnsworth refused to sell his patent to RCA for $100,000, the company sued him. The legal wrangling continued for many years and, though Farnsworth eventually earned royalties from his invention, he never did get wealthy from it.

By the time Farnsworth died in 1971, there were more homes on Earth with televisions than with indoor plumbing. Ironically, the man most responsible for television appeared on the small screen only once. It was a 1957 appearance on the game show *I've Got a Secret*. Farnsworth's secret was that "I invented electric television at the age of 15." When none of the panelists guessed Farnsworth's secret, he left the studio with his winnings—$80 and a carton of Winston cigarettes.

# Camelot 9-1-1: JFK's Secret Ailments

*The universal image of President John F. Kennedy is a young, athletic one: playing touch football, swimming a great distance after his PT boat was attacked, and rough-housing on the White House lawn with his children. But the popular image is false—in reality, Kennedy was a very sick man.*

✳ ✳ ✳ ✳

## State Secrets

THE STATUS OF presidential health is as zealously guarded as the formula for Coca-Cola. The image of a vigorous president is considered vital to the health of the nation, even if in reality he is incapacitated (Woodrow Wilson's debilitating stroke), seriously ill (Grover Cleveland had cancer surgery on his mouth), or just plain unhealthy (William Howard Taft weighed in at more than 300 pounds). To this day, many people still don't know that Franklin Roosevelt needed braces to stand because he and his staff hid his disability so well.

Kennedy was different. The youngest man ever elected a U.S. president, he projected an image of strength and vitality. Yet the further one gets from the idealistic façade of Camelot, the more one learns about it.

## A Lifetime of Medicating

Kennedy was a sickly child. He suffered from scarlet fever, bronchitis, measles, whooping cough, chicken pox, and ear infections—all before age 13. He had an operation for appendicitis in the early 1930s, and he was rushed to the hospital in the winter of 1936 where doctors feared he had leukemia. He also went to the Mayo Clinic that year to be treated for colitis, and repeatedly complained of abdominal pain.

Kennedy took steroids for his ailments, possibly as early as 1937 but certainly by 1947. When he ran for a seat in the

House of Representatives in 1946, he was described as looking "like a skeleton." Due to his many and varied illnesses, he received the Last Rites twice between 1947 and 1955. Robert Kennedy later said, "When we were growing up together we used to laugh about the great risk a mosquito took in biting Jack Kennedy—with some of his blood the mosquito was almost sure to die."

When Kennedy ran for president in 1960, an aide carrying a bag filled with medical supplies always followed him. Once the bag was misplaced in Connecticut. Kennedy frantically telephoned the state's governor to find the bag.

## Patient-in-Chief

After he was elected president, Kennedy felt it more important than ever to maintain the fiction that he was in good, robust health. Reporters who tried to pursue stories of his Addison's disease (a rare disorder that affects the adrenal gland's production of steroid hormones) were told that he had a mild adrenal deficiency, which was being handled by oral medication.

As Chief Executive, Kennedy outwardly portrayed a picture of tanned vitality. However, the truth was that he had numerous doctors available at any given time. Among the physicians caring for the president were an allergist, an endocrinologist, a gastroenterologist, an orthopedist, a urologist, and an internist.

Kennedy's medical problems during his first six months in office read like the script for a melodramatic medical movie: high fevers; problems with his colon, stomach, and prostate; abscesses; back troubles; adrenal ailments; periodic dehydration; high cholesterol; and sleeplessness. During this time, Kennedy took so many medications that Dr. Janet Travell, the internist, kept a list called the "Medicine Administration Record" to keep straight all the drugs he was receiving.

In addition, Kennedy also kept Dr. Max Jacobson close at hand. A German doctor known as "Dr. Feelgood" and "Miracle Max,"

Jacobson treated celebrities for depression and fatigue with injections laced with amphetamines, steroids, multivitamins, and other substances. In 1961, Jacobson accompanied the president on a trip to France, flying there on a chartered jet so that he could continue treating him. Kennedy dismissed questions about Jacobson's dubious injections with a curt, "I don't care if it's horse piss. It works."

## Side Effects

One long-term effect of steroids (unknown when Kennedy began taking them) is that they cause osteoporosis in the lower backbones. That, and several back surgeries, kept Kennedy in almost constant back pain for years. In the autumn of 1961, one of Kennedy's physicians, Admiral George Burkley, decided that the injections the president had been getting for his back, along with braces and other devices that he wore, were hurting rather than helping him. Burkley feared that Kennedy would soon be wheelchair-bound. He brought in orthopedic surgeon Hans Kraus, who warned Kennedy that he must begin immediate exercise to strengthen the muscles. Kennedy began exercising three times a week. By the spring of 1962, the president was doing better than he had in several years.

The million-dollar question is whether or not Kennedy's many medications affected his performance as president. Historians agree that it doesn't seem to be the case. While president, Kennedy was taking antibiotics (urinary tract infections), anti-spasmodics (colitis), steroids (Addison's disease), anti-histamines (allergies), and painkillers (back pain). Yet these medications probably helped him function at times when he otherwise could not have.

## The Great Question

History is filled with conjecture; one of the most intriguing theories concerns the stiff back brace Kennedy was wearing the day of his assassination in Dallas, Texas, on November 22, 1963. If he had not been wearing the brace, which was designed to hold him upright, perhaps he might have moved or slumped sideways when the first shot hit him. Perhaps he would have been able to avoid the fatal second shot. But that's the funny thing about conjecture: We'll never know for sure.

# All Choked Up

*Recollections of singer Mama Cass Elliot should include million-selling singles, garish garments, and a flamboyant stage presence. Instead, she is often remembered for dying with a hoagie gorged in her gullet. Let's satisfy the public's hunger and set her record straight.*

✳   ✳   ✳   ✳

A S RENOWNED FOR her prodigious girth as she was for the rich timbre of her singing voice, Ellen Naomi (Mama Cass) Cohen knew no half measures—she lived life to the fullest. Although the musical Mama had an appetite for substances of all quantities and assortments, the details surrounding her last hours and untimely demise have been greatly exaggerated.

Shortly after news of her death in a London apartment was announced to the public, rumors abounded that the corpulent chanteuse had punched her ticket to the great beyond by choking on a ham sandwich. The genesis for the gossip was a notation on the official police report, which stated that a half-eaten sandwich had been found near her expired form. However, the autopsy report, a far more reliable document, revealed that there was no evidence of food particles in her trachea.

The simple truth is that Mama Cass died a rather pedestrian death. The vocalist perished from heart failure, most likely because of her unhealthy habit of alternating periods of food and substance abuse with intervals of crash dieting.

# Why Is the Pirate Flag Called a Jolly Roger?

*With the 1883 publication of Robert Louis Stevenson's* Treasure Island, *the popular idea of the pirate germinated: a witty rogue with an eye patch, a peg-leg, and a smart-ass parrot, sailing the seven seas under the Jolly Roger, good-naturedly plundering booty and instigating a little plank-walking.*

\* \* \* \*

UNFORTUNATELY FOR THOSE romantics who long for the swashbuckling days of yore, most of Bob Lou Steve's details aren't particularly accurate. There is little evidence that something as dramatic as "walking the plank" happened much, and parrots were rarely recorded as ships' mascots. But calling the pirate flag the "Jolly Roger" was one of the details Stevenson got right.

For hundreds of years, ships have hoisted the colors of their home country to let other ships know from where they hail. In the golden age of piracy, pirates used this form of communication as well, though more deviously. Often, pirates would fly flags of certain countries as a form of deception, in order to get close to their prey. Once they were within striking distance, the buccaneers would lower their false flags and raise their own ensigns. These flags varied from pirate to pirate, but they all meant the same thing: "Surrender, hand over your booty, and we will not kill you." Though if the pirates raised a red flag, it meant, "We will kill you and take your booty." (One might say these flags were the original "booty call.")

French pirates most prominently used the red flag as a symbol of imminent death, and among these pirates, such a flag became known as a *joli rouge* ("pretty red"). The English, hewing to their long tradition of making no effort to correctly pronounce foreign words, turned this into the "Jolly Roger."

Another theory points to a legendary Tamil pirate by the name of Ali Raja. Raja ruled the Indian Ocean and had such a reputation that even English seamen had heard of the pirate captain. It's not hard to imagine how Europeans who were unfamiliar with Middle Eastern languages might corrupt "Ali Raja" into "Jolly Roger."

The least interesting hypothesis points to the fact that in England during piracy's glory days, the devil was often referred to as "Old Roger." That, combined with the grinning appearance of the skull symbol, led to the flag being called the "Jolly Roger." Unfortunately, there is no definitive evidence that supports one theory over another.

The origin of the familiar skull-and-crossbones image is also unclear. The image had been used as a general symbol of death long before pirates appropriated it—crusaders used the symbol in the 1100s, for example. The first recorded use of the skull-and-crossbones on a pirate flag was in 1700, when a French buccaneer named Emmanuel Wynne hoisted it. After that, the black flag with a variation of the image appeared more frequently and sometimes included hourglasses, spears, and dancing skeletons.

Once Stevenson published *Treasure Island*, the skull-and-crossbones—along with the mythical parrot—became forever associated with pirates in the popular mind. The novel is also famous for introducing the phrase, "Yo, ho, ho, and a bottle of rum" into pirate lore. We don't know what that means, either.

# The Secret Side of Elvis

*Being the King of Rock 'n' Roll is not all it's cracked up to be.*

✳    ✳    ✳    ✳

SPARKLING WHITE JUMPSUIT, shiny black pompadour, soulful eyes, and shimmying hips—that's the mythic image of Elvis Presley everyone knows and loves. But although he was a revolutionary recording artist and the King of Rock 'n' Roll, Elvis was also made of darker stuff. From his obsession with guns to his bizarre behavior regarding his mother's corpse and a long fascination with occult teachings, Elvis had a secret side that his publicists preferred to keep under blue suede wraps.

## I Remember Mama

Born on January 8, 1935, in Tupelo, Mississippi, to Vernon and Gladys Presley, Elvis Aaron came into the world along with a stillborn twin brother, Jesse Garon. It was an early tragedy that haunted Elvis for most of his life. The family was poor—a situation made worse when Vernon was sent to prison for forging a check. At age three, Elvis was suddenly the man of the house.

After Vernon's release in 1948, the family moved to Memphis, Tennessee. Even as his recording career began to take off in the mid-'50s, Elvis and his mother remained incredibly close and devoted to one another. She lived with him at his Graceland estate until her death in 1958. To say Elvis did not take his mother's death well would be an understatement, and his grief morphed into often bizarre behavior. Family and friends worriedly noted that he seemed obsessed with his mother's corpse. Later, he talked at length to friends about the technical details of the embalming process.

When Gladys's glass-topped coffin was brought to lie in state at the Graceland mansion, Elvis threw himself on the corpse. Elvis also threw himself on her coffin as it was being lowered into the ground. Recording artist Barbara Pittman said he was screaming and had to be restrained. Afterward, he carried his mother's nightgown everywhere for more than a week.

## Don't Be Cruel

When Elvis began dating 14-year-old Priscilla Beaulieu in 1959, he showed another unexpected side—the control freak. He asked her to dye her hair the same jet black as his own; the couple looked so similar that people believed they were twins.

He chose her wardrobe and once became upset over an imperfect polish job on one of her toenails. He also required her to carry a concealed handgun. Of course, Elvis sometimes carried as many as five guns himself, and was in the habit of shooting objects that irked him. A television with poor reception? *Blam!* Shattered console televisions were constantly dragged out of the Jungle Room at Graceland. Elvis once even shot his Ferrari after it stalled on the road.

## Got My Mojo Workin'

Elvis continued to feel haunted by the loss of his brother and mother, and he grew desperate for some sort of spiritual answer. For a time, he sought solace in the beliefs of a hair stylist named Larry Geller. Elvis confessed to Geller that as a young child, he often heard a voice and wondered if it was his dead brother. Geller, something of a New Age mystic, introduced Elvis to metaphysical books and to his own philosophy that—as redundant as it sounds—the main purpose of life was to find one's purpose in life. Presley staff member Alan Fortas said Elvis referred to Geller as his guru and to himself as "the divine messenger."

Elvis began carrying a numerology book with him that he consulted to help him decide which gifts to bestow on any given individual. His metaphysical journey ended after he tripped and hit his head in 1967, after which he was "deprogrammed" by his manager Colonel Tom Parker. In the end, Elvis apparently had enough, and his collection of metaphysical books wound up in flames in a burn pit on the grounds of Graceland. But when Elvis was found dead in his bathroom on August 16, 1977, he was wearing the symbols of three religions: an Egyptian ankh, a Jewish Star of David, and a Christian crucifix.

# From the Vaults of History

*Here are a few interesting tidbits they didn't teach you in high school history class: For example, did you know that condoms were incredibly important during the invasion of Normandy in World War II in 1944?*

## Safe War?

SURE, CONDOMS KEPT soldiers free of sexually transmitted diseases, and they no doubt helped to prevent a lot of out-of-wedlock pregnancies. But condoms were also used for more heavy-duty purposes. Soil samples collected on Omaha Beach were stored in the durable rubber receptacles. And when our boys bravely charged out of the flat-bottomed landing boats, their guns were protected from water damage by the condoms that covered their barrels. (Perhaps the director edited out that detail in *Saving Private Ryan*.)

## Things Unspoken

Queen of France Marie Antoinette may not have been a very nice person, and she may have made many foolish or unkind statements, but she almost surely never said the sentence that most people associate with her: "Let them eat cake." We know this because the phrase appears in Jean-Jacques Rousseau's *Confessions*, which was completed in 1769. Rousseau attributed the unsympathetic remark—supposedly said in response to the French people starving—to a "young princess," but the phrase had been ascribed to various other sovereigns for decades before Marie arrived in France in 1770.

While it is possible that Marie was familiar with *Confessions*, as it was published 20 years before the French Revolution began, it is highly doubtful that she actually read it—she wasn't exactly known as an intellectual. A more likely scenario is that someone on the side of the Revolution read Rousseau's work, decided the arrogant remark sounded like something the queen would say, and simply started spreading the rumor.

# Becoming Black Like Me

*Journalist and writer John Howard Griffin used deception to force America to take a closer look at racism.*

✳   ✳   ✳   ✳

IN 1959, JOHN Howard Griffin, a white Mansfield, Texas, native, pondered the issues of race in the United States. The Civil Rights Movement had started only four years prior, and Griffin decided the best way to find out how a black man lived was to transform himself into one and travel through the segregated Deep South. Griffin detailed his odyssey in a series of articles for *Sepia* magazine, a monthly black publication.

Before Griffin assumed his new persona, he visited Georgia, Alabama, Louisiana, and Mississippi as a white man. He reported meeting many friendly, hospitable people along his route. Next, with the aid of a dermatologist, Griffin ingested oral pigmentation medication followed by ultraviolet ray treatments, which greatly darkened his skin. He shaved the hair on his head and hands, lest they provide clues to his real identity.

When he returned to the same towns he had previously visited, now as a black man, he received a completely different reaction. He traveled for six weeks, later reporting that the daily difficulties of living as a black man outweighed even those moments of overt racism. Seemingly small tasks white people took for granted—getting a bite to eat, requesting water, using a restroom—took a large amount of time. Often he would be turned away from establishments and directed toward black-only diners and shops, and those would usually be located far away.

Griffin's story spread like wildfire. In 1961, he wrote a best-selling book, *Black Like Me*, which told of his journeys. Television interviews and magazine features followed. White Americans finally were able to realize what life was really like for a black man in the Deep South.

For his troubles, Griffin received criticism and protests. After he was hanged in effigy and confronted with death threats, Griffin moved his family to Mexico. He had peeled back the veneer of Southern society and provided an eye-opening look under its surface, but he paid a steep price for the revelation.

# Can People Get Fat Because of a Slow Metabolism?

*Your metabolism gets more blame than it should for that spare tire you call a stomach. The fact is, a slow metabolism is rarely the primary reason for excessive weight gain.*

✳    ✳    ✳    ✳

BROADLY SPEAKING, YOUR metabolism comprises all the chemical processes your cells undertake to sustain life. But when people talk about a fast or slow metabolism, they generally mean the basal metabolic rate—the rate at which the body turns nutrients into energy (burning calories) when at rest. While it's true that genetics plays a role in defining the baseline for this rate and that some people naturally burn more calories than others, very few folks have metabolic rates that are slow enough to single-handedly make them fat. The main culprit is almost always too many calories or too little exercise (or both).

The body's metabolic rate is highly flexible—it changes with your habits. For example, you can speed it up somewhat by adding more muscle; muscle burns more calories while you're at rest than fat does. On the other hand, you can slow your metabolism down through inactivity. And if your metabolism is naturally slow and you don't work out enough, you'll probably put on weight faster than somebody who has a quicker metabolism and doesn't exercise much. So if you haven't already gotten the hint, read the following words very, very carefully: Get off your keister and join a health club.

Oh, and one more thing: In a cruel twist of fate, serious dieting tends to slow down the metabolism. If you cut back drastically on your caloric intake, the body typically enters "starvation mode"—it reacts to a perceived lack of available food by storing fat. Ain't biology a bitch?

# Frequency Modulation (FM Radio)

*A fearless innovator's marvelous invention is tarnished by betrayal.*

✳   ✳   ✳   ✳

FAME AND RICHES are supposed to go to those visionaries that build the better mousetraps. But with the invention of frequency modulation (FM radio), things didn't quite work out that way. Edwin H. Armstrong (1890–1954) invented a new transmission medium that left the former giant, amplitude modulation (AM radio), quivering in its wake. For most people, such a lofty achievement would bring a degree of satisfaction—not to mention a stack of cash. For Armstrong, it would bring mostly heartache.

Before this underappreciated genius found his way to FM, he made other contributions. Two of Armstrong's inventions, the regenerative circuit of 1912 and the superheterodyne circuit of 1917, would set the broadcasting world on its ear. When combined, they would produce an affordable tube radio that would become an American staple. Armstrong was on his way.

Soon afterward, the inventor turned his attentions to the removal of radio static, an inherent problem in the AM circuit. After witnessing a demonstration of Armstrong's superheterodyne receiver, David Sarnoff, the head of the Radio Corporation of America (RCA) and founder of the National Broadcasting Company (NBC), challenged him to develop "a little black box" that would remove the static. Armstrong spent the late 1920s through the early 1930s tackling the problem.

Sarnoff backed the genius by allowing him use of a laboratory at the top of the Empire State Building. This was no small offering—in the broadcasting game, height equals might, and none came taller than this 1,250-foot giant, which has since been named one of the seven wonders of the modern world.

In 1933, Armstrong made a bold announcement. He had cracked the noise problem using frequency modulation. With a wider frequency response than AM and an absence of background noise, the new technology represented a revolutionary step in broadcasting.

Armstrong's upgraded system had the ability to relay programming from city to city by direct off-air pickup. But without knowing it, the inventor had effectively boxed himself in. NBC, and by extension Sarnoff, was the dominant force in conventional radio during this time. With America mired in an economic depression, NBC wasn't interested in tooling up for a new system. Even worse for Armstrong, television loomed on the horizon, and NBC was pouring most of its resources into that technology. Instead of receiving the recognition and financial rewards that he so rightly deserved, Armstrong was fired unceremoniously by his "friend" Sarnoff. It seemed like the end of the line—but Armstrong's battle was only just beginning.

In 1937, a determined Armstrong erected a 400-foot tower and transmitter in Alpine, New Jersey. Here, he would go about the business of perfecting his inventions. Unfortunately, without Sarnoff's backing, his operation found itself severely underfunded. To make matters infinitely worse, Armstrong became embroiled in a patent battle with RCA, which was claiming the invention of FM radio. The broadcasting giant would ultimately win the patent fight and shut Armstrong down. The ruling was so lopsided that it robbed Armstrong of his ability to claim royalties on FM radios sold in the United States. It would be hard to find a deal rawer than this.

To fully appreciate Armstrong's contribution, compare AM and FM radio stations: The difference in transmitted sound will be pronounced, with FM sounding wonderfully alive and AM noticeably flat in comparison. Even "dead air" sounds better on FM because the band lacks the dreaded static that plagues the AM medium. Without a doubt, FM technology is a tremendous breakthrough. But it came at a terrible cost. On January 31, 1954, Armstrong— distraught over his lack of recognition and dwindling finances—flung himself from the 13th-floor window of his New York City apartment.

# History's Grim Places of Quarantine

*Life has never been easy for lepers. Throughout history, they've been stigmatized, feared, and cast out by society. Such reactions—though undeniably heartless—were perhaps understandable because the disease was thought to be rampantly contagious. Anyone suspected of leprosy was forced into quarantine and left to die.*

✳ ✳ ✳ ✳

LEPROSY HAS AFFECTED humanity since at least 600 BC. This miserable disease, now known as Hansen's disease, attacks the nervous system primarily in the hands, feet, and face and causes disfiguring skin sores, nerve damage, and progressive debilitation. Medical science had no understanding of leprosy until the late 1800s and no effective treatment for it until the 1940s. Prior to that point, lepers faced a slow, painful, and certain demise.

Misinterpretations of Biblical references to leprosy in Leviticus 13:45–46, which labeled lepers as "unclean" and dictated that sufferers must "dwell apart . . . outside the camp," didn't help matters. (The "leprosy" cited in Leviticus referred to several skin conditions, but Hansen's disease was not one of them.)

It's really no surprise that society's less-than-compassionate response to the disease was the leper colony.

## Cast Out in Misery and Despair

The first leper colonies were isolated spots in the wilderness where the afflicted were driven, forgotten, and left to die. The practice of exiling lepers continued well into the 20th century. In Crete, for instance, lepers were banished to mountainside caves, where they survived by eating scraps left by wolves. More humane measures were adopted in 1903 when lepers were corralled into the Spinalonga Island leper colony and given food and shelter and cared for by priests and nuns. However, once you entered, you never left, and it remained that way until the colony's last resident died in 1957.

Still, joining a leper colony sometimes beat living among the healthy. It wasn't much fun wandering from town to town while wearing signs or ringing bells to warn of one's affliction. And you were always susceptible to violence from townsfolk gripped by irrational fear—as when lepers were blamed for epidemic outbreaks and thrown into bonfires as punishment.

## Life in the American Colony

American attitudes toward lepers weren't more enlightened. One of modern time's most notorious leper colonies was on the Hawaiian island of Molokai, which was established in 1866. Hawaiian kings and American officials banished lepers to a peninsula ringed by jagged rock and sea cliffs. Molokai became one of the world's largest leper colonies—its population peaked in 1890 at 1,174—and over 8,000 people were forcibly confined there before the practice was ended in 1969.

The early days of Molokai were horrible. The banished were abandoned in a lawless place where they received minimal care and had to fight with others for food, water, blankets, and shelter. Public condemnation led to improved conditions, but residents later became freaks on display as Hollywood celebrities flocked to the colony on macabre sightseeing tours.

## A Leper Haven in Louisiana

While sufferers of leprosy were being humiliated in Hawaii, they were being helped in Louisiana. In 1894, the Louisiana Leper House, which billed itself as "a place of treatment and research, not detention," opened in Carville. In 1920, it was transferred to federal authority and renamed the National Leprosarium of the United States. Known today as the National Hansen's Disease (leprosy) Program (NHDP), the facility became a leading research and rehabilitation center, pioneering treatments that form the basis of multidrug therapies currently prescribed by the World Health Organization (WHO) for the treatment of Hansen's disease.

It was here that researchers enlisted a common Louisiana critter—the armadillo—in the fight against the disease. It had always been difficult to study Hansen's disease. Human nerves are seldom biopsied, so direct data on nerve damage from Hansen's was minimal. But in the 1960s, NHDP researchers theorized that armadillos might be susceptible to the germ because of their low body temperature. They began inoculating armadillos with it and discovered that the animals could develop the disease systemically. Now the armadillo is used to develop infected nerves for research worldwide.

## A Thing of the Past?

In 1985, leprosy was still considered a public health problem in 122 countries. In fact, the last remaining leper colony, located in Croatia, didn't close until 2002. However, WHO has made great strides toward eradicating the disease and indicated in 2000 that the rate of infection had dropped by 90 percent. The therapies currently prescribed for the treatment of leprosy are available to all patients for free via WHO. Approximately four million patients have been cured since 2000.

# The Swastika: Sacred Good, Nazi Evil

*For thousands of years, it stood as a sacred symbol of fortune and vitality—until Adolph Hitler adopted its eye-catching geometry to lead his rise to power, turning the swastika into the 20th century's ultimate emblem of evil.*

✳    ✳    ✳    ✳

ORIGINATING IN INDIA and Central Asia, its name comes from the Sanskrit word *svastika*, meaning well-being and good fortune. The earliest known examples of the swastika date to the Neolithic period of 3000 BC. A sacred symbol in Hinduism, Buddhism, and Jainism, the symbol was most widely used in India, China, Japan, and elsewhere in Asia, though archaeological examples have also been found in Greco-Roman art and architecture, in Anglo-Saxon graves of the pagan period, in Hopi and Navajo art from the American Southwest, and in Gothic architecture in Europe. Synagogues in North Africa and Palestine feature swastika mosaics, as does the medieval cathedral of Amiens, France.

For thousands of years, the swastika was a symbol of life, the sun, power, and good luck, though in some cultures a counter-clockwise mirror image of the swastika, called a *sauvastika*, meant bad luck or misfortune. Pointing to evidence in an ancient Chinese manuscript, astronomer Carl Sagan theorized that a celestial phenomenon occurring thousands of years ago may have given rise to the swastika's use around the world, when gas jets shooting from the body of a passing comet were bent into forms hooked by rotational forces, creating a similar shape. Other scholars believe that it was so widely known because its geometry was inherent in the art of basket weaving.

The modern revival of the swastika in the Western world began with the excavation of Homer's Troy on the shores of the Dardanelles in the 1870s. German archaeologist Heinrich Schliemann discovered pottery and other artifacts at the site decorated with swastikas. Schliemann and other scholars associated his finds with examples of the symbol uncovered on ancient artifacts in Germany. They theorized that the swastika was a religious symbol linking their German-Aryan ancestors to the ancient Teutons, Homeric Greeks, and Vedic India. German nationalists, including anti-Semitic and militarist groups, began using the symbol at the end of the 19th century. But with its connotations of good fortune, the swastika also caught on in Western popular culture. Swastikas were used to decorate cigarette cases, postcards, coins, and buildings throughout Europe. In the United States, they were used by Coca-Cola, the Boy Scouts, and a railroad company. The U.S. Army's 45th Division used the symbol during WWI; and Charles Lindberg painted one inside the nose cone of the *Spirit of St. Louis* for good luck.

In 1920, Adolf Hitler adopted the symbol for the Nazi Party's insignia and flag—a black swastika inside a white circle on a field of red—claiming he saw in it "the struggle for the victory of the Aryan man." With Hitler's appointment as chancellor, the Nazi flag was raised alongside Germany's national flag on March 14, 1933, and became the nation's sole flag a year later. The symbol was used ubiquitously in Nazi Germany—on badges and arm bands, on propaganda material, and on military hardware. By the end of the war, much of the world identified the symbol only with Hitler and the Nazis. Its public use was constitutionally banned in postwar Germany. Though attempts have been made to rehabilitate its use elsewhere, the swastika is still taboo throughout the Western world.

In Asia, however, the swastika remains a part of several religious cultures and is considered extremely holy and auspicious. In India, it is a symbol of wealth and good fortune, appearing not only in temples and at weddings but on buses, on rickshaws, even on a brand of soap. Hindus in Malaysia,

Indonesia, and elsewhere in Southeast Asia also continue its use. In 2005, the government of Tajikistan called for adoption of the swastika as a national symbol.

# A Bigger Brain Doesn't Translate to a Smarter Person

*If you're someone who has an oversized noggin—and displays it like a trophy—we really hate to rain on your parade: You are not smarter than the rest of us. Scientific studies continue to show that size isn't everything where the human brain is concerned.*

✳   ✳   ✳   ✳

## History Lessons

SURE, IT MIGHT be easy to assume that a big cranium is capable of holding more intelligence—just by sheer mass. History suggests otherwise. William H. Calvin, a theoretical neurophysiologist and affiliate professor emeritus at the University of Washington School of Medicine, points to notable periods in the historical timeline when the brains of ancient humans greatly increased, but toolmaking smarts did not.

Although the *Homo sapiens* of 200,000 years ago had developed a brain size comparable to that of contemporary people, they continued to use the same crude, round-edged rocks for some 150,000 years before graduating to points, needles, harpoons, and hooks. You can't exactly say those bigger-brained primates were the sharpest tools in the shed.

## Modern Science Weighs In

As for modern people, advancements in magnetic resonance imaging (MRI)-based brain scans are giving researchers more pertinent data about the relationship between brain size and intelligence. (Before MRI, researchers had to measure the outside of a person's head to estimate brain size, or wait until that person died to get an accurate measurement.) A 2004 study conducted by researchers at the University of California-Irvine and the University of New Mexico was one of the first to use MRI technology to demonstrate that it's not overall brain size that counts, but brain organization.

How so? The researchers used MRI to get structural scans of the study participants' brains, and then compared those scans to respective scores on standard IQ tests. What they discovered was that human intelligence is less about total girth and more about the volume and specific location of gray-matter tissue across the brain. It appears there are several "smart" areas of the brain related to IQ, and having more gray matter in those locations is one of the things that makes us, well, smarter.

Undoubtedly, the relationship between brain size and intelligence will continue to be studied and debated, but some in the medical field now believe that brain size is purely a function of genetics and doesn't result in a greater intellect. Researchers at Harvard Medical School have even been able to identify two of the genes (beta-catenin and ASPM) that regulate brain size.

So if you've got a big head, don't be so quick to get a big head. It turns out that Albert Einstein's brain weighed only 2.7 pounds. That's 10 percent smaller than average.

# Clarifications on Kong

*The most famous inhabitant of Skull Island, he has elicited both screams and sympathy from moviegoers. But contrary to rumor, King Kong was never played by a man in an ape suit.*

✳ ✳ ✳ ✳

WE'VE ALL HEARD the term "800-pound gorilla" in reference to something considered big and bad, and in Hollywood, they don't get any bigger or badder. Standing a whopping 50 feet tall and weighing in excess of 800 pounds, Kong has captured the imaginations of millions since his premiere in 1933.

Much has been written and said about how Kong was brought to life, and for decades many believed that in some of his scenes, Kong was simply a man in a monkey suit. But such claims are patently false. With the exception of a few scenes that featured a life-size bust or a giant mechanical hand, Kong was made real through a meticulous and time-consuming process known as stop-motion animation. Despite his towering onscreen presence, the mighty Kong was nothing more than an 18-inch articulated metal skeleton (referred to as an armature) covered with rubber and rabbit fur.

## Birth of a King

When *King Kong* first hit theaters, moviegoers were awestruck. They watched in amazement as vicious dinosaurs came to life and a huge gorilla ravaged the streets of New York City until biplanes blasted him off the top of the Empire State Building. It was unlike anything they had seen before, and the movie raked in several times the $650,000 it cost to produce.

The myth that King Kong was a man in an ape suit was started by an inaccurate article in an issue of *Modern Mechanix and Inventions*, which featured illustrations showing how a stuntman was used for the scenes in which Kong scaled the Empire State Building.

## The Mighty Myth Grows

Thirty years later, a poorly researched AP wire story added to the myth by reporting that King Kong had been portrayed by Hollywood stuntman Carmen Nigro. In the article, Nigro made a number of outrageous claims, including the "fact" that Fay Wray was an animated doll and that Nigro had worn "fur-covered ballet slippers with suction pads" to help him stay on the skyscraper. Nigro also claimed to have starred in *Mighty Joe Young* (1949) as another supersize cinematic simian created through the artistry of stop-motion animation. (Both apes were animated by the gifted Willis O'Brien, who won an Academy Award for his special-effects work on *Mighty Joe Young*.)

Although the original King Kong was only a model, he has been portrayed by a man in a suit in other movies over the years. The Japanese monster smash *King Kong vs. Godzilla* (1962), for example, featured an embarrassingly bad gorilla suit and a storyline that had the famous ape duking it out with Japan's favorite superlizard. The movie is notable for having two endings: In the version shown in Japan, Godzilla wins. In the version seen by people in the United States, Kong is the victor.

# The Lizzie Borden Murder Mystery

*Most people know the rhyme that begins, "Lizzie Borden took an axe and gave her mother 40 whacks." In reality, approximately 20 hatchet chops cut down Abby Borden, but no matter the number, Lizzie's stepmother was very much dead on that sultry August morning in 1892. Lizzie's father was killed about an hour later. His life was cut short by about a dozen hatchet chops to the head. No one knows who was guilty of these murders, but Lizzie has always carried the burden of suspicion.*

✳   ✳   ✳   ✳

## Andrew Borden, an American "Scrooge"

ANDREW JACKSON BORDEN had been one of the richest men in Fall River, Massachusetts, with a net worth of nearly half a million dollars. In 1892, that was enormous wealth. Andrew was a shrewd businessman: At the time of his death, he was the president of the Union Savings Bank and director of another bank plus several profitable cotton mills.

Despite his wealth, Andrew was miserly. Though some of his neighbors' homes had running hot water, the three-story Borden home had just two cold-water taps. There was no water available above the first floor. The Bordens' only latrine was in the cellar, so they generally used chamber pots that were either dumped on the lawn behind the house or emptied into the cellar toilet. And, although most wealthy people used gas lighting, the Bordens lit their house with inexpensive kerosene lamps.

Worst of all, for many years, Andrew was an undertaker who offered some of the lowest prices in town. He worked on the bodies in the basement of the Borden home, and allegedly, he bent the knees of the deceased—and in some cases, cut off their feet—to fit the bodies into smaller, less expensive coffins in order to increase his business.

So, despite the brutality of Andrew's murder, it seems few people mourned his loss. The question wasn't why he was killed, but who did it.

## Lizzie vs. William

In 1997, when psychic Jane Doherty visited the murder site, she uncovered several clues about the Lizzie Borden case. Doherty felt that the real murderer was someone named "Willie." There is no real evidence to support this claim, but some say Andrew had an illegitimate son named William, who may have spent time as an inmate in an insane asylum. His constant companion was reportedly his hatchet. He talked to it as though it were a friend. Also, at least one witness reportedly saw William at the Borden house on the day of the murders. William was supposedly there to challenge Andrew about his new will.

Was William the killer? A few years after the murders, William took poison and then hung himself in the woods. Near his swinging body, he'd reportedly left his hatchet on the ground. So with William dead and Lizzie already acquitted, the Borden murder case was put to rest.

## Lizzie's Forbidden Romance

One of the most curious explanations for the murder involves the Bordens' servant Bridget Sullivan. Her participation has always raised questions. Like the other members of the Borden household, Bridget had suffered from apparent food poisoning the night before the murders. She claimed to have been ill in the backyard of the Borden home.

During the time Abby was being murdered, Bridget was apparently washing windows in the back of the house. Later, when Andrew was killed, Bridget was resting in her room upstairs. Why didn't she hear two people being butchered?

According to some theories, Lizzie and Bridget had been romantically involved. In this version of the story, their relationship was discovered shortly before the murders. Around this same time, Andrew was reportedly rewriting his will. His wife was now "Mrs. Borden," to Lizzie, not "Mother," as Lizzie had called her stepmother for many years. The reason for the estrangement was never clear.

Lizzie also had a strange relationship with her father and had given him her high school ring, as though he were her sweetheart. He wore the ring on his pinky and was buried with it.

Just a day before the murders, Lizzie had been attempting to purchase prussic acid—a deadly poison—and the family came down with "food poisoning" that night. Some speculate that Bridget was Lizzie's accomplice in the murders and helped clean up the blood afterward. This theory was bolstered when, a few years after the murders, Lizzie became involved with actress Nance O'Neil. For two years, Lizzie and the statuesque actress were inseparable. This prompted Emma Borden, Lizzie's sister, to move out of their home.

At the time, the rift between the sisters sparked rumors that either Lizzie or Emma might reveal more about the other's role in the 1892 murders. However, neither of them said anything new about the killings.

## Whodunit?

Most people believe that Lizzie was the killer. She was the only one accused of the crime, with good reason. Lizzie appeared to be the only one in the house at the time, other than Bridget. She showed no signs of grief when the murders were discovered. During questioning, Lizzie changed her story several times. The evidence was entirely circumstantial, but it was compelling enough to go to trial. Ultimately, the jury accepted her attorney's closing argument, that the murders were "morally and physically impossible for this young woman defendant." In other words, Lizzie had to be innocent because she was petite and well bred. In 19th-century New England, that seemed like a logical and persuasive defense. Lizzie went free, and no one else was charged with the crimes.

But Lizzie wasn't the only one with motive, means, and opportunity. The most likely suspects were family members, working alone or with other relatives. Only a few had solid alibis, and— like Lizzie—many changed their stories during police questioning. But there was never enough evidence to officially accuse anyone other than Lizzie.

So whether or not Lizzie Borden "took an ax" and killed her parents, she's the one best remembered for the crime.

## Lizzie Borden Bed and Breakfast

The Borden house has been sold several times over the years, but today it is a bed-and-breakfast—the main draw, of course, being the building's macabre history. The Victorian residence has been restored to reflect the details of the Borden home at the time of the murders, including the couch on which Andrew lay, his skull hideously smashed.

As a guest, you can stay in one of six rooms, even the one in which Abby was murdered. Then, after a good night's sleep, you'll be treated to a breakfast reminiscent of the one the Bordens had on their final morning in 1892. That is, if you get to sleep at all. (They say the place is haunted.) As with all good morbid attractions, the proprietors at the Lizzie Borden B&B don't take themselves too seriously. Before you leave, you can stop by the gift shop and pick up a pair of hatchet earrings or an ax-wielding Lizzie Borden bobble-head doll.

# The Curious Friendship of Cary Grant and Randolph Scott

*Today, gay characters are commonplace on television and in the movies, and stars are more likely to openly acknowledge their sexual orientation. But during Hollywood's Golden Age, when star images were carefully guarded by the studios, public perceptions regarding gay lifestyles could be quite biased. If a Hollywood star was so inclined, he hid the fact for fear that it would ruin his career. Nevertheless, whispers and rumors might persist.*

✳   ✳   ✳   ✳

## The Gossip Mill

DURING THE GOLDEN Age of Hollywood, when the major movie studios kept actors under contract, personas were constructed for actors, which they were expected to play on and off the screen. The studios were adamant that nothing be done to ruin or damage those carefully groomed personas, so they had publicity departments with press agents who fed free stories and photographs to magazines, which propagated the images of the major stars and presented their best sides. Any aspects of their lives that did not fit their image were hidden behind the studios' orchestrated promotion and propaganda.

Occasionally, an arrest, messy divorce, or scandal slipped through the gears of the star-making machine, but sometimes even those problems were covered up. The wild cards in this system were gossip columnists and nosy reporters, and it was this faction of the Hollywood dream machine that circulated veiled rumors about Cary Grant and Randolph Scott.

## Closer than Close

The two actors met on the set of *Hot Saturday* (1932) and formed a quick friendship. A short time later they acquired a Malibu beach house and moved in together—supposedly to save money. Dubbing the beach house "Bachelor Hall," the pair threw lavish parties and, according to witnesses, generally reveled in each other's company. They lived in this fashion, off and on, for several years, and during that time, suspicious tongues took to wagging. Had the two really paired up to save on expenses, as had been put forth, or was something more salacious occurring? The idea of the two living together to split expenses wasn't as far-fetched as it might now seem. Stars under contract to studios did not make the millions they do now. They made weekly salaries that went up only at the discretion of the studio. It wasn't unheard-of for up-and-coming actors to move in together. Yet something about the way Grant and Scott looked at each other suggested something deeper than friendship, at least to those who'd observed them up close.

Gossip columnist Jimmie Fiddler began to make veiled remarks about Grant and Scott's roommate status, and studio press agents only aggravated the situation when they tried to present the pair as the town's most eligible bachelors. Much later, gossip queen Hedda Hopper tried to "out" Grant in her column, but various people within the industry rallied around him, and Hopper backed off. The curious part was that neither man seemed much disturbed by the whisperings going on behind his back. In fact, each seemed indifferent to the potential backlash that might arise from their living arrangement.

So, were Grant and Scott gay? It depends on whom you choose to believe. Many friends thought the two were indeed gay. Director George Cukor supposedly revealed that the two were more than friends, and that Scott was willing to admit to it.

## Perhaps They Were

In William Mann's book *Behind the Screen: How Gays and Lesbians Shaped Hollywood, 1910–1969*, photographer Jerome Zerbe tells of "three gay months" spent taking photos of the pair. He implies that the two were gay or bisexual, based upon his lengthy observations. Fashion critic Richard Blackwell went Zerbe one better, claiming to have slept with both actors.

## But Then Again

On the "perhaps not" side, Grant more than once declared that he "had nothing against gays, I'm just not one myself." A book entitled *Whatever Happened to Randolph Scott*, penned by Scott's adopted son Christopher, puts forth similar, albeit somewhat predictable, denials about the famous duo's relationship. And director Budd Boetticher, who worked with Scott during the 1950s in some of the actor's most memorable Westerns, emphatically denied any rumors of the alleged romance. Further confusing the matter, Grant walked down the aisle a total of five times, and Scott took the plunge twice.

For their part, the actors let the insinuations slide past them the way a veteran actor sidesteps a bad review. If the two were gay or bisexual, they seemed comfortable with it. If they weren't, well, that too appeared to be okay. The most puzzling thing, however, was the fact that the Hollywood gossip machine didn't bring them down. Did the actors' prodigious charm and good looks neutralize writings about their romance? Had their studios suppressed information that proved conclusively that the two were gay? Were the actors just incredibly lucky? In Hollywood, anything seems possible, so any or all of these scenarios might be plausible. One thing is for certain: If their relationship took place in this day and age, there'd likely be no shame in admitting which team the boys were playing for.

More important are the films the two actors left behind. Grant's sophisticated, articulate, and well-mannered gentleman was the perfect comic foil for boisterous costars, providing audiences with classic films known for their snappy dialogue and wit, including *The Philadelphia Story* (1940), *His Girl Friday* (1941), and *The Bishop's Wife* (1947). Scott's image as the stoic Western hero who always retains his integrity was used to great effect by Boetticher in *Ride Lonesome* (1959) and Sam Peckinpah in Scott's last film, *Ride the High Country* (1962). Each represented an ideal of masculinity that overshadowed their personal sexual preferences, whatever they were.

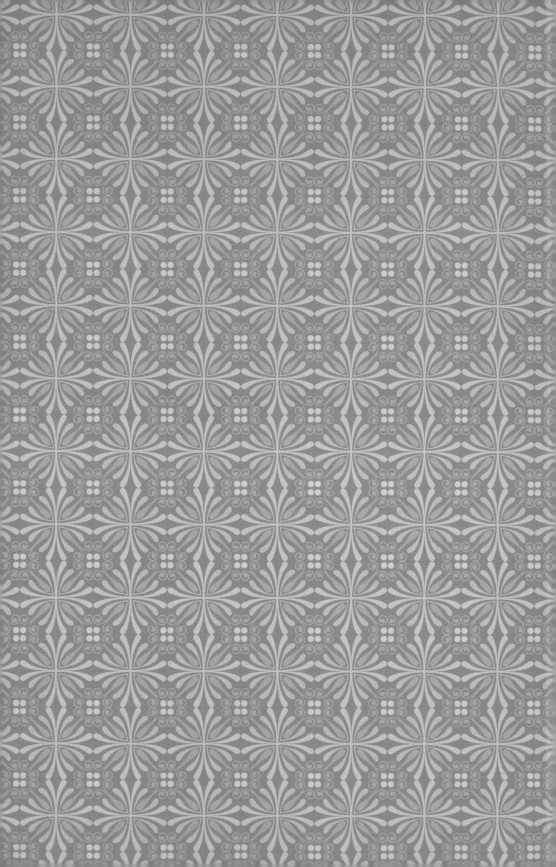